American Apparel, Inc.

CHAPTER 9
INTRODUCTION TO A STANDARD COST SYSTEM

Springfield Remanufacturing

CHAPTER 13
CONTROLLING COSTS IN THE
CHANGING WORKPLACE

CROWLEY
CANDY
CO.

CHAPTER 10
PROCESS COSTING

Teva Pharmaceutical

CHAPTER 14
RESPONSIBILITY ACCOUNTING AND TRANSFER
PRICING IN DECENTRALIZED OPERATIONS

Werthan Packaging

CHAPTER 11
CONTROLLING INVENTORY AND
PRODUCTION COSTS

Harnischfeger Industries, Inc.

CHAPTER 15
MEASURING AND REWARDING PERFORMANCE

CHAPTER 12
CONTROLLING NONINVENTORY COSTS

MANAGERIAL ACCOUNTING

THIRD EDITION

Cecily A. Raiborn

LOYOLA UNIVERSITY—NEW ORLEANS

Jesse T. Barfield

LOYOLA UNIVERSITY—NEW ORLEANS

Michael R. Kinney

TEXAS A&M UNIVERSITY

 South-Western College Publishing

an International Thomson Publishing company I(T)P®

Cincinnati • Albany • Boston • Detroit • Johannesburg • London • Madrid • Melbourne • Mexico City
New York • Pacific Grove • San Francisco • Scottsdale • Singapore • Tokyo • Toronto

ACCOUNTING TEAM DIRECTOR:	Richard K. Lindgren
SPONSORING EDITOR:	Alex von Rosenberg
DEVELOPMENTAL EDITOR:	Leslie Kauffman
PRODUCTION EDITOR:	Deanna Quinn
PHOTO MANAGER:	Cary Benbow
MARKETING MANAGER:	Matt Filimonov
MANUFACTURING COORDINATOR:	Gordon Woodside
PRODUCTION HOUSE:	Pre-Press Company, Inc.
INTERNAL DESIGN:	Hespenheide Design
COVER DESIGN:	Paul Neff Design
COVER PHOTOGRAPHY:	© 1998 Tony Stone Images

Library of Congress Cataloging-in-Publication Data

Raiborn, Cecily A.
    Managerial accounting / Cecily A. Raiborn, Jesse T. Barfield, Michael R. Kinney. — 3rd ed.
      p.   cm.
    Includes bibliographical references and index.
    ISBN 0-538-88512-2 (hard : alk. paper). — ISBN 0-324-00101-0 (looseleaf : alk. paper)
    1. Managerial accounting. I. Barfield, Jesse T. II. Kinney, Michael R. III. Title.
HF5657.4.R34 1999   98-28158
658. 15'11—dc21   CIP

2 3 4 5 6 7 8 9 WCBS 6 5 4 3 2 1 0 9

CECILY A. RAIBORN

Dr. Cecily A. Raiborn is Professor of Accounting at Loyola University New Orleans. She received her Ph.D. from Louisiana State University in 1975. Professor Raiborn teaches cost, managerial, intermediate, and advanced accounting at the undergraduate level, and financial and managerial accounting, cost management, and performance measurement at the graduate level. Her research interests include cost management, international, quality, and ethics issues. She has published articles in accounting, law, and ethics journals including *Management Accounting, Advances in Management Accounting, Journal of Accounting Case Research, Labor Law Journal,* and *Journal of Business Ethics.* She serves on the editorial board of *Advances in Management Accounting.* In 1991, she received the AICPA/Louisiana CPA Society Outstanding Educator Award. Her interests outside the classroom include traveling, reading, water activities, fishing, decorating, and cooking.

JESSE T. BARFIELD

Dr. Jesse T. Barfield is a Professor of Accounting at Loyola University New Orleans. He received his Ph.D. from Louisiana State University in 1971. He earned an undergraduate degree in accounting and a masters in accounting at Florida State University. He has practiced as a CPA and is licensed to practice in Florida and Louisiana. His research and professional interests include managerial and cost accounting, total quality management, and quality assessments for managers. He teaches accounting, quality management, and auditing in Loyola's undergraduate program and also teaches graduate courses in the MBA and MQM programs. He was chosen by the Loyola CBA undergraduates to receive the 1998 Award for Outstanding Teaching. He has published in the *Journal of Accountancy, Management Accounting, The Florida Certified Public Accountant,* and *The Louisiana CPA.*

MICHAEL R. KINNEY

Dr. Michael Kinney is a native of the rural, sandhills area of Nebraska and received a BA degree from Hastings College, Hastings, Nebraska in 1978. Following graduation, Professor Kinney worked as an insurance agent and broker and later as a commodity futures broker. He returned to graduate school in 1984, earning an MS in accounting from the University of Wyoming and a Ph.D. from the University of Arizona. Professor Kinney joined the faculty of accounting at Texas A&M in 1989, and is currently the Price Waterhouse Teaching Excellence Professor of accounting. He teaches undergraduate courses in cost and management accounting and graduate courses in management control systems, corporate tax, and tax strategies. He has received numerous teaching awards including the outstanding teacher of the Texas A&M College of Business from the College of Business Honors Society (twice), and Delata Iota Chapter's Beta Alpha Psi teaching excellence award in accounting (twice). Professor Kinney also received the Southwest Chapter of the Academy of International Business' Distinguished Paper Award for international research. Professor Kinney has authored and co-authored numerous articles in accounting, taxation, and finance. Professor Kinney is married with four children, and he spends his free time sailing the Gulf of Mexico.

CONTENTS IN BRIEF

CONTENTS

Accounting is often referred to as the "language of business." However, managers must be able to communicate their information needs to accountants and understand the resulting answers. This text provides a context for dialogue among all the business disciplines and emphasizes the practical rather than the theoretical. Thus, it stresses the techniques and procedures of greatest managerial importance. The perspective taken by *Managerial Accounting* is that managers and accountants must have a common understanding of the organizational role of accounting information, what techniques are available to provide that information, what details are needed to perform the techniques, and the benefits and limitations of the information provided by the various techniques in response to managers' needs. An integrated approach to information flow will create an atmosphere of trust, sharing, and cooperation.

We believe that it is critical for readers to understand that accounting is a cross-functional discipline that provides information useful to all management areas. It is also essential that readers recognize that managerial accounting information is necessary in all types of organizations (manufacturing, service, and not-for-profit), regardless of size. Substantial effort has been taken to illustrate all of these enterprise types, in both domestic and international operations. Rapid changes in the global business environment, such as the introduction in previously communist countries of profit-making operations, will create new demands for management information, and this information will be prepared in the international language of business: accounting.

AUDIENCE

This text is primarily directed toward students who have a basic familiarity with the informational content of financial statements. It may be used in a course under either the semester or the quarter system.

PEDAGOGY

This text is extremely student-oriented. The following text features have been designed to promote an ease of learning and provide a high interest level.

Learning Objectives   Each chapter provides an orderly framework for the material to be covered. Margin annotations indicate the text coverage of the learning objectives. *(See pages 2 and 6 for examples.)*

On-Site Openers   Each chapter begins with a vignette about a relevant aspect of a real-world organization. These openers show students how the chapter topics affect a business on a daily basis. The On-Sites feature organizations such as Coca-Cola, Exxon, Alaska Airlines, Riscky's Barbeque, Archway Cookies, Crowley Candy Co., American Apparel, and many more. *(See pages 3, 39, and 75 for examples.)*

News Notes   News Notes in the chapters provide selections from the popular business press and reflect the contemporary world of business activity. Four themes (general business, international, quality, and ethics) are used in the News Notes to illustrate how managerial accounting concepts affect various aspects of business. Logos are used to inform the reader of the News Note theme. There are over sixty references to organizations such as the Meridian Club, Toyota, Group Health Cooperative, Employment Canada, Terex Corp., Reebok, and Gelco Information Network. *(See pages 14, 46, 52, and 80 for examples.)*

General Business   International

Quality   Ethics

Key Terms   When a new term is introduced within a chapter, it is listed in boldface type, indicated in a margin annotation, and defined at that point. All key terms in each chapter are presented at the end of the chapter with page references for the definition. Additionally, a complete end-of-text glossary is provided.

NEW! Internet Links   Web site addresses for many real-world companies are listed in the margins throughout the text. *(See pages 22, 53, and 84 for examples.)*

Site Analysis   This chapter section continues discussion of the On-Site company's reaction to, or resolution of, the opening topic. *(See pages 28, 63, and 99 for examples.)*

Cross-Functional Applications   These strategies, written by Noel McKeon of Florida Community College—Jacksonville, follow the Site Analysis section and indicate how some tools presented in the chapter are applicable to business disciplines such as economics, finance, human resources, management, and marketing as well as to nonbusiness disciplines such as engineering, law, operations research, and public administration. For example, the applications in the chapter on capital budgeting indicate that capital budgets assist economists in planning an optimum production function, help financial managers analyze and predict profitability and cash flows, and aid attorneys in lease agreement negotiations. *(See pages 28, 63, and 100 for examples.)*

Chapter Summary   A summary of the most important concepts in each chapter is provided to promote student retention. *(See pages 29, 64, and 101 for examples.)*

Solution Strategies   In this section, students are provided with all relevant formulas and major computational formats from the chapter. These strategies may be used as guides to work end-of chapter materials or to refresh the memory. *(See pages 151 and 205 for examples.)*

Demonstration Problem   At the end of appropriate chapters, a demonstration problem and solution are given so that students can check their understanding of chapter computations before doing end-of-chapter assignments. *(See page 205 for an example.)*

End-of-Chapter Materials   Each chapter contains a variety of end-of-chapter materials (at different levels of difficulty) that include questions, exercises, problems, cases, and quality and ethics discussions. Some of the end-of-chapter materials are specifically designed to provide the opportunity for students to utilize their writing skills and/or emphasize the needs of different individuals in an organization (for instance, the marketing manager, finance officer, production supervisor, or human resource manager). Many of the ethics and quality discussions are taken from the popular business press and relate to actual business situations. Some of these discussion questions provide a current reference to an article that could help in answering the question or provide greater information about a situation.

   The ethics and quality items provide the dual benefit of indicating that choices are important to an organization's current and future existence as well as providing an additional avenue for written expression and logical thought.

Numerical end-of-chapter materials that are computer-solvable are indicated with a spreadsheet icon.

End-of-Text Appendices Appendix A provides a discussion of the management accounting profession and codes of ethics for the Institute of Management Accountants (U.S.) and the Society of Management Accountants of Ontario (Canada). Appendix B is a brief overview of the various ethical theories to help students analyze ethics situations and answer the chapter ethics discussion questions. Appendix C provides present and future value tables of $1 and an ordinary annuity of $1.

Glossary An end-of-text glossary is provided that includes all of the key terms in the text and their definitions.

MAJOR CHANGES IN THIRD EDITION

Although the prior editions of this text were very well received, the authors gathered comments from adopters and reviewers and made numerous changes to increase its teachability and student orientation. In addition, the Accounting Education Change Commission has been instrumental in providing guidance on improving and adding to the text's pedagogical features. The AECC has indicated that it is essential for students in accounting courses to possess strong communication, intellectual, and interpersonal skills as well as to understand ethics and make value-based judgments. Thus, to encourage students to improve their communication and intellectual skills, we have expanded the quantity of essay and logic problems in end-of-chapter materials, student study guide, and test bank. To improve the process of analyzing and making ethical decisions and value-based judgments, we have included more real-world discussion questions in the end-of-chapter materials. Additionally, to promote interpersonal skills, we encourage the use of student teams in answering some of the more complex problems, cases, and discussion questions. Teamwork is essential in today's business environment because flattened organizational structures result in the empowerment of employee teams with the authority, responsibility, and accountability for making positive changes and rational decisions.

The organizational and pedagogical changes to the second edition are listed below. Changes in the supplements are provided in the appropriate Instructor and Student Support Materials sections.

ORGANIZATION

⊙ Chapter 1 sets the stage for future chapters by focusing first on organizational strategy, influences on that strategy, and management functions. The chapter then addresses the global environment in which businesses operate. Tying these issues together, the chapter covers the role of accounting in organizational strategy and the influence of the value chain in an organization's existence. In summary, Chapter 1 is designed to help students understand the numerous forces that must be considered by businesspeople today and how those forces affect accounting and decision making. Some topics related to strategy that were covered in Chapter 10 of the second edition have been moved to this chapter.

⊙ Chapter 2 provides an introduction to information, control, and cost management systems. Within the context of a cost management system, the concepts of conversion, product and period costs, methods of product costing, and types of costing systems are discussed. This chapter allows students to understand the varying informational needs of managers and how those information attributes can be captured, analyzed, and utilized in an organization with a well-designed cost management system.

⊙ Chapter 3 is a revision of Chapter 2 from the second edition. Quality in service and not-for-profit organizations is addressed, and, as an integrally related topic, calculation of the cost of quality (previously in Chapter 12) is also included in this chapter.

⊙ Because both cost-volume-profit analysis and relevant costing involve short-run decisions and focus primarily on cost behavior, these topics have been combined into a new Chapter 6. Make-or-buy decisions have been moved to Chapter 13. Absorption/variable costing has been shortened and has been moved to become the first appendix to Chapter 6.

⊙ In response to significant reviewer feedback, budgeting (Chapter 7) and capital budgeting (Chapter 8) have been moved closer to the front of the text and placed together. Chapter 7 now contains information on the necessity of participation in the budgeting process, and an appendix to this chapter provides the computations for sales price and sales volume variances; all of these topics were in the second edition's Chapter 10.

⊙ Chapters 9 and 10 are, respectively, the chapters on standard and process costing.

⊙ The two chapters on cost control are now Chapter 11 (inventory and production) and Chapter 12 (non-inventory items).

⊙ Chapter 13 is a new chapter that focuses on controlling costs in a changing workplace. Topics are high-profile, real-world issues such as process reengineering, downsizing, workforce diversity, outsourcing, strategic alliances, and open-book management.

⊙ Chapter 14 corresponds to Chapter 15 in the second edition and covers decentralized operations, including transfer pricing. Chapter 15 corresponds to Chapter 16 in the second edition and covers the processes of measuring and rewarding performance.

PEDAGOGY

⊙ The theme of each opening vignette is carried through the chapter using a fictitious company within a related industry. Because of the need to maintain confidentiality of proprietary information, the On-Site company's actual data are not used, but example data are reflective of reality.

⊙ The end-of-chapter materials include discussion questions on both ethics and quality. As mentioned earlier, many of these questions address actual business situations. The quality discussion questions focus on the impacts of introducing (or choosing not to introduce) quality techniques on company costs, employee and customer behavior, and production/service processes.

⊙ Journal entries are, in many places, presented separately in chapter appendices. This placement allows faculty to include or exclude this accounting process information without interrupting the flow of the chapters.

⊙ Approximately 25 percent of the end-of-chapter material is new, and there are typically at least two exercises for each key concept in the chapter. Many of the end-of-chapter items ask the student to act as if he or she had a particular position in the firm in question to promote analysis and discussion from alternative perspectives.

INSTRUCTOR SUPPORT MATERIALS

The text is accompanied by a full range of support materials for the instructor.

Solutions Manual   This volume, prepared by the authors, has been independently reviewed and checked for accuracy. It contains complete solutions to each question, exercise, problem, and case in the text. This volume also contains a copy of the Student Check Figures.

Solution Transparency Acetates   Acetates are provided from the solutions manual for all numerical end-of-chapter materials.

Test Bank   The test bank (prepared by Chandra Schorg at Texas Woman's University) contains over one thousand multiple-choice, short exercise, and short discussion questions with related solutions.

Computerized Test Bank   A computerized version of the test bank includes edit and word-processing features that allow test customization through the addition, deletion, and scrambling of test selections.

Instructor's Manual   This manual (developed by Gregory K. Lowry of Macon Technical Institute and Athens Area Technical Institute) contains sample syllabi, a listing of chapter learning objectives and terminology, chapter lecture outlines, and some CMA exam multiple-choice questions for use as additional test materials or for quizzes. In addition to the inclusion of transparency masters for some of the text exhibits, the manual provides several teaching transparencies for items of interest that are not part of the text proper.

PowerPoint Teaching Transparency Slides   PowerPoint files (prepared by Marvin Bouillon of Iowa State University) are available on disk and provide entertaining and informative graphics and text for full-color, electronic presentations.

Videos   This text is accompanied by a wide selection of videos that illustrate text concepts. Several of the tapes produced by the Association for Manufacturing Excellence (AME) are available to qualified adopters. These tapes feature companies such as Hewlett-Packard, Motorola, Spectra-Physics, Whirlpool, Northern Telecom, and Oregon Cutting Systems. These videos illustrate automated processes, just-in-time/total quality management philosophies, manufacturing excellence at small and mid-sized companies, global business strategies, and teamwork skills. Short videos are also available that feature some companies that have been designated "Blue Chip Enterprises." This program for small businesses is sponsored by Connecticut Mutual Life Insurance Company, the U.S. Chamber of Commerce, and *Nation's Business* magazine. A third series of videos, *BusinessLink*, illustrates key management accounting concepts including activity-based costing, product costing, and total quality management. These videos feature companies such as Archway Cookies, World Gym, and Symbios Logic. A student workbook and instructor's manual are available to accompany these videos.

NEW! Web Resources   This text's supporting Web site at **raiborn.swcollege.com** provides downloadable versions of key instructor supplements, as well as an on-line study guide, selected readings, and virtual tours. As an adopter; you will also receive a complimentary subscription to Thomson Investors Network, a powerful business news and financial informational resource. For a preview, visit **www.thomsoninvest.net.**

STUDENT SUPPORT MATERIALS

Students are also provided with a comprehensive support package to enhance their learning experience.

Study Guide The student study guide (prepared by Alan Campbell, CPA) contains chapter learning objectives, chapter overviews, detailed chapter notes, and self-test questions.

Spreadsheet Applications for Managerial Accounting Prepared by Leslie Turner of Northern Kentucky University, this package allows students to use either Excel® or Lotus 1-2-3® to solve many in-text problems (which have been indicated with a computer disk icon).

Practice Sets Two practice sets are available for the text.

- Pennsylvania Containers: An Activity-Based Costing Case, developed by Bob Needham of Bucknell University, illustrates activity-based costing using a manufacturing company that produces garbage dumpsters and customized trash receptacles. This practice set concentrates on determination of cost drivers and their use in assigning overhead costs to products. It can be used when teaching Chapter 5 (Activity-Based Management) or in conjunction with several chapters from the text to show the student the impact of activity-based costing on decision making. A solutions manual is available for instructors.

- Pet Polygon Manufacturing Company is an IBM-compatible computerized practice set that was written by L. Murphy Smith of Texas A&M University and Dana Forgione of The University of Baltimore. It provides students with the opportunity to develop a complete master budget and make managerial decisions. A solutions manual indicates how the practice set can be used in conjunction with the budgeting chapter (Chapter 7) or as a continuing problem for the entire term.

Student Solutions Manual This student supplement, prepared from the instructor's Solutions Manual, provides complete solutions to alternate end-of-chapter exercises and problems.

ACKNOWLEDGMENTS

We would like to thank the many people who have helped us during the revision of this text. The constructive comments and suggestions made by the following reviewers were instrumental in developing, rewriting, and improving the quality and readability of this book.

Surenda P. Agrawal
University of Memphis

Uday Chandra
University of Oklahoma

Robert C. Elmore
Tennessee Technological University

Micah Frankel
California State University—Hayward

Ronald W. Halsac
Community College of Allegheny
County—Pittsburgh

George A. Heyman
Oakton Community College

Jerry Joseph
Indiana University of Pennsylvania

Celina L. Jozsi
University of South Florida

Noel McKeon
Florida Community College

Paul H. Mihalek
University of Hartford

Liz Mulig
University of Texas—Tyler

Sandra Pelfrey
Oakland University

Paulette A. Ratliff
University of Oklahoma

Barbara Reider
University of Alaska—Anchorage

Jack M. Ruhl
Western Michigan University

Marilyn Sagrillo
University of Wisconsin—Green Bay

Ann E. Selk
University of Wisconsin—Green Bay

P. K. Sen
SUNY—Buffalo

Thomas J. Stoffel
University of St. Thomas

Gerald A. Thalmann
North Central College

Kiran Verma
University of Massachusetts—Boston

Special mention must be given to Barbara Reider at University of Alaska—Anchorage for her hard work as a problem checker, to Joel Ridenour for securing the appropriate permissions, and to the many individuals who provided information related to the On-Sites and Site Analyses. Special thanks must also be made to the Institute of Management Accountants. This organization has been extremely generous in its permission to use numerous CMA problems and excerpts from its *Management Accounting* periodical and other publications. We also want to acknowledge the many publishers who granted permission for use of their materials as On-Site/Site Analysis/News Note excerpts.

Lastly, the authors thank all the people at South-Western College Publishing (especially Alex von Rosenberg, Leslie Kauffman, and Deanna Quinn) who have helped us on this project, and our families and friends, who have encouraged and supported us in this endeavor.

Cecily Raiborn
Jesse Barfield
Mike Kinney

PART 1

The Business Environment

Chapter 1   Operating in a Global Business Environment

LEARNING OBJECTIVES

After reading this chapter, you should be able to answer the following questions:

1. **WHAT** are the primary factors and constraints that influence an organization's strategy and why are these factors important?

2. **WHY** does an organization need to understand its core competencies before considering outsourcing?

3. **HOW** does an organization's competitive environment impact its strategy and how might an organization respond to competition?

4. **HOW** do the management functions affect strategic and tactical planning?

5. **WHAT** factors have influenced the globalization of businesses and why have these factors been significant?

6. **HOW** does the accounting function impact an organization's ability to successfully achieve its strategic goals and objectives?

7. **WHY** is a company segment's mission affected by product life cycle?

8. **WHAT** is strategic resource management and why is it important to managers?

The Coca-Cola Company

A vending machine on a narrow shopping street in Tokyo's Setagaya section tells a lot about the state of The Coca-Cola Company in Japan today. Although the big machine is emblazoned with the red "Coca-Cola®" logo, only three of the 25 cans behind the glass contain the familiar cola. The others are "Coke®" products that most of the world never sees: an Asian tea called "Sokenbicha™," an English tea called "Kochakaden™," a coffee drink called "Georgia™" and a fermented milk drink called "Lactia™."

While many foreign exporters are just discovering the Japanese consumer, The Coca-Cola Company has managed to prosper in Japan since it entered the market four decades ago. The payback for Coca-Cola is big: Japan is among the world's biggest soft-drink markets, with three trillion yen ($25.77 billion) in annual sales.

In introducing new products, the Company improves on competitors' product ideas. Consumer acceptance of The Coca-Cola Company's new products has been facilitated by its vending machine network. Coca-Cola controls 870,000 of the two million drink machines that stand on nearly every street corner and train platform in Japan and has plans to add another 150,000 machines over the next two years. Vending machines have been a key strategy for Coke in Japan, allowing the company to circumvent inefficient, insufficient distribution systems.

SOURCE: Norihiko Shirouzu, "For Coca-Cola in Japan, Things Go Better with Milk," *Wall Street Journal,* January 20, 1997, pp. B1, B2. Reprinted by permission of the *Wall Street Journal,* © 1997 Dow Jones & Company, Inc. All Rights Reserved Worldwide.

*T*o continue to prosper as a corporate giant, *Coca-Cola* managers need to understand the company's customer markets and desires. Such knowledge is more difficult now than in the past because, like many other businesses, the company now operates globally and thus confronts alternative tastes and buying preferences. For instance, in Japan Coca-Cola faces a difficult consumer marketplace: approximately a thousand new soft drinks are introduced each year, but only about 10 percent still exist after a few weeks![1]

strategy

Operating globally creates two primary considerations for an organization. First, the managers must understand the factors that influence the various international business markets so that the locations in which the company has the strengths and desire to compete can be identified. Second, a company must devise a business **strategy** or long-term, dynamic plan that fulfills organizational goals and objectives through satisfaction of customer needs or wants within the company's acknowledged operating markets.

This chapter first introduces organizational strategy formulation and the managerial functions. Because of the need to plan and operate in a global business environment, market structures, trade agreements, and legal and ethical considerations are discussed. The chapter also links strategy creation and implementation to the accounting information system. Although most of the discussion in the chapter addresses strategy in terms of a large profit-seeking business, many of the concepts also apply to small businesses, governmental and not-for-profit entities.

ORGANIZATIONAL STRATEGY

mission statement

An organization should begin its strategy formulation with a **mission statement**. This statement should (1) clearly state what the organization wants to accomplish and (2) express how that organization uniquely meets its targeted customers' needs with its products and services. This statement may change over time. For example, Toro used to be a "lawn mower" company, but has refocused itself as an "outdoor environmental problem-solver." This change in focus requires Toro to become more diverse in its product lines and its customer base.[2] Bell & Howell was a "consumer photography" company, making 8 millimeter cameras, microfilm machines, and film projectors. Now the company defines itself as being in the information-management and mail-processing businesses, making scanners and machines for the U.S. Postal Service.[3]

Strategy formulation is the foundation of organizational planning and links an organization's mission to actual activities. Strategy can be defined as follows:

http:// www.toro.com

http:// www.bhauto.com

---

[1] Norihiko Shirouzu, "For Coca-Cola in Japan, Things Go Better with Milk," *Wall Street Journal*, January 20, 1997, pp. B1.

[2] Richard Gibson, "Toro Charges into Greener Fields with New Products," *Wall Street Journal*, July 22, 1997, p. B4.

[3] Carl Quintanilla, "Bell & Howell Is Seeing Its New Image More Clearly," *Wall Street Journal*, May 28, 1997, p. B4.

Strategy is the art of creating value. It provides the intellectual frameworks, conceptual models, and governing ideas that allow a company's managers to identify opportunities for bringing value to customers and for delivering value at a profit. In this respect, strategy is the way a company defines its business and links together the only two resources that really matter in to-day's economy: knowledge and relationships or an organization's competencies and its customers.[4]

An organization's strategy tries to match its internal skills and resources to the opportunities found in the external environment.[5] Although small organizations may have a single strategy, larger organizations often have an overall entity strategy as well as individual strategies for each business unit (such as a division). The business units' strategies should flow from the overall strategy to ensure that effective and efficient resource allocations are made, an overriding corporate culture is developed, and organizational direction is enhanced. Exhibit 1-1 provides a checklist of questions that help indicate whether an organization has a comprehensive strategy in place. Smaller businesses may need to substitute "product lines" for "business segments" in answering the questions.

EXHIBIT 1-1
Does Your Organization Have a Good Strategy?

1. Who are your five most important competitors?
2. Is your firm more or less profitable than these firms?
3. Do you generally have higher or lower prices than these firms for equivalent product/service offerings? Is this difference due mainly to the mix of customers, to different costs, or to different requirements for profit?
4. Do you have higher or lower relative costs than your main competitors? Where in the cost structure (for example, cost of raw materials, cost of product, cost of selling, cost of distributing, cost of advertising and marketing) are the differences most pronounced?
5. What are the different business segments that account for 80 percent of your profits? [You will probably find that you are in many more segments than you thought, and that their profit variability is much greater.] If you cannot define the segments that constitute 80 percent of your total profits, you need to conduct a detailed product line profitability review.
6. In each of the business segments defined above, how large are you relative to the largest of your competitors? Are you gaining or losing relative market share?
7. In each of your important business segments, what are your customers' and potential customers' most important purchase criteria?
8. How do you and your main competitors in each segment rate on these market purchase criteria?
9. What are the main strengths of the company as a whole, based on aggregating customers' views of your firm in the segments that comprise most of your profits? What other competencies do you believe the firm has, and why do they seem to be not appreciated by the market?
10. Which are your priority segments; where is it most important to the firm as a whole that you gain market share? How confident are you that you will achieve this, given that other firms may have targeted the same segments for share gain? What is your competitive advantage in these segments and how sure are you that this advantage is real rather than imagined? (If you are not gaining relative market share, the advantage is probably illusory.)

SOURCE: Richard Koch, *The Financial Times Guide to Management and Finance* (London: Financial Times/Pitman Publishing, 1994), p. 359.

---

[4] Richard Normann and Rafael Ramirez, "From Value Chain to Value Constellation: Designing Interactive Strategy," *Harvard Business Review* (July–August 1993), p. 65.

[5] Thomas S. Bateman and Scott A. Snell, *Management: Building Competitive Advantage* (Chicago: Irwin, 1996), p. 117.

INFLUENCES ON ORGANIZATIONAL STRATEGY

LEARNING OBJECTIVE ❶
What are the primary factors and constraints that influence an organization's strategy and why are these factors important?

Each organization is unique and, therefore, even organizations in the same industries have unique strategies that are feasible and likely to be successful. Exhibit 1-2 provides a model of the major factors that influence an organization's strategy. These factors include organizational structure, core competencies, organizational constraints, management style and organizational culture, and environmental constraints.

Organizational Structure

goal

objective

http:// www.cocacola.com

An organization is composed of people, resources, and commitments that are acquired and arranged to achieve specified goals and objectives. **Goals** are desired results expressed in qualitative terms. For example, in profit-oriented firms, one typical goal is to maximize shareholder wealth. Goals are also likely to be formulated for other major stakeholders such as customers, employees, and suppliers. In contrast, **objectives** are quantitatively expressed results that can be achieved during a preestablished period or by a specified date. Objectives should logically measure progress in achieving goals. For example, Coca-Cola had a goal of being *the* soft-drink sponsor of the 1996 Summer Olympic Games and reportedly spent $40 million for that right. The objective following from that goal was to emphasize the drink's "universal appeal" and, thus, the company had daily themes for each of the seventeen days. Coca-Cola developed 100 different commercials to fit the daily themes and paid approximately $62 million for television advertising time during the Games' telecast.[6]

organizational structure

authority
responsibility

The **organizational structure** reflects the way in which authority and responsibility for making decisions is distributed in an organization. The right—usually by virtue of position or rank—to use resources to accomplish a task or achieve an objective is called **authority**. The obligation to accomplish a task or achieve an objective is called **responsibility**. The organizational structure normally evolves from its mission, goals, and managerial personalities.

EXHIBIT 1-2
Factors Influencing Organizational Strategy

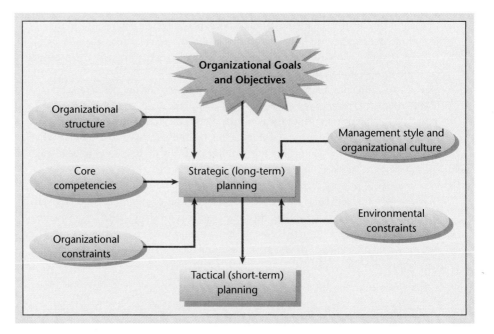

[6] Associated Press, "100 Different Ads, Most Running Only Once, Is Coke's Plan," *New Orleans Times-Picayune*, July 16, 1996, p. C2.

Line workers who oversee highly complex automated machinery generally have the greatest knowledge of how to solve problems or increase productivity of their equipment. Empowerment allows those individuals to exercise that knowledge to the company's benefit.

A continuum of feasible structures reflect the extent of authority and responsibility of managers and employees. At one end of the continuum is **centralization**, in which all authority for making decisions is retained by top management. Centralized firms often have difficulty diversifying operations because top management might lack the necessary and critical industry-specific knowledge. If higher-level management insists on maintaining all authority, then the people who deal directly with the issues (whether problems or opportunities), who have the most relevant information and who can best foresee the consequences, are not making the decisions.

centralization

At the other end of the continuum is **decentralization**, in which the authority for making decisions is distributed to various personnel, including lower-level managers and, possibly, line employees. In today's fast-changing and competitive operating environment, implementation of a decentralized organizational structure in a large firm is almost imperative and typically cost-beneficial. However, for decentralization to work effectively, there must be employee **empowerment**, which means that people are given the authority and responsibility to make their own decisions about their work. A decision to decentralize is also a decision to use responsibility accounting, as is discussed in Chapter 14.

decentralization

empowerment

Most organizations operate at some point on the continuum rather than at either end. Thus, a decision about where a new division will be located might be made by top management; when the new division is completed, the division manager might be empowered to make ongoing operating decisions. Long-term strategic decisions about the division might be made by the division manager in conjunction with top management.

Core Competencies

A second factor affecting feasible strategy is the organization's core competencies. A **core competency** is any critical function or activity in which one organization has a higher proficiency than its competitors. Core competencies are the roots of competitiveness and competitive advantage. "Core competencies are different for every organization; they are, so to speak, part of an organization's personality."[7] Technological innovation, engineering, product development, and after-sale service are some examples of core competencies. For instance, the Japanese electronics industry is viewed as having a core competency in miniaturization of electronics. MCI and Disney believe they have core competencies, respectively, in communications and

LEARNING OBJECTIVE ❷
Why does an organization need to understand its core competencies before considering outsourcing?

core competency

 www.mci.com

 www.disney.com

---

[7] Peter F. Drucker, "The Information Executives Truly Need," *Harvard Business Review* (January–February 1995), p. 60.

outsourcing

entertainment. However, management must realize that "knowing a little about a lot is not a core competency. Nobody should forget CBS's bid to become an 'entertainment' company in the 1960s and 1970s by getting into everything from toys and hi-fi shops to sports teams and pianos. All are long gone."[8]

When an organization does something better or less expensively than its competitors, it has a foundation for market success. Managers attempt to develop strategies that exploit the organization's core competencies. In doing so, firms have begun outsourcing activities that are not viewed as core competencies. **Outsourcing** means contracting with outside manufacturers or vendors for necessary goods or services rather than producing the goods or performing the services in-house.

In making outsourcing decisions, a company should first define its primary reasons for outsourcing, as indicated in Exhibit 1-3. By outsourcing non-core competencies, a company can further develop its core competencies and devote additional resources to those skills or expertise that represent potential sources of competitive advantage.

A company may develop partnerships, engage in joint ventures, form strategic alliances, or merge with another company with the intention of linking the core competencies of the two organizations. For example, in mid-1997, American Express Co. contracted with the U.S. Postal Service to process customer bill payments. The Postal Service is an obvious contract vendor because of its monopoly on first-class mail delivery—the manner in which over 90 percent of bills are paid.[9]

Although companies may gain the best knowledge, experience, and methodology available in a process through outsourcing, they also lose some degree of control. Thus, company management should carefully evaluate the activities to be outsourced. The pyramid shown in Exhibit 1-4 is one model for assessing outsourcing risk. Factors to consider include whether (1) a function is considered critical to the organization's long-term viability (such as product research and development); (2) the organization is pursuing a core competency relative to this function; or (3) issues such as product/service quality, time of delivery, flexibility of use, or reliability of supply cannot be resolved to the company's satisfaction. Analysis of outsourcing decisions is discussed in Chapter 13.

Organizational Constraints

A variety of organizational constraints may affect a firm's strategy options. In almost all instances, these hindrances are short term because they can be overcome by existing business opportunities. Three common organizational constraints involve monetary capital, intellectual capital, and technology. Decisions to minimize or eliminate

EXHIBIT 1-3
Top Ten Reasons to Outsource

> 1. Improve company focus.
> 2. Gain access to world-class capabilities.
> 3. Accelerate the benefits of reengineering.
> 4. Share risks.
> 5. Free non-capital resources.
> 6. Make capital funds available.
> 7. Reduce operating costs.
> 8. Obtain cash infusion.
> 9. Obtain resources not available internally.
> 10. Eliminate a function that is difficult to manage.
>
> SOURCE: Composite of the Outsourcing Institute survey of 1,200 companies, member experiences, and published research; reported in "Outsourcing: Redefining the Corporation of the Future." From a paid advertising section prepared for *Fortune* magazine's December 12, 1994 issue.

---

[8] "Multimedia's No-Man's Land," *Economist* (July 22, 1995), p. 58.

[9] "Postal Service Seeks Business of Processing Bills for Corporations," *Wall Street Journal*, June 11, 1997, p. A8.

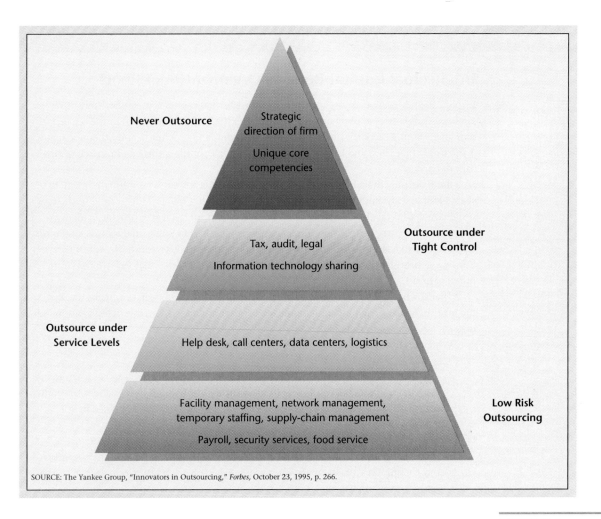

Never Outsource — Strategic direction of firm / Unique core competencies

Outsource under Tight Control — Tax, audit, legal / Information technology sharing

Outsource under Service Levels — Help desk, call centers, data centers, logistics

Low Risk Outsourcing — Facility management, network management, temporary staffing, supply-chain management / Payroll, security services, food service

SOURCE: The Yankee Group, "Innovators in Outsourcing," *Forbes*, October 23, 1995, p. 266.

EXHIBIT 1-4
Outsourcing Risk Pyramid

each of these constraints can be analyzed using capital budgeting analysis, covered in Chapter 8.

Strategy implementation generally requires a monetary investment, and all organizations are constrained by the level and cost of available capital. Although companies can almost always acquire additional capital through borrowings or equity sales, management should decide whether (1) the capital can be obtained at a reasonable cost or (2) reallocation of current capital would be more effective and efficient.

Another potentially significant constraint on organizational strategy is the level of the firm's **intellectual capital**, or "the intangible assets of skill, knowledge, and information."[10] Intellectual capital encompasses human and structural capital. Human capital is reflected in the knowledge and creativity of an organization's personnel and is a source of strategic innovation and renewal. Human capital provides the foundation for improvement opportunities that may, at least until adopted by others, provide the company a core competency. Without human capital, there would be few start-up companies with new products or services.

Structural capital, such as information systems, knowledge of market channels and customer relationships, and management focus, allows human capital to be utilized. In some respects, structural capital is more important: "It doesn't go home at night or quit and hire on with a rival; it puts new ideas to work; and it can be used again and again to create value, just as a die can stamp out part after part."[11] The following News Note describes the concept of intellectual capital and its components.

intellectual capital

---

[10] Thomas A. Stewart, "Your Company's Most Valuable Asset: Intellectual Capital," *Fortune*, October 3, 1994, p. 68.

[11] Ibid., pp. 71–72.

NEWS NOTE

Intellectual Capital Reflects Organizational Roots

Perhaps the best way to appreciate the role of intellectual capital is metaphorically. If we picture a company as a living organism, say a tree, then what is described in the organization charts, annual reports, quarterly statements, company brochures, and other documents is the trunk, branches, and leaves. The smart investor scrutinizes this tree in search of ripe fruit to harvest.

But to assume that this is the entire tree because it represents everything immediately visible is obviously a mistake. Half the mass or more of that tree is underground in the root system. And whereas the flavor of the fruit and the color of the leaves provide evidence of how healthy the tree is right now, understanding what is going on in the roots is a far more effective way to learn how healthy that tree will be in the years to come. The rot or parasite just now appearing thirty feet underground may well kill that tree that today looks in the prime of health.

That is what makes intellectual capital—the study of the roots of a company's value, the measurement of the hidden dynamic factors that underlie the visible company of buildings and products—so valuable.

http:// www.skandia.com

What are these factors? According to the Swedish company Skandia, these factors typically take two forms:

⊙ Human capital. The combined knowledge, skill, innovativeness, and ability of the company's individual employees to meet the task at hand. It also includes the company's values, culture, and philosophy. Human capital cannot be owned by the company.

⊙ Structural capital. The hardware, software, databases, organizational structure, patents, trademarks, and everything else of organizational capability that supports those employees' productivity—in a word, everything left at the office when the employees go home. Structural capital also includes customer capital, the relationships developed with key customers. Unlike human capital, structural capital can be owned and thereby traded.

SOURCE: Leif Edvinsson and Michael S. Malone, *Intellectual Capital* (New York: HarperBusiness, 1997), pp. 10–11.

Examples of the use of intellectual capital to promote core competencies and affect strategy include creating new pharmaceuticals through biotechnology developments, using the Internet to offer products and services electronically, and using automatic teller machine technology to produce machines that dispense tickets to sporting events. Companies lacking in intellectual capital find shifts in strategy difficult to pursue and will eventually cease to exist. As shown in Exhibit 1-5, even small businesses are aware of the need to make investments in intellectual capital to remain competitive and are doing so.

EXHIBIT 1-5
Intellectual Capital Investments

| | NUMBER OF EMPLOYEES | | |
TYPES OF IMPROVEMENTS BEING INVESTED IN	0–19	20–99	100–499
Developed new products/services	31%	44%	54%
Improved productivity	26%	54%	70%
Improved quality of products/services	26%	46%	51%
Increased investment in business	19%	50%	54%

SOURCE: Reprinted with permission of *Inc.* magazine, Goldhirsh Group, Inc., 38 Commercial Wharf, Boston, MA 02110. "What Improvements Companies Are Investing In," 1996, No. 1, p. 20 (http://www.inc.com). Reproduced by permission of the publisher via Copyright Clearance Center, Inc.

A third possible organizational constraint is a lack of technology, which explains why many current strategic decisions involve technology acquisition. When one company develops certain technology, that company's competitors seek to obtain, use, and possibly increase the value of that technology to minimize the development's long-run competitive advantage. "One of the most consistent patterns in business is the failure of leading companies to stay at the top of their industries when technologies or markets change."[12] Acquiring new technology is one way to create new strategic opportunities by allowing a company to do things better or faster—assuming the company has trained its human resources in the use of that technology. Exhibit 1-6 indicates how 150 senior executives are using information technology in their *Fortune 1000* companies.

Management Style and Organizational Culture

Going global, implementing employee empowerment, and investing in new forms of capital are all decisions that require organizational change. An organization's ability to change depends heavily on its management style and organizational culture. An organization's **management style** reflects the preferences of managers in how they interact with the entity's stakeholders. Management style is exhibited in organizational structure, decision-making processes, interpersonal and interorganizational relationships, resource allocations, level of risk adversity, pricing practices, organizational financing, and technology availability. Given the success of Japanese businesses, many Western managers are attempting to adopt or replicate some of the more distinctive Japanese management styles including empowering employees, engaging in supplier alliances, and seeking customer input for product/service improvements. Many managers are also becoming adept at forming and utilizing work teams, rather than relying on the traditional individual workers or work groups in the organization. Exhibit 1-7 (page 12) differentiates between the traditional view of a "group" with the current view of a "team." Adoption of new management styles will affect how products are made or services are performed, such as the use of just-in-time inventory, covered in Chapter 11; how information is communicated to employees, such as the utilization of open-book management techniques as discussed in Chapter 13; and how employee performance is measured and rewarded, covered in Chapter 15.

management style

USE	PERCENT RESPONDING "TO A VERY GREAT EXTENT"
Transaction processing tool	77%
Gain competitive edge	58%
As part of products/services	50%
Knowledge creation	48%
Creation of new products/services	33%
Worldwide communication tool	29%

Note: Ninety-two percent of the respondents cited information technology as the "key enabler" to essential changes in business operations. Efficiencies from information technology permitted 93 percent of the executives to deploy resources into other areas of their businesses.

SOURCE: Deloitte & Touche LLP, "Using Information Technology to Gain a Competitive Edge," *Deloitte & Touche Review* (May 13, 1996), p. 3.

EXHIBIT 1-6
Uses for Information Technology

[12] Joseph L. Bower and Clayton M. Christensen, "Disruptive Technologies: Catching the Wave," *Harvard Business Review* (January–February 1995), p. 43.

EXHIBIT 1-7
Differentiating between Groups
and Teams

WORK GROUP	TEAM
⊙ Strong, clearly focused leader	⊙ Shared leadership roles
⊙ Individual accountability	⊙ Individual and mutual accountability
⊙ Group's purpose is same as the broader organizational mission	⊙ Specific team purpose that the team itself delivers
⊙ Individual work-products	⊙ Collective work-products
⊙ Runs efficient meetings	⊙ Encourages open-ended discussion
⊙ Measures its effectiveness indirectly by its influence on others (e.g., financial performance of the business)	⊙ Measures performance directly by assessing collective work-products
⊙ Discusses, decides, and delegates	⊙ Discusses, decides, and does real work together

SOURCE: Reprinted by permission of *Harvard Business Review*. An excerpt from "The Discipline of Teams" by Jon R. Katzenbach and Douglas K. Smith, March–April 1993. Copyright © 1993 by the President and Fellows of Harvard College; all rights reserved.

organizational culture

Organizational culture is the set of basic assumptions about the organization, its goals, and its business practices. Culture describes an organization's norms in internal and external, as well as formal and informal, transactions.

> Culture refers to the values, beliefs, and attitudes that permeate a business. If strategy defines where a company wants to go, culture determines how— maybe whether—it gets there. Every business has some kind of culture, just because it's an organization of human beings. But most businesses never give the topic a second thought. Their culture is to do things the way they always have or the way everybody else does them.
>
> A few companies, by contrast, have explicit, highly distinctive cultures—strong, focused cultures that stick out from the crowd like the Grateful Dead at a marching-band convention. [For example, Southwest Airlines is] famous for its wild and woolly—not to say manic—culture. Everybody at Southwest, from CEO Herb Kelleher to the newest gate attendant, pitches in to make sure that customers have a good time and that airplanes get unloaded and reloaded and back in the air fast.[13]

http:// www.southwest.com

Management style and organizational culture are heavily influenced by the culture of the nation in which the organization is domiciled, extent of diversity in the

The workplace is not the only location to observe organizational culture. Getting employees together to provide a service to their community goes a long way toward solidifying a team culture and spirit.

workforce, and personal experiences and philosophies of the top management team. These variables have a significant role in determining whether the communication system tends to be formal or informal, whether authority is likely to be centralized or decentralized, whether relations with employees tend to be antagonistic or cooperative, and how control systems are designed and used. Like many of the other influences on organizational strategy, management style and organizational culture can be changed over time. In most cases, however, these variables are more likely to change because a company obtains new management than because existing management changes its ways of managing.

Environmental Constraints

A final factor affecting strategy is the environment in which the organization operates. An **environmental constraint** is any limitation on strategy caused by external cultural, fiscal (such as taxation structures), legal/regulatory, or political situations and by competitive market structures. Because environmental constraints cannot be directly controlled by an organization's management, these factors tend to be long-run rather than short-run. Managerial actions and organizational culture influence the firm and may work to affect the operating environment through numerous activities, including attempts to change laws.

> **environmental constraint**

The food industry provides many excellent examples of the influence of culture as one environmental constraint on organizational strategy. Many companies have recognized that culture may affect strategy because products and services that sell well in one locale may not be appropriate in another locale. For instance, Coca-Cola has not attempted to sell its fermented milk drink in the United States and, though sales of pigs' feet, oxtails, and pork ears may be popular staples in many Hispanic, Haitian, and Jamaican diets, these items are not available at most local grocery stores.

Market Structures

The market structure in which an organization operates can have a large impact on organizational strategy as well as on cost control (Chapters 11–13), cost–volume–profit analysis (Chapter 6), and budgeting (Chapter 7). The four primary market structures are pure competition, monopolistic competition, monopoly, and oligopoly.

> **LEARNING OBJECTIVE ❸**
> How does an organization's competitive environment impact its strategy and how might an organization respond to competition?

In **pure competition**, many firms exist, each having a small market share and all making identical products or performing identical services. Prices are set by the interaction of market demand for, and supply of, the product/service, rather than by any individual firm. Rarely will any firm be able to achieve and sustain a major market share; thus, strategically, maintenance of market share is a reasonable goal.

> **pure competition**

When many firms offer slightly differentiated products or services, there is **monopolistic competition**. Product differentiation is crucial, and advertising is used to create brand loyalty and consumer recognition. In such an environment, a firm's strategy is to build additional market share and to have purchasers pay a premium price for its products.

> **monopolistic competition**

A **monopoly** exists when there is only one seller of a product or provider of a service. The monopolistic firm has total control over its products, setting both market price and output level to maximize its profit. In the United States, federal antitrust laws restrict most monopolies; those that are allowed to exist are regulated and their prices are controlled (to some extent) by various levels of government. Other countries have been progressing rapidly in their establishment of antitrust laws; for instance, Korea recently enacted a Monopoly Regulation and Fair Trade Act. However, the specificity and administration of these laws differ dramatically among countries.

> **monopoly**

In an **oligopoly**, only a few firms exist whose products/services may be differentiated or standardized. If the goods can be differentiated (such as soft drinks or airline flights), large sums of money are spent on advertising and product development to build market share. Prices tend to be rigid, and price leadership is typical. Price decreases announced by one prominent firm are typically matched almost immediately by other members of the industry. For instance, in February 1998, a news article

> **oligopoly**

announcing a $199 maximum fare roundtrip to anywhere Southwest Airlines flew ended with, "Last time Southwest did this sale, other airlines flying the same routes matched the rates—at least briefly."[14] Occasionally, price increases are not followed, and the announcing firm is forced to return prices to previous levels to maintain market share.

Responses to Competition

Assuming that an organization operates in a competitive market structure, management may choose to avoid competition through compression of competitive scope, differentiation, or cost leadership.[15] A company deciding to compress its competitive scope focuses on a specific market segment to the exclusion of others. Many companies producing or selling luxury goods (such as Rolex watches and Concorde airline tickets) adopt this strategy. The same approach has, however, been adopted by some nonluxury entities, such as Chuck E. Cheese pizza restaurants.

 www.chuckecheese.com

differentiation

A company choosing a **differentiation** strategy distinguishes its product or service from that of competitors by adding enough value (including quality and/or features) that customers are willing to pay a higher price. Differentiation can be "based on the product itself, the delivery system by which it is sold, the marketing approach, or other factors."[16] The following News Note illustrates a slightly different version of differentiation strategy: including substantially fewer features and charging high prices.

cost leadership

Competition may also be avoided by establishing a position of **cost leadership**, that is by becoming the low-cost producer/provider and, therefore, being able to charge low prices that emphasize cost efficiencies. In this strategy, competitors cannot compete on price and must differentiate their products/services from the cost leader.

In the current business environment, maintaining a competitive advantage by avoiding competition is often difficult. Within a short time, competitors are generally able to duplicate the competencies that originally provided the competitive advantage. For many companies, the future key to success may be to confront competition by identifying and exploiting temporary opportunities for advantage. In a **confrontation strategy**, an organization tries to differentiate its products/services by introducing new features or tries to develop a price leadership position by dropping

confrontation strategy

NEWS NOTE

Less Costs More??

http:// www.meridian.com

For $675 a night, guests at the Meridian Club, on a private island in the Caribbean, get a room with no television, no radio, no telephone and no air conditioning —"almost like a motel room," says JoAnn Setzer, of Sacramento, Calif.

Call it downscale deluxe, and call it trendy. Ms. Setzer isn't complaining; she visits Meridian every year. And many well-heeled tourists apparently have similar tastes: These days, some of the most sought-after resorts are those that charge a whole lot but offer next to nothing in the way of amenities and nothing at all when it comes to technological innovations.

Deliberately distancing themselves from the far more numerous luxury hotels that boast every possible creature comfort and convenience, these spartan resorts proudly specialize in the experience of . . . *nada.*

Such resorts insist that simplicity is part of an industrywide trend in travel. But travel-industry consultants warn that the tactic is risky. The demand for less-is-more luxury is small, they say, and suited for only a few, mostly older resorts rather than a chain.

SOURCE: Lisa Miller, "Stifling Heat, No Room Service . . . and Sky-High Prices," *Wall Street Journal,* June 27, 1997, p. B1. Reprinted by permission of *Wall Street Journal,* © 1997 Dow Jones & Company, Inc. All Rights Reserved Worldwide.

---

[14] "$199 Airfare," *New Orleans Times-Picayune,* February 1, 1998, p. D1.

[15] Michael Porter, *Competitive Advantage: Creating and Sustaining Superior Performance* (New York: Free Press, 1985), p. 17.

[16] Richard J. Palmer, "Strategic Goals and Objectives and the Design of Strategic Management Accounting Systems," *Advances in Management Accounting* (Vol. 1, 1992), p. 187.

prices even though that organization knows that its competitors will rapidly bring out equivalent products and match price changes.[17] Although potentially necessary, a confrontation strategy is, by its very nature, less profitable for companies than differentiation or cost leadership.

To assess all of the internal and external factors that affect strategic planning, an organization needs to have a well-designed **business intelligence (BI) system**. This system represents the "formal process for gathering and analyzing information and producing intelligence to meet decision making needs."[18] A BI system requires knowledge of markets, technologies, and competitors, as shown in Exhibit 1-8. In addition to the need for information about external influences, the BI system should provide management with comprehensive information about internal functions and processes, including organizational strengths and constraints.[19] Information provided by this system will be of significant importance in helping managers perform their organizational functions, especially strategic and tactical planning.

business intelligence (BI) system

MANAGEMENT FUNCTIONS

Managers have multiple organizational functions, three of which are planning, controlling, and decision making. Translating the organization's mission and vision into the specific activities and resources needed for achievement is called **planning**. **Strategic planning** is generally performed by top-level management and provides plans (usually for five years or more) that state long-range organizational goals and related strategies and policies to achieve those goals.

Managers engaging in strategic planning should identify **key variables**, which are the factors believed to be direct causes of the achievement or failure to achieve organizational goals and objectives. Key variables can be internal and under management's control, such as high product quality. External key variables, such as the ability to operate in a free market, are normally noncontrollable.

LEARNING OBJECTIVE ❹
How do the management functions affect strategic and tactical planning?

planning
strategic planning
key variable

EXHIBIT 1-8
Levels of Intelligence Gathering

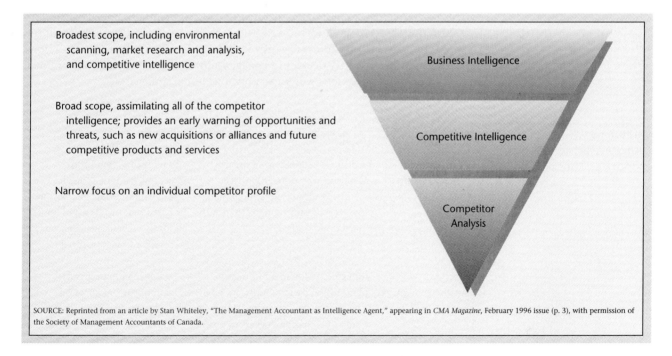

Broadest scope, including environmental scanning, market research and analysis, and competitive intelligence

Broad scope, assimilating all of the competitor intelligence; provides an early warning of opportunities and threats, such as new acquisitions or alliances and future competitive products and services

Narrow focus on an individual competitor profile

Business Intelligence

Competitive Intelligence

Competitor Analysis

SOURCE: Reprinted from an article by Stan Whiteley, "The Management Accountant as Intelligence Agent," appearing in *CMA Magazine*, February 1996 issue (p. 3), with permission of the Society of Management Accountants of Canada.

---

[17] Robin Cooper, *When Lean Enterprises Collide* (Boston: Harvard Business School Press, 1995), p. 11.

[18] "U.S. Companies Slow to Develop Business Intelligence," *Deloitte & Touche Review* (October 16, 1995), p. 1.

[19] For more information, see the Society of Management Accountants of Canada's *Management Accounting Guideline 39: Developing Comprehensive Competitor Intelligence*.

http:// www.enron.com

After the key variables are identified, information related to them can be gathered and appropriate assumptions made. Although much of the information will be historical, the assumptions must focus on a vision for the future and on the *next* opportunity for competitive advantage. For instance, Enron is a natural gas company that was instrumental in pushing for the deregulation of the industry. The company, by buying gas where it was cheap and shipping it to where it was needed, reduced "the cost of gas for some utilities by 30 percent to 50 percent."[20] This single company became an inspiration for an entire industry.

tactical planning

Tactical planning is based on the organization's strategic goals and objectives and results in detailed plans for the upcoming one to eighteen months. These plans are used by managers as one means to control and evaluate performance. Exhibit 1-9 illustrates the relationship between tactical and strategic planning.

controlling

Exerting managerial influence on operations so that they will conform to plans is **controlling**. Control cannot be exercised unless planning has occurred: there must be something against which to compare actual results. If actual results differ significantly from those expected, adjustments to operating activities may be needed. The best performance maximizes both **effectiveness**—successfully accomplishing a task— and **efficiency**—performing a task to produce the best outcome at the lowest cost from the resources used.

effectiveness
efficiency

decision making

An individual's ability to manage depends on good **decision making**—using information to choose the best alternative from the options available to reach a particular goal or objective:

> In today's corporations, oceans of data drown most decision makers. Eliminating irrelevant information requires the knowledge of what is relevant, the knowledge of how to access and select appropriate data, and the knowledge of how best to prepare the data by sorting and summarizing it to facilitate analysis. This is the raw material of decision making.[21]

The quantity of information needed by managers is related both to the decision's expected consequences and to the complexity of organizational activities. More important decisions and more complex activities require more information. Operating in a single localized environment (either because of contentment or financial constraints) is a fairly simple activity. However, a decision to expand operations to different sections of the same country forces the organization to face alternative cultures, habits, and tastes. When an entity decides to engage in international competition, numerous additional considerations will impact organizational strategy.

EXHIBIT 1-9
Relationship between Tactical and Strategic Planning

WHO?	WHAT?	HOW?	WHY?
Top and middle management	Tactical planning	Statement of organizational objectives and operational plans; short range (18 months or less)	Provide direction for the achievement of strategic plans; state strategic plans in terms that can be acted on; furnish a basis against which results can be measured
Top management	Strategic planning	Statement of organizational mission, goals, and strategies; long range (5 years or more)	Establish a long-range vision of the organization and provide a sense of unity and commitment to specified purposes

---

[20] Brian O'Reilly, "The Secrets of America's Most Admired Corporations: New Ideas/New Products," *Fortune,* March 3, 1997, p. 62.

[21] Edward G. Mahler, "Perform as Smart as You Are," *Financial Executive* (July–August 1991), p. 18.

THE GLOBAL ENVIRONMENT OF BUSINESS

Most of today's businesses participate in, or face competition from, the **global economy**, which encompasses the international trade of goods and services, movement of labor, and flows of capital and information.[22] The world has essentially become smaller through improved modes of communication and transportation as well as trade agreements that promote, rather than hinder, the international movement of goods and services among countries. Exhibit 1-10 indicates the results of a survey of *Fortune 1000* executives about the primary factors that encourage the globalization of business.

LEARNING OBJECTIVE ⑤
What factors have influenced the globalization of businesses and why have these factors been significant?

global economy

Trade Agreements

To encourage a global economy, government and business leaders around the world have made economic integration a paramount concern. **Economic integration** refers to creating "multicountry markets" through the development of transnational rules that reduce the fiscal and physical barriers to trade and thereby encourage greater economic cooperation among countries. Most economic integration occurs through the institution of trade agreements. Many of these agreements encompass a limited number of countries in close geographic proximity, but the General Agreement on Tariffs and Trade (GATT) involves over a hundred nations worldwide. Reductions in trade barriers mean that consumers have the freedom to choose from a significantly larger selection of goods than previously. Exhibit 1-11 (page 18) discusses some of the more well-known trade agreements.

economic integration

A new trade agreement may be on the horizon. Politicians and other policy makers are discussing the concept of TAFTA, or Transatlantic Free Trade Area. The TAFTA would consist of the members of NAFTZ, the EU, and some post-Communist countries. One primary reason behind the TAFTA "is that trade barriers are preventing the post-Communist countries from getting their exports accepted in the West."[23]

Trade agreements have created access to more markets with vast numbers of new customers, new vendor sources for materials and labor, and opportunities for new production operations. In turn, competitive pressures from the need to meet or beat prices and quality of international competitors force organizations to focus on cost control, quality improvements, rapid time-to-market, and dedicated customer service. As companies become more globally competitive, consumers' choices are often

FACTOR	PERCENT INDICATING FACTOR AS PRIMARY IN GLOBALIZATION TREND
Technology	43%
Competition	29%
The economy	21%
Better communications	17%
Need for new markets/growth	13%
Deregulation	11%
Access to information	9%
Legislation	7%
Easier to enter new market	5%

SOURCE: Deloitte & Touche LLP, *Survey of American Business Leaders: Information Technology* (November 1996), p. 1–11.

EXHIBIT 1-10
Factors Driving Business Globalization

[22] Paul Krugman, *Peddling Prosperity*, quoted by Alan Farnham in "Global—or Just Globaloney," *Fortune*, June 27, 1994, p. 98.

[23] Peter Brimelow, "Tafta?" *Forbes*, July 1, 1996, p. 52.

EXHIBIT 1-11
Economic Trade Agreements

- General Agreement on Tariffs and Trade (GATT)—over a hundred member countries; objective is to provide a "level playing field" for trade among the signees; uses the most-favored nation (MFN) principle; the average tariff among signees has been reduced to approximately 3 percent[24]; recent negotiations considered provisions about intellectual property, technical standards, import licenses, customs regulations, exchanges of services, and product dumping; recently established the World Trade Organization (WTO) as the arbiter of global trade and each signatory country has one vote in trade disputes
- European Union (EU)—twelve member countries (Belgium, Denmark, France, Germany, Greece, Ireland, Italy, Luxembourg, the Netherlands, Portugal, Spain, and the United Kingdom)[25]; eliminated almost all barriers to the flow of capital, labor, goods, and services among members and created the world's second largest single market (after NAFTZ); additional European market integration is likely to occur and may include countries in the former Soviet Bloc in Eastern Europe
- North American Free Trade Zone (NAFTZ)—members are Canada, Mexico, and the United States; provides for duty-free transfer of many goods but maintains some duties for up to fifteen years to protect industries sensitive to import competition (such as shoes and glassware)
- Association of Southeast Asian Nations (ASEAN)—six member countries (Brunei, Indonesia, Malaysia, the Philippines, Singapore, and Thailand); all nations have abundant natural resources (except Singapore), large international trade sectors, and liberal economic development
- Mercado Commun del Ser Mercosur (Mercosur)—four member countries (Argentina, Brazil, Paraguay, and Uruguay); may have a free trade agreement with the Economic Union by 2001
- Gulf Cooperation Council (GCC)—six member countries (Bahrain, Kuwait, Oman, Qatar, Saudi Arabia, and the United Arab Emirates); focuses on standardizing subsidies and negotiating with other regional trade organizations (such as the EU) to obtain favorable treatment

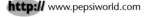 www.singapore.com

www.mercosur.com

made on the bases of price, quality, access (time of availability), and design rather than on whether the goods were made domestically or in another country.

Methods of Globalization

Organizations attempting to enter global markets need to consider how the globalization will occur. Some companies simply export their goods or services to foreign countries. Other companies engage in licensing arrangements with nondomestic companies. Still others establish plants and extensive sales infrastructures in other countries, engage in international joint-venture arrangements, or buy existing businesses that serve the desired markets. For example, in August 1996 Coca-Cola acquired 50 percent of a $400-million-a-year bottling company in Venezuela and "put Pepsi out of business there overnight."[26] In mid-1997, the company formed a joint venture with Coca-Cola Sabco and the Mozambique government in the Chimoio bottling facility. Future investment in Mozambique includes constructing a new bottling plant in Nampula and expanding the production capacity in Beira and Maputo.[27] The following News Note provides another example of joint ventures by one South Korean company.

www.pepsiworld.com

---

[24] "A Guide to GATT," *Economist* (December 4, 1993), p. 25.

[25] Turkey and Austria are also considering membership in the EU.

[26] Patricia Sellers, "How Coke Is Kicking Pepsi's Can," *Fortune*, October 28, 1996, p. 73.

[27] http://www.cocacola.com/co.news.html, "Coca-Cola Commitment to Southern Africa Extends to US $45 Million Investment In Mozambique" (July 17, 1997).

Daewoo's Diverse Investments

With wages in South Korea rising steeply and sales still low to picky buyers in quality-conscious markets such as the U.S. and the European Union, the former Soviet bloc offers Daewoo an inexpensive labor pool and a less-demanding consumer base more than 350 million strong. Eastern Europe is already Daewoo's largest car-export market. The 110,000 automobiles it sold there in 1996 were more than twice the combined sales to the U.S. and EU.

Daewoo's banner flies over a shipyard in Romania, banks in Budapest and Tashkent, Uzbekistan, automotive plants in Uzbekistan, Poland, Romania and the Czech Republic, hotels and office towers in Warsaw and Sofia, Bulgaria, electronics plants in Russia, Poland and Uzbekistan, and the list goes on. All told, the value of Daewoo's joint ventures with local governments and its wholly controlled projects in Eastern Europe and the former Soviet Union totals more than $15 billion, making the conglomerate a leading player in this part of the world.

Local officials often bend over backward to ensure that Daewoo gets favorable trade terms and ease the bureaucratic hurdles that frequently trip up investors in the former Soviet bloc. In tiny and isolated Uzbekistan, for instance, Daewoo's electronics and automotive units have spent more than $1 billion from 1992–1996, earning generous tax exemptions and protection against import tariffs levied against competitors. The preferential treatment has earned the Central Asian republic the nickname "Daewoostan."

SOURCE: Matthew Brzezinski, "Daewoo Boldly Invades Old Soviet Bloc," *Wall Street Journal*, May 7, 1997, p. A14. Reprinted by permission of *Wall Street Journal*, © 1997 Dow Jones & Company, Inc. All Rights Reserved Worldwide.

http:// www.daewoo.com

Globalization Risks

Operating in foreign markets may create some risks (see Exhibit 1-12, page 20) not found domestically. Political risks—such as the potential for expropriation or nationalization of assets—should be comprehensively evaluated prior to any global move. Others, such as cultural differences, are more subtle. In Brazil, for instance, retailers have a custom of "married sales" or buying soft drinks and beer from the same source. To compete, a local Coca-Cola bottler began manufacturing the beer that has become the market leader in São Paulo. Coca-Cola has made it clear that "being in the alcoholic-beverage business is not part of the company's global strategy," but it occurred in Brazil out of competitive necessity.[28]

Also, what might have appeared originally to be a country strength (high availability of labor) may become a difficulty. For example, Spain has approximately a 25 percent unemployment rate but extremely strict labor laws related to plant closings and layoffs in economic downturns. Suzuki Motor Corp. had severe difficulties when it wanted to close its Linares truck factory in 1994 after massive losses and determining that building a truck there cost 46 percent more than in Japan. Even after closure, workers blocked factory gates and refused to let finished trucks be shipped.[29]

http:// www.suzuki.com

Legal and Ethical Considerations

One important reality for businesses today is an ever-increasing legal and ethical responsibility. Domestic and international laws and treaties can significantly affect an organization's business strategy in matters such as how it may legally obtain new business or reduce costs or conduct operating activities. Courts are holding firms

[28] Matt Marshall, "In Brazil, Coke Sells Foam as Well as Fizz," *Wall Street Journal*, July 28, 1997, p. A12.

[29] Judith Valente and Carlta Vitzthum, "With Boom Gone Bust, Spain's Social Agenda Still Haunts Economy," *Wall Street Journal*, June 13, 1994, pp. A1, A8.

EXHIBIT 1-12
A Business Risk Framework

Strategic Risks—risks that relate to doing the wrong thing

Environmental Risks
- Natural and man-made disasters
- Political/country
- Laws and regulations
- Industry
- Competitors
- Financial markets

Organizational Risks
- Corporate Objectives and Strategies: planning; resource allocation; monitoring; mergers, acquisitions, and divestitures; joint ventures and alliances
- Leadership: vision; judgment; succession planning; tone at the top
- Management: accountability; authority; responsibility
- Corporate Governance: ethics; reputation; values; fraud and illegal acts
- Investor/Creditor Relations
- Human Resources: performance rewards; benefits; workplace environment; diversity

Operating Risks—risks that relate to doing the right things the wrong way
- Workforce: hiring; knowledge and skills; development and training; size; safety
- Suppliers: outsourcing; procurement practices; availability, price and quality of suppliers' products and services
- Physical Plant: capacity; technology/obsolescence
- Protection: physical plant and other tangible assets; knowledge and other intellectual property
- Products and Services: development; quality; pricing; cost; delivery; consumer protection; technology/obsolescence
- Customers: needs; satisfaction; credit
- Regulatory Compliance: employment; products and services; environmental; antitrust law

Financial Risks—risks that relate to losing financial resources or incurring unacceptable liabilities
- Capital/Financing: availability; interest rates; creditworthiness
- Investing: cash availability; securities; receivables; inventories; derivatives
- Regulatory Compliance: securities law; taxation

Information Risks—risks that relate to inaccurate or non-relevant information, unreliable systems, and inaccurate or misleading reports
- Information Systems: reliability; sufficiency; protection; technology
- Strategic Information: relevance and accuracy of measurements; availability; assumptions
- Operating Information: relevance and accuracy of measurements; availability; regulatory reporting
- Financial Information: relevance and accuracy of measurements; accounting; budgets; taxation; financial reporting; regulatory reporting

SOURCE: Deloitte & Touche LLP, *Perspectives on Risk* (New York: 1997), pp. 12, 24, 25.

responsible for not only the integrity of their financial statements but also for the integrity of their actions.

Legal Standards

Laws represent codified societal rules and change as the society changes. Globally, the fall of communism has resulted in new laws promoting for-profit businesses in the former Soviet Union countries; Japan is considering deregulating its economy by

It's important that business actions are tied to organizational strategy and supported by relevant information. Such linkages cannot eliminate, but can certainly help reduce, risk.

allowing better access to foreign competition and reducing bureaucracy;[30] and France has reached a trade agreement with Cuba.[31] These examples demonstrate how laws regarding business activities change as society changes.

Most government regulations seek to maintain a market environment that affords firms a viable business community in which to succeed. Regulatory agencies monitor various business practices to detect activities believed to be detrimental to healthy commerce. Many early business laws in the United States were concerned with regulating certain industries (such as telecommunications, utilities, airlines, and trucking) on which the public depended. As more industries in the United States are deregulated, American regulations are more concerned with issues such as fair disclosure of corporate information, product safety, and environmental protection.

Companies, especially in the food and health-related products industries, are increasingly being held accountable when their products adversely affect consumers. Similarly, manufacturing and extraction operations are particularly capable of harming the environment. One of the highest-profile environmental cases in recent years concerned an off-shore Alaskan oil spill by an Exxon tanker. Companies might even be held "liable for human rights abuses against indigenous people in foreign countries, even if the companies are not directly involved," if abuses take place near company operations.[32] Freeport-McMoRan Copper & Gold and Unocal Corp. have both been sued in the United States because of abuses allegedly committed by the military in Indonesia and Myanmar (formerly Burma), respectively.

 www.exxon.com

http:// www.fcx.com

http:// www.unocal.com

---

[30] Neil Weinberg, "First the Pain, Then the Gain," *Forbes*, May 5, 1997, p. 134.

[31] Associated Press, "Cuba, France to Trade," *New Orleans Times-Picayune*, April 15, 1997, p. A17.

[32] Stewart Yerton, "World Will Watch Lawsuits' Outcome," *New Orleans Times-Picayune*, May 11, 1997, p. F1.

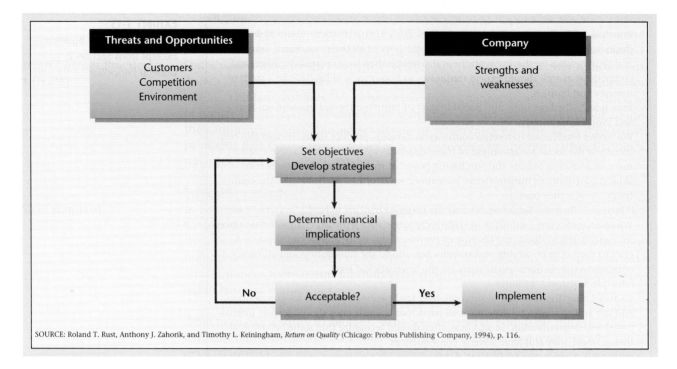

Threats and Opportunities	Company
Customers Competition Environment	Strengths and weaknesses

Set objectives
Develop strategies

Determine financial implications

No ← Acceptable? → Yes → Implement

SOURCE: Roland T. Rust, Anthony J. Zahorik, and Timothy L. Keiningham, *Return on Quality* (Chicago: Probus Publishing Company, 1994), p. 116.

EXHIBIT 1-14
The Planning Process

LEARNING OBJECTIVE 6
How does the accounting function impact an organization's ability to successfully achieve its strategic goals and objectives?

goal of profit generation so that the shareholders can obtain wealth maximization, employees can retain their jobs and increase their personal human capital, and creditors can be paid.

Because profits are a business necessity, management must consider the financial implications of its chosen strategies. Profitability is typically achieved by giving customers the products and services desired, delivered on time and at reasonable prices. Measurement of profitability is a function of the accounting information system. To best assess financial implications of organizational strategies, detailed, short-term tactical plans should be prepared in the form of a budget. If the projected financial results are unacceptable, management will make revisions to either the objectives or the strategies selected to achieve those objectives.

Although the financial accounting system is extremely important in assessing current or projected profitability, that system does not provide all the information needed by management to make decisions. "Exclusive focus on the financial results and budgets does not encourage managers to invest and build for longer-term competitive advantage."[35] Also, according to noted management author Peter Drucker:

> The standard concepts and tools of [traditional financial reporting] are inadequate to control operations because all they provide is a view of the skeleton of a business. What's needed is a way to examine the soft tissue.
>
> Financial accounting, balance sheets, profit-and-loss statements, allocations of costs, etc., are an X-ray of the enterprise's skeleton. But much as the diseases we most commonly die from—heart disease, cancer, Parkinson's—do not show in a skeletal X-ray, a loss of market standing or failure to innovate do not register in the accountant's figures until the damage is done.[36]

Organizations now have the technological capabilities to easily expand data collection activities to satisfy both external and internal information requirements. Professor Germain Böer, of Vanderbilt University, views the accounting information system as having a core set of data that satisfy financial, regulatory, and tax require-

[35] Michael Goold and John Quinn, *Strategic Control: Milestones for Long-Term Performance* (London: Economics Books Ltd/Hutchison, 1990); cited in Tony Barnes, *Kaizen Strategies for Successful Leadership* (London: Pitman Publishing, 1996), p. 135.

[36] "Drucker on Soft Tissue Metrics," *Datamation* (September 1, 1994), p. 64.

ments, surrounded by "rings of data" that allow individual managers to capture the distinct information that is relevant for their activities.[37]

Accounting information is often a primary basis for making strategic decisions and for measuring and evaluating managerial efficiency and effectiveness. To provide the correct management incentives, accounting measurements should be tied to the established mission. In large organizations, an individual segment or division may pursue one of three generic organizational missions: build, hold, and harvest, as defined in Exhibit 1-15.

Segments with a build mission require the most strategic planning because they are expected to be operated for the long run. Segments with a harvest mission require little strategic planning; their role is to generate cash and, at some point, they will probably be sold or spun off as other company segments begin to mature.

Segment mission is directly related to the **product life cycle** or the sequential stages that a product passes through from the time the idea is conceived until production of the product is discontinued. The five stages of the product life cycle are design and development, introduction, growth, maturity, and decline. The build mission is appropriate for products that are in the early stages of the product life cycle, and the harvest mission is appropriate for products in the final stages of the life cycle. Accordingly, long-term performance measures are more appropriate for build missions, and shorter-term performance measures are more appropriate for harvest missions. For example, increase in market share would be a long-term measure, whereas annual profitability would be a short-term measure.

Additionally, the measurement system will need adaptation when an organization begins to empower its employees and use work teams. Group—rather than only individual—performance will need to be assessed and often nonfinancial measures are more appropriate than dollar amounts. Accounting can help derive the new measurements, tie them to organizational goals and objectives, and integrate them with an organizational pay-for-performance plan.

The decision about the degree of decentralization to employ must reflect consideration of the following: the speed with which decisions need to be made, the willingness of upper management to allow subordinate managers to make potentially poor decisions, and the amount of training necessary to make workers understand and evaluate the consequences of their decisions. Decisions should be made only after comparing the costs of implementation, such as employee training, with the expected benefits, such as better communication, more rapid decisions, and higher levels of employee skills.

LEARNING OBJECTIVE ❼
Why is a company segment's mission affected by product life cycle?

product life cycle

- **Build**   This mission implies a goal of increased market share, even at the expense of short-term earnings and cash flow. A business unit that follows this mission is expected to be a net user of cash; that is, the cash flow from its current operations would usually be insufficient to meet its capital investment needs. Business units with "low market share" in "high growth industries" typically pursue a build mission.
- **Hold**   This mission is geared to the protection of the business unit's market share and competitive position. The cash outflows for a business unit that follows this mission generally equal the cash inflows. Businesses with "high market share" in "high growth industries" typically pursue a hold mission.
- **Harvest**   The harvest mission implies a goal of maximizing short-term earnings and cash flow, even at the expense of market share. A business unit that follows the harvest mission is a net supplier of cash. Businesses with "high market share" in "low growth industries" typically pursue a harvest mission.

SOURCE: Vijay Govindarajan and John K. Shank, "Strategic Cost Management: Tailoring Controls to Strategies." Reprinted with permission from *The Journal of Cost Management* (Fall 1992), © 1992 Warren Gorham & Lamont, 31 St. James Avenue, Boston, Mass. 02116. All rights reserved.

EXHIBIT 1-15
Generic Strategic Missions

---

[37] Germain Böer, "Management Accounting beyond the Year 2000," *Journal of Cost Management* (Winter 1996), pp. 46–47.

http:// www.lawson.com

http:// www.pwcglobal.com/ca

In evaluating core competencies, an organization must analyze its activities and compare them to internal or external benchmark measurements. Some comparison metrics will often relate to costs: how much does it cost an organization to make a product or perform a service compared to the amount for which that product or service could be acquired externally? To make fair comparisons, a company must be reasonably certain of the validity of its costs. Unfortunately, a recent survey of over two hundred financial and operating executives in North America by **Lawson Software** and **Price Waterhouse LLP** showed that less than half of the respondents "had confidence in the accuracy of the cost data available to them. . . . Operating executives in particular consistently asked for more accurate, timely, and detailed information from their systems."[38] To help overcome these defects in the accounting information system, some companies are now reporting additional information using activity-based costing (ABC). ABC (discussed in Chapter 5) traces costs more accurately to products and services than traditional costing systems do.

In assessing alternative strategies that require substantial monetary investments, such as investing in new technological capabilities or opening a production facility in a foreign country, managers compare the costs and benefits of the investment. Often, as with other strategic decisions, details about costs may be more attainable than details about benefits. Managers, with the assistance of financial personnel, must then make quantitative estimates of the qualitative benefits to be provided by new investments (for instance, being the first to bring a product or service to the market).

http:// www.mot.com

A mid-1997 strategy change by **Motorola** illustrates the nonfinancial benefits of decentralization and technology/reengineering investments. Recognizing the benefits of rapid time-to-market, Motorola divided its semiconductor sector into five groups, each with a specialized market focus to assess customers' needs and reduce product development time from three months to thirty days. Additionally, the company revamped its manufacturing processes to stress cycle time, or the speed at which products are produced. Such decisions obviously had an impact: after the announcement, Motorola's shares rose 2.1 percent on the **New York Stock Exchange**.[39]

http:// www.nyse.com

Although these changes cost money when implemented, they should provide substantial future benefits that could only be estimated before the changes were made.

From an accounting standpoint, there is frequently a mismatch in the timing of costs and benefits. Costs are recorded and recognized in the early years of many strategic decisions, whereas benefits created by these decisions are either recorded and recognized in later years or possibly not at all because they are nonmonetary in nature. For example, financial accounting does not recognize the qualitative organizational benefits of faster delivery time, customer satisfaction, and more rapid time-to-market of new products. Consequently, measurement methods other than traditional financial accounting are necessary to help managers better evaluate the strategic implications of organizational investments.

LEARNING OBJECTIVE 8
What is strategic resource management and why is it important to managers?

strategic resource management (SRM)

Strategic resource management (SRM) involves the organizational planning for deployment of resources to create value for customers and shareholders. Key attributes in the success of SRM are the management of information and change in responding to threats and opportunities. SRM is concerned with the following issues:[40]

- ⊙ how to deploy resources to support strategies;
- ⊙ how resources are used in, or recovered from, change processes;
- ⊙ how customer value and shareholder value will serve as guides to the effective use of resources; and
- ⊙ how resources are to be deployed and redeployed over time.

---

[38] Mary Lee Geishecker, "New Technologies Support ABC," *Management Accounting* (March 1996), p. 44.

[39] Quentin Hardy and Dean Takahashi, "Motorola Divides Semiconductor Sector in Five Groups to Hasten New Products," *Wall Street Journal*, May 28, 1997, p. B12.

[40] Adapted from W. P. Birkett, "Management Accounting and Knowledge Management," *Management Accounting* (November 1995), pp. 44–48.

These areas cannot be measured by financial accounting because they often relate to nonmonetary information and measurements. Thus, management accounting provides the necessary estimates to help managers address these issues and focus on strategic objectives.

The foundation of SRM is the **value chain** or the set of processes that convert inputs into products and services for the firm's customers. As shown in Exhibit 1-16, the value chain includes both internal and supplier processes. Managers can use the value chain to determine which activities create customer value as reflected in product/service prices and, thus, revenues earned. By reducing or eliminating activities that add no value within the value chain, firms can become more efficient and effective.

For their contributions to the value chain, employees earn compensation and suppliers earn revenues. Successful firms will gain the cooperation of everyone in the value chain and communicate a perspective that today's competition is between value chains more so than between individual businesses. Once this concept is accepted, members of the value chain become aware that information must be shared among all entities in the value chain.

The arrows in Exhibit 1-16 indicate information flows that provide the key linkage between managing resources and managing change in a business. Managers, as the agents of change, must understand internal organizational processes, external markets (customers), available and visionary technologies, current and future competitors, and operating environments. This knowledge helps managers to respond proactively to new market opportunities and to competitors' actions. Much of the information required by managers comes from the business intelligence system, which includes the accounting information system, discussed earlier in this chapter.

One of the most significant challenges of efficiently and effectively managing an organization is balancing the short-run and long-run demands for resources. Resources are composed of all organizational assets, including people. In the contemporary global competitive business environment, managers must be able to balance these considerations as well as recognize and prioritize strategic resource needs. In addition, managers must be careful to structure strategic initiatives to allow flexibility in day-to-day management. Stated another way, in making long-term commitments of resources, managers must consider how those commitments affect short-term management of resources. Information is the key to successfully analyzing and resolving all of these decision situations—and much of that information is provided by an organization's accounting system.

value chain

EXHIBIT 1-16
The Value Chain and Strategic Resource Management

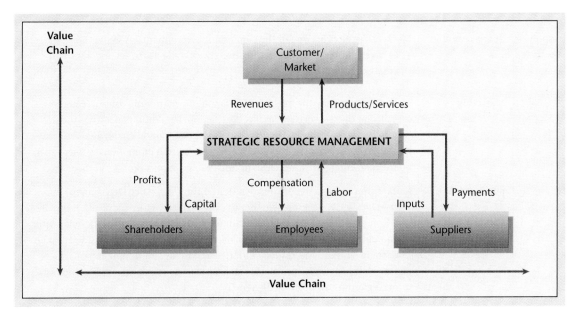

The Coca-Cola Company

The Coca-Cola Company makes mistakes, too (it will never live down New Coke). But in general, Coca-Cola devises strategies, oversees operations, and develops talent in ways virtually antithetical to PepsiCo's.

Nobody burrows as deeply into his business as Coca-Cola's president and CEO Doug Ivester. Coca-Cola's CEO started his career as an accountant at Ernst & Whinney (now Ernst & Young). Coca-Cola was Ivester's client, and the company plucked him from number-cruncher neverland in 1979. Ivester spent his first decade at Coca-Cola in the finance area, where he proved to be a wizard. His edge was the ability to analyze arcane problems, concoct clever solutions, and maximize returns on investment. "I look at business like a chessboard," says Ivester. "You always need to be seeing three, four, five moves ahead. Otherwise, your first move can prove fatal."

As CFO in 1986, Ivester devised the financial underpinnings of "the 49 percent solution." This innovative deal turned out to be the bedrock of Coca-Cola's global strategy: Coca-Cola bought a bunch of U.S. bottlers that weren't performing well and combined them with its own bottling network, calling the new outfit Coca-Cola Enterprises (CCE). Then it spun CCE off to the public but kept 49 percent of the stock and the right to throw its weight around.

Now Coca-Cola uses CCE to acquire weak bottlers, shake up their management, and increase their volume. (PepsiCo, having shunned the spin-off strategy, owns and operates most of its bottlers.) This is the real secret formula of Coca-Cola: senior management's intimate engagement in the core business.

Ivester visits some thirty overseas markets each year. He promotes what he calls "destination planning." This requires answering three questions, which Ivester asks at virtually every stop: "What's possible for your business? What are the barriers to achieving that? How can we remove the barriers?" Says Ivester: "We want to capture all the growth."

SOURCE: Patricia Sellers, "How Coke Is Kicking Pepsi's Can," *Fortune*, October 28, 1996, pp. 80, 84. © 1996 Time Inc. All rights reserved.

CROSS-FUNCTIONAL APPLICATIONS

TOPIC OF NOTE	DISCIPLINE	CROSS-FUNCTIONAL APPLICATIONS
Oligopoly, Monopoly, Pure and Monopolistic Competition, Market Structures	Microeconomics	Market structures are one of the paramount determinants of selling price. They give definition to the relative strength of the seller to set and maintain the market price of a product.
	Marketing	Market structures are the major consideration in determining control (channel captains) in the channels of product distribution. In addition, marketers use this concept to set and adjust their pricing policies. Distribution channels and pricing policies in conjunction with product specifications and promotional strategy make up the marketing mix of strategies necessary to position a product in the market.
	Business Law	Market structure is a major consideration of the U.S. Justice Department's Antitrust Division in deciding whether to invoke the Clayton Act or the Sherman Act. Competition benefits both consumers and society as a whole. A seller with the potential to dominate more than 65 percent of a market is considered to be in restraint of trade and is subject to legal action. In addition, many other federal regulatory agencies use market structures to determine the public interest prior to granting an operating license.

CROSS-FUNCTIONAL APPLICATIONS

TOPIC OF NOTE	DISCIPLINE	CROSS-FUNCTIONAL APPLICATIONS
Intellectual Capital	Financial Accounting	Generally accepted accounting principles recognize intellectual capital resources in a far more limited way than managerial accounting does. The costs are recorded upon acquisition, and the benefits to the organization are amortized over the useful life of the intellectual resource. However, the potential of intellectual capital is not recognized in financial statements because of the opportunity this would present for exaggerating a firm's future position.
	Business Law	Intellectual capital as a product has raised serious legal questions related to both equity and anticompetitive practices. Microsoft currently faces a legal challenge regarding whether its Windows software is part of a plan to dominate most of the software market.
	Marketing	Intellectual capital as a product suffers more heavily than any other product category from pirating—the practice of reproducing intellectual property without paying the associated research and development costs or royalties. The intangible nature of intellectual capital makes it very difficult to regulate.
Centralization, Decentralization	Transportation and Logistics Management	These concepts are used in management to describe not only the distribution of authority and responsibility throughout the organization but also the proximity of the distribution system to the customer. Decentralized distribution is most proximate to the customer and often more expensive than a centralized system, due to the economies of scale inherent in centralized processes.
	Financial Accounting	A major concern for the design of a general ledger accounting system is whether to centralize the process at a home office and have the various branches report data there, or decentralize the process in branch offices and integrate it through a common database. Decentralization often brings the branch manager closer to the information needed to make tactical decisions.
	Economics	Centralization or decentralization of the factors of production always implies a shift in the economies of scale. Centralization will increase the economies of scale, spreading the committed fixed cost over a greater number of units and thus lowering the unit cost. This spreading of fixed costs will reach a limit as centralization increases, and inefficiency caused by too many units will create diseconomies of scale.

CHAPTER SUMMARY

Strategy should be based on a mission that indicates what the organization wants to accomplish. Goals and objectives should flow from that statement. Strategy options may be constrained by internal or external factors. Organizational structure indicates the distribution of authority and responsibility in the entity. Core competencies indicate the organization's internal strengths and capabilities and, thus, help select appropriate business functions to outsource. Strategy may also be constrained by the level of capital (financial or intellectual) or technology available to the organization. Management style and organizational culture provide a foundation for normal business practices and protocol for interactions among employees, customers, and suppliers. Environmental factors such as market structures, government regulations and national cultures may help or hinder strategic options. Additionally, market structures—pure competition, monopolistic competition, monopoly, and oligopoly—will affect how an organization views and adapts to competitive forces. A business intelligence system can help management understand the factors that influence the organization's choice of strategies.

Managers perform numerous functions including planning, controlling, and decision making. Strategic planning provides long-term direction for an entity and a foundation for tactical, short-term planning.

Most companies must now adapt to operating in a globally competitive environment. Governments have established trade agreements, such as the General Agreement on Tariffs and Trade, European Union, and North American Free Trade Agreement, to reduce tariff barriers and foster global competition. Although an open global business environment provides new opportunities, it also creates some greater risks—strategic, operating, financial, and information—and requires knowledge of and adherence to differing legal requirements. Additionally, ethical standards may appear to vary by location, but a solid code of ethics should help a business operate in a consistent, moral way throughout the world.

The accounting function can contribute both to organizational strategic and tactical management. Strategic resource management (SRM) links organizational strategy and resource deployment as well as integrates involvement of the accounting function. The key focus in SRM is the value chain, or the string of activities that convert organizational inputs into outputs. The task of providing information relevant in strategic resource management has demanded that new ways of collecting and analyzing data be developed and that different types of data (such as nonfinancial) become a more common focus.

KEY TERMS

Authority (p. 6)
Build mission (p. 25)
Business intelligence (BI) system (p. 15)
Centralization (p. 7)
Confrontation strategy (p. 14)
Controlling (p. 16)
Core competency (p. 7)
Cost leadership (p. 14)
Decentralization (p. 7)
Decision making (p. 16)
Differentiation (p. 14)
Economic integration (p. 18)
Effectiveness (p. 16)
Efficiency (p. 16)
Empowerment (p. 7)
Environmental constraint (p. 13)
Ethical standard (p. 22)
Foreign Corrupt Practices Act
    (FCPA) (p. 22)
Global economy (p. 17)
Goal (p. 6)
Harvest mission (p. 25)

Hold mission (p. 25)
Intellectual capital (p. 9)
Key variable (p. 15)
Management style (p. 11)
Mission statement (p. 4)
Monopolistic competition (p. 13)
Monopoly (p. 13)
Objective (p. 6)
Oligopoly (p. 13)
Organizational culture (p. 12)
Organizational structure (p. 6)
Outsourcing (p. 8)
Planning (p. 15)
Product life cycle (p. 25)
Pure competition (p. 13)
Responsibility (p. 6)
Strategic planning (p. 15)
Strategic resource management (p. 26)
Strategy (p. 4)
Tactical planning (p. 16)
Value chain (p. 27)

END OF CHAPTER MATERIALS

⊙ QUESTIONS

1. Why is a mission statement important to an organization?

2. What is organizational strategy? Why would each organization have a unique strategy or set of strategies?

3. Distinguish between goals and objectives. What goals do you hope to achieve by taking this course? What objectives can you establish to measure the degree to which you achieve these stated goals?

4. Differentiate between authority and responsibility. Can you have one without the other? Explain.

5. In what types of organizations or under what organizational conditions would centralization be a more useful structure than decentralization? Decentralization more useful than centralization?

6. What is a core competency and how do core competencies impact the feasible set of alternative organizational strategies?

7. Why are many organizations relying more on outsourcing now than in the past?

8. "If an organization can borrow money or sell stock, it does not have a capital constraint." Is this statement true or false? Discuss the rationale for your answer.

9. Differentiate between human and structural aspects of intellectual capital. Which do you believe is more important in each of the following organizations: a start-up software development company, a car dealership, a university, a hospital, and Coca-Cola? Provide reasons for your answers.

10. Does the acquisition of new technology automatically overcome quality or speed problems that previously existed in an organization?

11. How does workforce diversity affect organizational culture? Include in your answer a discussion of both the potential benefits and potential difficulties in having workers with diverse backgrounds.

12. How can a change in governmental laws or regulations create a strategic opportunity for an organization? Give an example.

13. What are the four most common market structures? Give an example of a company operating in each type of market structure.

14. Describe how each market structure would affect strategy for a given product.

15. Define each of the three strategies an organization may pursue to avoid competition and discuss the benefits of each type of strategy.

16. Why would a useful business intelligence system contain substantial information about an organization's competitors?

17. Define and differentiate among the primary management functions. Provide several examples of instances in which a manager would need different information in order to perform these functions.

18. Compare and contrast strategic and tactical planning.

19. What are key variables, and how do they affect the planning process?

20. Differentiate between effectiveness and efficiency. Give an example of the two related to your life as a college student.

21. What is the role of information in decision making?

22. Why would operating in a global (rather than a strictly domestic) marketplace create a need for additional information? Discuss some of the additional information you think managers would need and why such information would be valuable.

23. Discuss the validity of the following statement, "Only large companies (such as those that are publicly held and listed on a major stock exchange) have the opportunity to operate in a global marketplace."

24. Why are economic trade agreements so important to the globalization of business?

25. What might be the most difficult factors to overcome in the implementation of a single market in Europe? Why did you choose these and what suggestions do you have for overcoming these difficulties?

26. What political and cultural issues might affect a British company considering opening a segment in Russia?

27. How do government regulations affect planning processes in the business organizations in your country?

28. Compare and contrast legal and ethical standards.

29. Why should businesses concern themselves about a clean environment when it might be substantially less expensive to pollute, thus making their products cheaper for consumers?

30. What factors impede the development of an international code of ethics for profit-oriented businesses? Do you believe these can be overcome through the passage of laws? Discuss the rationale for your answer.

31. Why is a code of ethics a necessity in any organization?

32. Are the financial implications of strategic planning more important in a business than in a not-for-profit organization? Why or why not?

33. What are the three generic segment missions and how are these missions related to product life cycle?

34. Why would employee empowerment generally require group as well as individual performance measurements?

35. "Most companies determine product or service price by adding a reasonable profit margin to costs incurred." Is this statement true or false? Provide a rationale for your answer.

36. What is the value chain of an organization and how does it interface with strategic resource management?

37. Why is it especially necessary to achieve a balance between short-term and long-term considerations in today's business environment?

⊙ EXERCISES

38. *(Terminology)* Match the following lettered items on the left with the appropriate numbered description on the right.

a. Authority	1. A target expressed in quantitative terms
b. Core competency	2. The right to use resources to accomplish something
c. Goal	3. A process that an organization does better than other organizations
d. Objective	
e. Responsibility	4. A process of choosing among alternatives
f. Decision making	5. A desired result, expressed qualitatively
g. Effectiveness	6. A factor that will determine the success or failure of an organization
h. Planning	
i. Key variable	7. The obligation to accomplish something
j. Efficiency	8. A measure of success of an endeavor
	9. The process of determining long-term and short-term strategy
	10. A measure of output achieved relative to resources consumed

39. *(Terminology)* Match the following lettered items on the left with the appropriate numbered description on the right.

a. Strategy	1. An organization's intangible assets of skill, knowledge, and information
b. Outsourcing	
c. Value chain	2. Basic assumptions about an organization, its goals, and its practices
d. Intellectual capital	
e. Organizational culture	3. A long-term plan related to organizational goals and objectives
f. Cost leadership	4. The way in which authority and responsibility are distributed in an organization
g. Tactical planning	
h. Differentiation	5. The attribute of being the low cost producer or service provider
i. Organizational structure	6. The process of contracting with external parties to provide inputs or services
j. Confrontation	
	7. The attribute of identifying and exploiting temporary opportunities for advantage
	8. The processes of an organization and its suppliers to convert inputs into products and services

9. The attribute of avoiding competition by distinguishing a product or service from that of competitors

√ 10. The process of preparing for the near future

40. *(Mission)* Obtain a copy of your college's mission statement. Draft a mission statement for this class that supports the college's mission statement.
    a. How does your mission statement reflect the goals and objectives of the college's mission statement?
    b. How can you measure the successful accomplishment of your objectives?
    c. Is there a difference between the effective and the efficient accomplishment of your objectives? Provide the rationale for your answer.

41. *(Empowerment)* Early this year, you started a house-cleaning service and now have twenty customers. Because of other obligations (including classes), you have had to hire three employees.
    a. What types of business activities would you empower these employees to handle and why?
    b. What types of business activities would you keep for yourself and why?

42. *(Core competencies)* As a team, make a list of the core competencies of your college or university and explain why you believe these items to be core competencies. Make appointments with the dean, one vice president, and, if possible, the president of your college or university and, without sharing your list, ask these individuals what they believe the core competencies to be and why. Prepare a written or video presentation that summarizes, compares, and contrasts all the lists. Share copies of your presentation with all the individuals you contacted.

43. *(Outsourcing)* You are the manager of an exclusive jewelry store that sells primarily on credit. The majority of your customers use the store's credit card rather than a bank or other major credit card.
    a. What would you consider to be the primary benefits of outsourcing the store's accounts collection function?
    b. What would you consider to be the primary risks of outsourcing the store's accounts collection function?

44. *(Competition strategy)* Choose a company that might utilize each of the following strategies relative to its competitors and discuss the benefits that might be realized from that strategy.
    a. Differentiation
    b. Cost leadership
    c. Confrontation

45. *(Strategy)* You are the manager of the local Toys 'R' Us store. Make a list of 10 key variables that you believe to be critical to your organization. (You might want to read "Can Toys 'R' Us Get on Top of Its Game?" in the April 7, 1997, issue of *Business Week*.)
    a. How would each of your key variables impact your tactical planning?
    b. How would each of your key variables impact your strategic planning?

46. *(Decision making)* You are the manager of a small restaurant in your hometown.
    a. What information would you want to have in making the decision whether to add chicken fajitas and Boston clam chowder to your menu?
    b. Why would each of the above information items be significant?

47. *(Globalization)* The 1996 annual report of Callaway Golf Company (headquartered in California) was slightly untraditional in that the opening "letter" to shareholders was given not only in English, but also in German, French, Spanish, Japanese, and Chinese.
    a. Discuss the costs and benefits to a U.S.-based company in taking the time to provide such translations.
    b. What additional information would you want to have to assess how such translations are related to Callaway's strategic plans?

48. *(Trade agreements)* You have been appointed to a business advisory group in your country to consider the implementation of the TAFTA. What issues relative to implementation concern you and why?

49. *(Business risks)* You have just been promoted to manage a branch location of a regional bank.
   a. Provide three examples of the strategic, operating, financial, and information risks that your organization faces.
   b. What might you do to minimize the impact of each of these risks?

50. *(Cost–benefit)* As the marketing manager for a small copying company, you have requested that your boss purchase a new high-speed, color copier that collates up to fifty sets of copies. The current color copier operates at approximately one-third the speed of the new one and only collates twenty-five sets of copies.
   a. How might you present the costs and benefits of this purchase to your boss?
   b. What additional information might you request from the marketing manager if you were the accounting or finance manager?

⊙ CASES

51. *(Mission statement)* You have owned Lee Construction for fifteen years and employ a hundred employees. Business has been profitable, but you are concerned that the locale in which your business is based may soon experience a downturn in growth. One way you have decided to help prepare for such an event is to engage in a higher level of strategic planning, beginning with a mission statement for your company. (Note: The December 1996 *Management Accounting* article "Measuring Your Mission" may provide a useful starting point.)
   a. How does a mission statement add strength to the strategic planning process?
   b. Who should be involved in developing a mission statement and why?
   c. What factors should be considered in the development of a mission statement? Why are these factors important?
   d. Prepare a mission statement for Lee Construction and discuss how your mission statement will provide benefits to tactical as well as strategic planning.

52. *(Benefits of successful planning)* Successful business organizations appear to be those that have clearly defined long-range goals and a well-planned strategy to reach those goals. These successful organizations understand their markets as well as their internal strengths and weaknesses. These organizations take advantage of this knowledge to grow, through internal development or acquisitions, in a consistent and disciplined manner.
   a. Discuss the need for long-range goals for business organizations.
   b. Discuss how long-range goals are set.
   c. Define the concepts of strategic planning and management control. Discuss how they relate to each other and contribute to progress toward the attainment of long-range goals.

(CMA adapted)

53. *(Strategy)* Dell Computer Co. has a straightforward business strategy: "Eliminate middlemen and don't build PCs until you have firm orders in hand." (Silvia Ascarelli, "Dell Finds U.S. Strategy Works in Europe," *Wall Street Journal*, February 3, 1997).
   a. Dell is gaining a large European market share using its uniquely American strategy. Provide some reasons why a U.S. strategy might not be accepted by overseas customers.
   b. Dell once tried to enter the retail sales market instead of relying on direct sales. Research Dell's attempt at a different strategic approach and discuss its outcome.
   c. Although strategic planning is essential to Dell's success, why would tactical planning also be tremendously important to this company?

54. *(Core competencies; outsourcing)* Outsourcing is a frequently used method of cost-cutting or of eliminating organizational activities that are not viewed as core competencies. However, outsourcing also creates new costs and, sometimes, new problems.
   a. Discuss some of the benefits and drawbacks of outsourcing the following activities in a large, publicly held corporation: (1) accounting; (2) data processing; (3) regulatory compliance; (4) research and development; and (5) travel arrangements.

   b. What effect might outsourcing each of the activities in part (a) have on the organization's corporate culture?

   c. In late 1996, General Motors was faced with a strike by the United Auto Workers over the issue of outsourcing. Obtain information about this "confrontation" and its settlement. How would you have reacted as the (1) lead labor negotiator for General Motors and (2) UAW president?

55. *(Organizational constraints)* Four common organizational constraints involve monetary capital, intellectual capital, technology, and organizational structure. Additionally, the environment in which the organization operates may present one or more types of constraints (cultural, fiscal, legal/regulatory, or political).

   a. Discuss whether each of these constraints might or might not be influential in the following types of organizations:

   (1) City Hall in a major metropolitan city.

   (2) a franchised quick-copy business.

   (3) a newly opened firm of attorneys, all of whom recently graduated from law school.

   (4) an international oil exploration and production company.

   Explain the rationale for each of your answers.

   b. For each of the previously listed organizations, discuss your perceptions of which of the constraints would be most critical and why.

   c. For each of the previously listed organizations, discuss your perceptions of whether human or structural capital would be most important and why.

56. *(Organizational culture)* The United States provides an ethnically, racially, and culturally diverse workplace. It has been argued that this plurality may be a competitive handicap for U.S. businesses. For example, communicating may be difficult because some workers do not speak English; motivating workers may be complicated because workers have diverse work ethics; and work scheduling may be difficult because of differing religions and ethnic holidays. Conversely, it has been argued that Japan has a competitive advantage because its population is much more homogeneous.

   a. What are the advantages of a pluralistic society in the global marketplace?

   b. On balance, does America's plurality give it a competitive advantage or place it at a competitive disadvantage? Discuss.

57. *(Competition)* You have recently come into a very large inheritance and have decided to buy an existing business or open a new one. Given your interests, you have narrowed your choices to the following:

   ⊙ Purchase the existing cable company in your regional area.

   ⊙ Purchase an airline that operates in most areas of the country.

   ⊙ Open a plant to manufacture and sell hot sauce domestically and in Central and South America.

   ⊙ Buy franchises for and open fifteen locations of a fast-food restaurant in areas of the former Soviet Union.

   a. Discuss the competitive influences that will impact each of your potential businesses.

   b. How would the tactics of compression of competitive scope, product/service differentiation, cost leadership, or confrontation work in each of your potential businesses?

   c. What would be the most important key variables for each of your potential businesses?

   d. Which business would you open and why?

58. *(Trade treaties)* The economic trade agreements described in Exhibit 1-11 are attempts to make the global marketplace an easier place in which to do business.

   a. Which trade agreement do you believe is *most* important to your home country and why?

   b. Why is it necessary for different countries to engage in separate trade agreements, given the global emphasis of the General Agreement on Tariffs and Trades?

   c. At production of this text, China was not a member of the World Trade Organization. Issues of human rights, workers' rights, and weapons proliferation have been used to justify denial of membership. Why are these issues of importance to free trade of goods among countries?

59. *(Value chain)* Strategic alliances are important parts of the value chain. In many organizations, suppliers are beginning to provide more and more input into customer activities. For example, in 1997 Chrysler announced that supplier ideas were expected to result in approximately $325 million in cost savings and, thus, increased profits.
   a. In the United States, when would a strategic alliance be considered illegal?
   b. What would you perceive the primary reasons for pursuing a strategic alliance to be?
   c. You are the manager of a catalog company that sells flowers and plants. With whom would you want to establish strategic alliances? What issues might you want to specify prior to engaging in the alliance?

⊙ ETHICS AND QUALITY DISCUSSIONS

60. Mission statements are supposed to indicate what an organization does and why it exists. Some of them, however, are simply empty words, with little or no substance and with few people using them to guide activities. (Note: The September 30, 1996, *Fortune* article "A Refreshing Change: Vision Statements That Make Sense" may provide a useful starting point.)
   a. Why does an organization need a mission statement? Or does it?
   b. How might a mission statement help an organization in its pursuit of ethical behavior from employees?
   c. How might a mission statement help an organization in its pursuit of production of quality products and provision of high customer service?

61. Broadstreet Deli and Bakery is known countrywide for its excellent bread and donuts. Sales have, however, been falling because of small but continuous price increases. The increases have been warranted because of increased costs for ingredients. The vice president of marketing wants to substitute low-grade animal fat for 95 percent of the vegetable shortening currently used and reduce the selling prices of the products to their old levels. She does not, however, want to change the slogan on the package ("Made with Pure Vegetable Shortening") since some vegetable shortening will still be used.
   a. From a strategic viewpoint, do you believe this is a wise decision? Discuss the rationale for your answer.
   b. You are the marketing manager for the bakery. How would you react to this proposal?

62. Today, many companies are outsourcing non-core competencies. Some companies are even becoming "virtual" organizations, like Amazon.com, which is a bookless, storeless bookstore. (Note: The July 7, 1997, *Forbes* article "The Plug-And-Play Economy" may provide a useful starting point.)
   a. How might product quality be improved through outsourcing?
   b. How might product quality be reduced through outsourcing?
   c. How might customer service be improved through outsourcing?
   d. How might customer service be reduced through outsourcing?

63. Intellectual capital is extremely important to the longevity of an organization. There are, however, "intellectual capital pirates" who make their livings from stealing.
   a. Assume you have made several popular recordings. These recordings are being pirated overseas. Discuss your feelings about these intellectual capital pirates and what (if anything) should be done to them. (Note: The April 24 and March 10, 1997, *Wall Street Journal* articles, "CP Piracy Flourishes in China, and West Supplies Equipment" and "Russian Copyright Lawyer is Leading Crackdown on Piracy in Music Industry," may provide a useful starting point.)
   b. Copying a computer software program is also intellectual capital piracy. Do you perceive any difference between this type of copying and the copying of recordings? Discuss the rationale for your answer.

64. You have just been elected president of the United States. One of your most popular positions was that you would reduce the costs of doing business in the United States. When asked how you intended to accomplish this, you replied, "By seeking to repeal

all laws that create unnecessary costs. Repealing these laws will be good not only for business but also for the consumer, since product prices will be reduced." Congress heard the message and has decided to repeal all environmental protection laws.

a. Discuss the short-term and long-term implications of such a policy.

b. How would such a policy impact the global competitiveness of U.S. companies?

c. What reactions would you expect to such a policy from (1) other industrialized nations and (2) third world countries?

65. "Few trends could so thoroughly undermine the very foundation of our free society," writes Milton Friedman in *Capitalism and Freedom*, "as the acceptance by corporate officials of a social responsibility other than to make as much money for their shareholders as possible."

a. Discuss your reactions to this quote from a legal standpoint.

b. Discuss your reactions to this quote from an ethical standpoint.

c. How would you resolve any conflicts that exist between your two answers?

66. The Foreign Corrupt Practices Act (FCPA) prohibits U.S. firms from giving bribes in foreign countries, although giving bribes is customary in some countries and non-U.S. companies operating in foreign countries may not be similarly restricted. Thus, adherence to the FCPA could make competing with non-U.S. firms more difficult in foreign countries.

Do you think that bribery should be considered so ethically repugnant to Americans that companies are asked to forego a foreign custom and, thus, the profits that could be obtained through observance of the custom? Prepare both a pro and a con position for your answer, assuming you will be asked to debate one position or the other. (Note: The September 9, 1995, *Wall Street Journal* article "How U.S. Concerns Compete in Countries Where Bribes Flourish" may provide a useful starting point.)

67. EraTech Corporation, a developer and distributor of business applications software, has been in business for five years. The company's sales have increased steadily to the current level of $25 million per year.

Andrea Nolan joined EraTech about one year ago as accounting manager. She has noticed that recently EraTech's sales have ceased to rise and in the past two months have actually declined, resulting in cash shortages. EraTech has also had to delay the introduction of a new product line because of delays in documentation preparation.

EraTech contracts most of its printing requirements to Web Graphic, Inc., a small company owned by Ron Borman. EraTech's contracts represent approximately 50 percent of Web Graphic's business. Nolan has known Borman for many years; in fact, she learned of EraTech's need for an accounting manager from Borman.

While preparing EraTech's most recent financial statements, Nolan became concerned about the company's ability to maintain steady payments to its suppliers; she estimated that payments to all vendors, normally made within thirty days, could exceed seventy-five days. Nolan is considering telling Borman about EraTech's cash problems.

a. Describe Andrea Nolan's ethical responsibilities in the previous situation. Use the IMA Code of Ethics (shown in Appendix A to the text) to support your answer.

b. Without prejudice to your answer in part (a), assume that Andrea Nolan learns that Ron Borman has decided to postpone a special paper order for an EraTech printing job. Nolan believes that Borman must have heard rumors about EraTech's financial problems. Should Nolan tell the appropriate EraTech officials that Borman has postponed the paper order? Explain your answer using the IMA Code of Ethics for support.

c. Without prejudice to your answers in parts (a) and (b), assume that Ron Borman has decided to postpone the special paper order for EraTech's printing job because he has learned of EraTech's financial problems. Jim Grason, EraTech's purchasing manager, knows of Nolan's friendship with Ron Borman. Nolan is concerned that Grason may suspect she told Borman of EraTech's financial problems when Grason finds out Borman has postponed the order. Describe the steps that Andrea Nolan should take to resolve this situation. Use the IMA Code of Ethics to support your answer.

(CMA adapted)

Chapter 2　Introduction to Cost Management Systems

LEARNING OBJECTIVES

After reading this chapter, you should be able to answer the following questions:

1　HOW
do control systems aid managers in achieving organizational goals and objectives?

2　WHAT
is a cost management system and what major factors influence its design?

3　HOW
are accounting systems influenced by both external and internal reporting requirements?

4　HOW
are product and period costs differentiated?

5　HOW
can product costing and valuation systems be compared and contrasted?

6　HOW
is an actual costing system different from normal and standard costing systems?

7　HOW
do the internal and external operating environments impact cost management systems?

8　HOW
does the product life cycle affect cost management strategies?

9　WHAT
three groups of elements affect the design of a cost management system and how are these elements used?

10　HOW
is gap analysis used in the implementation of a cost management system?

General Marble

Hans Wede, the president of General Marble, knew he had problems. The company's complaints from major customers included virtually every major aspect of operations: quality, shipping, billing, timeliness of delivery, and customer service. In addition, the company was only processing 53 percent of its orders correctly in the order entry process in the first pass—a miserable success rate. Manufacturing was hardly faring any better; only 52 percent of products were manufactured correctly in the first pass. Furthermore, 61 percent of manufacturing activities were nonvalue-adding.

The financial side of the business was also in disarray. The accounting inventory records provided only a vague reflection of the inventories that were identified in a physical audit; and consolidating records for financial reporting was nearly impossible, as several subsidiaries maintained separate general ledgers. The financial reporting burdens were dominating the time of the entire accounting staff, leaving no time for accountants to contribute expertise to the management of the business.

The nation's largest manufacturer of bathroom countertops and assembled vanities employed four hundred people and served some of the biggest names in the home builder supply market. However, unless the company could find ways to improve its operations, its survival was seriously in doubt. One positive factor for the company was that its employees recognized change was required and were willing to make it happen. To begin the process of change, the company had to listen to "the voice of the customer."

SOURCE: Charles M. Bokman, "Anatomy of a Turnaround," *Management Accounting* (December 1996), pp. 38–42. Reprinted from *Management Accounting*, published by the Institute of Management Accountants, Montvale, NJ. Visit our website at www.imanet.org.

*H*ans Wede realized that his company needed to change if it were to survive. The first change needed was to begin development of a customer-driven manufacturing strategy. Such a strategy would require vast improvements in efficiency, cost reduction, quality management and customer service; to realize such improvements, *General Marble* needed to develop reporting systems that tracked performance in all significant areas. System design would be crucial to the success of an integrated, structured approach to cost management.

This chapter begins with a broad introduction to control systems, which establishes a foundation and context for understanding the roles of the cost management system. Concepts relevant to the design of a cost management system as an essential part of an organization's overall control systems are discussed. An emphasis is placed on the main factors that determine the structure and success of a cost management system, the factors that influence the design of such a system, and the elements that comprise the system. The discussion builds on terms and concepts presented in Chapter 1.

INTRODUCTION TO MANAGEMENT INFORMATION AND CONTROL SYSTEMS

Competing in the global marketplace requires managers to have access to information that supports effective and efficient operation of their businesses. To remain solvent, maintain market share, and gain future growth, firms must find ways to satisfy their customers' needs by delivering quality products and services at competitive prices. Exhibit 2-1 presents a simple model of the value chain and basic product and information flows.

Exhibit 2-1 indicates that firms require information to manage relationships with suppliers and customers as well as internal processes. Customer information is necessary to determine which products and services are desired and how many units of each product or service must be produced, and to project demand levels for existing and future products and services. Effective management of supplier relationships is necessary so that firms can acquire the parts, materials, and services needed in the processes of generating goods and services for customers. Internal processes must be effectively managed so that the inputs purchased from suppliers are effectively and efficiently converted into outputs (goods and services) for customers.

EXHIBIT 2-1
The Value Chain and
Information Flows

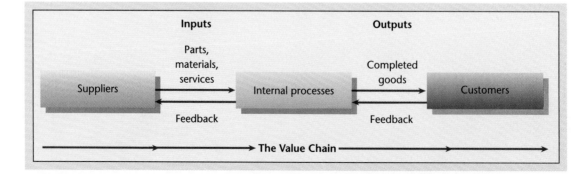

Exhibit 2-2 expands on the basic value chain information depicted in Exhibit 2-1 to include more of the types of information that need to be gathered and communicated among organizational stakeholders. Exhibit 2-2 indicates that many parties in addition to managers have an interest in the operations of a given organization. Competitors are interested in information about an organization that could be exploited in the market; for example, information about new products or new pricing and promotion strategies for existing products. Government is interested in many facets of operations, including profitability (for tax assessments) and conduct of operations (for compliance with laws and regulations). Creditors are interested in information that helps them establish the worthiness and assess the risk of the organization for borrowing.

Also depicted in Exhibit 2-2 are the inward flows of information from external parties to the organization. Exhibit 2-2 demonstrates that managers need information from, and about, parties other than customers and suppliers to manage their organizations. The inflow of external information allows managers to understand, anticipate, and respond to opportunities and threats in the market.

Managers require information so they may plan, control, evaluate performance, and make decisions. In planning, managers describe outcomes they hope to achieve in the future. Managers exert control by acting to bring operations into compliance with the plans. Performance is evaluated by measuring actual outcomes against plans, past performance levels and other performance benchmarks. Managers make decisions in the process of executing plans and controlling operations.

EXHIBIT 2-2

Information Flows and Types of Information

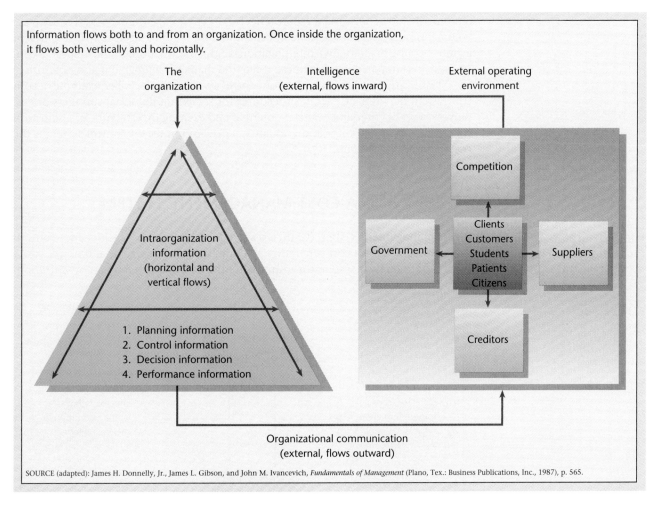

Information flows both to and from an organization. Once inside the organization, it flows both vertically and horizontally.

The organization   Intelligence (external, flows inward)   External operating environment

Intraorganization information (horizontal and vertical flows)

1. Planning information
2. Control information
3. Decision information
4. Performance information

Competition

Clients Customers Students Patients Citizens

Government   Suppliers

Creditors

Organizational communication (external, flows outward)

SOURCE (adapted): James H. Donnelly, Jr., James L. Gibson, and John M. Ivancevich, *Fundamentals of Management* (Plano, Tex.: Business Publications, Inc., 1987), p. 565.

[1]Robert N. Anthony and Vijay Govindarajan, *Management Control Systems* (Chicago: Irwin, 1995), p. 3. Reproduced with permission of The McGraw-Hill Companies.

Managers are charged with the responsibility of achieving organizational objectives. Therefore, managers develop plans for deploying their organizations' resources including employees, equipment and capital so that objectives are realized. However, once plans are made, managers bear the additional burden of seeing to it that the plans are followed. For this purpose, they develop control systems. **Control systems** are managerial tools for implementing plans. As illustrated in Exhibit 2-3, a control system has the following four primary components:

1. A *detector* or *sensor,* a measuring device that identifies what is actually happening in the process being controlled.
2. An *assessor,* a device for determining the significance of what is happening. Usually, significance is assessed by comparing the information on what is actually happening with some standard or plan regarding what *should* be happening.
3. An *effector,* a device that alters behavior if the assessor indicates the need for doing so. This device is often called "feedback."
4. A *communications network,* which transmits information between the detector and the assessor and between the assessor and the effector.[1]

It is through these system elements that information about actual organizational occurrences is gathered, actual data are compared to plans, changes are made when necessary, and information is gathered and provided to appropriate parties. For example, source documents (detectors) gather information about sales that is compared to the sales plan (assessor). If sales are below the planned level, management *may* issue (communications network) a report (effector) to encourage the sales staff to increase volume. However, given the same information, different managers may take different actions because of alternative interpretations of the information. In this respect, a control system is not merely mechanical; it requires managerial judgment and expertise.

Most businesses have a variety of control systems in place. For example, a control system may reflect a set of procedures for screening potential suppliers or employees, a set of criteria to evaluate potential and existing investments, or a statistical control process to monitor and evaluate quality. An important control system is the cost management system.

DEFINING A COST MANAGEMENT SYSTEM

A **cost management system (CMS)** is a set of formal methods developed for controlling an organization's cost-generating activities relative to its goals and objectives. A CMS is not merely a system for minimizing the costs incurred by an organization.

EXHIBIT 2-3
Elements of a Control System

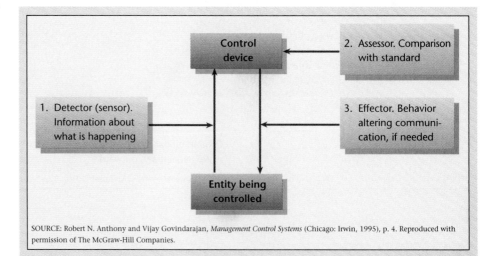

SOURCE: Robert N. Anthony and Vijay Govindarajan, *Management Control Systems* (Chicago: Irwin, 1995), p. 4. Reproduced with permission of The McGraw-Hill Companies.

Rather, it should help an organization obtain maximum benefits from incurring costs. More specifically, a CMS should help managers

- identify the cost of resources consumed in performing significant activities of the firm (accounting systems);
- determine the efficiency and effectiveness of the activities performed (performance measurement);
- identify and evaluate new activities that can improve the future performance of the firm (investment management); and
- accomplish the three previous objectives in an environment characterized by changing technology (manufacturing processes).[2]

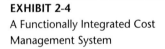

cost management system (CMS)

The information generated from the CMS should integrate and benefit all functional areas of the entity. As shown in Exhibit 2-4, the CMS should "improve the quality, content, relevance, and timing of cost information that managers use for [either strategic or tactical] decision making."[3]

By crossing all functional areas (not simply accounting), a cost management system can be viewed as having six primary goals: (1) to develop reasonably accurate product costs; (2) to assess product/service profitability over the entire life of the product/service; (3) to improve understanding of internal processes and activities; (4) to control costs; (5) to measure performance; and (6) to allow the pursuit of organizational strategies.

First and foremost, a CMS should provide the means to develop reasonably accurate product or service costs. Thus, the system must be designed to gather information in a manner that allows costs to be traced to products and services. It is not necessary that the system be "the most accurate one, but one which matches benefits of additional accuracy with expenses of achieving additional accuracy. The best

EXHIBIT 2-4

A Functionally Integrated Cost Management System

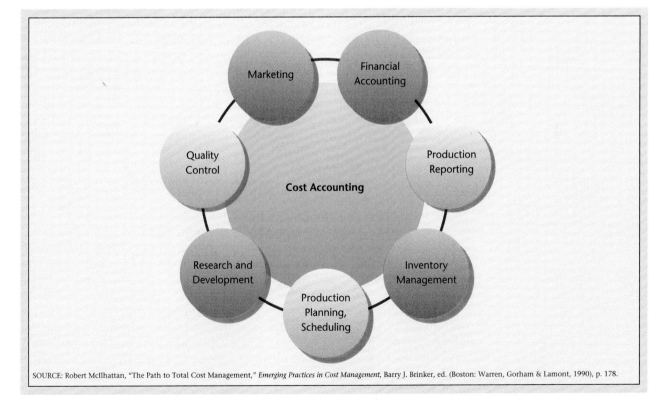

SOURCE: Robert McIlhattan, "The Path to Total Cost Management," *Emerging Practices in Cost Management*, Barry J. Brinker, ed. (Boston: Warren, Gorham & Lamont, 1990), p. 178.

---

[2]Callie Berliner and James A. Brimson, eds., *Cost Management for Today's Advanced Manufacturing* (Boston: Harvard Business School Press, 1988), p. 10.

[3]Steven C. Schnoebelen, "Integrating an Advanced Cost Management System into Operating Systems (Part 2)," *Journal of Cost Management* (Spring 1993), p. 60.

system will report approximate, but inaccurate, product costs, with the degree of approximation determined by the organization's competitive, product, and process environment."[4] Traceability has been made easier by improved information technology, such as bar coding.

The product/service costs generated by the cost management system are the input to managerial processes. These costs are used to plan, prepare financial statements, assess individual product/service and period profitability, establish prices for outputs, and create a basis for performance measurements. If the input costs accumulated and assigned by the CMS are not reasonably accurate, the information output of the CMS will be inappropriate for control and decision-making purposes.

Although product/service profitability may be calculated periodically as a requirement for external reporting, the financial accounting system does not reflect life-cycle information. The cost management system should provide information about the life-cycle performance of a product or service. Without life-cycle information, managers will not have a basis to relate costs incurred in one stage of the life cycle to costs and profitability of other stages. For example, managers may not recognize that increasing investment in the development and design stage of the life cycle could provide significant rewards in later stages by minimizing potential future costs caused by design, environmental pollution, or product recall. Further, if development/ design cost is not traced to the related product or service, managers may not be able to recognize organizational investment "disasters." Lastly, companies should take a long-term view and determine cost based on life-cycle, rather than period-by-period, relationships among price, profit margin, and cost.

A cost management system should help managers comprehend business processes and organizational activities. Only by understanding how an activity is accomplished and the reasons for cost incurrence can managers make cost-beneficial improvements in the production and processing systems. Managers desiring to implement new technology such as installing robotic assembly lines must identify the costs and benefits that will flow from such an action; these assessments can be made only if the managers understand how the processes, activities, and costs will differ after the change.

Cost control was the original purpose served by creating a cost accounting system, and given the current global competitive environment, it is still an important function of cost management systems. A cost can be controlled only when the activity causing the cost is known and monitored, and the information is available. For example, if units are spoiled (damaged) in a process, the CMS should provide information on spoilage quantity and cost rather than "burying" that information in the cost of good production. Additionally, the cost management system should allow managers to understand the process so that the underlying causes of the spoilage can be determined. Armed with this information, managers can compare the costs of fixing the process with the benefits to be provided.

The information generated from a cost management system should also help managers measure and evaluate human and equipment performance and assess future decision alternatives. Financial and nonfinancial measurements in a CMS can be captured at different organizational levels and can be combined and used for different purposes.

Lastly, to maintain a competitive position in an industry, a firm must generate information necessary to define and implement its organizational strategies. As discussed in Chapter 1, strategy is the set of long-term plans that provide the link between an organization's goals and objectives and the activities actually conducted by the organization. In the current global market, firms must be certain that such a linkage exists. Information provided by a CMS allows managers to perform strategic analyses on issues such as determining core competencies and managing organizational resources from a cost–benefit perspective, assessing the positive and negative financial and nonfinancial factors of investment and operational plans, and engaging in employee empowerment by utilizing new management techniques such as

---

[4]Robin Cooper and Robert S. Kaplan, *The Design of Cost Management Systems* (Englewood Cliffs, N.J.: Prentice-Hall, 1991), p. 4.

those discussed in Chapter 13. Thus, the cost management system is essential to the generation of information for effective resource management.

The world of business competition is dynamic, requiring the creation of innovative new business practices and competitive strategies. Such an environment mandates cost management systems that are designed to be responsive to evolutionary management practices.

DESIGNING A COST MANAGEMENT SYSTEM

Because a CMS is concerned with costs, it must be founded in part on accounting information. All accounting information is generated from one accounting system and one set of accounts. Although existing technology would allow companies to design different accounting systems for different purposes, most companies still rely on a single system to supply all accounting information. Historically, most accounting systems have been focused on providing information for financial accounting purposes, and their informational outputs must be adapted to meet most internal management requirements.

Integrating External and Internal Information Needs

Most firms, particularly those having stock traded on public exchanges, provide accounting data to parties outside of the firm. These parties include shareholders, debtholders and other parties shown in Exhibit 2-2. Capital markets and regulatory and taxing agencies also can mandate that firms provide certain financial data. Satisfying external reporting is the domain of financial accountants.

LEARNING OBJECTIVE ❸
How are accounting systems influenced by both external and internal reporting requirements?

Financial Accounting

Financial accounting focuses on external users and is generally required for obtaining loans, preparing tax returns, and reporting to the investment community how well or poorly the business is performing. The information used in financial accounting must comply with generally accepted accounting principles. Financial accounting information is usually quite aggregated and relates to the entire organization. In some cases, a regulatory agency (such as the Securities and Exchange Commission) or an industry commission (such as in banking or insurance) may prescribe specific financial accounting practices.

financial accounting

Management Accounting

Management accounting refers to the gathering and application of information used to plan, make decisions, evaluate performance, and control an organization. Management accounting can be applied in all types of organizations to provide information for internal users. Exhibit 2-5 (page 46) details differences between financial and management accounting.

management accounting

Managers are often concerned with individual parts or segments of the business rather than the organization as a whole. Therefore, management accounting information often focuses on particular segmental aspects of an entity rather than the big picture of financial accounting. Management accounting is flexible because it is not regulated by any organization or regulatory body. Often, managerial accountants provide forecasted, qualitative, and nonmonetary information. For instance, a manager debating whether to sell a piece of land now or in three years is not likely to use the land's historical cost to make the decision. Instead, he or she will need estimates about expected changes in land prices for the next three years as well as information about expected events, such as the possibility that a shopping center will be built on property adjoining the land.

A primary criterion for internal information is that it serves management's needs. A related criterion is the cost/benefit consideration that information should

EXHIBIT 2-5
Financial and Management
Accounting Differences

	FINANCIAL	MANAGEMENT
Primary users	External	Internal
Primary organizational focus	Whole (aggregated)	Parts (segmented)
Information characteristics	Must be	May be
	Historical	Forecasted
	Quantitative	Quantitative or qualitative
	Monetary	Monetary or nonmonetary
	Accurate	Timely and, at a minimum, a reasonable estimate
Overriding criteria	Generally accepted accounting principles	Situational relevance (usefulness)
	Consistency	Benefits in excess of cost
	Verifiability	Flexibility
Record keeping	Formal	Combination of formal and informal

be developed and provided only if the cost of producing it is less than the benefit gained from using the information.

The following News Note demonstrates how an accounting system that is adequate for meeting external reporting needs may be inadequate in meeting managerial needs.

Cost Accounting

conversion

All organizations transform inputs (acquired from suppliers) such as raw materials and parts into outputs. This transformation of inputs into outputs is called **conversion**. Exhibit 2-6 compares the levels of conversion activities of different types of organizations. A high level of conversion indicates that outputs are remarkably different from inputs—much transformation has occurred. A low level of conversion indicates that outputs appear little different from inputs. Although all manufacturers engage in high levels of conversion activities, so do some service companies. For

NEWS NOTE

http:// www.compana.com

Healing a Sick Cost Management System

Group Health Cooperative (GHC) of Puget Sound is a staff and network model HMO headquartered in Seattle. It serves 480,000 enrollees in the state of Washington. Typical of traditional approaches used by health-care organizations, the old cost management system of GHC originally was created to meet the financial reporting needs of a less competitive era.

Cost was managed along organizational lines—divisions and departments—and other expense classifications and accounts. Cost of service information was available only at the aggregate level for the total cost. Cost and service utilization information was location-specific with no organization-wide information available for any patient or group of patients.

The lack of systematic links among data from multiple information systems compelled management to make decisions based on less than complete information.

SOURCE: John Y. Lee and Pauline Nefcy, "The Anatomy of an Effective HMO Cost Management System," *Management Accounting* (January 1997) pp. 49–52, 54.

An automobile manufacturing plant is an example of a high degree of conversion.

example, firms of professionals (such as accountants, architects, attorneys, engineers, and surveyors) convert labor and other resource inputs (materials and supplies) into completed jobs (audit reports, building plans, contracts, blueprints, and property surveys). Companies that engage in conversion activities have a distinct need for **cost accounting**, which is comprised of tools and methods applied to determine the cost of making products or performing services.

Cost accounting bridges the financial accounting and management accounting functions as shown in Exhibit 2-7 (page 48). As part of financial accounting, cost

cost accounting

LOW DEGREE	MODERATE DEGREE	HIGH DEGREE
(adding only the value of having merchandise when, where, and in the assortment needed by customers)	(washing, testing, packaging, labeling)	(causing a major transformation from input to output)
Retailing companies that act as mere conduits between suppliers and consumers (department stores, gas stations, jewelry stores, travel agencies)	Retailing companies that make small visible additions to the output prior to sale or delivery (florists, meat markets, oil-change businesses)	Manufacturing, mining, construction, agricultural, and printing companies; architectural, engineering, legal, and accounting firms; restaurants

EXHIBIT 2-6
Degrees of Conversion in Organizations

EXHIBIT 2-7
Financial, Management and
Cost Accounting Overlap

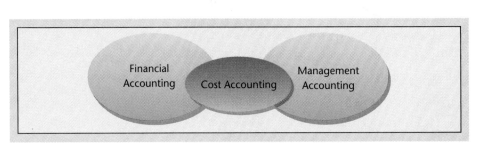

accounting provides product cost measurements for inventories and cost of goods sold on the financial statements. As part of management accounting, cost accounting provides some of the quantitative, cost-based information managers need to assess product profitability, prepare budgets, and make investment decisions. Cost accounting measurements often depend on classification of costs as product or period costs.

Product Costs and Period Costs

LEARNING OBJECTIVE ❹
How are product and period
costs differentiated?

product cost
period cost

Costs associated with making or acquiring inventory are **product costs** and are generally incurred in the production or conversion portion of the value chain. All other costs incurred outside the production or conversion areas are **period costs**.

Product Costs

Product (or inventoriable) costs for a merchandising company are fairly easy to determine. Most retailers buy goods in finished or almost finished condition and do not have significant conversion activities. The primary product cost is the purchase amount (including freight charges) of the merchandise that has been bought for resale. Retailers ordinarily have only a single inventory account, called Merchandise Inventory, which represents the cost of inventory that has been purchased but not sold. As the merchandise is sold, the product cost is transferred to Cost of Goods Sold (an expense).

In contrast, manufacturers and service companies engage in many value chain activities involving the physical change of inputs into finished products and services. Costs of these activities must be gathered and assigned as product costs to the outputs. This assignment allows the company to determine inventory costs and the cost of goods sold or cost of services rendered.

If control is to be maintained over the production process, manufacturers must account for purchased materials and supplies, goods in the process of conversion (referred to as work in process), and finished goods. Each product classification requires its own inventory account. Costs remain in the inventory accounts until the goods are sold. The costs are then charged to Cost of Goods Sold. A service provider has an inventory account for supplies used in the conversion process and may also have a Work in Process Inventory account for the cost of jobs not yet completed. However, such a firm would rarely have a Finished Goods Inventory account. Services are not normally warehoused; upon completion and acceptance, the costs related to performance are expensed on the income statement.

Period Costs

Period costs are not associated with production activities and are therefore noninventoriable. These costs are commonly associated with periods of time and relate to business operations such as sales and administration. Period costs that have been incurred and have future benefit are classified as assets. Period costs that have no determinable future benefit (such as secretaries' salaries and current period advertising) are expensed as incurred. For example, prepaid insurance on an administration building represents an asset; as the premium period passes, the insurance becomes insurance expense. Exhibit 2-8 provides some additional examples of product and period costs. As is evident in the examples, the defining criterion is whether the cost item is

PRODUCT COSTS	PERIOD COSTS
⊙ Purchased materials	⊙ Salaries of office personnel
⊙ Factory insurance premium	⊙ Depreciation on office building
⊙ Factory utility costs	⊙ Cost of shipping finished goods
⊙ Depreciation on factory building	⊙ Insurance premium on office building
⊙ Property taxes on factory	⊙ Property taxes on office building
⊙ Supplies used in factory	⊙ Advertising/Promotion costs
	⊙ Costs of recruiting sales personnel

EXHIBIT 2-8
Cost Classifications for
Financial Reporting

associated with manufacturing a product or generating a service. If so, the cost item is a product cost; otherwise, the cost item is a period cost.

Similar types of costs are classified as product or period for merchandising, manufacturing, and service companies, although some of the account titles differ. Exhibit 2-9 (page 50) compares these costs and account titles. Although both merchandise and manufacturing firms have a Cost of Goods Sold account for expensing product costs, service firms have a Cost of Services Rendered account for this purpose. All three types of firms have similar account titles for period costs.

For any of the firm types presented in Exhibit 2-9, information from the accounts can be used to analyze company profitability and answer a variety of managerial questions. For instance, a manager of a service company might want to know how much it costs to purchase the supplies needed to provide a specific service. An answer can be obtained by reviewing information in the Supplies Inventory account, but that answer is based on historical information and may not reflect current or future conditions. Supply costs change for a variety of factors, including where, and from whom, the purchase was made.

One specific type of period cost is that associated with distribution. A **distribution cost** is any cost incurred to fill an order for a product or service. Distribution costs include all amounts spent on warehousing, delivering, or shipping products to customers. Total distribution cost changes with changes in product or service volume. Although these costs directly relate to products and services, distribution costs are expensed as incurred for financial accounting purposes. When making decisions, managers cannot take an "out of sight, out of mind" attitude about these costs simply because they have been charged off in a selling expense category for financial accounting purposes.

distribution cost

Because advertising expense is incurred to increase sales rather than increase production, it is a period cost.

	COST CLASSIFICATION ON	
	BALANCE SHEET (ASSET/EXPENSE)	INCOME STATEMENT (ASSET/EXPENSE)
Merchandising Company		
Product Costs (Inventoriable)—incurred through purchases of merchandise for resale	Merchandise Inventory	⟶ Cost of Goods Sold
Period Costs (Noninventoriable)—incurred through payment or accrual for variety of nonmerchandise-related costs	Prepaid Expenses	⟶ Selling, General, & Administrative (SG&A) Expenses
Manufacturing Company		
Product Costs (Inventoriable)—incurred through purchase of raw materials; converted through incurrence of direct labor and factory overhead costs; completed and transferred out of the factory; sold	Raw Materials Inventory to Work in Process Inventory to Finished Goods Inventory	⟶ Cost of Goods Sold
Period Costs (Noninventoriable)—incurred through payment or accrual for a variety of nonproduction-related costs	Prepaid Expenses; Nonproduction Assets	⟶ SG&A Expenses
Service Company		
Product Costs (Inventoriable)—incurred through using direct labor and overhead to convert supplies into services; acceptance of service by customers	Supplies Inventory possibly to Work in Process Inventory possibly to Completed Services Inventory*	⟶ Cost of Services Rendered
Period Costs (Noninventoriable)—incurred through payment or accrual for a variety of nonservice-revenue-related costs	Prepaid Expenses; Nonproduction Assets	⟶ SG&A Expenses

*It is possible for service companies to have WIP Inventory and Completed Services Inventory on the balance sheet, although generally these accounts would not appear because services usually cannot be warehoused.

EXHIBIT 2-9
Comparison of Product and Period Costs

http://www.fedex.com

http://www.ups.com

http://www.smucker.com

Successful management of the distribution function requires not only efficiently managing costs, but developing distribution channels to deliver products and services to customers in a reliable and timely manner. An entire industry has evolved as firms have been created to provide new distribution channels. Some firms, such as Federal Express and United Parcel Service, have developed worldwide distribution services. Because of the level of competition in the distribution service industry, transportation and distribution is one of the most efficient segments of the U.S. economy. High quality delivery is now available via several modes: air, rail, truck, and ship.

Manufacturers can use one or a combination of these modes to deliver their products. For example, J.M. Smucker Co. of Orrville, Ohio, cut its transportation costs by 7 percent in 1996. It did so by using fewer carriers and opting to use a combination of rail and truck delivery services.[5]

Methods of Product Costing

LEARNING OBJECTIVE ❺
How can product costing and valuation systems be compared and contrasted?

One cost management requirement is to determine the cost of the products made or the services performed by an organization. Product costing is concerned with identi-

[5]Wilde Mathews, "Low Shipping Prices May Curb Inflation," *Wall Street Journal,* June 24, 1997, p. A2.

In the United States, product distribution is one of the most competitive and efficient areas of the economy.

fying, assigning, and managing costs. Just as a variety of methods exist to assign costs to inventory and cost of goods sold in a retail company, different methods are available to calculate product cost in a manufacturing or service environment. The method chosen depends on the nature of the product or service and the company's production or service process.

Before products can be costed, the type of product costing system and the method of cost measurement to be used must be determined. The product costing system used specifies what is to be the cost object and how costs are to be assigned to production. The method of measurement specifies how product costs will be determined.

Costing Systems

Job order and process costing are the two primary costing systems. **Job order costing** is used by entities that produce limited quantities of custom-made goods or services that conform to specifications designated by the purchaser. For instance, job order costing is appropriate for a printing firm that prepares advertisements for numerous clients, a commercial construction firm that builds skyscrapers, or an accountant who has her own tax practice. In general, services are highly user-specific so job order costing systems are usually appropriate for such businesses. Job order costing is discussed in detail in Chapter 4.

job order costing

Process costing, the other primary product costing system, is used by entities engaged in the continuous, mass production of large quantities of homogeneous goods. For example, companies manufacturing soft drinks, saltwater taffy, or gasoline would use process costing systems. In a company using process costing, the output of a single process is homogeneous; thus, specific units of output cannot be readily identified with specific input costs within a given time frame. Process costing is covered in depth in Chapter 10.

process costing

Measurement Methods

The three primary methods of measurement are actual, normal, and standard costing. A company that uses the actual costs of production to determine the cost of Work in Process (WIP) Inventory is employing an **actual cost system**. Actual cost

LEARNING OBJECTIVE 6
How is an actual costing system different from normal and standard costing systems?

actual cost system

systems are less than desirable because they require that all cost information for the period be known before any cost assignment can be made to products or services. Waiting for the information reduces management's ability to make timely operating decisions, for example, determining the price to be charged for products.

standard cost system

Rather than using actual costs, companies may employ standards (or predetermined benchmarks) for costs to be incurred and/or quantities to be used. In a **standard cost system**, unit norms are developed for production costs. Then, both actual and standard costs are recorded in the accounting records to provide an essential element of cost control: having norms against which actual costs of operations can be compared. Standard costs are used to plan for future activities and to measure inventories. Standard costing is discussed in detail in Chapter 9.

normal cost system

A third type of costing system is a normal cost system. A **normal cost system** uses a combination of actual and budgeted costs. Some material and labor costs are assigned to products at actual amounts; other costs are assigned at estimated or budgeted amounts. The normal costing system has several advantages over an actual costing system. The most obvious advantage is that the cost of a particular product can be determined at an earlier point in time, which facilitates better decision making. Normal costing is introduced in Chapter 4.

Critical Factors in Designing a Cost Management System

LEARNING OBJECTIVE ❼
How do the internal and external operating environments impact cost management systems?

A costing system is necessary to determine product or service cost, to manage a business, and to meet external reporting requirements. However, as highlighted in the following News Note, other information must be gathered if managers are to control costs. In designing or improving a cost management system, managers and accountants must be attuned to the unique characteristics of their firms.

An effective cost management system is one that successfully implements the strategies and plans of an organization and, consequently, achieves the organization's goals and objectives. A generic cost management system cannot be pulled off the shelf and applied to any organization. Each firm warrants a custom-tailored cost management system. Some overriding factors that are critical to designing any cost management system are described in the following sections.

1ˢᵗ NEWS NOTE

http:// www.conairnet.com

How to Measure Success

Conair-Franklin is a small company that manufactures bulk systems such as conveyors, dryers and blenders for other manufacturers. The company's accounting system had traditionally provided information to managers regarding cost categories such as direct materials, direct labor, overhead, and selling and administrative expenses. However, the managers found that this information was not very useful for day-to-day management of the business.

For example, the traditional profit and loss statement, balance sheet and cost accounting reports measured only the "score" at the end of each period, posted the "way it had always been posted," even though the "business game" and its rules were in constant, dynamic change. What were the P&Ls telling us about changes in market share, about customer satisfaction, or about the four fundamentals of customer-measured value: quality, service, delivery, and price competitiveness? Nothing. Our P&Ls looked okay (not great), but customers were complaining about all four "QSDP" areas. Everything was slow and laborious throughout our process, office, and plant. We were not measuring speed.

SOURCE: Jack Downie and Gail Pastoria, "Measuring Change at Conair-Franklin," *Management Accounting* (June 1997), pp. 30–32, 34, 35.

Organizational Form, Structure, and Culture

An entity's legal nature reflects its **organizational form**. Selecting the organizational form is one of the most important decisions made by business owners because that choice affects the costs of raising capital, operating the business (including taxation issues), and, possibly, of litigating. In recent years, organizational form alternatives have increased remarkably. The following News Note discusses how one firm's decision to change its organizational form was reconsidered and revoked after the passage of a new tax law.

Most large, publicly traded businesses employ the corporate organizational form. Smaller businesses or cooperative ventures between large businesses may be formed as general or limited partnerships. Most recently, as a result of new federal, state, and international legislation, some companies have chosen to organize as limited liability partnerships (LLPs) and limited liability companies (LLCs). These two forms provide some enhanced legal protections to the owners that are not available in the traditional partnership form.

Once the organizational form is selected, top managers are responsible for creating a structure that is best suited to achieving the firm's goals and objectives. Top managers make judgments about how to organize subunits and the extent to which authority will be decentralized. Although the current competitive environment is conducive to a high degree of decentralization, top managers usually retain authority over operations that can be performed more efficiently at a central location. For example, financing, personnel, and certain accounting functions may be maintained at headquarters rather than being delegated to organizational subunits.

In designing the organizational structure, top managers normally will try to group subunits either geographically or by similar missions or natural product clusters. These aggregation processes provide effective cost management because of proximity or similarity of units under a single manager's control.

The extent to which firms decentralize also determines who will be accountable for cost management and organizational control. An information system must provide relevant and timely information to the people who are making decisions that have cost control implications, and a control system must be in place to evaluate the quality of those decisions.

An entity's culture also plays an important role in designing a cost management system. To illustrate the effect of organizational culture on the cost management system, consider AT&T prior to its division into several separate firms: it was an organization characterized by "bureaucracy, centralized control, nepotism, a welfare mentality in which workers were 'taken care of,' strong socialization processes, [and] little concern

organizational form

 www.att.com

NEWS NOTE

Law Change Taxes Prior Decision

The financial wizards employed by master limited partnerships have been sharpening their pencils and studying their income statements—trying to determine whether those companies should keep their current form in light of last week's passage of new tax laws.

Recently, Borden Chemicals & Plastics LP joined a handful of other publicly traded partnerships in announcing that it will drop plans to become a corporation and will remain a partnership.

Borden, one of about twenty-four remaining "grandfathered" partnerships that were facing the expiration of a tax exemption at the end of the year, is one of a number of companies that earlier said it would convert to corporate form.

SOURCE: Phyllis Plitch, "Master Limited Partnerships Weigh Status," *Wall Street Journal*, August 19, 1997, p. A6. Reprinted by permission of *Wall Street Journal*, © 1997 Dow Jones & Company, Inc. All Rights Reserved Worldwide.

for efficiency. . . ."[6] In such a culture, the requirements of a cost management system would have been limited because few individuals needed information, decisions were made at the top of the organization, and cost control was not a consideration because costs were passed along through the rate structure to customers. After the breakup, the company's culture changed to embrace decentralized decision making, cost efficiency, and individual responsibility and accountability; supporting such a changed culture requires different types, quantities, and distributions of cost management information.

The values-based aspects of organizational culture are also extremely important in assessing the cost management system. For example, one part of Conair-Franklin's mission statement is "to be the Best Company in our industry segment as measured by the customer satisfaction index."[7] Without a well-designed cost management system, Conair-Franklin could not evaluate how well it is progressing toward the accomplishment of that mission. Thus, the cost management system is instrumental in providing a foundation for companies with an organizational culture that strives for the highest quality in all aspects of operations.

Organizational Mission and Critical Success Factors

Knowledge of the organization's mission is a key consideration in the design of a cost management system. The mission provides a long-term goal toward which the organization wishes to move. If the entity's mission is unknown, it does not matter what information is generated by the cost management system—or any other information system!

In pursuing the business mission, companies may avoid or confront competition. For example, companies may try to avoid competition by attempting to be more adept in some business dimension than other entities. As discussed in Chapter 1, generic paths a company may take to avoid competition include compression of competitive scope, differentiation, and cost leadership.[8] Companies may also decide to meet competition head-on.

critical success factor (CSF)

Clarification of mission can be served by identifying the organization's **critical success factors (CSFs)**, which are dimensions of operations that are so important to an organization's survival that, with poor performance in these areas, the entity would cease to exist. Most organizations would consider timeliness, quality, customer service, efficiency and cost control, and responsiveness to change as five critical success factors. Once managers have gained consensus on the entity's CSFs, the cost management system can be designed to (1) gather information related to measurement of those items and (2) generate output about those CSFs in forms that are useful to interested parties such as top managers.

Integrating Operating and Competitive Environment with Strategies

Once the organizational big picture has been established, managers can assess internal specifics related to the design of a cost management system. A primary consideration is the firm's **cost structure** or relative proportions of variable and fixed costs. A **variable cost** is one that changes in total in direct proportion to changes in the volume of activity, for example, the number of units produced and sold. A **fixed cost** is one that remains constant when the activity level changes.

cost structure
variable cost
fixed cost

Exhibit 2-10 shows graphically how variable and fixed costs change with changes in activity level. The behaviors of fixed and variable costs shown in the exhibit indicate that the total variable cost rises and falls as the activity level rises and falls; the fixed cost does not react to a change in activity level.

---

[6]Thomas S. Bateman and Scott A. Snell, *Management: Building Competitive Advantage* (Chicago: Irwin, 1996), p. 268.

[7]Jack Downie and Gail Pastora, "Measuring Change at Conair Franklin," *Management Accounting* (July 1997), p. 31.

[8]Michael Porter, *Competitive Advantage: Creating and Sustaining Superior Performance* (New York: Free Press, 1985), p. 17.

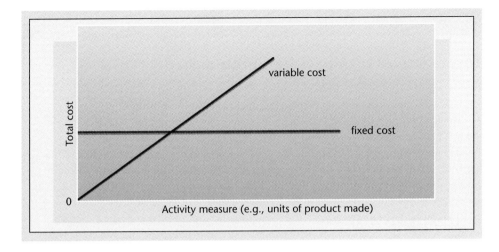

EXHIBIT 2-10
Variable and Fixed Cost
Behavior Relative to Activity

Organizational cost structures have changed dramatically in recent years, largely because of increased use of technology. Many fixed costs are associated with plant, equipment, and infrastructure investments that provide the capacity to produce goods and services. Higher proportions of these costs are most evident in industries that depend on technology for competing on the bases of quality and price. Because of the greater extent of their conversion processes, manufacturing and service firms have been better able to leverage technology than most retailing businesses.

The cost management implications of a shift in cost structure to a higher proportion of fixed costs are significant. Most importantly, fewer costs are susceptible to short-run control by managing product volume, so cost management efforts are increasingly directed toward the longer term. Also, managing fixed costs is partly a matter of capacity management: high capacity utilization (if accompanied by high sales volumes) allows a firm to reduce its per-unit fixed costs in pursuing a low-cost producer strategy. **Capacity utilization** is a measure of the extent to which actual production volume approaches potential production volume (capacity). Capacity is limited by factors such as the quantity and quality of workers and the output capacity of production technology.

capacity utilization

A second implication of the increased proportion of fixed costs is a limitation on a firm's ability to respond to changes in short-term conditions. The firm has less flexibility to take short-term actions to effect a change in the level of fixed costs. Additionally, most efforts to change costs in the short term will have long-term consequences.[9]

To pursue either a differentiation or cost leadership strategy, companies with an ever-increasing fixed cost structure must bring new products to market more rapidly than competitors. Being first to market may allow a company to price the product such that a large market share can be obtained, allowing the fixed costs to be spread over a greater number of units—and providing an industry position of cost leadership. Alternatively, the leading-edge company may set a product price that provides a substantial per-unit profit for all sales generated before competitors are able to offer similar or substitute products. Rapid time-to-market requires that new products be developed quickly.[10]

The auto industry is one in which time-to-market offers substantial advantages. For example, General Motors "aims to cut its costs of bringing new cars and light trucks to market 25 percent by 1997 by speeding up its product-development activities."[11] Chrysler Corporation and Dassault Systèmes of France have developed

http:// www.gm.com

http:// www.chrysler.com

http:// www.dsweb.com

---

[9]Many of the new fixed costs would be regarded as "committed" rather than "discretionary." See Chapter 11 for additional details.

[10]The concept of product life cycle is introduced in Chapter 1.

[11]Robert L. Simison, "GM Plans to Speed Vehicle Development and Reduce Such Costs 25% by 1997," *Wall Street Journal*, August 11, 1995, p. A2.

NEWS NOTE

http:// www.toyota.com

Toyota Drives Up Stakes in Auto Industry

Toyota Motor Corp., already a world standard-setter in vehicle quality and factory efficiency, has set a goal of nearly doubling its operating profits in the next few years.

Analysts say that Toyota's operating profit goal is roughly equivalent to targets set by the U.S. Big Three automakers to earn net income equal to 5 percent of sales. In recent years Toyota's profitability has fallen far short of its own goals and has lagged behind that of the Big Three, partly because it wasn't an overriding management focus. But because Toyota is already one of the strongest automakers financially, its determination to substantially increase its earnings power is sobering news for its rivals.

In recent presentations to analysts in New York, Boston, London and Stockholm, senior Toyota financial executives said they plan to boost profitability through "a new generation of cost savings" and continuing gains in sales volume. Ryuji Araki, Toyota's managing director for finance and accounting, acknowledged that the company could cut another 25 percent or so out of the costs of building future new vehicles.

In addition to active programs targeted at reducing costs, Toyota is a leader in technological competition in the industry. For example, the firm has pursued technologies to reduce gas consumption, reduce emissions, and create new fuel sources. By being the first to bring these technologies to market, Toyota can continue to build on its strong market-share position and differentiate its products from those of its competitors.

SOURCE: Robert L. Simison, "Toyota Aims to Double Profit Margin," *Wall Street Journal*, August 19, 1997, pp. A3, A4; Toyota Motor Corporation 1997 Annual Report. Reprinted by permission of *Wall Street Journal*, © 1997 Dow Jones & Company, Inc. All Rights Reserved Worldwide.

a computer-aided design system that will slash approximately 20 percent off the factory time needed to retool to produce a new model.[12] As indicated in the News Note above, the U.S. auto industry, to remain viable, must compete with Japan's Toyota Motor Corporation—and Toyota has ambitious plans.

LEARNING OBJECTIVE 8
How does the product life cycle affect cost management strategies?

Reducing time-to-market is merely one of many ways a company can reduce costs; other ways are listed in Exhibit 2-11. Most cost reduction actions are associated with the early part of a product's life cycle. Thus, as previously mentioned, product profitability is largely determined by an effective design and product development process.

Getting products to market quickly and profitably requires a compromise between the advantages associated with speed of product innovation and superior product design. Rapid time-to-market may mean that a firm incurs costs associated with design flaws (such as the costs of future changes) that could have been avoided if more time had been allowed for the product's development. Also, if a flawed product is marketed, some costs will likely be incurred for returns, warranty work, or customer skepticism regarding the firm's reputation for product quality.

Another aspect of an organization's operating environment is supplier relations. Many companies that have formed long-term alliances with suppliers have found such relationships to be effective cost control mechanisms. For example, by involving suppliers early in the design and development stage of new products, a better design for manufacturability will be achieved and the likelihood of meeting target costs will be improved.

Another operating environment consideration in the designing of a cost management system is the need to integrate the organization's current information systems. The feeder systems (such as payroll, inventory valuation, budgeting, and costing) that are in place should be evaluated to determine answers to the following questions:

---

[12]Neal Templin, "Chrysler Co-Designs a Computer-Aided Manufacturing Plan," *Wall Street Journal*, August 2, 1995, p. B3.

EXHIBIT 2-11
Actions to Substantially Reduce
Product Costs

⊙ Develop new production processes
⊙ Capture learning curve and experience effects
⊙ Increase capacity utilization
⊙ Use focused factory arrangement
    reduces coordination costs
⊙ Design for manufacturability
    reduces assembly time
    reduces training costs
    reduces warranty costs
    reduces required number of spare parts
⊙ Design for logistical support
⊙ Design for reliability
⊙ Design for maintainability
⊙ Adopt advanced manufacturing technologies
    reduces inventory levels
    reduces required production floor space
    reduces defects, rework and quality costs

SOURCE: Adapted from Gerald I. Susman, "Product Life Cycle Management," *Journal of Cost Management* (Summer 1989), pp. 8–22.

⊙ What data are being gathered and in what form?
⊙ What outputs are being generated and in what form?
⊙ How do the current systems interact with one another and how effective are those interactions?
⊙ Is the current chart of accounts appropriate for the cost management information desired?
⊙ What significant information issues (such as material spoilage and rate of product defects) are not presently being addressed by the information system and could those issues be integrated into the current feeder systems?

With knowledge of the above information, managers must analyze the cost–benefit tradeoffs that relate to the cost management system design. As the costs of gathering, processing, and communicating information decrease, or as the quantity and intensity of competition increase, more sophisticated cost management systems are required. Additionally, as companies focus on customer satisfaction and expand their product or service offerings, more sophisticated cost management systems are needed. In these conditions, the generation of better cost information is essential to long-run organizational survival and profitability.

Even with appropriate information systems in place, managers might fail to make decisions that are consistent with organizational strategies. Proper incentives and reporting systems must be incorporated into the CMS for managers to make appropriate decisions. This will be discussed in the following section.

ELEMENTS OF A COST MANAGEMENT SYSTEM

A cost management system is composed of a set of three primary elements: motivational, informational, and reporting. These elements are detailed in Exhibit 2-12 (page 58). Managers develop a cost management system by selecting appropriate items from each of the three categories of elements. The selected elements must be consistent with the strategies and missions of the subunits. The purpose in selecting individual control elements is to successfully implement the firm's strategies that have been formulated for the overall organization and individual subunits.

LEARNING OBJECTIVE ⑨
What three groups of elements affect the design of a cost management system and how are these elements used?

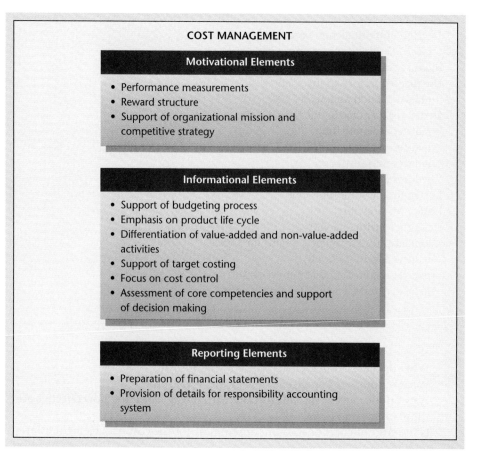

Motivational Elements

Performance measurements should be selected to be consistent with organizational goals and objectives, and to drive managers toward designated achievements. These measurements, which are discussed in depth in Chapters 14 and 15, may be quantitative or nonquantitative, financial or nonfinancial, and short term or long term. For example, if a subunit is expected to generate a specified annual profit amount, the established performance measure is quantitative, financial, and short term. A longer-term performance measure would be the change in profit over a five- to ten-year period.

The performance measurement system should be designed to encourage managers to act in the best interest of the organization and its subunits, and in support of the organizational mission and competitive strategies. Once defined, the criteria used to measure performance should be linked to the organizational incentive system because typically, "You get what you measure." Establishing a performance–reward linkage assures that managers will be rewarded in line with the quality of their organizational and subunit decisions, and thereby, for their contributions to achieving the organizational mission.

In addition to performance measures, different forms of rewards have different incentive effects and can reflect different time orientations. In general, longer-term incentives encourage managers to be more long-term-oriented in their decisions, and short-term incentives encourage managers to be focused on the near future.

To illustrate, cash is the most obvious reward that can be used to reward short-term performance. All managers receive some compensation in cash so they may pay ordinary living expenses. However, once a manager receives a cash reward, its value is not dependent on future performance. In contrast, a stock option that is not exercisable until a future time encourages a manager to be concerned about long-term performance. The ultimate value of the stock option is determined in the future when it is exercised, rather than on the date it is received.

Performance rewards for top management may consist of both short-term and long-term incentives. Normally, a major incentive is performance-based pay that is tied to the firm's stock price. The rewards for subunit managers should be based on the specific subunit's mission. Managers of subunits charged with a build mission should receive long-term incentives. These managers need to be concerned about long-term success and willing to make short-term sacrifices for long-term gains. Alternatively, managers of subunits charged with a harvest mission must be more oriented to the short term. These subunits are expected to produce as much cash and profit as possible from their operations. Accordingly, incentives should be in place to encourage managers in these subunits to have a short-term focus in decision making.

Managers will evaluate decision alternatives based on how the outcomes may impact the specified performance (measurement and reward) criteria. Because higher performance equates to a larger reward, the cost management system must have specified performance yardsticks and provide measurement information to the appropriate individuals for evaluation purposes. Performance measurement is meaningful only in a comparative or relative sense. Typically, current performance is assessed relative to past or expected performance.

Informational Elements

An organization's accounting function is expected to support the planning, controlling, performance evaluation, and decision-making functions. All of these roles converge in a system designed for cost management.

Relative to the planning role, the cost management system should provide a sound foundation for the budgeting process. Budgets provide both a specification of expected achievement as well as a benchmark against which to compare actual performance. A CMS, like a traditional cost-accounting system, should provide the financial information needed for budget preparation. But in addition, a well-designed CMS will help identify the factors that cause costs to be incurred so that more useful simulations of alternative scenarios can be made. The same system can highlight any activities in the budgeting process that provide no tangible benefits so that these activities can be reduced or eliminated and, thus, reduce the time needed for budget preparation. "By reducing the length of the budgeting cycle and making the process more efficient, the informational benefit of semiannual or quarterly budgeting may become practical."[13]

As a competitive advantage becomes more and more difficult to maintain, firms must place greater emphasis on management of the product life cycle. Firms often use innovative tools—such as target costing, first developed by the Japanese—to provide information relevant to assessing their competitive positions. As discussed earlier in this chapter, most actions available to managers to control costs are concentrated in the earliest part of the product life cycle. Accordingly, information relevant to managing costs must be focused on decisions made during that time—that information will be provided by a well-designed and integrated cost management system.

The life cycle of many products will shorten as firms become more adept at duplicating (without pirating) their competitors' offerings. In this type of environment, firms will be forced to squeeze cash from their older and more mature products to support new product development. Additionally, a greater emphasis will be placed on a firm's ability to adapt to changing competitive conditions. Flexibility will be an important organizational attribute and will cause managers to change the emphasis of control systems, as shown in Exhibit 2-13 (page 60).

To provide information relevant to product design and development, the accounting information system must relate resource consumption and cost to alternative product and process designs. In addition, managers will be more concerned about investing in research and development or acquiring new technology. Such decisions will need to be analyzed relative to effects on a firm's future cost structure, long-range competitive benefits, and organizational cash flow. Then, consideration

---

[13]Ibid.

EXHIBIT 2-13
Shift in Control Emphasis in Future Competitive Environment

	FROM		TO
Strategic Focus	Achieving financial results: sales, costs, and profits	----------▶	Achieving critical success factors: low cost, high quality, sales mix variety, on-time delivery, and high capacity usage
Product Sales	Submitting bids and taking orders	----------▶	Developing partnerships and creating sales opportunities
Budgeting	Developing annual plans	----------▶	Ongoing planning and frequent budget revisions
Culture	Meeting project expectations	----------▶	Learning and improving upon processes

SOURCE: Ralph E. Drtina and Gary A. Monetti, "Controlling Flexible Business Strategies," *Journal of Cost Management* (Fall 1995), pp. 42–49.

must be given to the level of flexibility the firm will maintain if short-run changes create new competitive challenges or opportunities.

The information required to support decisions depends on the unique situational factors of the firm and its subunits. The information system must allow the decision maker to evaluate how alternative decision choices would impact the items that are used to measure and evaluate the decision maker's performance.

Reporting Elements

The reporting elements of a cost management system refer to methods of providing information to persons in evaluative roles. First and foremost, the CMS must be effective in generating fundamental external financial statement information including inventory valuation and cost of goods sold. This information will not necessarily be used for internal planning, control, performance evaluation, or decision-making purposes. But if the feeder systems to the CMS have been appropriately integrated and the system has been designed to minimize informational distortions, generating both external and internal product or service costs will not be difficult.

In addition to financial statement valuations, the reporting elements of the cost management system must address the internal needs of a **responsibility accounting system**. This system provides information to top management about the performance of organizational subunits and their managers.[14] For each subunit, the responsibility accounting system separately tracks costs and, if appropriate, revenues.

Performance reports are useful only to the extent that the actual performance can be compared to a meaningful baseline of expected performance. Expected performance can be denoted in financial terms (such as budgetary figures) or in nonfinancial terms (such as customer satisfaction measures, capacity utilization, and research and development activities). By comparing actual and expected performance information generated from the cost management system, top managers are able to determine which managers and subunits exceeded, met, or failed to meet expectations. This information can then be linked to managerial decisions about performance rewards.

The movement toward decentralization has increased the importance of an effective reporting system. With decentralization, top managers must depend on the

responsibility accounting system

---

[14]Responsibility accounting concepts are discussed in detail in Chapter 14.

reporting system to keep all organizational subunits striving to achieve their subunit missions and organizational goals and objectives. A cost management system is not designed to cut costs. It exists to ensure that a satisfactory outcome is realized from the incurrence of costs. Accordingly, cost management begins with an understanding that different costs are incurred for different purposes. Some costs are incurred to yield immediate benefit; others are expected to yield a benefit in the near or distant future.

Only by linking activities to strategies and costs to activities can the benefits of cost incurrence be understood. Thus, a starting point in achieving effective cost management is sorting organizational activities according to their strategic roles. This logic suggests organizational management is made easier by dividing operations into subunits. By so doing, top managers can assign responsibility and accountability for distinct subunit missions to a particular manager. In turn, by creating the correct incentives for each subunit manager, top management will have set the stage for each subunit manager to act in the best interest of the overall organization. This linkage focuses the attention of a specific subunit manager on a set of costs and activities that uniquely relate to the subunit's organizational mission.

For subunit managers to be effective in managing costs, each must be provided with relevant information. Because the nature and time horizon of decisions made by managers vary across subunits, each manager requires unique information. Additionally, a manager needs to know how each alternative decision is likely to impact his or her performance.

A reporting system provides a comparison of expected to actual performance for each manager. This comparison is the basis for distinguishing strong from weak or unacceptable performance. The comparison is also a basis for determining the relative rewards (bonus pay, stock options, etc.) of each manager. The better the performance, the greater the reward that is earned. Accordingly, the reporting system provides motivation for subunit managers to act in the best interest of the organization so that their rewards are maximized.

Optimal organizational performance is realized only if there is consistency for each subunit across the elements of motivation, information, and reporting. Managers of subunits with growth-oriented missions need information tailored to appropriate competitive strategies and focused on the early part of the product life cycle. Incentives for these managers to control costs need to be relatively long term, and reward structures should emphasize success in the areas of product development and design. Alternatively, subunit managers of mature businesses need more information pertaining to short-term competition. The reward and reporting structures for these managers should emphasize near-term profit and cash flow.

IMPLEMENTING A COST MANAGEMENT SYSTEM

Because most businesses have a CMS in place, CMS design and implementation issues typically relate to modifications of existing cost management systems. Once the organization and its subunits have been assessed and the structure of the cost management system determined, the current information system(s) should be evaluated. A gap analysis is necessary to compare the information needed to the information that is currently available, or how well desired outputs coincide with current outputs. Any difference represents a gap to be overcome. Exhibit 2-14 (page 62) demonstrates how gap analysis is used to design changes in the CMS.

In many situations, eliminating all system gaps is impossible in the short term, potentially because of software or hardware capability or availability. Methods of reducing or eliminating the gaps, including all related technical requirements and changes to existing feeder systems, should be specified in detail. These details should be expressed, qualitatively and quantitatively, in terms of costs and benefits.

LEARNING OBJECTIVE ❿
How is gap analysis used in the implementation of a cost management system?

EXHIBIT 2-14
Design of a Cost Management System

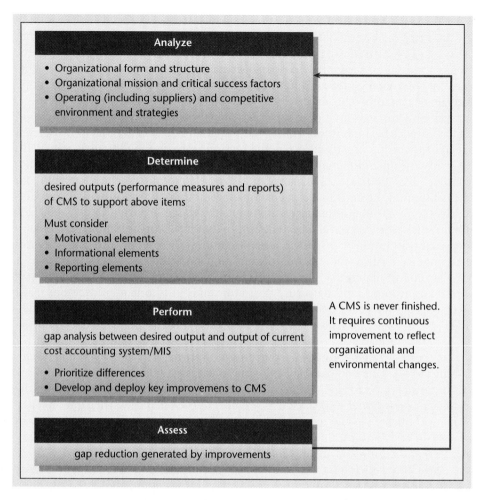

In the event of limited resources, top management may then prioritize the differences as to which gap issues to address and in which order. As system implementation proceeds, management should assess the effectiveness of the improvements and evaluate the need for other improvements. Once the CMS has been established, previously identified gaps may become irrelevant or may rise in priority. It is only through continuous improvement efforts that the cost management system will provide an ongoing, viable network of information to users.

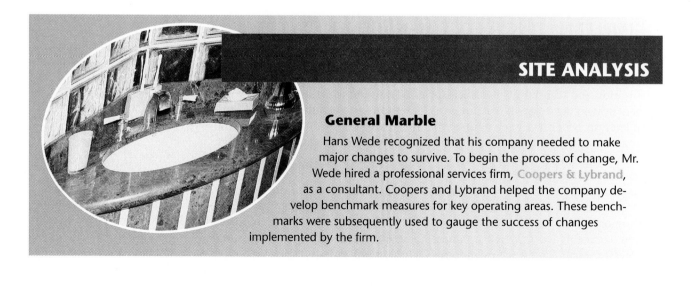

SITE ANALYSIS

General Marble

Hans Wede recognized that his company needed to make major changes to survive. To begin the process of change, Mr. Wede hired a professional services firm, Coopers & Lybrand, as a consultant. Coopers and Lybrand helped the company develop benchmark measures for key operating areas. These benchmarks were subsequently used to gauge the success of changes implemented by the firm.

SITE ANALYSIS

The company organized teams to lead changes in six areas: order filling, inventory procurement, value engineering, financial processes, accounts receivable, and inventory analysis. Common objectives were established for the teams. These objectives included reducing inventory by $2 million, reducing costs of order filling by $1.5 million, reducing defects and returns by $2 million, and achieving other cost reductions of $600,000.

After attacking the problems with consolidation, the closing cycle for the accounting system was reduced from fifteen days to four days. This reduction was achieved within the first eight months. Changes made encompassed everything from the chart of accounts to the accounting systems. By reducing closing time, the accounting function was able to free staff to concentrate on managerial concerns. A new reporting system was developed that tracked improvements in important business processes such as cost of processes, unit costs, fill rates, on-time shipments, first run yield, and adherence to schedule.

Next, the accounting function attacked other areas of financial management, such as reinforcing continuous improvement, consolidating billing and cash management, and reducing the costs of goods damaged during shipping. The accounting function had become a valuable aid to managing the process of change and in providing managers information they needed to function effectively.

So, how successful have been the changes made at the company? Following are a few of the relevant statistics:

- Inventory turnover increased from .2 to 5.7.
- On-time delivery increased from 40 percent to 100 percent.
- Headcount dropped from 400 to 269.
- Inventory dropped by $2.1 million.
- Order fulfillment increased to 100 percent.

Mr. Wede believes that the company is making substantial progress. By concentrating on improving its core competencies, the company is developing skills that will allow it to be successful in its traditional business lines and to grow by entering new markets with new products.

SOURCE: Charles M. Bokman, "Anatomy of a Turnaround," *Management Accounting* (December 1996), pp. 38–42. Reprinted from *Management Accounting*, published by the Institute of Management Accountants, Montvale, NJ. Visit our website at www.imanet.org.

CROSS-FUNCTIONAL APPLICATIONS

TOPIC OF NOTE	DISCIPLINE	CROSS-FUNCTIONAL APPLICATIONS
Product Costs	Marketing	Marketers use product costs to determine a product's competitiveness in the marketplace. A product cost is necessary to design the marketing strategies, especially pricing, research, and distribution strategies.
	Financial Accounting	Product costs are necessary to determine cost of goods sold and project gross margins as well as inventories. Most firms project their financial statements into the future for planning purposes. These are called "pro-forma" financial statements.
	Engineering	Reduction of product costs through innovative technology and less expensive material and processes is a major goal of industrial engineers. In addition, improvement of a product's features, attributes, and benefits is constrained by considerations of product cost. Engineers' efforts to improve a product's utility and competitiveness is ultimately constrained by those same considerations.

CROSS-FUNCTIONAL APPLICATIONS

TOPIC OF NOTE	DISCIPLINE	CROSS-FUNCTIONAL APPLICATIONS
Product Costs *(continued)*	Microeconomics	Product costs are a primary determinant of selling price. Certain products are sensitive to a change in selling price, causing the market to find a ready substitute product when the selling price exceeds some limit. This is a condition known as "elasticity."
Period Costs	Microeconomics	When a cost cannot be traced as a factor of production into a product, then it is associated with the period of time that the product was produced or sold. The value-added concept of product cost can never explain the total cost of producing a product for sale. Therefore, an accounting period is used as a second parameter of total cost.
	Financial Accounting	All costs of operating a business except for those associated with providing a product are termed operating costs and are often subdivided into general, administrative, and selling expenses. These operating costs appear on the income statement as a deduction from gross margin if they are associated with the firm's main line of business, or as other expenses if they are related to a secondary line of business in which the firm engages.
	Marketing	"Distribution costs in marketing" is usually a loosely defined term for all costs necessary to position a product for sale, excluding the cost of the product itself. Distribution costs are usually quoted as a percentage of the sales dollar, although many of these costs are controllable by marketing managers.
Cost Behavior— Fixed, Variable	Business Law	Management attempts to stabilize cost behavior through contractual arrangements, thus locking in certain aspects of the cost structure. Future costs that are not predictable are limited by contingency contracts, which relate future costs to some fixed event.
	Engineering	Engineers often project cost behavior based upon the inputs into the manufacturing process—such as material specifications, power consumption, and efficiency of the process. This approach depends more on the physical measurements of the factors of production to determine cost than would traditional accounting. However, when new or unproven processes are being evaluated, this method is indispensable. Also, it could be coordinated with the more traditional approaches once the firm has some baseline experience with the new process.
	Management	Management is attempting to mitigate the trend in many organizations toward a greater relative fixed cost component by sharing those costs with willing suppliers or customers. The key term in management is "cooperative." Advertising can be thought of as a committed fixed cost. Cooperative advertising could spread the burden among the supplier, the firm offering the product for sale, and even some other firms with complementary products.

CHAPTER SUMMARY

Managerial accountants provide information for managers' planning, controlling, performance evaluation and decision-making needs. A cost management system is a part of a firm's control systems. Control systems exist to guide organizations to achievement of their goals and objectives by implementing plans and strategies.

Control systems have four primary components: detectors, assessors, effectors, and communications networks.

A cost management system consists of a set of formal methods developed for planning and controlling an organization's cost generating activities relative to its goals and objectives. This system serves multiple purposes: develop product costs, assess product/service profitability, improve understanding of how processes affect costs, facilitate cost control, measure performance, and implement organizational strategies.

A cost management system is built on many subsystems that gather and classify financial and nonfinancial data. These systems support not only the cost management system but all demands for financial and managerial accounting information. One of the most important subsystems is the product costing system.

Product costs are associated with buying a product for resale, manufacturing a product, or providing a service. Period costs are incurred in sales and administration areas. Product cost assignments may utilize job order, process, or hybrid systems. Such systems may assign actual, standard, or normal costs to products.

It is not possible to simply adopt a generic, off-the-shelf cost management system. Managers must be sensitive to the unique aspects of their organizations. Three factors that should be taken into account in designing a control system are the organizational form, structure, and culture; organizational mission and critical success factors; and the competitive environment.

A cost management system must be designed using elements from three groups of management control tools: motivational, informational, and reporting elements. The selected elements of the system should be consistent with the missions of the individual subunits.

The motivational elements provide managers the incentive to take the actions that are in the best interest of their subunits and the overall organization. Managers are motivated to do the right thing when their rewards are linked to the quality of decisions they make on behalf of the organization and their specific subunits.

The informational elements provide relevant data that are useful in measuring the performance of managers and their subunits and in making managerial decisions. To compete in the global environment, firms need a variety of informational techniques to assess their relative competitive positions.

The reporting elements provide information regarding managerial performance. A responsibility accounting system provides information to top management about the performance of an organizational subunit and its manager. The information provided by the reporting elements is the basis for rewarding managers.

Gap analysis is the key to identifying differences, gaps, between the ideal cost management system and the existing system. By prioritizing the order in which gaps are to be closed, managers can proceed in an orderly manner with updating the cost management system. Because business processes are constantly evolving, the cost management system must be continuously evaluated and updated so that it is able to provide the information and motivation required by managers.

KEY TERMS

Actual cost system (p. 51)

Capacity utilization (p. 55)

Control system (p. 41)

Conversion (p. 46)

Cost accounting (p. 47)

Cost management system (p. 43)

Cost structure (p. 54)

Critical success factors (p. 54)

Distribution cost (p. 49)

Financial accounting (p. 45)

Fixed cost (p. 54)

Job order costing (p. 51)

Management accounting (p. 45)

Normal cost system (p. 52)

Organizational form (p. 53)

Period cost (p. 48)

Process costing (p. 51)

Product cost (p. 48)

Responsibility accounting system (p. 60)

Standard cost system (p. 52)

Variable cost (p. 54)

END OF CHAPTER MATERIALS

⊙ QUESTIONS

1. Why is an effictive management information system a key element of an effective management control system?

2. Why do managers require both internal and external information to manage effectively?

3. What are the four components of a control system? To what devices would each of these relate in one of an automobile's systems?

4. Why would an organization have multiple control systems in place?

5. Why is cost management different from cost minimization?

6. How can a cost management system help in investment management activities?

7. Identify examples of useful information that could be provided *to* a cost management system by each of the functional areas shown in Exhibit 2-4.

8. Why would management be willing to accept "inaccurate" costs from the cost management system? What sacrifices would be necessary to obtain "accurate" costs?

9. What are examples of costs that a cost management system might treat differently for internal and external purposes? Why would these treatments be appropriate?

10. How is managerial accounting related to financial accounting? To cost accounting?

11. Why is it important for managers and accountants to distinguish between product and period costs?

12. On which financial statement would you find assets? On which financial statement would you find expenses? Explain.

13. How are manufacturing firms significantly different from merchandising firms with regard to conversion activities?

14. Why do some firms use job order costing while other firms use process costing? Is this an arbitrary choice? Explain.

15. How is normal costing a significant improvement over actual costing in terms of providing timely product cost information?

16. Why is the choice of organizational form a cost management decision?

17. Discuss ways in which organizational culture could be used as a control mechanism.

18. List five types of cost management information that would be most useful to an organizational subunit that is (a) expected to achieve growth and (b) expected to generate cash.

19. What benefits are gained by an organization that has a high level of variable costs and a low level of fixed costs? A high level of fixed costs and a low level of variable costs?

20. How has technology increased the levels of fixed (or long-term variable) costs in companies?

21. How might the cost management systems of an organization that has a high level of variable costs and a low level of fixed costs differ from that of an organization with a high level of fixed costs and a low level of variable costs?

22. Give three examples of industries in which time-to-market is critical. Give three examples of industries in which time-to-market is almost irrelevant. Discuss the reasons for importance or lack thereof in each industry.

23. What are feeder systems and why are they important in the design of a cost management system?

24. Why is product life-cycle stage such an important consideration in managing production costs?

25. Which is most important in the design of a cost management system: motivational elements, informational elements, or reporting elements? Discuss the rationale for your answer.

26. "A firm cannot be successful unless short-term profits are achieved." Is this statement true or false? Why?

27. Provide three examples from your academic career of the truthfulness of the statement, "You get what you measure."

28. How does the nature of the performance reward provided affect the incentives of a manager to be either short-term or long-term oriented in making decisions?

29. What is gap analysis? How is gap analysis used in updating cost management systems?

⊙ EXERCISES

30. *(Terminology)* Match each item in the right-hand column with a term in the left-hand column.

   a. Process costing
   b. Cost structure
   c. Normal cost system
   d. Responsibility accounting system
   e. Cost accounting
   f. Job order cost system
   g. Actual costing
   h. Control system
   i. Cost management system
   j. Financial accounting

   1. Provides information mainly to external users
   2. Is a bridge between financial and managerial accounting
   3. Uses a combination of actual and estimated costs
   4. Is a costing system used by custom manufacturers
   5. Is the costing system that is most likely to provide untimely information
   6. Is used to manage costs relative to organizational strategy
   7. Is a managerial tool to implement organizational plans
   8. Is relative amounts of fixed and variable costs
   9. Is a costing system that would be used by a brick maker
   10. Is a source of information regarding managerial performance

31. *(Difference between financial and management accounting)* The following words and phrases describe or are associated with either financial or managerial accounting. Indicate for each item whether it is more closely associated with financial (F) or management (M) accounting.
   a. Verifiable
   b. Historical
   c. Relevant
   d. Internally focused
   e. FASB
   f. Forecasted
   g. Formal
   h. Focus is on organizational segments
   i. Cost/benefit analysis
   j. Focus is on serving external users
   k. Emphasis is on timeliness
   l. Emphasis is on consistency
   m. Future oriented
   n. Flexible

32. *(Degree of conversion)* Next to each of the following descriptions of firms, indicate whether the firm is best described as engaging in a high (H), moderate (M), or low (L) degree of conversion. Also indicate whether the firm is best described as a manufacturing (M), merchandising (MD), or service (S) enterprise.
   a. Fish processor
   b. Commercial lending department of a bank

    c. Fast-food franchise

    d. Department store

    e. Hair salon

    f. City street cleaning department

    g. Labor union

    h. Freight company

    i. Insurance company

    j. News organization

    k. Cotton farm

    l. Street newspaper vendor

    m. Flower shop

    n. Butcher shop

    o. Accounting firm

33. *(Type of organization)* Indicate whether each of the following accounts is likely to be associated with a manufacturing (M), merchandising (MD), or service (S) business. Note that there may be more than one correct answer for each item.

    a. Income tax expense

    b. Raw materials inventory

    c. Cost of goods sold

    d. Finished goods inventory

    e. Administrative expenses

    f. Work in process inventory

    g. Shipping expense

    h. Merchandise inventory

    i. Cost of services rendered

    j. Rent expense

    k. Factory depreciation expense

    l. Selling expense

34. *(Inventory types)* Manufacturing firms typically have three different types of inventory: raw materials (RM), work in process (WIP), and finished goods (FG). For each of the following items, indicate which, if any, inventory would be affected by the given transaction. Note that some transactions may involve more than one type of inventory.

    a. A clothes manufacturer incurs freight costs to ship shirts to its customers.

    b. A clothes manufacturer sells a thousand pairs of denim slacks.

    c. A contractor acquires fence posts it uses in making commercial fencing.

    d. A hose manufacturer completes the production of two thousand feet of custom-made hose.

    e. A lamp manufacturer purchases three thousand light bulbs.

    f. A lamp manufacturer installs electric cords in four hundred lamps on the production floor.

    g. A lamp manufacturer ships five hundred lamps from the production floor to a warehouse pending shipment to wholesalers.

    h. A restaurant chain purchases three thousand pounds of ground beef.

    i. A farmer sprays his corn crop with insecticide to prevent insect damage.

    j. A commercial bakery adds yeast to its bread mix.

    k. A bakery incurs monthly sales commissions in marketing its products.

35. *(Product or period cost)* For each of the following, indicate whether the transaction involves a product (PR) or period (PD) cost.

    a. A retail firm pays $1,200 to advertise its special sale of winter clothes.

    b. An engineering firm pays salaries of $100,000 to engineers who are working on four different design contracts.

    c. A manufacturing firm incurs $48,000 of conversion costs in its factory.

    d. An accounting firm incurs $62,000 of administrative costs.

    e. A grocer pays $25 to repair a display shelf.

    f. A manufacturer records $98,000 of depreciation on its factory building.

g. A restaurant pays $400 in electricity costs to operate its stoves and other cooking equipment.

h. A hardware store pays $200 to have its windows cleaned.

i. A marketing executive pays $3,000 to entertain prospective clients.

j. An ice-cream company buys milk from a local dairy for $2,100.

k. A California fruit farm pays $18,000 to ship fruit to the East Coast.

l. A tire manufacturer records $40,000 of depreciation on its finished goods inventory warehouse.

36. *(Source documents)* Assume that you have been hired by a large manufacturing firm to develop a payroll cost control system. Identify which source documents you would need to develop this system and how those source documents would be used to support the system.

37. *(Product and period costs)* Identify ten firms in ten different industries. For each of these firms for a given year, compute the following ratio:

   Product cost ratio = Cost of goods sold ÷ Sales

   Write a report in which you discuss why this ratio is not the same across the industries and firms that you investigated.

38. *(Product cost management)* A ratio that provides information about inventory management is called inventory turnover. This ratio can be computed as cost of goods sold divided by the ending inventory balance. Find five manufacturing firms and compute the inventory turnover ratio using financial statement data for each of the following years: 1980, 1985, 1990, and 1995. Next, compute the mean (average) ratio for each year for the five firms. Then, write a report in which you describe how the ratio has changed over the period 1980 through 1995 and discuss the reasons you believe are responsible for the change.

39. *(Managerial information requirements)* Assume that you are an accountant who is considering employment with one of two firms. The first firm is a fast-growing technology firm. Its sales are $500 million per year, with annual sales projected to grow at a rate of 22 percent over the next five years. The other firm is in a mature industry in which approximately twelve firms are fiercely competing to maintain market share and profitability. This firm has annual sales of $2 billion. Prepare a brief oral report in which you discuss how your job focus and daily activities would likely vary between the two firms.

40. *(Role of accounting information)* In a team of three, prepare an oral presentation discussing how accounting information can (a) help and (b) hinder an organization's progress toward its mission and objectives.

⊙ CASES

41. *(Designing cost management systems)* Taking the stage at Agco Corp.'s annual product show, Robert J. Ratliff makes a brazen prediction: The seven-year-old farm-equipment maker will threaten to unseat 160-year-old Deere & Co. as the industry giant.

   A new tractor maker? Go on, laugh. That's what bankers did when Mr. Ratliff was trying to start the company. For years, their Sunday drives in the country had shown them that farm equipment came in three colors: green (Deere), red (Case Corp.), and blue (Amsterdam-based New Holland NV). Why would farmers, a cautious breed, choose something new?

   To keep manufacturing costs low, Agco employs a strategy unusual in the farm-equipment industry: It makes barely 50 percent of its own products and gets the rest from suppliers, which ship to Agco assembly plants entire transmissions, engines, and axles, like pieces of a giant jigsaw puzzle. At its tractor plant in Independence, Mo., for example, workers simply bolt the components together and send the machine through a paint booth. The time needed to make a tractor: three days. "We're an assembler, not a manufacturer," Mr. Ratliff says. By contrast, Agco's rivals, such as Deere, make almost everything, down to building engines and mixing paint.

Agco differs in other ways too. Case and Deere routinely spend 3 percent to 4 percent of sales—hundreds of millions of dollars—on research and development to improve engines or electronic controls. Mr. Ratliff is spending barely $65 million this year.

"We're not technological leaders," says Mr. Shumejda, Agco's executive vice president of technology and development, "and we shouldn't be. But we're quick followers." Today, he adds, technological advances in farm equipment are essentially luxury items. "Most of our customers don't need a Mercedes. They just need a top-end Buick." [SOURCE: Carl Quintanilla, "A Remarkable Gamble in an Industry Slump Pays Off Fast for Agco," *Wall Street Journal*, August 19, 1997, pp. A1, A8. Reprinted by permission of *Wall Street Journal*, © 1997 Dow Jones & Company, Inc. All Rights Reserved Worldwide.]

a. Describe, contrast, and discuss the apparent strategies of Agco and Deere.

b. Based on your answer in part (a), how would the focus of the cost management systems of the two firms be different?

c. Assume you are a market analyst. How would you evaluate Ratliff's prediction that Agco will overtake Deere & Co., given Agco's present strategy?

42. *(Cost management strategies)* In Digital Equipment Corp.'s 1994 reorganization, its second in as many years, the company eliminated hundreds of sales and marketing jobs in its health-industries group, which had been bringing in $800 million of annual revenue by selling computers to hospitals and other health-care providers worldwide.

Digital says it cut [costs and positions] because it had to act fast. It was losing about $3 million a day, and its cost of sales was much higher than that of its rivals. Robert B. Palmer, the chief executive officer of the Maynard, Mass., company, saw across-the-board cuts in all units, regardless of profitability, as the way to go . . .

But in the health-industries group, the cutbacks imposed unexpected costs. Digital disrupted longstanding ties between its veteran salespeople and major customers by transferring their accounts to new sales divisions. It also switched hundreds of smaller accounts to outside distributors without notifying the customers.

At the industry's annual conference, "I had customers coming up to me and saying, 'I haven't seen a Digital sales rep in nine months. Whom do I talk to now?'" recalls Joseph Lesica, a former marketing manager in the group who resigned last year. "That really hurt our credibility. I was embarrassed."

Resellers of Digital computers, who account for most of its health-care sales, also complained about diminished technology and sales support. "There were months when you couldn't find anybody with a Digital badge," complains an official at one former reseller who had been accustomed to Digital sales reps accompanying him on customer calls. "They [Digital] walked away from large numbers of clients."

Adds Richard Tarrant, chief executive of IDX Systems Corp., a Burlington, Vt., reseller that used to have an exclusive arrangement with Digital: "Now, they're just one of several vendors we use."

Many Digital customers turned to International Business Machines Corp. [IBM] and Hewlett-Packard Co. and so did some employees of Digital's downsized health-care group. Mr. Lesica says some laid-off workers went to Hewlett-Packard and quickly set about bringing Digital clients with them. "That's another way [Digital] shot itself in the foot," he says. [SOURCE: Alex Markels and Matt Murray, "Call It Dumbsizing: Why Some Companies Regret Cost-Cutting," *Wall Street Journal*, May 4, 1996, pp. A1, A6. Reprinted by permission of *Wall Street Journal*, © 1996 Dow Jones & Company, Inc. All Rights Reserved Worldwide.]

a. What is the implied mission of the health-industries group of Digital? Explain.

b. As a stock analyst, how would you evaluate across-the-board cuts as an approach to reducing costs?

c. When Digital decided to cut costs, what were the apparent criteria used to determine which costs were to be cut?

d. How could a better, integrated cost management system have helped Digital avoid the adverse effects of its cost cutting efforts?

43. *(Incentives and performance measurement)* Flatland Metals Co. produces steel products for a variety of customers. One division of the company is Residential Products Division. This division was created in the late 1940s; its principal products since that time have been galvanized steel components used in garage door installations. The division has been continuously profitable since 1950 and in 1996 generated profits of $10 million on sales of $300 million.

However, over the past ten years, growth in the division has been slow; profitability has become stagnant, and few new products have been developed, although the garage door components market has matured. The president of the company, John Stamp, has asked his senior staff to evaluate the operations of the Residential Products Division and to make recommendations for changes that would improve its operations. The staff uncovered the following facts:

- Tracinda Green, age 53, has been president of the division for the past fifteen years.
- Ms. Green receives a compensation package that includes a salary of $175,000 annually plus a cash bonus based on achievement of the budgeted level of annual profit.
- Growth in sales in the residential metal products industry has averaged 12 percent annually over the past decade. Most of the growth has occurred in ornamental products used in residential privacy fencing.
- Nationally, the division's market share in the overall residential metal products industry has dropped from 12 percent to 7 percent during the past ten years and it has dropped from 40 percent to 25 percent for garage door components.
- The division maintains its own information systems. The systems in use today are mostly the same systems that were in place fifteen years ago; however, some of the manual systems have been computerized (e.g., payroll, accounts payable, accounting).
- The division has no customer service department. A small sales staff solicits and takes orders by phone from national distribution chains.
- The major intra-division communication tool is the annual operating budget. No formal statements have been prepared in the division regarding strategies, mission, values, goals, or objectives, or identifying core competencies or critical success factors.

You have been hired as a consultant for the Residential Products Division. Given the introductory paragraphs and the facts from the staff of the company's president, prepare a report in which you identify the major problems in the Residential Products Division and develop recommendations to address the problems you have identified.

44. *(Cost management and service quality)* A joke making the rounds in Philadelphia-area doctors' lounges goes like this:

Leonard Abramson, chief executive officer of U.S. Healthcare Inc., the big health-maintenance company, dies and goes to heaven, where he tells God what a great place it is. "Don't get too comfortable," God advises. "You're only approved for a three-day stay."

That's the kind of cost control that the messianic Mr. Abramson understands. In the past two years, U.S. Healthcare has slashed the fees it pays to specialists and hospitals by 12 percent to 20 percent and sometimes more, these providers say. In the past year, it has cut members' days in hospitals by 11 percent. Increasingly, it asks specialists and hospitals to assume the financial risk for procedures that cost more than anticipated.

U.S. Healthcare is widely considered one of the country's toughest HMO companies, and one of the most innovative. It keeps 30 cents of every premium dollar to pay for salaries, marketing, administration and shareholder dividends, nearly 10 cents more than the industry average. It zealously tracks the performance of doctors and hospitals, paying more to those whose quality scores are high. It is earning robust profits—up 99 percent in the past 24 months—while rocking the tradition-bound health-care markets along the East Coast.

"Unless you change the culture of the community you're working in, you're not changing health care," Mr. Abramson declares.

In the health-care community, U.S. Healthcare has both staunch supporters and critics. Consider the following additional information:

⊚ Last year, Mr. Abramson earned $9.8 million in salary, bonuses and stock options. Critics suggest this is excessive pay and takes resources that could otherwise have been applied to benefit patients. Mr. Abramson says that in a free market economy, large rewards flow to those who provide superior performance.

⊚ Critics claim U.S. Healthcare selects service providers based on price rather than quality.

⊚ The company pays doctors to take training courses, such as one in breast cancer screening.

⊚ The company has an information system that allows it to rank hospitals according to infection rates of urology patients, the length of stay for coronary-bypass surgery, or the number of babies delivered by cesarean. The company shows the comparative data to its service providers and uses it as leverage in negotiations.

⊚ The company is increasingly using performance-based pay contracts for its service providers.

⊚ All of U.S. Healthcare's HMOs have earned three-year accreditation from the National Committee for Quality Assurance; this is the best performance of any U.S. managed-care company.

Assume that you sit on a regulatory board that monitors health-care providers. Examine the preceding information and determine your opinion as to whether U.S. Healthcare is developing superior methods of delivering health care to U.S. citizens, or, alternatively, uses its market power and information resources to exploit members and service providers. Support your conclusion with arguments by applying concepts provided in the chapter to the information provided in this case.

⊙ ETHICS AND QUALITY DISCUSSION

45. When a machine tried out for her job reading electricity meters earlier this year, Vicki Barsczak hoped it would fail. It didn't.

So, in April, Kansas City Power & Light Co., her employer, became the first big U.S. utility to begin installing a tiny electronic device in each of its 420,000 meters. The automatic reader, which broadcasts data on electricity usage every few minutes, is dooming Ms. Barsczak's $15-an-hour job—and probably those of all of the nation's 35,000 human meter readers.

She admits to feeling "animosity toward this inanimate object."

The number of people displaced by technology—modern-day John Henrys—is becoming legion. Automation has been shrinking manufacturing payrolls for years, but now it is spreading rapidly into the much larger service sector. Smart machines and networks born of a marriage of computing and communications are raising service productivity, but also destroying many jobs, destabilizing others, and constraining growth in new jobs.

Since services provide most of the jobs in any mature economy, the new information networks raise doubts about the commonly held belief that technology always creates more jobs than it destroys.

[SOURCE: Pascal Zachary, "Service Productivity Is Rising Fast—and So Is the Fear of Lost Jobs," *Wall Street Journal*, June 8, 1995, pp. A1, A10. Reprinted by permission of *Wall Street Journal*, © 1995 Dow Jones & Company, Inc. All Rights Reserved Worldwide.]

a. One of the key success factors of most companies is quality output. Often, new technology is acquired for the sake of improving efficiency and quality. However, when new technology is installed, it often displaces existing employees. Knowledge of the impact of technology acquisitions on employment may make employees fearful of new technology and distrustful of management. In turn, the lack of trust may impair quality initiatives, including the very quality initiatives for which new technology is sought.

What actions would you take as a manager in acquiring new technology to maintain the loyalty of workers and maintain or improve the overall quality of operations?

b. What are the ethical responsibilities of managers to workers in instances where new technology displaces existing workers?

46. [John] Strazzanti is the president of Com-Corp Industries, a $13 million, 100 employee metal-stamping shop he incorporated in Cleveland in 1980. He'd started out as a machine operator with a tool-and-die manufacturer, rapidly climbing the ladder to become general manager of another stamping company. Along the way, he didn't just dream about what he'd change if he were a company president. He figured out ways to make his dreams a reality.

   [Dateline: Cleveland, 1977]. Packie Presser was vice president of the notoriously demanding local chapter of the teamsters' union. The chapter controlled a metal-stamping plant where Strazzanti had just been promoted from floor supervisor to general manager. Strazzanti recalls:

   > Two coworkers marched into my office. It was a hot summer day; they had had a few beers at lunch and were fired up. They worked hard in the warehouse and saw the engineers working in the air-conditioning and getting paid a lot more. They didn't think it was fair and wanted more money. I knew I was in a no-win situation. If I told them I thought they were being paid fairly, that's what they expected; they were going to argue, and they weren't going to be happy with the results. If I gave them more money, I was being unfair to everybody else.
   >
   > So I took out a legal pad and I told them to write down whatever they wanted to be paid. Thirty days from that date, they would get that pay—with one caveat. During the thirty days, I would shop for replacements for them. If I could get highly qualified people to work for anything less than that number, they would have to take a hike. They asked for time to think about it and never came back with a number.
   >
   > A lot of these guys think that if a company fills an order for a million dollars, it earns a million dollars in profit. I realized that if workers understood how a company earned a profit and how it had to be competitive, a lot of the resentment between managers and employees could be eliminated. And they needed to understand that if they improved their job skills, they could receive a higher wage.
   >
   > [SOURCE: Reprinted with permission of *Inc.* magazine, Goldhirsh Group, Inc., 38 Commercial Wharf, Boston, MA 02110. "If I Were President . . ." April 1995, pp. 56–61 (http://www.inc.com). Reproduced by permission of the publisher via Copyright Clearance Center, Inc.]

   a. How does the sharing of information in an organization contribute to the empowerment of employees in a decentralized organizational structure to enhance their performance and that of the organization?

   b. In a decentralized organization, how does the sharing of information allow employees to better understand their organizational roles relative to the roles of others?

   c. In a decentralized organization, how does quality control depend on widespread distribution of information?

47. Some people may view an organization's culture as a mechanism to eliminate diversity in the workplace. Is it ethical to attract and retain only individuals who accept an organization's culture and value system? In responding, be sure to discuss the positive and negative aspects of conformity as part of organizational culture.

Chapter 3 Operating in a Quality Environment

Archway Cookies, Inc.

Founded in 1936, Archway Cookies, Inc. annually produces over a billion cookies in over 60 varieties, including homestyle, gourmet, fat free, sugar free, and holiday. Archway is one of the largest cookie manufacturers in the U.S., and the nation's leading oatmeal cookie maker. The company is headquartered in Battle Creek, Michigan, and operates through two company-owned and four licensed bakeries throughout the United States and Canada.

Archway's mission statement expresses a philosophy of producing only high-quality cookies. In pursuing this mission, company employees have instituted quality measures prior to and during raw material acquisition, during production, and during and after delivery of finished products.

The company ensures high quality of raw material by forming long-term relationships and working closely with suppliers. Although price is a significant purchasing criterion, the quality of raw materials and supplier service are ranked by Archway as the first two purchasing criteria. Because the company emphasizes strong supplier relationships, only random samples of raw materials are subject to in-house inspection and testing to ascertain the continuance of high-quality inputs.

Production quality is enhanced because Archway's workforce is highly trained both in job functions and in decision making; additionally, the workers are provided with tools and resources to perform effectively and to make efficient use of time. Workers strive to eliminate downtime, reduce scrap, and maintain consistently high production quality.

Output quality is also monitored through sampling procedures, which allow the company to be sure that the production output conforms to organizational quality standards of moisture, texture, color, and size; and, most importantly, taste.

For Archway, the concurrent implementation of all these techniques results in high levels of customer satisfaction, employee morale, and operating efficiencies—and very tasty cookies!

SOURCE: Archway Cookies, Inc. Headquarters, 5451 W. Dickman Road, P. O. Box 762, Battle Creek, Michigan.

*S*everal decades ago, business literature stated that the primary goal of business owners should be to maximize profits. More recently, the literature has indicated that maximizing shareholder wealth is the appropriate business owners' goal. Today, many scholars believe that the primary goal of business should be to satisfy customer wants and needs for quality, with long-run stockholder profits and wealth confirming that quality has been achieved.

The quality movement is having a profound worldwide effect on business culture. Managers are redirecting some of their focus from short-run profits to long-run growth in market share and long-run profitability. Within this context, new markets and competitors emerge, customer satisfaction standards increase, and management is introducing different styles and organizational structures.

Understanding the role of management accounting in business requires a comprehension of how business is practiced. As business practices evolve, so must the discipline of management accounting. Changes in the business environment affect the information needed by managers to fulfill their organizational functions. Management accounting's goal is to provide managers with information that is relevant to their decisions in the contemporary business climate. Thus, accounting practices must adapt to generate information that satisfies management's needs. These emerging practices have arisen as the demand for them has occurred.

This chapter discusses quality as a key element in the current operating environment, regardless of whether those operations are related to a for-profit, not-for-profit, manufacturing, or service organization. More and more frequently, changes in organizational practices are being driven by the demand for quality and the increased abilities provided by technology. These factors affect an organization's capacity for long-run market success and its need to introduce strategically based cost management practices. Thus, managers of all organizations are seeking to refine information so that the benefits and costs of product/service quality can be routinely captured by the cost management system and used to make better decisions. As the next chapter more thoroughly discusses, **cost** is the monetary measure of the resources given up to acquire a good or a service or to achieve an objective. Today, the work of many accountants has expanded to include a greater consulting role in assisting managers in developing, maintaining and continuously improving quality systems for their businesses. This chapter provides a foundation for that expanded consulting role.

cost

WHAT IS QUALITY?

Quality must initially be viewed by management from the perspective of the user, rather than the provider, of a product or service. A quality product or service must reflect both performance and value. Thus, management must first define quality before trying to improve it. An all-inclusive definition of **quality** is the sum total of all characteristics that influence a product's or service's ability to meet a customer's stated or implied needs, within that product's or service's grade. **Grade** refers to the addition or removal of product or service characteristics to satisfy additional needs, especially price. All customers cannot afford the same grade of product or service and, therefore, make assessments about quality by comparing equivalent types of items. For example, costume jewelry is not part of the grade of jewelry made from precious gems and precious metals. The quality of costume jewelry must be evaluated within the context of its own grade rather than being compared to the quality of fine jewelry.

Consumer perception of the quality of an organization's products or services distinctly impacts profitability and longevity. Given issues of greater competition, heightened public interest in product safety, and increased product safety litigation, quality can no longer be viewed as simply a production issue. All entity processes (production, procurement, distribution, financial, and promotion) must be involved in quality improvement efforts. (A **process** is a network of repetitive activities arranged to produce a particular output.) Therefore, a management perspective of quality should reflect (1) customer satisfaction with a product or service and (2) the totality of internal processes that generate the product or service.

Exhibit 3-1 provides eight characteristics that would commonly be included in any customer's definition of product quality. An obvious difference exists between the first six and the last two characteristics. The first six characteristics can be reasonably evaluated through objective methods and are, therefore, fairly susceptible to control by the organization providing the product. The last two characteristics are strictly subjective and out of the realm of control by the organization.

Five commonly acknowledged characteristics of high-quality service are presented in Exhibit 3-2 (page 78). Several of these, such as reliability, are the same as or similar to product quality characteristics. However, determination of service quality is much more subjective than objective.

LEARNING OBJECTIVE ❶
How and by whom is quality defined for products and services?

quality
grade

process

---

1. Performance—relates to a product's primary operating characteristics
2. Features—describes the secondary characteristics that supplement a product's basic function
3. Reliability—addresses the probability of a product's likelihood of performing within a specified period of time
4. Conformance—relates to the degree to which preestablished standards are matched by the product's performance and features
5. Durability—measures a product's economic and technical life
6. Serviceability—measures the ease with which the product is repaired
7. Aesthetics—relates to a product's appeal to the senses
8. Perceived quality—relates to image, brand names, and other indirect measures of quality

SOURCE: Reprinted from "What Does 'Product Quality' Really Mean?" by David Garvin, *Sloan Management Review* (Fall 1984), pp. 25–43, by permission of publisher. Copyright 1984 by Sloan Management Review Association. All rights reserved.

EXHIBIT 3-1
Characteristics of Product Quality

EXHIBIT 3-2
Characteristics of
Service Quality

1. Reliability—the ability to provide what was promised, dependably and accurately
2. Assurance—the knowledge and courtesy of employees, and their ability to convey trust and confidence
3. Tangibles—the physical facilities and equipment, and the appearance of personnel
4. Empathy—the degree of caring and individual attention provided to customers
5. Responsiveness—the willingness to help customers and provide prompt service

SOURCE: A. Parasuraman, Valarie Zeithaml, and Leonard L. Berry, "Servqual: A Multiple-Item Scale for Measuring Customer Perceptions of Service Quality," Working Paper of the Marketing Science Institute Research Program, Cambridge, Mass., 1986.

THE DEMAND FOR QUALITY

LEARNING OBJECTIVE ❷
How are companies addressing the demand for product and service quality?

Today, business managers are scrambling to attract customers and to offer them more choices than were available in the past. Additionally, consumers recognize the enhanced extent of their options for quality, price, service, and promptness of delivery. Customers are more likely to select products because of their perceived value than because of where they were produced. If a foreign manufacturer provides the greatest product quality or customer service, business will be taken away from a local producer until that company provides equivalent quality and service. The foreign manufacturer is then motivated to exceed the attributes offered by the local producer. This ongoing competition among foreign and local producers has caused many firms to adopt a dynamic approach toward the continuous improvement of product and/or service quality to better satisfy consumers' demands.

In the past, managers often focused on fostering market growth and creating company strengths to differentiate their firms from all the others. Recently, managerial emphasis has additionally been placed on product and service quality and the creation of customer value. This new attitude refines, blends, and extends prior competitive strategies. A quality perspective merges the concepts of increased market share and differentiated products by using customer focus as the key integrating factor. This focus causes managers to keep one eye on improving their processes and the other on how well their products satisfy customers. By meeting or exceeding the wants and needs of specific customers, firms create customer satisfaction.

A firm is part of an extensive value chain, within which all participants (including the firm's internal processes) are expected to add value. Internally, a firm's work is accomplished in a horizontal flow across functional areas rather than vertically within each functional area. Increased attention is being given to the design and flow of internal processes through improving process quality, decreasing process costs, eliminating any processes or costs that do not provide customer value, and increasing a product's or service's value to customers by modifying design or adding features. In making operational improvements, contemporary management has revised its perception of what constitutes a "customer." In today's value chain perspective, workers have upstream providers of resources and downstream "customers," who may be either internal (other workers) or external (consumers). Thus, **customer** is a generic term for an external or internal recipient or beneficiary of a process's output.[1]

customer

Total Quality Management

LEARNING OBJECTIVE ❸
What underlying factors support the concept of total quality management?

The current challenge to improve quality in products and processes has led many firms to look closely at their fundamental business practices. Some companies have

[1]Jack Hagan, *Management of Quality* (Milwaukee: ASQC Quality Press, 1994), p. 73.

concluded that quality must be the key focus in every facet of operations for growth in profitability to be realized. Thus, many companies have adopted total quality management as their basis for operating activity.

Total quality management (TQM) is a "management approach of an organization, centered on quality, based on the participation of all its members and aiming at long-term success through customer satisfaction, and benefits to all members of the organization and to society."[2] The word *total* in TQM implies involvement of all levels of managment in establishing and maintaining quality in all of an organization's functions. As shown in Exhibit 3-3, TQM is a philosophy of organizational management and change with an objective of continuous improvement. TQM's underlying principles are customer focus, process improvement, and total organizational involvement. Management has the responsibility to provide employees with the necessary resources to support the achievement of this objective and these principles.

total quality management (TQM)

Ethically, when a company sells goods or services to customers, there is either an expressed or implied understanding that the company will do its best to meet those customers' needs. The News Note on page 80 indicates that TQM is not only a system to improve performance but also to promote ethical business behavior.

All members of an organization seeking total quality management must accept continuous improvement as a routine goal of the work environment: it must become a way of life. Improvements should be expected rather than viewed as unusual. As targets are met, new ones should be established.

The concepts of continuous improvement and innovation differ. **Continuous improvement** refers to small, ongoing efforts to make positive adjustments in the status quo; **innovation** involves dramatic improvements in the status quo caused by radical new ideas, technological breakthroughs, or large investments in new technology. Whereas continuous improvement efforts can be accomplished at all organizational levels, innovation typically results from research and development projects. Both concepts are necessary for long-term survival.

continuous improvement

innovation

Customer Focus

Customer expectations, which are continuously rising, have been designated as the ultimate motivators for quality in a total quality management approach to business. Thus, pursuing quality requires chasing a moving target. TQM focuses attention on the relationship between the production/service process and the customer (whether internal or external). Customer-driven quality first requires recognition of

EXHIBIT 3-3
Concepts Underlying TQM

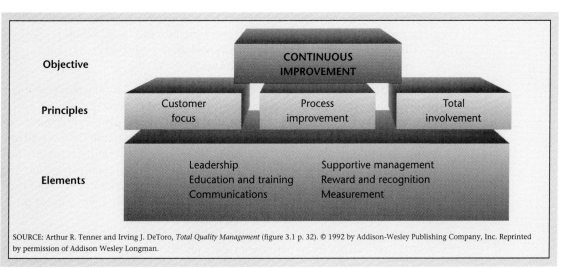

SOURCE: Arthur R. Tenner and Irving J. DeToro, *Total Quality Management* (figure 3.1 p. 32). © 1992 by Addison-Wesley Publishing Company, Inc. Reprinted by permission of Addison Wesley Longman.

[2]ISO 8402, *Total Quality Management* (1994), definition 3.7, p. 6.

TQM: Just What the Ethicist Ordered

Total quality management (TQM) has become a basic business practice in organizations throughout the world. Implementation of TQM in these organizations has been driven by the desire to increase profits in the highly competitive business world. Total quality management techniques are designed to improve performance.

TQM encompasses concepts and practices that are in the best organizational interest for all stakeholders. Additionally, TQM promotes activities that encourage high moral behavior. To support this notion, consider the following six important concepts that provide a foundation for TQM:

Empowerment of employees

Throughput that is prompt and without defects

Helpfulness of managers and employees in task accomplishment

Integrity of products, services and people

Change in process and behavior

Stakeholder emphasis (stockholders, customers, and equity)

Viewed in the above form, TQM is simply good ethics put into practice.

SOURCE: Cecily Raiborn and Dinah Payne, "TQM: Just What the Ethicist Ordered," *Journal of Business Ethics* (Netherlands: Kluwer Academic Publishers, 1996), p. 963. With kind permission from Kluwer Academic Publishers.

who the process customers are and identification of their product or service needs and expectations.

After determining who its customers are, a company must understand what they want and need for two reasons. First, external customer needs and expectations change throughout the product or service life. For instance, after purchase and delivery, customers focus their needs and expectations more on areas such as durability, reasonably priced preventive maintenance and parts, and/or prompt and efficient service availability. Second, as a product or product group matures, customer needs and expectations rise. For instance, not long ago a computer containing a CD-ROM was viewed as a very innovative oddity. This feature has now become, for most buyers, a basic need. Service features are changing too; for example, in the medical industry, waiting times for doctors, lab results, surgery, or appointments have become noticeably reduced. Consider the following observation:

> Doctors and hospitals are realizing there is a price to pay if they leave their patients stranded. Promptness is becoming a coveted value, and the changed medical market, which places a premium on profits, is fiercely competitive and wants to be more user-friendly.[3]

It is clear that the primary characteristics currently desired by external customers are quality, value, and "good" service, given their specific grade of product. Good service is an intangible, meaning different things to different people. But most customers would agree that good service reflects a positive interaction between themselves and organizational employees. Frequently, only service quality separates one product from its competition. Poor service can be disastrous. Data indicate that "70 percent of customers stop doing business with companies because of perceived rude or indifferent behavior by an employee—over three times the total for price or product quality (20 percent)."[4]

External customers want to maximize their satisfaction within the context of their willingness and ability to pay. They view a product or service as a **value** when it

value

---

[3]Meriam Uhlman, "Competition in Medicine May End Patients' Waiting," *Wall Street Journal*, August 3, 1997, p. A28.

[4]Scott J. Simmerman, "Improving Customer Loyalty," *B&E Review* (April–June 1992), p. 4.

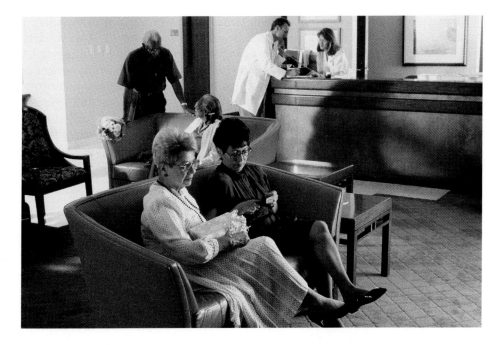

Medical waiting rooms have become less crowded as medical personnel attempt to minimize waiting time.

meets the highest number of their needs at the lowest possible cost (which includes an item's purchase price plus its operating, maintenance, and disposal costs).

In addition to focusing on external customers, companies engaging in total quality management must also consider their internal customers. If the quality of the output provided to an internal customer is flawed, satisfying the external customer is highly improbable. In partial recognition of the importance of internal customers, managers in TQM companies have begun instituting higher degrees of decentralization and employee empowerment.

Decentralization refers to the downward delegation, by top management, of decision-making authority. This process eliminates tiers of middle managers and, in general, causes organizational structures to become flatter. Decentralization can work effectively in TQM-based organizations because employees are "empowered" or given greater rights and responsibilities. **Empowerment** refers to all practices that give workers the training and authority they need to manage their own jobs. The TQM philosophy supports the concept that the individuals who are closest to a process are the ones who are most able to determine when things go wrong and most often know the best ways to fix the problem. The concept of empowerment was born in 1961 when Taiichi Ono (a self-taught Toyota engineer) "installed a cord above every work station and instructed workers—all workers—to stop the [production] line immediately if they spotted a problem."[5] He rationalized that if errors were allowed to continue uncorrected to downstream internal customers, they would simply multiply and become more expensive to fix.

For empowerment to be effective, employees must (1) understand how their jobs fit into the "big picture"; (2) recognize customer needs; (3) have the knowledge, skills, and resources to properly perform their jobs; (4) be educated to make appropriate judgments; (5) be held responsible for the outcomes of their decisions; and (6) believe that they are trusted by and can trust management. If these conditions are met, empowered employees can make valuable contributions to their organizations, especially in process improvements. For instance, at Ford, an executive estimated that employee ideas related to the manufacturing process for the Taurus often were "worth more than $300,000 each."[6]

decentralization

empowerment

http:// www.toyota.com

http:// www.ford.com

---

[5]Jerry Bowles and Joshua Hammond, *Beyond Quality* (New York: Berkley Books, 1991), p. 31.

[6]James W. Dean, Jr., and James R. Evans, *Total Quality* (Minneapolis/St. Paul: West Publishing Company, 1994), p. 199.

Empowered workers within a given organizational area establish self-managed teams to set their own goals and interact on issues with a common purpose. Workers may also form interdepartmental or cross-functional teams to solve quality-related problems. In the not-too-distant past, organizations often viewed work as occurring vertically within each functional area, meaning that managers were almost oblivious to the existence of "white spaces," or gaps where work was handed off at functional interfaces. Now, the use of cross-functional teams forces work to be viewed as flowing horizontally through the company. These teams can analyze the white spaces and make valid suggestions to eliminate such gaps and to improve process quality and effectiveness.

Activity Analysis and Process Improvement

Evaluating customer needs and expectations allows managers and workers to better understand the organization's value chain and to assess the contribution of each internal process to that value chain. Using this information, managers can estimate the cost of each process, compare that cost with the customer value created by that process, and devote a higher level of attention to processes that have poor value-to-cost relationships.

non-value-added activity

value-added activity

A process must be understood and analyzed before attempts are made to improve it. Flowcharting a process and obtaining consensus about the accuracy of that flowchart from the people who carry out the process is one of the best ways to understand a process. The flowchart can then provide a basis for analyzing the process to remove errors, redundancies, and waste. Some activities in a process can be classified as **non-value-added**: they increase the time spent on a product or service but do not increase its worth to the customer. The flowchart can also help identify and streamline other process activities that are value-added. **Value-added activities** are those that increase the worth of a product or service and for which the customer is willing to pay. Process understanding also helps employees recognize who "owns" each organizational process—a necessity explained by the following News Note.

Before improvements can be made, the company's processes and procedures must be defined, standardized, and documented. The definition should indicate the inputs and outputs of each process as well as its beginning and end. Standardization is necessary so that variations can be identified. Statistics indicate that processes will have natural variations over time, but errors are typically produced at points where variation causes the process to be out of control. These errors typically take the form of defective

NEWS NOTE

This Process Is Mine!

The process owners at the Employment Canada office in Scarborough now know who their internal customers and suppliers are, and they have invested time and effort in finding the requirements of their customers. This has enabled them to focus on the requirements where problems exist and then work on eliminating those problems.

Process ownership ensures that all people in the organization understand which processes are their responsibility, and who their customers and suppliers are.

Why is process ownership so important? Over half of the processes in your organization do not have clear ownership—and without clear ownership you don't have internal customers or suppliers talking to each other—and if your customers and suppliers are not talking to each other, then they are not agreeing on requirements—and without agreeing on requirements you cannot deliver quality.

SOURCE: Reprinted from an article appearing in *CMA* magazine by Peter Merrill, April 1997, with permission of The Society of Management Accountants of Canada.

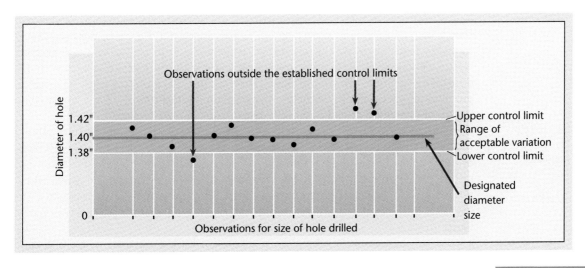

EXHIBIT 3-4
Control Chart

goods or poor service. Documentation is necessary so that all personnel will conduct procedures consistently. Process documentation helps communicate new and revised procedures to all appropriate personnel, provides a basis for training new personnel, and affords task performance continuity even when there are personnel changes.

To identify and analyze process variations, **control charts** (such as the one in Exhibit 3-4) can be prepared that graphically present the actual results of a specified activity and indicate upper and lower control limits. Workers monitoring a process can decide whether the process is out of control either if actual observations fall outside the established control limits or if groupings of observations within the control limits follow predetermined patterns. Workers may also be able to predict when the process might go out of control and therefore prevent adverse consequences from process deviations. Company personnel who prepare control charts must do so consistently and accurately so that intelligent analyses can be made.

The results base selected should be a reasonable performance measure for the activity. Possible measures include number of defective products, errors in tolerance levels, and unexpected work slowdowns or stoppages.

The source of variation is classified as either special cause or common cause. A special cause variation is created by some specific, nonrandom condition or event, such as inferior quality raw material; it is most easily corrected by shop floor workers. In contrast, a common cause variation is systemic or inherent in the system; common causes, such as poor lighting, underlie random variation in the system. Correcting common cause variations sometimes requires resources to modify or re-engineer the system. Therefore, although workers may be heavily involved in such common cause improvements, top management frequently must also be involved because of the long-term commitment of resources.

After processes have been defined, standardized, documented, and are stabilized with little variation, workers can make significant, practical improvements. All processes cannot be improved at once, so specific targets for improvement should be chosen. Selection of targets can be based on ease of or critical need for improvement. Some companies may first want to make housekeeping improvements to build confidence in the quality movement before addressing more difficult process variations. Other companies may find that improvement of particular processes is critical to organizational success and should be addressed early.

Benchmarking

Companies can improve processes by relying on employee suggestions or by looking to others for information and assistance in the form of benchmarking. Simply put, **benchmarking** means learning from others. More completely, it is the process of investigating, comparing, and evaluating a company's products, processes, or services

control chart

benchmarking

against those of organizations (or organizational subunits) believed to be the "best in class." Such comparisons allow a company to understand other production and performance methods, so that it can identify its own strengths and weaknesses. The success of benchmarking efforts is frequently gauged by progress in key, measurable dimensions or indicators of a process. For example, a key indicator for a particular production process might be the pounds of scrap produced by the process relative to the number of good units produced.

LEARNING OBJECTIVE ❹
How do process benchmarking and results benchmarking differ?

process benchmarking

http:// www.xerox.com

results benchmarking

There are two major types of benchmarking: process and results. **Process benchmarking** assesses the quality of key internal processes by comparing them with those of other firms. Process benchmarking focuses on individual processes or functions rather than an organization's entire operation. Additionally, the firms against which an organization compares its processes should be those that have established the highest quality results for a given practice or process, regardless of industry or global location.

Process benchmarking helps companies learn about their own strengths and weaknesses and those of their competitors. For example, Xerox's benchmarking efforts indicated that it had nine times as many suppliers as the best companies, ten times as many assembly line rejects, and seven times as many defects per hundred machines—and Xerox's unit manufacturing cost equaled the Japanese selling price of a similar unit in the United States.[7] Armed with benchmarked information, companies like Xerox have been able to adapt the best practices to their own operations.

In **results benchmarking**, a company examines the end product or service of another company, focusing on product/service specifications and performance results. Results benchmarking helps companies determine which other companies are the best in class. Also, by use of reverse engineering (disassembling a product), one company can often ascertain another company's product design, process, and costs.

Benchmarking is consistent with a customer-oriented focus of business and its concept of market-defined quality. By identifying the fundamentals of success of firms achieving the highest quality in specific processes, companies can reengineer and adapt the benchmark practices in their own processes to achieve greater quality. Although benchmarking against direct competitors is often necessary, these direct competitors tend to resist the process as indicated in the following discussion:

> Typically, there is no charge for benchmarking visits. The idea is to foster a free exchange of information—it's the business-world equivalent of doctors' sharing their findings with the medical community at large. Of course, this enlightened attitude doesn't generally extend to competitors.[8]

Since each company has its own unique philosophy, products, and people, copying is neither appropriate nor feasible. Therefore, each company should imitate only readily transferable ideas and, more importantly, upgrade its own effectiveness and efficiency by improving on methods in use by others.

Although the concept of benchmarking may superficially appear to benefit only one party, the flow of information should, in the long run, be two-directional. To illustrate, assume that Company B benchmarks itself against Company A, the best in class. After Company B implements process improvements, it becomes the best in class. It is only appropriate that Company B then share its improvements with Company A.

Benchmarking has risen in popularity because it benefits organizational quality and profitability. Another source for the emphasis on benchmarking has been the establishment of various quality awards, one of which specifically features benchmarking in its criteria.

---

[7]James R. Evans and William M. Lindsay, *The Management and Control of Quality* (Minneapolis/St. Paul: West Publishing Company, 1993), p. 144.

[8]Justin Martin, "Are You as Good as You Think You Are?" *Fortune*, September 30, 1996, p. 142.

Quality Awards

The ultimate affirmation of TQM in the United States is the 1987 Malcolm Baldrige National Quality Improvement Act, which established a program to encourage U.S. businesses to pursue quality initiatives. The program is administered by the U.S. Department of Commerce. At the heart of the program is the Malcolm Baldrige Quality Award or **Baldrige Award**, named after the late Malcolm Baldrige, a former Secretary of Commerce. Awards are given annually to winners in manufacturing, service, and small businesses. The winners have demonstrated quality achievements in the following seven categories: Leadership, Strategic Planning, Customer and Market Focus, Information and Analysis, Human Resource Focus, Process Management, and Business Results.

http:// www.doc.gov

Baldrige Award

Baldrige Award applicants undergo a quality evaluation by a review board of experts from the public and private sectors. One significant benefit of the evaluation process, other than the possibility of winning the award, is the review board's feedback about the company's operations. This benefit is described by Patrick Mene of the Ritz Carlton, a Baldrige Award winner in 1992:

http:// www.ritzcarlton.com

> We thought we were doing a very good job when we submitted our application. When the Baldrige team came in, they left us a report that mentioned 75 areas where we could make improvements. From the point of view of improving your business, how could you ask for more than that?[9]

The Baldrige Award evaluation process is modeled after the **Deming Prize**, an award instituted in Japan in 1950. This award, named for the late W. Edwards Deming, is Japan's highest form of industrial recognition. The Deming Prize emphasizes the conformity of products to a standard; there is not even a category related to customer satisfaction. In comparison, the Baldrige Award is more focused on the customer than on the product.

Deming Prize

To compete effectively in the global market, companies must recognize and willingly comply with a variety of international standards. Standards have essentially become the international language of trade; they are formalized agreements that define the various contractual, functional, and technical requirements that ensure that products, services, processes, and/or systems perform as expected. Global quality standards have also been set, although they are not as demanding as those of the Baldrige Award or the Deming Prize.

Most notable among the international quality initiatives is the **ISO 9000** series, initially developed in 1987 and revised in 1994 by the International Organization for Standardization, based in Geneva, Switzerland. This organization is comprised of members of quality standards boards from more than ninety countries. Key objectives for a company following the ISO 9000 series are (1) seeking and achieving continuous improvement of the quality of its products in relationship to quality requirements, (2) continuously meeting all customers' and other stakeholders' needs by improving operations, and (3) assuring managers and customers that quality requirements are being fulfilled and improved.

ISO 9000

http:// www.iso.ch.com

The ISO 9000 series of five standards are written in a general manner and prescribe the design, material procurement, production, quality control, and delivery processes necessary to produce high-quality products and services.[10] Although these standards are primarily concerned with meeting customer needs, they do address *process*, rather than *product*, quality.

Beginning in 1993, companies must have had an approved quality system to sell certain products (such as toys, weighing machines, gas appliances, and certain medical equipment) in Europe. The system described in the ISO series is the only one that

---

[9]Ronald Fink, "Group Therapy—Not a Fad or a Quick Fix, but a Way of Managing Change: That's Benchmarking," *Financial World* (September 28, 1993), p. 46.

[10]The ISO 9000 standards are equivalent to the American Society for Quality Control (ASQC) Q-90 quality series, issued in 1987. Companies that currently meet the Q-90 standards also meet the ISO 9000 standards.

meets the European Economic Area requirements.[11] More than forty countries have adopted the ISO standards as either a component of or a stand-alone national quality standard.[12]

quality audit

After an internal review, a company deciding that it can meet the standards may apply for ISO registration. To be registered, the company must undergo a **quality audit** by a third-party assessor. The quality audit reviews product design activities (although not for individual products), manufacturing processes and controls, quality documentation and records, and management quality policy and philosophy. The audit is conducted by an accredited, third-party registrar. No international organization administers the program, so companies must use an internationally accepted registration program administered by a national registrar.

Quality audits are quite expensive, costing between $800 and $3,000 per person-day plus expenses. Audit teams usually consist of between two and six people who work up to ten days between the initial review and follow-up. After registration, teams visit the company biannually to monitor compliance.

Although the costs are high, certified companies believe the benefits exceed the costs. Externally, ISO 9000 certified companies gain an important distinguishing characteristic over noncertified competitors. Additionally, certified companies are listed in a registry of approved suppliers, which should increase business opportunities. Internally, certification helps ensure higher process consistency and quality, and should reduce costs. Under ISO 9000, the cost–benefit relationships of the quality system must be measured, documented, and reported.

ISO registration is not required to do business in the United States. However, even companies that do not sell overseas should investigate ISO registration because of its operational and competitive benefits. And, if a company's competitors are ISO registered, good business sense would indicate the necessity of becoming ISO certified as indicated by the following News Note.

NEWS NOTE

ISO 9000—It's Not Just for Europe!

Customers demand that suppliers and contractors speak the language of quality—hence the rush of businesses worldwide to comply with ISO 9000. Companies that don't implement ISO 9000 guidelines put themselves at serious risk in the global marketplace.

⊙ In North America, ISO 9000 registration is widespread. A new industry is emerging to help businesses comply with ISO 9000 specifications. The Big Three automakers have their own industry-specific version of ISO 9000. North American suppliers of these automakers must be in compliance by Dec. 31, 1997.

⊙ Europe used ISO 9000 as a means of uniting the EU into one homogeneous market. While ISO 9000 requirements never became part of official EU law, these standards are applied in fact throughout member countries.

⊙ In Asia, the Chinese government has embraced ISO 9000, and is applying it to specific industries on a prioritized basis. The toy industry was the first to be legally required to have ISO 9000 certification in order to export. Progress has been slower in Japan, but the country plans to make ISO registration a requirement for all software manufacturers doing business there.

SOURCE: H. James Harrington, "A Global View of ISO 9000," *Executive UpSide* (Ernst & Young, April 1997), p. 7.

[11]The European Economic Area includes the twelve countries belonging to the European Union (Belgium, Denmark, France, Germany, Greece, Ireland, Italy, Luxembourg, the Netherlands, Portugal, Spain, and the United Kingdom) and the seven countries that belong to the European Free Trade Association (Austria, Finland, Iceland, Liechtenstein, Norway, Sweden, and Switzerland).

[12]Gary Spizizen, "The ISO 9000 Standards: Creating a Level Playing Field for International Quality," *National Productivity Review* (Summer 1992), p. 333.

ISO standards are also becoming a part of some U.S. federal rules and regulations. For example, in revising its 1978 Good Manufacturing Practices, the U.S. Food and Drug Administration incorporated certain ISO 9001 design control and service standards. In addition, "in Canada, some of the provincial governments and certainly the federal government are seriously considering a requirement for ISO 9000 certification by their suppliers."[13]

http:// www.fda.gov

The ISO 9000 standards are currently undergoing revisions that will lead to greater consistency in the registration process and remove some ambiguities in the individual standards. Additionally, "comparisons show ISO at best meets 40 percent of the criteria used by the U.S. Baldrige Award. So companies are pressuring the International Standards Organization to upgrade the guidelines by 1996."[14]

In 1996, the International Organization for Standardization issued the ISO 14000 series, which provides criteria for an effective environmental management system. The standards in this series are designed to support a company's environmental protection and pollution prevention goals in balance with socioeconomic needs. One part of the series, ISO 14001, establishes requirements for certification or self-declaration regarding a firm's environmental management system.

Total Involvement

Because all processes in a firm are interdependent, a company will not be able to earn the Baldrige Award or Deming Prize, or be ISO certified without total employee involvement. TQM recognizes that everyone in an organization shares the responsibility for product/service quality. Thus, all members of the organization must accept a personal role and participate in continuously improving their work efforts.

Consistent and committed top management leadership is the catalyst for moving the company culture toward an *esprit de corps* in which all individuals feel compelled to meet or exceed customer expectations. Such an attitude should also permeate everything a company does—including customer relations, marketing, research and development, product design, production, and information processing. Upper-level management must be involved in the quality process, develop an atmosphere that is conducive to quality improvements, and set an example of commitment to TQM. Although workers were historically blamed unfairly for many problems in the workplace, they should, today, be made to feel that they are part of the process of success, not creators of problems.

In addition, a management information system for planning, controlling, and decision making must exist. This system should be capable of providing information about process quality to both managers and workers. Historically, the consideration of quality has not been part of the planning process but rather has involved an after-the-fact measurement of errors. Action was not triggered until a predetermined threshold was exceeded. In contrast, a total quality system should promote a reorientation of thinking from an emphasis on inspection to an emphasis on prevention. The system should identify existing quality problems so that managers can set goals and methods for improving quality. The system should also be capable of measuring quality and providing feedback on quality improvements. Finally, the system should encourage teamwork in the quality improvement process. In summary, a TQM system should move an organization away from product inspection (finding and correcting problems at the end of the process) to process control (designing and monitoring the process so that either problems do not occur or, if they do, taking corrective and preventive measures to eliminate their causes).

Another part of the management information system should also address the issue of supplier relationships. Suppliers are an integral part of an organization's value chain and can directly affect production costs as well as process and product quality.

[13]William J. L. Swirsky, "Focus on: ISO 9000," *Journal of Accountancy* (February 1994), p. 61.

[14]Jonathan B. Levine, "Want EC Business? You Have Two Choices," *Business Week*, October 19, 1992, p. 59.

NEWS NOTE

Q-1 Preferred Quality Award

As early as 1990, Ford Motor Company recognized outstanding quality and demonstrated management commitment to continuous improvement for its suppliers of production and service products with the Q-1 Award. This award indicates that the supplier has in place processes and systems meeting and exceeding customer needs and expectations. The criteria include

1. Adequacy of supplier quality system,
2. Management quality awareness and commitment, and
3. Quality products and services.

Suppliers receiving this award become partners with Ford and achieve a preferred status in new product development and source selection. Ford relies upon the supplier's own quality system, exempting the supplier from certain requirements imposed on non-Q-1 suppliers.

The Q-1 award process has been administered worldwide by Ford's purchasing offices in association with its quality and engineering departments.

Ford, in conjunction with General Motors and Chrysler, has developed the QS9000 quality standard. QS9000 is the "new" quality standard for automotive suppliers.

SOURCE: Holly McMunn and Rob Depasquale, "Everyone an Internal Auditor," *Management Accounting* (March 1997), p. 44.

http:// www.gm.com

http:// www.chrysler.com

Therefore, managers should carefully screen suppliers, standardize and reduce the number and variety of components needed from suppliers, and reduce the total number of suppliers. For example, in screening suppliers, Ford Motor Company has developed specific supplier criteria, as indicated in the News Note above, for its Preferred Quality Award.

Exhibit 3-5 depicts the quality continuum along which companies move toward achieving world-class status. At the most basic level, a company simply opts for quality assurance by inspecting products for defects and/or monitoring employees and surveying customers to find poor service. When a company implements quality assurance techniques to eliminate the possibility of defective products or poor service, the company has become quality conscious. When an organization's quality system has progressed to a high level of sophistication, that organization may choose to compete against others for quality honors. Finally, when the concept of quality has become a distinct element of the organizational culture to the point where no defective product or poor service is tolerated, the company has achieved world-class status and can be viewed as the benchmark for others. But achieving world-class status does not mark an ending point. TQM is not a static concept; when one problem has been solved, there is always another problem waiting for a solution.

LEARNING OBJECTIVE 5
How can a company's move along the quality continuum be assessed?

MEASURING THE COSTS OF QUALITY

prevention cost

quality of design

http:// www.archway.com

A company can increase its product and service quality by investing in **prevention costs**, which are intended to improve quality by preventing product defects that might result from dysfunctional processing. Amounts spent on improved production equipment, training, engineering and modeling are considered prevention costs. The quality of design is especially important in the prevention costs category. **Quality of design** reflects how well a product is conceived or designed for its intended use. Extensive training at Archway Cookies improves its employees' abilities to make good decisions and enhances their capacity to operate more efficiently and effectively.

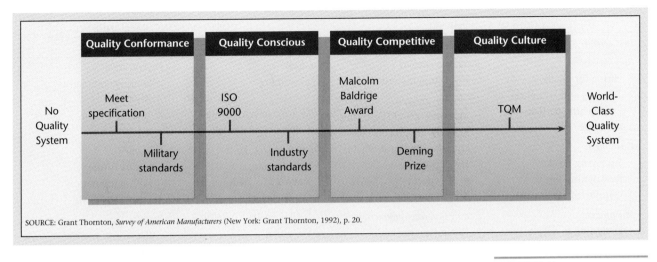

SOURCE: Grant Thornton, *Survey of American Manufacturers* (New York: Grant Thornton, 1992), p. 20.

EXHIBIT 3-5
Quality Continuum

appraisal cost

Appraisal costs are a complement to prevention costs. Appraisal costs represent quality control costs incurred for monitoring; these costs compensate for mistakes not eliminated through prevention activities. Archway uses statistical sampling to monitor the quality of both its raw material inputs and its finished goods, the baked cookies. Both prevention and appraisal costs can be expected to cause a reduction in another group of costs known as failure costs. Taken together, prevention costs and appraisal costs address the firm's efforts toward ensuring the quality of conformance. The **quality of conformance** is the extent to which a product meets the specifications of its design.

quality of conformance

Failure costs represent internal losses, such as scrap or rework, and external losses, such as warranty costs, handling customer complaints, litigation, and recalling defective products. The results of TQM indicate that the ultimate net effect of these cost tradeoffs is an overall decline in costs. Also, productivity increases when non-value-added activities are eliminated and technologically advanced equipment is installed.

failure costs

Lower costs mean that the company can contain (or reduce) selling prices and that customers, pleased with the higher quality at the same (or lower) price, perceive they have received good value and will buy more. These factors create larger profits for the company, which can be reinvested in research and development activities to generate new high-quality products or services. The profits can also be used to train workers to provide even higher quality products and services than are currently available. This cycle of benefits will continue in a company that is profitable and secure in its market share—two primary goals of an organization

As mentioned, the TQM philosophy indicates that total costs will decline, rather than increase, as quality improvements are made in an organization. "Zero defects" means that there is nothing to correct and customers are happy with the conformity of the products to technical specifications. Thus, total quality management also includes the idea that it is the *lack* of quality that is expensive, rather than its presence. Understanding the types and causes of quality costs can help managers prioritize improvement projects and provide feedback that supports and justifies improvement efforts.

Two types of costs make up the total quality cost of a firm: (1) the cost of quality compliance, or assurance, and (2) the cost of noncompliance, or quality failure. The cost of compliance equals the sum of prevention and appraisal costs. Compliance cost expenditures are incurred with the intention of eliminating the present costs of failure and maintaining that zero level in the future; thus, they are proactive on management's part. Furthermore, effective use of prevention costs can even minimize the costs of appraisal. Alternatively, the cost of noncompliance results from production imperfections and is equal to internal and external failure costs. Exhibit 3-6 (page 90) presents specific examples of each type of quality cost.

LEARNING OBJECTIVE 6
How is the cost of quality measured?

COSTS OF COMPLIANCE		COSTS OF NONCOMPLIANCE	
Prevention Costs	*Appraisal Costs*	*Internal Failure*	*External Failure*
Employees:	*Before production:*	*Product:*	*Organization:*
⊙ Hiring for quality	⊙ Inspecting materials	⊙ Reworking	⊙ Staffing complaint
⊙ Training and awareness		⊙ Waste	departments
⊙ Establishing participation	*Production process:*	⊙ Storing and disposing	⊙ Staffing warranty claims
programs	⊙ Monitoring and inspecting	⊙ Reinspecting rework	departments
	⊙ Keeping the process con-		
Customers:	sistent, stable, and reliable	*Production process:*	*Customer:*
⊙ Surveying needs	⊙ Using procedure	⊙ Reprocessing	⊙ Losing future sales
⊙ Researching needs	verification	⊙ Having unscheduled	⊙ Losing reputation
⊙ Conducting field trials	⊙ Automating	interruptions	⊙ Losing goodwill
		⊙ Experiencing unplanned	
Machinery:	*During and after production:*	downtime	*Product:*
⊙ Designing to detect	⊙ Having quality audits		⊙ Repairing
defects			⊙ Replacing
⊙ Arranging for efficient	*Information process:*		⊙ Reimbursing
flow	⊙ Recording and reporting		⊙ Recalling
⊙ Arranging for monitoring	defects		⊙ Litigation
⊙ Incurring preventive	⊙ Measuring performance		
maintenance			*Service:*
⊙ Testing and adjusting	*Organization:*		⊙ Providing unplanned
equipment	⊙ Administering quality		service
⊙ Fitting machinery for	control department		⊙ Expediting
mistake-proof operations			⊙ Serving after service
Suppliers:			
⊙ Arranging for quality			
⊙ Educating suppliers			
⊙ Involving suppliers			
Product design:			
⊙ Developing specifications			
⊙ Engineering and modeling			
⊙ Testing and adjusting for:			
conformity, effective and			
efficient performance,			
durability, ease of use,			
safety, comfort, appeal,			
and cost			

EXHIBIT 3-6
Types of Quality Costs

Information about production quality or lack thereof is contained in inspection reports, control charts, and customer returns or complaints. Information about the costs of quality, on the other hand, is partially contained in the accounting records and supporting documentation. However, since the accounting records are commonly kept with an eye toward financial accounting, other specific information about quality costs must be developed or estimated for quality management purposes. The behavior of quality costs relative to changes in activity as well as the appropriate drivers for these costs must be developed or estimated for quality management purposes. The need to estimate quality costs makes it essential for the management accountant to be involved in all activities—from system design to cost accumulation of quality costs.

Historically, quality costs have not been given separate recognition in the accounting system. In most instances, the cost of quality has been buried in a variety of general ledger accounts, including the Work in Process Inventory and the Finished Goods Inventory (for rework, scrap, preventive maintenance, and other overhead costs); marketing/advertising expense (for product recall, image improvement after poor products were sold, or surveys to obtain customer information); personnel costs (for training); and engineering department costs (for engineering design change orders and redesign).

In trying to determine the cost of quality, actual or estimated costs are identified for each item listed in Exhibit 3-6. If these costs were plotted on a graph, they would appear similar to the cost curves shown in Exhibit 3-7. If the firm spends larger amounts on prevention and appraisal costs, the number of defects is lower and the costs of failure are smaller. If less is spent on prevention and appraisal, the number of defects is greater and failure costs are larger. The external failure costs curve begins moving toward vertical when a certain number of defects are encountered by customers. The ultimate external failure cost is reached when customers will no longer buy a given product or any other products made by that firm because they perceive that it produces poor-quality work.

By developing a system in which quality costs are readily available or determinable, the management accountant is able to provide useful information to managers trying to make spending decisions, pinpointing the areas that would provide the highest cost–benefit relationships. Additionally, quality cost information will indicate how a shift in one or more curves will affect the others.

Exhibit 3-8 (page 92) shows the location in the production-sales cycle where the types of quality costs are usually incurred. Note in this exhibit that an information feedback loop (indicated by the bold line) should be in effect to link the types and causes of failure costs to prevention costs to be subsequently incurred. Alert managers and employees continuously monitor the nature of failures to discover their causes and adjust prevention activities to close the gaps that allowed the failures to occur. These continuous rounds of action, reaction, and action are essential to continuous improvement initiatives.

ANALYZING QUALITY COST RELATIONSHIPS

Theoretically, if prevention and appraisal costs were prudently incurred, failure costs would become zero. However, prevention and appraisal costs would still be incurred to achieve zero failure costs. Thus, total quality costs can never be zero. This is not to disregard the knowledge that the benefits of increased sales and greater efficiency should exceed all remaining quality costs. In this sense, the cost of quality is free. Management needs to analyze the quality cost relationships and spend money for

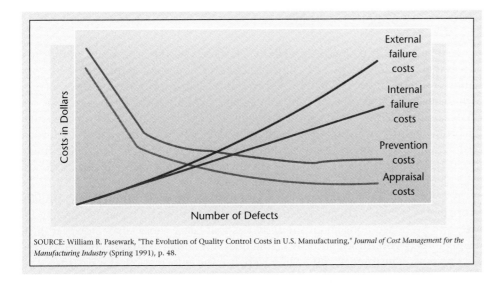

EXHIBIT 3-7
Relationships among
Quality Costs

SOURCE: William R. Pasewark, "The Evolution of Quality Control Costs in U.S. Manufacturing," *Journal of Cost Management for the Manufacturing Industry* (Spring 1991), p. 48.

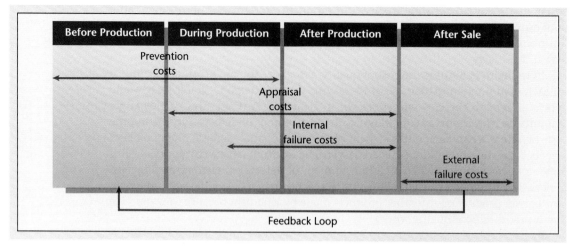

Before Production	During Production	After Production	After Sale

Prevention costs

Appraisal costs

Internal failure costs

External failure costs

Feedback Loop

EXHIBIT 3-8

Time-Phased Model for Quality Costs

Pareto analysis

quality in ways that will provide the greatest benefit. Such an analysis requires that the cost of quality be measured to the extent possible and practical and the benefits of quality costs be estimated.

Pareto analysis is one way management can decide where to concentrate its quality prevention cost dollars. This technique classifies the causes of process problems according to impact on an objective. For example, a company that makes dishwashing machines might subclassify its warranty claim costs for the past year according to the type of product failure as follows:

COST OF TYPE OF FAILURE

Model	Electrical	Motor	Structural	Mechanical	Total Dollars
Mercury	$12,000	$16,000	$13,000	$ 3,000	$ 44,000
Comet	11,000	14,000	7,000	3,000	35,000
All other	8,000	10,000	3,000	4,000	25,000
Total	$31,000	$40,000	$23,000	$10,000	$104,000

Model	Dollars	Percent of Total	Cumulative Percent Total
Mercury	$ 44,000	42%	42%
Comet	35,000	34	76%
All other	25,000	24	100%
Total	$104,000	100%	

Listing the total failure costs of all models in descending order of magnitude indicates that models Mercury and Comet account for 76 percent of total warranty cost claims. Also, the largest single source of warranty claims cost is caused by problems with dishwasher motors. Therefore, management should focus further analysis on what causes models Mercury and Comet, and the motors on all models, to generate the greatest warranty claims costs. Such knowledge permits management to devote the appropriate portion of its prevention efforts to minimizing or eliminating these specific problems. This kind of analysis should be conducted often enough for trends to be detected quickly and adjustments made rapidly.

A company desiring to engage in TQM and continuous improvement should record and report its quality costs separately so that managers can plan, control, evaluate, and make decisions about the activities that cause those costs. However, just having quality cost information available does not enhance quality. Managers and workers must consistently and aggressively use the information as a basis for creatively and intelligently advancing quality.

A firm's chart of accounts can be expanded to accommodate either separate tracing or allocating quality costs to new accounts. Exhibit 3-9 lists some suggested accounts that will help management focus on quality costs. Opportunity costs—including forgone future sales and a measure of the firm's reputation—are also associated with poor quality. Although opportunity costs are real and may be estimated, they are not recorded in the accounting system because they do not result from specific transactions.

If the firm has a data-based management system, the information resulting from an expanded chart of accounts can alternatively be generated by coding transactions representing quality costs. Coding will permit these transaction types and amounts to be reformatted so that reports detailing the costs of quality can be provided as shown (using assumed numbers) in Exhibit 3-10 (page 94). This report makes two important assumptions: stable production and a monthly reporting system. If wide fluctuations in production or service levels occur, period-to-period comparisons of absolute amounts may not be appropriate. Amounts may need to be converted to percentages to have any valid meaning. Additionally, in some settings (such as a just-in-time environment), a weekly reporting system would be more appropriate because of the need for continuous monitoring.

Exhibit 3-11 (page 95) provides formulas for calculating an organization's total cost of quality, using prevention, appraisal, and failure categories. Some amounts used in these computations are, by necessity, estimates; however, it is a well-accepted business approach to use reliable estimates rather than choosing not to perform the calculations because of the lack of verifiable or precise amounts. This situation reflects the idea discussed in Chapter 2 that management accountants are more apt to use estimated figures than financial accountants because management needs timely information more than it needs totally precise information.

Consider the following July 1999 operating information for the Wing Company:

Defective units (D)	800	Units reworked (Y)	400
Profit per good unit (P_1)	$25	Profit per defective unit (P_2)	$15
Cost to rework defective unit (r)	$5	Defective units returned (D_r)	100
Cost of handling return (w)	$8	Prevention cost (K)	$20,000
Appraisal cost (A)	$5,400		

Substituting these values into the formulas provided in Exhibit 3-11 provides the following results:

$$Z = (D - Y)(P_1 - P_2) = (800 - 400)(\$25 - \$15) = \$4,000$$
$$R = (Y)(r) = (400)(\$5) = \$2,000$$
$$W = (D_r)(w) = (100)(\$8) = \$800$$
$$F = Z + R + W = \$4,000 + \$2,000 + \$800 = \$6,800 \text{ total failure cost}$$
$$T = K + A + F = \$20,000 + \$5,400 + \$6,800 = \$32,200 \text{ total quality cost}$$

EXHIBIT 3-9
New Quality Accounts

PREVENTION COSTS	APPRAISAL COSTS
Quality Training	Quality Inspections
Quality Participation	Procedure Verifications
Quality Market Research	Measurement Equipment
Quality Technology	Test Equipment
Quality Product Design	
INTERNAL FAILURE COSTS	EXTERNAL FAILURE COSTS
Reworking Products	Complaints Handling
Scrap and Waste	Warranty Handling
Storing and Disposing Waste	Repairing and Replacing Returns
Reprocessing	Customer Reimbursements
Rescheduling and Setup	Expediting

EXHIBIT 3-10
Cost of Quality Report

	Cost of Current Period	Cost of Prior Period	% Change from Prior Period	Current Period Budget	% Change from Budget
Prevention Costs					
Quality Training	$ 9,400	$ 9,000	+ 4	$ 10,000	− 6
Quality Participation	16,400	16,800	− 2	16,000	+ 3
Quality Market Research	22,000	17,600	+ 25	24,000	− 8
Quality Technology	19,200	21,600	− 11	30,000	− 36
Quality Product Design	33,200	24,400	+ 36	33,000	+ 1
Total	$100,200	$ 89,400	+ 12	$113,000	−11
Appraisal Costs					
Quality Inspections	$ 6,600	$ 7,000	− 1	$ 6,000	+ 10
Procedure Verifications	2,400	2,800	− 14	3,000	− 20
Measurement Equipment	5,400	6,000	− 10	6,400	− 16
Test Equipment	3,000	2,400	+ 25	3,000	0
Total	$ 17,400	$ 18,200	− 4	$ 18,400	− 5
Internal Failure Costs					
Reworking Products	$ 17,000	$ 16,600	+ 2	N/A*	
Scrap and Waste	4,400	4,800	− 8	N/A	
Storing and Disposing Waste	8,800	11,400	− 23	N/A	
Reprocessing	3,600	3,200	+ 13	N/A	
Rescheduling and Setup	1,800	2,400	− 25	N/A	
Total	$ 35,600	$ 38,400	− 7		
External Failure Costs					
Complaints Handling	$ 11,600	$ 12,400	− 6	N/A	
Warranty Handling	21,400	18,600	+ 15	N/A	
Repairing and Replacing Returns	54,000	58,400	− 8	N/A	
Customer Reimbursements	24,000	21,400	+ 12	N/A	
Expediting	2,200	2,600	− 15		
Total	$113,200	$113,400	+ 0		
Total Quality Costs	$266,400	$259,400	+ 3	$131,400	+ 103

*TQM advocates planning for zero defects; therefore, zero failure costs would be included in the budget.

Of the total quality cost of $32,200, Wing Company managers will seek to identify the causes of the $6,800 failure costs and work to eliminate them. The results may also affect the planned amounts of prevention and appraisal costs for future periods.

High quality allows a company to improve current profits, either through lower costs or, if the market will bear, higher prices. But management is often more interested in business objectives other than short-run profits. An example of an alternative, competing objective is that of increasing the company's market share. Indeed, if increasing market share were an objective, management could combine the strategies of increasing quality while lowering prices to attract a larger market share. When quality is increased by giving greater attention to prevention and appraisal activities, overall costs decline and productivity increases. This has been the experience of Archway Cookies. Lower costs and greater productivity support lower prices that, in turn, often stimulate demand. The result is greater market share, higher long-run profits, and, perhaps, even greater immediate profits.

EXHIBIT 3-11
Formulas for Calculating
Total Quality Cost

CALCULATING LOST PROFITS

Profit Lost by Selling Units as Defects = (Total Defective Units − Number of
Units Reworked) × (Profit for Good Unit − Profit for Defective Unit)

$$Z = (D - Y)(P_1 - P_2)$$

CALCULATING TOTAL COSTS OF FAILURE

Rework Cost = Number of Units Reworked × Incremental Cost to Rework Defective Unit

$$R = (Y)(r)$$

Cost of Processing Customer Returns = Number of Defective Units Returned ×
Incremental Cost of a Return

$$W = (D_r)(w)$$

Total Failure Cost = Profit Lost by Selling Units as Defects + Rework Cost
+ Cost of Processing Customer Returns

$$F = Z + R + W$$

CALCULATING THE TOTAL QUALITY COST

Total Quality Cost = Defect Control Cost + Failure Cost

$$T = \text{(Prevention Cost + Appraisal Cost)} + \text{Failure Cost}$$

$$T = K + A + F$$

Prevention and appraisal costs (represented respectively by symbols K and A above) are
total estimated amounts; no formulas are appropriate. As the cost of prevention rises, the
number of defective units should decline. Additionally, as the cost of prevention rises, the
cost of appraisal should decline; however, appraisal cost should never become zero.

SOURCE: James T. Godfrey and William R. Pasewark, "Controlling Quality Costs," *Management Accounting* (March 1988), p. 50.
Reprinted from *Management Accounting*, published by the Institute of Management Accountants, Montvale, NJ. Visit our website
at www. imanet.org.

OBTAINING INFORMATION FROM THE
COST MANAGEMENT SYSTEM

Today's business strategy of focusing on customers and quality requires a firm to
manage organizational costs so a reasonable value-to-price relationship can be
achieved. Although prices are more commonly set by the competitive market than
necessarily by internal organizational costs, companies lacking appropriate cost management skills cannot expect to succeed in the long run. Thus, it can be said that organizations need to engage in **strategic cost management (SCM)**.

    SCM can be viewed as the managerial use of management accounting informa-
tion for the purposes of setting and communicating organizational strategies; establishing, implementing, and monitoring the success of methods to accomplish the
strategies; and assessing the level of success in meeting the promulgated strategies.[15]
Thus, an organization's management accounting system should be designed and
used to accumulate and report information related to organizational success in meeting or exceeding customer needs and expectations—and quality-related goals and objectives. Managers can analyze and interpret such information in order to plan and
control current activities and to make decisions about current as well as long-term
future courses of action, including expansion of the company's market base and/or
technology installation.

    In designing such a management accounting system, planners must consider
cost accumulation and process measurement activities. Costs that are accumulated

**strategic cost management
(SCM)**

[15]The term *strategic cost management* was coined by Professors John K. Shank and Vijay Govindarajan of Dartmouth College. A full discussion of the concept is provided in their book, *Strategic Cost Management* (New York: Free Press, 1993).

LEARNING OBJECTIVE 7
Why is a strategically based management accounting system needed in addition to a financial accounting system?

for financial accounting purposes may be inadequate for strategy-based decisions. For example, financial accounting requires that research and development costs be expensed as incurred. However, a product's cost is largely determined during design. Product design has implications for its perceived value, the complexity and variety of components required for its production, its ease of manufacture, and its durability and likelihood of success. Consequently, strategy-based cost management would suggest that design cost be accumulated as part of product cost. It is not necessary that this cost appear on the financial accounting statements, but it must exist in the management accounting system for decision making.

On the other hand, financial accounting accumulates all production costs as inventoriable and makes no distinction as to whether they add value in the eyes of the customer. A strategically based cost management system would provide a way to distinguish costs that add value from those that do not, so that managers and employees alike could work to reduce the latter such costs. In this way, the objective of continuous improvement would be enhanced.

Another example of the abilities of a strategically based management accounting system is in the area of process measurement rather than cost accumulation. Financial accounting is monetarily based and, therefore, does not measure nonfinancial organizational activities. However, as indicated earlier in the chapter, many activities critical to success in a quality-oriented, global marketplace are related to time—a nonmonetary characteristic. A useful management accounting system would ensure that information related to nonmonetary occurrences (such as late deliveries or defect rates) would be available. Such information could then, if necessary, be translated into financial terms so that its significance to the company's profitability could be objectively analyzed.

Finally, financial accounting reflects a short-term perspective toward operating activity. An organizational goal of continuous improvement is not short term; it is ongoing. Gathering monetary information and forcing it into a particular annual period of time does not necessarily provide managers with a clear indication of how today's decisions will affect the organization's long-run financial success. For example, deciding not to invest in research and development would cause a company's short-run profitability to improve, but could be disastrous in the long run.

Thus, a strategically based management accounting system would report a greater number of the costs and benefits of organizational activities. Having this information in a form designed to meet managerial needs would allow managers to make informed assessments of the company's performance in its value chain, position of competitive advantage (or disadvantage), and progress toward organizational goals.

INCREASED TECHNOLOGICAL ABILITIES

LEARNING OBJECTIVE 8
What recent changes in technology are affecting current business practices?

 www.amanet.org/
worldint.htm

In the current business environment, the firm with the highest level of technology *and* the employees able to employ that technology to its fullest is often one step ahead of its competitors. For instance, according to an American Management Association survey of 1,441 companies:

> [A] strong correlation [exists] between increased training budgets and increased profits and productivity following a workforce reduction. In the long term, firms that increased training budgets after workforce reductions were almost 75 percent more likely to show increased profits and nearly twice as likely to improve worker productivity than those that cut training budgets. An even stronger correlation exists between quality improvements in product/service and increased profits.[16]

---

[16]"Job Creations Outpace Eliminations," *Deloitte & Touche Review* (December 9, 1996), pp. 2–3.

Information Systems

Companies have entered what could be termed the Information Revolution. New information technologies are becoming successively less expensive and, at the same time, successively more powerful. Even in 1993, it was estimated that there was an expected improvement of 15 to 25 percent annually in the cost-to-performance ratio.[17]

One current trend is to integrate all fundamental business systems, such as accounting, production, inventory, marketing, and product design. Such integration provides a more accurate and complete picture of organizational operations. It also provides the ability to obtain and retain important market information and stay informed about customer requirements. Furthermore, systems integration eliminates duplicate systems, allows managers to identify and respond to problems more quickly, and facilitates more rapid decision making. As new technology is developed, this systems integration trend is likely to accelerate.

Electronic Data Interchange

Technology has greatly benefited various modes of communication. The most noteworthy recent advances in information technology are those that have made it possible to integrate one company's information system with the electronic systems of other companies. These systems reflect electronic data interchange (EDI) capability.

Electronic data interchange (EDI) refers to the almost instantaneous computer-to-computer transfer of information. EDI systems allow firms to eliminate paperwork and communicate with their suppliers and customers electronically. Typical communications involve ordering goods and services and acknowledging receipt of orders for goods and services. Frequently, such transactions and communications are triggered by external information systems that monitor and control inventory levels, record sales, and account for purchases and sales. Archway Cookies and most of its customers are connected by EDI, which is one reason Archway is able to respond so rapidly to customer sales orders.

electronic data interchange (EDI)

Electronic communication reduces the likelihood of errors in communication, decreases the time needed to prepare and send written communication through traditional modes such as the postal services, and eliminates the manual data entries that would otherwise be required to update inventory records and related accounting records. Paying for goods and services by electronic transfer rather than bank drafts or checks is becoming common. "In fact, any company that plans to remain aggressive and profitable—and in business—[in 1999] had better start looking at what it needs to become EDI-capable."[18]

Production Systems and Management

In a customer-focused manufacturing environment, each product or service should be defect free. A starting point for this objective is to demand that all material inputs and conversion processes be virtually flawless. Employee training and empowerment, documented procedures, strong supplier relationships, and technologically advanced production equipment are important factors in helping an organization attain total quality.

Bar coding is probably the technology with which people are most familiar. **Bar codes** are groups of lines and spaces arranged in a special machine-readable pattern. For example, manufacturers can use bar codes to gain information about raw material receipts and issuances, products as they move through an assembly area, and quality problems. Bar codes have reduced clerical costs, paperwork, and inventory, and simultaneously made processing faster, less expensive, and more reliable.

bar code

---

[17]R. C. Heterick, "Paradigms and Paradoxes," *Higher Education Product Companion* (Vol. 3, Number 1, 1993), p. 10.

[18]Allan Snow, "EDI: Made to Order," *CMA Magazine* (November 1994), p. 22.

http:// www.symbol.com

Conventional bar codes carry information in a single dimension: the width. But one company, Symbol Technologies of Bohemia, N.Y., has developed a two-dimensional bar code that can store even more information in a very small space. "The entire Gettysburg Address, for example, can be stored in less than a two-inch square on one of Symbol's PDF 417s."[19] These codes have been put to use in all economic sectors: military personnel will soon have identification cards with two-dimensional bar codes that will not be susceptible to forgery and that will contain their entire medical history; and Volvo is using the PDF in its electronic data interchange applications.

http:// www.volvo.com

Bar coding is only the most visible of the many technologies used in manufacturing. Modern manufacturing equipment often uses computerized technology to schedule, control, and monitor production with little or no human intervention. In highly integrated systems, computer programs oversee each production process and develop statistical data on both the component and process reliability. These data are used to evaluate the reliability of components obtained from internal and external suppliers as well as to aid in the design of new products and processes.

Because of this intense oversight process, production defects should be promptly discovered and their causes identified and corrected. Sometimes the computer-generated statistical data are used to identify problem situations. Other times, elements of the production system are designed to be self-checking.

In Japan, such techniques are called *poka-yoke*, a phrase meaning "mistake proofing." Many *poka-yoke* techniques are low-cost and relate to a primary checklist of functions needed to perform an activity. If possible, devices should be devised to discover disorders automatically, without the workers' having to attend to minute details and measurements. Examples of *poka-yoke* are the following:

- If operation A was to machine a diameter, the fixture at operation B would receive the part as machined in operation A. If the diameter was undersized or oversized, the part would not fit on the fixture at operation B.
- Socket wrenches are dipped in red paint so that torqued parts are seen visually. Untorqued parts are thus easily spotted at subsequent operations.
- A machine does not start if a part is not mounted properly on a fixture.[20]

New high-technology equipment has raised quality levels on two fronts. It has provided substantial opportunities to reduce defective production and to attain a higher level of satisfaction of customer wants and expectations. A global economy has made consumers more aware of the breadth and depth of the competition vying for their attention in the market. Such a vast amount of competition has allowed consumers to be more discriminating in their purchases. In the customer-oriented market, firms have tried to distinguish their products and services from those of competitors by offering the prices and features that appeal to specific consumer profiles. One of the predictable consequences of this type of competition is that it leads firms to focus on needs and wants of individual consumers rather than the market as a whole. In the manufacturing sector, accomplishing this task requires that firms be able to change rapidly from one production run to another and use standard components to produce the variety and quality of products desired by consumers.

flexible manufacturing system (FMS)

Rapid changeover is a feature of a **flexible manufacturing system (FMS)**. These systems allow a single factory to produce numerous variations of products through the use of computer-controlled robots, which are becoming a new kind of labor force.

A firm's success in a global, quality-based competitive environment will reflect consumers' perceptions of the value-to-price relationship for the firm's products and services. Customers perceive a product or service to have high value relative to that item's price if it meets most of their needs at the lowest possible price. When that relationship occurs, the product or service is likely to be a market success. Alternatively, if consumers perceive a product to have a low ratio of value to price, then the prod-

---

[19]Srikumar S. Rao, "Tomorrow's Rosetta Stones," *Financial World* (November 22, 1994), p. 71.

[20]Mark C. DeLuzio, "The Tools of Just-in-Time," *Journal of Cost Management* (Summer 1993), p. 19.

Use of high-tech equipment, such as this computer-controlled robot that welds airplane fuselages, reduces the risk of defective products, which, in turn, results in greater customer satisfaction.

uct is likely to be a market failure, regardless of how it measures up on a singular scale of quality, such as lack of defects.

Companies that have shifted their focus to customers and quality have been forced to take a longer-run perspective on their business operations. This perspective has necessitated an in-depth review of types and timing of information provided by the management accounting system.

SITE ANALYSIS

Archway Cookies, Inc.

Archway employees are proud of the high quality of their products. Workers form improvement suggestion groups, task forces, and quality teams. Such employee empowerment has led to low employee turnover and significant gains in efficiency and effectiveness.

The company has experienced that higher quality has resulted in lower costs. Purchasing high-quality ingredients not only ensures more conformity to high-quality specifications but also reduces scrap and waste. To assure suppliers' capabilities, Archway visits their plants, observes their procedures, and inspects their work.

The company makes sure of the freshness of raw material ingredients by using a just-in-time (JIT) inventory management system. Because inventory levels are lower under JIT, the costs of handling and storing ingredients are lower.

A JIT system is also used for finished goods. Finished goods are baked to order and shipped within forty-eight hours of receiving an order. Rapid responses to customer orders and strictly practiced procedures for withdrawing products from grocery shelves beyond prescribed time limits result in enhanced product freshness. Greater freshness is an important characteristic of a higher quality cookie and this gives Archway a significant competitive advantage.

SOURCE: Archway Cookies, Inc. Headquarters, 5451 W. Dickman Road, P.O. Box 752, Battle Creek, Mich.

CROSS-FUNCTIONAL APPLICATIONS

TOPIC OF NOTE	DISCIPLINE	CROSS-FUNCTIONAL APPLICATIONS
Value-Added Activity Costing	Financial Accounting	Financial accounting guidelines permit only manufacturing costs to be included in cost of goods sold while other costs that contribute to the product such as research and development, or distribution costs are treated under different, often special, rules for operating costs. This process distorts internal decision making concerning product profitability over the long run. The value-added approach can correct this distortion by including these additional activity costs in the long-run product profitability analysis.
	Public Finance	Many states levy a standing inventory tax on finished goods, and some have proposed a value-added tax on products. The government has a vested interest in identifying a common measurable basis on which to tax inventories and the value-added approach is the leading method being considered.
	Management	A value-added analysis can avoid distortions created by inappropriate allocation among strategic business units (SBU) or arbitrary assignment of common costs to SBU's. These practices can hide inefficiencies by causing more efficient operations to shoulder some of the cost burden of less efficient ones. The value-added approach will focus management's attention on the resources used by each operation and permit greater control.
Quality Cost	Business Law	In civil lawsuits involving product liability, quality cost is often measured by an argument as to the "state of the art." Manufacturers are responsible for the safety of their products for up to twenty years after the sale, even though the state of the art may have significantly advanced or the customer may have modified the product. The "big four" manufacturers of general aviation aircraft (small aircraft) decided to relocate to Canada because they could not afford the product liability litigation in the United States. That may be quality cost at the extreme, but many firms face a similar situation.
	Economics	The consumer price index has been adjusted downward to incorporate the quality improvements in products that increase their utility or durability. A blue ribbon committee of economists advised President Clinton of the need for this change, saying that otherwise the real product cost would be overstated by the amount of quality improvement added to the product over the years.
	Marketing	Quality cost is a principal determinant of a product strategy which includes design, features, accessories, durability, etc. Also, many activities in the channel of distribution—such as debulking, grading, and sorting—are influenced by quality cost.
	Engineering	A quality cost report should alert engineers to problem areas in design, production, or packaging. Such a report can also serve as a baseline for future activities or for evaluating alternatives in design or manufacturing.

CHAPTER SUMMARY

Modern managers are now trying to balance both short-run and long-run considerations in conducting their planning, controlling, performance evaluating, and decision-making functions. Globalization of business has increased competition, which, in turn, has led managers to find ways to improve quality and lower costs. The quality movement focuses on meeting or exceeding customer expectations and promotes a long-run continuous improvement effort. It requires total employee involvement; TQM has also fostered decentralization through worker empowerment. Empowerment challenges all employees to be involved, manage their own jobs, and work in teams to solve group problems.

In focusing on the quality of internal processes, firms have established benchmarking practices. Benchmarking requires identifying firms having the highest-quality processes in specific operational areas. Managers then try to emulate and improve the successful practices of the benchmark organizations in their own companies.

Governments have also encouraged a focus on quality by establishing awards for achievements in quality. The premier quality awards in the United States and Japan, respectively, are the Baldrige Award and the Deming Prize. International quality standards are established by the ISO 9000 standards. Such increased scrutiny places even greater importance on controlling the quality of internal processes and the quality of products and services produced.

Strategically based cost management views management accounting as a means of assisting managers in setting and communicating organizational strategies and establishing and monitoring methods of accomplishing the intended results of those strategies. This type of cost management system differs from financial accounting by taking a longer-range perspective, including an alternative view of product costs. For instance, a strategically based cost management system would include research and development costs in total product cost, but would exclude costs of activities that create no value in the value chain.

Technological innovations are also having a continuing impact on business operations. Advances in technology have substantially enhanced the abilities of firms to process information and have allowed electronic linkages among firms and the linkage of production and control systems within companies. Electronic data interchange systems diminish paperwork and speed up communications with suppliers and customers. Bar codes, robotics, and other forms of automation can enhance the quantity and quality of business output and the value-to-price relationship of a company's goods and services for customers.

KEY TERMS

Appraisal cost (p. 89)

Baldrige Award (p. 85)

Bar code (p. 97)

Benchmarking (p. 83)

Continuous improvement (p. 79)

Control chart (p. 83)

Cost (p. 76)

Customer (p. 78)

Decentralization (p. 81)

Deming Prize (p. 85)

Electronic data interchange (EDI) (p. 97)

Empowerment (p. 81)

Failure cost (p. 89)

Flexible manufacturing system (p. 98)

Grade (of product or service) (p. 77)

Innovation (p. 79)

ISO 9000 (p. 85)

Malcolm Baldrige Quality Award
   see Baldrige Award (p. 85)

Non-value-added activity (p. 82)

Pareto analysis (p. 92)

Prevention cost (p. 88)

Process (p. 77)

Process benchmarking (p. 84)

Quality (p. 77)

Quality audit (p. 86)

Quality of conformance (p. 89)

Quality of design (p. 88)

Results benchmarking (p. 84)   **Value** (p. 80)
Strategic cost management (SCM) (p. 95)   **Value-added activity** (p. 82)
Total quality management (TQM) (p. 79)

END OF CHAPTER MATERIALS

⊙ QUESTIONS

1. Why are high-quality products and services so important in today's global business environment?

2. What is meant by the term *quality*? In defining quality, from what two perspectives may a definition be formulated? Why are both important?

3. List and explain the eight characteristics of product quality from the perspective of the customer.

4. List and explain the five characteristics of service quality from the perspective of the customer.

5. What is *total quality management*? Why does adoption of TQM require a fundamental change in the way a company considers quality in its operations?

6. Why must a quality standard be regarded as a moving target rather than a static objective?

7. For the sake of protecting profitability, why would a business be willing to stop serving certain groups of customers?

8. Top managers at Global Manufacturing Company are considering the possibility of decentralizing control of all foreign operating divisions. The firm has traditionally maintained very tight control over these operations. What are some of the major benefits that the company stands to gain from decentralization?

9. Many companies are now empowering their employees. What is employee empowerment? What additional costs might a company incur to empower employees?

10. How can statistical process controls be utilized to monitor quality?

11. How does benchmarking allow a company to evaluate the quality of its products and services?

12. How do process benchmarking and results benchmarking differ? How are they similar?

13. What is the Baldrige Award? What are the award categories?

14. Why do countries establish quality standards? Why is it desirable to have a common set of global quality standards?

15. What role is served by the International Organization for Standardization?

16. What are the advantages and disadvantages of having only one (or a few) supplier sources?

17. What are the four stages or levels on the quality continuum? Where is TQM located on the continuum?

18. What are the two types of costs that comprise the total quality cost of a firm? What are the two subtypes within each type? Given the tradeoffs between the two main types of quality costs, is quality ever free? Explain.

19. How can Pareto analysis help focus managerial efforts in reducing the costs of quality-related problems?

20. How does strategic cost management link information management to corporate strategies?

21. How has the evolution of technology dramatically affected the processing of information?

22. Why should businesses be concerned about electronic data interchange? Wouldn't it be better for them to continue to use paper transactions and checks? Discuss the advantages and disadvantages of each type of system.

23. What is *poka yoke*? Provide three examples not given in the text of how such a concept could be used. The examples can be related to home, business, or school.

24. Choose any product that is produced in at least ten varieties (such as calendars). What kinds of additional costs would a company incur to produce such variety?

25. What is a flexible manufacturing system? How do such systems provide greater capability to produce a variety of products quickly?

⊙ EXERCISES

26. *(Terminology)* As a prospective employee of a firm that uses TQM, you have been asked to demonstrate your knowledge of quality by matching each numbered item on the right with a lettered item on the left.

    a. Deming Prize
    b. Baldrige Award
    c. ISO 9000
    d. Bar codes
    e. Electronic data interchange
    f. Flexible manufacturing system
    g. Process benchmarking
    h. Results benchmarking
    i. Strategic cost management
    j. Empowering
    k. Process

    1. Comparing the quality of end products or services
    2. A network of repetitious activities to accomplish a desired output
    3. Machine readable lines and spaces
    4. Comparing the quality of internal procedures and techniques
    5. Aligning information system to report on organizational strategies
    6. Giving workers the training and authority to manage their own jobs
    7. The primary Japanese quality award
    8. A set of international quality standards
    9. Computer-to-computer transfer of information
    10. Production using computer-controlled robots
    11. U.S. quality award

27. *(True/false)* Your college friend has asked your help in completing the following homework assignment. Mark each of the following statements as true or false and explain why the false statements are incorrect.

    a. Adoption of TQM leads to more stability in organizational processes.
    b. Accounting practices, like laws, once created remain in effect forever.
    c. A focus on quality allows companies to engage in economies of scale by producing the best of a single type of product.
    d. By reducing the number of suppliers, companies should achieve better relations with the suppliers that are retained.
    e. Smart companies are willing to drop some customers.
    f. The information revolution has allowed computers to do things at least a million times better than people can do them manually.
    g. Benchmarking is the same as copying another company's products or processes.
    h. TQM requires participation by everyone in the organization and can only be successful with top management support.
    i. Poor quality of products cause greater loss of customers than poor quality of service.

28. *(Work restructuring) To build a factory of the future, Sony Corp. is taking a page from the workshops of the past.*

    At a plant here, men are dismantling conveyor belts on which as many as 50 people assembled camcorders. Nearby, Sony has set up tables to form a snail-shaped shop for four people. Walking through this "spiral line," workers assemble an entire camera themselves, doing everything from soldering to testing.

This is progress, Sony says. Output per worker on the experimental line is 10 percent higher than on a conventional one. The spiral performs better, Sony says, because it frees efficient assemblers to churn out more product instead of limiting them to a conveyor belt's speed. It reduces handling time, the seconds consumed as goods under production are passed from worker to worker. And if something goes wrong, only a small section of the plant is affected.

"There is no future in conventional conveyor lines," says Hitoshi Yamada, a consultant to Sony and other companies. "They are a tool that conforms to the person with the least ability."

With the spiral line reducing assembly time to fifteen minutes per camera from seventy, the plant is moving closer to a goal sought by many manufacturers: Making goods only as customers order them, instead of basing output on estimates. That change would slash inventory close to zero.

[SOURCE: Michael Williams, "Some Plants Tear Out Long Assembly Lines, Switch to Craft Work," *Wall Street Journal*, October 24, 1994, pp. A1, A4. Reprinted by permission of *Wall Street Journal*, © 1994 Dow Jones & Company, Inc. All Rights Reserved Worldwide.]

A colleague in your company is developing an in-house course on modern management techniques. She has asked your help in answering the following questions:

a. If craft-type work or small-group manufacturing is more efficient than mass manufacturing, why did mass manufacturing evolve in the industrial revolution as a (presumably) more efficient replacement for craft-work?

b. Is the small-group work cell approach described at Sony likely to be a more efficient work configuration for all types of products? Explain.

c. Why does the emerging emphasis on quality favor small-group production over mass manufacturing?

d. How does the evolution of computer-based manufacturing, including flexible manufacturing systems, provide a competitive edge for small-group manufacturing over mass manufacturing?

29. *(Sourcing) Nothing is certain yet, but it increasingly looks as if Texas Municipal Power Agency, in east-central Texas, will change its power contract to Western coal, mined in Wyoming, at the expense of Navasota Mining Co. lignite, a local Texas coal. The benefits include the following:*

The Wyoming fuel, 35,000 tons of which was test burned December 26–31, burns stronger and has less sulphur and ash than Navasota Mining's locally produced fuel.

The coal's heat is good, its power is more intense, and the TMPA furnace would not require major modification if a fuel switch took place.

While there may be transportation delays since the mine is about 1,500 miles from the power plant, triple railroad tracks are under construction to alleviate train bottlenecks leaving the mine.

[SOURCE: David Howell, "Power Company Considering Fuel Change," *Bryan-College Station Eagle*, January 13, 1995, p. A9.

a. As stated or implied in the article, what are the apparent important dimensions of coal quality to the Texas power plant?

b. As manager of the Texas power plant, what would be your greatest concern in purchasing the Wyoming coal?

c. Should the potential loss of income and jobs at the Texas Navasota Mining Co. affect this sourcing decision? Why or why not?

d. What factors favor sourcing the coal locally, even if it is of lower quality?

30. *(Technological change)* Although technological change has dramatically affected practices in many industries, its impact on the entertainment industry is extraordinary. Paul Tagliabue, Commissioner of the National Football League (NFL), describes how technological change has impacted the NFL:

"Sports was still local in the '40s and '50s. It started to become national in the '60s and '70s, and then in the '80s, it started to become really international. The evolution is now the information technology, really. We can't stand still. I think it's more competitive

now. There's more and more sports and more and more programming chasing fewer network viewers and fewer network advertisers."

Even so, the popularity of the NFL has continued under Tagliabue. At last year's Super Bowl in Pasadena, for example, there were 2,164 media credentials issued to 652 news organizations, 372 of which were for international media from 21 countries. The game was shown on television in a record 100 countries, including live telecasts for the first time to China and Brazil.

At their recent meeting in Chicago, the NFL team owners decided to set up a football league based solely in Europe beginning in 1995.

[SOURCE: Manny Topol, "In a League of His Own," *Sky* (January 1994), pp. 49ff.]

As their consultant, you have been asked to answer the following questions:

a. Why has technology affected the NFL to a much greater extent than other organizations?

b. Which specific technologies have had the greatest impact on the growing popularity of the NFL?

c. What would be major impediments to globalizing the NFL?

d. Are all parts of the American entertainment industry likely to enjoy the same market benefits from technology as the NFL? Explain.

31. *(Control chart)* Wells Cookies has recently hired several college students to work part-time making special-order oatmeal cookies. Tom Wells, the owner, has a policy of baking ingredients to result in a 3.6-inch oatmeal cookie, but (given variations in dough, yeast, and baking times) he sometimes gets cookies between 3.4 and 3.8 inches. After observing the students for a day, Tom gathered the following data on cookie sizes:

11:00 AM to 5:00 PM: one dozen cookies were made resulting in the following sizes measured in inches (3.5, 3.7, 4.1, 3.3, 3.6, 3.6, 3.5, 3.9, 4.4, 3.7, 3.6, 3.6)

5:00 PM to 11:00 PM: two dozen cookies were made containing the following dimensions measured in inches (3.5, 3.5, 3.7, 4.1, 4.2, 3.6, 3.9, 4.4, 4.3, 4.4, 3.7, 4.8, 3.6, 3.5, 4.0, 3.9, 4.1, 2.9, 3.6, 3.6, 4.2, 4.5, 4.4, 3.7)

a. Prepare a control chart for cookie dimensions in inches.

b. What information does the chart provide Tom?

32. *(Cost of quality)* Downing Manufacturers has gathered the following data on its quality costs for 1998 and 1999:

Defect prevention costs	1998	1999
Quality training	$8,000	$9,500
Quality technology	6,000	8,000
Quality production design	4,000	9,000
External failure costs		
Warranty handling	$15,000	$10,000
Customer reimbursements	11,000	7,200
Customer returns handling	7,000	4,000

Downing's vice-president of finance has enlisted your help to accomplish the following:

a. Compute the percentage change in the two quality cost categories from 1998 to 1999.

b. Write a brief explanation for the pattern of change in the two categories.

33. *(Cost of quality)* Frederick Machine Tools Inc.'s accounting system reflected the following costs related to quality for 1999 and 2000:

	1999	2000
Customer refunds for poor product quality	$ 6,000	$ 4,500
Fitting machines for mistake-proof operations	2,100	3,200
Educating suppliers	2,000	2,500
Disposal of waste	11,000	9,000
Quality training	7,000	7,500
Litigation claims	18,000	14,000

Bill Frederick, the company owner, is your neighbor. He dropped by your house with the hope that you would help him with the following:

a. Which of these are costs of compliance and which are costs of noncompliance?

b. Calculate the percentage change in each cost and for each category.

c. Discuss the pattern of the changes in the two categories.

34. *(Cost of quality)* The Pearson Company wants to determine its cost of quality. The company has gathered the following information from records pertaining to June 1998:

Defective units	6,000	Prevention costs	$10,000
Units reworked	5,500	Profit per good unit produced	
Customer units returned	200	and sold	$30
Appraisal costs	$9,000	Profit per defective unit sold	$10
Cost per unit for rework	$6	Cost to handle returned units	$12

As a new employee on the company's management team, you are asked to compute the following:

a. lost profits from selling defective work.

b. total costs of failure.

c. total quality cost.

35. *(Cost of quality)* Paradise Sailbag Company has gathered the following information pertaining to quality costs of production for November 2000:

Total defective units	240
Number of units reworked	140
Number of sailbags returned	25
Total prevention cost	$10,000
Total appraisal cost	$12,000
Per unit profit for defective units	$12
Per unit profit for good units	$30
Cost to rework defective units	$14
Cost to handle returned units	$18

Since you are the newest member of the quality management team, you have been assigned to find:

a. total cost to rework.

b. profit lost from not reworking all defective units.

c. cost of processing customer returns.

d. total failure costs.

e. total quality cost.

36. *(Technology changes)* *A lot of people would just as soon stay behind as America charges full speed into the electronic information age. Surveys show that substantial minorities of people are still uncomfortable with videocassette recorders, answering machines, compact disc players and even digital alarm clocks— not to mention home computers. The thought of trying to send mail, consult an encyclopedia, order a movie or chat with strangers over a computer network leaves them scared, hostile or indifferent.*

[SOURCE: Robert S. Boyd, "Technology: Fear Keeps Some Living in Past," New Orleans *Times-Picayune*, May 3, 1994, p. A10.]

Assume you are the manager of a medium-sized business. Prepare a report that addresses the following issues:

a. Why are some people experiencing technophobia?

b. If several people in your organization were technophobes, how would you attempt to eliminate this fear?

c. If technophobia could not be eliminated, what problems might arise in the areas in which the technophobes worked? (Assume that one was in production operations, one in accounting, and one in marketing.)

37. *(Benchmarking) Oregon, a perennial innovator among the states, has come up with an inventive way to measure how well it's doing. The approach, borrowed from the corporate* *world, is called "Benchmarks." Benchmarks began in 1988. Hundreds of Oregonians—from business, labor, education, environmental groups, state and local government, the health care system and grass-roots organizations—developed the official set of benchmarks for the state.*

Then, in 1991, the legislature enacted the benchmarks into law. The lawmakers also created an Oregon Progress Board *to make sure the process stays alive and on target. Each two years, the board has to report publicly on progress toward each benchmark goal.*

Altogether, Oregon has 272 benchmarks. For practicality, they've been divided into two classes—priority standards related to acute questions (health care access, drugs, reducing teenage pregnancy, for example) and core benchmarks (for more long-term fundamental issues, such as the base of the state's economy and basic literacy of the population). All are, however, based on measurable outcomes.

[SOURCE: Neal Peirce, "Benchmarks for State, Local Governments Good Idea," New Orleans *Times-Picayune*, April 11, 1994, p. B5.]

You are a politician running for office in Oregon. Your future constituency wants information about the use of benchmarking in a political setting. Develop a presentation for a paid political announcement that would address the following issues:

a. why benchmarks are as useful in government as they are in business.

b. the benefits that (1) the Oregon government and (2) Oregonians might expect from the use of benchmarks.

c. any potential hazards that might exist in using benchmarks in a governmental setting.

⊙ PROBLEMS

38. *(Pareto analysis)* High-Tech Computer Co. has identified the following failure costs during 1999:

COST OF TYPE OF FAILURE

Model	CPU	Internal Drive	External Drive	All Other	Total
Laptop	$ 8,000	$ 7,000	$ 5,000	$ 3,000	$23,000
Desktop	7,000	6,000	12,000	5,000	30,000
Mini	3,000	1,000	8,000	3,000	15,000
Total	$18,000	$14,000	$25,000	$11,000	$68,000

You let it slip to your boss that you knew something about Pareto analysis and she has requested that you address the following:

a. Rearrange the above rows in descending order of magnitude based on the total dollars columns and prepare a table using Pareto analysis with the following headings: Model, Dollars, Percent of total, and Cumulative percent of total.

b. Which models account for almost 80 percent of all failure costs?

c. Focusing on the models identified in part b, prepare a table using Pareto analysis to identify the types of failure causing the majority of failure costs. (Hint: rearrange the cost of failure types in descending order of magnitude.) Use the following headings for your table: Failure type, Dollars, Percent of total, and Cumulative percent of total.

d. Describe the problem areas that require preventive measures first. How, if at all, does this answer reflect the concept of leverage?

39. *(Cost of quality)* Specialty Lumber Company manufactures cedar doghouses for the discerning canine homeowner. The firm produced 3,000 doghouses during its first year of operations. At year end, there was no inventory of finished goods. The company sold 2,700 through regular market channels (some after rework), but 300 units were so defective that they had to be sold as scrap. For this first year, the firm spent $30,000 on prevention costs and $15,000 on quality appraisal. There were no customer returns. An income statement for the year follows:

Sales (regular channel)	$270,000	
(scrap)	12,000	$282,000
Cost of Goods Sold		
Original production costs	$150,000	
Rework costs	22,000	
Quality prevention and appraisal	45,000	217,000
Gross margin		$ 65,000
Selling and administrative expenses (all fixed)		90,000
Net loss		$ (25,000)

Because you are the newly appointed director of quality, the owner has asked you to:

a. Compute the total profits lost by the company in its first year of operations by selling defective units as scrap rather than selling the units through regular channels.

b. Compute the total failure costs for the company in its first year.

c. Compute total quality costs incurred by the company in its first year.

d. Discuss the evidence that indicates the firm is dedicated to manufacturing and selling high-quality products.

40. *(Cost of quality)* Golf courses are demanding in their quest for high-quality carts because of the critical need for lawn maintenance. Ride-in-Style manufactures golf carts and is a recognized leader in the industry for quality products. In recent months, company managers have become more interested in trying to quantify the costs of quality in the company. As an initial effort, the company was able to identify the following costs for 2000, by category, that are associated with quality:

Prevention costs

Quality training	$15,000
Quality technology	$50,000
Quality circles	$32,000

Appraisal costs

Quality inspections	$18,000
Test equipment	$14,000
Procedure verifications	$ 9,000

Internal failure costs

Scrap and waste	$ 6,500
Waste disposal	$ 2,100
Rework cost	$ 6,000

External failure costs

Warranty handling	$ 9,500
Customer reimbursements/returns	$ 7,600

Managers were also aware that in 1999, 250 of the 8,000 carts that were produced had to be sold as scrap. These 250 carts were sold for $80 less profit per unit than "good" carts.

As a college student, you work between semesters and in the summer in the accounting office. The company accountant wants you to use the above data to find Ride-in-Style's 1999 expenses for:

a. lost profits from scrapping the 250 units.

b. total failure costs.

c. total quality costs.

d. Assume that the company is considering expanding its existing full 5-year warranty to a full 7-year warranty in 2000. How would such a change be reflected in quality costs?

⊙ CASES

41. *(Change in competitive environment)* *[There are two major producers of railroad locomotives for the U.S. market: General Motors (GM) and General Electric (GE). For most of the*

recent past, GM has dominated the market with a market share of about 70 percent. However, in the late 1980s, 39-year-old Michael Lockhart became head of GE's locomotive division.]

Before Mr. Lockhart arrived in January 1989, he attended GE's annual Christmas dinner for railroad presidents. At the dinner, "I asked them what I could do to help them. They told me I could make our locomotives work." Subsequent visits to railroads confirmed that GE had a problem. At CSX [Railway], Mr. Taylor [vice-president of CSX] recounts, he told Mr. Lockhart: "I need help. I've got this installed fleet that's killing me."

Shocked, Mr. Lockhart returned to the production plant. He moved the locomotive headquarters from the perimeter of the sprawling plant to a building in the middle of assembly operations. He set up a task force of a hundred engineers to fix a dozen problems, drawing experts from around GE's empire. GE's locomotive marketing manager, who had antagonized some railroad officials, left the company.

"Lockhart shook things up," says Michael Iden, director of motive power engineering at the Chicago & Northwestern. "At General Electric it used to be, 'Here's my product,' but now they're listening to customers and building more reliable units."

[After making many changes, GE has cut the time to build a locomotive from ninety-two days to forty-six days and has earned a 60 percent market share.]

Just as General Electric began improving its performance, GM was encountering setbacks. Having dominated the locomotive business, some GM officials became arrogant, rail executives say. Mimicking a GM official, one rail official juts his jaw out and says: "I'm here to take orders."

With the world's biggest locomotive plant in LaGrange, GM also was stuck with costly overcapacity when orders fell. And because the parent has suffered huge losses on autos in recent years, the corporation isn't giving the locomotive unit funds to make its plants smaller and more efficient. In fact, GM has put a majority stake in its locomotive business for sale, with no takers thus far.

[SOURCE: William M. Carley, "GE Locomotive Unit, Long an Also-Ran, Overtakes Rival GM," *Wall Street Journal*, September 3, 1993, pp. A1, A4. Reprinted by permission of *Wall Street Journal*, © 1993 Dow Jones & Company, Inc. All Rights Reserved Worldwide.]

a. Identify changes that were made in the GE locomotive plant that are consistent with changes occurring in business today as described in the chapter.

b. Why would GM be so (apparently) complacent about its position in the locomotive market?

c. What do you recommend that the GM locomotive unit consider in its efforts to return to its market dominance?

d. The article says that GE's Lockhart assembled a significant number of engineers to resolve problems in GE's locomotives. The ultimate output of the engineers' efforts was a new locomotive design. Carl Taylor, vice-president of CSX Railway, described the new locomotives: "They work." What does the story suggest about the importance of product design and engineering to product quality and perceived customer value?

42. *(Coping with technological innovations)* In ten years, *Hopper Specialty Co.* had grown from a small storefront into the biggest distributor of industrial hardware in northwest New Mexico, catering especially to oil and gas drillers. In May 1988, *NCR Corp.'s* highly touted Warehouse Manager computer package promised even better things to come. When up and running, the computer system would track the thousands of items in a huge inventory, keep prices current, warn when items were running low, punch up invoices in seconds, and even balance the monthly books—all at the touch of a few keystrokes. Particularly for drilling customers who lose money every minute their equipment isn't working, anything that could get orders for parts filled faster would indeed be cause for celebration.

NCR began installing hardware and countertop terminals for Hopper. During sales demonstrations, Mr. Hopper had been impressed that the terminals could punch up a customer invoice in a fraction of a second. But when Hopper Specialty actually switched on its new system in September 1988, the response time ranged from half a minute to several minutes, leaving Hopper's customers waiting in increasingly long lines. Additional delays were caused by twenty to thirty terminal lockups a day.

At Hopper, Warehouse Manager couldn't even be relied on to keep prices straight. A piece of industrial hose that should have been listed at $17 a foot showed up as costing $30 a foot.

By far the most damaging problem stemmed from huge gaps between what the computer told Hopper Specialty was in stock and what actually was there. The Warehouse Manager might show 50 parts in stock, for instance, when in fact Hopper needed to order 50. Other times, it would show that items were on order when they were sitting on the shelf.

The chaos seemed to compound itself. Six times in two months during 1989, Hopper employees hand-counted every item in the building, only to find the tally didn't match what NCR's computer said was there.

NCR kept records of complaints from Hopper and the nearly identical ones from many others using Warehouse Manager. But at Hopper and other locations, users say NCR told them that their problems were isolated. When he called for technical help, Mr. Hopper says, NCR blamed his employees' inexperience in using the system. In one instance, Mr. Hopper says, NCR technicians blamed problems on static electricity from office manager Tracy Irwin's nylon stockings.

Ms. Irwin, the office manager, began logging fourteen-hour days and coming in on weekends with her children to work out problems with the system. But she couldn't keep customers from taking their business two doors down, to Advance Supply Pump Co., *which now was boasting superior inventory and service. As Hopper Specialty's customer base eroded, it couldn't afford to carry as big an inventory. The shrinking inventory and confusion over what was in stock in turn further hurt Hopper's reputation for reliability. "The whole thing just snowballed," says Mr. Hopper.*

[SOURCE: Milo Geyelin, "How an NCR System for Inventory Turned into a Virtual Saboteur," *Wall Street Journal,* August 8, 1994, pp. A1, A4. Reprinted by permission of *Wall Street Journal,* © 1994 Dow Jones & Company, Inc. All Rights Reserved Worldwide.]

a. What procedures could Mr. Hopper have used to evaluate Warehouse Manager before purchasing the system?

b. In general, how can managers reduce uncertainty about whether an emerging technology is appropriate for use in their companies?

c. What internal factors are likely to affect the success of adopting a new technology? What external factors?

d. How can the quality of a new technology be assessed by nonexpert managers?

⊙ ETHICS AND QUALITY DISCUSSIONS

43. Grumman Corp., *in a move to avert criminal charges of defrauding the* Navy, *has agreed to a precedent-setting $20 million civil settlement that greatly expands federal supervision of the company's ethics compliance programs.*

The agreement . . . mandates the most extensive involvement yet by federal agencies in a major defense contractor's internal compliance efforts. It also is expected to allow the Bethpage, N.Y., contractor to avoid being suspended or barred from receiving new federal contracts.

Law enforcement officials said that the settlement, which gives Justice Department *and Pentagon officials a direct say in sensitive legal and personnel decisions facing Grumman's top management, is likely to serve as a model for future agreements with other companies.*

The settlement . . . ends a five-year criminal investigation of the company that was part of the nationwide Pentagon corruption inquiry dubbed Operation Ill Wind. The investigation . . . uncovered a pattern of overcharges, fraud and other violations involving some $17 million in business . . .

[SOURCE: Andy Pasztor, "U.S., Grumman Reach Accord in Pentagon Case," *Wall Street Journal,* November 23, 1993, pp. A3, A4. Reprinted by permission of *Wall Street Journal,* © 1993 Dow Jones & Company, Inc. All Rights Reserved Worldwide.]

A journalist friend of yours has asked you to assist her by addressing the following:

a. What does this story suggest about the costs of legal and ethical compliance relative to the costs of legal and ethical noncompliance?

b. Discuss whether the federal government should have the right to monitor compliance with ethical codes in addition to federal laws.

c. What does the story suggest about the importance of complying with both ethical codes and laws in governing organizations?

44. *A senior Toyota Motor Corp. official sharply criticized U.S. auto-parts suppliers [because] American suppliers still produce lower-quality parts than their Japanese competitors. In addition, U.S. suppliers are slower than Japanese suppliers. For instance, Japanese suppliers met every deadline when producing part prototypes for the Avalon sedan. U.S. suppliers, however, met their deadlines just 47 percent of the time. Toyota said it was forced to modify its product-development schedule to accommodate the slower U.S. suppliers.*
[SOURCE: Krystal Miller, "Toyota, Alleging Low Quality, Says It Won't Expand U.S. Parts Purchases," *Wall Street Journal*, June 17, 1994, p. A2.]

A fellow graduate of yours from your university has been pondering this article and seeks your help in understanding the implications. He wants to know:

a. Why would a delay in Toyota's product-development schedule be of extreme concern to the company?

b. What reasons might a U.S. company give for the lower quality and time delays?

c. What techniques might the American companies employ to raise quality and reduce lead times?

45. *A new voice-activated robot could enable quadriplegics and other severely disabled people to work at office jobs, researchers at Southwestern Pennsylvania Human Services said.*

The researchers led by K.G. Engelhardt and others formerly associated with Carnegie Mellon University, spent the past three years designing a version of the robot for use in the customer service department at Pittsburgh National Bank [PNB], a unit of Pittsburgh Financial Corp.

PNB has hired Scott Ferguson, a 31-year-old who became quadriplegic after a motorcycle accident ten years ago, to use the robot to answer customers' questions about credit card accounts.

The technology is timely, since the Americans with Disabilities Act requires businesses with twenty-five or more employees to provide "reasonable accommodation" to disabled workers by July 26 [1992]. It's unclear what "reasonable" means. But companies that can employ quadriplegics will be easily able to accommodate employees, "with less severe disabilities," Ms. Engelhardt said.

It's too early to tell how important the robot will be to PNB. The company plans to test the robot for a year before deciding whether to buy more, at an estimated cost of $50,000 each.
[SOURCE: Joan E. Rigdon, "Robot Could Help Quadriplegics Work at Jobs in Offices," *Wall Street Journal*, January 22, 1992, p. B6. Reprinted by permission of *Wall Street Journal*, © 1992 Dow Jones & Company, Inc. All Rights Reserved Worldwide.]

You have a quadriplegic friend who read this article and has asked you to consider the following to help him understand the situation:

a. What ethical obligations do business firms bear to employ disabled workers, given the assumption that the cost to employ a disabled worker will exceed the cost to employ other workers?

b. In your opinion is $50,000 per employee a "reasonable" cost to incur to accommodate a disabled employee? Explain.

c. What do companies stand to gain by hiring disabled workers? What do they stand to lose in doing so?

PART 2

The Basics of Managerial Accounting

Chapter 4 Cost Terminology and Cost Flows

LEARNING OBJECTIVES

After reading this chapter, you should be able to answer the following questions:

1 WHAT
is the relationship between cost objects and direct costs?

2 HOW
do you classify product costs into direct materials, direct labor, and factory overhead categories?

3 HOW
does the conversion process work in manufacturing and service companies?

4 WHAT
are the assumptions accountants make about cost behavior and why are these assumptions necessary?

5 HOW
can mixed costs be analyzed using the high–low method and (Appendix) least-squares regression analysis?

6 WHAT
is the usefulness of flexible budgeting to managers?

7 HOW
are predetermined factory overhead rates developed and how does the selection of a capacity measure affect factory overhead application?

8 HOW
is underapplied or overapplied factory overhead accounted for at year-end and why are these accounting techniques appropriate?

9 WHY
are separate predetermined overhead rates generally more useful than combined rates?

10 HOW
is cost of goods manufactured calculated?

Riscky Barbeque

Jim Riscky's grandmother began selling smoked meats in 1927 as a way to dispose of inventory from her husband's butcher shop at the end of the week. In time, the butcher shop became a family-owned supermarket that continued grandmom's sideline barbecue business. When Jim Riscky's father was killed in an accident, the 33-year old took over the family enterprise and additionally started a barbeque restaurant. Jim rapidly realized that the profit margin on barbeque was much higher than it could ever be on groceries. He began to convert the old supermarket to the center of a catering business that supplied "barbeque and fixin's" to events in the Fort Worth/Dallas area.

Today Riscky Barbeque has 10 locations in Fort Worth/Dallas. Other Riscky restaurant locations have different themes, such as "RisckyRita" with Southwestern style food and "Riscky's Steak House." Because cost control is so important in the restaurant business, Jim Riscky relies on a centralized commissary operation to prepare or process food items (such as barbeque, baked beans, potato salad, and vegetables) that can travel easily to the various restaurant sites. This organizational characteristic allows Riscky to control his direct labor and overhead costs to a much greater extent than if each restaurant was independently responsible for cooking food that is more easily prepared in mass quantities.

Even with investor offers of financing, Jim Riscky has resisted taking his operations to locations outside Fort Worth. He understands that long-distance locations do not currently fit in his organizational strategy. "The centralized preparation location is one secret to the success of my restaurants. I can have large amounts of food prepared on a daily basis and yet retain such consistently high quality that customers cannot tell if the food was prepared on- or off-site. Thus, I only do business in the local area."

SOURCE: Interview with Jim Riscky, Fort Worth, Texas (1997).

*C*ost is a major factor both in competing effectively and in operating profitably. It is of interest to everyone. A student is concerned about the cost of a Saturday night dinner and movie. Parents are concerned about the cost of their child's college education. College administrators are concerned about the costs associated with equipping and operating new computer labs. Jim Riscky is concerned about the costs of ingredients, equipment, and product quality assurance.

However, simply referring to "the cost" is inappropriate because numerous conditions must be specified before the cost can be determined. Is the student considering a fast-food or a four-star restaurant? Will the child want to attend a public or private college, in-state or out-of-state? Are the computer labs going to be open beyond normal class hours and how will they be staffed? At Riscky's, how many meals are to be prepared and what does it cost the company to deliver each meal?

Effective managers must be able to understand and communicate about costs using common management accounting terms. **Cost** is an often-used word and reflects a monetary measure of the resources given up to acquire a good or service. But the term cost is seldom used without a preceding adjective to specify the type of cost being considered. Different types of costs are used in different situations. For instance, an asset's historical or acquisition cost is used to prepare a balance sheet, but its replacement cost is used to estimate insurance value.

A cost can be viewed in many ways, depending on the information desired. Exhibit 4-1 presents a number of different cost categories and the types of costs included in each. These categories are not mutually exclusive; a cost may be included in different categories at different times. A variety of costs will be discussed throughout the text. At this time, it is sufficient to understand that the term cost can have many different meanings.

cost

COMPONENTS OF PRODUCT COST

LEARNING OBJECTIVE ❶
What is the relationship between cost objects and direct costs?

cost object
direct cost
indirect cost
allocate

Costs are classified as either product or period costs. Product costs relate to the products or services that generate an entity's revenues. These costs are either direct or indirect to a particular cost object. A **cost object** is anything to which management desires to attach costs or to which costs are related. A cost object can be a product or service, a department, a division, or a territory. Any costs that are clearly traceable to the cost object are called **direct costs**. Costs that cannot be traced are **indirect** (or common) **costs** and these costs can only be **allocated**, or assigned, to cost objects by

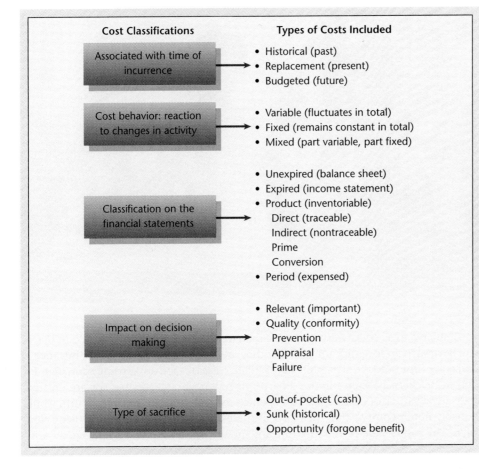

EXHIBIT 4-1
Cost Classification Categories

use of one or more appropriate drivers, predictors, or arbitrarily chosen bases.[1] Product cost components can be designated as direct materials, direct labor, and factory overhead (a set of indirect costs).

Direct Materials

Any readily identifiable, physical part of a product that is clearly, conveniently, and economically traceable to that product is a **direct material.** Direct materials may be purchased raw materials or manufactured components.[2] Direct materials cost should theoretically include the cost of all materials used in manufacturing a product or performing a service. For example, the cost of the tomato paste, corn syrup, vinegar, molasses, food starch, flavoring, salt, and water would theoretically make up the direct materials cost for Riscky's barbeque sauce.

However, management may decide that the benefit of treating an insignificant cost as direct is not worth the clerical cost involved. Such costs are treated and classified as indirect costs. For instance, most accountants would agree that the costs of the flavoring, salt, and water are neither economically traceable nor monetarily significant to the sauce's production cost. Thus, these costs would probably be deemed indirect materials and therefore would be included as a part of overhead.

LEARNING OBJECTIVE ❷
How do you classify product costs into direct materials, direct labor, and factory overhead categories?

direct material

---

[1]Different cost objects may be designated for different decisions. As the cost object changes, the direct and indirect costs may also change. For instance, if a production division is specified as the cost object, the division manager's salary is direct. If, instead, the cost object is a sales territory and the production division operates in more than one territory, the division manager's salary is indirect.

[2]Outside processing cost may also be considered a direct material cost. For example, a furniture manufacturer may want a special plastic laminate on tables. Rather than buying the necessary equipment, the manufacturer may send the tables to another company that specializes in this process. The amount paid for this process may be considered a direct material cost by the manufacturer.

Direct labor occurs in both manufacturing and service environments. At a tailor shop, direct labor personnel measure and pin garments that are then given to a seamstress (another direct labor person) to sew.

Similarly, in a service business, some materials that could be traced to a cost object may have such an insignificant cost that they are not considered direct. For instance, a marketing firm needs to separately accumulate costs of each advertising campaign for each of its clients. When dummy boards, or mock-ups, of possible ads are created, artists use a variety of colored pens and pencils for design purposes. But the firm would probably not attempt to trace the costs of these items to a particular advertising campaign. The costs would be too insignificant and would be treated as overhead.

Direct Labor

LEARNING OBJECTIVE ❷
How do you classify product costs into direct materials, direct labor, and factory overhead categories?

direct labor

Direct labor refers to the individuals who work specifically on manufacturing a product or performing a service. Their labor transforms raw materials or supplies into finished goods or completed services. Another perspective on direct labor is that it directly *adds* value to the final product or service. The food preparer and the chef at Riscky's represent direct labor.

Direct labor cost consists of wages or salaries paid to employees who work on a product or perform a service. Direct labor cost should include basic compensation, production efficiency bonuses, and the employer's share of social security taxes. In addition, when a company's operations are relatively stable, direct labor cost should include all employer-paid insurance costs, holiday and vacation pay, and pension and other retirement benefits.[3]

Even though direct labor cost is clearly traceable to a particular cost object, a given cost must also be conveniently and economically traceable to the product or service to be considered direct. As with some materials, some labor costs that should theoretically be considered direct are treated as indirect for two reasons.

First, it might be cost inefficient to trace the labor costs. For example, some employee fringe benefits should conceptually be treated as direct labor cost, but many companies do not have stable work forces and cannot develop a reasonable estimate of fringe benefit costs. Thus, the time, effort, and cost of trying to trace the fringe benefit costs might not be worth the additional accuracy that would be provided. In contrast, when fringe benefit costs are extremely high (such as for professional staff

---

[3]Institute of Management Accountants (formerly National Association of Accountants), *Statements on Management Accounting Number 4C, Definition and Measurement of Direct Labor Cost* (Montvale, N.J.: National Association of Accountants, June 13, 1985), p. 4.

in a service organization), tracing them to products and services may provide more useful management information.

Second, erroneous information about product or service costs might result from handling such costs in the theoretically correct manner. An assumed payroll for production workers who make barbeque sauce for one week at Riscky's commissary can illustrate this possibility. If each of these six sauce-production employees earns $6 per hour, overtime pay would be $9 per hour or time-and-a-half pay. One week prior to a holiday, the employees worked a total of 300 hours, including 60 hours of overtime to complete all the orders. Exhibit 4-2 presents the determination of how much of this portion of the commissary's weekly payroll is direct labor and how much is indirect factory cost (known as *overhead*—to be discussed subsequently).

Barbeque sauce production is scheduled based on the expected current demand. If the $3 per hour overtime premium were assigned to the sauce produced during the overtime hours, the labor cost for this sauce would appear to be 50 percent greater than that for sauce manufactured during regular working hours. Since scheduling is random, the sauce made during overtime hours should not be forced to bear the overtime charges. Therefore, amounts incurred for costs such as overtime or shift premiums are usually considered overhead rather than direct labor cost and are allocated to all products made by the Riscky commissary.

There are occasions, however, when allocating costs such as overtime to all units is not appropriate. If a customer who is to be catered requests a job to be scheduled during overtime hours or is in a rush and requests that overtime be worked, overtime or shift premiums should be considered direct labor and be attached to the job that created the costs.

The proportion of direct labor cost to total product cost has been slowly declining in many industries, especially over the past 25 years.[4] Now, in many highly automated production environments, it is not uncommon to find that direct labor accounts for a very small proportion of total cost at many manufacturers. Eventually, managers may find that almost all direct labor cost is replaced with a new cost of production—the cost of robots and other fully automated machinery. Thus, while labor may still be an essential element of production in some industries, managers should avoid overestimating the importance of labor cost in a technically advanced setting.

EXHIBIT 4-2

Payroll Analysis for Direct Labor and Overhead

Week's payroll information:

- 300 hours worked, of which 60 hours are overtime at time-and-a-half pay
- $6 per hour regular pay rate; applies to all hours worked (considered direct labor cost)
- $3 per hour overtime premium; applies only to the overtime hours (considered overhead)

Total hours for week	300	Overtime hours for week	60
× Regular pay rate per hour	× $6	× Overtime premium rate per hour	× $3
Direct labor cost (1)	$1,800	Factory overhead (2)	$180

Total payroll = $1,800 + $180 = $1,980

(1) The $1,800 direct labor cost is assigned directly to all sauce made during the week, regardless of whether it was made during regular hours or overtime hours.

(2) The $180 of factory overhead cost is considered overhead and will be assigned, by indirect means that are described later, to all products made by the Riscky commissary over a longer period.

[4]Germain Böer, "Five Modern Management Accounting Myths," *Management Accounting* (January 1994), pp. 22, 24.

Factory Overhead

factory overhead

Factory overhead is any factory or production cost that is not directly or conveniently traceable to manufacturing a product or providing a service.[5] Factory overhead costs are essential to the process of converting raw materials into finished goods. "The great part of most companies' costs (other than those for purchased materials) typically occurs in overhead categories. Even in manufacturing, more than two-thirds of all nonmaterial costs tend to be indirect or overhead expenses."[6]

The sum of direct materials, direct labor, and overhead costs comprises total product cost.[7] Product costs can also be classified as either prime or conversion costs. According to generally accepted accounting principles, product costs are inventoriable until the products are sold or otherwise disposed of.

Prime and Conversion Costs

prime cost

conversion cost

The total cost of direct materials and direct labor is referred to as **prime cost** because these costs are most convincingly associated with and traceable to a specific product. **Conversion cost** is defined as "the sum of direct labor and factory overhead which is directly or indirectly necessary for transforming raw materials and purchased parts into a salable finished product."[8] Because direct labor is included as part of both prime cost and conversion cost, prime cost plus conversion cost does not sum to product cost. Otherwise, direct labor would be double-counted. Exhibit 4-3 shows the typical components of product cost for a manufacturing company in terms of prime and conversion costs.

EXHIBIT 4-3
Components of Product Cost

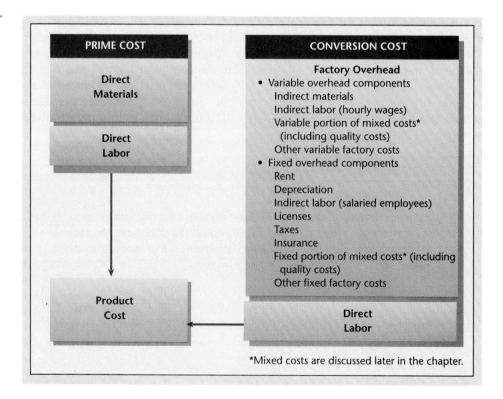

---

[5]Another term used for overhead is *burden*. The authors believe that this term is unacceptable, as it connotes costs that are extra, unnecessary, or oppressive.

[6]James Brian Quinn et al., "Beyond Products: Services-Based Strategy," *Harvard Business Review* (March–April 1990), p. 65.

[7]This definition of product cost is traditionally accepted and is also referred to as *absorption costing*. Another product-costing method, called *variable costing*, excludes the fixed factory overhead component from inventories. Absorption and variable costing are compared in Appendix 2 of Chapter 6.

[8]Institute of Management Accountants (formerly National Association of Accountants), *Statements on Management Accounting Number 2: Management Accounting Terminology* (Montvale, N.J.: National Association of Accountants, June 1, 1983), p. 24.

STAGES OF PRODUCTION

Production processing or conversion can be viewed as existing in three stages: (1) work not started (raw materials), (2) work in process, and (3) finished work. The stages of production in a manufacturing firm and some costs associated with each stage are illustrated in Exhibit 4-4. In the first stage of processing, the cost incurred reflects the prices paid for raw materials and/or supplies. As work progresses through the second stage, accrual-based accounting requires that costs related to the conversion of raw materials or supplies be accumulated and attached to the goods. These costs include wages paid to people producing the goods as well as overhead charges. The total costs incurred in stages 1 and 2 are equal to the total production cost of finished goods in stage 3.

Cost accounting provides the means for accumulating the processing costs and allocating the costs to the goods produced. The primary accounts involved in the cost accumulation process are (1) Raw Materials, (2) Work in Process, and (3) Finished Goods. These accounts relate to the three stages of production shown in Exhibit 4-4 and form a common database for cost, management and financial accounting.

Service firms ordinarily do not have the same degree of cost complexity as manufacturers. The work-not-started stage of processing normally consists of the cost of

LEARNING OBJECTIVE ❸
How does the conversion process work in manufacturing and service companies?

EXHIBIT 4-4
Stages and Costs of Production

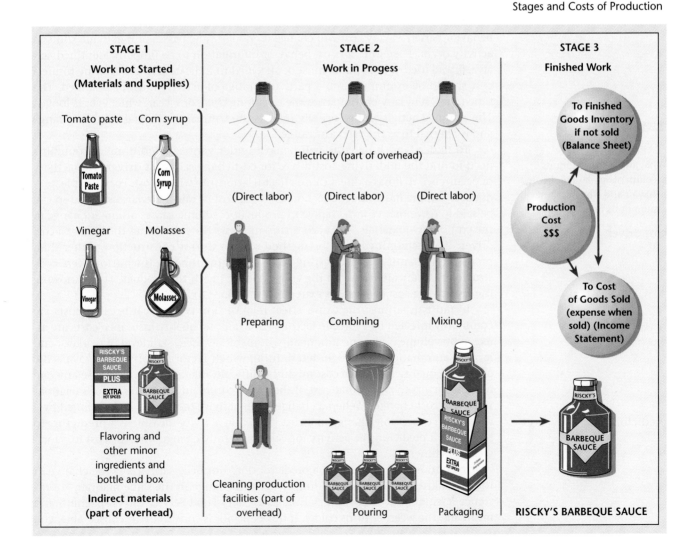

STAGE 1	STAGE 2	STAGE 3
Work not Started (Materials and Supplies)	**Work in Progess**	**Finished Work**

Tomato paste   Corn syrup

Vinegar   Molasses

Flavoring and other minor ingredients and bottle and box

Indirect materials (part of overhead)

Electricity (part of overhead)

(Direct labor)   (Direct labor)   (Direct labor)

Preparing   Combining   Mixing

Cleaning production facilities (part of overhead)

Pouring   Packaging

To Finished Goods Inventory if not sold (Balance Sheet)

Production Cost $$$

To Cost of Goods Sold (expense when sold) (Income Statement)

RISCKY'S BARBEQUE SAUCE

supplies necessary for performing services. Supplies are inventoried until they are placed into a work-in-process stage. At that point, labor and overhead are added to achieve finished results. Developing the cost of services is extremely important and useful in service-oriented businesses. For instance, cost accounting is very useful in hospitals that need to accumulate the costs incurred by patients in their hospital stays and in architectural firms that need to accumulate the costs incurred for designs and models of individual projects.

The product and service costs accumulated in the inventory accounts are composed of three cost components: direct materials, direct labor, and factory overhead. Each of these components is discussed in the preceding section of this chapter. Precise classification of some costs into one of these categories may be difficult and judgment may be required in the classification process.

COST BEHAVIOR

cost behavior

In any period, a cost may change from a prior period because of changes in activity. The way a cost responds to a change in activity is known as its **cost behavior**. For Riscky Barbeque, activity measures can include sales; production volume; machine hours; number of purchase orders sent; or number of grocery stores and restaurants selling Riscky products, meals using barbeque sauce, or other Riscky products. The way a *total* (rather than unit) cost reacts to a change in activity reflects that cost's behavior pattern. Every cost will change if enough time passes or if extreme shifts in activity occur. Therefore, for cost behavior information to be properly identified, analyzed, and used, a time frame must be specified to indicate how far into the future a cost should be examined, and a particular range of activity must be assumed. The time frame generally encompasses the operating cycle or a year, whichever is longer. The assumed activity range usually reflects the company's normal operating range and is referred to as the **relevant range**.

relevant range

LEARNING OBJECTIVE 4
What are the assumptions accountants make about cost behavior and why are these assumptions necessary?

cost driver

To understand how costs will behave under various conditions, accountants need to find the underlying cost driver for cost changes. A **cost driver** is an activity or occurrence that has a direct cause-effect relationship with a cost. For example, production volume has a direct effect on the total cost of raw materials used and so can be said to drive that cost. A change in production volume causes a similar change in the cost of raw materials. The accompanying News Note illustrates the idea of a cost driver: IBM determined that the method of laser mirror construction, rather than production quantity, caused testing costs. Changing the way the mirrors were constructed dramatically changed the cost associated with the product. Thus, knowing the underlying cost drivers was extremely important to IBM.

In most situations, the cause–effect relationship is less clear because costs are commonly affected by multiple factors. For example, quality assurance costs are affected by volume of production, quality of materials used, skill level of workers, and level of automation. Although determining which factor actually *caused* a specific change in quality assurance cost might be difficult, managers could choose any one of these factors to *predict* that cost, if they were confident about the factor's relationship with cost changes. When a change in an activity measure is accompanied by a consistent, observable change in a cost item, that activity measure is a **predictor**. To be used as a predictor, the activity measure need only change with the cost in a foreseeable manner.

predictor

In contrast to a cost driver, a predictor does not necessarily *cause* the change in the related item; the two items simply need to change in the same manner. For instance, assume that almost every time University Food Service offers spaghetti and meatballs, the weather turns colder. If this behavior is consistent and observable, you

Change the Process—Change the Cost

International Business Machines Corp. said it has developed a low-cost way to make tiny lasers, a technology now dominated by Japanese electronics companies.

The new process allows IBM to test the lasers in batches of as many as 20,000 units; testing is a major expense in laser-making. IBM estimated that its method will be 50 percent cheaper than current processes, and said it will also be faster and more efficient.

IBM said it used a chip-making process to etch small trenches into 3-inch-diameter wafers of laser material. Then it covered the trenches with a reflective material that turned them into tiny mirrors. After each wafer was tested, it was cut into as many as 20,000 separate lasers.

By contrast, current laser-making methods form mirrors by breaking the wafer into tiny pieces; the broken edges then act as reflecting surfaces. Since the lasers aren't finished until their mirrors are made, devices must then be tested one at a time.

Daniel Wilt, a technical supervisor at AT&T's Bell Laboratories, estimated that IBM's method, if done well, could cut the cost of each semiconductor laser from $10 to $1.

SOURCE: Laurence Hooper, "IBM Finds Way to Reduce Costs of Small Lasers," *Wall Street Journal*, January 31, 1991, p. B5.

http:// www.ibm.com

may use it to predict colder weather—but the offering of spaghetti and meatballs itself does not cause colder weather, and colder weather may occur when University Food Service does not offer spaghetti and meatballs or is not even open for business.

The difference between a cost driver and a predictor is important. A cost driver reflects the *actual* cause–effect relationship; a predictor reflects a *possible* relationship or perhaps even a totally *random* occurrence that simply *seems* to be related. However, managers often use both cost drivers and predictors to estimate how changes in activity will influence cost behavior.

Variable and Fixed Costs

Cost behavior patterns will be referred to throughout the text because they are so helpful in many management accounting situations requiring analysis and decision making. The two most common types of cost behaviors are variable and fixed. The respective total cost and unit cost definitions for variable and fixed cost behaviors are presented in Exhibit 4-5.

	Total Cost	Unit Cost
Variable Cost	Varies in direct proportion to changes in activity	Is constant throughout the relevant range
Fixed Cost	Remains constant throughout the relevant range	Varies inversely with changes in activity throughout the relevant range

EXHIBIT 4-5
Comparative Total and Unit Cost Behavior Definitions

variable cost

A cost that varies in total in direct proportion to changes in activity is classified as a **variable cost**. Because the total cost varies in direct proportion to the changes in activity, a variable cost is a constant amount per unit.[9]

Direct labor cost is commonly viewed as a variable cost in Western cultures, but not necessarily in others. For example, in Japan, many workers have lifelong employment contracts; thus, companies often treat direct labor costs as fixed. Because of a downturn in the Japanese economy, some companies are trying to modify this situation and trade these fixed costs for variable ones, as indicated in the accompanying News Note.

Other examples of variable costs and their drivers include raw materials costs and production volume, units-of-production depreciation and production volume, sales commissions and number or price of products sold, and gasoline cost and miles driven. Variable costs are extremely important to a company's total profit picture because every time a particular activity takes place, a specific amount of variable cost is incurred.

fixed cost

In contrast, a cost that remains constant *in total* within the relevant range of activity is a **fixed cost**. Such a cost varies inversely on a per-unit basis with changes in activity: the per-unit fixed cost decreases with increases in activity and increases with decreases in activity.

While direct materials and direct labor are generally variable in relation to production volume, factory overhead costs may be variable, mixed, or fixed. Variable factory overhead includes the cost of indirect materials and indirect labor paid on an hourly basis, such as wages for forklift operators, material handlers, and others who support the production, assembly, or service process. Also included in variable fac-

NEWS NOTE

Lifetime Contracts Make Labor Cost Fixed

Recent business publications contend that Japan's current economic woes are compounded by the inability of companies to reduce their work forces due to lifetime employment practices.

Most Japanese companies understand the nature of their current problem. The typical Japanese company still views almost all of its costs, including labor, as fixed. To steer their way through the current recession, however, Japanese companies must focus on reducing all costs, which means changing their view on the fixed nature of personnel expenses.

One manufacturer is toying with the idea of putting everyone in its Japanese operations on a temporary contract. That is, anyone in the work force could be laid off as economic conditions dictate. To make this work, at the end of five months and twenty-nine days, a worker would be dismissed for a day, then reemployed under a new five-month, twenty-nine-day contract. (Under Japanese labor practices, at the end of six months a worker becomes a "permanent" employee.) The company concedes that this would be easiest to apply to factory-floor workers. At any rate, the company says it will probably not be able to implement such a program because it is "too American" and it would be impossible to recruit and retain quality workers.

SOURCE: Douglas T. Shinsato, "Japan Tries to Get the Size Right," *Wall Street Journal*, June 28, 1993, p. A16.

---

[9]An accountant's view of a variable cost is, in fact, a slight distortion of reality. Variable costs usually increase at a changing rate until a range of activity is reached in which the average variable cost rate per unit becomes fairly constant. Within this range, the slope of the cost line becomes less steep because the firm benefits from operating efficiencies such as price discounts on materials, improved worker skills, and increased productivity. Beyond this range, the slope becomes quite steep as the firm enters an activity range in which some operating inefficiencies (such as worker crowding and material shortages) cause the average variable cost rate to trend sharply higher. Because of the curves on each end of the graph, accountants choose as the relevant range that range of activity in which the variable costs per unit are constant.

For this Domino's, the fixed cost of depreciation is taken not on a "fixed" asset, but rather on a moveable store and its equipment. The gas used to move the store to Biloxi's "Cruisin' the Coast Weekend" is a variable cost.

tory overhead are the costs of oil and grease used for machine maintenance, paper towels used in the factory rest rooms, and the variable portion of utility charges (or any other mixed cost) for the conversion area. Depreciation calculated with the units-of-production method is a variable factory overhead cost.

Fixed factory overhead comprises costs such as straight-line and declining-balance depreciation and insurance and property taxes on production/service-providing assets. Fixed indirect factory labor cost includes salaries for production supervisors, shift superintendents, and service managers. The fixed portion of mixed costs (such as maintenance and utilities) incurred in the conversion area is also part of fixed factory overhead.

Each fixed cost is basically independent of production or sales volume as long as a relevant range is specified. However, if production or sales volume were to rise to a point at which additional supervisors, plant space, or equipment were needed, the related salaries, depreciation, and insurance costs would also rise.

The need to define a relevant range of activity in order to determine variable and fixed cost levels can be illustrated as follows. Assume that Riscky Barbeque has the cost structures for tomato paste and building rent shown in the graphs in Exhibit 4-6 (page 126). The exhibit indicates that actual cost for tomato paste is curvilinear rather than linear and that, over a wide range of activity, several levels of fixed cost will actually exist for rent.

The curves on the raw materials cost graph (Graph A) reflect suppliers' pricing policies. If Riscky's purchasing agent buys tomato paste in less than 2,000-gallon lots, the price per gallon is $1.10. If tomato paste is purchased in lots between 2,000 and 10,000 gallons, the price falls to $.95 per gallon. Quantities over 10,000 gallons may be purchased for only $.85 per gallon. The company always buys tomato paste in quantities of 2,000 to 10,000 gallons; therefore, this activity level becomes the relevant range for tomato paste purchases. The tomato paste cost is variable because total cost varies in direct proportion to the quantity purchased within the relevant range. If Riscky Barbeque buys 4,000 gallons, it will pay $3,800 for its purchases; if it buys 8,000 gallons, the cost will be $7,600. In each instance, the volume is within the relevant range and, thus, the cost remains constant at $.95 per gallon. Under these circumstances, the per-gallon cost of tomato paste is a truly linear variable cost.

A decision about the relevant range of activity must also be made for fixed costs. Rent is the fixed cost shown in Exhibit 4-6. Riscky Barbeque management has determined that a building that can be rented for $1,000 per month is large enough to

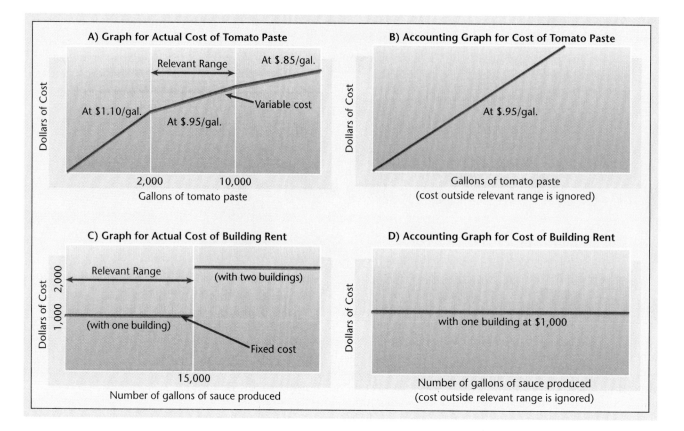

EXHIBIT 4-6

Relevant Range of Activity for
Riscky Barbeque

house the equipment needed to produce between 1 and 15,000 gallons of sauce per month. However, if monthly production exceeds 15,000 gallons, additional facilities will be required. If another similar building is acquired, an additional $1,000 of monthly building rent will be incurred. The company always produces between 2,000 and 5,000 gallons per month, so the fixed cost for building rent is $1,000 per month.

In some businesses and for some items, managers can decide to trade variable and fixed costs for one another. For instance, a company may reduce the variable cost of postage by investing in a fixed cost for a machine to presort mail. Or a company may reduce the fixed cost of salaried employees by hiring part-time workers who are paid an hourly wage. Shifting from costs exhibiting one type of cost behavior to costs exhibiting a different type of behavior changes a company's basic cost structure and can significantly affect profits.

http:// www.saralee.com

http:// www.terex.com

Companies may decide to outsource, or hire external providers to perform certain tasks that were previously done in-house. Sara Lee is an example of a company that does extensive outsourcing. It has decided "to become an 'assetless' company—one that outsources virtually everything and concentrates on managing its brands."[10] Companies that outsource will realize additional profit if the costs paid to external providers are less than the costs that were incurred internally. As indicated in the accompanying News Note, Terex Corporation has chosen to trade substantial fixed costs for lower variable costs by increasing its use of outside contractors, outsourcing all its operations.

Mixed Costs

mixed cost

Some costs are not strictly variable or fixed. For example, a **mixed cost** (also called a semivariable cost) has both a variable and a fixed component. This type of cost does not fluctuate in direct proportion to changes in activity, nor does it remain constant

[10]Robert B. Reich, "Brand-Name Knowledge—Manager's Journal," *Wall Street Journal*, October 13, 1997, p. A22.

Terex's Fortunes Improve after Tough Cost-Cutting

http:// www.terex.com

At the end of Ronald M. DeFeo's first day as an executive at Terex Corp. [in 1992], the chairman pulled him aside and dropped a bombshell: The company didn't have enough money to make the next loan payment. [Terex is a manufacturer of heavy equipment for the construction industry.]

"Not having enough cash to pay the bills really focused us on the fundamentals," says Mr. DeFeo, now 45 years old and Terex's president and chief executive officer.

The results have been promising. . . . This year, analysts expect the company to earn in the neighborhood of $25 million, or $1.45 a share, on sales of about $850 million.

Terex has tried to cut fixed costs in all its operations by increasing the use of outside contractors. Frames for cranes assembled in the U.S., for example, are now shaped, welded and painted in Mexico, where costs are lower, while the company concentrates its own manufacturing efforts on the unique parts used in its products. Terex is also buying and making more standardized parts, such as hydraulic cylinders, which can be used on a variety of cranes and lifts.

But the company's efforts to remake itself are not confined to the factory floor. It has slashed its sales staff and, instead of visiting many of its customers, sends them air tickets for an annual visit to one of Terex's factories.

Mr. DeFeo has also trimmed the company's engineering staff. "Engineers add complexity and cost," says Mr. DeFeo. "When you're selling to the rental market, you have to keep your product simple."

SOURCE: Gordon Fairclough, "Corporate Focus: Terex's Fortunes Improve after Tough Cost-Cutting," *Wall Street Journal*, September 30, 1997, p. B4. Reprinted by permission of *Wall Street Journal*, © 1997 Dow Jones & Company, Inc. All Rights Reserved Worldwide.

with changes in activity. Electricity is a good example of a mixed cost. Electricity bills are commonly computed as a flat charge (the fixed component) for basic service plus a stated rate for each kilowatt hour (kwh) of electricity used (the variable component). Exhibit 4-7 shows a graph for Riscky's electricity charge, which consists of a flat rate of $100 per month plus $.02 per kwh. If Riscky uses 20,000 kwhs of electricity in a month, its total electricity bill is $500 [$100 + ($.02 × 20,000)]. If the company uses 30,000 kwhs, the electricity bill is $700. Management accountants generally separate mixed costs into their variable and fixed components so that the behavior of these costs is more readily apparent.

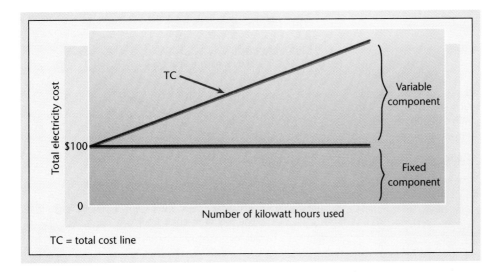

EXHIBIT 4-7
Graph of a Mixed Cost

All costs are treated by accountants as linear rather than curvilinear. Because of this treatment, the general formula for a straight line is used to describe any type of cost (variable, fixed, or mixed) within a relevant range of activity. The straight-line formula is:

$$y = a + bx$$

where y = total cost
a = fixed portion of total cost
b = variable portion of total cost (the rate at which total cost changes in relation to changes in x; when a graph is prepared to depict the straight line, b represents the slope of the line)
x = activity base (or cost driver) to which y is being related

Exhibit 4-8 illustrates the use of the straight-line formula for each type of cost behavior. An entirely variable cost is represented as $y = \$0 + bx$. Zero is shown as the value for the a term because there is no fixed cost. A purely fixed cost is formulated as $y = a + \$0x$. Zero is the b term in the formula since no cost component varies with activity. A mixed cost has formula values for both the a and b unknowns. Thus, mixed costs must be separated into their variable and fixed components before separate variable and fixed overhead rates can be calculated. The simplest method of separation is the high–low method.

EXHIBIT 4-8

Uses of the Straight-Line
Cost Formula

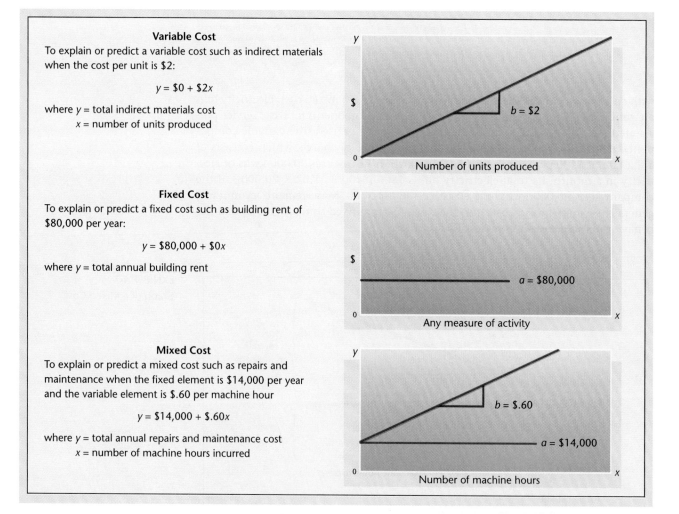

Variable Cost

To explain or predict a variable cost such as indirect materials when the cost per unit is $2:

$$y = \$0 + \$2x$$

where y = total indirect materials cost
x = number of units produced

$b = \$2$

Number of units produced

Fixed Cost

To explain or predict a fixed cost such as building rent of $80,000 per year:

$$y = \$80,000 + \$0x$$

where y = total annual building rent

$a = \$80,000$

Any measure of activity

Mixed Cost

To explain or predict a mixed cost such as repairs and maintenance when the fixed element is $14,000 per year and the variable element is $.60 per machine hour

$$y = \$14,000 + \$.60x$$

where y = total annual repairs and maintenance cost
x = number of machine hours incurred

$b = \$.60$

$a = \$14,000$

Number of machine hours

High–Low Method

LEARNING OBJECTIVE ⑤
How can mixed costs be analyzed using the high–low method and (Appendix) least-squares regression analysis?

high–low method

The **high–low method** is a cost estimation technique for separating a mixed cost into its variable and fixed components. The high–low method uses activity and cost information from an actual set of cost observations to calculate the variable and fixed cost estimates. The highest and lowest activity levels are selected from the data set, *if* these two levels are within the relevant range. The reason for selecting the high and low activity levels rather than high and low costs is that the analysis is undertaken to estimate how *costs* change in relation to *activity* changes. Activities cause costs to change; costs do not cause activities to change.

The high–low method is used to develop an equation that predicts the unknown values of a dependent variable (*y* term) from the known values of one or more independent variables (*x* term). An **independent variable** is an amount that, when changed, will cause consistent, observable changes in another variable. A **dependent variable** is an unknown amount that can be predicted by the use of one or more independent variables.

independent variable
dependent variable

Total mixed cost increases or decreases with changes in activity. The change in cost is equal to the change in activity multiplied by the unit variable cost; the fixed cost element does not fluctuate with changes in activity. The variable cost per unit of activity reflects the average change in cost for each additional unit of activity. Finding the changes in activity and cost simply involves subtracting the observation values of activity and cost at the low activity from the observation values of activity and cost at the high level of activity. These differences are then used to calculate the *b* term in the $y = a + bx$ formula as follows:

$$b = \frac{\text{Change in total cost}}{\text{Change in activity level}}$$

The *b* term represents the unit variable cost per measure of activity. At either the low or high level of activity, the *b* value can be multiplied by the activity level to determine the amount of total variable cost contained in the total mixed cost.

Since a mixed cost has both a variable and a fixed component, the latter is found by subtracting total variable cost from total cost: $y - bx = a$. Either the high or the low level of activity can be used to determine the fixed portion of the mixed cost. Both activity levels are assumed to be on the same straight line and, thus, fixed cost would be constant at all activity levels within the relevant range.

The high–low method is illustrated in Exhibit 4-9 (page 130) using assumed cups of coffee served and utility cost information for RisckyRita Restaurant. The restaurant's normal operating range of activity is between 8,000 and 11,600 cups of coffee per month. For RisckyRita Restaurant, the variable cost is $.10 per can of coffee and the fixed cost is $569 per month.

Note that the July data for RisckyRita Restaurant are outside the relevant range; this unusually high activity was analyzed and found to be caused by a promotional campaign in which RisckyRita's gave cups of coffee to passersby to make the community aware of a new brand of coffee available. A nonrepresentative point that falls outside of the relevant range of activity or that is a distortion of normal costs within the relevant range is known as an **outlier**. Outliers should be disregarded in analyzing mixed costs under the high–low method.

outlier

Regression analysis is another technique used to separate mixed costs into their variable and fixed cost elements. Regression (discussed in the appendix to this chapter) often results in a better estimate of the cost formula than does the high-low method. Performing it by hand is tedious; however, many software packages are available to do regression analysis.

Regardless of which method is used to separate mixed costs, it is important to recognize the following three points. First, high–low and regression are simply cost estimation techniques; neither provides exact costs of future activities. Second, the

EXHIBIT 4-9

High–Low Analysis of
Utility Cost

The following information on cups of coffee and utility cost is available from the prior year:

MONTH	LEVEL OF ACTIVITY IN CUPS OF COFFEE	UTILITY COST
January	11,300	$1,712
February	11,400	1,716
March	9,000	1,469
April	11,500	1,719
May	11,200	1,698
June	10,100	1,691
July	12,200	1,989

Step 1: Select the highest and lowest levels of activity within the relevant range and obtain the costs associated with those levels. These levels and costs are 11,500 and 9,000 cups of coffee and $1,719 and $1,469, respectively.

Step 2: Calculate the change in activity and the change in cost.

	CUPS OF COFFEE	ASSOCIATED UTILITY COST
High activity—April	11,500	$1,719
Low activity—March	9,000	1,469
Changes	2,500	$ 250

Step 3: Determine the relationship of cost change to activity change to find the variable cost element.

$$b = \frac{\text{Change in total cost}}{\text{Change in activity volume}} = \frac{\$250}{2,500} = \$.10 \text{ per cup}$$

Step 4: Compute total variable cost (TVC) at either level of activity.

High level of activity: TVC = $.10 (11,500) = $1,150

or

Low level of activity: TVC = $.10 (9,000) = $900

Step 5: Subtract total variable cost from total cost at either level of activity to determine fixed cost.

High level of activity: $a = \$1,719 - \$1,150 = \$569$

or

Low level of activity: $a = \$1,469 - \$900 = \$569$

Step 6: Substitute the fixed and variable cost values in the straight-line formula to get an equation that can be used to estimate total cost at any level of activity within the relevant range.

$$y = \$569 + \$.10x$$

where x = number of cups of coffee

---

correlation

appropriateness of the cost formula depends on the validity of the activity measure chosen to predict the variable cost. The activity base selected should be logically related to the incurrence of overhead cost and should reflect significant correlation. (**Correlation** is a statistical measure of the strength of relationship between two variables.) Third, when significant changes are occurring in a business (such as the introduction of new production techniques or new product lines or expansion into new locales), historical information may not be extremely useful in attempting to predict future costs.

PREPARING FLEXIBLE BUDGETS

After all overhead costs are analyzed as to their cost behavior, managers can use the various $y = a + bx$ cost formulas to prepare a flexible budget. A **flexible budget** is a series of individual financial plans that detail the individual costs comprising total cost and present those costs at different levels of activity.[11] In a flexible budget, all costs are treated as either variable or fixed; thus, mixed costs must be separated into their variable and fixed components.

flexible budget

LEARNING OBJECTIVE ⑥
What is the usefulness of flexible budgeting to managers?

The activity levels shown on a flexible budget usually cover management's contemplated range of activity for the upcoming period. If all activity levels are within the relevant range, costs at each successive level should equal the amount of the previous level plus a uniform dollar increment for each variable cost factor. The increment is the variable cost per unit of activity multiplied by the quantity of additional activity.

An analysis of hypothetical past data for individual overhead costs for Columbia River Barbeque (a fictitious company intended to be similar to Riscky Barbeque) for 1997 has generated the information shown in Exhibit 4-10. This information is used to illustrate the preparation of a flexible budget. The company's activity base is pounds of barbeque smoked, and its contemplated range of activity for the upcoming year is between 1,000,000 and 1,500,000 pounds of barbeque.

All cost factors are presented in terms of the a (fixed) and b (variable) values of the straight-line formula. Note that the information in Exhibit 4-10 indicates that both supervision and equipment maintenance contract costs increase at an activity

EXHIBIT 4-10
Analysis of Overhead Costs

The formulas are based on pounds of barbeque smoked as the independent variable (x).

	a = FIXED COST	b = VARIABLE COST
Purely Variable Costs		
Indirect materials		$.11
Indirect labor:		
Support workers		.07
Idle time		.02
Fringe benefits		.03
Total variable cost per pound		$.23
Purely Fixed Costs		
Supervision	$ 90,000*	
Depreciation	100,000	
Maintenance contract	30,000‡	
Insurance	4,256	
Total fixed cost per pound	$224,256	
Mixed Costs		
Utilities	6,832	.01
Totals for flexible budget formula		
(for x < 1,400,000 pounds)	$231,088	$.24

Flexible budget formulas (where y = total production overhead):
  (If x < 1,400,000 pounds of barbeque) $y = \$231,088 + \$.24x$
  (If $x \geq 1,400,000$ pounds of barbeque) $y = \$267,088 + \$.24x$

*Supervision is expected to be $120,000 when $x \geq 1,400,000$ pounds.
‡Equipment maintenance contract will increase to $36,000 when $x \geq 1,400,000$ pounds.

[11]Flexible budgets can be prepared for all types of costs (both product and period), not just for overhead.

level of 1,400,000 pounds of barbeque. These costs are said to be step-fixed or long-term variable costs. Columbia River Barbeque needs two flexible budget formulas (given at the bottom of the exhibit), since the analysis indicates the existence of changes in the fixed costs within the contemplated range of activity.

With the formulas derived in Exhibit 4-10, a flexible budget (shown in Exhibit 4-11) can be prepared for Columbia River Barbeque's production overhead costs. The owner expects to produce 1,372,800 pounds of barbeque in 1998; therefore, a cost column for this level of activity is provided.

Presenting a flexible budget is a good way to show any steps that exist for the categories of expected fixed costs. Exhibit 4-11 also illustrates the stable behavior of variable cost per pound of barbeque compared with the irregular behavior of fixed cost per pound.

Two factors cause the irregular behavior of Columbia River Barbeque's fixed cost per pound of barbeque: a change in activity level and the steps in the fixed costs. As pounds of barbeque increase, fixed cost per pound should decrease, assuming total fixed cost does not change. However, in this company, total fixed cost increases by $36,000 at 1,400,000 pounds of barbeque. The irregular behavior of fixed cost per pound requires that a specific level be chosen to calculate a predetermined fixed overhead rate per unit for product costing purposes.

step cost

Another type of cost shifts upward or downward when activity changes by a certain interval or step. **Step costs** can be variable or fixed. Step variable costs have small steps and are treated for analysis purposes as variable costs. A water bill computed at $.002 per gallon for 1 to 1,000 gallons, $.003 per gallon for 1,001 to 2,000 gallons, $.005 per gallon for 2,001 to 3,000 gallons, and so on, is an example of a step variable cost. In contrast, step fixed costs have large steps and are commonly treated as fixed costs. An example of a step fixed cost would be salaries for computer data-entry clerks. Each clerk can handle 800 lines of input per day and is paid $2,000 per month. For each additional 800 lines of input per day that occur (on an extended basis), another clerk is needed, requiring an additional $2,000 per month in salary. A relevant range of activity must be specified for step variable and step fixed costs to allow their treatment, respectively, as variable or fixed.

EXHIBIT 4-11
Overhead Flexible Budget

	POUNDS OF BARBEQUE			
Variable Overhead Costs	*1,000,000*	*1,100,000*	*1,372,800*	*1,400,000*
Indirect materials	$110,000	$121,000	$151,008	$154,000
Indirect labor:				
Support workers	70,000	77,000	96,096	98,000
Idle time	20,000	22,000	27,456	28,000
Fringe benefits	30,000	33,000	41,184	42,000
Utilities	10,000	11,000	13,728	14,000
Total variable costs	$240,000	$264,000	$329,472	$336,000
Variable cost per pound	$ .24	$ .24	$ .24	$ .24
Fixed Overhead Costs				
Supervision	$ 90,000	$ 90,000	$ 90,000	$120,000
Depreciation	100,000	100,000	100,000	100,000
Maintenance contract	30,000	30,000	30,000	36,000
Insurance	4,256	4,256	4,256	4,256
Utilities	6,832	6,832	6,832	6,832
Total fixed costs	$231,088	$231,088	$231,088	$267,088
Fixed cost per pound (rounded)	$ .23	$ .21	$ .17	$ .19
Total cost	$471,088	$495,088	$560,560	$603,088
Total cost per pound of barbeque	$ .47	$ .45	$ .41	$ .43

Separating mixed costs and specifying a relevant range for step costs allows accountants to *treat their perceptions of the cost behaviors that occur in the relevant range as if they were fact.* A variable cost is assumed to be perfectly linear and equal to the average variable unit cost within the relevant range, while a fixed cost is assumed to be constant in total within the relevant range. These treatments of variable and fixed costs are justified for two reasons. First, the assumed conditions approximate reality: if the company operates only within the relevant range of activity, the cost behaviors reflect the expected and actual cost patterns. Second, selection of a constant variable cost per unit and a constant fixed cost in total provides a convenient, stable measurement for use in planning and decision making.

Although all costs do not strictly conform to the categories just described, the categories represent the types of cost behavior typically encountered in business. Managers who understand cost behavior can better estimate total costs at various levels of activity.

DEVELOPING AND USING PREDETERMINED OVERHEAD RATES

With the information provided in the flexible budget, a company can compute separate overhead rates for variable and fixed overhead costs.

Variable Overhead Rate

Variable overhead (VOH) changes proportionately in total with some measure of volume or activity. A **predetermined overhead rate** should be computed for each variable overhead cost pool (a set of costs—found on the flexible budget—for a preselected activity). The information needed for these computations can be taken from any level of activity shown on the flexible budget that is within the relevant range. Total cost for each cost pool is then divided by the level of activity on which the estimate was based to determine a per unit cost of the activity. Variable factory overhead is applied to production, using the result of multiplying the related activity base by the cost per unit of the activity.

predetermined overhead rate

Since VOH is constant per unit at all activity levels within the relevant range, the activity level chosen for budgeting total variable cost is unimportant. For example, Columbia River Barbeque budgets $121,000 of indirect materials cost at 1,100,000 pounds of barbeque. These budget amounts give a predetermined variable overhead rate for indirect materials of $.11 per pound ($121,000 ÷ 1,100,000). Correspondingly, if the indirect materials cost is truly variable, the company would budget a total cost of $154,000 for 1,400,000 pounds, or the same $.11 per pound.

The activity measure selected to apply overhead to production should provide a logical relationship between the measure and the overhead cost incurrence. The activity measure that generally first comes to mind is production volume. However, unless a company makes only one type of output (such as Columbia River Barbeque), production volume is not really a feasible activity measure for any overhead cost. If multiple products or services are produced, overhead costs are incurred because of numerous factors, including the differing nature of the items, product variety, and product complexity.

The concept of homogeneity (uniform common attribute of all items included in a set) underlies all cost allocation. Some measure of activity that is common to all costs in a given cost pool must be used to allocate overhead to heterogeneous (unlike) products. The most frequently used volume-based allocation measures include direct labor hours, direct labor dollars, machine hours, production orders, and production-related physical measures such as pounds and gallons. In addition, companies often use only a single total overhead cost pool or two overhead cost pools (total variable and total

LEARNING OBJECTIVE ❼
How are predetermined factory overhead rates developed and how does the selection of a capacity measure affect factory overhead application?

fixed). Alternatively, some companies apply overhead to products separately in each department and develop predetermined departmental overhead rates for this purpose.

As technology and the manufacturing environment change, companies must recognize that they may need to change their cost information systems. Using a less-than-appropriate allocation base and a minimal number of cost pools can result in poor managerial information. The failure of traditional labor-based allocation systems, with a small number of cost pools, to accurately assign costs is becoming more apparent as companies automate, increase the number and variety of product lines, and incur higher overhead costs than ever before.

An emerging production environment is occurring in which new manufacturing methods based on computer-driven, automated machinery and information technology are changing a number of accounting practices. For example, using direct labor to allocate overhead costs in highly automated plants results in extremely large overhead rates because the costs are applied over an ever-decreasing number of labor hours (or dollars). When automated plants allocate overhead on the basis of labor, managers are frequently concerned about the high rates per labor hour. On occasion, some managers have concluded that the way to reduce overhead is to reduce labor. This conclusion is erroneous. The overhead charge is high because labor is low; further reducing labor will simply increase the overhead rate.

If only a single type of activity base is to be used for overhead allocations in highly automated plants, machine hours are a more appropriate base than either direct labor hours or direct labor dollars. However, machine hours and overhead costs should be accumulated by machine type to develop a predetermined overhead rate per machine. In this way, overhead can be assigned in a cause-and-effect manner to products as they move through the various machine processes.

Many companies are looking at multiple cost pools and new activity measures for overhead allocation, including number or time of machine setups, number of different parts, material handling time, and quantity of product defects.[12] But regardless of how many cost pools are created or which activity base is chosen, the *method* of overhead application is the same. In a typical cost system, overhead is assigned to Work in Process Inventory, using the predetermined rate multiplied by the actual quantity of the activity base. For simplicity, at this time, separate cost pools for variable and fixed overhead will be assumed, as will a single activity measure for allocating each.

Columbia River Barbeque's total predetermined variable overhead rate was given in Exhibit 4-10. From this exhibit, the owner selected 1,372,800 pounds of barbeque as the estimated annual production volume. At that level of activity, estimated variable overhead costs of $329,472 were shown in the flexible budget. Dividing this cost estimate by the production volume estimate gives the predetermined variable overhead rate of $.24, as follows:

$$\text{Predetermined VOH rate} = \frac{\text{Budgeted VOH cost}}{\text{Budgeted output in pounds}} = \frac{\$329,472}{1,372,800} = \$.24$$

This computation produces the necessary information for product costing purposes, but it does not provide the detail needed by managers to plan or control each of the individual variable overhead costs. For these purposes, managers need individual costs per type of activity resource consumption, as shown in Exhibit 4-12. This information allows the actual and budgeted costs of each type to be compared. Significant **variances** (or deviations) from budgets can be investigated and their causes determined.

variance

Remember that predetermined overhead rates are always calculated in advance of the year of application. So the 2000 rate for Columbia River Barbeque was computed in 1999, on the basis of budgeted variable overhead costs and production volume for 2000. As production occurs in 2000, overhead will be assigned to the Work in Process

---

[12]Use of such nontraditional activity measures to allocate overhead and the resultant activity-based costs are discussed in Chapter 5.

Estimated indirect materials	$151,008 ÷ 1,372,800 =	$.11
Estimated indirect labor		
Support workers	$ 96,096 ÷ 1,372,800 =	.07
Idle time	$ 27,456 ÷ 1,372,800 =	.02
Fringe benefits	$ 41,184 ÷ 1,372,800 =	.03
Estimated utilities	$ 13,728 ÷ 1,372,800 =	.01
Total variable overhead rate		$.24

EXHIBIT 4-12
Detailed Predetermined
Variable Overhead Rate
Calculation

Inventory account. The process of making this assignment is described after the discussion of fixed overhead rates.

Fixed Overhead Rate

Fixed overhead (FOH) is that portion of total overhead that remains constant in total with changes in activity within the relevant range. For product costing purposes, all fixed factory overhead costs must be budgeted and assigned to appropriate cost pools to comprise the numerators of the predetermined fixed factory overhead rate calculations.

Since fixed overhead is constant in total, it varies inversely on a per-unit basis with changes in activity. Therefore, a different unit cost is associated with each different level of activity. For this reason, calculating the predetermined FOH rate per unit requires that a specific activity level be chosen for the denominator. The level of activity selected is usually the firm's expected activity. **Expected annual capacity** is a short-run concept representing the anticipated level of activity of the firm for the upcoming year. If actual results are close to expected or budgeted results (in both dollars and volume), this measure of **capacity** (either according to production volume or volume of some other specified cost driver) should result in product costs that most closely reflect actual costs. Except where otherwise indicated throughout the text, the expected annual capacity level has been chosen as the level at which to calculate the predetermined fixed factory overhead rate because it is believed to be the most prevalent practice.[13]

Companies may choose to use an activity level other than expected annual capacity to compute their predetermined fixed overhead rates. Alternative measurement bases include theoretical capacity, practical capacity, and normal capacity. The estimated maximum productive activity that could occur in an organization during a specified time frame is the ideal or **theoretical capacity**. This measure assumes that all production factors are maximum and operating perfectly; as such, it disregards probable occurrences such as machinery breakdowns and reduced or halted plant operation on holidays.

These assumptions were traditionally considered unrealistic and, until recently, theoretical capacity has generally been considered an unacceptable basis for overhead application. Reducing theoretical capacity by factors such as unused resources and ongoing, regular operating interruptions (such as holidays, downtime, and start-up time) provides the **practical capacity** that could be efficiently achieved during normal working hours. The accompanying News Note (page 136) provides a perspective on valid reasons why practical capacity (rather than expected activity) may be a more appropriate base to calculate a predetermined overhead rate.

Sometimes managers wish to consider historical and estimated future production levels as well as cyclical and seasonal fluctuations in the computation of a predetermined fixed overhead rate. In such an instance, a **normal capacity** measure that encompasses the anticipated long-run average production activity (over five to ten

LEARNING OBJECTIVE ❼
How are predetermined factory overhead rates developed and how does the selection of a capacity measure affect factory overhead application?

expected annual capacity

capacity

theoretical capacity

practical capacity

normal capacity

---

[13]Although many firms use expected annual capacity to compute their predetermined fixed overhead rates, this choice of activity level may not be the most effective for planning and control purposes because it ignores the effects of unused capacity. This issue is discussed further in Chapter 9 in regard to standard cost variances.

Use of Practical Capacity Can Highlight Low Usage of Resources

Practical capacity should be used as the relevant capacity level because it reveals the cost of unused resources. The concept of unused resources makes a distinction between the cost of resources available for manufacturing and the cost of resources actually used for that purpose.

The cost of supplying the productive resources is largely fixed in the short run, does not vary with usage, and provides information relevant for predicting near-term spending. The cost of resources used provides information relevant for predicting changes in resource requirements as a function of changes in demand, technology, and product design. The difference between these two costs is called the cost of unused resources.

By using the practical capacity available in determining the fixed [overhead] rate, the cost of each unit produced contains only the cost of the resource used and, unlike the cost computed using [expected activity], does not include the cost of unused resources. Hence, each identical item of production is assigned the same cost, regardless of the number of such items produced or the number of changes in the product mix.

In addition, using practical capacity highlights the fact that some capacity is idle. (Note: Idle capacity is indicated by the size of the underapplied overhead at the end of the period. This concept is discussed later in the chapter.) Since world-class manufacturing must be flexible enough to respond to changing market conditions, corporate management must be informed when its facilities are not being used efficiently so that appropriate action can be taken.

SOURCE: Marinus DeBruine and Parvez R. Sopariwala, "The Use of Practical Capacity for Better Management Decisions," *Journal of Cost Management* (Spring 1994), pp. 26–27.

years) may be used. This measurement does represent a reasonably attainable level of activity, but does not generally provide estimates that are most similar to actual costs in a given annual period. When normal capacity is used, distortions of cost would arise when activity levels vary significantly within the long-run period.

The budgeted fixed overhead costs for Columbia River Barbeque were given in Exhibit 4-11. Because Columbia River Barbeque is highly automated, the company's accountant has determined that fixed costs are more appropriately related to barbeque smoking hours (BSHs) than to production volume. To produce the budgeted 1,372,800 pounds of barbeque in 2000 will require 114,400 BSHs. Based on these budgeted figures, the predetermined fixed overhead rate is calculated as $2.02 per BSH:

$$\frac{\text{Budgeted FOH costs for 2000}}{\text{Budgeted BSHs to produce 1,372,800 pounds of barbeque}} = \frac{\$231,088}{114,400} = \$2.02 \text{ per BSH}$$

OVERHEAD APPLICATION

Once the predetermined variable and fixed overhead rates have been calculated, they are used throughout the following year to apply (or assign) overhead to Work in Process Inventory. Production overhead is assigned to goods being transferred from one processing department to another or as goods are transferred to Finished Goods Inventory so that a complete product cost can be obtained. Additionally, overhead must be applied at the end of each period so that the Work in Process Inventory account contains costs for all three product elements (direct materials, direct labor, and production overhead).

Applied overhead is the amount of overhead assigned to Work in Process Inventory as a result of the occurrence of the activity that was used to develop the application rate. Application is based on the predetermined overhead rates and the actual level of activity. For example, assume that during January 1998, Columbia River Barbeque produces 108,000 pounds of barbeque and its smoking equipment operates 9,100 hours. The previously calculated rates of $.24 for variable production overhead and $2.02 for fixed production overhead result in the following applications to Work in Process Inventory: $25,920 of variable production overhead (108,000 pounds × $.24 per pound) and $18,382 of fixed production overhead (9,100 BSHs × $2.02 per BSH). The journal entry to record this overhead application is:

applied overhead

Work in Process Inventory	44,302	
Variable Factory Overhead		25,920
Fixed Factory Overhead		18,382

To apply factory overhead to production in January.

Underapplied and Overapplied Overhead

Although companies may be able to budget future overhead costs and expected activity with some degree of accuracy, it simply is not humanly possible to precisely project future events. Thus, actual overhead incurred during a period probably never equals applied overhead. The difference between the two total amounts represents underapplied or overapplied overhead. When the amount of overhead applied to Work in Process Inventory is less than actual overhead, overhead is **underapplied.** When the amount applied is more than actual overhead, overhead is **overapplied.**

underapplied overhead
overapplied overhead

It is important to note that the incurrence of actual factory overhead costs does not affect the process of overhead application. Actual factory overhead costs may be recorded in an overhead account on a daily, weekly, or monthly basis. Those overhead costs are created because activity takes place in the production area of the company. That same actual activity is used by the accountant to apply overhead periodically to Work in Process Inventory; that application is based on the *predetermined* overhead rate multiplied by the *actual* quantity of activity. Thus, applied overhead is directly related to the amount of *actual activity* that took place, but only indirectly related to the amount of *actual overhead cost* incurred by a company.

The factory overhead accounts used for recording actual and applied overhead amounts are temporary accounts. Any balances in these accounts are closed at year-end because an annual period was used to develop the predetermined overhead rates.

Disposition of Underapplied and Overapplied Overhead

In a typical costing system, actual overhead costs are debited to the variable and fixed overhead general ledger accounts and credited to the various sources of overhead costs. (These entries are presented in a subsequent section of this chapter.) Applied overhead is debited to Work in Process Inventory using the predetermined rates and actual levels of activity, and credited to the variable and fixed overhead general ledger accounts. Applied overhead is added to actual direct materials and direct labor costs in the computation of cost of goods manufactured. The end-of-period balance in each overhead general ledger account represents underapplied (debit) or overapplied (credit) overhead.

LEARNING OBJECTIVE ⑧
How is underapplied or over-
applied factory overhead
accounted for at year-end and
why are these accounting
techniques appropriate?

Variable or Fixed Overhead		Work in Process Inventory		
Actual OH costs XXX*	Applied OH costs YYY	DM	✓✓✓	
		DL	✓✓✓	
		Applied OH costs YYY		

*Offsetting these debits are credits to various sources of OH costs, such as Accumulated Depreciation, Accounts Payable, Supplies Inventory, and Wages Payable.

Disposition of underapplied or overapplied overhead depends on the materiality of the amount involved. If the amount of the variance is small, it is closed to Cost of Goods Sold in a manufacturing firm or to Cost of Services Rendered in a service firm. When underapplied overhead is closed, it causes Cost of Goods Sold (or Cost of Services Rendered) to increase since not enough overhead was applied to production during the year. Alternatively, closing overapplied overhead causes Cost of Goods Sold (or Cost of Services Rendered) to decrease because too much overhead was applied to production during the year.

If the amount of underapplied or overapplied overhead is large, it should be allocated among the accounts containing applied overhead (Work in Process Inventory, Finished Goods Inventory, and Cost of Goods Sold or Cost of Services Rendered). Allocation to the accounts may be based on the relative amounts of overhead contained in the accounts or the relative ending account balances. A large amount of underapplied or overapplied overhead means that the balances in these accounts vary significantly from what they would have been if actual overhead costs had been assigned to production. The underapplied or overapplied amount is allocated among the affected accounts so that their balances conform more closely to actual historical costs as required by generally accepted accounting principles for external financial statements.

Exhibit 4-13 uses assumed amounts for Columbia River Barbeque to illustrate the technique of apportioning overapplied variable overhead among the necessary accounts. Had the amount been underapplied, the accounts debited and credited in the journal entry would have been reversed. The computational process would be the same if the overhead were fixed rather than variable.

If predetermined overhead rates are based on valid cost drivers, those rates provide a rational and systematic way for accountants to assign overhead costs to products for external financial statement preparation. Separate cost pools as well as separate variable and fixed overhead rates should be used to obtain the most refined

LEARNING OBJECTIVE ❾

Why are separate predetermined overhead rates generally more useful than combined rates?

EXHIBIT 4-13

Apportioning Overapplied Overhead

VARIABLE OVERHEAD		AMOUNT OF VOH IN ACCOUNT BALANCE	
Actual	$73,400	Work in Process Inventory	$ 58,500
Applied	94,400	Finished Goods Inventory	97,500
Overapplied OH	$21,000	Cost of Goods Sold	234,000

1. Add overhead amounts in accounts and determine proportional relationships:

	VOH Balance	Proportion	Percentage
Work in Process Inventory	$ 58,500	$ 58,500 ÷ $390,000	15%
Finished Goods Inventory	97,500	$ 97,500 ÷ $390,000	25%
Cost of Goods Sold	234,000	$234,000 ÷ $390,000	60%
Total	$390,000		100%

2. Multiply percentages times overapplied variable overhead amount to determine the amount of adjustment needed:

Amount	Percentage	×	Overapplied VOH	=	Adjustment
Work in Process Inventory	15%	×	$21,000	=	$ 3,150
Finished Goods Inventory	25%	×	$21,000	=	5,250
Cost of Goods Sold	60%	×	$21,000	=	12,600

3. Prepare journal entry to close variable overhead account and assign adjustment amount to appropriate accounts:

Variable Overhead	21,000	
Work in Process Inventory		3,150
Finished Goods Inventory		5,250
Cost of Goods Sold		12,600

information for planning, controlling, and decision making. In spite of this fact, companies may (and commonly do) choose to use combined overhead rates rather than separate ones for variable and fixed overhead.

COMBINED OVERHEAD RATES

Combined overhead rates are traditionally used in businesses for three reasons: clerical ease, clerical cost savings, and absence of any formal requirement to separate overhead costs by cost behavior. The process of computing a combined predetermined overhead rate is essentially the same as that of computing separate rates. The difference is that only one type of activity can be selected for the cost pool (rather than different activities for the variable and fixed components). Once the activity base is chosen, management specifies the level of activity at which costs are to be budgeted. Variable and fixed costs are computed for that activity using the appropriate cost formulas, and the costs are totaled and divided by the activity level to yield the single overhead application rate.

Assume that Columbia River Barbeque decides to use a combined predetermined factory overhead rate based on expected production volume. With the previously specified 1,372,800 pounds of barbeque as its expected activity level, the company's combined predetermined overhead rate is calculated as follows:

Total budgeted VOH at 1,372,800 pounds of barbeque (from Exhibit 4-11)	$ 329,472
Total budgeted FOH (from Exhibit 4-11)	231,088
Total budgeted overhead cost	$ 560,560
Divided by expected activity in pounds of barbeque	÷ 1,372,800
Predetermined overhead rate per pound (rounded)	$ .41

Note that this single rate is equal to the sum of the variable and fixed rates calculated earlier in Exhibit 4-11.

For each pound of barbeque produced by Columbia River Barbeque in 2000, the company's Work in Process Inventory account will be charged with $.41 of overhead. If Columbia River Barbeque produces 108,000 pounds of barbeque in January, $44,280 (108,000 × $.41) of overhead would be added to the Work in Process Inventory account as follows:

Work in Process Inventory	44,280	
Factory Overhead		44,280
To apply January overhead to production.		

Although the use of a combined overhead rate achieves the necessary function of assigning overhead costs to production, it reduces a manager's ability to determine the causes of underapplied or overapplied overhead. Exhibit 4-14 (page 140) provides an example in which the overapplied overhead is solely related to fixed costs—a fact not observable from the combined rate.

When companies use a single overhead application rate, the rate can be related to a particular cost pool (such as machine-related overhead) or to overhead costs in general. As more cost pools are combined, the underlying cause-effect relationships between activities and costs are blurred. This factor may contribute to an inability to reduce costs, improve productivity, or discover the causes of underapplied or overapplied overhead. The lack of detailed information hinders managers' abilities to plan operations, control costs, and make decisions. Thus, although some clerical cost savings may be achieved, the ultimate costs of poor information are probably significantly greater than the savings generated.

Using separate departmental and cost pool activity bases is superior to using a combined plantwide base. Since most companies produce a wide variety of products or perform a wide variety of services, different activity measures should be used to

Actual 2000 production volume   1,378,800

Actual 2000 barbeque smoking hours   114,900

Assume that actual 2000 overhead costs were exactly as budgeted by Columbia River
Barbeque:

Variable ($.24 per pound × 1,378,800) $330,912

Fixed   231,088

Total $562,000

Applied 2000 overhead using a single rate:

1,378,800 pounds × $.40833* per pound = $563,005

Actual OH − Applied OH = $562,000 − $563,005 = $1,005 overapplied OH

Applied 2000 overhead using separate OH rates:

Variable (1,378,800 pounds × $.24 each) $330,912   (same as actual)

Fixed (114,900 BSHs × $2.02 per BSH)   232,098   ($1,010** greater than actual)

Total $563,010

Where BSH stands for barbeque smoking hour

*Presented earlier as a rounded number
**Difference due to rounding

calculate overhead rates for different departments and for different types of overhead costs. Machine hours may be the most appropriate activity base for many costs in a department that is highly automated. Direct labor hours may be the best basis for assigning the majority of overhead costs in a labor-intensive department. In the quality control area, number of defects may provide the best allocation base. In contrast to focusing on a heterogeneous set of plantwide activities, using separate bases for overhead computations allows management to accumulate and apply costs for distinct homogeneous groups of activities. Different rates provide better information for planning, control, performance evaluation, and decision making.

ACCUMULATION OF PRODUCT COSTS

The financial accounting concept of periodicity requires that financial statements be prepared at regular intervals. The balance sheet lists all assets owned by an entity, while the income statement reflects income for a specified period of time. Assets are items of future benefit, having either an exchange value or an ability to generate revenues or reduce costs. Because of the financial accounting requirement to produce financial statements, costs must be designated as unexpired (assets) or expired (expenses or losses). As assets (unexpired costs) are exchanged, consumed, or lost, they become expenses or losses (expired costs). Such costs must be properly classified on the financial statements. Unexpired period costs are typically shown as prepaid assets or plant and equipment. Expired period costs are operating expenses and comprise the selling and administrative expense categories. Unexpired product costs that reflect raw materials, goods in process, or completed goods must be shown as inventory; upon sale, these assets become expired product costs and are shown as cost of goods sold in determination of gross profit or gross margin. Other unexpired product costs may be shown as prepaid expenses (for example, prepaid insurance or taxes on a factory building) or as plant and equipment costs.

Product costs may be accumulated for inventory purposes and expensed to Cost of Goods Sold using either a periodic or a perpetual inventory system. In either system, all product costs flow through Work in Process Inventory to Finished Goods Inventory and, ultimately, to Cost of Goods Sold. The periodic system provides beginning-of-the-period information in the inventory accounts during the period;

information is updated only after physical inventories have been taken (or estimates of these quantities made) at financial statement dates. In contrast, the perpetual system continuously provides current inventory and cost of goods sold information for financial statement preparation and for inventory planning, cost control, and decision making. Because the costs of maintaining a perpetual system have fallen significantly as computerized production, bar coding, and information processing have become more pervasive, this text will assume that all companies discussed use the perpetual inventory method.

Hypothetical information for Columbia River Barbeque is used to illustrate the flow of product costs in a manufacturing organization. The June 1, 2000, inventory account balances for the company are as follows: Raw Materials (all direct), $2,500; Work in Process, $6,000; and Finished Goods, $9,000. The company uses separate variable and fixed accounts to record the incurrence of overhead. Such separation of information improves the accuracy of tracking and controlling costs. Overhead costs are transferred at the end of the month to the Work in Process Inventory account. The following transactions, keyed to the journal entries in Exhibit 4-15, represent Columbia River Barbeque's activity for a month.

During June, Columbia River Barbeque's purchasing agent bought $85,000 of direct materials on account (entry 1), and $81,600 of materials were transferred into the production area; of these, $69,000 represented direct materials and $12,600 represented indirect materials (entry 2). Production wages for the month totaled $18,800; direct labor accounted for $5,000 of that amount (entry 3). The June salaries for production supervisors was $7,500 (entry 4). The total utility cost for June was $1,870; analyzing this cost indicated that $1,200 of this amount was variable and $670 was fixed (entry 5). Contract maintenance of $2,692 was recognized (entry 6). Columbia also accrued depreciation on the factory assets of $8,333 (entry 7), and recorded the expiration of $355 of prepaid insurance on the factory assets (entry 8). Entry 9 shows the application of variable and fixed overhead to Work in Process Inventory. During June, $122,150 of goods were completed and transferred to Finished Goods (entry 10). Sales on account of $242,000 were recorded during the month (entry 11); the goods that were sold had a total cost of $120,150 (entry 12).

As illustrated in the T-accounts in Exhibit 4-16 (page 142), the perpetual inventory system provides detailed information about the cost of raw materials used, goods completed, and goods sold. From this information, formal financial statements can be prepared.

(1)	Raw Materials Inventory	85,000	
	Accounts Payable		85,000
	To record cost of direct materials purchased on account.		
(2)	Work in Process Inventory	69,000	
	Variable Factory Overhead	12,600	
	Raw Materials Inventory		81,600
	To record transfer of direct and indirect materials.		
(3)	Work in Process Inventory	5,000	
	Variable Factory Overhead	13,800	
	Salaries and Wages Payable		18,800
	To accrue factory wages for direct and indirect labor.		
(4)	Fixed Factory Overhead	7,500	
	Salaries and Wages Payable		7,500
	To accrue production supervisors' salaries.		

EXHIBIT 4-15

Flow of Product Costs through Accounts

(5)	Variable Factory Overhead	1,200	
	Fixed Factory Overhead	670	
	Utilities Payable		1,870
	To record mixed factory utility cost in its variable and fixed proportions.		
(6)	Fixed Factory Overhead	2,692	
	Cash		2,692
	To record payments for contract maintenance for the period.		
(7)	Fixed Factory Overhead	8,333	
	Accumulated Depreciation-Factory Equipment		8,333
	To record depreciation on factory assets for the period.		
(8)	Fixed Factory Overhead	355	
	Prepaid Factory Insurance		355
	To record expiration of prepaid insurance on factory assets.		
(9)	Work in Process Inventory	47,150	
	Variable Factory Overhead		27,600
	Fixed Factory Overhead		19,550
	To record the transfer of predetermined overhead costs to Work in Process Inventory.		
(10)	Finished Goods Inventory	122,150	
	Work in Process Inventory		122,150
	To record the transfer of work completed during the period.		
(11)	Accounts Receivable	242,000	
	Sales		242,000
	To record the sale of goods on account during the period.		
(12)	Cost of Goods Sold	120,150	
	Finished Goods Inventory		120,150
	To record cost of goods sold for the period.		

EXHIBIT 4-16
Selected T-Accounts for
Columbia River Barbeque

RAW MATERIALS INVENTORY				VARIABLE FACTORY OVERHEAD			
Beg. bal.	2,500	(2)	81,600	(2)	12,600	(9)	27,600
(1)	85,000			(3)	13,800		
End bal.	5,900			(5)	1,200		

WORK IN PROCESS INVENTORY				FIXED FACTORY OVERHEAD			
Beg. bal.	6,000	(10)	122,150	(4)	7,500	(9)	19,550
(2)	69,000			(5)	670		
(3)	5,000			(6)	2,692		
(9)	47,150			(7)	8,333		
End bal.	5,000			(8)	355		

FINISHED GOODS INVENTORY				COST OF GOODS SOLD			
Beg. bal.	9,000	(12)	120,150	(12)	120,150		
(10)	122,150						
End bal.	11,000						

COST OF GOODS MANUFACTURED AND SOLD

In merchandising businesses, cost of goods sold (CGS) is presented as the beginning merchandise inventory plus net purchases minus ending merchandise inventory. Manufacturing businesses cannot use such a simplistic approach to calculate cost of goods sold. The production costs incurred during the period relate both to goods that were completed and to goods that are still in process. Therefore, a manufacturer prepares a schedule of **cost of goods manufactured (CGM)** as a preliminary step to the presentation of CGS. CGM represents the total production cost of the goods that were completed and transferred to Finished Goods Inventory during the period. This amount does not include the cost of work still in process at the end of the period. The schedule of cost of goods manufactured allows managers to see the relationships among the various production costs and to know the results of the cost flows through the inventory accounts. It is prepared only as an internal schedule and is not provided to external parties.

cost of goods manufactured (CGM)

Using the information given in the previous section, the CGM and CGS schedules for Columbia River Barbeque are shown in Exhibit 4-17 (page 144). The schedule of cost of goods manufactured reflects the manufacturing activity as summarized in the Work in Process Inventory account. It first presents the beginning balance of the Work in Process Inventory; the details of all product cost components added during the period (direct materials, direct labor, variable overhead, and fixed overhead) are shown next. Following are brief descriptions of each element of the CGM schedule.

LEARNING OBJECTIVE ⑩
How is cost of goods manufactured calculated?

The cost of direct materials used in production during the period is equal to the beginning balance of Raw Materials Inventory plus raw materials purchased minus the ending balance of Raw Materials Inventory. Direct labor cost is determined from payroll records of the period and is added to the cost of direct materials used. Since direct labor cannot be warehoused, all charges for direct labor during the period become part of Work in Process Inventory. Variable and fixed overhead costs are added to the prime costs of production to represent total current period manufacturing costs.

Adding the beginning Work in Process Inventory and total current period manufacturing costs provides a subtotal that can be referred to as "total costs to account for." The value of the ending Work in Process Inventory is calculated (through techniques discussed later in the text) and subtracted from the subtotal to provide the Cost of Goods Manufactured during the period.

To calculate Cost of Goods Sold, Cost of Goods Manufactured is first added to the beginning balance of Finished Goods Inventory to determine the cost of goods available for sale during the period. Ending Finished Goods Inventory is subtracted next to yield Cost of Goods Sold. The amount of ending finished goods inventory is calculated by multiplying a physical unit count times a unit cost. Under a perpetual inventory system, the balance shown in Finished Goods Inventory at the end of the period should be compared with the inventory that is actually on hand. Any differences can be attributed to loss factors such as theft, breakage, or recording errors. Major differences between the amount of inventory shown in the accounting records and the actual amount of inventory on hand should be investigated.

ACCUMULATION OF PRODUCT COSTS IN A JOB ORDER COSTING SYSTEM

Actual, normal, or standard costing can be used in a job order costing environment. In a job order system, costs are accumulated individually by **job.** The output of a given job can be a single unit or group of units identifiable as being produced to distinct customer specifications. Each job in a job order system is treated as a unique cost object.

job

EXHIBIT 4-17

Cost of Goods Manufactured
and Cost of Goods Sold
Schedules

COLUMBIA RIVER BARBEQUE

Schedule of Cost of Goods Manufactured
for Month Ended June 30, 2000

Beginning balance of Work in Process, 6/1/00			$ 6,000
Manufacturing costs for the period:			
Raw Materials			
Beginning balance	$ 2,500		
Purchases of materials	85,000		
Raw materials available for use	$87,500		
Ending balance	(5,900)		
Total raw materials used	$81,600		
Less indirect materials	(12,600)		
Total direct materials used		$ 69,000	
Direct Labor		5,000	
Variable Overhead Applied		27,600	
Fixed Overhead Applied		19,550	
Total current period manufacturing costs			121,150
Total costs to account for			$127,150
Ending balance of Work in Process, 6/30/00			(5,000)
Cost of goods manufactured			$122,150

COLUMBIA RIVER BARBEQUE

Schedule of Cost of Goods Sold
for Month Ended June 30, 2000

Beginning balance of Finished Goods, 6/1/00	$ 9,000
Cost of Goods Manufactured	122,150
Cost of Goods Available for Sale	$131,150
Ending balance of Finished Goods, 6/30/00	(11,000)
Cost of Goods Sold	$120,150

If a job's output is a single product, the total costs of the job are assigned to the individual unit. For multiple outputs, a unit cost may be computed only if the units are similar. In such a case, the total accumulated job cost is averaged over the number of units produced to determine a cost per unit. If the output consists of dissimilar units, no cost per unit can be determined, although it is still possible to know the total cost of the job. Costs of different jobs are maintained in separate subsidiary ledger accounts and are not added together or commingled in those ledger accounts.

materials requisition

When materials are needed for a job, a **materials requisition** is prepared so that raw materials can be released from the warehouse and sent to the production area. This source document links the types and quantities of materials to be placed into production (or used in performing a service) to specific jobs and provides a way to trace responsibility for materials cost. Material requisitions release warehouse personnel from further responsibility for the issued materials and assign responsibility to the department that issued the requisition. As materials are issued, their costs are transferred from Raw Materials Inventory and, if the materials are direct to the job, are added to Work in Process Inventory. If Raw Materials Inventory also contains indirect materials, costs for issuances of those materials are assigned to an overhead account.

job order cost sheet

When direct materials are first issued to production, a job is considered to be "in process." Then accumulating product costs on a **job order cost sheet** can begin. This source document provides virtually all financial information about a particular job. The set of all job order cost sheets for uncompleted jobs makes up the Work in Process Inventory subsidiary ledger. The job order cost sheet includes the job number, a description of the job, customer identification, scheduling information, delivery instructions, and contract price. Details about costs are provided on the cost sheet with separate sections for direct materials, direct labor, and factory overhead. The job order cost sheet might also include budgeted cost information, especially if such information was used to estimate the job's selling price.

Production workers, both direct and indirect, may keep track of the jobs they work on each day and the time they spend on each job using **employee time sheets** (or time tickets). Alternatively, in today's highly automated factories, machine time can be tracked on machine clocks or counters. As jobs are transferred from one machine to another, the machine's clock or counter can be reset to record the start and stop times. Another convenient way to track employee time is through bar coding. Bar coding also allows the company to trace machine depreciation to specific products by using a time-related depreciation measure (such as depreciation per hour of use). The accompanying News Note indicates the versatility of this tool.

employee time sheet

Labor information is recorded on the job order cost sheet in both time and cost amounts. Labor cost equals the time spent on a job multiplied by the employee's wage rate. If total actual labor costs for the job differ significantly from the original estimate, the manager responsible for labor cost control can be asked to clarify the reasons underlying the situation.

Actual factory overhead of a period is accumulated in a factory overhead control account. If actual overhead is applied to jobs, the management accountant must wait until after the end of the period to assign overhead costs. Actual overhead incurred would be divided by some related measure of activity or cost driver to obtain the actual overhead rate. Then, that rate would be multiplied by the actual measure of activity associated with each job to calculate the amount of overhead to assign to each job. More commonly, factory overhead is applied to jobs by use of predetermined overhead application rates under a **normal cost system**. Such a system applies actual direct material and actual direct labor but applies factory overhead based on predetermined rates to jobs or products.

normal cost system

NEWS NOTE

Bar Coding: Not Just for Grocery Stores Anymore

Bar coding is among the most accurate data collection technologies. As cost systems are revised to meet management's need for timely information, bar coding often becomes the data collection method of choice from both a price and performance perspective.

Aside from point-of-sale applications, bar code systems were initially implemented to track and control product movement through the receipt, storage, and shipping functions of large warehouse facilities. More and more firms are adopting the JIT philosophy and are seeking to reduce inventories, improve quality, and eliminate waste. Many of these firms realize that having ready access to timely, accurate information is the key to maintaining *total* control of the business and that bar code systems are best able to supply this information to management.

Carefully designed pilot projects in visible, highly successful applications enable bar coding to reveal its many benefits to management and systems users. For example, one large plumbing manufacturer in the Midwest recently implemented time-and-attendance and shop-floor-control systems that use bar coding. The pilot project was begun in a rather simple two-stage labor process involving furnace heating and quality inspection. In less than two years, the company eliminated eleven different forms that were used when time and inspection data were recorded manually. Inspector efficiency improved by 10 to 12 percent, in part because the inspector never touched a piece of paper other than a bar code label.

SOURCE: Thomas Tyson, "The Use of Bar Coding in Activity-Based Costing," *Journal of Cost Management* (Winter 1991), pp. 52–53.

SITE ANALYSIS

Riscky Barbeque

With his "gimme" hat pulled down, shirttail flapping, and grease on his jeans from crawling under a piece of restaurant equipment, Jim Riscky doesn't look much like the CEO of a Fort Worth, Texas, business. But his willingness to understand and tinker with every detail of his varied enterprises is the secret to the success of Riscky Barbeque: in 1997, Riscky's restaurant business had $10 million in sales.

To maintain profitability in his restaurants, Jim Riscky must understand what his costs are and how they will behave under alternative conditions. By purchasing meat in large quantities, he can control a significant direct material cost. Less control can be maintained over the cost of direct labor because of the government-imposed minimum wage law. Overhead costs are controlled through the use of the centralized commissary and, additionally, through relatively low-cost, but high-traffic, restaurant locations.

Riscky's business philosophy is easy: "The best way to see if something works is to try it—to not be afraid to change things. Some people may find it hard to operate that way, but I find it's usually cheaper to try something and carefully watch it in operation than to spend a lot of time planning. To me, time is money and the worrying before implementation just seems excessively costly."

SOURCE: Interview with Jim Riscky, Fort Worth, Texas (1997).

CROSS-FUNCTIONAL APPLICATIONS

TOPIC OF NOTE	DISCIPLINE	CROSS-FUNCTIONAL APPLICATIONS
Flexible Budget	Marketing	The primary concern of marketers is to provide an adequate amount of product that will yield a profit per unit and yet avoid the cost of excessive inventory, as well as the possibility of losing a sale due to inadequate stock. Flexible budgets permit marketers to negotiate contracts with suppliers that permit alternatives to seasonal or unpredictable sales patterns.
	Business Statistics	A Bayesian analysis matches the probability of a certain level of sale or production occurring with the sales/cost consequence of that activity. This tool, known as systems-contingency theory, permits management to anticipate alternative plans in response to the uncertainties of a changing market.
	Finance	Financial managers depend upon flexible budgets to project the resources needed and the cost of capital required for the operation of their organizations.
	Economics	Economists employ flexible budgeting to quantify the relationship between the selling price and volume of sales so sales of products that are sensitive to price changes can be estimated from this relationship.

CROSS-FUNCTIONAL APPLICATIONS

TOPIC OF NOTE	DISCIPLINE	CROSS-FUNCTIONAL APPLICATIONS
Flexible Budget (continued)	Engineering	Flexible budgets guide manufacturing engineers on how to calculate the efficiency of their equipment and processes with respect to alternative levels of output. In addition, the appropriate level of technology, comparing various labor to capital equipment blends, and sourcing, can be evaluated with this tool. Design engineers, who are often responsible for product specifications, require flexible budgets to constrain their decisions concerning features, accessories, materials, and bulk packaging.
Predetermined Overhead Rates (POR)	Marketing	Marketers of heterogeneous, made-to-specification type of products must use POR to estimate job costs and profitability. If overhead cost is underestimated it will have a negative impact on profits, and overestimation will reduce competitive advantage along price or quality lines.
	Economics	POR represent estimates that economists can use to structure cost models, and analyze and predict the impact of marginal costs on overall efficiency. These models can be used to make routine decisions such as order size or out-sourcing to clarify management's view of the playing field.
	Management	POR estimates are used by management to plan the flow of costs and control the cost drivers. Production or sales activities can be simulated before they are actually incurred. This serves to focus management's attention on the most critical activities/cost drivers. POR can be an early warning system for management trouble shooters.
	Business Law	Many purchase/sale agreements, where future selling price cannot be accurately determined, are tied to POR. Since direct costs are traceable, it is only the overhead component of total cost that must be estimated in such contractual pricing arrangements.

CHAPTER SUMMARY

This chapter introduces terminology used by managers and management accountants and presents the flow of costs in a manufacturing environment. Variable costs are constant per unit but fluctuate in total with changes in activity levels within the relevant range. Fixed costs are constant in total as activity levels change within the relevant range, but vary inversely on a per-unit basis with changes in activity levels. The relevant range is generally the company's normal operating range. Step variable costs have small steps and are treated as variable costs; step fixed costs have large steps and are treated as fixed costs. Mixed costs have both a variable and a fixed element.

A predictor is an activity measure that changes in a consistent, observable way with changes in a cost. A cost driver is an activity measure that has a direct causal effect on a cost.

Direct costs are so defined because they are traceable to a specific cost object. Although indirect costs cannot be explicitly traced to a cost object, allocation techniques can be used to assign such costs to related cost objects. Materials and labor may be directly or indirectly related to particular products, but factory overhead costs are indirect and must be allocated to the products produced.

If separate variable and fixed overhead rates are to be calculated, mixed costs must be separated into their variable and fixed components. One technique that can be used to make this separation is the high–low method. The high–low method uses two points of actual activity data (the highest and lowest) to determine the change in cost and activity. Dividing the cost change by the activity change gives the per-unit variable cost portion of the mixed cost. Fixed cost is found by subtracting total variable cost from total cost at either the high or the low level of activity.

After mixed costs have been separated into their variable and fixed elements, flexible budgets that indicate costs at various activity levels can be prepared. All costs in the flexible budget can be calculated by use of the formula $y = a + bx$, where y = total cost, a = fixed cost, b = variable cost per unit of activity, and x = the level of activity.

Given the overhead cost formulas, accountants can calculate predetermined overhead rates by dividing budgeted overhead costs by a selected level of activity. Such rates assign overhead cost to goods or services based on the actual quantity of activity used to produce the goods or services. The use of predetermined rates eliminates the delays and distortions that occur when actual overhead is applied. Separate rates computed according to cost behavior yield costs that best reflect the resources sacrificed to make a product or perform a service.

Since unit variable costs remain constant over the relevant range of activity, total variable overhead can be divided by any level of activity to compute the predetermined rate. The predetermined fixed overhead rate is computed as budgeted fixed overhead at a specific level of activity divided by that level of activity. Most companies select the expected annual capacity level as the activity measure.

Using predetermined rates normally results in either underapplied or overapplied overhead at year-end. If the total amount of underapplied or overapplied overhead is small, it is closed to Cost of Goods Sold or Cost of Services Rendered. If the amount is large, it is allocated to Work in Process Inventory, Finished Goods Inventory, and Cost of Goods Sold/Services Rendered.

Cost of goods manufactured is the total cost of the goods completed and transferred to finished goods during the period. This computation is prepared for internal management information and is presented on a schedule that supports the cost of goods sold computation on the income statement.

APPENDIX

LEAST-SQUARES REGRESSION ANALYSIS

LEARNING OBJECTIVE ⑤
How can mixed costs be analyzed using the high–low method and (Appendix) least-squares regression analysis?

least-squares regression analysis

The chapter illustrates the high–low method of separating mixed costs into their variable and fixed elements. A potential weakness of the high–low method is that outliers may be inadvertently used in the calculation. Outliers are not representative of actual costs and are generally not good predictors of future costs. Thus, a cost formula derived from outlier data will probably not be very useful.

This appendix introduces a statistical technique known as **least-squares regression analysis**, another method of mixed cost analysis. The least-squares method makes it possible to mathematically determine the cost formula of a mixed cost by considering the best fit to all representative data points rather than only two points. (Outliers should be excluded from the set of data points.)

Like the high–low method, least-squares separates the variable and fixed cost elements of any type of mixed cost. When multiple independent variables exist, least-squares regression also helps managers to select the independent variable that has the strongest correlation with—and thus is the best predictor of—the dependent variable. For example, least-squares can be used by managers trying to decide if machine hours, direct labor hours, or number of parts per product best explain and predict changes in a certain factory overhead cost pool.

All chapter examples assume that a linear relationship exists between the independent and dependent variables. Thus, each one-unit change in an independent variable produces a specific unit change in the dependent variable. When only one independent variable is used to predict the dependent variable, the process is known as **simple regression** analysis.[14]

simple regression

Simple linear regression employs the same straight-line formula ($y = a + bx$) used in the high–low method. First, the available data set consisting of the actual values of the independent variable (x) and actual values of the dependent variable (y) is analyzed for outliers, which are eliminated from consideration. Next, a **regression line** is mathematically developed that represents the line that best fits the data observations. This line minimizes the sum of the squares of the vertical deviations between itself and the actual observation points.

regression line

Exhibit 4-18 graphically illustrates least-squares regression. Graph A of the exhibit presents a set of actual observations. These observed values from the data set are designated as y values. Graph B indicates that many lines could be drawn through the data set, but most would provide a poor fit. The y values are used, along with the actual activity levels (x values), to mathematically determine the regression line of best fit. This regression line represents values computed for the dependent variable for all actual activity levels. The dependent values that comprise the regression line are designated as y_c values.

The vertical line segments from the actual observation points (y values) to the regression line (y_c values) in Graph B of Exhibit 4-18 are called deviations. The amount of a deviation is determined by subtracting the y_c value at an activity level from its related y value. Deviations above the regression line are positive amounts, while deviations below the line are negative. By squaring the deviations, the negative signs are eliminated. The positive sum of the squared deviations [$(y - y_c)^2$] can be mathematically manipulated to yield the regression line of best fit. This regression line minimizes the sum of the squared deviations (hence, the name least-squares). The least-squares regression line can then be used to estimate cost formula values for fixed (a) and variable (b) terms. This equation can then be used by the cost analyst to make predictions and analyses.

The RisckyRita Restaurant data for cups of coffee and utility cost from Exhibit 4-9 are used here to illustrate the calculation of the least-squares regression line. The equations necessary to compute b and a values using the method of least squares are as follows:[15]

$$b = \frac{\Sigma xy - n\bar{x}\bar{y}}{\Sigma x^2 - n\bar{x}^2}$$

$$a = \bar{y} - bx$$

EXHIBIT 4-18

Illustration of Least-Squares Regression Line

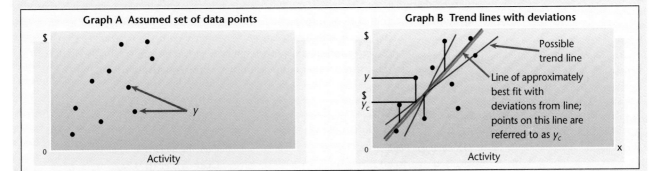

Graph A Assumed set of data points

$

0   Activity

Graph B Trend lines with deviations

$

y

$

y_c

0   Activity   x

Possible trend line

Line of approximately best fit with deviations from line; points on this line are referred to as y_c

---

[14]In **multiple regression**, two or more independent variables are used.

[15]These equations are derived from mathematical computations beyond the scope of this text but found in many statistics books. The symbol Σ means "the summation of."

multiple regression

where x = mean (or arithmetic average) of the independent variable
y = mean (or arithmetic average) of the dependent variable
n = number of observations

The RisckyRita Restaurant data must be restated in an appropriate form for substitution into the equations for b and a. Because of the magnitude of the x values, calculations are made for each one hundred cups of coffee to avoid working with extremely large numbers. At the completion of the calculations, the resulting values are converted to a per-unit b value by dividing by 100. These restatements are as follows:

x	y	xy	x^2
113	$ 1,712	$ 193,456	12,769
114	1,716	195,624	12,996
90	1,469	132,210	8,100
115	1,719	197,685	13,225
112	1,698	190,176	12,544
101	1,691	170,791	10,201
645	$10,005	$1,079,942	69,835

(Note that the outlier for July of 12,200 cups of coffee has once again been ignored.) The mean value for the data in the x column is 107.5 (or 645 ÷ 6) and the mean value for the data in the y column is $1,667.50 (or $10,005 ÷ 6).

Substituting appropriate amounts into the formulas yields the b (variable) and a (fixed) cost values. The b value is calculated first, since it is used to compute a.

$$b = \frac{\Sigma xy - n\bar{x}\bar{y}}{\Sigma x^2 - n\bar{x}^2}$$

$$= \frac{\$1,079,942 - 6(107.5)(\$1,667.50)}{69,835 - 6(107.5)(107.5)}$$

$$= \frac{\$4,404.50}{497.5} = \$8.85 \text{ per hundred or } \$.09 \text{ per cup}$$

$$a = \bar{y} - b\bar{x}$$
$$= \$1,667.50 - \$8.85(107.5)$$
$$= \$1,667.50 - \$951.38$$
$$= \$716.12$$

Thus, the cost formula under least-squares regression is:

Total utility cost = $716.12 + $.09 per cup of coffee

Notice that the least-squares method gives a different cost formula than did the high–low method demonstrated in Exhibit 4-9. Regression information yields more reliable results— a characteristic that is very important to managers seeking to understand and control costs based on changes in activity. Because of the many computer packages that are able to do least-squares regression quickly and accurately, it has become virtually costless to do this type of analysis using a variety of possibilities as the independent variable.

KEY TERMS

Allocate (p. 116)
Applied overhead (p. 137)
Capacity (p. 135)
Conversion cost (p. 120)
Correlation (p. 130)
Cost (p. 116)

Cost behavior (p. 122)
Cost driver (p. 122)
Cost object (p. 116)
Cost of goods manufactured (CGM) (p. 141)
Dependent variable (p. 129)

Direct cost (p. 116)
Direct labor (p. 117)
Direct material (p. 117)
Employee time sheet (p. 145)
Expected annual capacity (p. 135)
Factory overhead (p. 120)
Fixed cost (p. 124)
Flexible budget (p. 131)
High–low method (p. 129)
Independent variable (p. 129)
Indirect cost (p. 116)
Job (p. 143)
Job order cost sheet (p. 145)
Least-squares regression analysis (p. 149)
Materials requisition (p. 144)
Mixed cost (p. 126)
Multiple regression (p. 149)

Normal capacity (p. 135)
Normal cost system (p. 146)
Outlier (p. 129)
Overapplied overhead (p. 137)
Practical capacity (p. 135)
Predetermined overhead rate (p. 133)
Predictor (p. 122)
Prime cost (p. 120)
Relevant range (p. 122)
Regression line (p. 149)
Simple regression (p. 149)
Step cost (p. 132)
Theoretical capacity (p. 135)
Underapplied overhead (p. 137)
Variable cost (p. 124)
Variance (p. 134)

SOLUTION STRATEGIES

High–Low Method (example using assumed amounts)

	(Independent Variable) Activity	(Dependent Variable) Associated Total Cost	=	Total Variable Cost (Rate × Activity)	+	Total Fixed Cost
High level of activity	28,000	$36,000	=	$22,400	+	$13,600
Low level of activity	18,000	28,000	=	14,400	+	13,600
Differences	10,000	8,000				

$.80 variable cost per unit of activity

Flexible Budget (at any activity level within the relevant range)

$$y = a + bx$$

or

Total cost = Total fixed cost + (Variable cost per unit of activity × Level of activity)

Predetermined Overhead Rate

Predetermined OH rate = Budgeted overhead ÷ Budgeted level of activity
  (Should be separated into variable and fixed rates and by related cost pools)

Underapplied and Overapplied Overhead

Variable/Fixed Factory Overhead	XXX
Various accounts	XXX

Actual overhead is debited to the overhead general ledger
account and credited to the sources of the overhead costs.

Work in Process Inventory*	YYY
Variable/Fixed Factory Overhead	YYY

Applied overhead is debited to WIP Inventory and credited
to the overhead general ledger account.

*Can be debited directly to Cost of Services Rendered (CSR) in a service company

A debit balance in Variable/Fixed Factory Overhead at the end of the period is underapplied overhead; a credit balance is overapplied overhead. An immaterial underapplied or overapplied balance in the OH account is closed at the end of the period to CGS or CSR; a material amount is prorated to WIP Inventory, FG Inventory, and CGS or CSR.

Cost of Goods Manufactured

Beginning balance of Work in Process Inventory			XXX
Manufacturing costs for the period			
Raw materials (all direct)			
Beginning balance	X		
Purchases of materials	+ XX		
Raw materials available for use	XXX		
Ending balance	− XX		
Total raw materials used		XXX	
Direct labor		+ XX	
Variable factory overhead		+ XX	
Fixed factory overhead		+XXX	
Total current period manufacturing costs			+XXXX
Total costs to account for			XXXX
Ending balance of Work in Process Inventory			− XX
Cost of goods manufactured			XXXX

Cost of Goods Sold

Beginning balance of Finished Goods Inventory	XX
Cost of goods manufactured	+XXXX
Cost of goods available for sale	XXXX
Ending balance of Finished Goods Inventory	− X
Cost of goods sold	XXXX

Flow of Costs

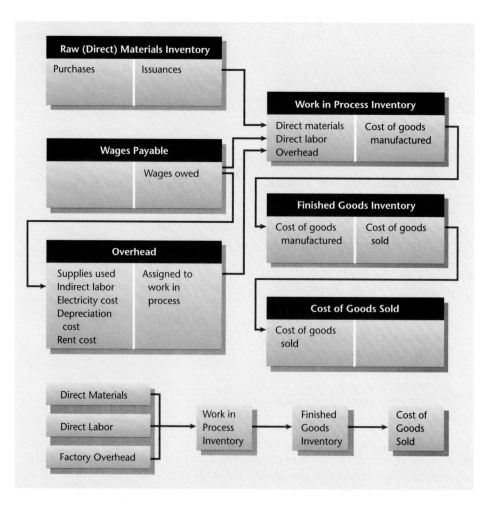

END OF CHAPTER MATERIALS

⊙ QUESTIONS

1. Why must the word *cost* be accompanied by an adjective to be meaningful?

2. With respect to a specific cost object, what is the difference between a direct cost and an indirect cost?

3. What is a product cost? What are the three general categories of product costs?

4. What specific costs are usually included in direct labor cost?

5. Over the past decade or so, which product cost category has been growing most rapidly? Why?

6. What is meant by the term *conversion cost* and what product costs does the term include?

7. "Prime costs and conversion costs are components of product cost; therefore, the sum of these two cost categories is equal to product cost." Is this statement true or false? Explain.

8. At year-end, where on the balance sheet would the costs appear for products that had been placed into production but were not finished?

9. Why is the relevant range important to managers?

10. How do predictors and cost drivers differ? Why is the distinction important?

11. What is the distinction between a fixed cost and a variable cost?

12. What is a mixed cost? How do mixed costs behave with changes in the activity measure?

13. What is a step cost? Explain the distinction between a step fixed and a step variable cost.

14. What are the two major types of overhead cost? Which of these categories has been increasing in recent years?

15. Why is it necessary to separate mixed costs into their variable and fixed cost elements for product costing purposes?

16. What is a flexible budget? Why is it necessary to separate mixed costs into fixed and variable components to prepare a flexible budget?

17. Why must a particular level of activity be specified to calculate a predetermined fixed overhead rate? Why is such specificity not required to calculate a predetermined variable overhead rate?

18. What is the primary criterion for selecting an overhead application base? Explain.

19. Why do some companies use multiple cost pools, rather than a single cost pool, to allocate overhead costs?

20. What are the four capacity measures that may be used for overhead application? Which capacity measure do you think will result in the greatest underapplication of overhead? Why?

21. Why may overhead for a given period be underapplied? What are the alternative methods for disposing of the underapplied overhead?

22. What is included on the Cost of Goods Manufactured schedule? Why is it said that this schedule shows the flow of costs in a manufacturing company?

23. Describe the difference between Cost of Goods Manufactured and the Cost of Goods Sold.

24. *(Appendix)* How does the least-squares regression method improve upon the high–low method for separating mixed costs into their fixed and variable components?

25. *(Appendix)* Differentiate between an independent and a dependent variable.

⊙ EXERCISES

26. *(Terminology)* Your cousin is taking managerial accounting at another university than you and has asked for your help with this exercise. Match the definitions on the right with the terms on the left. Definitions may be used more than once or not at all.

   a. Cost of goods manufactured
   b. Applied overhead
   c. Overhead
   d. Conversion cost
   e. Mixed cost
   f. Dependent variable
   g. Indirect cost
   h. Product cost
   i. Period cost
   j. Direct cost
   k. Prime cost
   l. Outsourcing
   m. Cost driver

   1. The sum of direct labor and factory overhead
   2. A cost outside the production area
   3. A factor that causes a cost to be incurred
   4. A cost that has both a variable and a fixed component
   5. Buying rather than internally making
   6. The sum of direct materials and direct labor costs
   7. A cost that cannot be traced to a particular cost object
   8. Any unknown that needs to be predicted
   9. The total cost of products finished during the period
   10. A cost that is clearly traceable to a particular object
   11. The total of all nontraceable costs necessary to make a product or perform a service
   12. Expenses and losses
   13. Overhead assigned to Work in Process

27. *(Product cost category)* Classify the following factory costs incurred in manufacturing potato chips as direct materials, direct labor, or manufacturing overhead.
   a. Wages of a packaging machine operator
   b. Wages of maintenance and clean-up personnel
   c. Potato costs
   d. Cooking oil costs (considered to be significant)
   e. Seasoning costs (considered to be significant)
   f. Packaging material costs
   g. Packing carton costs
   h. Heating and energy costs
   i. Potato storage costs
   j. Production supervisor's salary

28. *(Product cost category)* Indian Summer Company makes aluminum canoes. Following are some costs incurred in the factory in 1998:

Material Costs

Aluminum	$371,000
Oil and grease for equipment	6,000
Chrome rivets to assemble canoes	23,600
Wooden ribbing and braces	18,400

Labor Costs

Equipment operators	$120,000
Equipment mechanics	54,000
Factory supervisors	28,000

As an intern with this company, you have been asked to ascertain the following:
a. What is the direct material cost for 1998?
b. What is the direct labor cost for 1998?
c. What are the indirect labor and indirect materials costs for 1998?

29. *(Direct labor cost)* Old West Restaurant Supply operates two shifts, paying a late-shift premium of 10 percent and an overtime premium of 50 percent. Labor premiums are included in service overhead. The May 1998 factory payroll is as follows:

Total wages for May for 7,000 hours	$66,000
Normal hourly wage for early-shift employees	$8
Total regular hours worked, split evenly between	
the early and late shifts	5,000

All overtime was worked by the early shift during May.

Assume that you are a management trainee being cross-trained in the payroll department. You are asked to ascertain the following:
a. How many overtime hours were worked in May?
b. How much of the total labor cost should be charged to direct labor? To service overhead?
c. What amount of service overhead was for late-shift premiums? For overtime premiums?

30. *(Cost behavior, product cost category)* Classify the following factory costs incurred in manufacturing bicycles as direct materials, direct labor, or factory overhead; and indicate whether each cost is most likely fixed, mixed, or variable (using number of units produced as the activity measure).
a. Factory supervision
b. Aluminum tubing
c. Rims
d. Emblem
e. Gearbox
f. Crew supervisor's salary
g. Fenders
h. Inventory clerk's salary
i. Inspector's salary
j. Handlebars
k. Metal worker's wages
l. Roller chain
m. Spokes (assume costs are considered significant)
n. Paint (assume costs are considered significant)

31. *(Cost behavior)* Indicate whether each of the following items is a variable (V), fixed (F), or mixed (M) cost with respect to production volume; and whether it is a product or service cost or a period cost. If some items have alternative answers, indicate the alternatives and the reasons for them.
a. Wages of forklift operators who move materials along the assembly line
b. Hand soap used in factory restrooms
c. Utility costs incurred at manufacturing company headquarters
d. Drafting paper used in an architectural firm
e. Cost of company labels attached to shirts made by the firm
f. Wages of quality control inspectors at a factory
g. Insurance premiums on raw materials warehouses
h. Salaries of staff auditors in a CPA firm
i. Cost of clay to make pottery
j. Wages of carpenters in a construction company

32. *(Direct versus indirect costs)* Veritas State University's College of Business has six departments: Accounting, Finance, International Business, Management, Marketing,

and Decision Sciences. Each department chairperson is responsible for the department's budget preparation. The following costs are incurred in the International Business Department:

a. International business faculty salaries
b. Chairperson's salary
c. Cost of computer time of campus mainframe used by members of the department
d. Cost of equipment purchased by the department from allocated state funds
e. Cost of travel by department faculty paid from externally generated funds contributed directly to the department
f. Cost of secretarial salaries (secretaries are shared by the entire college)
g. Depreciation allocation of the college building cost for the number of offices used by department faculty
h. Cost of periodicals and books purchased by the department

The dean has asked you, a new faculty member with a fresh outlook, to indicate whether each of these costs is direct or indirect to the International Business Department.

33. *(Prime cost and conversion cost)* A small construction company's accounting records showed the following construction costs and operating costs for the year 2000:

Direct materials	$718,000
Direct labor	421,000
Indirect materials	102,000
Indirect labor	129,000
Construction utilities	103,000
Selling and administrative expenses	317,000

You have been asked by the company's business manager to determine:
a. What amount of prime cost was incurred in 2000?
b. What amount of conversion cost was incurred in 2000?
c. What was total product cost for 2000?

34. *(Cost behavior)* Merry Old Games produces croquet sets. The company incurred the following costs to produce 2,000 sets last month:

Wooden cases (1 per set)	$ 4,000
Balls (6 per set)	6,000
Mallets	12,000
Wire hoops (12 per set including extras)	4,800
Straight-line depreciation	2,400
Supervisors' salaries	4,400
Total	$33,600

The firm's accountant has requested that you assist her by answering the following:
a. What did each croquet set component cost? What did each croquet set cost?
b. What type of behavior would you expect each of these costs to exhibit?
c. This month, the company expects to produce 2,500 sets. Would you expect each type of cost to increase or decrease relative to last month? Why? What will be the total cost of 2,500 sets?

35. *(Cost behavior)* A-1 Printers pays $200 per month for a photocopy machine maintenance contract. In addition, variable charges average $.04 per page copied. You are negotiating with the city and have been requested to address the following:
a. Determine the total cost and the cost per page if the municipality makes the following number of photocopies (pages):
   1. 1,000
   2. 2,000
   3. 4,000
b. Why is the cost per page different in the three previous cases?

36. *(CGM and CGS)* Precision Machine Shop had the following inventory balances at the beginning and end of September 1999:

	9/1/99	9/30/99
Raw Materials Inventory	$16,000	$18,000
Work in Process Inventory	94,000	72,000
Finished Goods Inventory	36,000	22,000

All raw materials are direct to the production process. The following is also available about manufacturing costs incurred during September:

Costs of raw materials used	$ 94,000
Direct labor costs	181,000
Factory overhead	258,000

As the company accountant, you have been asked to
a. Calculate the cost of goods manufactured for September.
b. Determine the cost of goods sold for September.

37. *(Cost of services rendered)* The following information is related to the Painless Animal Clinic for April 2000, the firm's first month in operation:

Veterinary salaries for April	$23,000
Assistants' salaries for April	7,200
Medical supplies purchased in April	3,200
Utilities for month (80% related to animal treatment)	900
Office salaries for April (50% of time spent in animal treatment)	3,400
Medical supplies at April 30	1,800
Depreciation on medical equipment for April	2,100
Building rental (80% related to animal treatment)	1,700

The doctor has asked you to compute the cost of services rendered.

38. *(CGM and CGS)* Little Rock Custom Mirror's December 2000 cost of goods sold was $900,000. December 31 work in process was 80 percent of the December 1 work in process. Overhead was 100 percent of direct labor cost. During December, $220,000 of raw materials were purchased. All raw materials are direct to the production process. Other December information follows:

	DECEMBER 1	DECEMBER 31
Raw Materials Inventory	$108,000	$ 95,400
Work in Process Inventory	180,000	?
Finished Goods Inventory	419,000	411,200

You have been engaged as a consultant to address the following:
a. Prepare a schedule of the cost of goods sold for December.
b. Prepare the December cost of goods manufactured schedule.
c. What was the amount of prime costs incurred in December?
d. What was the amount of conversion costs incurred in December?

39. *(High–low method)* Paley Appliances incurred the following expenses for utilities during the first six months of 2000:

MONTH	SALES VOLUME	UTILITIES
January	$60,000	$600
February	35,000	350
March	40,000	400
April	50,000	450
May	30,000	150
June	42,500	425

a. Using the high–low method, develop a budget formula for utilities expense.
b. Describe any unusual features of your solution in part a. Give a probable explanation for the result.

40. *(High–low method)* The owner of the Saltydog Catfish Shop wants to estimate a cost function for its supplies expense. The restaurant has been operating for six months and has had the following activity (customer volume) and costs:

MONTH	CUSTOMER VOLUME	SUPPLIES
March	3,400	6,100
April	3,100	5,850
May	3,400	6,200
June	3,600	6,400
July	3,000	5,500
August	2,800	5,400

a. In a restaurant, what types of supplies are in the variable expense category? The fixed expense category?

b. Using the high–low method, estimate the cost equation for supplies expense.

c. What amount of supplies expense would the company expect to incur in a month in which 3,300 customers were served?

41. *(Flexible budget)* CD's R Us used the following values of *a* and *b* for preparing its flexible budget for selling and administrative expense in the past year: $y = \$3,500 + \$1.85x$, where x = number of compact disks sold. The company is expecting to expand into a new relevant range in the coming year. Accordingly, fixed costs are expected to remain at $3,500 for a volume under 6,000 units; at a volume equal to or exceeding 6,000 units fixed costs are expected to increase to $5,200. Variable costs will remain at $1.85 per unit for volume at or below 7,000 units. Above 7,000 units variable costs are expected to decline to $1.75 per unit.

a. Prepare a flexible budget for the new relevant range: 5,000, 7,000 and 9,000 units of sales.

b. Calculate the unit costs at each level of sales.

42. *(Flexible budget)* The Howling Success is in the business of dog grooming. It has determined the following formulas for its costs:

Grooming supplies (variable): $y = \$0 + \$4.00x$
Direct labor (variable): $y = \$0 + \$12.00x$
Overhead (mixed): $y = \$8,000 + \$1.00x$

Wailing Jenson, the owner, has determined that direct labor is the cost driver for all three cost categories.

a. Prepare a flexible budget for each of the following activity levels: 550, 600, 650, and 700 direct labor hours.

b. Determine the total cost per direct labor hour at each of the levels of activity.

c. Groomers at Howling Success normally work a total of 650 direct labor hours during a month. Each grooming job typically takes a groomer one and one-quarter hours. Jenson wants to earn a profit equal to 40 percent of the costs incurred. What should she charge each pet owner for grooming?

43. *(Predetermined OH rates with different bases)* Pardo's Precision Parts prepared the following abbreviated flexible budget for 2000:

	MACHINE HOURS			
	10,000	11,000	12,000	13,000
Variable costs	$40,000	$44,000	$48,000	$52,000
Fixed costs	15,000	15,000	15,000	15,000

The company has set 11,000 machine hours as the 2000 expected annual capacity and expects to operate at one-twelfth of the expected annual capacity each month. It takes two machine hours to produce each product.

a. Calculate separate variable and fixed overhead rates using (1) machine hours and (2) units of production.

b. Calculate the combined overhead rate using (1) machine hours and (2) units of production.

c. Assume that in May 2000, the company produced 442 units. During May, $3,360 of variable overhead and $1,310 of fixed overhead was incurred, and 884 actual machine hours were recorded. Based on the preceding information and your answers in Parts a and b, determine:

1. the amount of fixed factory overhead to be applied to production in May 2000.
2. the amount of variable factory overhead to be applied to production in May 2000.
3. the overapplied or underapplied variable and fixed overhead amounts for May 2000.

44. (*Overhead application with multiple rates*) Miami Technologies has determined that a single overhead application rate no longer results in a reasonable allocation of overhead to its diverse products. Accordingly, the company has restructured its overhead application. It has established six cost pools and identified appropriate cost drivers. The new cost pools and allocation bases and rates follow:

COST POOL	APPLICATION RATE
Setup costs	$37 per setup
Machine costs	$15 per machine hour
Labor-related costs	$ 7 per direct labor hour
Material handling costs	$ 1 per pound of material received
Quality costs	$80 per customer return
Other costs	$ 4 per machine hour

During 2000, the company experienced the following volume for each cost application base:

Setups	300
Machine hours	9,000
Direct labor hours	8,000
Pounds of material received	100,000
Customer returns	250

a. Determine the amount of overhead applied in 2000.
b. Assuming the company incurred $362,000 in actual overhead costs in 2000, compute the company's underapplied or overapplied overhead.
c. Why are more firms adopting multiple application rates to apply overhead?

45. (*Predetermined OH rates and underapplied/overapplied OH*) Crystal Glassworks had the following information in its Work in Process Inventory account for June 2000:

WORK IN PROCESS INVENTORY

Beginning balance	5,000	Transferred out	167,500
Materials added	75,000		
Labor (10,000 DLHs)	45,000		
Applied overhead	60,000		
Ending balance	17,500		

All workers are paid the same rate per hour. Factory overhead is applied to Work in Process Inventory on the basis of direct labor hours. The only work left in process at the end of the month had a total of 1,430 direct labor hours accumulated to date.

a. What is the total predetermined overhead rate per direct labor hour?
b. What amounts of material, labor, and overhead are included in the ending Work in Process Inventory balance?
c. If actual total overhead for June is $61,350, what is the amount of underapplied or overapplied overhead?

46. (*Selecting capacity measure*) Green Paper Supply Company manufactures recycled paper. The company has decided to use predetermined factory overhead rates to apply factory overhead to its products. To set such rates, the company has gathered the following budgeted data:

Variable factory overhead at 12,000 machine hours	$72,000
Variable factory overhead at 14,000 machine hours	84,000
Fixed factory overhead at all levels between 12,000 and 20,000 machine hours	72,000

Practical capacity is 20,000 machine hours; expected capacity is 75 percent of practical capacity.

a. What is the company's predetermined variable factory overhead rate?

b. Compute the company's fixed factory overhead rate based on expected capacity. Using practical capacity, compute the company's predetermined fixed factory overhead rate.

c. If the company incurred a total of 13,500 machine hours during a period, what would be the total amount of applied factory overhead, assuming fixed factory overhead was applied based on expected capacity? Practical capacity? If actual factory overhead during the period was $155,000, what was the amount of underapplied or overapplied factory overhead, assuming fixed factory overhead was applied based on expected capacity? Practical capacity? (Use your answers to Parts a and b.)

d. Based on your answers in Part c, explain why most firms use expected capacity as the factory overhead allocation base. What is the benefit of using practical capacity?

47. *(Disposition of underapplied/overapplied OH)* Schultz Research Services Company has an overapplied overhead balance of $31,000 at the end of 1998. The amount of overhead contained in other selected account balances at year-end are:

Work in Process Inventory	$ 27,000
Finished Goods Inventory	60,000
Cost of Goods Sold	213,000

a. Prepare the necessary journal entries to close the overapplied overhead balance assuming that:
   1. the amount is material.
   2. the amount is immaterial.

b. Which approach is the better choice, and why?

48. *(Cost drivers and cost predictors)* To explain or predict the behavior of costs, accountants often use factors that change in a consistent pattern with the costs in question. What are some factors you might select to predict or explain the behavior of the following costs? Would these same factors be considered cost drivers as well as predictors? If not, why not? What other items could be used as cost drivers?

a. Inspection costs

b. Equipment maintenance

c. Salespersons' travel expenses

d. Indirect factory labor

49. *(Cost drivers and changing technology) Consumers are demanding new diversified products in short intervals. Due to factory automation, robots and computer-controlled manufacturing systems are replacing the conventional production lines. What all these changes mean is the traditional standard costing systems, which emphasize cost control in the manufacturing phase of the product life cycle, are no longer effective. With a one-year product life, controlling costs in the manufacturing phase simply doesn't accomplish much. Once the product is developed and designed, there is a limit to how much cost cutting companies can do in the manufacturing stage.*
[SOURCE: John Y. Lee, "Use Target Costing to Improve Your Bottom Line," *CPA Journal* (January 1994), p. 68.]

With the preceding article in mind, your company president has asked you to discuss the following propositions:

a. Why is determining the cost to manufacture a product a quite different activity from determining how to control such costs.

b. Does the advancement of technology appear to make costs more difficult to control? Discuss.

c. For many production costs, why should "number of units produced" not be considered a cost driver even though it is certainly a valid cost predictor?

50. *(Cost predictors)* The following are graphical representations of the relationships between four different costs and production volume. Briefly discuss for each cost why production volume is, or is not, a good predictor for the cost. Also, identify a specific cost item that may be represented by each graph.

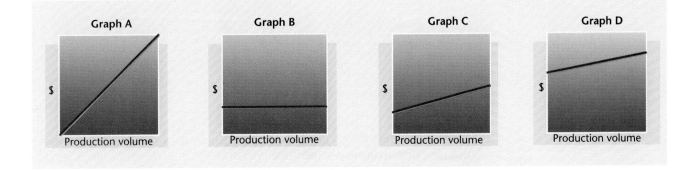

⊙ PROBLEMS

51. *(Cost behavior)* A company's cost structure may contain many different cost behavior patterns. Descriptions of several different costs follow. Your professor wants you to identify, by letter, the graph on page 162 that illustrates each of the following cost behavior patterns. Graphs may be used more than once. On each graph, the vertical axis represents cost and the horizontal axis represents level of activity or volume.

1. Cost of raw materials, where the cost decreases by $.06 per unit for each of the first 150 units purchased, after which it remains constant at $2.75 per unit.

2. City water bill, which is computed as follows:

First 750,000 gallons or less	$1,000 flat fee
Next 15,000 gallons	$.002 per gallon used
Next 15,000 gallons	$.005 per gallon used
Next 15,000 gallons	$.008 per gallon used
Etc.	Etc.

3. Rent on a factory building donated by the city, where the agreement provides for a fixed-fee payment, unless 250,000 labor hours are worked, in which case no rent needs to be paid.

4. Cost of raw materials used.

5. Electricity bill—a flat fixed charge of $250 plus a variable cost after 150,000 kilowatt hours are used.

6. Salaries of maintenance workers if one maintenance worker is needed for every 1,000 hours or less of machine time.

7. Depreciation of equipment using the straight-line method.

8. Rent on a factory building donated by the county, where the agreement provides for a monthly rental of $100,000 less $1 for each labor hour worked in excess of 200,000 hours. However, a minimum rental payment of $20,000 must be made each month.

9. Rent on a machine that is billed at $1,000 for up to 500 hours of machine time. After 500 hours of machine time, an additional charge of $1 per hour is paid up to a maximum charge of $2,500 per period.

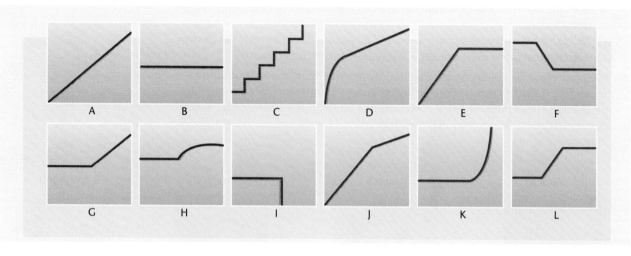

(AICPA adapted)

52. *(Cost behavior)* Tom Rankin has been elected to handle the local Little Theater summer play. He is trying to determine the price to charge little theater members for attendance at this year's presentation of *My Fair Lady.* He has developed the following cost estimates associated with the play:
   - Cost of printing invitations will be $260 for 100 to 500; cost to print between 500 and 600 will be $280.
   - Cost of readying and operating the theater for three evenings will be $1,000 if attendance is below 500; this cost rises to $1,200 if attendance is 500 or above.
   - Postage to mail invitations will be $.30 each.
   - Cost of building stage sets will be $1,215.
   - Cost of printing up to 1,000 programs will be $250.
   - Cost of security will be $110 per night plus $30 per hour; five hours will be needed each night.
   - Costumes will be donated by several local businesses.

   The Little Theater has 200 members, and each member is allowed two guests. Ordinarily, only 75 percent of the members attend the summer offering, each bringing the two allowed guests. The play will be presented from 8 to 11 PM. Invitations are mailed to those members calling to say they plan to come and also to each of the guests they specify. Tom wants you to:
   a. Indicate the type of behavior exhibited by all the items Tom needs to consider.
   b. If the ordinary attendance occurs, what will be the total cost of the summer offering of the play?
   c. If the ordinary attendance occurs, what will be the cost per person attending?
   d. If 90 percent of the members attend and each invites two guests, what will be the total cost of the play? The cost per person? What primarily causes the difference in the cost per person?

53. *(Cost behavior)* Celestial Delights prepares dinners for several airlines, and sales average 300,000 meals per month. The significant costs of each dinner prepared are for the meat, vegetables, and plastic trays and utensils. (No desserts are provided, because passengers are more calorie-conscious than in the past.) The company prepares meals in batches of 1,000. The following data are shown in the company's accounting records for April 1999:

Cost of meat for 1,000 dinners	$900
Cost of vegetables for 1,000 dinners	360
Cost of plastic trays and utensils for 1,000 dinners	120
Direct labor for 1,000 dinners	950

Overhead charges total $1,200,000 per month; these are considered fully fixed for purposes of cost estimation. Company management has asked you to address the following:

a. What is the cost per dinner based on average sales and April prices?

b. If sales increase to 400,000 dinners per month, what will be the cost per dinner (assuming that cost behavior patterns remain the same as in April)?

c. If sales are 400,000 dinners per month but the company does not want the cost per dinner to exceed its current level (based on Part a), what amount can the company pay for meat, assuming all other costs are the same as in April?

d. The company's major competitor has bid a price of $10.96 per dinner to the airlines. The profit margin in the industry is 100 percent of total cost. If Celestial Delights is to retain the airlines' business, how many dinners must the company produce each month to reach the bid price of the competitor and maintain the 100 percent profit margin? Assume April cost patterns will not change and dinners must be produced in batches of 1,000.

54. *(Cost classification, cost object)* Vincent Dimatto, a painter, incurred the following costs during September 1998 when he painted three houses. He spent $600 on paint, $50 on mineral spirits, and $65 on brushes. He also bought two pair of coveralls for $12 each; he wears coveralls only while he works. During the first week of September, Vincent placed a $10 ad for his business in the classifieds. Vincent had to hire an assistant for one of the painting jobs; he paid her $8 per hour, and she worked 25 hours.

Being a very methodical person, Vincent keeps detailed records of his mileage to and from each painting job. His average operating cost per mile for his van is $.25. He found a $15 receipt in his van for a Mapsco that he purchased in September; he uses it to find addresses when he is first contacted to give an estimate on a painting job. He also had $6 in receipts for bridge tolls ($1 per trip) for a painting job he did across the river.

Near the end of September, Vincent decided to go camping, and he turned down a job on which he had bid $1,800. He called the homeowner long-distance (at a cost of $3.60) to explain his reasons for declining the job.

Using the following headings, Vincent has asked you to indicate how each of the September costs incurred by Vincent would be classified. Assume that the cost object is a house-painting job.

COST	VARIABLE	FIXED	DIRECT	INDIRECT	PERIOD	PRODUCT

55. *(Cost flows, prime costs and conversion costs)* Huitt Contractors had the following inventory balances at the beginning and end of May 1999:

	MAY 1	MAY 31
Raw Materials	$16,900	$21,700
Work in Process	32,100	29,600
Finished Goods	25,800	22,600

During May, the company purchased $90,000 of raw materials. All raw materials are considered direct materials. Total labor payroll for the month was $78,000. Direct labor employees were paid $9 per hour and worked 6,800 hours in May. Total factory overhead charges for the period were $109,300. Mr. Ken Huitt, company president, has asked your help in the following:

a. Determine the prime cost added to production during May.

b. Determine the conversion cost added to production in May.

c. Determine the cost of goods manufactured in May.

d. Determine the cost of goods sold in May.

56. *(CGM; journal entries)* Weatherguard manufactures a single product: mailboxes. The following data represent transactions and balances for December 1998, the company's first month of operations.

The firm produces one style of sofa, which can be covered in a variety of fabrics. Each sofa requires one hour of machine time and three hours of direct labor. Next year, Westwego Upholstery plans to produce 6,000 sofas, which is 1,000 more than normal capacity.

a. Give the a and b values for the cost formula for each department.

b. Predict next year's factory overhead for each department.

c. Using normal capacity, calculate the predetermined total factory overhead per sofa. Using expected activity, calculate the predetermined total factory overhead per sofa.

d. Management wants to earn a gross margin of 50 percent on cost. Which of the two activity measures used in Part c would you select to determine total cost per sofa, and why?

62. *(Capacity measures and underapplied/overapplied OH)* McQueen Enterprises makes only one product. It has a theoretical capacity of 50,000 units annually. Practical capacity is 80 percent of theoretical capacity, and normal capacity is 80 percent of practical capacity. The firm is expecting to produce 36,000 units next year. The company president, Kendall Howington, has budgeted the following factory overhead costs for the coming year:

⊙ Indirect materials: $2.00 per unit
⊙ Indirect labor: $144,000 plus $2.50 per unit
⊙ Utilities for the plant: $6,000 plus $.04 per unit
⊙ Repairs and maintenance for the plant: $20,000 plus $.34 per unit
⊙ Material handling costs: $16,000 plus $.12 per unit
⊙ Depreciation on plant assets: $.06 per unit
⊙ Rent on plant building: $50,000 per year
⊙ Insurance on plant building: $12,000 per year

a. Determine the cost formula for total factory overhead.

b. Assume that McQueen produces 35,000 units during the year and that actual costs are exactly as budgeted. Calculate the overapplied or underapplied overhead for each possible measurement base.

c. Which information determined in Part b would be the most beneficial to management, and why?

63. *(Flow of costs)* After preparing for your managerial accounting exam, you confidently turn to your roommate and declare, "I think I've finally figured out how product costs flow through the various accounts and how they are reflected on income statements and balance sheets."

On hearing this wonderful news, your roommate responds, "Hey, if you really want to test your understanding of product costing, try working a problem my old prof gave me." After rummaging for 15 minutes through various files, folders, and shelves, your roommate slaps a sheet of paper in front of you and explains that the sheet contains information pertaining to one year of operations for the Peterson Manufacturing Company. The sheet contains the following information:

Beginning inventory, direct material	$ 20,000
Ending inventory, direct material	40,000
Direct material used	400,000
Sales	900,000
Beginning Work in Process Inventory	100,000
Ending Work in Process Inventory	160,000
Cost of products completed during the year	800,000
Actual factory overhead costs incurred	190,000
Selling and administrative expenses	140,000
Beginning Finished Goods Inventory	200,000
Ending Finished Goods Inventory	170,000
Beginning balance—Property, Plant and Equipment	450,000
Ending balance—Property, Plant, and Equipment	480,000
Applied factory overhead = 60% of direct labor cost	

At the bottom of the sheet was the following information: Peterson uses a normal costing system. Using the information just given, compute the following:

a. cost of direct materials purchased.

b. cost of direct labor.

c. applied factory overhead.

d. Cost of Goods Sold before closing underapplied or overapplied factory overhead.

e. net income or net loss before closing underapplied or overapplied factory overhead.

64. *(Appendix)* Irving Enterprises has compiled the following data to analyze its utility costs in an attempt to improve cost control:

MONTH	MACHINE HOURS	UTILITY COST
January	200	$150
February	325	220
March	400	240
April	410	245
May	525	310
June	680	395
July	820	420
August	900	450

a. Determine the *a* and *b* values for the utility cost formula using the high–low method.

b. Determine the *a* and *b* values for the utility cost formula using least-squares regression analysis.

c. Assuming September's machine hours are expected to be 760, what is the expected utility cost for September based on your answers to Part a? Based on your answer to Part b? Why do these answers differ?

d. Which of the answers, to Part a or to Part b, is preferable, and why?

e. As a manager, what questions might you ask about the data just compiled?

⊙ CASES

65. *(Direct labor cost)* Some of the costs incurred by businesses are designated "direct labor costs." As used in practice, the term *direct labor cost* has a wide variety of meanings. Unless the meaning intended in a given context is clear, misunderstanding and confusion are likely. A user who does not understand the elements included in direct labor cost may interpret the numbers incorrectly and poor management decisions may result.

In addition to understanding the conceptual definition of *direct labor cost*, management accountants must understand how direct labor cost should be measured.

a. Distinguish between direct labor and indirect labor.

b. Discuss why some nonproductive labor (such as coffee breaks and personal time) can be and often is treated as direct labor, while other nonproductive time (such as downtime or training) is treated as indirect labor.

c. Following are three labor cost categories used by a company and some costs it has included in each category:

⊙ Direct labor: Included in the company's direct labor cost are cost production efficiency bonuses and certain benefits for direct labor workers, such as FICA (employer's portion), group life insurance, vacation pay, and workers' compensation insurance.

⊙ Manufacturing overhead: Included in the company's overhead are costs for wage-continuation plans in the event of illness, the company-sponsored cafeteria, the personnel department, and recreational facilities.

⊙ Direct labor or manufacturing overhead depending on the situation: Included in the "situational" category are maintenance expenses, overtime premiums, and shift premiums.

Explain the rationale used by the company in classifying these costs in the three categories.

d. The two aspects of measuring direct labor costs are (1) the quantity of labor effort that is to be included (the types of hours to be counted) and (2) the unit price by which each of these quantities is multiplied to arrive at monetary cost. Why are these considered separate and distinct aspects of measuring labor cost?

(CMA adapted)

66. *(Missing data)* Alabama Yarn Company experienced a flood on May 21 of the current year that destroyed the company's work in process inventory. For the purposes of submitting an insurance claim, the company needs an estimate of the inventory value. Management found the following information in some records that were salvaged:

Raw materials, May 1	$1,000
Work in process, May 1	5,000
Accounts payable, May 1	5,500
Accounts payable, May 20	8,000
Direct labor hours from May 1 to May 20	1,750
Direct labor hourly rate	6
Estimated fixed overhead, May 1 to May 20	3,500
Estimated variable overhead, May 1 to May 20	5,250

On May 22, the company took a physical inventory and found $2,500 of raw materials on hand. The accounts payable account is used only for purchases of raw materials. Payments made on account from May 1 through May 20 were $6,500.

a. Determine the value of the work in process inventory that was destroyed by the flood if $16,000 of goods had been transferred to finished goods from May 1 to May 20.

b. What other information might the insurance company require? How would management determine or estimate this information?

67. *(Cost management)* Litchfield Inc.'s main business is the publication of books and magazines. Alan Shane is the production manager of the Bridgton plant, which manufactures paper used in all of Litchfield's publications. The Bridgton plant has no sales staff and limited contact with outside customers since most of its sales are to other divisions of Litchfield. As a consequence, the Bridgton plant is evaluated by merely comparing its expected costs to its actual costs to determine how well costs were controlled.

Shane perceives the accounting reports that he receives to be the result of a historical number-generating process that provides little information that is useful in performing his job. Consequently, the entire accounting process is perceived as a negative motivational device that does not reflect how hard or effectively he works as a production manager. In discussions with Susan Brady, controller of the Bridgton plant, Shane said, "I think the cost reports are misleading. I know I've had better production over a number of operating periods, but the cost reports still say I have excessive costs. Look, I'm not an accountant; I'm a production manager. I know how to get a good quality product out. Over a number of years, I've even cut the raw materials used to do it. The cost reports don't show any of this; they're always negative, no matter what I do. There's no way you can win with accounting or the people at headquarters who use these reports."

Brady gave Shane little consolation when she stated that the accounting system and the cost reports generated by headquarters are just part of the corporate game and almost impossible for an individual to change. "Although these reports are used to evaluate your division and are the means headquarters uses to determine whether you have done the job they want, you shouldn't worry too much. You haven't been fired yet! Besides, these cost reports have been used by Litchfield for the last fifteen years."

From discussions with the operations people at other Litchfield divisions, Shane knew that the turnover of production managers at the company was high, even though relatively few were fired. A typical comment was: "The accountants may be quick with numbers, but they don't know anything about production. I wound up completely ignoring the cost reports. No matter what they say about not firing people, negative cost reports mean negative evaluations. I'm better off working for another company."

A copy of the most recent cost report for the Bridgton plant follows:

Bridgton Plant Cost Report
For the Month of November 1998
(in thousands)

	EXPECTED COST	ACTUAL COST	EXCESS COST
Raw materials	$ 400	$ 437	$ 37
Direct labor	560	540	(20)
Factory overhead	100	134	34
Total	$1,060	$1,111	$ 51

Discuss Alan Shane's perception of
a. the business role of Susan Brady, controller.
b. corporate headquarters' reasons for issuing cost reports; and
c. himself, as a production manager.
d. How could the cost report be changed to make it more useful to Mr. Shane?

(CMA)

68. *(Quality costs and overhead application)* Moss Manufacturing has just completed a major change in its quality control (QC) process. Previously, products were reviewed by QC inspectors at the end of each major process, and the company's ten QC inspectors were charged as direct labor to the operation or job. In an effort to improve efficiency and quality, the company purchased a computerized video QC system for $250,000. The system consists of a minicomputer, 15 video cameras, other peripheral hardware, and software.

The new system uses cameras stationed by QC engineers at key points in the production process. Each time an operation changes or there is a new operation, the cameras are moved, and a new master picture is loaded into the computer by a QC engineer. The camera takes pictures of the units in process, and the computer compares them with the picture of a "good" unit. Any differences are sent to a QC engineer, who removes the bad units and discusses the flaws with the production supervisors. The new system has replaced the ten QC inspectors with two QC engineers.

The operating costs of the new QC system, including the salaries of the two QC engineers, have been included as factory overhead in calculating the company's plantwide factory overhead rate, which is based on direct labor dollars.

The company's president is confused. His vice-president of production has told him how efficient the new system is, yet there is a large increase in the factory overhead rate. The computation of the rate before and after automation is as follows:

	BEFORE	AFTER
Budgeted overhead	$1,900,000	$2,100,000
Budgeted direct labor	1,000,000	700,000
Budgeted overhead rate	190%	300%

"Three hundred percent," lamented the president. "How can we be competitive with such a high factory overhead rate?"
a. 1. Define factory overhead, and cite three examples of costs typically included in factory overhead.
   2. Explain why companies develop factory overhead rates.

    b. Explain why the increase in the overhead rate should not have a negative financial impact on Moss Manufacturing.

    c. Explain, in the greatest detail possible, how Moss Manufacturing could change its overhead accounting system to eliminate confusion over product costs.

(CMA)

⊙ ETHICS AND QUALITY DISCUSSIONS

69. You are the chief financial officer for a small manufacturing company that has applied for a bank loan. In speaking with the bank loan officer, you are told that two minimum criteria for granting loans are (1) a 40 percent gross margin and (2) income of at least 15 percent of sales. Looking at the last four months' income statements, you find that gross margin has been between 30 and 33 percent and income has ranged from 18 to 24 percent of sales. You discuss these relationships with the company president, who suggests that some of the product costs included in Cost of Goods Sold be moved to the selling, general, and administrative categories so that the income statement will conform to the bank's criteria.

    a. Which types of product costs might be most easily reassigned to period cost classifications?

    b. Since the president is not suggesting that any expenses be kept off the income statement, do you see any ethical problems with the request? Discuss.

    c. Write a short memo to convince the banker to loan the company the funds in spite of its noncompliance with the loan criteria.

70. A cost of operating any organization in the contemporary business environment is computer software. Most software can be purchased on either a per-unit basis (making it a variable cost) or a site-license basis (making it a fixed cost). You are a manager in a marketing company that engages in a great deal of market research. You have asked the company to acquire a copy of a statistical analysis package that would cost $400 per package for each of the twenty people in your department. Alternatively, the software company will give a site license at a cost of $12,000. The package is essential to the organization's ability to perform research, but the controller does not have funds in the budget for twenty copies. Therefore, the controller purchases four copies and tells you to duplicate the other necessary copies. You resist, saying that to do so would violate the copyright law, which allows only one copy to be made for backup purposes.

    a. Since the fixed cost for the site license exceeds the cost for 20 copies, can you think of any reason to incur that $12,000 cost? Discuss.

    b. Assume you are currently working on a marketing research project for Mighty Midget Toy Company. Proper analysis requires the use of this software package. Is the cost of the software a direct or an indirect cost to the Mighty Midget project? If direct, what amount do you believe could be attached to the project? If indirect, should the cost be allocated to the project in some way? If so, how?

    c. How would you handle this situation? What might be the consequences of your actions?

71. Assigning overhead costs to products is necessary to more accurately estimate the cost of producing a good or performing a service. One "product" that takes on an exceptional number of additional charges for overhead is an aspirin dose (two units) in a hospital. Following is an estimate of why a patient is charged $7 for a dose of aspirin. Some costs are referred to as "shared and shifted costs"; others are called overhead. In all cases, this simply means that these costs are not covered by revenue dollars elsewhere and so must be covered for the hospital to do all of the things a hospital charges for—including administering aspirin.

County Community Hospital Product Costing Sheet

	UNIT	UNIT COST	TOTAL UNITS	TOTAL COST
Raw Material				
Aspirin	each	$ 0.006	2	$0.012
Direct Labor				
Physician	hour	60.000	0.0083	0.500
Pharmacist	hour	30.000	0.0200	0.603
Nurse	hour	20.000	0.0056	0.111
Indirect Labor				
Orderly	hour	12.000	0.0167	0.200
Recordkeeping	hour	12.000	0.0167	0.200
Supplies				
Cup	each	0.020	1	0.020
Shared and Shifted Costs				
Unreimbursed Medicare		0.200	1	0.200
Indigent Care		0.223	1	0.223
Uncollectible Receivables		0.084	1	0.084
Malpractice Insurance*		0.034	2	0.068
Excess Bed Capacity		0.169	1	0.169
Other Operating Costs		0.056	1	0.056
Other Administrative Costs		0.112	1	0.112
Excess Time Elements		0.074	1	0.074
PRODUCT COST				$2.632
HOSPITAL OVERHEAD COSTS @ 32.98%				.868
FULL COST (including Overhead)				$3.500
PROFIT (@ 50%)				3.500
PRICE (per dose)				$7.000

*Note that the dose is charged twice for malpractice insurance—once for each aspirin!

[SOURCE: Based on David W. McFadden, "The Legacy of the $7 Aspirin," *Management Accounting* (April 1990), p. 39. Reprinted from *Management Accounting*, published by the Institute of Management Accountants, Montvale, NJ. Visit our website at www.imanet.org.]

a. Discuss the reasons why such cost shifting is necessary.

b. What other kinds of costs might be included in the additional overhead charge at the rate of 32.98 percent?

c. Discuss the ethical implications of shifting costs such as those for indigent care, uncollectible receivables, and excess bed capacity to a patient receiving a dose of aspirin.

d. Are you willing to accept a $7 charge for a dose of aspirin, knowing what costs are considered in developing such a charge if you are (1) a paying customer or (2) the hospital manager? Discuss the reasons behind your answers.

Chapter 5 Activity-Based Management

Volkswagen Canada

The only Volkswagen manufacturing plant in either Canada or the United States is located in Barrie, Ontario, and makes aluminum wheels, catalytic converters, and die cast engine parts. The plant once sold parts only to its parent company, but then VW made a decision to buy from the least expensive producers. This policy led to a 25–30 percent decrease in prices, a need to reduce costs, and a need to find new third-party business to fill the gaps from declining parent company orders.

Massive changes in technology and competition have caused VW to take drastic actions to continue being profitable, including aggressive pricing and selling policies, cost cutting, and downsizing. Activity-based costing (ABC) has helped VW management make tough decisions, with a degree of clarity that otherwise would not have been possible.

An ABC pilot project was undertaken in the die casting area at the Barrie plant. This study indicated that, overall, the area was profitable but only because two parts were making most of the profit, and five parts were making all the profit. The other 15 parts were losing money or, at best, breaking even. The pilot was so successful that the plant launched a full-scale implementation two years later.

To track progress, ABC analyses as well as information on progress toward certain cost, quality, and cycle-time goals are shared among managers. The ABC information is used for determining product and customer profitability, pricing, budgeting, calculating cost of quality, justifying process improvement initiatives, and making outsourcing decisions. The cost and economic data provided by ABC ensure that the process improvement team concentrates on what is important and allows it to prioritize its improvement targets. VW management hopes that the activity-based costing and activity-based management (ABM) information will help the company achieve its goal of becoming the ultimate, cost-conscious, world-class, customer-focused supplier.

Source: Jim Gurowka, "ABC, ABM, and the Volkswagen Saga," *CMA Magazine* (May 1996), p. 30–32.

*L*ike many other companies, *Volkswagen Canada* has numerous, complex processes that generate a wide variety of products and services. Overhead allocations in such organizations are best made using multiple predetermined overhead rates rather than a single one. These rates should be developed and based on the underlying drivers of the overhead costs.

As global competitiveness increases, companies will need to understand the causes of cost, work harder to control costs, and be acutely aware of product line profitability. For VW Canada to meet the competition's prices and remain profitable, the most "convenient" method of overhead allocation no longer provides adequate product or service cost information. To overcome this deficiency, plant management piloted the implementation of a new costing system, activity-based costing (ABC), to help managers obtain the best possible estimates of product and service costs.

ABC falls under the umbrella heading of activity-based management (ABM). The simple difference between ABC and ABM has been defined as follows: "ABC is about gathering cost information. ABM shows you how to do something about it."[1] This chapter defines ABM and ABC, illustrates the process of analyzing organizational activities and cost drivers, and shows how the analysis results can be used to more appropriately allocate overhead costs to products and services. The chapter also discusses the conditions under which ABC systems provide better information than traditional overhead allocations.

DEVELOPING PRODUCT/ SERVICE COST INFORMATION

Product or service costs are developed to: (1) have information for financial and regulatory reporting; (2) help management make product pricing and product line expansion/contraction decisions; and (3) allow management to monitor and control operations. In many organizations, the first purpose has often overridden the other purposes for two reasons. First, external parties (such as the SEC, FASB, IRS, and other regulatory agencies) have established rules about what should be included in or excluded from determining product cost; there have been no mandates, however, about how product costs should be determined for internal management purposes. Second, it is often easier to use the same product costing system for all three purposes. Using the mandated definitions may diminish the resulting costs' internal usefulness as summarized by the following quote: "Today's management accounting information, driven by the procedures and cycles of the organization's financial reporting system,

---

[1]Daniel J. McConville, "Start with ABC," *Industry Week* (September 6, 1993), p. 33.

To get from one point to another, the easiest route is the
most direct one. Determining
product cost is also easiest if
costs incurred can be traced
directly to related products.
Allocating costs to products is
similar to wandering aimlessly
through a mall—the costs may
finally get to the right place,
but oftentimes it's quicker to
stop at the most convenient
location.

is too late, too aggregated, and too distorted to be relevant for managers' planning
and control decisions."[2]

Although it is impossible to determine exact product costs, managers should develop the best possible cost estimates. The best estimate occurs when the majority of
production or service costs can be traced directly to the resulting products or services.
Direct tracing requires the use of valid measures of resource consumption called cost
drivers. Direct material and direct labor costs have always been traced easily to products because, by definition, these costs must be physically and conveniently traceable to cost objects.

If the best estimate results when the largest number of costs are traced directly,
then the best estimate will also be obtained when the least number of costs are assigned arbitrarily. However, because overhead cannot be directly traced to individual
products or services, it must be attached to products or services using a valid cost predictor (or driver) or an arbitrary method. In the past, factory overhead was often attached to products using direct labor hours. Although this base may not have been
the *most accurate* measure of resource consumption, it was generally considered a reasonable, rather than arbitrary, allocation method.

The modern manufacturing environment is more machine-intensive, with low
direct labor and high overhead costs. Attempts to use direct labor as the overhead allocation base in such an environment can lead to significant product cost distortions. Most overhead costs in these environments are machine-related: depreciation
on high-cost machinery; utilities to run that machinery; and repair and maintenance
to keep that machinery operating. As illustrated in Exhibit 5-1 (page 176), overhead
allocation rates based on direct labor can be very high and will assign primarily
machine-related overhead costs to products using high amounts of direct labor rather

LEARNING OBJECTIVE ❶
How can reasonably accurate
product and service cost information be developed?

[2]H. Thomas Johnson and Robert S. Kaplan, *Relevance Lost* (Boston: Harvard Business School Press, 1987), p. 1.

Overhead costs per month, primarily machine-related	$600,000
Total direct labor hours (DLHs)	800
Overhead rate per DLH ($600,000 ÷ 800)	$750
Total machine hours (MHs)	2,400
Overhead rate per MH ($600,000 ÷ 2,400)	$250

PRODUCT A (10,000 UNITS PER MONTH)		PRODUCT B (10,000 UNITS PER MONTH)	
Total DLHs 600		*Total DLHs 200*	
OH assigned using DLHs	$450,000	OH assigned using DLHs	$150,000
OH per unit	$45	OH per unit	$15
Total MHs 400		*Total MHs 2,000*	
OH assigned using MHs	$100,000	OH assigned using MHs	$500,000
OH per unit	$10	OH per unit	$50

than to the products that are truly creating the costs to be incurred—those products that use the machine technology. Thus, a more sophisticated method of overhead cost allocation is needed.

Machine time is often a useful overhead allocation base in the modern manufacturing environment. But even machine hours may not be adequate as the sole allocation base for overhead costs. If overhead is created by factors such as product variety, product complexity, or other cost drivers, multiple allocation bases will result in more accurate estimates of product or service cost. Because companies now have the technology to collect, process, analyze, and use a much greater quantity of information than in the past, it is possible to obtain greater accuracy in product costing by using multiple cost pools to accumulate and to rationally allocate, rather than arbitrarily assign, overhead costs.

ACTIVITY ANALYSIS

The development of product or service cost may be designated as an accounting function, but this task concerns all managers. Costs should be computed in a systematic and rational manner so that they are as accurate as possible and may be relied on for planning, controlling, and decision-making purposes. For example, product costs affect decisions on corporate strategy (Is it profitable to be in a particular market?), marketing (What is the relationship between product cost and product price?), production (Should a component be made or purchased?), and finance (Should money be invested in additional plant assets to manufacture this product?).

In theory, it would not matter how much it cost to make a product or perform a service if enough customers were willing to buy that item at a price that would cover a company's costs and provide a reasonable profit margin. In reality, there are two problems with this concept. First, customers usually only purchase items that provide acceptable value for the price being charged. Second, prices are often set by competitive market forces rather than specific companies. Thus, management should be concerned about whether customers perceive selling price and value to be equal. This concern is normally addressed by ascertaining that the product meets customer quality and service expectations. Additionally, management must decide whether the company can make a reasonable profit, given external prices and internal costs. If the market price is considered a given, then cost becomes the controlling variable in profitability.

Activity-Based Management

Managers can use **activity-based management (ABM)** to help enhance customer value and organizational profits by increasing organizational efficiency and effectiveness and producing more accurate costs. ABM concepts overlap with numerous other disciplines as shown in Exhibit 5-2. Depending on one's perspective, ABM could be viewed as part of a total quality management or business process reengineering effort. Alternatively, total quality management and business process reengineering could result from implementing activity-based management. But, most importantly, activity-based management should be integrated with management's strategic planning and with the organization's cost management system. Without this integration factor, activity-based management is like "a book on a shelf. The book is brought down off the shelf when needed (e.g., for a process improvement project). Once the project is complete, the book can be placed back on the shelf next to the other books (improvement tools)."[3] Integration into the planning process and the cost management system indicates that all the concepts under the ABM umbrella are viewed as integral parts of the organization's customer focus and long-range fiscal success (see Exhibit 5-3, page 178).

activity-based management (ABM)

The use of activity-based management first requires an analysis of an organization's activities. An **activity** is any repetitive action, movement, or work sequence performed to fulfill a business function. Each activity should be able to be described with a verb and a noun. For example, *lift material, open door, insert document* are all activities.

activity

The activities performed in making or doing something can be detailed on a flowchart or grid called a **process map**. These maps should include *all* activities performed to accomplish a specific task or process, not just the obvious ones. For example, walking from the front desk with a change drawer and breaking open rolls of coins would not be on a typical list of "Steps in Cash Register Operation." However, these activities must be performed each time a new clerk opens a register. Many activities that require significant time are not viewed as true parts of the process. By detailing *all* activities, process maps allow duplication, waste, and unnecessary work to be identified. These maps can also be used as benchmarking guides to assist all departments or divisions in an organization to adopt the best possible practices. Detail from a process map is included in the value chart shown in Exhibit 5-4 (page 179).

process map

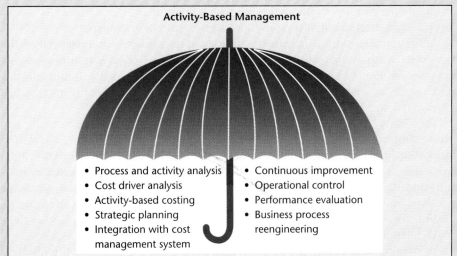

EXHIBIT 5-2

The Activity-Based Management Umbrella

[3]James Reeve, "Projects, Models, and Systems—Where Is ABM Headed?" *Journal of Cost Management* (Summer 1996), p. 7.

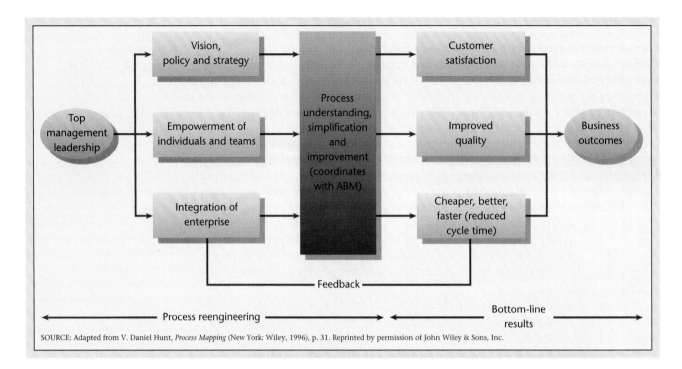

SOURCE: Adapted from V. Daniel Hunt, *Process Mapping* (New York: Wiley, 1996), p. 31. Reprinted by permission of John Wiley & Sons, Inc.

EXHIBIT 5-3
Process-Driven Improvement

LEARNING OBJECTIVE ❷
What are the differences among value-added, non-value-added, and business-value-added activities?

value chart
value-added (VA) activity
value-added processing (service) time

non-value-added (NVA) activity

transfer time

idle time

Value-Added and Non-Value-Added Activities

Some process maps are called **value charts** because they indicate the time spent in each activity from the beginning to end of a process and assess the value of each activity. Activities may be value-added, non-value-added, or business-value-added. A **value-added (VA) activity** increases the worth of a product or service to customers and is one for which customers are willing to pay. VA activities are functions absolutely necessary to manufacture a product or perform a service. The time spent in these activities is the **value-added processing** (or **service**) **time**. For example, a telecommunications company in Plano, Texas, makes a product that recognizes whether a call is being made by human voice or by data transmission (as is necessary for fax, Internet, and other modem telecommunications traffic). The manufacturing time needed to incorporate this ability into the product is value-added processing time and the second spent in making the voice/data determination is value-added service time for customers.

Other activities simply increase the time spent on a product or service but do not increase its worth to the customer. These **non-value-added (NVA) activities** create unnecessary additional costs which, if eliminated, would decrease costs without affecting the product's or service's market value or quality. NVA activities exist throughout an organization and, in general, are extremely expensive.

Processing or service time may be non-value-added if activities are being performed simply to keep people and machines busy. Also, any processing time spent in unnecessarily packaging a product is non-value-added. For example, packaging a man's dress shirt into a cellophane package would most likely be viewed as non-value-added although packaging medicines for health and safety reasons would be perceived as value-added by customers. Many companies are focusing attention on minimizing or eliminating packaging to help reduce time and cost as well as to be environmentally conscious.

Non-value-added activities also include moving and waiting. Moving products or components from one place to another constitutes **transfer time**; storage time and time spent waiting at the production operation for processing are referred to as **idle** (or **wait**) **time**. Although this time is non-value-added, few companies can eliminate all transfer or idle time.

Compounding

Operations	Receiving	Quality control	Storage	Move to production facility	Wait for use	Set up machine	Compounding	Quality control	Move to packaging
Average time (days)	1	2	15–20	.5	5	.5	3.5	1	.5

Packaging

Operations	Receiving	Storage	Move to production facility	Wait for use	Set up machine	Packaging	Quality control	Move to finished goods warehouse	Storage	Move to shipping dock	Sit on shipping dock	Ship to customer
Average time (days)	.5	5–15	.5	5	.5	.5	2	.5	0–20	1	.5	1–3

Total time in compounding: 36.0–41.0 days   Total value-added time: 3.5 days
Total time in packaging: 17.0–49.0 days   Total value-added time: .5 days
Total processing time: 53.0–90.0 days   Total value-added time: 4.0 days
                        Non-valued-added time: 49–86 days

Non-Value-Added Activities ▮   Value-Added Activities ▮

Performing quality assurance activities results in **inspection time**. In most instances, quality control inspections are considered non-value-added if the concept of total quality management is adopted. Under a TQM system, the goal is zero defects by both people and machines. If this goal is being met or being strived for, inspections are simply a matter of looking for a needle in a haystack. A company, such as

EXHIBIT 5-4
Value Chart

inspection time

Chatting at the water cooler appears to be a good example of a non-value-added activity. However, if these individuals were attorneys discussing legal strategy for a case, the time would definitely be value-added. The perception of an activity's value to a customer is not always the same as fact . . . investigate before categorizing!

http:// www.mot.com

Motorola, with a 6 sigma achievement (incurring only 3.4 defects per million units) does not need to spend time inspecting: there is no cost-benefit justification. Alternatively, customers purchasing food or pharmaceuticals or buying seats on an airplane may view quality control inspections as very value-added.

The value chart in Exhibit 5-4 illustrates the manufacturing activities of Elyssa Corporation. Only four days of value-added production time are needed in the entire sequence; even within this sequence, as mentioned earlier, the company may question the time spent in packaging. Additionally, there is an excessive amount of time consumed in storing and moving materials. Understanding the non-value-added nature of these functions should motivate managers to minimize such activities as much as possible.

business-value-added (BVA) activitiy

Some NVA activities exist that are essential to business operations, but for which customers would not willingly choose to pay. These activities are known as **business-value-added (BVA) activities.** For instance, publicly held companies must have an audit at the end of their fiscal years. Customers know that this activity must occur and that it creates costs. However, because the audit adds no direct value to companies' products or services, customers would prefer not to have to pay for this activity.

The accompanying News Note provides one bank's classification scheme for its activities. This Note indicates that, regardless of the terminology used, there is a high degree of importance in analyzing activities.

Cycle Efficiency

cycle time

In a manufacturing environment, the total **cycle time** reflects the time from the receipt of an order to completion (or delivery) of a product. Thus, total cycle time is equal to value-added processing time plus total non-value-added time. Dividing value-added processing time by total cycle time gives **manufacturing cycle efficiency (MCE)**, a measure of how well a firm's manufacturing capabilities use time resources. In a manufacturing environment,

LEARNING OBJECTIVE ❸
What might cause decreased manufacturing cycle efficiency?

manufacturing cycle efficiency (MCE)

NEWS NOTE

Activity Analysis Takes a Customer Focus

ABC requires identification and classification of activities. In banking, activities are classified first as customer order-driven activities and ongoing-concern activities. The customer order-driven activities include such things as sales, services, processing, and administration. The ongoing-concern activities include areas considered as overhead such as accounting and finance, personnel, general counsel, and purchasing among others. A major effort is made to minimize the cost of these activities using the value-added, non-value-added activities analysis. These analyses have been renamed mission-related activities and nonmission-related activities analysis. Mission-related activities are defined as the things we do to satisfy the needs of our constituents, while nonmission-related activities are those things we do that increase the elapsed time of various processes, such as inspection, movement, storage, and error correction. The objective is to eliminate or at least reduce the amount of nonmission activities. A major reason for using the word mission instead of value in classifying activities is psychological. We do not want to imply that an activity, such as correcting errors, has no value. Rather, we want to convey the idea that by avoiding errors we can achieve our mission and avoid the correction activity.

SOURCE: Robert B. Sweeney and James W. Mays, "ABM Lifts Bank's Bottom Line," *Management Accounting* (March 1997), p. 24. Reprinted from *Management Accounting*. Copyright by Institute of Management Accountants, Montvale, N.J.

[t]ypically, cycle time efficiency at most companies is 10%. In other words, value is added to the product only 10% of the time from receipt of the parts until shipment to the customer. Ninety percent of the cycle time is waste. A product is much like a magnet. The longer the cycle time, the more the product attracts and creates cost.[4]

In a retail environment, cycle time refers to the time from when an item is ordered to when that item is sold to a customer. Non-value-added activities in retail include shipping time from the supplier, receiving department delays for counting merchandise, and storage time between receipt and sale.

In a service company, cycle time refers to the time between the service order and service completion. All activities other than actual service performance and nonactivity (such as delays in beginning a job, unless specifically requested by the customer) are considered non-value-added *for that job*.

The following example illustrates non-value-added activities in a service environment. On Monday at 9:00 AM, the telephone company is asked to install a telephone line for a customer. The job is scheduled for Tuesday at 3:30 PM. Upon arriving at the customer's house, the service technician spends 20 minutes installing the telephone jack, 5 minutes writing an invoice, and 5 minutes chatting with the homeowner. The total cycle time is 31 hours (9:00 AM Monday to 4:00 PM Tuesday) or 1,860 minutes—of which only 20 to 25 minutes is value-added time for that particular job! (The 5 minutes spent writing the invoice could be perceived as value-added because, if a problem occurs, the invoice shows that the work was performed by a telephone company employee.) Thus, the service cycle efficiency is a mere 1.3 percent (25 minutes ÷ 1,860 minutes). Alternatively, if the customer did not want the line installed on Monday and *asked* for the delay until 3:30 PM on Tuesday, the total cycle time is 30 minutes and the cycle efficiency is 66 or 83 percent (depending on the classification of the invoice-writing time).

Non-value-added activities can be attributed to systemic, physical, and human factors. For example, a system may require that products be manufactured in large batches to minimize machinery setup costs or that service jobs be taken in order of importance. A building's layout does not always provide for the most efficient transfer of products, especially in multistory buildings in which receiving and shipping are on the ground floor and storage and production are on other floors. People may be responsible for NVA activities because of improper skills, improper training, or a need to be sociable (as when workers discuss weekend sports events on Monday morning). Attempts to reduce non-value-added activities should focus on those activities that create the most unnecessary costs.

In a perfect environment, the manufacturing or service cycle efficiency would be 100 percent because all NVA time would be eliminated. Such an environment will never exist, but companies are moving toward higher cycle efficiencies. One means by which companies can move toward such an optimized environment is through the use of **just-in-time (JIT)** inventory. Under JIT, inventory is manufactured or purchased only as it is needed or in time to be sold or used. JIT eliminates a significant portion of the idle time consumed in storage and transfer processes.

just-in-time (JIT)

Preparing process maps or constructing value charts for each product or service would be quite time-consuming. A few such charts, however, can quickly indicate where a company is losing time through NVA activities. A cost estimate of that time can be made by totaling costs such as depreciation on storage facilities, wages for warehouse employees, and an interest charge on working capital funds that are tied up in inventory. This information allows managers to make more informed decisions about how much costs could be reduced if NVA activities were minimized or eliminated and, thus, how company profitability would be improved. Exhibit 5-5 (page 182) indicates the various opportunities that exist to improve activities.

---

[4]Tom E. Pryor, "Activity Accounting: Key to Waste Reduction," *Accounting Systems Journal* (Fall 1989), p. 34.

EXHIBIT 5-6

Relationship between ABM and ABC

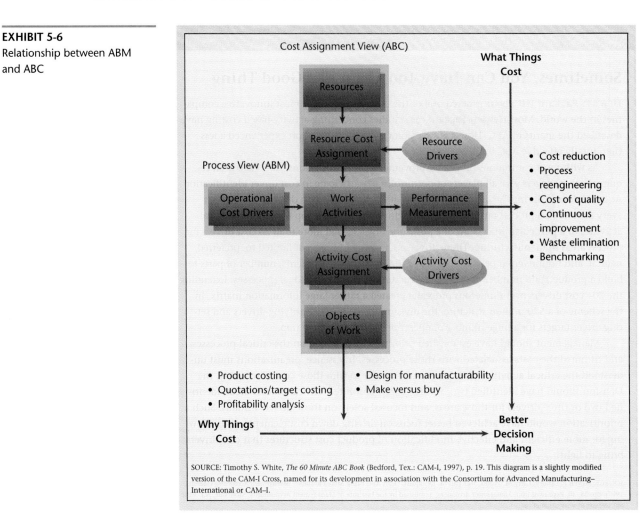

SOURCE: Timothy S. White, *The 60 Minute ABC Book* (Bedford, Tex.: CAM-I, 1997), p. 19. This diagram is a slightly modified version of the CAM-I Cross, named for its development in association with the Consortium for Advanced Manufacturing–International or CAM–I.

Level of Cost Incurrence

In complex production or service environments, reclassifying costs based on the resources consumed provides better information for decision making. In addition, in such environments the accounting system should accumulate activities and their related costs based on their "level" of incurrence. Traditionally, activities and costs were primarily assessed only in relation to how they reacted to changes in volume of production or sales.

EXHIBIT 5-7

Traditional versus ABM Focus on Sales Order Department Activities

TRADITIONAL FOCUS ON RESOURCES		ABM FOCUS ON ACTIVITIES	
Salaries	$460,000	Take orders	$300,000
Space	50,000	Expedite orders	70,000
Depreciation	50,000	Correct errors	60,000
Supplies	30,000	Issue credits	80,000
Other	10,000	Amend orders	30,000
	$600,000	Answer queries	20,000
		Supervise employees	40,000
			$600,000

SOURCE: Tom Pryor, "Making New Things Familiar and Familiar Things New," *Journal of Cost Management* (Winter 1997), p. 39. Reprinted with permission from *The Journal of Cost Management* (Winter 1997), © 1997, Warren Gorham & Lamont, 31 St. James Avenue, Boston, Mass. 02116. All rights reserved.

Some costs are, in fact, strictly variable **unit-level costs** created by the production or acquisition of a single unit of product or the delivery of a single unit of service. But an activity-based system recognizes that costs may vary at activity levels "higher" than the unit level. These higher levels include batch, product or process, and organizational or facility levels.[5] Examples of the kinds of costs that occur at the various levels are given in Exhibit 5-8.

A **batch-level cost** is created when a group of similar things are made, handled, or processed at the same time. Assume that VW Canada has a casting machine that is used for only two of the company's products. The machine casts thin dies for customer X and thick dies for customer Y. The machine's setup cost is $150; two setups are made one day for a total cost of $300. The first run generated 500 thin dies; the second run generated 100 thick dies. If a unit-based cost driver (such as number of dies cast) is used to allocate the setup cost, the setup cost per die is $.50 ($300 ÷ 600). This method would assign the majority of the setup cost to the thin dies (500 × $.50 = $250). However, setup is a batch-level cost, so $150 should be spread over the 500 thin dies for a cost of $.30 per piece, and $150 should be spread over 100 thick dies for a cost of $1.50 per piece. A batch-level perspective shows the commonality of the cost to units within the batch and indicates more clearly the relationship between the activity (setup) and the driver (different casting runs).

unit-level cost

batch-level cost

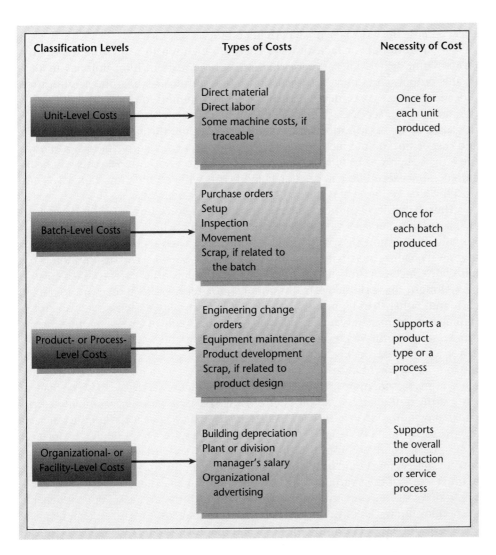

EXHIBIT 5-8
Levels of Costs

Classification Levels	Types of Costs	Necessity of Cost
Unit-Level Costs	Direct material / Direct labor / Some machine costs, if traceable	Once for each unit produced
Batch-Level Costs	Purchase orders / Setup / Inspection / Movement / Scrap, if related to the batch	Once for each batch produced
Product- or Process-Level Costs	Engineering change orders / Equipment maintenance / Product development / Scrap, if related to product design	Supports a product type or a process
Organizational- or Facility-Level Costs	Building depreciation / Plant or division manager's salary / Organizational advertising	Supports the overall production or service process

[5]This hierarchy of costs was introduced by Professor Robin Cooper in "Cost Classification in Unit-Based and Activity-Based Manufacturing Cost Systems," in the *Journal of Cost Management* (Fall 1990).

product-level cost
process-level cost

A cost incurred in support of different products or processes is a **product-** or **process-level cost**. These costs are created by activities such as developing products, processing engineering change orders, or maintaining production specifications. "The costs of these activities can be assigned to individual products, but the costs are independent (i.e., fixed) regardless of the number of batches or the number of units of each product produced."[6] Product/process-level costs vary with increases in the number of products or processes that need to be sustained in an organization.

To illustrate a product/process-level cost, assume that VW Canada's Billing Department revised five forms during May. Of these forms, four related to casting customers (Group One) and one related to aluminum wheel customers (Group Two). None of the form changes related to catalytic-converter customers (Group Three). Each form revision costs $3,000 to issue. During May, the company billed 2,000 Group One customers, 3,000 Group Two customers, and 10,000 Group Three customers. If form-revision cost is treated as a unit-level cost, the total $15,000 cost would be spread over the 15,000 forms produced for a cost of $1 per unit. However, this method inappropriately assigns $10,000 of form-revision cost to Group Three, which had no form revisions for the month! Treating form-revision cost as a product/process level cost results in the assignment of $12,000 and $3,000 of cost, respectively, to Group One and Group Two customers. These cost amounts would be assigned not only to bills issued in the current month, but to all Group One and Group Two customer bills produced during the entire time that the revisions are in effect because the costs benefit all current and future issuances.

organizational-level cost
facility-level cost

Organizational- or **facility-level costs** are incurred to support and sustain a business unit such as a department, division, or headquarters. If the unit has an identifiable output, costs may be attachable to that output in a reasonable allocation process. But if the costs incurred at this level are common to many different activities, products, or services, these costs can only be assigned arbitrarily. For instance, the salary of the organization's executive officers, cost of the annual corporate audit, and cost of stockholder meetings are company-wide organizational costs. Although these costs appear to be fixed, as the organization grows, additional costs will be incurred: more executives will be added; audit costs will become more expensive; and stockholder meetings will require larger space and greater costs.

Thus, batch-level, product/process-level, and organizational/facility-level costs are all variable, but they vary with causes other than changes in production or service volume. Accounting traditionally assumed that costs which did not vary with unit level changes in activity were fixed rather than variable. This assumption is too narrowly conceived. In contrast, activity-based systems often refer to fixed costs as being **long-term variable costs**. Essentially, long-term variable costs are step fixed costs and, rather than ignoring the steps, ABC acknowledges their existence. Professor Robert Kaplan of Harvard University refers to the "Rule of One": any time there is more than one unit of a resource, that resource is variable and the appropriate cost driver simply needs to be identified. Knowledge of the driver may help to eliminate the source of a potential cost change.

long-term variable cost

For this reason, more accurate estimates of product or service cost can be made if costs at the unit-, batch-, and product/process activity levels are accumulated separately. If organizational/facility-level costs are related to a particular product or service, the costs should be assigned to that product or service. For example, the focus of BMW's Design and Engineering Center at Gaydon, Great Britain, is on Rovers. Thus, costs of this center should be allocated to all Rover production facilities. In the same manner, costs of the Spartanburg, USA, plant should be assigned to BMW Z3 roadsters—that facility's only output. Costs for these facilities are reasonably attachable to specific output. Use of this methodology means that cost assignment can be made relative to the activities causing the costs and that total product (or service) cost can be developed and matched with sales revenues.

http:// www.bmw.com

---

[6]Robin Cooper, "Cost Classification in Unit-Based and Activity-Based Manufacturing Cost Systems," *Journal of Cost Management* (Fall 1990), p. 6.

In contrast, organizational- and facility-level costs may not be product- or service-related. If these costs cannot be associated with specific products or services, they should be subtracted in total from net product margin. An activity-based costing system will not normally try to assign organizational-level costs to products because the allocation base would be too arbitrary.

Exhibit 5-9 indicates how cost accumulation at the various levels can be used to determine a total unit product cost. Each product's total unit cost is multiplied by the number of units sold, and that product's cost of goods sold is subtracted from its

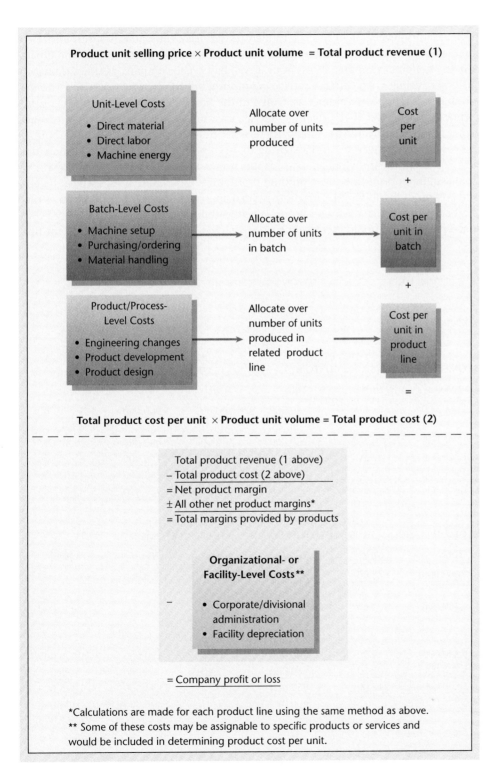

EXHIBIT 5-9
Determining Product Profitability and Company Profits

total product revenue, yielding a net product margin. After these computations are performed for each product line, the product-line profits are summed to determine net product revenues. The unassigned organizational-level costs are subtracted to find company profit or loss. In this model, the traditional distinction between product and period costs is not visible because the emphasis is on analyzing product profitability for internal management decision making rather than financial statement presentation.

An assumed company, TeleConnect, will be used to illustrate the effect of recognizing multiple activity and cost levels on the information available to management. Data from TeleConnect's Billing Department are provided in Exhibit 5-10. Before recognizing that some costs were incurred at the batch-, product/process-, and organizational/facility-levels, TeleConnect totaled its service overhead costs and allocated them among its three lines of business (local service, long-distance service, and broadcast service) on a computer access hour (CAH) basis. The company assumes that each customer averages two CAHs of service per month, but the broadcast service customer group is extremely low volume. As shown in the first section of Exhibit 5-10, cost information indicated that broadcast service customers were a profitable customer group for TeleConnect. After analyzing its activities, the company began accumulating costs at different levels and assigning them to products based on appropriate drivers. Although the individual details for this overhead assignment are not shown, the final assignments and resulting product profitability figures are presented in the second section of Exhibit 5-10. This more refined approach to assigning costs shows that the broadcast service customer group is unprofitable. Such information may mean that TeleConnect should increase the price charged to broadcast service users or find

EXHIBIT 5-10

Profitability Analysis for TeleConnect Co.

Total OH cost = $8,113,000

Total CAHs = 1,330,000

OH rate per CAH = $8,113,000 ÷ 1,330,000 = $6.10

	LOCAL (600,000 CUSTOMERS)		LONG DISTANCE (50,000 CUSTOMERS)		BROADCAST (15,000 CUSTOMERS)		
	Unit	Total	Unit	Total	Unit	Total	Total
Service Revenue	$20.00	$12,000,000	$25.00	$1,250,000	$60.00	$900,000	$14,150,000
Service Costs							
Direct	$ 3.80	$ 2,280,000	$ 4.60	$ 230,000	$32.00	$480,000	$ 2,990,000
OH per 2 CAHs	12.20	7,320,000	12.20	610,000	12.20	183,000	8,113,000
Total	$16.00	$ 9,600,000	$16.80	$ 840,000	$44.20	$663,000	$11,103,000
Company Profit		$ 2,400,000		$ 410,000		$237,000	$ 3,047,000

	LOCAL (600,000 CUSTOMERS)		LONG DISTANCE (50,000 CUSTOMERS)		BROADCAST (15,000 CUSTOMERS)		
	Unit	Total	Unit	Total	Unit	Total	Total
Service Revenue	$20.00	$12,000,000	$25.00	$1,250,000	$60.00	$900,000	$14,150,000
Service Costs							
Direct	$ 3.80	$ 2,280,000	$ 4.60	$ 230,000	$32.00	$480,000	$ 2,990,000
Overhead							
Unit-level	6.00	3,600,000	7.20	360,000	24.00	360,000	4,320,000
Batch-level	2.00	1,200,000	4.00	200,000	8.00	120,000	1,520,000
Product-level	1.20	720,000	1.20	60,000	2.40	36,000	816,000
Total	$13.00	$ 7,800,000	$17.00	$ 850,000	$66.40	$996,000	$ 9,646,000
Service Line Margin		$ 4,200,000		$ 400,000		$ (96,000)	$ 4,504,000
Organizational-Level Costs							(1,457,000)
Company Profit							$ 3,047,000

ways to reduce the costs of having and serving broadcast service users. Alternatively, this business venture may be unprofitable when first established and TeleConnect management will have to give the venture time to grow—especially if this service is viewed as a future core competency and a necessity to organizational survival.

Two-Step Allocation

After initial recording, costs are accumulated in activity center cost pools. An **activity center** is any segment of the production or service process for which management wants separate information about the costs of the activities performed. In defining these centers, management should consider the following issues: geographical proximity of equipment; defined centers of managerial responsibility; magnitude of product costs; and a need to maintain a manageable number of activity centers. Costs having the same driver are accumulated in pools reflecting the appropriate level of cost incurrence (unit, batch, or product/process). If a relationship exists between a cost pool and a cost driver, then reducing or eliminating that cost driver should also reduce or eliminate the related cost.

In the past, most companies accumulated overhead using a vertical or functional approach. For example, all Sales Department costs were grouped together and separated from costs incurred in other parts of the organization. But production and service activities are horizontal by nature. A product or service flows *through* an organization, affecting numerous departments along the way. Gathering costs in pools reflecting the same cost drivers allows managers to better recognize these organizational cross-functional activities and focus on their cost impacts. Exhibit 5-11 provides an example of the horizontal nature of organizational work; in this case, all activities have occurred because the Sales Department received an order from a customer.

After accumulation, costs are allocated out of the activity center cost pools and assigned to products and services by use of an activity cost driver. An **activity cost driver** measures the demands placed on activities as well as the resources consumed by products and services; thus, an activity driver often indicates an activity's output. Exhibit 5-12 (page 190) provides some common activity cost drivers.

activity center

activity cost driver

EXHIBIT 5-11
Horizontal Work Activities

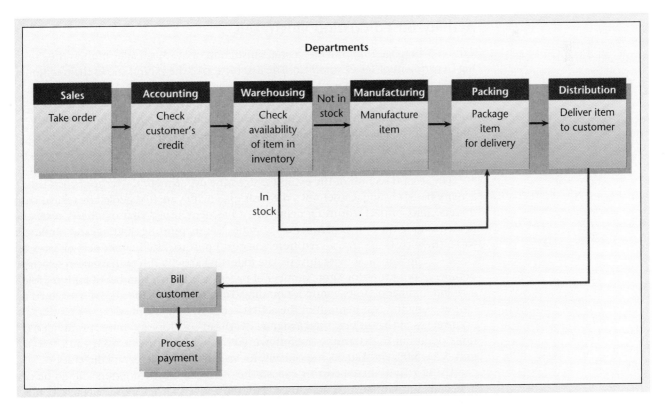

EXHIBIT 5-12
Activity Drivers

ACTIVITY CENTER	ACTIVITY COST DRIVERS
Accounting	Reports requested; dollars expended
Personnel	Job change actions; hiring actions; training hours; counseling hours
Data processing	Reports requested; transactions processed; programming hours; program change requests
Production engineering	Hours spent in each shop; job specification changes requested; product change notices processed
Quality control	Hours spent in each shop; defects discovered; samples analyzed
Plant services	Preventive maintenance cycles; hours spent in each shop; repair maintenance actions
Material services	Dollar value of requisitions; number of transactions processed; number of personnel in direct support
Utilities	Direct usage (metered to shop); space occupied
Production shops	Fixed per-job charge; setups made; direct labor; machine hours; number of moves; material applied

Source: Michael D. Woods, "Completing the Picture: Economic Choices with ABC," *Management Accounting* (December 1992), p. 54. Reprinted from *Management Accounting*, published by the Institute of Management Accountants, Montvale, NJ. Visit our website at www.imanet.org.

The process of cost assignment is the same as the overhead application process illustrated in Chapter 4. Exhibit 5-13 illustrates this two-step process of tracing costs to products and services in an ABC system. As indicated in the exhibit, cost drivers used for the collection stage may differ from the activity drivers used for the allocation stage. Some activity center costs are not traceable to lower levels of activity. Costs at the lowest (unit) activity level should be allocated to products using volume- or unit-based drivers. Costs incurred at higher (batch and product/process) levels may also be allocated to products by use of volume-related drivers, but the volume measure should include only those units associated with the batch or the product/process—not total production or service volume.

Activity-Based Costing Illustrated

Exhibit 5-14 (page 192) provides a brief illustration of overhead allocation in the Printing Department of TeleConnect Co. The first section of the exhibit shows the traditional allocation of departmental overhead costs among the departmental outputs (customer letters, advertising pieces about TeleConnect's various services, and specialized telephone directories). This assignment is based on number of pages (a unit-level driver) and provides an allocated overhead cost of $.16, respectively, for each page. Thus, each letter and ad piece has an overhead cost of $.16, and each directory has an overhead cost of $2.40.

The second section of the exhibit assigns the departmental overhead costs using activity-based costing. Under ABC, the costs of activities are first pooled by related cost drivers. TeleConnect's printing department has determined that overhead costs are pooled among the four departmental activities (setup, printing, folding, and binding). Next, these costs are transferred from the cost pools to specific products or services based on appropriate activity drivers. The following activity drivers have been selected: number of print runs for setup; number of pages for printing; number of folds for folding; and number of units bound for binding. Each type of overhead cost is assigned to output using the cost per unit of the activity cost driver multiplied by the number of occurrences of that driver. Total assigned overhead cost for each output is divided by units of output to determine the following Printing Department overhead costs per unit: $.11, $.08, and $20.90, respectively, for each letter, ad piece, and directory.

Using activity-based costing caused the overhead costs for letters and ad pieces to decline substantially (31 and 50 percent, respectively) from those calculated under

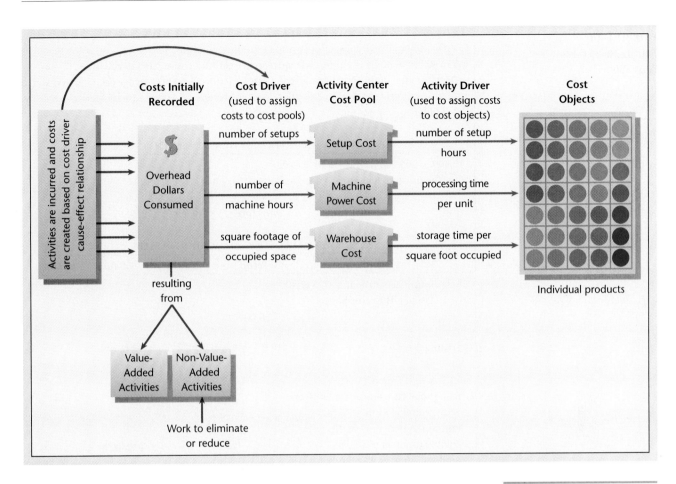

EXHIBIT 5-13

Tracing Costs in an Activity-Based Costing System

a traditional allocation system. In contrast, the overhead cost for directories increased approximately 771 percent! The primary difference is that the letters and ad pieces were previously absorbing all of the binding costs when these costs should have been attributed solely to the directories.

One consequence of relying on the inaccurate traditional cost figures could have been that TeleConnect would seek additional work in printing specialized directories. Should the company bid on these jobs based on inaccurate costs, management would make poor decisions regarding how to price directories or whether to outsource the printing work. Planning, control, and evaluation should also be more effective with the better information generated under ABC.

Discrepancies in costs between traditional and activity-based costing are not uncommon. Activity-based costing systems indicate that significant resources are consumed by low-volume products and complex production operations. Activity-based costing typically shifts substantial overhead costs away from the standard, high-volume products to which those costs have been assigned under more traditional methods to premium special-order, low-volume products, as shown in Exhibit 5-15 (page 193). The ABC costs of moderate products and services (those that are neither extremely simple nor complex, nor produced in extremely low or high volumes) tend to remain approximately the same as the costs calculated using traditional costing methods.

DETERMINING WHETHER ABC IS APPROPRIATE

Not every accounting system that uses direct labor or machine hours as the cost driver provides inadequate or inaccurate cost information. Activity-based costing is a useful tool, but is not necessarily appropriate for all companies. There are two primary assumptions that underlie ABC: (1) the costs in each cost pool are driven by

LEARNING OBJECTIVE ⑥

When is the use of activity-based costing appropriate?

EXHIBIT 5-14

Activity-Based Costing
Illustration

⊙ 4 departmental activities: setup; printing; folding; binding
⊙ $42,400 total budgeted annual departmental overhead cost related to activities
⊙ Departmental outputs: confirmation of service letters (50,000 @ 1 page each; tri-folded);
   ad pieces (200,000 @ 1 page each; bi-folded); directories (1,000 @ 15 pages each); total
   265,000 pages of output

TRADITIONAL ALLOCATION SYSTEM—BASED ON PAGES

$42,400 ÷ 265,000 pages = $.16 per page

Thus, the printing department cost per letter (1 page) is $0.16
                                       ad piece (1 page) is $0.16
                                   directory (15 pages) is $2.40

ACTIVITY-BASED COSTING ALLOCATION SYSTEM

	Setup	*Printing*	*Folding*	*Binding*
Total printing department cost: $42,400				
Step 1: Assign OH to cost pools				
Setup	$8,000			
Printing		$7,950		
Folding			$11,000	
Binding				$15,450
Step 2: Assign OH cost in cost pool				
to cost objects using activity drivers				
Setup (number of print runs)	8			
Printing (number of pages)		265,000		
Folding (number of folds)			550,000	
Binding (number of items bound)				1,000
Cost per unit of activity cost driver	$1,000	$.03	$.02	$15.45

Cost Allocation to Products

Letters (50,000): require 1 run, 50,000 pages, 150,000 folds, and no binding.
Ad pieces (200,000): require 2 runs, 200,000 pages, 400,000 folds, and no binding.
Directories (1,000): require 5 runs, 15,000 pages, no folds, and 1,000 items bound.

	Letters	*Ad Pieces*	*Directories*
Print runs (1, 2, and 5) @ $1,000	$ 1,000	$ 2,000	$ 5,000
Pages (50,000, 200,000, and 15,000) @ $.03	1,500	6,000	450
Folds (150,000, 400,000, and 0) @ $.02	3,000	8,000	0
Units bound (0, 0, and 1,000) @ $15.45	0	0	15,450
Total Dept. OH cost assigned to product	$ 5,500	$16,000	$20,900
Divided by number of units of product	÷50,000	÷200,000	÷1,000
Dept. OH cost per unit of product	$ .11	$ .08	$ 20.90

---

homogeneous activities and (2) the costs in each cost pool are strictly proportional
to the activity.[7] If these assumptions are true, then ABC will be advantageous under
the following conditions:

⊙ there is significant product/service variety or complexity;
⊙ there is a lack of commonality in the creation and use of overhead;
⊙ there are problems with current cost allocations; and
⊙ there has been significant change in the environment in which the organization operates.

---

[7]Harold P. Roth and A. Faye Borthick, "Are You Distorting Costs by Violating ABC Assumptions?" *Management Accounting* (November 1991), p. 39.

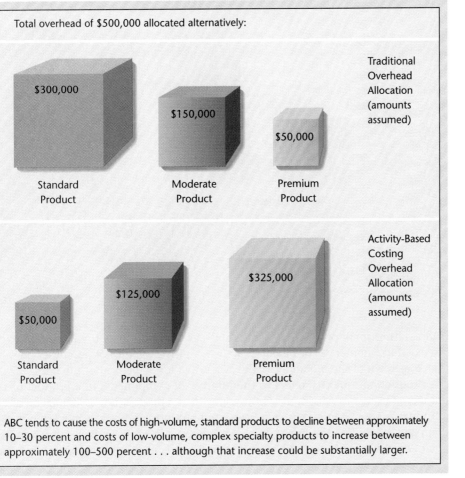

Product/Service Variety or Complexity

Two factors commonly associated with a need to consider activity-based costing are product/service variety and complexity. **Product (service) variety** refers to the number of different types of products made (or services provided). The items may be variations of the same product line (such as Hallmark's different types of greeting cards or the local bank's different types of checking accounts), or they may be in numerous product families (such as Procter & Gamble's detergents, diapers, fabric softeners, and shampoos or the local energy company's offerings of gas, electric, telephone, and broadcast services). In either case, product/service additions cause numerous overhead costs to increase. Exhibit 5-16 (page 194) illustrates the potential for increased overhead with an increase in product variety. In addition, the changes in overhead costs resulting from increased product variety show that seemingly fixed costs (such as warehousing, purchasing, and quality control) are in fact long-term variable costs.

In the quest for product variety, many companies are striving for **mass customization** of products. This production method refers to the use of a flexible manufacturing system to mass produce, relatively inexpensively, unique products for individual customers. There are four primary approaches to customization, as indicated in the News Note (page 195).

Although such customization may please some customers, it does have some drawbacks. First, there may simply be too many choices. For instance, in Louisiana, there are almost a hundred special license plates that include (to name just a few) designations of regular and disabled veterans, firefighters, senators, antique cars, street rods, ham operators, and various colleges and universities. Second, mass customization creates a tremendous opportunity for errors. And third, most companies have found that customers, given a wide variety of choices, typically make selections

product (service) variety

mass customization

Production overhead at P&G is significant—costs are created not only because of multiple varieties of the same type of product (detergent, diapers, etc.) but because of numerous product lines. In such a situation, using a single cost pool and driver would be efficient but *highly* ineffective for product cost determination.

http:// www.toyota.com

product complexity

EXHIBIT 5-16
Product Variety Creates
Overhead Costs

from a rather small percentage of the total—an application of the Pareto principle discussed in Chapter 3. For instance, at Toyota, investigation of purchases revealed that 20 percent of the product varieties accounted for 80 percent of the sales.[8]

Product complexity refers to the number of components in a product or the number of processes or operations through which a product flows. Management can minimize product complexity by redesigning products and processes to standardize them and reduce the number of different components, tools, and processes required. Again, Pareto analysis generally reveals that 20 percent of the components are used

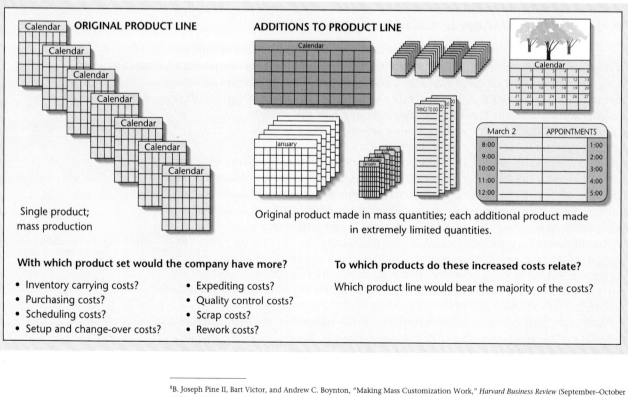

[8]B. Joseph Pine II, Bart Victor, and Andrew C. Boynton, "Making Mass Customization Work," *Harvard Business Review* (September–October 1993), p. 108.

How Do My Customers Want My Product?

Virtually all executives today recognize the need to provide outstanding service to customers. Focusing on the customer, however, is both an imperative and a potential curse. In their desire to become customer driven, many companies have resorted to inventing new programs and procedures to meet every customer's request. But as customers and their needs grow increasingly diverse, such an approach has become a surefire way to add unnecessary cost and complexity to organizations.

Companies throughout the world have embraced mass customization in an attempt to avoid those pitfalls and provide unique value to their customers in an efficient manner. There are four distinct approaches to customization: collaborative, adaptive, cosmetic, and transparent.

- Collaborative customizers conduct a dialogue with individual customers to help them articulate their needs, to identify the precise offering that fills those needs, and to make customized products for them. For example, Paris Miki is a Japanese eyewear retailer that has developed a design system that eliminates the customer's need to review a myriad of choices when selecting a pair of rimless glasses. The system takes a picture of each consumer's face, analyzes its attributes as well as a set of statements about the kind of look the customer desires, recommends a distinctive lens size and shape, and displays the lenses on the digital image of the consumer's face. Adjustments can be made, options (for the nose bridge, hinges, and arms) selected, and the eyeglasses are ground and assembled in the store in as little as one hour.

- Adaptive customizers offer one standard, but customizable, product that is designed so that users can alter it themselves. For example, Lutron Electronics Company of Coopersburg, Pennsylvania, offers a lighting system that connects different lights in a room and allows the user to program settings for different effects such as a party, romantic moments, or quiet evenings of reading.

  http:// www.lutron.com

- Cosmetic customizers present a standard product differently to different customers. For example, the Planters Company used this methodology when it retooled its old plant in Suffolk, Virginia, to satisfy demands of its retail customers. Now the company can quickly switch among different sizes, labels, and shipping containers, responding to each retailer's desires on an order-by-order basis.

- Transparent customizers provide individual customers with unique goods or services without letting them know explicitly that those products or services have been customized for them. For example, ChemStation of Dayton, Ohio, independently analyzed the type of industrial soaps used by its customers so that it can custom-formulate the right mixture and deliver it before the customer has to ask.

  http:// www.chemstation.com

SOURCE: Reprinted by permission of *Harvard Business Review*. An excerpt from "The Four Faces of Mass Customization" by James H. Gilmore and B. Joseph Pine II, January–February 1997. Copyright © 1997 by the President and Fellows of Harvard College.

in 80 percent of the products. If this is the case, then companies need to consider two other factors. First, are the remaining components used in key products? If so, could equal quality be achieved by using the more common parts? If not, can the products be sold for a premium price to cover the costs associated with the use of low-volume components? Second, are the nonstandard parts used in products purchased by important customers who are willing to pay a premium price for the products? If so, the benefits from the complexity may be worth the cost. However, would customers be equally satisfied if more common parts were used and the product price were reduced? Parts complexity is acceptable only if it is value-added from the customer's point of view.

Process complexity may develop over time, or it may exist because of a lack of sufficient planning in product development. Processes are complex when they create difficulties for the people attempting to perform production operations (physical straining, awkwardness of motions, or wasted motions) or for the people using manufacturing machinery (multiple and/or detailed setups, lengthy transfer time between machine processes, or recalibration of instruments). Process complexity reflects numerous non-value-added activities that cause time delays and cost increases.

simultaneous (concurrent) engineering

A company can employ simultaneous engineering to reduce both product and process complexity. **Simultaneous** (or **concurrent**) **engineering** refers to involving all the primary functional areas and personnel that contribute to a product's origination and production from the beginning of a project. Multifunctional teams are used to design the product by considering customer expectations, vendor capabilities, parts commonality, and production process compatibility. Such an integrated design effort is referred to as a design-for-manufacturability approach. Simultaneous engineering helps companies shorten the time to market for new products and minimize complexity and cost.

business process reengineering (BPR)

Even when simultaneous engineering is used in process development, processes may develop complexity over time. One way to overcome this type of complexity is **business process reengineering (BPR)** or process innovation and redesign. BPR's goal is to find and implement radical changes in how things are made or how tasks are performed to achieve substantial cost, service, or time reductions. Emphasizing continuous improvement, BPR ignores the way it is and looks instead for the way it should be. BPR may redesign old processes or design new ones to eliminate complexity.

> Process redesign takes a current process, improves its effectiveness, and can bring about improvements that range from 300 to 1000 percent. This technique is the right choice for about 70 percent of the business processes. [In contrast, new process design] completely ignores the present process and organizational structure. This technique takes advantage of the latest mechanization, automation, and information techniques available. New process design can lead to improvements that range from 700 to 2000 percent. New process design costs more and takes more time to implement than process redesign. It also has the highest degree of risk . . . and is very disruptive to the organization.[9]

Many traditional cost systems were not designed to account for information such as how many different parts are used in a product, so management may not be able to identify products made with low-volume or unique components. Activity-based costing systems are more flexible and gather such details, thereby providing important information about relationships among activities and cost drivers. Armed with these data, people can focus reengineering efforts on the primary causes of process complexity and those that create the highest level of waste.

Lack of Commonality in Overhead Costs

Certain products, services, or types of customers create substantially more overhead costs than others. Although some of these additional overhead costs may be caused by product variety or process complexity, others may be related to support services. For example, some products require substantially more advertising than others; some use higher cost distribution channels; and some necessitate the use of high-technology machinery. In addition, some companies' output volumes differ significantly among their products and services. Each of these differences creates additional overhead costs. If only one or two overhead pools are used, overhead related to specific products will be spread over all products. The result will be increased costs for products that are not responsible for the increased overhead.

---

[9]H. James Harrington, "Process Breakthrough: Business Process Improvement," *Journal of Cost Management* (Fall 1993), pp. 36, 38.

Problems in Current Cost Allocations

If a company has undergone one or more significant changes in its products, processes, or customer base, then managers and accountants need to investigate whether the existing cost system still provides a reasonable estimate of product or service cost. Many companies that have automated their production processes have experienced large reductions in labor cost and large increases in overhead. In such companies, using direct labor as an overhead allocation base tends to charge products made by automated equipment with insufficient overhead, and products made with high proportions of direct labor with too much overhead.

Traditional cost allocations also tend to assign product costs (direct material, direct labor, and manufacturing overhead) to products and expense the majority of period costs when incurred. ABC recognizes that some period costs may be distinctly and reasonably associated with specific products and therefore should be traced and allocated to those products. This recognition changes the traditional view of product versus period cost.

Changes in Business Environment

A change in the competitive environment in which a company operates may also require better cost information. Increased competition may occur for several reasons: (1) other companies have recognized the profit potential of a particular product or service, (2) the product or service has become cost-feasible to make or perform, or (3) an industry has been deregulated. If many new companies are competing for old business, the best estimate of product or service cost must be available to management so that profit margins and prices can be reasonably set.

Changes in management strategy can also signal a need for a new cost system. For example, if management wants to begin new operations, the cost system must be capable of providing information on how costs will change. The traditional variable versus fixed cost classifications may not allow the effective development of such information. The use of ABC offers a different perspective about how the planned operational changes will affect activities and costs through its analysis of costs as short-term versus long-term variables as well as its emphasis on the use of cost drivers.

Many companies are currently engaging in continuous improvement efforts that recognize the need to eliminate non-value-added activities so as to reduce lead time, make products or perform services with zero defects, reduce product costs on an ongoing basis, and simplify products and processes. Activity-based costing, by promoting an understanding of cost drivers, allows the NVA activities to be identified and their causes eliminated or reduced—thereby enhancing operational performance.

The choice to implement activity-based costing should mean that management is willing to accept the new information and use it to plan, control, and evaluate operating activities. If this is the case, then management must have some ability to set prices relative to cost changes; accept alternative business strategies—such as eliminating or expanding product or service offerings—if the new costs should so indicate; and reduce waste where necessary, including downsizing or job restructuring. If management is powerless to institute changes for whatever reason (for example, centralized control or industry regulation), then the ABC-generated information is nothing more than an exercise in futility—and probably a fairly costly one.

Regardless of why there is a need for change in their costing systems, companies at least now have the technological capability to implement ABC systems. Introduction of the personal computer, bar coding, generic software packages, and other advanced technologies means that significantly more information can be readily and cost effectively supplied. In the past, ABC implementation would have been prohibitively expensive or technologically impossible for most companies.

OPERATIONAL AND STRATEGIC PLANNING AND CONTROL USING ABC

LEARNING OBJECTIVE 7
What are the benefits and limitations of using activity-based costing?

Activity-based management and costing provide many benefits for production and service organizations. The list of companies using activity-based costing is large and impressive and includes Hewlett-Packard, American Express, AT&T, Caterpillar, Parker Hannifin, Harris Semiconductor, and USWEST. A recent survey by the Institute of Management Accountants of companies that were upgrading their cost management systems provided the following information: forty-one percent of the companies surveyed were using ABC-type systems. Of the remaining 59 percent that were using a method other than ABC, almost one-third felt that they should also be using ABC.[10] These companies are using ABC to make both operational and strategic decisions such as more effectively controlling costs; adjusting product, process, or marketing strategy; influencing behavior; and evaluating performance.

To control costs, managers must understand where costs are being incurred and for what purpose. This understanding is provided by more appropriate tracing of overhead costs to products and services. Viewing fixed costs as long-term variable costs provides useful information for assessing the cost–benefit relationship of obtaining more customers or providing more goods and services. Additionally, differentiating between value-added and non-value-added activities helps managers visualize what needs to be done to control these costs, implement cost reduction activities, and plan resource utilization.

Traditional accounting systems concentrate on controlling cost incurrence, while ABC focuses on controlling the cause of the cost incurrence. Concentrating on the *causes* of costs makes cost reduction efforts more successful because they can be directed at specific cost drivers. It is critical, however, to understand that simply reducing cost drivers or activities will not cause a decline in total costs unless excess resources are eliminated or reassigned to value-adding areas.

Managers who better understand the underlying cost of making a product or performing a service can obtain new insight into product or service profitability:

> Often managers can see, for the first time, the cost of nonconformance, the cost of design activities, the cost of new product launches, and the cost of administrative activities, such as processing customer orders, procurement, and handling special requests. The high cost of these activities can stimulate companies to adopt the TQM, JIT, and business process improvement programs that will produce a leaner and more responsive enterprise.[11]

This improved information can result in management decisions about expanding or contracting product variety, raising or reducing prices, and entering or leaving a market. For example, managers may decide to raise selling prices of low-volume specialty output. Or they may decide to discontinue such production because that output consumes disproportionately more resources than does high-volume output.

ABC information can even affect decisions about plant and equipment investments and highlight the benefits that can be obtained if high-technology processes are implemented. Installing computerized equipment may reduce non-value-added production activities and increase efficiency. Activity-based costing helps managers understand the effects of the various activities that are needed in the changing business environment (especially relative to technology) and provide flexibility in designing systems that are able to cope with this environment. Although activity-based

---

[10]Cost Management Group, Institute of Management Accountants, "4th Annual Activity-Based Cost Management Survey Results," *Cost Management Update* (February 1994), pp. 1–4.

[11]Robert S. Kaplan, "In Defense of Activity-Based Cost Management," *Management Accounting* (November 1992), p. 60.

costing only *indirectly* changes the cost accumulation process, it *directly* changes the cost assignment process, making it more realistic regarding how and why costs are incurred.

Thus, activity-based costing is more than a system to generate product costs for financial statements; it is employed as a tool to improve performance through an integration with organizational strategy. One survey indicated that ABC information was used in 24 percent of the strategic decisions about insourcing versus outsourcing, 72 percent of the strategic decisions about pricing and product discontinuation, and 36 percent of the strategic decisions about customer profitability.[12] The following News Note provides information on the additional need to link ABC information with an organization's type of competitive strategy.

CRITICISMS OF AND CONCLUSIONS ABOUT ABC

No currently existing accounting technique or system can provide management with exact cost information for every product or with all the information needed to make consistently perfect decisions. Activity-based costing, although it can provide better information than a traditional overhead allocation process, is not a panacea for

LEARNING OBJECTIVE ❼
What are the benefits and limitations of using activity-based costing?

NEWS NOTE

Linking ABC Information to Competitive Strategy

ABC should be linked to a company's competitive strategy regarding organizational design, new product development, product mix and pricing, and technology. Here are some examples:

- ⊙ *Competing based on cost or custom design.* If a company chooses to compete based on the design of custom or low-cost products, its ABC systems should provide designers with accurate estimates of product or process costs. These costs should be available both before and during the design process. Designers should also know the costs of customization.
- ⊙ *Competing based on scale economies.* If a company competes based on manufacturing scale economies and efficiencies for commodity products, its ABC systems should focus on measuring the costs of manufacturing activities and plant capacity.
- ⊙ *Competing based on distribution and logistics.* If a company competes based on superior distribution and logistics, its ABC systems should focus on measuring the costs of those activities rather than manufacturing costs.

Additionally, an organization may specify quality and continuous improvement as part of its competitive strategy. ABC information can play important roles in helping a company achieve continuous improvement. It can be used to identify potential economic gains from improving quality and speed. It also can be used to measure economic progress toward improving quality and time-based performance.

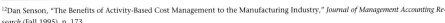

[12]Dan Senson, "The Benefits of Activity-Based Cost Management to the Manufacturing Industry," *Journal of Management Accounting Research* (Fall 1995), p. 173.

all managerial difficulties. The following points should be noted as some of this method's shortcomings.

First, implementing ABC requires a significant investment in terms of time and cost. If implementation is to be successful, substantial support is needed throughout the firm. An environment for change must be created, and creating such an environment requires overcoming a variety of individual, organizational, and environmental barriers. Individual barriers are typically related to fear of (1) the unknown or a shift in the status quo, (2) a possible loss of status, or (3) the need to learn new skills. Organizational barriers may be related to territorial, hierarchical, or corporate-culture issues. Environmental barriers are often built by employee groups including unions, regulatory agencies, or other stakeholders.

To overcome barriers, managers first must recognize that those barriers exist; second, managers need to investigate the causes of the barriers; and third, managers must communicate information about ABC to all concerned parties. It is essential that top management be involved with and support the implementation process. Lack of commitment or involvement by top management will make achieving meaningful progress very slow and difficult. Additionally, employees and managers must be educated in some nontraditional techniques, including new terminology, concepts, and performance measurements. Such an educational process cannot occur overnight. Assuming that top management supports the changes in the internal accounting system and employees are educated about the system, additional time will be required to analyze the activities taking place in the activity centers, trace costs to those activities, and determine the appropriate cost drivers. At VW Canada, for example, thousands of person-hours were spent in developing training materials and providing workshops on what ABC was, what was expected from its implementation, and why it would provide information not available from the existing accounting system.

Another shortcoming of ABC is that it does not conform specifically with generally accepted accounting principles (see Exhibit 5-17). ABC would suggest that some traditionally designated period costs, such as research and development costs and some service department costs, be allocated to products and that some traditionally designated product costs, such as factory building depreciation, not be allocated to products. Because of the differing perspectives, many companies implemented ABC as a supplemental system for internal reporting while continuing to use a more traditional system to account for product and period costs, allocate indirect costs, and prepare external financial statements. It is possible that, as ABC systems become more widely used, either the differences between GAAP and ABC cost accumulation will narrow or companies will become more adept at making the appropriate adjustments at the end of a period to bring internal information into compliance with GAAP's external reporting requirements. In either event, the need for two costing systems would be eliminated.

As indicated by the following quote, another criticism that has been leveled at activity-based costing is that it does not promote total quality management and continuous improvement:

> Activity-based prescriptions for improved competitiveness usually entail steps that lead to selling more or doing less of what should not be sold or done in the first place. Indeed, activity-based cost information does nothing to change old remote-control, top-down management behavior. Simply because improved cost information becomes available, a company does not change its commitment to mass produce output at high speed, to control costs by encouraging people to manipulate processes, and to persuade customers to buy output the company has produced to cover its costs. American businesses will not become long-term global competitors until they change the way managers think. No cost infor-

INVENTORIABLE INDIRECT COST	GAAP	ABC
Marketing, selling, advertising, and distribution costs	E	I
Interest	E	I, E
Research and experimental costs	E	I, E
General and administrative costs	E	I
Costs of strikes	P	E
Rework labor, scrap, and spoilage	P	I
Insurance	P	I, E
Distribution and warehousing	E	I

I = inventoriable; E = expensed; P = practice varies

SOURCE: Extracted from Richard B. Troxel, "The Relationship between Activity-Based Costing and Generally Accepted Accounting Principles," *Handbook of Cost Management: 1998 Edition* (Boston: Warren, Gorham & Lamont/RIA Group), p. C5-10. Reprinted from *Handbook of Cost Management*, with permission of the publisher, Research Institute of America Group.

EXHIBIT 5-17

Differences in Inventoriable Indirect Costs under GAAP and ABC

mation, not even activity-based cost management information, will do that.[13]

Companies attempting to implement ABC as a cure-all for product failures, volume declines, or financial losses will quickly recognize that the statement above is true. However, companies can implement ABC and its related management techniques in support of and in conjunction with TQM, BPR, JIT, and any other world-class methodology. The customers of these companies will be provided with the best variety, price, quality, service, and cycle time of which they are capable. Not coincidentally, they should find their businesses booming. Activity-based costing and activity-based management can effectively support continuous improvement, short lead times, and flexible manufacturing by helping managers to do the following:

- Identify and monitor significant technology costs
- Trace many technology costs directly to products
- Promote achievement of market share through use of target costing (discussed in Chapter 14)
- Identify the cost drivers that create or influence cost
- Identify activities that do not contribute to perceived customer value (i.e., non-value-added activities or waste)
- Understand the impact of new technologies on all elements of performance
- Translate company goals into activity goals
- Analyze the performance of activities across business functions
- Analyze performance problems
- Promote standards of excellence

Activity-based costing, in and of itself, does not change the amount of overhead costs incurred, but it distributes those costs in a more equitable manner. ABC does not change the cost accumulation process, but it makes that process more realistic through a reflection of how and why costs are incurred. Finally, activity-based costing does not eliminate the need for assigning indirect overhead costs to products and services, but it uses a more appropriate means of doing so than has been possible under traditional methods. In summary, ABC is an improved cost accounting tool that helps managers know how the score is kept so that they can play the game more competitively.

---

[13]H. Thomas Johnson, "It's Time to Stop Overselling Activity-Based Concepts," *Management Accounting* (September 1992), pp. 31, 33.

SITE ANALYSIS

Volkswagen Canada

Although the ABC information and its uses are invaluable to many functions and improvement initiatives, in the end, ABC simply helps managers and employees do their jobs better and with more certainty. It tells you not only what your organization does but also how well it is being done.

For example, the die cast pilot project indicated which products were profitable and which were not. Unfortunately, the two big moneymakers were in an extremely competitive market and the company was forced to reduce their prices by approximately 75 percent, making the profit margin close to zero. Then, two of the other three profit-producing parts were discontinued. Even the numerous improvements that had been made were not enough to turn the die cast area around. The ABC model showed that, even under the most optimistic scenario, the die cast area would not be profitable in the near future. Management therefore made a decision to move die-casting operations to another VW plant.

In this case, the ABC data were used to help make the toughest decision management ever has to make—the decision to close down an operation, with all its effects on employees and the community at large. For the remaining manufacturing functions at the Barrie plant, ABC and ABM are being used to improve processes and explain the underlying rationale for change.

Volkswagen's experience has shown that the road to implementing activity-based management is difficult and requires a strong, dedicated leadership team to drive the project forward. The rewards of such perseverance, however, are worth it. ABC and ABM information cannot tell management what to do to improve results but, rather, point out potential opportunities, thus dramatically altering the way a company does business. As a decision-making tool, ABC and ABM information provides the most potentially valuable data that decision makers can have in their toolbox of resources.

SOURCE: Jim Gurowka, "ABC, ABM, and the Volkswagen Saga," *CMA Magazine* (May 1996), p. 33.

CROSS-FUNCTIONAL APPLICATIONS

TOPIC OF NOTE	DISCIPLINE	CROSS-FUNCTIONAL APPLICATIONS
Activity-Based Costing	Marketing	ABC can drastically affect pricing policies and as such, the marketing mix, especially in a competitive environment where bids and offers cannot be easily changed. When competitors in the industry charge extraordinarily different prices for similar products, ABC should be used to determine possible over/understatement of costs.
	Management	ABC can focus management's attention on the activities that require more control or improvement by identifying the activity that is driving excess costs. Overhead rates often obscure the actual cost driver that needs attention, especially when combined rates are used.
	Engineering	Engineers often model costs based on ideal conditions of operation by evaluating material alternatives, labor/machine usage, utilities, or efficiency of each production process. ABC shows engineers practical conditions of operation where inefficiencies exist. The difference between the two approaches suggests design or specification changes to planners.

CROSS-FUNCTIONAL APPLICATIONS

TOPIC OF NOTE	DISCIPLINE	CROSS-FUNCTIONAL APPLICATIONS
Activity-Based Costing *(continued)*	Economics	ABC can be used in tandem with economic models of cost structure to improve predictions or troubleshoot. Because each approach proceeds from different assumptions and measurements of cost behavior, one system can check on the accuracy of the other.
	Management of Service Firms	Many medical care facilities, health insurance companies, and financial service institutions have implemented ABC in an effort to control their costs. Service industries such as medical care vary substantially in the activities that they provide for their customers. Their need is to identify and control the activity that is driving a particular cost, and ABC is useful in this matter. Also, health insurance companies are imposing their cost control standards on the health care providers, which may not be relevant for management decision making.
Manufacturing Cycle Efficiency (MCE)	Production/ Operations Management	Non-value-added activities that lengthen the time between starting a product into production and completing the product for shipment can be identified by MCE. Management can then decide whether the non-value-added activity is necessary to the company's overall objectives.
	Marketing	Short lead times create a competitive advantage associated with place utility. A marketer can build long-term relationships with customers by reducing lead times and, thus, the customers' carrying costs. Cycle efficiency is a performance measurement that can monitor flow-through time for either a manufacturer or a retailer.
	Engineering	The MCE permits engineers to compare alternative production processes or labor-equipment blends to identify which methods yield the greatest value contribution to the product.

CHAPTER SUMMARY

In a highly competitive business environment, companies need to reduce costs to make profits. One way to reduce costs without reducing quality is to decrease the number of non-value-added organizational activities. Value is added to products only during production (manufacturing company), performance (service company), or display (retail company). Most other activities, such as inspecting, moving, storing, and waiting, are non-value-added.

Activity-based management views organizational processes as value-added and non-value-added activities. Process mapping can be used to determine all the activities that take place in the production of a product or the performance of a service. Each activity is designated as value-added or non-value-added on a value chart. Management should strive to minimize or eliminate non-value-added activities because they create unnecessary costs and longer lead times without providing extra worth for customers.

A third category of activities, known as business-value-added activities, also exists. While customers would not want to pay for these activities, they are currently necessary to conduct business operations.

Activity-based management is also concerned with finding and selecting an appropriate number of activity cost pools and then identifying the cost drivers that best represent the firm's activities and are the underlying causes of costs. The activities chosen by management are those judged to reflect the major and most significant company processes. These activities normally overlap several functional areas and are said to occur horizontally across the firm's departmental lines. Cost drivers can also be used to evaluate the efficiency and effectiveness of the firm's activities.

Costs incurred in one area often result from activities in other areas—for instance, poor product quality or defects may be related to engineering design. Activity-based management highlights and provides feedback about relationships between and among functional areas as well as suggests areas that might benefit from process improvements or waste elimination. ABM allows and encourages the use of non-financial measures, such as lead time, as indicators of activity and performance.

Product and process variety and complexity often cause a business's costs to increase because of unobserved increases in non-value-added activities. Simultaneous engineering and business process reengineering can help firms to accelerate the time to market of new products as well as reduce design or process complexity and the related costs (both direct and indirect) of these new products and of the processes by which they are made.

Traditional costing systems often accumulate costs in one cost pool (or very few cost pools) and allocate those costs to products using one cost driver (generally related to direct labor or machine hours). Activity-based costing accumulates costs for activity centers in multiple cost pools at a variety of levels (unit, batch, product/process, and organizational/facility). ABC then allocates these costs to output using appropriate cost drivers (both volume-related and non-volume-related). Thus, costs are assigned more accurately, and managers can focus on controlling activities that create costs rather than trying to control the resulting costs themselves. Activity-based costing provides a more accurate way to assign overhead costs to products than what has been used traditionally.

KEY TERMS

Activity (p. 177)
Activity-based costing (ABC) (p. 183)
Activity-based management (ABM) (p. 177)
Activity center (p. 189)
Activity cost driver (p. 189)
Batch-level cost (p. 185)
Business process reengineering (BPR) (p. 196)
Business-value-added activity (p. 180)
Concurrent engineering (p. 196)
Cycle time (p. 180)
Facility-level cost (p. 185)
Idle time (p. 178)
Inspection time (p. 179)
Just-in-time (JIT) (p. 181)
Long-term variable cost (p. 186)
Manufacturing cycle efficiency (MCE) (p. 180)

Mass customization (p. 193)
Non-value-added activity (p. 178)
Organizational-level cost (p. 185)
Process-level cost (p. 185)
Process map (p. 177)
Product complexity (p. 194)
Product-level cost (p. 185)
Product variety (p. 193)
Service variety (p. 193)
Simultaneous engineering (p. 196)
Transfer time (p. 178)
Unit-level cost (p. 185)
Value-added activity (p. 178)
Value-added processing time (p. 178)
Value-added service time (p. 178)
Value chart (p. 178)

SOLUTION STRATEGIES

1. Determine the activity centers of the organization.
2. Determine activities and the efforts needed to conduct those activities—the cost drivers.
3. Determine the resources the organization consumes in conducting its activities and the level at which those resources are consumed (unit, batch, product/process, organizational/facility).
4. Allocate the resources to the activity centers based on the cost drivers.
5. Allocate unit-, batch-, and product/process-level costs to products and services based on activities and activity cost drivers involved.
6. Treat organizational/facility-level costs as nonattachable to products.

DEMONSTRATION PROBLEM

Casper Manufacturing Co. uses a traditional approach to overhead allocation. The company produces two types of products: a regular (Model R) and a programmable (Model P) thermostat. For 2000, the company incurred $300,000 of factory overhead and produced 40,000 units of Model R and 20,000 units of Model P. The predetermined factory overhead rate used was $10 per direct labor hour. Based on this rate, the unit cost of each model in 2000 was as follows:

	MODEL R	MODEL P
Direct material	$6	$10
Direct labor	5	5
Factory overhead	5	5
Total	$16	$20

The market is becoming more competitive, so the firm is considering the use of activity-based costing in 2001. Analysis of the 2000 data revealed that the $300,000 of overhead could be assigned to three activities as follows:

	SETUPS	MATERIAL HANDLING	EQUIPMENT OPERATIONS	TOTAL
2000 overhead	$20,000	$60,000	$220,000	$300,000

Management determined that the following activity drivers were appropriate for each overhead category:

	ACTIVITY DRIVER	2000 ACTIVITY VOLUME
Setups	Number of setups	160 setups
Material handling	Pounds of material	120,000 pounds
Equipment operations	Machine hours	40,000 MHs

Activity drivers and units produced in 2000 for each product were:

	MODEL R	MODEL P
Number of units	40,000	20,000
Number of setups	100	60
Pounds of material handled	60,000	60,000
Machine hours	14,000	26,000

Requirements:

a. In 2000, the company used the traditional allocation based on direct labor hours. How much total factory overhead was allocated to Model R units and to Model P units?

b. For 2000, how much total factory overhead would have been allocated to each model if ABC had been used? Calculate a unit cost for Model R and Model P.

c. Casper Manufacturing has a policy of setting selling prices with the unit costs in mind. What direction do you think the prices of Model R and Model P will take if the company begins using activity-based costing? Why?

Solution to Demonstration Problem

a. Model R: 40,000 units × $5 $200,000
     Model P: 20,000 units × $5   100,000
        Total allocated overhead $300,000

b. Cost per setup: $20,000 ÷ 160 = $125
   Cost per pound: $60,000 ÷ 120,000 = $.50
   Cost per machine hour: $220,000 ÷ 40,000 = $5.50

MODEL R		MODEL P	
100 setups × $125	$ 12,500	60 setups × $125	$ 7,500
60,000 pounds × $.50	30,000	60,000 pounds × $.50	30,000
14,000 MHs × $5.50	77,000	26,000 MHs × $5.50	143,000
Assignable factory OH	$119,500	Assignable factory OH	$180,500
Divided by units	÷ 40,000	Divided by units	÷ 20,000
Factory OH per unit	= ≈$2.99	Factory OH per unit	=≈$9.03

	MODEL R	MODEL P
Direct material	$ 6.00	$10.00
Direct labor	5.00	5.00
Factory overhead	2.99	9.03
Total activity-based product cost	$13.99	$24.03

c. Because the cost of Model R is $13.99 under ABC and $16 under traditional costing, the price of Model R should be reduced; this pricing decision will probably make Model R more competitive and increase its sales volume. In contrast, because the cost of Model P is $20 based on the traditional approach and $24.03 using ABC, Model P's price should be raised. ABC provides more accurate costing information so that management's abilities to plan, control, solve problems, and evaluate choices should be enhanced.

END OF CHAPTER MATERIALS

⊙ QUESTIONS

1. Why does management need product cost information?

2. Why has information developed for external uses become a primary source for internal decision making? Is this rationale valid? Explain.

3. Why is it not possible to develop totally accurate product or service costs?

4. Describe the system known as activity-based management. What cost management tools fall under the activity-based management umbrella?

5. What does a process map show and why is it useful?

6. Distinguish between a process map and a value chart.

7. Define value-added activity and non-value-added activity. Compare these types of activities and give examples of each.

8. Why is the concept of value-added activities a customer-oriented notion?

9. To what factors can non-value-added activities be attributed? Why would customers perceive these factors as not adding value?

10. What is a business-value-added activity? Why is it not always possible to eliminate this type of activity? Give an example, other than the one in the text, of a business-value-added activity that would not be possible to eliminate.

11. Define *cycle efficiency* and explain how it is calculated in a manufacturing environment and in a service environment.

12. What is a cost driver and how is it used?

13. Does conventional cost accounting use cost drivers? If so, explain how. If not, explain why.

14. Why is ABM considered a process view and ABC considered a cost assignment view of an organization?

15. What are the four levels of cost drivers? Which level is the focus in traditional costing systems?

16. Briefly describe the cost accumulation and assignment process in an ABC system.

17. Why do the more traditional methods of overhead assignment overload standard products with overhead costs, and how does ABC improve overhead assignments?

18. What operating characteristics of a company might indicate that ABC could provide improved information to the company's managers?

19. The chapter identified several underlying *causes* of a company's need for a new cost system. List and discuss some *symptoms* that might be visible reflections of these underlying causes.

20. Explain why product or service variety creates substantial overhead costs.

21. What are the primary methods of mass customization? Provide an example of each.

22. How can (a) simultaneous engineering and (b) business process reengineering help reduce process complexity? What types of costs are likely to be reduced if these approaches are adopted successfully?

23. Why can control in an activity-based management system be more effective than control in a conventional system?

24. Explain this comment: "Identifying non-value-added activities provides management with a distinct control opportunity."

25. Why is ABC often adopted as a stand-alone control system rather than as the main product costing system?

26. Should ABC be considered for adoption by all firms? Why or why not?

27. Can some firms expect to benefit more than others from adopting ABC? Why or why not?

28. What are the shortcomings of activity-based costing as an accounting system methodology? How might these be overcome?

29. "If a company institutes activity-based costing, its profits will rise substantially." Discuss the validity of this statement.

30. Why does the implementation of activity-based costing not reduce the amount of overhead costs incurred by an organization? How would such a reduction have to be achieved?

⊙ EXERCISES

31. *(Terminology)* Match each item in the right-hand column with a term in the left-hand column.

a. Activity-based costing	**1.** Something that increases the worth of a product to a customer
b. Value chart	**2.** A measure of the demands placed on an activity
c. Process map	**3.** A measure of processing efficiency
d. Activity driver	**4.** Something that increases the time and cost of production, but not the worth of a product to a customer
e. Manufacturing cycle efficiency	
f. Long-term variable cost	**5.** A cost created by a group of things processed at a single time
g. Value-added activity	
h. Business process reengineering	**6.** Process innovation and redesign
i. Non-value-added activity	**7.** A cost that has been traditionally viewed as fixed
j. Batch level cost	**8.** A flowchart indicating all steps in producing a product or performing a service
	9. A representation of the value-added and non-value-added activities and the time spent in these activities from the beginning to the end of a process
	10. A system that collects costs according to the nature and extent of activities

32. *(Terminology)* Match each item in the right-hand column with a term in the left-hand column.

a. Activity center	**1.** A process that involves all design and production personnel from the beginning of a project
b. Pareto principle	
c. Product complexity	**2.** A methodology that focuses on activities to improve the value delivered to customers
d. Transfer time	
e. Activity-based management	**3.** The number of components, operations, or processes needed to make a product
f. Simultaneous engineering	
g. Mass customization	**4.** The relatively low-cost bulk production of products to customer specifications
h. Activity	
i. Idle time	**5.** The time spent in storage or waiting for processing
j. Product variety	**6.** The time spent moving products or components from one place to another
	7. A repetitive action performed to fulfill a business function
	8. A part of the organization for which management wants separate reporting
	9. The different types of products produced in an organization
	10. A fundamental principle often referred to as the 20:80 rule

33. *(VA and NVA activities)* You and your friend from law school opened a legal practice ten months ago. You have been discussing with Bob McKnight, a friend who graduated with a degree in accounting, all the different tasks you perform during a week. Bob has suggested that you list your and your partner's activities for a typical week. This list follows:

ACTIVITY	TIME (HOURS)
Take depositions	10.4
Do legal research for cases	14.2
Make calls concerning cases	6.6

ACTIVITY	TIME (HOURS)
Travel to/from court	7.8
Litigate cases	11.9
Write correspondence	9.9
Eat lunch with clients	6.8
Eat dinner at office while watching *Jeopardy*	2.5
Contemplate litigation strategies	10.7
Play golf	3.2
Write wills for clients	4.9
Assign tasks to the firm secretary	6.7
Fill out time sheets for client work	10.1

a. List the value-added activities and explain why they are value-added.

b. List the non-value-added activities and explain why they are non-value-added.

c. Why might it be more difficult for a small, start-up law firm to reduce the non-value-added activities listed as your answer to Part c than it might be for a large, well-established law firm?

34. *(VA and NVA activities)* Paradise Construction Company constructs beach-front vacation homes. You have developed the following information about the average length of time it takes to complete one home:

OPERATION	AVERAGE NUMBER OF DAYS
Receive materials	1
Store materials	6
Move materials to job site	2
Measure and cut materials	7
Set up and move scaffolding	5
Wait for crew that is completing previous job	6
Frame structure	4
Cut and frame doors and windows	3
Build gas fireplace	4
Attach siding and seal joints	5
Construct inside of home	9
Inspect home (by county inspectors)	1

a. What are the value-added activities and their total time?

b. What are the non-value-added activities and their total time?

c. How did you classify the inspection time? Why? Could this have been classified in another manner? Why?

35. *(VA and NVA activities)* Rockport Manufacturing Company is investigating the costs of schedule changes in its factory. Following is a list of the activities, estimated times, and average costs required for a single schedule change.

ACTIVITY	ESTIMATED TIME	AVERAGE COST
Review impact of orders	30 min.–2 hrs.	$ 300
Reschedule orders	15 min.–24 hrs.	800
Reschedule production orders	15 min.–1 hr.	75
Contact production supervisor; stop production and change over; generate paperwork to return materials	5 min.–2 hrs.	45
Return excess inventory and locate new materials	20 min.–6 hrs.	1,500
Generate new production paperwork change routings; change bill of materials	15 min.–4 hrs.	500
Change purchasing schedule	10 min.–8 hrs.	2,100
Collect paperwork from the floor	15 min.	75
Review new line schedule	15 min.–30 min.	100
Account for overtime premiums	3 hrs.–10 hrs.	1,000
Total		$6,495

a. Which of the previous activities, if any, are value-added?

b. What is the cost driver in this situation?

c. How can the cost driver be controlled and the activities eliminated?

36. *(VA and NVA activities)* You are planning a weekend trip to San Francisco. You will be traveling by plane and will need a hotel room when you arrive. These two reservations will be made by you through 1-800 numbers. Because you are planning to stay in the city, you will take the airport shuttle service to and from your hotel and will not need a car.

a. Describe the process of preparing for this trip by listing the activities in which you would engage.

b. Indicate which of the above listed activities are value-added and which are non-value-added.

c. How might you reduce or eliminate the time spent in non-value-added activities?

37. *(VA and NVA activities)* The College of Business has recently selected you as its representative on a committee to improve the preregistration process at your university.

a. Describe the activities composing the current preregistration process.

b. Estimate the time required for the various activities listed in Part a.

c. What activities do you perceive as not adding value and why?

d. How would you improve the registration process?

38. *(VA & NVA activities; cycle time; cycle efficiency)* Carol Schmidt is a front desk clerk at the Westwego Mansion Hotel. Carol performs the following functions when a guest checks into the hotel:

FUNCTION	TIME (MINUTES)
Greet guest and ask for name	1.0
Find reservation in computer system	1.0
Ask guest to fill in card with personal information: name, address, credit card number	.5
Wait for guest to fill in card	3.0
Answer and talk on phone to another guest	2.5
Ask guest what type of room he/she prefers and listen to response	1.5
Check computer system for this preferred room type	1.5
Obtain plastic key card and program it	.5
Put key card in paper sleeve and write guest room number on it	1.0
Ask guest if he/she needs help with luggage	.5
Get bellhop if help is needed	2.0
Wish guest a pleasant stay	.5

a. Indicate whether each activity is value-added or non-value-added.

b. Calculate the cycle time and service cycle efficiency of this process.

c. Make recommendations to increase the service cycle efficiency.

39. *(VA & NVA activities; cycle time; cycle efficiency)* The following functions are performed in making barbeque sauce at Logan's Food Company.

FUNCTION	TIME (MINUTES)
Receiving ingredients	45
Moving ingredients to stockroom	15
Storing ingredients in stockroom	7,200
Moving ingredients from stockroom	15
Mixing ingredients	50
Cooking ingredients	185
Bottling ingredients	90
Moving bottled sauce to warehouse	20
Storing bottled sauce in warehouse	10,080
Moving bottled sauce from warehouse to trucks	30

a. Indicate whether each activity is value-added or non-value-added.

b. Calculate the cycle time and manufacturing cycle efficiency of this process.

c. Make some recommendations to Mr. Logan that would improve the company's manufacturing cycle efficiency.

40. *(Cost drivers)* Following is a list of the overhead cost pools in Dinah Corp. For each cost pool, identify a cost driver and explain why it is appropriate.

a. Equipment maintenance

b. Factory utilities

c. Factory depreciation

d. Machinery rent

e. Quality inspection labor

f. Computer operations

g. Material handling

h. Setup

i. Engineering changes

j. Advertising

k. Freight for materials

l. Scheduling meetings

m. Obtaining purchase order quotes

n. Filing purchase orders

o. Checking on overdue purchase orders

41. *(Cost drivers)* Your mother is the owner of a pizza delivery franchise. You and your older sister have been working as order taker and delivery person for several years. This year, your sixteen-year-old brother has started working in the family business. Overhead costs seem to be rising and your mother has asked you to determine the cost drivers for the following activities.

a. Pizza oven electricity

b. Delivery vehicle repair, maintenance, and insurance

c. Building insurance

d. Plastic cups for side orders of anchovies or jalapeños

e. Property taxes

f. Gasoline for delivery vehicles

42. *(Cost levels)* Katie's Kopies is a self-service photocopy store that has 25 photocopy machines for customer use. A manager is always on duty to handle complaints or problems and monitor the machines. Determine whether each of the following costs for Katie's Kopies is a unit-level (U), batch-level (B), product/process-level (P), or organizational-level (O) cost.

a. Store manager's salary

b. Electricity expense

c. Depreciation on the photocopy machines

d. Property taxes on the building

e. Order costs for purchasing paper and toner

f. Cost of paper

g. Cost of toner

h. Cost of labor to place paper and toner in machines

i. Repairs expense

j. Insurance expense on photocopy machines

k. Advertising and promotion expense

43. *(Cost levels)* Classify each of the following costs as being incurred at a unit-level (U), batch-level (B), product/process-level (P), or organizational/facility-level (O).

a. Cost of printing books at a publishing house

b. Cost of preparing payroll checks

c. Cost of supplies used in research and development on an existing product

d. Salary of the vice-president of marketing

e. Cost of developing an engineering change order
f. Depreciation on camera at Drivers' License Office in the Department of Motor Vehicles
g. Salary of guard for five-story headquarters building
h. Cost of paper and cover for a passport

44. *(Activity-based costing)* Phan Publishing is concerned about the profit generated by its regular paperback dictionaries. Company managers are considering producing only the top-quality, hand-sewn dictionaries with gold-edged pages. Phan currently uses production hours to assign its $500,000 of production overhead to both types of dictionaries. Some additional data follow.

	REGULAR	HAND-SEWN
Direct costs	$2,500,000	$1,200,000
Number produced	1,000,000	700,000
Production hours	85,000	15,000
Square feet of space occupied	1,500	2,500
Inspection hours	5,000	25,000

The $500,000 of production overhead is composed of $100,000 of utilities, $100,000 of factory/storage rent, and $300,000 of quality control inspectors' salaries.
a. How much production overhead is currently being assigned to the regular and to the hand-sewn dictionaries?
b. Determine the production overhead cost that should be assigned to each type of dictionary, using the activity driver appropriate for each type of overhead cost.
c. Should Phan Publishing stop producing the regular dictionaries? Explain.

45. *(Activity-based costing)* As the manager of the five-employee Purchasing Department at Vancouver Ltd., you have decided to implement an activity-based product costing system. Annual departmental costs are $710,250 per year. Finding the best supplier takes the majority of the department's effort and creates the majority of the department's costs.

ACTIVITY	ALLOCATION MEASURE	NUMBER OF PEOPLE	COST
Find best supplier	Number of telephone calls	3	$450,000
Issue purchase orders	Number of purchase orders	1	150,000
Review receiving reports	Number of receiving reports	1	110,250

During the year, the Purchasing Department makes 150,000 telephone calls, issues 10,000 purchase orders, and reviews 7,000 receiving reports. Many purchase orders are received in a single shipment.

One product manufactured by the company required the following activities in the Purchasing Department over the year: 118 telephone calls, 37 purchase orders, and 28 receipts.
a. What amount of Purchasing Department cost should be assigned to the manufacturing of this product?
b. If 200 units of the product are manufactured during the year, what is the Purchasing Department cost per unit?
c. This analysis has caused you to investigate the need for such complexity in this product. After engaging in discussions with Vancouver Ltd.'s engineering design personnel and some of the company's best suppliers, it has been agreed that the number of parts in this product can be reduced and that suppliers will monitor parts supply levels on an ongoing basis. If the same type of analysis is performed for other products, you estimate that departmental costs, on average, will decrease by 25 percent. You have also estimated that, under the new circumstances, making 200 units of this product next year will only require 20 telephone calls, 15 purchase orders, and 8 receipts. What would be the Purchasing Department's new cost per unit for this product next year?

46. *(Activity-based costing)* For the past twenty years, Dauterive Corp. has maintained an internal Research and Development (R&D) Department that provides services to in-

house manufacturing departments. Costs of operating this department have been rising dramatically. You have suggested instituting an activity-based costing system to control costs and charging service users for product and process development. The principal departmental expense is professional salaries. Activities in this department fall into three major categories. These categories, estimated related professional salary costs, and suggested allocation bases follow:

ACTIVITY	SALARY COST	ALLOCATION BASE
Evaluation of market opportunities	$ 600,000	Hours of professional time
Product development	1,800,000	Number of products developed
Process design	2,400,000	Number of engineering changes

In the year 2000, the R&D Department worked 15,000 hours evaluating market opportunities, aided in the development of 100 new products, and responded to 500 engineering-process change requests.

a. Determine the allocation rate for each activity in the R&D Department.
b. How can the rates developed in Part a be used for evaluating output relative to cost incurred in the R&D Department?
c. How much cost would be charged to a manufacturing department that had consumed 1,000 hours of market research time, received aid in developing 14 new products, and requested 75 engineering process changes?
d. What alternative does the firm have to maintaining an internal R&D department? What potential benefits and problems might arise if the company pursued this alternative?

47. *(Activity-based costing)* Pennington Plastics makes large plastic water bottles and plastic composite control panels for aircraft. Plastic bottles are relatively simple to produce and are made in large quantities. The control surfaces are more complicated to produce because they must be customized to individual plane types. Pennington sells 200,000 plastic bottles annually and 5,000 control panels. A variety of information follows related to the annual production and sale of these products.

	PLASTIC BOTTLES	CONTROL PANELS
Revenues	$6,000,000	$13,000,000
Direct labor hours	2,000	53,000
Machine hours	120,000	86,250
Direct material	1,360,000	1,200,000

Labor is paid $14 per hour. Production overhead consists of $9,500,000 of supervisors' salaries, labor fringe benefits, design and engineering, and other human-related costs and $2,500,000 of machine-related costs. Administrative costs total $1,200,000 and are allocated to individual product lines.

a. Calculate the profit or loss on each product if total overhead (production and administrative) is assigned according to direct labor hours.
b. Calculate the profit or loss on each product if total overhead (production and administrative) is assigned according to machine hours.
c. Calculate the profit or loss on each product if human-related overhead is assigned according to direct labor hours, machine-related overhead is assigned according to machine hours, and administrative overhead is assigned according to dollars of revenue.
d. Calculate the profit or loss on each product if administrative overhead is deducted from total company income rather than being allocated to products.
e. Does your answer in Part a, b, c, or d provide the best representation of the profit contributed by each product? Explain.

⊙ PROBLEMS

48. *(Value chart)* You are the new controller of a small job shop that manufactures special-order desk nameplate stands. As you review the records, you find that all the orders are shipped late, the average process time for any order is three weeks, and the

67. Activity-based management implementations appear to succeed better in organizations that want to become and are striving toward becoming world-class competitors. Companies that emphasize techniques such as total quality management, employee empowerment, and benchmarking seem to view ABM as a "natural fit" and believe these types of initiatives reinforce one another. One other key to success is the commitment and support of top management to these initiatives. (Note: The Fall 1995 *Journal of Cost Management* article "Some Human Aspects of Implementing Activity-Based Management" may be a useful starting point.)

   a. How might activity-based management and activity-based costing help a company in its quest to achieve world-class status?

   b. Would it be equally as important to have top management support if a company were instituting activity-based costing rather than activity-based management? Discuss the rationale for your answer.

   c. Assume you are a member of top management in a large organization. Do you think implementation of ABM or ABC would be more valuable? Explain the rationale for your answer.

68. As the chief executive officer of a large corporation, you have made a decision, after discussion with production and accounting personnel, to implement activity-based management concepts. Your goal is to reduce cycle time and, thus, costs. A primary way to accomplish this goal is to install highly automated equipment in your plant; in doing so, approximately 60 percent of your work force would be displaced. Your company is the major employer in the area.

   a. Discuss the pros and cons of installing the equipment from the perspective of your (1) stockholders, (2) employees, and (3) customers.

   b. How would you explain to a worker that his/her job is non-value-added?

   c. What alternatives might you have that could accomplish the goal of reducing cycle time without creating economic havoc for the local area?

PART 3

Using Managerial Accounting Information for Planning

Chapter 6 Cost-Volume-Profit Analysis and Relevant Costing

LEARNING OBJECTIVES

After reading this chapter, you should be able to answer the following questions:

① **HOW** is breakeven point computed and what does it represent?

② **HOW** do costs, revenues, and contribution margin interact with changes in an activity base (volume)?

③ **HOW** does cost-volume-profit (CVP) analysis in single-product and multiproduct firms differ?

④ **WHAT** are the underlying assumptions of CVP analysis and how do these assumptions create a short-run managerial perspective?

⑤ **HOW** do quality decisions affect the components of CVP analysis?

⑥ **WHAT** constitutes relevance in a decision-making situation?

⑦ **HOW** can management best utilize a scarce resource?

⑧ **WHAT** is the relationship between sales mix and relevant costing problems?

⑨ **HOW** can pricing decisions be used to maximize profit?

⑩ **HOW** can product margin be used to determine whether a product line should be retained or eliminated?

⑪ **HOW** are breakeven and profit-volume graphs prepared? (Appendix 1)

⑫ **WHAT** are the differences between absorption and variable costing? (Appendix 2)

⑬ **WHY** is linear programming a valuable tool for managers? (Appendix 3)

Rogar International Corporation

In 1975 Bob Crist started Rogar Manufacturing Corporation (RMC) in Abilene, Texas, to manufacture parts for the Department of Defense, based on his experience as a USAF pilot and his knowledge from a recently earned MBA. By 1987 the firm had grown to sixty-five people. However, during the mid-to-late 1980s, a severe economic depression caused either the FDIC or RTC to close five of the six Abilene banks. One of those closed banks was due about $1,000,000 from RMC on a twenty-year mortgage. In 1988, the RTC gave Rogar 45 days to pay this loan, and the company became one of the many financial casualties of the Texas economic depression of the 1980s. By 1990, RMC's building and equipment were auctioned by the RTC.

In 1989, Bob Crist started a new company, Rogar International Corporation [RIC], in Richmond, Virginia, with three employees, some worn-out equipment, and a crucial $350,000 line of credit from the firm's major supplier, Mr. C. T. Fung of Hong Kong. Bob Crist gained the distinction of being the only person in the world who had been granted this type of credit by any of Mr. Fung's companies.

Today, RIC produces two product line categories: wine accessories and decorative kitchen storage racks. The wine accessories line includes replicas of wine bottle openers dating back to the 1800s. Rogar's catalog lists over 100 items.

The company uses continuous processing of small lots, which Bob Crist has named "lot processing." Firm management is very aware of the importance of cost behavior and cost control, and uses up-to-date standard costs so that RIC can assure delivery of value for its customers. In today's market, value is the key word. It is the relationship between quality and price, and all customers want the highest value. Dropping quality to lower price will destroy your market.

SOURCE: Information provided by Bob Crist of Rogar International Corporation of Richmond, Virginia, 1998.

*S*ince covering costs is a matter of operational survival (regardless of whether you manage Rogar International Corporation, the Denver Broncos, Radio City Music Hall, or a medical practice), the first part of this chapter discusses determining an organization's breakeven point, which is the level of activity at which total revenues equal total costs. At breakeven, a company experiences neither profit nor loss on its operating activities. Managers, however, generally do not want to operate at a volume level that merely covers costs; they want to make profits. Cost-volume-profit analysis adds a profit element to breakeven calculations so that managers are better able to plan for volume goals that should generate income rather than losses. The chapter then extends cost-volume-profit analysis to the use of relevant costing to solve a series of frequently encountered short-run business problems.

THE BREAKEVEN POINT

LEARNING OBJECTIVE ❶
How is breakeven point computed and what does it represent?

breakeven point (BEP)

The level of activity, in units or dollars, at which total revenues equal total costs is called the **breakeven point (BEP)**. Although most business managers hope to do better than just break even, the breakeven point is an important point of reference by which the manager can judge either the company's level of risk of not exceeding the BEP or the company's level of comfort in exceeding the BEP. Managers make this determination by comparing the magnitude of the company's current or planned sales with the BEP. Finding the breakeven point requires an understanding of an organization's revenue and cost functions.

Basic Assumptions

LEARNING OBJECTIVE ❷
How do costs, revenues, and contribution margin interact with changes in an activity base (volume)?

As noted in Chapters 4 and 5, certain assumptions are made about cost behavior so that cost information can be used in accounting computations. The following list summarizes these simplifying assumptions about revenue and cost functions.

Relevant range: A primary assumption is that the company is operating within the relevant range of activity specified in determining the revenue and cost information used in each of the following assumptions.

Revenue: Total revenue fluctuates in direct proportion to units sold. Revenue per unit is assumed to remain constant, and fluctuations in per-unit revenue for factors such as quantity discounts are ignored.

Variable costs: Total variable costs fluctuate in direct proportion to level of activity or volume. On a per-unit basis, variable costs remain constant. Variable costs exist in all functional business areas including production, distribution, selling, and administration.

Fixed costs: Total fixed costs remain constant; thus, per-unit fixed cost decreases as volume increases and increases as volume decreases. Fixed costs include both fixed factory overhead and fixed selling and administrative expenses.

Mixed costs: Mixed costs must be susceptible to separation into their variable and fixed elements. Any method (such as high-low or regression analysis) that validly separates these costs in relation to one or more predictors may be used.

Because these basic assumptions treat selling prices and costs as *known and constant,* any analysis based on the assumptions is valid for only the short term. Long-range planning must recognize the possibilities of price and cost fluctuations.

An important amount in breakeven analysis is contribution margin. On a per-unit basis, **contribution margin (CM)** is equal to selling price minus per-unit variable production, selling, and administrative costs. Contribution margin reflects the revenue remaining after all variable costs have been covered. Contribution margin per unit is constant, because both revenue and variable costs per unit have been defined as being constant. Total contribution margin fluctuates in direct proportion to sales volume.

To illustrate the computation of the breakeven point, 2000 income statement information for Better Homes Ice Buckets is presented in Exhibit 6-1. The current relevant range of production and sales for the company is between 6,000 and 30,000 ice buckets per year. The costs given in the exhibit are the expected costs for all income statement elements.

contribution margin (CM)

Formula Approach

The formula approach uses an algebraic equation to calculate the breakeven point. However, the answer to the equation is not always acceptable and may need to be rounded to a whole number. For instance, items may be sold only in specified lot sizes, and some partial units cannot be sold.

Algebraic breakeven computations use an equation representing the income statement. This equation groups costs by behavior and shows the relationships among revenue, volume, variable cost, fixed cost, and profit as follows:

where

$$R(X) - VC(X) - FC = PBT$$
$$R = \text{revenue (selling price) per unit}$$
$$X = \text{number of units sold or to be sold}$$
$$R(X) = \text{total revenue}$$
$$VC = \text{variable cost per unit}$$
$$VC(X) = \text{total variable cost}$$
$$FC = \text{total fixed cost}$$
$$PBT = \text{profit before tax}$$

Since the equation represents an income statement, PBT can be set equal to zero for the formula to indicate a breakeven situation. BEP in units can be found by solving the equation for X.

	TOTAL	PER UNIT	PERCENT OF SALES
Sales (10,000 ice buckets)	$400,000	$40	100%
Variable Costs:			
Production	$200,000	$20	50%
Selling	40,000	4	10%
Total variable cost	(240,000)	$24	60%
Contribution Margin	$160,000	$16	40%
Fixed Costs:			
Production	$100,000		
Selling and administrative	20,000		
Total fixed cost	(120,000)		
Profit before Tax	$ 40,000		

EXHIBIT 6-1

Better Homes Ice Buckets, 2000 Income Statement

$$R(X) - VC(X) - FC = \$0$$
$$R(X) - VC(X) = FC$$
$$(R - VC)(X) = FC$$
$$X = FC \div (R - VC)$$

Breakeven volume is equal to total fixed cost divided by the difference between revenue per unit and variable cost per unit. Since revenue minus variable cost equals contribution margin, the formula can be abbreviated as follows:

$$X = FC \div CM$$

where CM = contribution margin per unit

For Better Homes Ice Buckets, Exhibit 6-1 indicates a unit selling price of $40, a unit variable cost of $24, and total fixed cost of $120,000. The company's contribution margin is $16 per unit ($40 − $24). Substituting these values into the equation yields the following breakeven point:

$$\$40X = \$24X + \$120,000$$
$$\$40X - \$24X = \$120,000$$
$$\$16X = \$120,000$$
$$X = \$120,000 \div \$16$$
$$X = 7,500 \text{ ice buckets}$$

As mentioned, breakeven point can be expressed either in units or in dollars of revenue. One way to convert a unit breakeven point to dollars is to multiply the breakeven point in units by the selling price per unit. For Better Homes Ice Buckets, the breakeven point in sales dollars is $300,000 (7,500 units × $40 per unit). Another method of computing breakeven point in sales dollars requires the computation of a contribution margin ratio.

contribution margin ratio (CM%)

The **contribution margin ratio (CM%)**, calculated as contribution margin divided by revenue, indicates what proportion of selling price remains after variable costs have been covered. The CM ratio can be computed with either per-unit or total cost information and allows the BEP to be determined even if multiple products are involved or if unit selling price and unit variable cost are not known. Dividing total fixed cost by the CM ratio gives the breakeven point in sales dollars.

$$X_\$ = FC \div CM\%$$

where $X_\$$ = breakeven point in sales dollars
$$CM\% = \text{contribution margin ratio} = (R - VC) \div R$$

The contribution margin for Better Homes Ice Buckets is given in Exhibit 6-1 as 40 percent ($16 ÷ $40). Thus, based on the CM ratio, the company's breakeven point in dollars equals $120,000 ÷ .40 = $300,000—the same amount shown in the earlier calculation. The breakeven point in units equals the BEP in sales dollars divided by the unit selling price, or $300,000 ÷ $40 = 7,500 units.

As indicated in the accompanying News Note, knowledge of the BEP can help managers plan for future operations although managers want to earn profits, not just cover costs. Substituting an amount other than zero for the profit (P) term converts the breakeven formula to cost-volume-profit analysis.

LEARNING OBJECTIVE ❸
How does cost-volume-profit (CVP) analysis in single-product and multiproduct firms differ?

cost-volume-profit (CVP) analysis

CVP ANALYSIS

Cost-volume-profit (CVP) analysis is the process of examining the relationships among revenues, costs, and profits for a relevant range of activity and for a particular time. This technique is applicable in all economic sectors (manufacturing, whole-

NEWS NOTE

BEP Helps Businesses Plan for Profits

"Breakeven point." Does the term ring a bell? It should. That's the magic number that tells you when your revenue will cover your expenses. Although entrepreneurs often fail to realize the significance of recognizing and reaching the breakeven point, understanding what it takes to breakeven is critical to making any business profitable.

Failing to calculate your breakeven point early in your business life is a grave mistake that could lead to an entrepreneurial nightmare. Poor financial planning is certainly a major culprit in the untimely demise of many of these businesses.

Incorporating accurate and thorough breakeven analysis as a routine part of your financial planning will keep you abreast of how your business is really faring. Determining how much business is needed to keep the door open will help improve your cash-flow management and your bottom line.

Because most small businesses remain severely undercapitalized, entrepreneurs have little or no margin for error. If they don't plan for profit early on, their chances of surviving three years are almost nil. After you've determined your breakeven point, adds Louis Hutt, Jr., managing partner of a Columbia, Md., accounting firm, "the profit factor can be built into your business."

SOURCE: Kevin D. Thompson, "Planning for Profit," *Black Enterprise* (April 1993), pp. 93–94.

saling, retailing, and service industries) because the same types of managerial functions are performed in all types of organizations.

When known amounts are used for selling price per unit, variable cost per unit, volume of units, and fixed costs, the algebraic equation given in the previous section can be solved to give the amount of profit generated under specified conditions. A more frequent and significant application of CVP analysis is to set a desired target profit and focus on the relationships between that target and specified income statement amounts to find an unknown. Volume is a common unknown in such applications because managers want to achieve a particular level of profit and need to know what quantity of sales must be generated for this objective to be accomplished. Managers may want to use CVP analysis to determine how high variable costs can be (given fixed costs, selling price, and volume) and still provide a given profit level. Variable cost may be increased or decreased by modifying product design specifications, the manufacturing process, or grade of material.

Profit may be stated as either a fixed or a variable amount and on either a before-tax or an after-tax basis. The following situations requiring various levels of desired profit continue the Better Homes Ice Buckets example.

Fixed Amount of Profit before Tax

If desired profit is stated as a before-tax amount, it is treated in CVP analysis simply as an additional cost to be covered. The following equation yields before-tax profit in units:

$$R(X) - VC(X) - FC = PBT$$
$$R(X) - VC(X) = FC + PBT$$
$$X = (FC + PBT) \div (R - VC)$$
$$\text{or}$$
$$X = (FC + PBT) \div CM$$

where $PBT = \text{profit before tax}$

If sales dollars are desired, the formula is as follows:

$$R(X) = (FC + PBT) \div CM\%$$

Assume that Better Homes Ice Buckets wants to generate a before-tax profit of $64,000. To do so, the company must sell 11,500 units, which will provide $460,000 of revenue. These calculations are shown in Exhibit 6-2.

Fixed Amount of Profit after Tax

Both production costs and income taxes are important in analyzing organizational profitability. Income taxes represent a significant aspect of business decision making, and managers need to be aware of tax effects when specifying a profit amount.

A company desiring a particular amount of after-tax net income must first determine the equivalent amount on a before-tax basis, given the applicable tax rate. The CVP formulas needed to calculate a desired after-tax net income amount are as follows:

$$R(X) - VC(X) - FC = PBT$$

and

$$[(PBT)(TR)] = \text{Tax Expense}$$
$$PBT - [(TR)(PBT)] = PAT$$

where

$$TR = \text{tax rate}$$
$$PAT = \text{profit after tax}$$

The profit after tax is equal to the profit before tax minus the applicable tax. Thus defined, PAT can be integrated into the original before-tax CVP formula:

$$PBT - [(TR)(PBT)] = PAT$$
$$PBT (1 - TR) = PAT$$
$$PBT = PAT \div (1 - TR)$$

Assume that Better Homes Ice Buckets wants to earn $49,000 of profit after taxes and the company's tax rate is 30 percent. The number of ice buckets and dollars of sales needed are calculated in Exhibit 6-3.

Rather than specifying a fixed amount of profit to be earned, managers may state profit as a variable amount. Then, as units sold or sales dollars increase, profit will increase proportionally. Variable profit may be stated on either a before-tax or an after-tax basis and either as a percentage of revenues or a per-unit amount. If the variable amount is stated as a percentage, it is convenient to convert that percentage into a per-unit amount. When variable profit is used, the CVP formula must be adjusted to recognize that profit is related to volume of activity.

EXHIBIT 6-2

CVP Analysis—Fixed Amount of Profit before Tax

PBT desired = $64,000

In Units:

$$R(X) - VC(X) = FC + PBT$$
$$\$40X - \$24X = \$120,000 + \$64,000$$
$$X = \$184,000 \div \$16$$
$$= 11,500 \text{ ice buckets}$$

In Sales Dollars:

$$X\$ = (FC + PBT) \div CM\%$$
$$= \$184,000 \div .40$$
$$= \$460,000$$

EXHIBIT 6-3
CVP Analysis—Fixed Amount
of Profit after Tax

PAT desired = $49,000; tax rate = 30%

In Units:

$$PBT = PAT \div (1 - \text{Tax rate})$$
$$= \$49,000 \div (1 - .30)$$
$$= \$49,000 \div .70$$
$$= \$70,000$$

$$R(X) - VC(X) = FC + PBT$$
$$CM(X) = FC + PBT$$
$$\$16X = \$120,000 + \$70,000$$
$$\$16X = \$190,000$$
$$X = \$190,000 \div \$16$$
$$= 11,875 \text{ ice buckets}$$

In Sales Dollars:

$$X_s = (FC + PBT) \div CM\%$$
$$= (\$120,000 + \$70,000) \div .40$$
$$= \$190,000 \div .40$$
$$= \$475,000$$

Variable Amount of Profit before Tax

Managers may want desired profit to be equal to a specified variable amount of sales. The CVP formula for computing the unit volume of sales necessary to earn a specified variable rate or per-unit profit before tax is as follows:

$$R(X) - VC(X) - FC = P_uBT(X)$$

where $\quad P_uBT = \text{profit per unit before tax}$

Solving for X (or volume) gives the following:

$$R(X) - VC(X) - P_uBT(X) = FC$$
$$X = FC \div (R - VC - P_uBT)$$
$$X = FC \div (CM - P_uBT)$$

The profit is treated in the CVP formula as if it were an additional variable cost to be covered. If the profit is viewed in this manner, the original contribution margin and contribution margin ratio are effectively adjusted downward to reflect the desired net margin or profit per unit.

When the desired profit is set as a percentage of selling price, that percentage cannot exceed the contribution margin ratio. If it does, an infeasible specification is created, since the effective contribution margin is a negative percentage. In such a case, the actual contribution margin percentage plus the desired profit percentage would exceed 100 percent of the selling price—a condition that cannot occur.

Assume that the president of Better Homes Ice Buckets wants to know what sales level (in units and dollars) would be required to earn a 25 percent before-tax profit on sales. The calculations in Exhibit 6-4 (page 236) provide the answer.

Variable Amount of Profit after Tax

Adjusting the CVP formula to determine a return on sales on an after-tax basis involves stating profits in relation to both volume and the tax rate. The algebraic manipulations are as follows:

EXHIBIT 6-4

CVP Analysis—Variable Amount of Profit before Tax

P_uBT desired = 25% on sales revenues

This is equal to the following per unit net margin:

P_uBT per unit = .25($40) = $10

In Units:

$$R(X) - VC(X) - PBT(X) = FC$$
$$\$40X - \$24X - \$10X = \$120,000$$
$$X = \$120,000 \div [(\$40 - \$24) - \$10]$$
$$X = \$120,000 \div (\$16 - \$10)$$
$$= \$120,000 \div \$6$$
$$= 20,000 \text{ ice buckets}$$

In Sales Dollars:

The following relationships exist:

	PER UNIT	PERCENT OF SALES
Selling price	$40	100%
Variable costs	(24)	(60%)
25% net margin on sales	(10)	(25%)
Effective contribution margin	$ 6	15%

$$X_\$ = FC \div \text{Effective CM ratio*}$$
$$= \$120,000 \div .15$$
$$= \$800,000$$

*Note that it is not necessary to have per-unit data; all computations can be made with percentage information only.

$$R(X) - VC(X) - FC = P_uBT(X)$$

and

$$[P_uBT(X)](TR) = \text{Tax Expense}$$
$$P_uBT(X) - [P_uBT(X)](TR) = P_uAT$$
$$P_uBT(X)[(1 - TR)] = P_uAT$$
$$P_uBT(X) = P_uAT \div (1 - TR)$$

$$R(X) - VC(X) - FC = P_uBT(X)$$
$$R(X) - VC(X) = FC + P_uBT(X)$$
$$CM(X) = FC + P_uBT(X)$$
$$CM(X) - P_uBT(X) = FC$$
$$X(CM - P_uBT) = FC$$
$$X = FC \div (CM - P_uBT)$$

where P_uBT = desired profit per unit before tax

P_uAT = desired profit per unit after tax

Assume that Better Homes Ice Buckets wishes to earn a profit after tax of 14 percent on revenue and has a 30 percent tax rate. The necessary sales in units and dollars are computed in Exhibit 6-5.

All the previous illustrations of CVP analysis used a variation of the formula approach. Solutions were not accompanied by mathematical proofs; however, income statements are effective means of developing and presenting solutions and/or proofs for solutions to CVP applications.

The answers provided by breakeven and CVP analysis are valid only in relation to specific selling prices and cost relationships. Changes in the company's selling price or cost structure will cause changes in the breakeven point and in the sales needed for the company to achieve a desired profit figure.

EXHIBIT 6-5
CVP Analysis—Variable Amount
of Profit after Tax

PAT desired = 14% of revenue = .14($40) = $5.60; tax rate = 30%

In Units:

$$PBT(X) = [\$5.60 \div (1 - .3)](X)$$
$$= [\$5.60 \div .7]X$$
$$= \$8X$$

$$R(X) - VC(X) - PBT(X) = FC$$
$$CM(X) = FC + PBT(X)$$
$$\$16X = \$120{,}000 + \$8X$$
$$\$8X = \$120{,}000$$
$$X = \$120{,}000 \div \$8$$
$$= 15{,}000 \text{ ice buckets}$$

In Sales Dollars:

	PER UNIT	PERCENT OF SALES
Selling price	$40	100%
Variable costs	(24)	(60%)
Net margin on sales before taxes	(8)	(20%)
Effective contribution margin	$ 8	20%

$$X_\$ = FC \div \text{Effective CM ratio}^*$$
$$= \$120{,}000 \div .20$$
$$= \$600{,}000$$

*Note that it is not necessary to have per-unit data; all computations can be made with percentage information only.

CVP ANALYSIS IN A MULTIPRODUCT ENVIRONMENT

Companies typically produce and sell a variety of products or services. To perform CVP analysis in a multiproduct company, it is necessary to assume a constant product sales mix and to use its corresponding average contribution margin ratio. The constant mix assumption can be referred to as the bag or package assumption. This analogy compares the sales mix to a bag or package of items that are sold together. For example, whenever some of Product A is sold, specified quantities of Products B and C are also sold.

Use of the constant sales mix assumption allows the computation of a weighted average contribution margin ratio, which is useful for CVP analysis. The CM ratio is *weighted* on the basis of the quantity of each item included in the group. The contribution margin ratio of the item that makes up the largest proportion of the bag has the greatest impact on the average contribution margin of the bag mix. Without the assumption of a constant sales mix, the breakeven point cannot be calculated, nor can CVP analysis be used effectively.[1]

The Better Homes Ice Buckets example is continued. Because of the success of the ice buckets, company management has decided to begin producing metal serving sets comprised of ice tongs and a tray. The vice-president of marketing estimates that for every five ice buckets sold, the company will sell two serving sets. Therefore, the bag of products has a 5:2 ratio. The company must incur $30,000 in additional fixed costs related to plant assets (depreciation, insurance, and

LEARNING OBJECTIVE 3
How does cost-volume-profit (CVP) analysis in single-product and multiproduct firms differ?

[1]Once the constant percentage contribution margin in a multiproduct firm is determined, all of the situations regarding income points can be treated the same as they were earlier in the chapter—remembering that the answers reflect the bag assumption.

so on) to support a higher relevant range of production and additional licensing fees. Exhibit 6-6 provides relevant company information and shows the breakeven computations.

Any shift in the proportion of sales mix of products will change the weighted average contribution margin and the breakeven point. If the sales mix shifts toward products with lower contribution margins, there will be an increase in the BEP; furthermore, there will be a decrease in profits unless there is a corresponding increase in total revenues. A shift toward higher-margin products without a corresponding decrease in revenues will cause increased profits and a lower breakeven point.

EXHIBIT 6-6
CVP Analysis—
Multiple Products

PRODUCT COST INFORMATION	ICE BUCKETS		SERVING SETS	
Selling price	$40	100%	$24	100%
Total variable cost	(24)	(60%)	(12)	(50%)
Contribution margin	$16	40%	$12	50%

Total Fixed Costs ($120,000 previous + $30,000 additional) = $150,000

	ICE BUCKETS		SERVING SETS		PER BAG TOTAL	PERCENT
Number of units	5		2			
Revenue per unit	$40		$24			
Total revenue per bag		$200		$48	$248	100.0%
Variable cost per unit	(24)		(12)			
Total variable per bag*		(120)		(24)	(144)	(58.1)%
Contribution margin per unit	$16		$12			
Contribution margin per bag		$ 80		$24	$104	41.9%

*Note that this works out to a variable cost of 60% for ice buckets and 50% for serving sets.

BEP in units:

$$CM(B) = FC$$
$$\$104B = \$150,000$$
$$B = 1{,}443 \text{ bags to break even (rounded)}$$

where B = Bag of products

NOTE: Each bag is made up of 5 ice buckets and two serving sets; thus, it will take 7,215 ice buckets and 2,886 serving sets to break even.

BEP in sales dollars:

$$B_\$ = FC \div CM \text{ ratio}$$
$$B_\$ = \$150,000 \div .419$$
$$= \$357,995 \text{ (rounded)}$$

where CM ratio = Weighted average for bag

NOTE: The breakeven sales dollars also represent the assumed constant sales mix of $200 of ice buckets sales to $48 of serving set sales or an 80.6% to 19.4% ratio. Thus, the company must have approximately $288,544 ($357,995 × 80.6%) of ice bucket sales and $69,451 ($357,995 × 19.4%) of serving set sales to break even.

Proof of above computations is made using an income statement format as follows:

	ICE BUCKETS	SERVING SETS	TOTAL
Sales	$288,544	$69,451	$357,995
Variable costs*	(173,126)	(34,726)	(207,852)
Contribution margin	$115,418	$34,725	$150,143
Fixed costs			(150,000)
Profit before tax			$ 143 (rounding difference)

*These amounts are determined by taking the previously calculated variable cost percentages of 60% for ice buckets and 50% for serving sets.

A Gunfighter with the Soul of a Management Accountant

Most people today know Wyatt Earp as one of the most respected and feared lawmen of the Old West. He helped bring law and order to Dodge City and Wichita, the toughest of frontier towns. He became the stuff of legend at the O.K. Corral in Tombstone, Arizona, where he joined his brothers Morgan and Virgil, and his friend, Doc Holliday, in a deadly face-to-face gun battle with the notorious Clanton gang. Wyatt survived and lived to old age, never having been grazed by a bullet.

Wyatt's earlier career pursuits, though perhaps just as dangerous, are not as well known: teamster, gambler, and buffalo hunter. In fact, during the period 1871–74, he made quite a tidy profit in buffalo hunting using methods that were revolutionary at the time. He developed his methods by observing what more experienced hunters were doing and making improvements—improvements aimed at ensuring that his hunts were more efficient and profitable. In doing so, Wyatt made efficient use of cost-volume-profit analysis, a key analytical tool for the 20th-century management accountant. Wyatt's approach was surprisingly sophisticated for its time and circumstances.

SOURCE: Reprinted from an article appearing in *CMA* magazine by Thomas L. Barton, William G. Shenkir, and John E. Hess, "Wyatt Earp, Frontier Accountant" (June 1995), p. 48, with permission of The Society of Management Accountants of Canada.

It is also possible to calculate the weighted average contribution margin ratio by multiplying the sales mix percentage (relative to sales dollars) by the CM ratio for each product and summing the results. According to the note in Exhibit 6-6, the relationship of dollars of ice bucket sales to dollars of serving set sales is 80.6 percent to 19.4 percent. Based on this information, the CM ratio for the bag of products is computed by multiplying these percentages by the CM%s of the respective individual products (also from Exhibit 6-6) and adding the results as follows:

$$
\begin{array}{rl}
\text{Ice buckets} & 80.6\% \times 40\% = .322 \\
\text{Serving sets} & 19.4\% \times 50\% = \underline{.097} \\
\text{Total CM ratio} & \underline{.419}
\end{array}
$$

To break even at the level indicated, Better Homes Ice Buckets must sell products in exactly the relationships specified in the original sales mix. If sales are at the specified level but not in the specified mix, the company will experience either a profit or a loss, depending on whether the mix is shifted toward the product with the higher or the lower contribution margin ratio.

CVP analysis is not a new tool as is indicated in the accompanying News Note, entitled "A Gunfighter with the Soul of a Management Accountant."

UNDERLYING ASSUMPTIONS OF CVP ANALYSIS

LEARNING OBJECTIVE ❹
What are the underlying assumptions of CVP analysis and how do these assumptions create a short-run managerial perspective?

The CVP model is a useful planning tool that can provide information on how profits are affected when changes are made in the costing structure or in sales levels. Like any model, however, it reflects reality but does not duplicate it. Cost-volume-profit analysis is a tool that focuses on the short run, partially because of the assumptions that underlie the computations. Although these assumptions are necessary, they limit the results' accuracy. These assumptions follow; some of them were also provided at the beginning of the chapter.

1. All variable cost and revenue behavior patterns are constant per unit and linear within the relevant range.
2. Total contribution margin (total revenue − total variable cost) is linear within the relevant range and increases proportionally with output. This assumption follows directly from assumption 1.
3. Total fixed cost is a constant amount within the relevant range.
4. Mixed costs can be accurately separated into their fixed and variable elements. Such accuracy is particularly unrealistic, but reliable estimates can be developed from the high-low method or regression analysis (discussed in Chapter 4 and its appendix).
5. Sales and production are equal; thus there is no material fluctuation in inventory levels. This assumption is necessary because otherwise fixed costs might be allocated to inventory at different rates each year. The assumption is more realistic as more companies begin to use just-in-time inventory systems.
6. There will be no capacity additions during the period under consideration. If such additions were made, fixed (and possibly variable) costs would change. Any changes in fixed or variable costs would invalidate assumptions 1–3.
7. In a multiproduct firm, the sales mix will remain constant. If this assumption were not made, no useful weighted average contribution margin could be computed for the company for purposes of CVP analysis.
8. There is no inflation, or inflation affects all cost factors equally, or, if factors are affected unequally, the appropriate effects are incorporated into the CVP figures.
9. Labor productivity, production technology, and market conditions will not change. If any of these factors changed, costs would change correspondingly, and it is possible that selling prices would change. Such changes would invalidate assumptions 1–3.

These nine premises are the traditional assumptions associated with cost-volume-profit analysis and reflect a basic disregard of possible (and probable) future changes. Accountants have generally assumed that cost behavior, once classified, remained constant over periods of time as long as operations remained within the relevant range and in the absence of evidence to the contrary. Thus, for example, once a cost was determined to be fixed, it would be fixed next year, the year after, and from then on.

As mentioned in Chapter 5, however, it may be more realistic to regard fixed costs as long-term variable costs. Companies can, over the long run and through managerial decisions, lay off supervisors and sell plant and equipment items. Alternatively, companies may grow and increase their fixed investments in people, plant and equipment. Fixed costs are not fixed forever. In many companies, some costs considered to be fixed "have been the most variable and rapidly increasing costs."[2] Part of this cost "misclassification" problem has occurred because of improper specification of cost drivers. As companies become less focused on production and sales volumes as cost drivers, they will begin to recognize that fixed costs only exist under a short-term reporting period perspective.

In addition, certain costs may arise that are variable in the first year of providing a product or service to a customer but will not recur in future years. Differing current and future period costs are very important concerns in various service businesses. Getting new customers requires a variety of one-time costs for things such as advertising, mailing, and checking customers' credit histories. As companies and customers become more familiar with one another, services can be provided more

---

[2]Robin Cooper and Robert S. Kaplan, "How Cost Accounting Distorts Product Costs," *Management Accounting* (April 1988), p. 27.

efficiently or higher prices can be charged for the trusted relationship. Failure to consider such changes in costs can provide a very distorted picture of how profits are generated and, therefore, can lead to an improper analysis of the relationships of costs, volume, and profits.

COSTS AND QUALITY

While cost, price, and volume are the three major factors in determining a company's profits, it is necessary to recognize that these three factors work hand in hand with a fourth factor—quality. High-quality products are typically able to command higher selling prices, and often sales volume increases simply through quality recognition. For example, a substantial part of the popularity of Seiko and Coca-Cola is quality-based. Quality improvements are especially important for companies that wish to compete in export markets.

Achieving higher quality, however, will affect costs. Some costs may decline because products or parts are redesigned to simplify processing or standardize components. Other costs may increase. Some of the increasing costs may be variable (such as costs for higher-grade materials and components, training courses for employees, and preventive maintenance), while others (such as costs of supplier certification programs, computer-integrated machines to better monitor quality, and implementation of quality-circle programs) may be treated as fixed or long-term variable costs.

It would seem that the costs of ensuring quality should, in the long run, outweigh the costs of having poor quality. At Rogar International, controlling costs does not simply mean obtaining the lowest cost. For instance, significant variable and fixed costs are incurred for training employees, educating the company's distributors about corporate products, purchasing state-of-the-art equipment that improves product quality, and investing in the community in which the company operates. While such practices may create higher variable and fixed costs currently, they lower other costs (such as those attributable to rework, redesign, and product failure). Thus, company management is well aware of the adage, "You get what you pay for."

Breakeven point and the volume levels needed to achieve desired profits do not necessarily increase as a result of quality-enhancing measures. It may be possible to charge higher selling prices for a high-quality product and thus maintain a constant contribution margin. And even if the BEP volume levels do rise, these levels may be

LEARNING OBJECTIVE ⑤
How do quality decisions affect the components of CVP analysis?

http:// www.seiko-usa-ecd.com

http:// www.cocacola.com

World-class companies strive to ensure that their quality endeavors are enduring—unlike names written in the sand on a beach.

more attainable because of the higher quality of the products. All in all, considering the implications of quality changes for cost, price, and volume should help focus managers' attention more on the long run and less on the short run.

ANALYZING EFFECTS OF SHORT-RUN OPERATIONAL CHANGES

Accounting information can improve, but not perfect, management's understanding of the consequences of resource allocation decisions. To the extent that this information can reduce management's uncertainty about the economic facts, outcomes, and relationships involved in various courses of action, the information is valuable for decision-making purposes and necessary for conducting business.

Many decisions are made on the basis of incremental analysis. Such analysis encompasses the concept of relevant costing, which allows managers to focus on pertinent facts and disregard extraneous information. This chapter illustrates the use of relevant costing in decisions about allocating scarce resources, determining the appropriate sales or production mix, and product line decisions. While these decisions are often viewed by managers as short-run, each decision also has significant long-run implications that must be considered.

THE CONCEPTS OF RELEVANCE AND RELEVANT COSTING

relevant cost

Managers routinely make decisions concerning alternatives that have been identified as feasible solutions to problems or feasible methods for the attainment of objectives. In doing so, they must weigh the relevant costs and benefits associated with each course of action and then determine the best course. **Relevant costs** are those costs that are pertinent to or logically associated with a specific problem or decision and that differ between alternatives.

LEARNING OBJECTIVE ⑥
What constitutes relevance in a decision-making situation?

Information is relevant when it logically relates to a decision about a future endeavor. Costs provide information, and different costs can be used for many different purposes. No single cost can be relevant in all decisions or to all managers. Two general rules for short-run decision making are that (1) most variable costs are relevant and (2) most fixed costs are not. The reasoning behind this rule is that, as sales or production volume change, variable costs change but fixed costs do not. As with most general rules, though, there are some exceptions that must be acknowledged in the decision-making process.

relevant costing

Accountants can assist managers in determining which costs are relevant to the objectives and decisions at hand. To the extent possible and practical, **relevant costing** allows managers to focus on pertinent facts and disregard extraneous information by comparing the differential, incremental revenues and costs of alternative decisions. *Differential* refers to the different costs between or among the choices. *Incremental* means the additional or extra amount associated with some action. Thus, **incremental revenue** is the additional revenue resulting from a contemplated sale or provision of service. An **incremental cost** is the additional cost of producing or selling a contemplated additional quantity of output.

incremental revenue
incremental cost

Differential and, therefore, incremental costs are relevant costs. These costs may be variable or fixed. For example, the direct material cost of a product is a relevant incremental variable cost in a decision to make each additional unit. In contrast, the fixed cost of the available production machinery would not be relevant to the production of each additional unit. However, the cost of buying new machinery is an incremental fixed cost relevant to the decision to produce a new product line or expand an existing one beyond the current relevant range.

Some relevant costs, such as sales commissions and the prime costs of production (direct material and direct labor), are easily identified and quantified. These factors are integral parts of the accounting system. Other factors (such as opportunity costs) may be relevant and quantifiable but are not recorded in the accounting system. (An **opportunity cost** represents the benefits foregone when one course of action is chosen over another. For example, by choosing to attend college a student incurs an opportunity cost of the foregone earnings that he or she could have made by spending his/her time at a paying job instead.) Such factors cannot be overlooked simply because they may be more difficult to obtain or may require the use of estimates.

opportunity cost

The difference between the incremental revenue and incremental cost of a particular alternative is the positive or negative incremental benefit of that course of action. When evaluating alternative courses of action, managers should select the alternative that provides the highest incremental benefit to the company. Such a comparison may superficially appear simple but often is not, because relevance is a concept that is inherently individual. For example, an investment proposal might provide a high rate of return for a company but might also create a future potential environmental hazard. One unit manager might view the potential hazard as very relevant, while another manager might minimize the relevance of that possibility. In some instances, all alternatives result in incremental losses, and managers must choose the one that creates the smallest incremental loss.

One alternative course of action often considered is defensive avoidance, or the "change nothing for the moment" option. While other alternatives have certain incremental revenues and costs associated with them, the change nothing alternative represents current conditions. It may serve as a baseline against which all other alternatives can be measured. However, even the change nothing alternative may involve the risk of loss of competitive advantage. If a firm chooses this alternative while its competitors upgrade processes, that firm may incur the ultimate incremental loss—losing its market. Also, the opportunity costs associated with the status quo may result in less benefit than another alternative.

The change nothing alternative should be chosen only when it is perceived to be the best decision choice. Often, however, this alternative is selected only because it is easier than making changes. At other times, this selection is made because decision makers, lacking information, perceive uncertainty to be so great that they consider the risk of making a change to be greater than the risk of continuing the current course of action. When this condition exists, the results achieved from the change nothing alternative (current results) are thought to be more advantageous than the potential incremental benefit of any other alternative.

In some situations, such as those involving government regulations or mandates, a change nothing alternative does not truly exist. For example, if a company were polluting river water and a governmental regulatory agency issued an injunction against that company, it (assuming it wished to continue in business) would be forced to correct the pollution problem. The company could, of course, delay installation of the pollution control devices at the risk of fines or closure—creating additional incremental cost effects that would have to be considered. Managers in this situation must make decisions using a now-versus-later attitude and may determine that now is better regardless of the cost.

Since a comprehensive evaluation of all alternative courses of action is part of rational management behavior, the chosen course should be the one that will make the business and its stakeholders better off in the future. This means that managers must provide some mechanism for including all nonmonetary or inherently non-quantifiable considerations in the decision process. They can do that by attempting to quantify items or simply by making instinctive value judgments about nonmonetary benefits and costs.

To illustrate this point, consider the factors that should be evaluated when a labor-intensive company analyzes the labor savings that would result from replacing employees with robots or, as discussed in the News Note below, by changing locales. Company managers need to weigh potential future cost reductions and increases in productivity against possible short- and long-range negative public reaction toward the company because of the layoffs. Although public reactions are difficult to measure and quantify and may not be immediately noticeable, such reactions should still be factored into the decision. In addition, there may be very relevant but highly nonquantifiable costs resulting from ethical considerations, such as the moral obligations the firm has toward the displaced workers. Such costs must be estimated in a reasonable manner if the decision to replace workers is to be based on a truly valid analysis.

The need for specificity in information depends on how important that information is relative to management objectives. If all other factors are equal, more precise information is given greater weight in the decision-making process. However, if information is important but qualitative and imprecise, management should find a way to estimate the impact such information may have on known, monetary details and company profits.

Information can be based on past or present data but is relevant only if it relates to a future choice and creates a differential effect in regard to alternative choices. All managerial decisions are made to affect future events, so the information on which decisions are based should reflect future conditions. The future may be the short run (two hours from now or next month) or the long run (five years or more from now).[3]

Future costs are the only costs that can be avoided, and the longer into the future a decision's time horizon extends, the more costs are avoidable, controllable, and relevant. *Only information that has a bearing on future events is relevant in decision making.* But people too often forget this basic truth and try to make decisions using inappropriate data.

NEWS NOTE

Yankee Shoes in the Caribbean

Charles Lindbergh was wearing Bass shoes from Maine when he flew across the Atlantic, and Hollywood legend James Dean made Bass footwear a fashion statement with his rolled-up jeans and white T-shirt.

 www.ghbass.com

For 122 years, G.H. Bass and Co. has boasted of New England quality and durability while evoking images of Maine's rugged wilderness. That history will come to an end soon, leaving hundreds of people to pick up the pieces and recall a time when shoemaking was king in Maine.

The company will move the manufacturing operations to factories in Puerto Rico and the Dominican Republic, far from the Yankees who made the shoes popular. The Wilton, Maine, factory was Bass's only plant in the continental United States.

Closing the mill and consolidating some of its warehouses will save New York's Phillips-Van Heusen (Bass's parent company), which also owns Izod and Gant, about $40 million in the next three years, Chairman Bruce Klatsky said.

Charles Colgan, professor of public policy and management at the University of Southern Maine, said that with lowered tariffs, a strong dollar, and weak foreign currencies, "the result was that foreign shoes got much cheaper."

SOURCE: The Associated Press, "Bass Shoes to Leave U.S.," *Wall Street Journal,* February 8, 1998, p. F-2. Reprinted with permission of the Associated Press.

---

[3]Short-run decisions typically focus on a measure of accounting income that excludes some past costs, such as depreciation on old assets. Long-range decision analysis commonly uses cash flow as its decision criterion; this topic is covered in Chapter 8.

One common error is trying to use a previously incurred, historical cost to make a current decision. Costs incurred in the past to acquire an asset or a resource—called **sunk costs**—are not recoverable and cannot be changed, regardless of what current circumstances exist or what future course of action is taken. A current or future selling price may be present for an asset, but that is the result of current or future conditions and is not a recouping of an historical cost.

sunk cost

RELEVANT COSTS IN SCARCE RESOURCE DECISIONS

Managers are frequently confronted with the short-run problem of making the best use of **scarce resources** that are essential to production activity but are available only in limited quantity. Scarce resources create constraints on producing goods or providing services. These resources may include money, machine hours, skilled labor hours, raw materials, and production capacity. In the long run, management may desire and be able to obtain a greater abundance of a scarce resource—for example, by purchasing additional machines to increase availability of machine hours. However, in the short run, management must make the best current use of the scarce resources it has.

scarce resource

Determining the best use of a scarce resource requires that specific company objectives be recognized. If management's objective is to maximize company contribution margin and profits, the best use of a scarce resource is for the production and sale of the product that has the highest contribution margin per unit of the scarce resource. This strategy assumes that the company is faced with only one scarce resource.

LEARNING OBJECTIVE ❼
How can management best utilize a scarce resource?

Exhibit 6-7 presents information on two products made by Better Homes Products on its plastic molding machines. Better Homes Products, which produces a variety of kitchen and serving products, is a wholly owned subsidiary of Better Homes Ice Buckets (a separate company presented earlier in the chapter). Better Homes Products has only 4,000 machine hours available per month to make plastic housings for ice crushers, juice extractors, or some combination of both. Demand is unlimited for both products. Assume there are no variable selling, general, or administrative costs related to either product.

The ice crusher's $15 unit selling price minus its $10 unit variable cost provides a contribution margin of $5 per unit. The juice extractor's contribution margin per unit is $6 ($12 − $6). Fixed overhead totals $160,000 and is allocated to products on a machine hour basis for purposes of inventory valuation. However, fixed overhead does not change with production levels within the relevant range and, therefore, is not a relevant cost for a decision on scarce resource mix.

Since fixed overhead per unit is not relevant in the present case, unit contribution margin rather than unit gross margin is the appropriate measure of profitability of the two products. Unit contribution margin is multiplied by the number of units of output per unit of the scarce resource (in this case, machine hours) to obtain the

	ICE CRUSHER	JUICE EXTRACTOR
Selling price per unit (*a*)	$ 15	$ 12
Variable production cost per unit:		
Direct material	$ 3	$ 3
Direct labor	4	2
Variable overhead	3	1
Total variable cost per unit (*b*)	(10)	(6)
Unit contribution margin [(*c*) = (*a*) − (*b*)]	$ 5	$ 6
Units of output per machine hour (*d*)	× 30	× 20
Contribution margin per machine hour [(*c*) × (*d*)]	$150	$120

EXHIBIT 6-7
Scarce Resource—
Machine Hours

contribution margin per unit of scarce resource. The last line in Exhibit 6-7 shows contribution margins per machine hour of $150 ($5 × 30) for ice crushers compared with $120 ($6 × 20) for juice extractors. Ice crushers are the more profitable items for Better Homes Products to produce.

At first, it would appear that juice extractors would be more profitable, since their $6 unit contribution margin is higher than the $5 unit contribution margin for ice crushers. However, since one hour of machine time produces one-and-one-half as many ice crushers as juice extractors, a greater amount of contribution margin per hour of scarce resource is generated by the production of ice crushers. If Better Homes Products wanted to achieve the highest possible profit, it would dedicate all machine time to the production of ice crushers. If all units produced were sold, this strategy would provide a total contribution margin of $600,000 per month.

linear programming

When one limiting factor is involved, the outcome of a scarce resource decision will always indicate that a single type of product should be manufactured and sold. Most situations, though, involve several limiting factors that compete with one another. One method used to solve problems that have several limiting factors is **linear programming**. Analysts use this method to find the optimal allocation of scarce resources when there is one objective and multiple restrictions on achieving that objective.[4]

Managers must be concerned about the quantitative effects of scarcity of resources, but they must also remember that not all factors involved in the decision alternatives can be readily quantified. Company management must consider qualitative aspects of the problem in addition to quantitative ones. For example, to achieve the maximum possible profit, Better Homes Products would have to produce only ice crushers during the available time on the molding machines. Before choosing such a strategy, managers would need to assess the potential damage to the company's reputation and image from limiting its market assortment of products by providing one product to the exclusion of another. Concentrating on a single product might also create market saturation and cause future sales to decline.

Other situations can also make providing multiple products desirable: the products may be complementary (serving sets and silver polish), one product may not be usable without the other (razors and razor blades), or one product may be the key to high revenue generation in future periods. To illustrate the latter possibility, consider **Mattel, Inc.**, the producer of Barbie dolls. Would it be reasonable for Mattel to produce only Barbie dolls and none of the related accessories (clothes, dream house, car, camper, and so forth)? While the sale of Barbie dolls is profitable, the income flow from the total group of Barbie products is enormous.

http:// www.service.mattel.com

Not-for-profit entities are constantly faced with the issue of scarce resources. In putting on this 5K Race for the Cure in Dallas, scarce resources include money, space, volunteers . . . but not participants!

---

[4]Linear programming is briefly discussed in Appendix 3 to this chapter and is covered in depth in most management science courses.

For all of the above reasons, management may decide that some less profitable products are necessary components in the company's product mix. Production mix translates into sales mix on the revenue side. The next section addresses the issue of sales mix.

RELEVANT COSTS IN SALES MIX AND SALES PRICE DECISIONS

Management continuously strives to satisfy a variety of company goals such as maximization of company profit, improvement of relative market share, and generation of customer goodwill and loyalty. These goals are achieved through selling products or performing services. Regardless of whether the company is a retailer, manufacturer, or service organization, **sales mix** refers to "the relative combination of quantities of sales of the various products that make up the total sales of a company."[5] One way a company can achieve its goals is to manage its sales mix effectively. Some important factors affecting the appropriate sales mix are product selling prices and advertising expenditures. A change in one or both of these factors may cause a company's sales mix to shift. The Better Homes Products data presented in Exhibit 6-8 are used to illustrate the effects on sales mix of these factors. In addition to plastic housings, the company produces three types of kitchen appliances.

LEARNING OBJECTIVE 8
What is the relationship between sales mix and relevant costing problems?

sales mix

Sales Price Changes and Relative Profitability of Products

Managers must continuously monitor the selling prices of company products, in relation to each other as well as to competitors' prices. This process may provide information that causes management to change one or more selling prices. For example, if Better Homes Products found that microwave ovens sold better at the beginning of the year than at other times, it might increase the sales price of them during this period. Factors that might influence price changes include fluctuations in demand, production/distribution costs, economic conditions, and competition. Any shift in the selling price of one product in a multiproduct firm will normally cause a change in the sales mix of that firm because of the economic law of demand elasticity with respect to price.[6]

	BLENDER	FOOD PROCESSOR	MICROWAVE OVEN
Unit selling price	$50.00	$65.00	$75.00
Variable unit costs:			
Direct material	$ 7.00	$10.00	$19.00
Direct labor	5.00	8.00	15.00
Variable factory overhead	2.00	3.00	8.00
Total variable production cost	$14.00	$21.00	$42.00
Variable selling expense*	5.00	6.50	7.50
Total variable cost	(19.00)	(27.50)	(49.50)
Contribution margin per unit	$31.00	$37.50	$25.50

*The only variable selling expense is a sales commission, which is always 10% of unit selling price.

EXHIBIT 6-8
Product Information for Various Sales Mix Decisions

---

[5]Institute of Management Accountants (formerly National Association of Accountants), *Statements on Management Accounting Number 2: Management Accounting Terminology* (Montvale, N.J.: National Association of Accountants, June 1, 1983), p. 94.

[6]The law of demand elasticity indicates how closely price and demand are related. Product demand is highly elastic if a small price reduction generates a large demand increase. If demand is less elastic, large price reductions are needed to bring about moderate sales volume increases.

LEARNING OBJECTIVE ⑨
How can pricing decisions be
used to maximize profit?

Better Homes Products' management has set profit maximization as the primary corporate goal. This strategy does not necessarily mean selling as many units as possible of products with the highest selling prices and as few as possible of products with lower selling prices. The product with the highest selling price per unit does not necessarily yield the highest contribution margin per unit or per unit of scarce resource. In Better Homes Products' case, microwave ovens yield the lowest unit contribution margin of the three products. The microwave oven also requires more direct labor cost and machine time, given that variable overhead is applied on a machine hour basis. But even making the simplistic assumption that no resources are scarce, it is more profit-beneficial to sell food processors than either blenders or microwave ovens, since a food processor provides the highest unit contribution margin of the three products. Even a blender is more profitable than a microwave oven, because, although the blender has the lowest unit selling price, its unit contribution margin is greater than that of the microwave oven.

Unit contribution margin and sales volume should be considered together when profitability is evaluated. Total company contribution margin is equal to the combined contribution margins provided by all the products' sales. Exhibit 6-9 indicates the respective total contribution margins of Better Homes Products' three types of appliances. While the blenders do not have the highest unit contribution margin, they do generate the largest total product line contribution margin because of their sales volume. To maximize profits, Better Homes Products' management must maximize total contribution margin rather than per-unit contribution margin.

The sales volume of a product or service is usually directly related to its selling price. When selling price is increased and demand is elastic with respect to price, demand for that good decreases.[7] Thus, if Better Homes Products management, in an attempt to increase profits, decides to raise the price of the blenders to $60, there should be some decline in demand. Assume that consultation with marketing research personnel indicates that such a price increase would cause demand for the product to drop from 20,000 to 12,000 blenders per period. Exhibit 6-10 shows the effect of this pricing decision on total contribution margin.

Even though the contribution margin per unit of the blenders increased from $31 to $40, the total dollar contribution margin generated by sales of the product has declined because of the decrease in sales volume. This example assumes that customers did not switch their purchases from blenders to other Better Homes Products appliances when the price of the blender was raised. Price increases normally cause customers to switch from a company's high-priced products to its lower-priced products or to a competitor's product. In this instance, switching within the company was ignored because none of the other products is a perfect substitute for blenders. It is *unlikely* that customers would stop buying blenders because of a $10 price increase and begin buying food processors that cost even more.

In making decisions to raise or lower prices, the relevant quantitative factors include (1) prospective or new contribution margin per unit of product, (2) both short-

EXHIBIT 6-9

Relationship between
Contribution Margin and
Sales Volume

	UNIT CONTRIBUTION MARGIN (FROM EXHIBIT 6-8)	CURRENT SALES VOLUME IN UNITS	TOTAL
Blenders	$31.00	20,000	$ 620,000
Food Processors	$37.50	13,000	487,500
Microwave Ovens	$25.50	8,000	204,000
Total contribution margin of product sales mix			$1,311,500

[7]Such a decline in demand generally does not occur when the product in question has no close substitutes or is not a major expenditure in consumers' budgets.

	UNIT CONTRIBUTION MARGIN	NEW SALES VOLUME IN UNITS	TOTAL
Blenders	$40.00*	12,000	$ 480,000
Food Processors	$37.50	13,000	487,500
Microwave Ovens	$25.50	8,000	204,000
Total contribution margin of product sales mix			$1,171,500

*Calculated as:

New selling price	$60
Total variable production cost (from Exhibit 6-8)	(14)
Total variable selling expense (10% of selling price)	(6)
Contribution margin	$40

EXHIBIT 6-10
Relationship between Sales Price and Demand

term and long-term changes in product demand and production volume caused by the price increase or decrease, and (3) best use of any scarce resources. Some relevant qualitative factors involved in decisions regarding price changes are (1) influence on customer goodwill, (2) customer product loyalty, and (3) competitors' reactions.

When deciding to change the price of current products or to introduce new products that will compete with current products and may affect their sales volumes, managers need to be certain that their assumptions about consumer behavior are rational. Comparisons are typically made against a base case scenario, which estimates how consumers will behave if no new projects are carried out. "Often companies implicitly assume that the base case is simply a continuation of the status quo, but this assumption ignores market trends and competitor behavior. Using the wrong base case is typical of product launches in which the new product will likely erode the market for the company's existing product line."[8] Failure to diversify as product demand for current products and services wanes can be costly. The News Note on page 250 makes such a point.

Special Order Pricing

In **special order pricing**, management must determine a sales price to charge for manufacturing or service jobs that are outside the company's normal production or service realm. Special order situations include jobs that require a bid, are taken during slack periods, or are made to a specific buyer's specifications. Typically, the sales price quoted on a special order job should be high enough to cover the variable costs of the job, any incremental (additional) fixed costs caused by the job, and to generate a profit. Special order pricing requires knowledge of the relevant costs associated with the specific problem or decision at hand.

Better Homes Products has been given the opportunity to bid on a special order for 1,000 food processors. Company management wants to obtain the order as long as the additional sale will provide a satisfactory contribution to profit. The company has machine and labor hours that are not currently being used, and raw materials can be obtained from the supplier. Also, Better Homes Products has no immediate opportunity to use its current excess capacity in another way, so an opportunity cost is not a factor.

The information necessary to determine a bid price on the food processor is presented in Exhibit 6-8 (page 247). Direct material, direct labor, and variable factory overhead costs are relevant to setting the bid price because these variable production costs will be incurred for each additional food processor manufactured. While all variable costs are normally relevant to a special pricing decision, the variable selling expense is

special order pricing

---

[8]In regard to this last item, consider what occurs when one airline raises or lowers its fares between cities. It typically does not take very long for all the other airlines flying that route to adjust their fares accordingly. Thus, competitive advantage often exists only for a short time.

NEWS NOTE

Misjudgment Kills a Monument Company

In 1990 a new owner with little or no experience in the industry bought Apperson & Dent, a monument-carving company in Alexandria, Va. But the venture was doomed from the start. Although the funeral industry has thrived over the past six years, demand for upright markers from the country's three thousand or so monument-carving shops has slowed in the past decade.

One factor contributing to that decline is cemetery consolidation. The large management companies that are buying up small cemeteries slash maintenance costs by installing markers flush to the ground. The three largest cemeteries in Alexandria mandate flat markers. It's not surprising, then, that sales of flat marble and cast bronze markers are what's growing. But Apperson & Dent didn't diversify into that market. And the company's revenues, which in the mid-1980s had reached as high as $400,000, dwindled as cemeteries started selling their own monuments, some adding "installation" fees of up to $500 if customers purchased monuments elsewhere.

Company management made several unfortunate decisions, including the outsourcing of low-margin work. That move—outsourcing of some of the work—proved fatal, as complaints about poor work began pouring in. After too many complaints about unfinished work, Arlington National Cemetery finally quit referring customers to Apperson & Dent in 1995. In October 1996 Apperson & Dent filed for bankruptcy.

SOURCE: Reprinted with permission of *Inc.* magazine, Goldhirsh Group, Inc., 38 Commercial Wharf, Boston, MA 02110. "Monument Co. Misjudges Funeral Industry, Pays with Its Life," Phaedra Hise (January 1997), p. 17 (http://www.inc.com). Reproduced by permission of the publisher via Copyright Clearance Center, Inc.

irrelevant in this instance because no sales commission will be paid on this sale. Fixed production overhead and fixed selling and administrative expenses are not expected to increase because of this sale, so these expenses are not included in the pricing decision.

Using the available cost information, the relevant cost used to determine the bid price for the food processor is $21 (direct material, direct labor, and variable overhead). This cost is the minimum special order price at which the company should sell a food processor. If the existing fixed costs have been covered by regular sales, any price set higher than $21 will provide the company some profit.

Assume that Better Homes Products is currently experiencing a $5,000 net loss. Company managers want to set a bid price that would cover the net loss generated by other sales and create a $2,000 before-tax profit. In this case, Better Homes Products would spread the total $7,000 desired amount over the 1,000 food processors at $7 per food processor. This would give a bid price of $28 per food processor ($21 variable cost + $7). However, any price above the $21 variable cost will contribute toward reducing the $5,000 loss.

In setting the bid price, management must decide how much profit it would consider reasonable on the special order. As another example, since Better Homes Product's usual selling price for a food processor is $65, each sale provides a normal contribution margin of $37.50 or approximately 58 percent. Setting the bid price for the special order at $50.00 would cover the variable production costs of $21 and provide a normal 58 percent contribution margin. This computation illustrates a simplistic cost-plus approach to pricing, but ignores both product demand and market competition. Better Homes Products' bid price should also reflect the latter considerations. In addition, company management should consider the effect that the special order will have on all company activities (for example, purchasing, receiving, and warehousing) and whether these activities will create additional, unforeseen costs.

There are situations in which a company will depart from its typical price-setting routine. For example, a company may low-ball bid some jobs. A low-ball bid may only cover variable costs or it may be below such costs. The rationale behind making low-ball bids is to obtain the job in order to introduce company products or services to a particular market segment. Another special pricing concession may also be justi- fied when orders are of an unusual nature (because of the quantity, method of deliv- ery, or packaging) or because the products are being tailor-made to customer instructions. Further, special pricing can be used when producing goods for a one- time job, such as an overseas order that will not affect domestic sales.

Advertising Budget Changes

Another factor that may cause shifts in the sales mix involves either increasing the total company advertising budget or reallocating the budget among the products the company sells. This discussion uses the original sales mix data for Better Homes Prod- ucts (Exhibit 6-8, page 247) and examines a proposed increase in the company's total advertising budget.

Better Homes Products' advertising manager, George Smith, has proposed dou- bling the advertising budget from $15,000 to $30,000 per year. George thinks the in- creased advertising will result in the following additional unit sales during the coming year: blenders, 200; food processors, 500; and microwave ovens, 100.

If the company spends the additional $15,000 for advertising, will the additional 800 units of sales raise profits? The original fixed costs as well as the contribution margin generated by the old sales level are irrelevant to the decision. The relevant items are the increased sales revenue, increased variable costs, and increased fixed cost—the incremental effects of the change. The difference between incremental rev- enues and incremental variable costs is the incremental contribution margin. The in- cremental contribution margin minus the incremental fixed cost is the incremental benefit (or loss) resulting from the decision.

Exhibit 6-11 shows how the increased advertising expenditures are expected to affect contribution margin. The $27,500 of additional contribution margin far ex- ceeds the $15,000 incremental cost for advertising, so Better Homes Products should definitely increase its advertising budget by $15,000.

RELEVANT COSTS IN PRODUCT LINE DECISIONS

To facilitate performance evaluations, operating results in multiproduct environ- ments are often presented in terms of separate product lines. In reviewing these disaggregated statements, managers must distinguish relevant from irrelevant infor- mation for each product line. If all costs (variable and fixed) are allocated to product lines, a product line or segment may be perceived to be operating at a loss when ac- tually it is not. Such perceptions may be caused by the commingling of relevant and irrelevant information on the statements.

In addition to its Better Homes Products subsidiary, Better Homes Ice Buckets also owns a Cooking Products Division which makes a variety of kitchen products. Ex- hibit 6-12 presents earnings information for the Cooking Products Division's three most popular product lines: electric skillets, convection ovens, and steamers. The format

	BLENDERS	FOOD PROCESSORS	MICROWAVE OVENS	TOTAL
Increase in volume	200	500	100	800
Contribution margin per unit	× $ 31	× $ 37.50	× $25.50	
Incremental contribution margin	$6,200	$18,750	$2,550	$27,500
Incremental fixed cost of advertising				(15,000)
Incremental benefit of increased advertising expenditure				$12,500

EXHIBIT 6-11
Incremental Analysis of Increasing Advertising Cost

EXHIBIT 6-12
Product Line Income Statement

	ELECTRIC SKILLETS	CONVECTION OVENS	STEAMERS	TOTAL
Sales	$75,000	$42,500	$190,000	$307,500
Total direct variable costs	(43,750)	(27,625)	(114,000)	(185,375)
Total contribution margin	$31,250	$14,875	$ 76,000	$122,125
Total fixed costs*	(39,500)	(17,500)	(38,000)	(95,000)
Profit before tax	$ (8,250)	$ (2,625)	$ 38,000	$ 27,125
*Total fixed costs:				
(1) Avoidable fixed costs	$25,000	$16,000	$ 24,000	$ 65,000
(2) Unavoidable fixed costs	4,500	500	3,000	8,000
(3) Allocated common costs	10,000	1,000	11,000	22,000
Total	$39,500	$17,500	$ 38,000	$ 95,000

of the information at the top of the exhibit makes it appear that the electric skillet and convection oven lines are operating at a net loss ($8,250 and $2,625, respectively). Managers reviewing such results might reason that the Cooking Products Division would be $10,875 ($8,250 + $2,625) more profitable if both of these products were eliminated. This conclusion may be premature, however, because of the mixture of relevant and irrelevant information in the income statement presentation. This problem results from the fact that *all* fixed costs have been allocated to the individual product lines.

Fixed cost allocations are traditionally based on one or more measures that are presumed to provide an "equitable" division of costs. These measures might include square footage of the manufacturing plant occupied by each product line, number of machine hours incurred for production of each product line, or number of employees directly associated with each product line. Regardless of the allocation base, allocations may *force* fixed costs into specific product line operating results even though those costs may not have actually been caused by the making or selling of the product line. This inequity results from the fact that most cost allocation schemes currently used by managers are arbitrary.

The detail in Exhibit 6-12 separates the Cooking Products Division's fixed costs into three categories: (1) those that could be avoided by elimination of the product line; (2) those that are directly associated with the product line but are unavoidable; and (3) those that are incurred for the division as a whole (**common costs**) and allocated to the individual product lines. The latter two categories are irrelevant to the question of whether to eliminate a product line.

common cost

An unavoidable cost will be shifted to another product line if the product line with which it is associated is eliminated. For example, the division has several senior employees who work in the electric skillet area. If that product line were eliminated, those employees would be transferred to the convection oven or steamer area. Similarly, depreciation on factory equipment used to manufacture a specific product is an irrelevant cost in product line decisions. If the equipment will be kept in service and used to produce other products, the depreciation expense on it is unavoidable. However, if the equipment can be sold, the *selling price* is relevant because it would increase the marginal benefit of a decision to discontinue the product line.

As to common costs, they will be incurred regardless of which product lines are retained. One example of a common cost is the insurance premium on a manufacturing facility that houses all product lines.

product margin

If the division eliminated both electric skillets and convection ovens, its total profit would decline by $5,125. This amount represents the combined lost **product margin** of the two product lines, shown in Exhibit 6-13. Product margin represents the excess of revenues over direct variable costs and avoidable fixed costs. It is the amount remaining to cover unavoidable direct fixed costs and common costs and

EXHIBIT 6-13
Product Line Income Statement

	ELECTRIC SKILLETS	CONVECTION OVENS	STEAMERS	TOTAL
Sales	$75,000	$42,500	$190,000	$307,500
Total direct variable cost	(43,750)	(27,625)	(114,000)	(185,375)
Product contribution margin	$31,250	$14,875	$ 76,000	$122,125
(1) Avoidable fixed cost	(25,000)	(16,000)	(24,000)	(65,000)
Product margin	$ 6,250	$(1,125)	$ 52,000	$ 57,125
(2) Unavoidable direct fixed cost (see Exhibit 6-12)				(8,000)
Product line operating results				$ 49,125
(3) Common cost				(22,000)
Profit before tax				$ 27,125

LEARNING OBJECTIVE 10
How can product margin be used to determine whether a product line should be retained or eliminated?

then to provide profits.[9] The product margin is the appropriate figure on which to base a decision to continue or eliminate a product, since that figure measures the product's ability to help cover indirect and unavoidable costs. For the Cooking Products Division, the decrease in total before-tax profit from eliminating both electric skillets and convection ovens can be shown in the following alternative computations:

Current before-tax profit	$27,125
Increase in profit due to elimination of convection oven product line (product margin)	1,125
Decrease in profit due to elimination of electric skillet product line (product margin)	(6,250)
New before-tax profit	$22,000

or

Product contribution margin of steamer line	$76,000
Minus avoidable fixed expenses of steamer line	(24,000)
Product margin of the steamer line	$52,000
Minus all remaining expenses shown on Exhibit 6-13 ($8,000 + $22,000)	(30,000)
Remaining profit with one product line	$22,000

Based on the quantitative information in Exhibit 6-13, the Cooking Products Division should eliminate only the convection oven line. That product line is generating a negative product margin and thus is not even covering its own costs. If that product line were eliminated, total divisional profit would increase by $1,125, the amount of the negative product margin. Before making decisions to discontinue a product line or sell off a segment, management should also carefully consider what it would take to turn that product line or division around.

The other decision relative to product lines is expansion or extension. Expansion refers to the introduction of totally new products. Extension refers to the introduction of offshoots of current products because the company decides that the market needs to be more highly segmented. The segmentation might focus on price, size, operating costs, or aesthetics issues; alternatively, extensions may be necessary to meet competitive pressures.

Extensions have often been viewed as fairly low-cost endeavors—especially if a company has excess capacity. However, sometimes unanticipated incremental costs of expansions and extensions (other than the variable costs of the product) become necessary; these costs include market research, product and packaging development, product introduction, and advertising.

---

[9]It is assumed here that all common costs are fixed costs; this is not always the case. Some common costs are variable, such as costs of processing purchase orders and computer time-sharing costs for payroll or other corporate functions.

SITE ANALYSIS

Rogar International Corporation

The U.S. Chamber of Commerce accorded Rogar International (RIC) the "Blue Chip Award" for 1997 as one of four companies in Virginia that had overcome extreme adversity. RIC sells only wholesale directly to approximately 1,600 retailers in the USA. The company also sells to distributors in six foreign countries. Based in large part on the company's reputation for value, RIC achieved a sales volume of $3 million in 1997 and estimates $4.25 million for 1998.

Although some of RIC's product line is capital intensive, most is labor intensive. Labor cost is the most important cost to contain at Rogar. Unless counted and monitored on a daily basis, productivity can suffer and unit costs can elevate.

Another key variable in company success is prompt delivery. RIC management believes that a company either delivers on time or is not used. This is especially true for giant retailers like Wal-Mart and Target. When a small company sells to one of the very large customers, it must have a plan for increasing production quickly and the capital required to put the plan in action. If one of the large retailers wants more product because they underestimated the sales demand, a company must ship on time or its vendor number becomes inactive.

Management believes that any small business that does not continually analyze cost behavior is a disaster waiting to happen. The biggest threat to a small business is the lack of capital to overcome adversity. Problems are continuously occurring and it takes both intellectual and economic resources to solve them. Today, Rogar International Corporation has grown to thirty-two employees and produces over a hundred types of products for its customers. The company plans to grow to $5 million in revenue within twenty-four months. Rogar is financially strong and plans for market expansion and new products.

SOURCE: Information provided by Bob Crist of Rogar International Corporation of Richmond, Virginia, 1998.

CROSS-FUNCTIONAL APPLICATIONS

TOPIC OF NOTE	DISCIPLINE	CROSS-FUNCTIONAL APPLICATIONS
Cost-Volume-Profit Analysis (CVP)	Marketing	In a competitive environment, especially for price sensitive products, CVP analysis guides market researchers in decisions involving pricing policies, promotional strategies, and product line assortment. Pricing policies can be a decisive competitive advantage; however, the marketer must have a clear understanding of the profitability per unit of product sold prior to implementing price changes, discounts, coupons, trade-ins, etc. The contribution margin format of an income statement assists marketers in targeting their promotional budgets toward products that yield the greatest contribution to overall profits. Product line and merchandising decisions involving the introduction or culling of products from the assortment offered are heavily influenced by CVP analysis.
	Microeconomics	CVP analysis originated as an economic theory of the great economist Alfred Marshall and it still remains a major concept of price formation in the marketplace. Economists use the concept to verify research on price formations determined by other quantifiable theories such as supply-demand equilibrium, utility-preference theory, and value-added models.

TOPIC OF NOTE	DISCIPLINE	CROSS-FUNCTIONAL APPLICATIONS
Cost-Volume-Profit Analysis (CVP) (continued)	Production Management	CVP analysis guides production cost decisions concerning the use of technology or manufacturing processes to spread fixed costs over the production run. Routine, short run decisions may be determined by production managers based on production capacity and the impact of the short run on reducing the fixed production cost per unit.
	Research and Development (R&D)	It is pointless for a design engineer to develop a product that is not salable in the marketplace in quantities necessary to assure an acceptable profit. Engineers must work within the constraints of CVP analysis to make decisions concerning cost/quality of materials, assortment of features in the product design, as well as processing, storing and packaging. Most engineering schools currently recommend managerial accounting as a business elective to develop a practical appreciation of cost constraints in research, design, and environmental and manufacturing engineering.
	Public Administration	Both federal and state legislative bodies have governmental operation committees that are under great public pressure to produce public services and transfer payment activities more efficiently. Public administrators are currently using CVP analysis to make outsourcing decisions. In the area of transfer payments, comparative studies of the cost of administration between large insurance and public entities influence organizational decisions in government.
		A revival of zero-based budgeting in government has caused public administrators to rethink notions of relevant and sunk costs. Traditional public budgeting depended upon estimations of the budget's dynamic margins to project new budgets. Often, relevant costs were buried in programs as sunk costs which were then increased by the amount of the budgetary estimate. This practice limits the decision-making alternatives of the administrator.
	Finance	Financial managers use CVP analysis to assist in the projection of costs, profitability and cash flows, budgets, and pro-forma (future projection) financial statements and incorporate CVP information to estimate operational, cash, and capital equipment needs, as well as the resources available to meet them.
Relevant Cost versus Irrelevant Cost	Information Theory and Common Databases	The paradox of information theory is how to serve the informational requirements of diverse users within the same organization and simultaneously enhance overall goal congruence. Managers within the strategic business units (SBU) of an organization can "flag" certain costs as relevant to the decisions of their SBUs. This will improve decisions not only on a particular SBU basis but also foster an understanding of the impact of an SBU's decision on cooperating units. An irrelevant cost in one SBU's decision could have a major impact on another unit or the organizational goals as a whole.
	Contract Law	Attorneys frequently are the key players in negotiating sales, purchase or leasing contracts. They must be made aware of the relevant costs, conditions, and contingencies that benefit the seller or consumer unit in order to structure the most favorable contract. A relevant cost which is variable in managerial planning could turn out to be a sunk cost if negotiators are not properly informed.

CROSS-FUNCTIONAL APPLICATIONS

TOPIC OF NOTE	DISCIPLINE	CROSS-FUNCTIONAL APPLICATIONS
Relevant Cost versus Irrelevant Cost (continued)	Environmental Management	Responsibility accounting in part has created a narrow perspective on relevant costs. Managers must apply the concept of relevant and irrelevant costs to the environment in which they conduct their business. Decisions concerning waste sites, cheap labor, or nonrenewable sources may imply costs that must be estimated as relevant although the impact is external. Quality costs, for example, were generally considered irrelevant 20 years ago.
	Production Management	Production managers often see all costs in terms of some fixed physical measurement such as floor space or machine capacity. The concept of relevant and irrelevant costs assists production decisions by presenting the range of alternatives available for consideration separate from the usual concepts of fixed, variable, and semi-variable costs. This reduces the confusion of relevant costs with variable costs and fixed costs with sunk costs.
	Health Care	Health care administrators use relevant costs in patient assessment systems to target resources toward a patient's most critical needs for diagnosis, therapy, or emergency services. Often insurance carriers of Medicaid define relevant costs with respect to particular diagnostic results in an attempt to hold down escalating health care costs based on excessive, inappropriate or experimental treatment. This practice has been particularly effective in countering the abuses of defensive medicine and unnecessary treatment.

CHAPTER SUMMARY

Management planning for company success includes planning for price, volume, fixed and variable costs, quality, contribution margins, and breakeven point. The interrelationships of these factors are studied in breakeven point (BEP) and cost-volume-profit (CVP) analysis.

The BEP is that quantity of sales volume at which the company will experience zero profit or loss. Total contribution margin (sales minus all variable costs) is equal to total fixed costs at the BEP.

Since most companies want to operate above breakeven, CVP analysis extends the BEP computation by introducing a desired profit factor. A company can determine the sales necessary to generate a desired amount of profit by adding the desired profit to fixed costs and dividing that total by contribution margin or contribution margin ratio. After fixed costs are covered, each dollar of contribution margin generated by company sales will produce a dollar of before-tax profit.

In a multiproduct firm, all BEP and CVP analyses are based on an assumed constant sales mix of products or services. This sales mix requires the computation of a weighted average contribution margin (and, thus, contribution margin ratio) for a *bag* of products. Answers to breakeven or CVP computations are in units or dollars of these bags of products. The number of bags can be converted to individual items by use of the sales mix relationship.

CVP analysis is short-range in focus because it assumes linearity of all functions. Managers need to include in their considerations the effects of changes in quality and other types of changes on both current and future costs to make better, more realistic decisions. While CVP analysis provides one way for a manager to reduce the risk of uncertainty, the model is based on several assumptions that limit its ability to reflect reality.

Management's task is to effectively and efficiently allocate its finite stock of resources to accomplish its chosen set of corporate goals and objectives. Managers should explain how requested information will be used so that accountants can make certain that relevant information is provided in an appropriate form. In this way, managers will have a reliable quantitative basis on which to analyze problems, compare viable solutions, and choose the best course of action.

For information to be relevant, it must (1) relate to the decision at hand, (2) be important to the decision, and (3) have a bearing on a future endeavor. Relevant costing compares the incremental, or additional, revenues or costs associated with alternative decisions.

Relevant information may be quantitative or qualitative. Variable costs are generally relevant to a decision; they are irrelevant only when they cannot be avoided under any possible alternative or when they do not differ between (or among) alternatives. Direct avoidable fixed costs are also relevant to decision making. Sometimes costs seem relevant when they actually are not. Examples of such irrelevant costs include sunk costs and arbitrarily allocated common costs.

Managers use relevant cost information to determine the incremental benefits of alternatives. One option often available is to "change nothing." This option, however, may be strategically risky if competitors gain advantage by upgrading their processes. After rigorous analysis of the quantifiable factors associated with each alternative, a manager must assess the merits and potential risks of the qualitative factors involved so that the best possible course of action is chosen.

Relevant costing is essential in many decision-making situations, including those related to further processing of a product, scarce resource allocations, sales mix distributions, and retentions or eliminations of product lines. The following points are important to remember:

1. In a decision involving a single scarce resource, if the objective is to maximize company contribution margin and profits, then production and sales should be focused toward the product with the highest contribution margin per unit of the scarce resource.

2. In a sales mix decision, changes in selling prices and advertising costs normally affect sales volume, thus changing the company's total contribution margin. Special order prices may be set using variable costs as a starting point.

3. In a product line decision, product lines should be evaluated on their product margins rather than their income amounts. Product margin includes relevant direct costs but excludes allocated common costs.

Quantitative analysis is short-range in perspective. Additional, qualitative factors should be reviewed by management in each case. Some of these qualitative factors may have long-range planning and policy implications. Others may be short-range in nature. Managers must decide the relevance of individual factors based on experience, judgment, knowledge of economic theory, and logic.

APPENDICES

1. GRAPHIC APPROACHES TO BREAKEVEN ANALYSIS

To graphically depict the relationships among revenues, variable costs, fixed costs, and profits (or losses), a **breakeven graph** may be used. The breakeven point is located at the point where the total cost and total revenue lines cross. The following steps are necessary in preparing a breakeven graph.

breakeven graph

costing. This approach treats the costs of all manufacturing components (direct material, direct labor, variable factory overhead, and fixed factory overhead) as inventoriable or product costs. Absorption costing considers costs incurred in the nonmanufacturing (selling and administrative) areas of the organization as period costs and it expenses these costs in a manner that properly matches them with revenues. Exhibit 6-17 depicts the absorption costing model.

An organization incurs costs for direct material (DM), direct labor (DL), and variable factory overhead (VOH) only when goods are produced or services are rendered. Since total DM, DL, and VOH costs increase with each additional product made or unit of service rendered, these costs are considered product costs and inventoried until the product or service is sold. Fixed factory overhead (FOH) cost, on the other hand, may be incurred even when production or service facilities are idle. Although total FOH cost does not vary with units of production or level of service, this cost provides the basic capacity necessary for production or service to occur. Because production could not take place without the incurrence of fixed factory overhead, absorption costing considers this cost to be inventoriable.

Thus, when absorption costing is used, the financial statements show the Work in Process Inventory, Finished Goods Inventory, and Cost of Goods Sold accounts as including variable per-unit production costs as well as a per-unit allocation of fixed factory overhead. Absorption costing also presents expenses on an income statement according to their functional classifications. A **functional classification** is a grouping of costs that were all incurred for the same basic purpose. Functional classifications include categories such as cost of goods sold, selling expenses, and administrative expenses.

functional classification

variable costing

Variable costing is a cost accumulation method that includes only variable production costs (direct material, direct labor, and variable factory overhead) as inventoriable, or product costs. Thus, variable costing defines product costs solely as costs of *actual production*. Since fixed factory overhead will be incurred even if there is no production, variable costing proponents believe this cost does not qualify as a product cost. Fixed factory over-

EXHIBIT 6-17
Absorption Costing Model

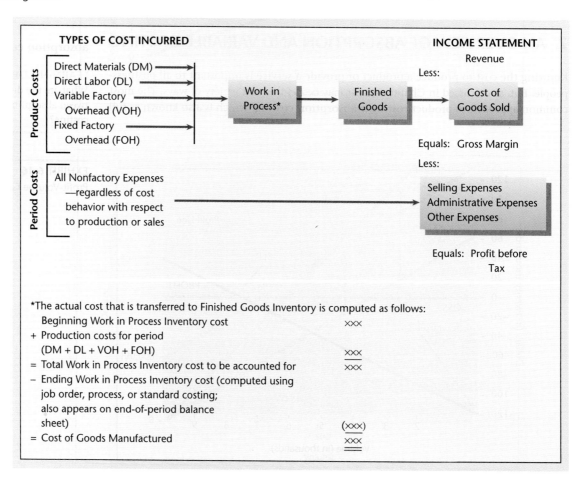

head costs are therefore treated as period expenses by being charged against revenue as incurred. Variable costing is also known as direct costing and is illustrated in Exhibit 6-18.[10]

A variable costing income statement or management report separates costs by cost behavior, although it may also present expenses by functional classifications within the behavioral categories. Under variable costing, Cost of Goods Sold is more appropriately called *Variable* Cost of Goods Sold because it is composed only of the variable production costs related to the units sold. Revenue minus Variable Cost of Goods Sold is called **product contribution margin** and indicates how much revenue is available to cover all period expenses and to provide net income.

product contribution margin

EXHIBIT 6-18
Variable Costing Model

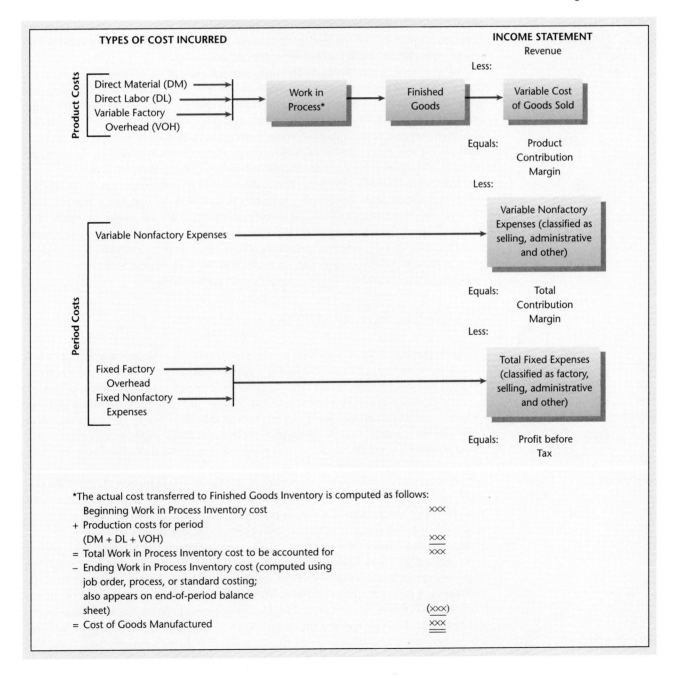

[10]Direct costing is, however, a misnomer for variable costing. All variable *manufacturing* costs, whether direct or indirect, are considered product costs under variable costing.

total contribution margin

Variable nonfactory period expenses (such as a sales commission set at 10 percent of product selling price) are deducted from product contribution margin to determine the amount of **total contribution margin**. Total contribution margin is the difference between total revenues and total variable expenses. This amount represents the dollar figure available to "contribute" to the coverage of all fixed expenses, both factory and nonfactory. After fixed expenses are covered, any remaining contribution margin provides income to the company. Variable costing financial statements are also known as contribution income statements.

Major authoritative bodies of the accounting profession, such as the Financial Accounting Standards Board and Securities and Exchange Commission, apparently believe that absorption costing provides external parties with the most informative picture of earnings. This belief is indicated by the fact that the accounting profession has unofficially disallowed the use of variable costing as a generally accepted inventory measurement method for external reporting purposes commencing at the time when the IRS began requiring absorption costing for tax purposes.[11] The rationale for this position reflects the importance of the matching concept in that absorption costing expenses all product costs in the period that the related revenue is recognized.

On the other hand, managers attempting to use absorption costing information for internal decision making find that combining costs into functional classifications obscures important cost behavior patterns (relative to changes in activity). Therefore, while companies must prepare external statements using absorption costing, internal reports are also often prepared to show cost behaviors to facilitate management analysis and decision making. Variable costs may figure more prominently in short-run decisions because, for ongoing operations, these costs are normally more controllable than fixed costs.

Even with their differences, the two costing methods have some underlying similarities. First, both methods use the same basic cost information. Second, the treatment of direct material, direct labor, and variable factory overhead is the same under absorption and variable costing; these costs are always considered product costs. Third, selling and administrative expenses are considered period costs under both costing methods. Fourth, there are no differences between accounts other than in Work in Process Inventory, Finished Goods Inventory, and the expense accounts under the two methods.

3. LINEAR PROGRAMMING

LEARNING OBJECTIVE 13
Why is linear programming a valuable tool for managers?

objective function

constraint

feasible solutions

Linear programming (LP) is a method used to solve problems with one objective and multiple limiting factors. LP is used to find the optimal allocation of scarce resources when the objective and restrictions on achieving that objective can be stated as linear equations.

The objective in an LP problem is to either maximize or minimize some measure of performance. The mathematical equation stating that objective is called the **objective function**. For example, Rogar's objective could be to maximize product contribution margin or to minimize product cost. A linear programming problem can have only one goal, expressed as the objective function.

A restriction on management's pursuit of its objective is a **constraint**. There are several types of constraints. Resource constraints involve limited availability of labor time, machine time, raw materials, space, or production capacity. Demand or marketing constraints restrict the quantity of the product that can be sold during a time period. Constraints can also take the form of technical product requirements. For example, management of a company preparing frozen meals for a hospital may be constrained in the production requirements for frozen meals by caloric or vitamin content. A final constraint in all LP problems is a non-negativity constraint. This constraint specifies that physical quantities cannot have negative values. Constraints, like the objective function, are specified in mathematical equations and represent the limits imposed on optimizing the objective function.

Almost every allocation problem has a number of **feasible solutions** that do not violate any of the problem constraints. Different solutions generally give different values for the objective function. In some problems, several solutions provide the same value for the

---

[11]Robert W. Koehler, "Triple-Threat Strayegy," Management Accounting (October 1991), p. 34.

objective function. Solutions may also be generated that contain fractional values. The **optimal solution** to a maximization or minimization goal is the one that provides the best answer to the allocation problem. Some LP problems have more than one optimal solution.

optimal solution

Linear programming problems may be solved by a graphical approach or the simplex method. Graphs are simple to use and provide a visual representation of the problem. However, because it is virtually impossible to accurately draw and interpret graphs in three or more dimensions, graphical approaches to solving LP problems lose their appeal when the number of unknowns exceeds two. In such cases, the computer-adaptable simplex method can be used.

Simplex is an iterative (sequential) algorithm used to solve multivariable, multiconstraint LP problems. (An algorithm is a logical step-by-step problem-solving technique that continuously searches for an improved solution until it achieves the optimal one.) Simplex solutions also provide valuable additional information that may be used in budgeting and production analyses.

simplex method

Detailed solutions to linear programming problems are beyond the scope of this text.

KEY TERMS

Absorption costing (p. 259)
Breakeven graph (p. 257)
Breakeven point (BEP) (p. 230)
Common cost (p. 252)
Constraint (p. 261)
Contribution margin (CM) (p. 231)
Contribution margin ratio (CM%) (p. 232)
Cost-volume-profit (CVP) analysis (p. 232)
Feasible solution (p. 262)
Functional classification (p. 260)
Incremental cost (p. 242)
Incremental revenue (p. 242)
Linear programming (p. 246)
Objective function (p. 261)

Opportunity cost (p. 243)
Optimal solution (p. 262)
Product contribution margin (p. 261)
Product margin (p. 252)
Profit-volume (PV) graph (p. 259)
Relevant cost (p. 242)
Relevant costing (p. 242)
Sales mix (p. 247)
Scarce resource (p. 245)
Simplex method (p. 263)
Special order pricing (p. 249)
Sunk cost (p. 245)
Total contribution margin (p. 261)
Variable costing (p. 260)

SOLUTION STRATEGIES

⊙ COST-VOLUME-PROFIT

Most CVP problems are solvable by use of the numerator/denominator approach. All numerators and denominators and the type of problem each relates to are listed below. The formulas relate to both single-product and multiproduct firms, but results for multiproduct firms are per bag and must be converted to units of individual products.

PROBLEM SITUATION	NUMERATOR	DENOMINATOR
Simple BEP in units	FC	CM
Simple BEP in dollars	FC	CM%
CVP with lump-sum profit in units	FC + P	CM
CVP with lump-sum profit in dollars	FC + P	CM%
CVP with variable profits in units	FC	$CM - P_u$
CVP with variable profit in dollars	FC	$CM\% - P_u\%$

where   FC   = fixed cost
            CM   = contribution margin per unit
            CM% = contribution margin percentage

P   = total profit (can be on before-tax or on an after-tax basis converted to before-tax)

P_u = profit per unit

$P_u\%$ = profit percentage per unit

To convert after-tax profit to before-tax profit, divide after-tax profit by $(1 - \text{tax rate})$.

     General rule of decision making: Choose the alternative that yields the greatest incremental benefit (or the smallest incremental loss).

Incremental (additional) revenues
 − Incremental (additional) costs
 = Incremental benefit (positive or negative)

Relevant Costs

Direct material and direct labor

Variable production overhead

Variable selling expenses related to each alternative (may be greater or less than under the "change nothing" alternative)

Avoidable fixed production overhead

Avoidable fixed selling/administrative costs (if any)

Opportunity cost of choosing some other alternative (will either increase one alternative's cost or reduce the cost of the other)

Single Scarce Resource

1. Determine the scarce resource.
2. Determine the production quantity per unit of the scarce resource.
3. Determine the contribution margin (CM) per unit of the scarce resource.
4. Multiply units of production times CM per unit of the scarce resource to obtain total CM provided by the scarce resource. Production and sale of the product with the highest CM per unit of scarce resource will maximize profits.

DEMONSTRATION PROBLEM

Equalizer Corporation makes and sells jar lid openers. Cost information for one unit is as follows:

Direct material	$1.00
Direct labor	.50
Variable factory overhead	.25
Variable selling expenses	.05
Total variable costs	$1.80
Total fixed cost	$194,400

Each lid opener sells for $4.50. Current annual production and sales volume is 150,000 lid openers. A predetermined fixed factory overhead rate can be computed based on this activity level.

Required

a. Compute the unit contribution margin and contribution margin ratio for Equalizer Corporation's product.

b. Compute the breakeven point in units for Equalizer Corporation, using contribution margin.

c. Compute the breakeven point in sales dollars for Equalizer Corporation, using contribution margin ratio.

d. If Equalizer Corporation wants to earn $43,200 of before-tax profits, how many openers will it have to sell?

Send note to Brindha Formula Sheet?

e. If Equalizer Corporation wants to earn $40,500 after taxes and is subject to a 25 percent tax rate, how many units will it have to sell?
f. If Equalizer Corporation's fixed costs increased by $7,560, how many units would it need to sell to break even? (Use original data.)
g. Equalizer Corporation can sell an additional 12,000 openers overseas for $3.50. Variable costs will increase by $.20 for shipping expenses, and fixed costs will increase by $25,000 because of the purchase of a new machine. This is a one-time-only sale and will not affect domestic sales this year or in the future. Should Equalizer Corporation sell the additional units?

Solutions

a. CM = Selling Price − Variable Cost = $4.50 − $1.80 = $2.70

CM% = Selling Price − Variable Cost ÷ Selling Price = $2.70 ÷ $4.50 = 60%

b. BEP = Fixed Cost ÷ CM = $194,400 ÷ $2.70 = 72,000
c. BEP = Fixed Cost ÷ CM% = $194,400 ÷ 60% = $324,000
(Note: This answer is also equal to 72,000 units × $4.50 per unit selling price.)
d. BEP = (FC + Desired Profit) ÷ CM = ($194,400 + $43,200) ÷ $2.70 = 88,000 units
e. Profit after tax ÷ (1 − Tax rate) = Profit before tax

$40,500 ÷ .75 = $54,000

BEP = (FC + Desired Profit) ÷ CM = ($194,400 + $54,000) ÷ $2.70 = 92,000 units

f. Additional units to break even = Increase in FC ÷ CM = $7,560 ÷ $2.70 = 2,800; new BEP = 72,000 + 2,800 = 74,800 units
g. New CM for these units = $3.50 − $2.00 = $1.50; 12,000 × $1.50 = $18,000, which is $7,000 below the additional $25,000 fixed costs. Equalizer Corporation should not sell the additional units.

Product Lines

   Sales
− Direct variable expenses
= Product contribution margin
− Avoidable fixed expenses
= Product margin*

*Make decision to retain or eliminate based on this line item.

END OF CHAPTER MATERIALS

QUESTIONS

1. Since managers in commercial entities aspire to make a profit, why do these managers care about the breakeven point?
2. Why does contribution margin fluctuate in direct proportion to sales volume?
3. How is breakeven analysis related to CVP?
4. If the variable costs associated with a product increase per unit but selling price and fixed costs remain constant, what will happen to (a) contribution margin and (b) breakeven point? Explain.
5. What is the bag assumption and why is it necessary in a multiproduct company?
6. What do you think are the three most fundamental CVP assumptions? Why should managers who use CVP analysis keep these assumptions in mind when using the answers provided by the model?

7. What effect would specifying the quality of a product be likely to have on each of the CVP factors?

8. The president of Henry's Hamburgers has just been informed that the chain is operating at 8 percent above the breakeven point. What should his course of action be and why?

9. Why is it necessary to consider qualitative factors when solving problems using CVP?

10. Why is the perspective of managers using CVP a short-term one, and what are the implications of such a perspective?

11. What are the three characteristics that a cost must possess to be relevant to a decision? Why are these characteristics important?

12. What is meant by the term *incremental* as it applies to costs and revenues?

13. Are future variable costs always relevant costs? Discuss the rationale for your answer.

14. What category of costs is often relevant in decision making, but is probably never directly recorded in a company's cost records? Explain.

15. Evaluate the merit of the following statement: "In the long run, the only binding constraint on a firm's output is capital; in the short run, nearly any resource can be a binding constraint."

16. In allocating a scarce production resource in a multiproduct corporation whose goal is to maximize the total corporate contribution margin, why would management not simply produce the product that generates the highest contribution margin per unit?

17. Why are some direct fixed costs irrelevant to the decision to eliminate a product line?

18. *(Appendix 1)* What is a breakeven graph? How is it similar to and different from a profit-volume graph?

19. *(Appendix 2)* Which of the following are defined as product costs when absorption costing is used? When variable costing is used?
    a. Direct material
    b. Variable factory overhead
    c. Selling expenses
    d. Direct labor
    e. Fixed factory overhead
    f. Administrative expenses

20. *(Appendix 2)* Which approach (variable or absorption) classifies costs by behavior? Which classifies costs by functional categories? Are these mutually exclusive?

21. *(Appendix 2)* What is the difference between absorption and variable costing in the treatment of fixed factory overhead? Why is this difference important?

22. *(Appendix 3)* Why is linear programming used in business organizations?

23. *(Appendix 3)* What is the difference between a feasible solution and an optimal solution?

⊙ EXERCISES

24. *(BEP)* Even Steven Co. has the following revenue and cost functions:

    Revenue = $15 per unit
    Fixed costs = $400,000
    Variable costs = $11 per unit

    Even Steven has asked you to determine the breakeven point, both in units and in dollars.

25. *(BEP)* In each of the following situations, you have been asked by the company owner to determine how many units must be sold for the company to break even.
    a. Total fixed costs are $45,000, and the unit contribution margin is $9.
    b. Unit selling price is $8, unit variable cost is $5, and total fixed costs are $48,000.
    c. Unit selling price is $12, contribution margin is 25 percent of revenue, and total fixed costs are $30,000.

d. Unit variable cost is 80 percent of the unit selling price, total fixed costs are $48,000, and unit selling price is $12.

e. Unit variable cost is $5, contribution margin per unit is $3, and total fixed costs are $24,000. Compute total sales at the breakeven volume in addition to total number of units.

26. *(BEP)* Lucky Tots Co. publishes paperback cartoon books. The following operational data relate to a typical month:

Unit sales price	$10.00
Unit variable cost	$ 4.60
Fixed costs	$16,200
Current volume of books	3,200

   The company is considering an expansion that would increase monthly fixed costs by $5,400. If it does, production and sales will increase by 2,000 books. You are the company's newest employee and the only employee who has had a course in managerial accounting. You have been asked to do the following:

   a. Without considering the expansion, calculate the firm's breakeven point and its monthly before-tax profit.

   b. Recalculate breakeven point in books and monthly before-tax profit assuming that the company undertakes the expansion.

27. *(CVP with before-tax profit)* We Supply U is planning to make and sell 10,000 computer disk trays. Fixed costs are $40,000, and variable costs are 60 percent of the selling price. Your neighbor, who works for the firm, wants you to help him determine what the selling price must be for the company to earn $10,000 of before-tax profit on the trays.

28. *(CVP with after-tax profit)* Domestic Steel, Inc., manufactures home furnaces that sell for $1,000. The unit costs are:

Direct material	$375
Direct labor	250
Variable factory overhead	130
Variable selling expense	45

   Annual fixed factory overhead is $100,000 and fixed selling and administrative expenses are $120,000. The company is in a 30 percent tax bracket.

   You have been enlisted to determine how many furnaces the company needs to make and sell to earn $140,000 in after-tax profit.

29. *(CVP analysis)* A local company has learned about the CVP model but has not yet gained confidence in using it. As a friend of the owner, you have been engaged to compute the number of units that must be sold and the total sales in each of the following situations:

   a. The company's profit goal is $40,000. Total fixed costs are $80,000, unit contribution margin is $5, and unit selling price is $8.

   b. The company's profit goal is $25,000 after tax, and its tax rate is 40 percent. Unit variable cost is $6, unit contribution margin is $4, and total fixed costs are $40,000.

   c. The company's after-tax profit goal is $54,000, and the tax rate is 40 percent. Unit variable cost is 70 percent of the $10 unit selling price, and total fixed costs are $60,000.

   d. The company's after-tax profit goal is $30,000, and the tax rate is 50 percent. Unit contribution margin is $3, unit variable cost is 70 percent of the unit selling price, and total fixed costs are $60,000.

   e. The company's after-tax profit goal is $40,000 and the tax rate is 50 percent. Unit variable cost is $9, unit contribution margin is 25 percent of selling price, and total fixed costs are $25,000.

30. *(CVP analysis)* Exotic Rugs has annual sales of $2,000,000, variable expenses of 60 percent of sales, and fixed expenses of $80,000 monthly. Haabeeba, the store manager, has asked you to tell her how much sales will have to increase so that Exotic Rugs will have before-tax profit of 20 percent of sales.

31. *(CVP; incremental analysis)* Hans Neuschwanstein is an architect. He charges $100 per client hour. His monthly expenses are:

Office rent	$ 800
Office staff	1,200
Utilities	400
Total fixed expenses	$2,400

In addition to the above expenses, Mr. Neuschwanstein must have 60 hours of continuing education (CE) annually to maintain his certification. He has determined that this CE costs him $400 a month. Monthly variable costs average $20 per client hour, and Mr. Neuschwanstein is in a 20 percent tax bracket. Hans is a good architect but never took managerial accounting. He has hired you to determine the following:

a. How many client hours per month must Mr. Neuschwanstein generate to break even?

b. How many client hours per month must Mr. Neuschwanstein generate to earn $8,000 per month after tax? Use incremental analysis based on your answer to Part a.

c. Mr. Neuschwanstein enjoys bowling and flying his private plane and wonders if he could work six-hour days and four-day weeks and still earn $8,000 after tax. Could he do this? Show computations and prove your answer (assume that there are four weeks per month). Use incremental analysis based on your answer to Part a.

32. *(Multiproduct BEP)* Retsey Boss Co. sells flags and sun visors at the entrances to local sporting events. The firm sells two flags for each sun visor. A flag sells for $3 and costs $1. A sun visor sells for $1.50 and costs $1. The company's monthly fixed costs are $4,500. You have been asked to calculate how many flags the company will sell at the BEP. Prove your answer.

33. *(Multiproduct CVP)* Fairway Zephyrs manufactures two types of golf carts, which are sold to golfers throughout the country. The compact cart is sold for an average price of $2,000 per unit; variable manufacturing costs are $1,800 per unit. The standard-size cart is sold for an average price of $3,500 per unit; variable manufacturing costs are $3,000 per unit. Total fixed costs are estimated to be $360 million per year. As the company's new accountant, you have been asked to:

a. Determine the breakeven volume for the company if the expected sales mix is one-third compact carts and two-thirds standard carts.

b. Because of a battery shortage, the management team expects the sales mix to shift to 50 percent compact carts and 50 percent standard carts. Determine the breakeven volume based on the new sales mix, and explain why your answer differs from the one you gave in Part a.

c. It is expected that if the firm produced more than 50 percent compact carts, fixed costs would increase by $65 million. Determine the breakeven volume based on a sales mix of 60 percent compact carts and 40 percent standard carts.

34. *(Scarce resource)* Because of a labor strike in the plant of its major competitor, Johnson Tool Co. has found itself operating at peak capacity. The firm makes two electronic woodworking tools: sanders and drills. At this time, the company can sell as many of either product as it can make. The firm's machines can be run only 90,000 hours per month. Data on each product follow:

	SANDERS	DRILLS
Sales	$45	$28
Variable costs	(30)	(19)
Contribution margin	$15	$ 9
Machine hours required	8	6

Fixed costs are $110,000 per month. You are on a consulting engagement with the firm and have been requested to tell management the following:

a. How many of each product the company should make. Explain your answer.

b. How much profit the company would expect to make per month based on your recommendation in Part a.

35. *(Scarce resource)* Belle Ringers makes holiday bells. The firm produces three types of bells: bass, baritone, and tenor. Because of political turmoil in Australia, a critical raw material, gonganese, is in very short supply and is restricting the number of bells the firm can produce. For the coming year, the firm will be able to purchase only 30,000 pounds of gonganese (at a cost of $5 per pound). The firm needs to determine how to allocate the gonganese to maximize profits. The following information has been gathered for your consideration:

	BASS	BARITONE	TENOR
Sales demand in units	200,000	300,000	100,000
Sales price per unit	$15.00	$10.00	$4.00
Gonganese cost	6.25	5.00	2.50
Direct labor cost	6.00	3.00	1.00
Variable overhead cost	2.00	1.00	.25

Fixed production costs total $200,000 per year, fixed selling costs are $28,000, and there are no variable selling costs. Management has enlisted you to help them determine the following:
   a. How should Belle Ringers allocate the scarce gonganese?
   b. Based on the optimal allocation, what is the company's projected contribution margin for the coming year?

36. *(Sales mix)* Martha's Doggy Do provides two types of services to dog owners: bathing and trimming. All company personnel can perform either service equally well. To expand sales and market share, Martha's relies heavily on radio and billboard advertising. For 2000, advertising funding is expected to be very limited. Information on projected operations for 2000 follows:

	BATHING	TRIMMING
Projected billable hours for 2000	10,000	8,000
Revenue per billable hour	$15	$25
Variable cost of labor	5	10
Material costs per billable hour	1	2
Allocated fixed costs per year	100,000	90,000

The last time you took your dog in to Martha for grooming, she asked you, the most well-known accountant in the community, the following:
   a. What is her projected profit or loss for 2000?
   b. If $1 spent on advertising could increase either bathing revenue or trimming revenue by $20, on which service should the advertising dollar be spent?
   c. If $1 spent on advertising could increase bathing billable time or trimming billable time by one hour, on which service should the advertising dollar be spent?

37. *(Sales mix)* Among many products made by Creative Toys is a plastic wagon. You are the company accountant. The company's projections for this product for 2000 follow:

Projected volume in units	100,000
Sales price per unit	$ 62
Variable production costs per unit	42
Variable selling costs per unit	8
Total fixed production costs	500,000
Total fixed selling and administration costs	200,000

The company president wants you to address the following:
   a. Compute the projected profit to be earned on the wagon during 2000.
   b. Corporate management estimates that unit volume could be increased by 15 percent if the sales price were decreased by $4. How would such a change affect the profit level projected in Part a?
   c. Rather than cutting the sales price, management is considering holding the sales price at the projected level and increasing advertising by $200,000. Such a change would increase volume by 20 percent. How would the level of profit under this alternative compare with the profit projected in Part a?

38. *(Special order)* Star Company produces a plastic courtroom set that includes a judge's bench, witness stand, jury box, and 25 people. The set is sold to exclusive children's toy stores for $200. Plant capacity is 20,000 sets per year. Production costs are as follows:

Direct material cost per set	$ 20
Direct labor cost per set	30
Variable overhead per set	40
Variable selling cost per set	10
Fixed overhead per year	1,100,000

A prominent Washington D.C. store, which has not previously purchased from Star Company, has approached the marketing manager about buying 5,000 sets for $170 each. No selling expenses would be incurred on this offer, but the Washington D.C. store wants the set to include five plastic briefcases. This request means that Star Company will incur an additional $2 cost per unit. The company is currently selling 18,000 courtroom sets, so acceptance of this job would require the company to reject some of its current business. The company engages you as its consultant to address the following:

a. What is the current operating profit of Star Company?

b. If the company accepted this offer, what would be its operating profit? Should the company accept the offer?

c. If Star Company were currently selling only 10,000 sets per year and wanted to earn $150,000 of profit for the year, what selling price would the company have to quote the Washington D.C. store?

39. *(Special order)* The manufacturing capacity of Poston Company's plant is 70,000 units of product per year. A summary of operations for the year ended December 31, 2000, is as follows:

Sales (36,000 units at $75 per unit)		$2,700,000
Variable manufacturing costs	$1,440,000	
Variable selling costs	180,000	(1,620,000)
Contribution margin		$1,080,000
Fixed costs		(1,000,000)
Operating profit		$ 80,000

A French distributor has offered to buy 32,000 units at $60 per unit during 2001. As company consultant you have been instructed to assume that all costs (including variable selling expenses) will be at the 2000 level during 2001. Management wants you to advise them regarding what would be the total operating profit for 2001 if Poston accepts this offer and also sells as many units to regular customers as it did in 2000? Normal variable selling costs will be incurred on this and all transactions as a result of a sales contract.

40. *(Product line)* Speakers R Us is in the business of hiring celebrities and marketing their services. The firm has three operating segments: country-western (CW) entertainment, humorous speakers, and inspirational speakers. The owner, a former comedian and inspirational speaker, has engaged you to help her with some financial matters. Projected income statements for the fourth quarter of this fiscal year follow:

	CW	HUMOROUS	INSPIRATIONAL
Sales	$600,000	$250,000	$300,000
Variable costs of professional services	(200,000)	(150,000)	(162,500)
Variable marketing costs	(100,000)	(37,500)	(50,000)
Direct fixed costs	(200,000)	(75,000)	(62,500)
Allocated fixed costs	(30,000)	(15,000)	(15,000)
Profit before tax	$ 70,000	$ (27,500)	$ 10,000

a. Assuming that $35,000 of the direct fixed costs of the humorous segment can be avoided if the segment is eliminated, what would be the effect of its elimination on Speakers R Us' overall profit?

b. Before the humorous segment is eliminated, what qualitative factors should be considered?

41. *(Product line)* The management of Gulf Pipe Company is currently contemplating the elimination of one of its products, product N, because this product is now showing a loss. The president of the company is upset and asks for you, the company's chief accountant, to address the issues. An annual income statement follows:

GULF PIPE COMPANY
INCOME STATEMENT
FOR YEAR ENDED AUGUST 1, 2000
(IN THOUSANDS)

| | *Product* | | | |
	M	N	O	Total
Sales	$2,200	$1,400	$1,800	$5,400
Cost of sales	1,400	800	1,080	3,280
Gross margin	$ 800	$ 600	$ 720	$2,120
Avoidable fixed and				
variable marketing costs	$ 630	$ 525	$ 520	$1,675
Allocated fixed costs	90	80	105	275
Total avoidable and allocated costs	$ 720	$ 605	$ 625	$1,950
Operating profit	$ 80	$ (5)	$ 95	$ 170

a. Should the Gulf management team stop sales of product N? Support your answer with appropriate schedules.

b. How would the operating profit of the company be affected by the decision?

42. *(Appendix 1)* Cajun Candy Co. makes and sells boxes of Cajun candies. The firm's income statement for 1997 follows:

Sales (25,000 boxes @ $12)		$300,000
Variable costs		
Production (25,000 × $3)	$75,000	
Sales commissions (25,000 × $1.20)	30,000	(105,000)
Contribution margin		$195,000
Fixed costs		
Production	$58,000	
General, selling, and administrative	20,000	(78,000)
Profit before tax		$117,000

You are considering buying an interest in the company and decide you need to do the following:

a. Prepare a cost-volume-profit graph for Cajun Candy Co.

b. Prepare a profit-volume graph for Cajun Candy Co.

43. *(Appendix 2; product cost under AC and VC)* The Brown Cow Shoe Company produced 100,000 pairs of shoes and sold 70,000 in its first year of operations. There was no Work in Process Inventory at year-end. Its costs for that year were:

Direct material	$ 400,000
Direct labor	300,000
Variable factory overhead	150,000
Variable selling and administrative	210,000
Fixed factory overhead	250,000
Fixed selling and administrative	175,000
Total	$1,485,000

You have just been hired as the company's accountant. For this company's first year of operations, compute the cost of one unit of product if the company uses (a) absorption costing and (b) variable costing.

44. *(Appendix 2; product cost under AC and VC)* The Allison Electric Company is considering switching to variable costing. In an effort to better understand the significance of the possible change, the management team has asked that ending inventories be costed on both an absorption and a variable costing basis. Production for the year was 200,000 units, of which 25,000 units remained in ending inventory. Additional information concerning production follows:

Direct material costs	$600,000
Direct labor costs	450,000
Factory overhead costs	600,000

Factory overhead has not been separated into fixed and variable components, but the fixed factory overhead rate approximates $6 per direct labor hour. The current direct labor rate is $10 per hour. As consultant to the team, you have been asked to calculate the total costs to be assigned to ending inventory under both absorption and variable costing.

45. *(Appendix 2; defining cost)* Your neighbor, Tom Allen, wants to do some home improvements but finds that the power drill he owns is inadequate for the job. You are a vice-president of the Zoomby Corporation, which manufactures the Zoomby Power Drill 2000. Tom knows that you can purchase tools from the company at "cost plus 10 percent"—a tremendous discount from what he would have to pay in a retail store. Discuss the variety of ways that Zoomby could compute "cost" in selling tools to company employees and which one or ones would be the most appropriate.

46. *(Appendix 3)* The contribution margins for three different products of a company are $12.50, $9.00, and $7.30. Your fellow managers know that you have studied linear programming and have requested that you state, in words, the objective function that would communicate a goal of maximizing the company's contribution margin.

47. *(Appendix 3)* The variable costs for four different products are $.56, $.93, $2.12 and $1.98. You have been asked by your management colleagues to state, in words, the objective function that would communicate a goal of minimizing the company's variable costs.

⊙ PROBLEMS

48. *(BEP; CVP before and after tax)* High School Traditions operates a shop that makes and sells class rings for local high schools. Operating statistics follow:

Average selling price per ring	$250
Variable costs per ring	
Rings and stones	$90
Sales commissions	18
Variable overhead	8
Annual fixed costs	
Selling expenses	$42,000
Administrative expenses	56,000
Production expenses	30,000

The company's tax rate is 30 percent. You are doing a finance internship with the company and have been asked to address the items below.
   a. What is the firm's breakeven point in rings? In revenue?
   b. How much revenue is needed to yield $140,000 before-tax profit?
   c. How much revenue is needed to yield an after-tax profit of $120,000?
   d. How much revenue is needed to yield an after-tax profit of 20 percent of revenue?
   e. The firm's marketing manager believes that by spending an additional $12,000 in advertising and lowering the price by $20 per ring, he can increase the number of rings sold by 25 percent. He is currently selling 2,200 rings. Should he make these changes?

49. *(Multiproduct CVP)* Upscale Computers manufactures three types of computers, all of which are sold at wholesale to dealers throughout the world. Laptop models manufactured by Upscale sell at an average price of $2,200, and variable costs per unit total $1,900. Standard-size Upscale computers sell at an average price of $3,700, and vari-

able costs per unit equal $3,000. Luxury models manufactured by Upscale sell at an average price of $6,000, and the variable costs per unit are $5,000. Total fixed costs for the company are estimated at $1,080,000,000. As a consultant for the firm, you are requested to give your attention to the issues following.

a. The company's marketing department estimates that next year's unit sales mix will be 30 percent laptop, 50 percent standard, and 20 percent luxury. What is the breakeven point in units for the firm?

b. If the company has an after-tax profit goal of $1 billion and the tax rate is 50 percent, how many units of each type of computer must be sold for the goal to be reached?

c. Assume the sales mix shifts to 50 percent laptop, 40 percent standard, and 10 percent luxury. How does this mix affect your answer to Part b?

d. If the company sold more luxury computers and fewer laptop computers, how would your answers to Parts a and b change?

50. *(Multiproduct company)* Enchanting Sounds makes portable CD players, CDs, and batteries, which follow a normal sales mix pattern of 1:3:6. The following are the company's costs:

	CD PLAYERS	CDS	BATTERIES
Variable product costs	$ 62	$1.20	$.22
Variable selling expenses	14	.50	.10
Variable administrative expenses	3	.05	.03
Selling prices	140	5.00	.50
Annual fixed factory overhead	$110,000		
Annual fixed selling expenses	60,000		
Annual fixed administrative expenses	16,290		

The firm is in a 40 percent income tax bracket. As the new owner of the firm, you are interested in fine-tuning the performance of the company and need to devote some attention to the questions listed below.

a. What is the annual dollar breakeven point?

b. How many CD players, CDs, and batteries are expected to be sold at the breakeven point?

c. If the firm desires a before-tax profit of $114,640, how much total revenue is required and how many units of each item must be sold?

d. If the firm desires an after-tax profit of $103,176, how much total revenue is required and how many units of each item must be sold?

51. *(Multiproduct company)* The Arts & Crafts Emporium makes carved wooden mallard hens and ducklings. For every hen the firm sells, it sells two ducklings. The following are the company's revenues and costs:

	HENS	DUCKLINGS
Selling price	$12	$6
Variable cost	(4)	(4)
Contribution margin	$ 8	$2

Monthly fixed costs are $12,000. You have just inherited this firm and have decided that you need to focus on the following issues.

a. What is the average contribution margin ratio?

b. Calculate the breakeven point. At the breakeven point, identify the total units of each product sold and sales dollars of each product.

c. If the company wants to earn $24,000 in before-tax profit per month, how many hens and how many ducklings must it sell?

d. The company specifies $9,000 of after-tax profit as its objective, is in a 40 percent tax bracket, and believes that the mix has changed to five ducklings for every hen. How much total revenue is needed, and in what product proportions, to achieve its profit objective?

52. *(Multiproduct CVP; incremental analysis)* Bill Gunther owns a travel agency. He receives commission revenue based on the total dollar volume of business he generates for various client-firms in the travel and entertainment industries. His rates of commission currently are 20 percent of total hotel fees, 15 percent of total car rental fees, and 10 percent of airline ticket fees. Bill is your friend and has asked for your help. Data for a normal month's operations are as follows:

COSTS		FEES GENERATED FOR CLIENTS	
Advertising	$1,000	Hotel fees	$10,800
Rent	800	Car rental fees	3,600
Utilities	300	Airline ticket fees	14,200
Other expenses	1,400		$28,600

a. Given the stated commission percentages, what is Bill's normal total monthly commission? The normal monthly before-tax profit?

b. Bill can increase the amount of hotel fees he generates by 40 percent if he spends an additional $200 on advertising. Should he do this?

c. Sally Westin has offered to merge her bookings with Bill's and become his employee. She would receive a base salary of $600 a month plus 20 percent of the commissions on client fees she generates, which, for a normal month, are

Hotel fees	$5,000
Car rental fees	2,000
Airline ticket fees	2,000

Should Bill accept the proposal?

d. Use the information in Part c. During Sally's first month, she generated $10,000 of total fees, but they were as follows:

Hotel fees	$3,000
Car rental fees	2,000
Airline ticket fees	5,000

Will Bill be pleased? Why or why not?

53. (Scarce resource) The Premier Bakery produces three types of cakes: birthday, wedding, and special occasion. The cakes are made from scratch and baked in a special cake oven. During the holiday season (roughly November 15 through January 15), total demand for the cakes exceeds the capacity of the cake oven. The cake oven is available for baking 690 hours per month, but because of the size of the cakes, it can bake only one cake at a time. Management must determine how to ration the oven time among the three types of cakes. Information on costs, sales prices, and product demand follows:

	BIRTHDAY CAKES	WEDDING CAKES	SPECIAL OCCASION CAKES
Required minutes of oven time per cake	10	80	18
Sales price	$25	$100	$40
Variable costs:			
Direct material	5	30	10
Direct labor	5	15	8
Variable overhead	2	5	4
Variable selling	3	12	5
Fixed costs (monthly)			
Factory	$1,200		
Selling and administrative	800		

The chief baker and shop owner is trying to maximize her profits. She lives next door to you and has discussed the situation with you. You have agreed to develop answers to the following questions.

a. If demand is essentially unlimited for all three types of cakes during the holiday season, which cake or cakes should Premier bake during the holiday season? Why?

b. Based on your answer in Part a, how many cakes of each type will be produced? What is the projected level of monthly profit for the holiday season?

c. If you were the marketing manager for Premier, how would your marketing efforts differ between the holiday season and the rest of the year?

54. *(Sales mix)* One year ago, Tim Powers gave up his position as the movie critic and sportswriter of the local paper and purchased the rights (under a five-year contract) to sell concessions at a local municipal football stadium. After analyzing the results of his first-year operations, Tim is somewhat disappointed. His two main products are "dogs" and "burgers." He had expected to sell about the same number of each product over the course of the year. However, his sales mix was approximately two-thirds dogs and one-third burgers. Tim feels this combination is less profitable than a balanced mix of dogs and burgers. He is now trying to determine how to improve profitability for the coming year and is considering strategies to improve the sales mix. His first year operations are summarized below:

DOGS:

Sales (100,000 @ $1.50)	150,000	
Less: Direct material	(40,000)	
Direct labor	(15,000)	
Fixed costs	(45,000)	
Net profit		$ 50,000

BURGERS:

Sales (50,000 @ $2.50)	$125,000	
Less: Direct material	(55,000)	
Direct labor	(10,000)	
Fixed costs	(15,000)	
Net profit		45,000
Total profit		$ 95,000

If Tim takes no action to improve profitability, he expects sales and expenses in the second year to mirror the first-year results. Tim is considering two alternative strategies to boost profitability.

Strategy 1: Add point-of-sale advertising to boost burger sales. The estimated cost per year for such advertising would be $29,000. Tim estimates the advertising would decrease dog sales by 6,000 units and increase burger sales by 22,000 units.

Strategy 2: Provide a sales commission to his employees. The commission would be paid at a rate of 10 percent of the product contribution margin (sales less variable production costs) generated on all sales. Tim estimates this strategy would increase dog sales by 10 percent and burger sales by 25 percent.

Tim was a college classmate of yours and asks you to help him with the items below.
  a. Determine what action Tim should take: no action, strategy 1, or strategy 2. Show your supporting calculations.
  b. Assuming Tim decided to implement either of the new strategies, what behavioral concerns should he be prepared to address? Explain.

55. *(Special order)* Mary Ann Fisher makes and sells the "Pillow Pal," her famous stuffed bunny for young children. These toys are sold to department stores for $50. The capacity of the plant is 20,000 Pillow Pals per year. Costs to make and sell each stuffed animal are as follows:

Direct material	$ 6.00
Direct labor	6.50
Variable overhead	10.00
Fixed overhead	12.00
Variable selling expenses	3.00

An English import/export company has approached Mary Ann about buying 2,000 Pillow Pals. She is currently making and selling 20,000 Pillow Pals per year. The English firm wants its own label attached to each stuffed animal, which will raise costs by $.50 each. No selling expenses would be incurred on this offer. Mary Ann feels she must make an extra $1 on each stuffed animal to accept the offer. Assume that Mary Ann is your mother and has just paid for you to take a managerial accounting course. She asks you the following:

a. What is the opportunity cost per unit of selling to the English firm?
b. What is the minimum selling price Mary Ann should set?
c. Predict how much more operating profit Mary Ann will have if she accepts this offer at the price determined in Part b.
d. Prove your answer to Part c by providing operating profits without and with the new offer.

56. *(Product line)* Le Roi Paper Products makes three types of consumer products: computer paper, legal pads, and custom stationery. The firm has become increasingly concerned about the profitability of the custom stationery line. A segmented income statement for the most recent quarter follows:

	COMPUTER PAPER	LEGAL PADS	CUSTOM STATIONERY
Sales	$800,000	$400,000	$1,000,000
Variable costs:			
Production	(200,000)	(150,000)	(550,000)
Selling	(150,000)	(100,000)	(200,000)
Fixed costs:			
Production	(160,000)	(80,000)	(300,000)
Selling	(200,000)	(60,000)	(180,000)
Profit (loss) before tax	$ 90,000	$ 10,000	$ (230,000)

Because of the significance of the loss on custom stationery products, the company is considering the elimination of that product line. Of the fixed production costs, $400,000 are allocated to the product lines based on relative sales value; likewise, $250,000 of fixed selling costs are allocated to the product lines based on relative sales value. All of the other fixed costs charged to each product line are direct and would be eliminated if the product line was dropped.

As the company chief accountant, recast the income statements in a format more meaningful for deciding whether the custom stationery product line should be eliminated. Based on the new income statements, determine whether any product line should be eliminated.

57. *(Appendix 1)* The Senior Citizens Club has enlisted your help in developing a presentation for a group of local business executives who have previously given generously to support the club's efforts. Investigation reveals that each member pays dues of $8 per month, monthly variable costs per member are $1, and the club's monthly fixed expenses are $2,100. Most of the club's workers are volunteers.
a. Prepare a breakeven graph for the club.
b. Prepare a profit-volume graph for the club.
c. Which graph would you recommend that the club use in its presentation?

⊙ CASES

58. *(BEP; CVP)* Kalifo Company manufactures a line of electric garden tools that are sold in general hardware stores. The company's controller, Sylvia Harlow, has just received the sales forecast for the coming year for Kalifo's three products: weeders, hedge clippers, and leaf blowers. Kalifo has experienced considerable variations in sales volumes and variable costs over the past two years, and Harlow believes the forecast should be carefully evaluated from a cost-volume-profit viewpoint. The preliminary forecast information for 2000 is as follows:

	WEEDERS	HEDGE CLIPPERS	LEAF BLOWERS
Unit sales	50,000	50,000	100,000
Unit selling price	$28	$36	$48
Variable manufacturing cost per unit	13	12	25
Variable selling cost per unit	5	4	6

For 2000, Kalifo's fixed factory overhead is estimated at $2,000,000, and the company's fixed selling and administrative expenses are forecasted to be $600,000. Kalifo has an effective tax rate of 40 percent.

a. Determine Kalifo Company's forecasted net profit for 2000.

b. Assuming the sales mix remains as budgeted, determine how many units of each product Kalifo Company must sell to break even in 2000.

c. Determine the total dollar sales Kalifo Company must have in 2000 to earn an after-tax profit of $450,000.

d. After preparing the original estimates, Kalifo Company determined that the variable manufacturing cost of leaf blowers would increase 20 percent and the variable selling cost of hedge clippers would increase $1 per unit. However, Kalifo has decided not to change the selling price of either product. In addition, Kalifo has learned that its leaf blower has been perceived as the best value on the market; so it can expect to sell three times as many leaf blowers as any other product. Under these circumstances, determine how many units of each product Kalifo Company would have to sell to break even in 2000.

e. Explain the limitations of cost-volume-profit analysis that Sylvia Harlow should consider when evaluating Kalifo Company's 2000 forecast.

(CMA adapted)

59. *(BEP; CVP)* Southern States Airline is a small local carrier that flies among the gulf coast states. All seats are coach, and the following data are available:

Average full passenger fare	$150
Number of seats per plane	120
Average load factor (seats occupied)	70%
Average variable cost per passenger	$40
Fixed operating costs per month	$1,800,000

Southern States Airline has engaged you to answer the questions listed below.

a. What is the breakeven point in passengers and revenues?

b. What is the breakeven point in number of flights?

c. If Southern States raises its average full passenger fare to $200, it is estimated that the load factor will decrease to 55 percent. What will be the breakeven point in number of flights?

d. The cost of fuel is a significant variable cost to any airline. If fuel charges increase $8 per barrel, it is estimated that variable cost per passenger will rise to $60. In this case, what will be the new breakeven point in passengers and in number of flights? (Refer to original data.)

e. Southern States Airline has experienced an increase in variable cost per passenger to $50 and an increase in total fixed costs to $2,000,000. The company has decided to raise the average fare to $180. What number of passengers is needed to generate an after-tax profit of $600,000 if the tax rate is 40 percent?

f. Southern States is considering offering a discounted fare of $120, which the company feels would increase the load factor to 80 percent. Only the additional seats would be sold at the discounted fare. Additional monthly advertising costs would be $100,000. How much before-tax profit would the discounted fare provide Southern States if the company has 40 flights per day, 30 days per month? (Use the original data.)

g. Southern States has an opportunity to obtain a new route. The company feels it can sell seats at $175 on the route, but the load factor would be only 60 percent. The company would fly the route 20 times per month. The increase in fixed costs for additional crew, additional planes, landing fees, maintenance, and so on, would total $100,000 per month. Variable cost per passenger would remain at $40.

   (1) Should the company obtain the route?

   (2) How many flights would Southern States need to earn pretax profit of $57,500 per month on this route?

(3) If the load factor could be increased to 75 percent, how many flights would the company need to earn before-tax profit of $57,500 per month on this route?

(4) What qualitative factors should Southern States consider in making its decision about acquiring this route?

60. *(Special pricing)* McHenry Co. builds custom motor homes, which range in price from $100,000 to $400,000. For the past twenty-five years, the company's owner, Bob McHenry, has determined the selling price of each vehicle by estimating the costs of material, labor, and prorated overhead, and adding 25 percent to these estimated costs. For example, a recent price quotation was determined as follows:

Direct material	$ 50,000
Direct labor	80,000
Overhead	20,000
Cost	$150,000
Plus 25%	37,500
Selling price	$187,500

Overhead is allocated to all orders at 25 percent of direct labor. The company has traditionally operated at 80 percent of full capacity. Occasionally, a customer would reject a price quote and, if the company were in a slack period, McHenry Co. would often be willing to reduce the markup to as little as 10 percent over estimated costs. The average markup for the year is estimated to be 20 percent.

Bob McHenry has recently completed a course on pricing with an emphasis on the contribution margin approach to pricing. He thinks that such an approach would be helpful in determining the selling prices of custom vehicles.

Total overhead, which includes selling and administrative costs for the year, is estimated to be $1,500,000. Of this amount, $900,000 is fixed and the remainder is variable in direct proportion to direct labor.

a. Assume the customer in the example rejected the $187,500 bid and also rejected a $165,000 bid. The customer countered with a $150,000 offer.

(1) What is the difference in pretax profit for the year (assuming no replacement offer) between accepting and rejecting the customer's offer?

(2) What is the minimum selling price McHenry Co. could have quoted the customer without reducing or increasing net income for the year?

b. What advantage does the contribution margin approach to pricing have over the approach McHenry Co. is currently using?

c. What pitfalls are there, if any, to contribution pricing?

(CMA adapted)

⊙ ETHICS AND QUALITY DISCUSSIONS

61. The president of a large automotive firm was asked to attend a congressional hearing to specify the breakeven point for his firm in either units or sales dollars. The president of the firm replied that this was not possible because of the many variables that had to be taken into consideration in determining a breakeven point. The congressional investigator replied that the president was being evasive and expressed doubt that the stockholders of the firm were being adequately served by a management team that did not even know the firm's breakeven point. As a financial advisor to the Congress, you are asked the following:

a. What are some of the variables that the president of the firm had in mind?

b. How could the congressional investigator have reached the stated conclusion about the management team of the firm?

62. Hanson Chemical Company's new president has learned that for the past four years, the company has been dumping its industrial waste into the local river and falsifying reports to authorities about the levels of suspected cancer-causing materials in that waste. His plant manager says that there is no proof that the waste causes cancer, and there are only a few fishing towns within a hundred miles downstream. If the company has to treat the substance to neutralize its potentially injurious effects and then transport it to

a legal dumpsite, the company's variable and fixed costs would rise to a level that might make the firm uncompetitive. If the company loses its competitive advantage, 10,000 local employees could become unemployed, and the town's economy could collapse.

a. What kinds of variable and fixed costs can you think of that would increase (or decrease) if the waste were treated rather than dumped? How would these costs affect product contribution margin?

b. What are the ethical conflicts the president faces?

c. What rationalizations can you detect that have been devised by plant employees?

d. What options and suggestions can you offer the president?

63. Peter Klein is a sales representative for a heavy construction equipment manufacturer. He is compensated by a moderate fixed salary plus an 8 percent bonus on sales. Klein is aware that some of the higher-priced items earn the company a lower contribution margin and some of the lower-priced items earn the company a higher contribution margin. He learned this information from the variable costing financial statements produced by the company for management-level employees. One of Klein's best friends is a manager at the company.

Klein has recently started pushing sales of the high-priced items (to the exclusion of lower-priced items) by generously entertaining receptive customers and offering them gifts through the company's promotion budget. He feels that management has not given him adequate raises in the 20 years he has been with the company, and now he is too old to find a better job. As Klein's best friend and as a manager of the company, you are being asked to contemplate the following:

a. Are Klein's actions legal?

b. What are the ethical issues involved in the case from Klein's standpoint?

c. Are there ethical issues in the case from company management's standpoint?

d. What do you believe Klein should do? Why?

64. In Japan, the decision to stop production of a product or to close down a plant has different cost consequences than in the United States. One principal difference is that Japanese managers are much less likely to fire workers who are displaced by an event such as a plant closing. Japanese managers simply try to move the displaced workers to active plants. However, this concept of permanent or lifetime employment can be awkward to manage when economic times become difficult and prudent financial management suggests that activities, including employment, be scaled back to cut costs. Several years ago, one Japanese company found a unique solution:

> Nissan Motor Co., in a sign that its severe slump may be worsening, is taking the unusual step of loaning some of its idle factory workers to a rival automaker.
>
> Nissan said it will assign 250 of its production employees to work for six months at factories run by Isuzu Motors Ltd., a 37% owned affiliate of General Motors Corp.
>
> Nissan's spokesman, Koji Okuda, called the move an attempt to deal with the company's sharp drop in auto output in Japan. In May, Nissan's Japanese auto production fell 26% from a year earlier. "Demand is low," Mr. Okuda said. "We have to adjust our operations."
>
> [SOURCE: Michael Williams, "Nissan Will Loan Workers to Rival Amid Low Demand," *Wall Street Journal*, June 24, 1994, p. A4.]

As an economic journalist of a large international publication, you have been asked to contemplate the following issues.

a. What specific types of costs might Nissan have considered relevant in its decision to lend employees to Isuzu?

b. Why would Isuzu be interested in hiring, on a temporary basis, workers of Nissan?

c. What were the likely impacts of this arrangement on the quality of the output at Isuzu? The quality of output at Nissan?

Chapter 7   The Budget Process

Penn Fuel Gas

In 1994, Penn Fuel Gas, Inc. (PFG) initiated its first annual and long-range operating budget process. PFG is a public utility holding company with consolidated revenues of $125 million and 550 employees. In addition to selling natural gas, the company provides natural gas storage and transportation services, merchandise services, and has a propane business. PFG's utility operations are split between two subsidiaries, each with multiple locations.

The motivation for budgeting came jointly from PFG's bankers, its board of directors, and its management. The information needs of all three users were fairly similar. All three were interested in cash flow projections and future earnings potential. The board was interested in improving PFG's return on equity (ROE), and it wanted to analyze the prospects of reinstituting a common stock dividend. In addition, management wanted segmented profit and loss statements and improved departmental expense and cash flow tracking. PFG's segments are regions, lines of business (utility, propane, merchandise), and types of customer (commercial, industrial, residential).

Budgeting for natural gas and propane operations is difficult because a significant amount of demand for these products is dependent upon Mother Nature. Penn Fuel experienced two abnormal winters in its first two years of budgeting. In 1994, Pennsylvania had its coldest, iciest winter in history. In 1995, it had one of its warmest. But forecasting is difficult for many rapidly growing companies. They must be flexible. For example, PFG budgets use the normal winter weather forecast, but the company also provides sensitivity analyses and budget reprojections at least quarterly. Company and budget personnel realize that capital spending is partially a function of the winter season's revenues, which won't be known until the first quarter is over. The first quarter is particularly important in the utility and propane business as it represents 40 percent of the total annual product delivered.

SOURCE: Robert N. West and Amy M. Snyder, "How to Set Up a Budgeting and Planning System," *Management Accounting* (January 1997), pp. 20, 21. Published by Institute of Management Accountants, Montvale, NJ. Visit our website at www.imanet.org.

When a company's environment is relatively stable, budgeting factors are fairly predictable and the budgeting process is less challenging than when environmental factors are highly uncertain. For companies such as *Penn Fuel Gas* (PFG), some of the underlying budget assumptions, such as the severity of winter temperatures, are extremely unpredictable. In these situations, factors that can significantly affect the budget require an ongoing monitoring process as the year progresses. Although budgeting is important for all organizations, entities that have significant amounts of cash and other resources should prepare and use detailed budgets for both planning and control purposes.

Regardless of the type of endeavor in which you engage, it is necessary at some point to visualize the future, imagine what results you want to achieve, and determine the activities and resources required to achieve those results. Even individuals frequently must engage in budgeting. For example, Tim Brown, who is a sophomore at Ivy University, has been invited to spend his spring vacation week at his college dorm roommate's home in Fort Lauderdale. Tim has only $180 available and asks his dad for supplemental money for the trip. His dad requires that Tim prepare a budget. Tim provides the following budgetary estimates for his proposed vacation:

TIM'S VACATION BUDGET

Gasoline (2,000 miles ÷ 25 mpg) × ($1.30 per gallon) ÷ 2 persons*	$ 52	
Meals and lodging for round trip (10 meals @ $15) + (4 nights @ $50)	350	
Beach clothes, sunglasses, and suntan oil	40	
Admissions, entertainment, and snacks	100	
Total cost of trip		$542
Less the money Tim already has		(180)
Money needed from dad		$362

*Tim's roommate agrees to pay for half the gasoline.

Fortunately for Tim, he had just received his midterm grades, and they were all quite favorable. He mailed both his budget request and midterm grades to his dad. By return mail, Tim received a check for $362 and a note from his parents congratulating him on his grades.

Most budgeting situations are more complex than the simplistic example just given. When the budgeting process requires the integration of large amounts of funds, people, and organizational units, budgets and budgetary results should be committed to paper or input to a computer. This is because of the human tendency to forget and the difficulty of mentally processing many facts and relationships at the same time.

budget　　　　Detailed plans that are monetarily enumerated are called **budgets**. This chapter not only describes some of the managerial aspects of budgeting but also covers quantitative aspects of the process and the preparation of a master budget.

PURPOSES OF BUDGETING

Budgeting is the process of devising a financial plan for future operations. Budgeting is a management task, not an accounting task. The accounting function simply assembles the information provided into a known and consistent format. Budgeting is an important part of an organization's planning and controlling processes; and as indicated in Exhibit 7-1, the resulting budgets may serve many different roles.

Budgets can be used to indicate direction and priorities; measure individual, divisional, and corporate performance; encourage achievement and continuous improvement efforts; and identify areas of concern. The process itself can be performed in a variety of ways: top-down, bottom-up, or a combination of the two. The basics of the budgeting process are illustrated in the flow diagram in Exhibit 7-2 (page 284); the individual steps are discussed in the remainder of this chapter.

Like any other planning activity, budgeting helps managers focus on one direction chosen from many future alternatives. Management generally defines the chosen path using some accounting measure of financial performance, such as net income, earnings per share, or sales level in dollars or units. Such accounting-based measures provide specific quantitative criteria against which future performance (also recorded in accounting terms) can be compared. Budgets, then, are a type of standard, and variances from budget can be computed.

Budgeting can also help identify potential problems in achieving specified goals and objectives. For example, assume that a particular company has objectives of generating $55 million in revenues and $2.5 million of net income for the year 2000. The budget might indicate that, based on current prices and expenses, such objectives cannot be obtained. Managers could then brainstorm to find ways to increase revenues or reduce costs so that these objectives can be reached. By quantifying potential difficulties and making them visible, budgets can help stimulate managers to think of ways to overcome those difficulties.

budgeting

LEARNING OBJECTIVE ❶
What is the importance of the budgeting process?

- ⊙ Planning—By linking objectives and resources, budgets serve as primary planning documents and project expected or pro forma results.
- ⊙ Motivation—Motivation of workers can be affected by several key elements of both the budgeting process and the budget's content, such as degree of participation and reasonableness of financial goals.
- ⊙ Evaluation—Considerable care must be exercised to ensure that performance evaluations are fair and productive; like motivation, this budget role is affected by elements such as degree of participation and reasonableness of financial goals.
- ⊙ Coordination—Coordination among the various interest or functional areas in an organization is essential in the budgeting process and budget preparation because of the financial interaction of those areas.
- ⊙ Communication—Communication must take place among the various interests or functional areas in an organization if coordination is to occur.
- ⊙ Education—Managers and staff will learn from their involvement in the budgeting process. A major educational component can be the discovery of changes in cost structure as cost behavior and cost drivers are analyzed.
- ⊙ Ritual—In some organizations, the budgeting process is simply a ritual that occurs periodically, in which all players merely go through the motions. While the ritual aspect creates financial and emotional costs for the participants, it delivers few real benefits.

SOURCE: Adapted from Stephen V. Senge, "A Curricular Model for Short-Term Budgeting," *Accounting Instructor's Report* (Fall 1994), p. 6.

EXHIBIT 7-1
Different Roles of the Budgeting Process and of Budgets

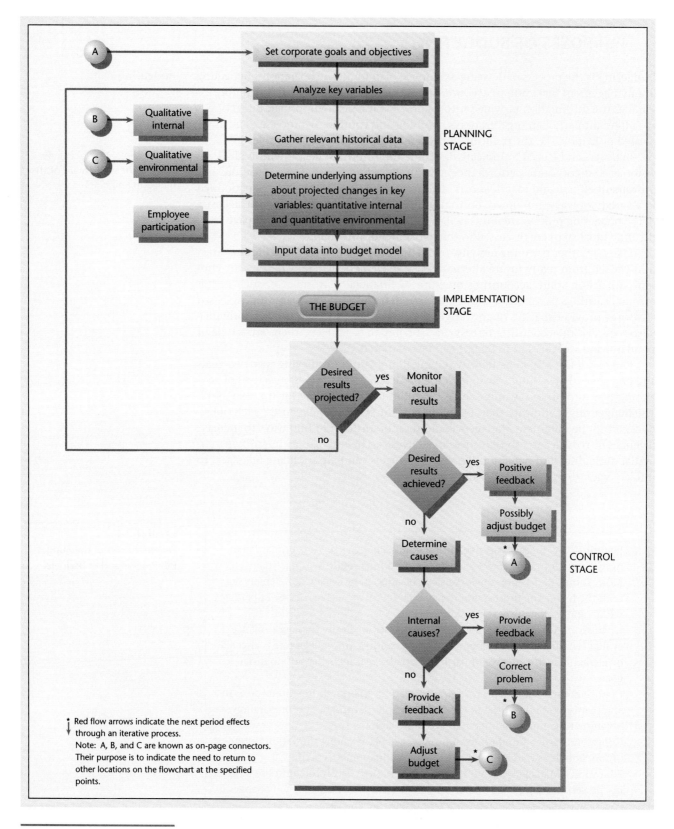

EXHIBIT 7-2
The Budgeting Process

A well-prepared budget can be an effective device to communicate objectives, constraints, and expectations to people throughout an organization. Such communication helps everyone understand exactly what is to be accomplished, how those accomplishments are to be achieved, and how resources are to be allocated. Decisions about resource allocations are made, in part, through a process of obtaining information, justifying requests, and negotiating compromises. Allowing managers to participate in the budgeting process motivates them and instills a feeling of teamwork. Employee participation is needed to effectively integrate necessary information from various sources as well as to obtain individual managerial commitment to the resulting budget.

The budget indicates the resource constraints under which managers must operate for the upcoming budget period. Thus, the budget becomes the basis for controlling activities and resource usage. Periodic budget-to-actual comparisons allow managers to determine how well they are doing and to assess how well they understand their operations.

While budgets are typically expressed in financial terms, the budgeting and planning processes are concerned with all organizational resources—raw materials inventory, supplies, personnel, and facilities. These processes can be viewed from a long-term or a short-term perspective. Exhibit 7-3 provides a checklist for the budgeting process.

PARTICIPATION IN THE BUDGETING PROCESS

Once management has evaluated the operating environment and relevant product life cycles and decided on the organization's strategic plan, budgeting activity should begin for future periods. The budgeting process requires carefully integrating a complex set of facts and projections with human relationships and attitudes. Therefore, no single system of budgeting is right for all organizations. However, it is recognized that there are basically two ways by which budgets can be derived: from the top down (**imposed budgets**) or from the bottom up (**participatory budgets**).

For decades, budgets in governmental and not-for-profit organizations, such as the Red Cross, have had the primary goals of monetary control and fiscal responsibility. Business budgets originally maintained the same focus and were prepared by top management with little or no input from operating personnel. Such budgets were simply imposed on the operating personnel, who had to work within the budgeted figures and constraints. In such a budgeting environment, operating personnel may be given an opportunity to suggest changes to the budget, but such suggestions are not always seriously considered. As indicated in Exhibit 7-4 (page 286), imposed budgets are effective and provide some distinct advantages under certain circumstances; but they involve disadvantages as well.

imposed budget
participatory budget

LEARNING OBJECTIVE ❷
How do the advantages and disadvantages of imposed budgets and participatory budgets compare?

http:// www.redcross.org

EXHIBIT 7-3
Checklist for a Successful Budgeting Process

Questions to ask about the budgeting process and the budget:
- ⊙ Is it realistic, accurate, and internally consistent?
- ⊙ Does it plan the best results achievable for the company that are consistent with acceptable risk and long-term health?
- ⊙ Does it contain the information most useful for management?
- ⊙ Is it consistent with a strategy that reassures employees that the company is moving in a good direction?
- ⊙ Does it facilitate goal setting and measurement at all levels?
- ⊙ Does it communicate strategy, plans, and required outputs?
- ⊙ Does it communicate operating plans, including support needs, across functions?
- ⊙ Will it be beaten?
- ⊙ Will it be approved?
- ⊙ Does it give every organizational unit the resources it needs to accomplish what is needed?

SOURCE: Robert G. Finney, "Budgeting: From Pain to Power," p. 28. Reprinted by permission of the publisher from *Management Review*, September 1993. © 1993 American Management Association, New York. http://www.amanet.org. All rights reserved.

EXHIBIT 7-4
Imposed Budgets

Best Times to Use:
- In start-up organizations
- In extremely small businesses
- In times of economic crisis
- When operating managers lack budgetary skills or perspective
- When organizational units require precise coordination of efforts

Advantages of Imposed Budgets:
- Increase probability that the organization's strategic plans will be incorporated in planned activities
- Enhance coordination among divisional plans and objectives
- Use top management's knowledge of overall resource availability
- Reduce the possibility of input from inexperienced or uninformed lower-level employees
- Reduce the time frame for the budgeting process

Disadvantages of Imposed Budgets:
- May result in dissatisfaction, defensiveness, and low morale among individuals who must work under the budget
- Reduce the feeling of teamwork
- May limit the acceptance of the stated goals and objectives
- Limit the communication process between employees and management
- May create a view of the budget as a punitive device
- May result in unachievable budgets for international divisions if local operating and political environments are not adequately considered
- May stifle the initiative of lower-level managers

Businesspeople slowly recognized the disadvantages of imposed budgets and the dissatisfaction they caused. Thus, participation at various management levels was introduced. From the standpoint of operational managers, participation can be viewed on a spectrum. At one end is the right to comment on budgets before their implementation; at the other is the ultimate right to set budgets. Neither end of the spectrum is quite appropriate. Simply giving managers the right to comment on the handed-down budget still reflects an imposed budgeting system, while giving each individual manager the right to set his or her own budget ignores the fact that cooperation and communication among areas are essential to the functioning of a cohesive organization.

A participatory budget is generally defined as one that has been developed through a process of joint decision making by top management and operating personnel. The degree to which lower-level operating management is allowed to participate in budget development usually depends on two factors: top management's awareness of the advantages of the participation process and its confidence in those advantages. Both the advantages and disadvantages of participatory budgets are listed in Exhibit 7-5.

budget slack

Managers may introduce **budget slack** (the intentional underestimation of revenues and/or overestimation of expenses) into the budgeting process. Slack, if it exists, is usually built into the budget during the participation process; it is not often found in imposed budgets. Having slack in the budget allows subordinate managers to achieve their objectives with less effort than if there were no slack. Budget slack creates problems because of the significant interaction of budgeting factors. If sales are understated, for example, problems can arise in the production, purchasing, and personnel areas.

To reduce the possibility of slack, management may wish to consider basing the budget on activities rather than costs. Activity-based budgets require an analysis of cost drivers and the relating of budget line items to activities performed. Some benefits of using activity-based budgets are discussed in the News Note on page 288.

EXHIBIT 7-5
Participatory Budgets

Best Times to Use:
- In well-established organizations
- In extremely large businesses
- In times of economic affluence
- When operating managers have strong budgetary skills and perspectives
- When organizational units are quite autonomous

Advantages of Participatory Budgets:
- Provide information from persons most familiar with the needs and constraints of organizational units
- Integrate knowledge that is diffused among various levels of management
- Lead to better morale and higher motivation
- Provide a means to develop fiscal responsibility and the budgetary skills of employees
- Develop a high degree of acceptance of and commitment to organizational goals and objectives by operating management
- Are generally more realistic
- Allow organizational units to coordinate with one another
- Allow subordinate managers to develop operational plans that conform to organizational goals and objectives
- Include specific resource requirements
- Blend overview of top management with operating details
- Provide a social contract that expresses expectations of top management and subordinates

Disadvantages of Participatory Budgets:
- Require significantly more time than imposed budgets
- Create a level of dissatisfaction with the process similar to that occurring under imposed budgets when the effects of managerial participation are negated by top-management changes
- Create an unachievable budget when managers are ambivalent or unqualified to participate
- May cause lower-level managers to introduce slack into the budget
- May support "empire building" by subordinates
- May start the process earlier in the year when there is more uncertainty about the future year

Since the functions of operating personnel are affected by the budget and these individuals must work under the budget guidelines, input from the operating level is often invaluable in the planning process. While there is no concrete evidence as to how well participatory budgeting works in all circumstances, such participation by operating managers also seems to create a higher commitment to the budget's success. To the extent that participation reduces the precarious aspect of projections by providing managers with a greater quantity and quality of information, better budgets will result.

The budgeting process, as mentioned, represents a continuum with imposed budgets on one end and participatory budgets on the other. Currently, most business budgets are prepared through a coordinated effort including input from operating personnel and revision by top management. In this manner, plans of managers at all levels can be considered. Top management first sets strategic objectives for lower-level management; then lower-level managers suggest and justify their operations' performance targets. Upper-level managers combine all component budgets, evaluate the overall results, and provide feedback on any needed changes to the lower-level managers.

Regardless of whether the process is top-down or bottom-up, management must review the completed budget before approving and implementing it. This process is necessary to determine (1) if the underlying assumptions on which the budget is based

Activity-Based Budgeting Focuses on Work, Not Costs

http:// www.jnj.com

http:// www.chrysler.com

A budget should be based on knowledge of how good the organization can be and should be. Developing an achievable budget is often difficult because most managers develop a budget on what they spend, not on what they do (activities) that consumes the budgeted costs.

Many organizations, such as Johnson & Johnson and Chrysler Corporation, are looking to their existing activity-based cost systems as the basis for re-engineering their budgeting process. Unlike conventional budgeting that focuses on resource cost, the re-engineered budget process should assume that the focus will center on activities and business processes. Activity-based budgeting (ABB) is a process of planning and controlling the expected activities of an organization. ABB links work (activity) with the strategic cost, time, and quality objectives of the organization. ABB focuses on activities. Costs are determined after the activity workload is defined.

The following list compares traditional and activity-based budgeting:

Top 10 Weaknesses of Traditional Budgeting	vs.	Top 10 Advantages of Activity-Based Budgeting
1. Does not provide a common language that supports common sense.		1. Uses a common (verb + noun) activity language.
2. Focuses on costs, not quality or time.		2. Focuses on activity cost, time, and quality.
3. Focuses on input (costs), not output.		3. Focuses on activity input and output.
4. Does not link to the strategic plan.		4. Strategic goals are linked to the activity's cost, time, and quality.
5. Does not identify levels of service.		5. Focuses on required versus discretionary activity output.
6. Does not identify root causes of costs.		6. Aids in identifying the cost drivers of activities and processes.
7. Focuses on functions, not processes.		7. Focuses on functional activities and business processes.
8. Focuses on cuts, not continuous improvement.		8. Focuses on the unending improvement of activity output.
9. Does not identify work or workload.		9. Focuses on activity and output.
10. Does not identify or quantify waste.		10. Quantifies non-value-added activity costs.

SOURCE: Tom Pryor, "The Budget Is Not the Best You Can Be," *Focus on ABM* (Winter 1993), pp.1–2. www.icms.net/1993

are reasonable and (2) if the budgeted results are acceptable and realistic. The budget may indicate that the results expected from the planned activities do not achieve the desired objectives. In this case, planned activities should be reconsidered and revised to more appropriately aim the company toward the desired outcomes expressed during planning for the intermediate term (assuming they are not overly ambitious).

THE BUDGETING PROCESS

The budget is normally prepared on an annual basis and detailed first by quarters and then by months within those quarters. At a *minimum*, budget preparation should begin two to three months before the period to be covered, but management must keep two things in mind: (1) participatory budget development will take longer than an imposed budget process and (2) the larger and more complex the company is, the longer the budgeting process will take.

Some companies use a **continuous** (or rolling) **budget**, an ongoing twelve-month budget that adds a new budget month (twelve months into the future) as each current month expires. As shown in Exhibit 7-6, at any point, management is working within the present one-month component of a full twelve-month annual budget. Continuous budgets make the planning process less sporadic and disruptive. Rather than "going into the budgeting period" at a specific point in time, managers are continuously involved in planning and budgeting. Continuous budgets also provide a longer-range focus, so that no surprises occur at year-end. Surprises within the budgeting process can also be minimized through the use of a detailed budget manual.

continuous budget

The evolution of electronic spreadsheets has dramatically affected the budgeting process. Computerized spreadsheets allow companies to quickly and inexpensively examine "what if" scenarios and adjust interrelated budgets to reflect environmental or internal changes. These spreadsheets are also helpful to a company's ability to maintain a continuous budget. Once the set of budget headings, budget formulas, and current twelve months of budget figures have been tested and entered on a spreadsheet, each new month's figures can be developed as the month just concluded is deleted.

A good budget requires a substantial amount of time and effort from the persons engaged in preparing it. This process can be improved by the availability of an organizational **budget manual**, a detailed set of documents that provide information and guidelines about the budgetary process. The manual should include the following:

budget manual

1. Statements of the budgeting purpose and its desired results
2. A listing of specific budgetary activities to be performed
3. A calendar of scheduled budgetary activities
4. Sample budget forms
5. Original, revised, and approved budgets

LEARNING OBJECTIVE ❸
Why does a budget manual facilitate the budgeting process?

The *statements of budgeting purpose and desired results* communicate the reasons behind the process and should flow from general statements to specific details. An example of a general statement of budgeting purpose is: "The cash budget provides a

EXHIBIT 7-6
Continuous Budget

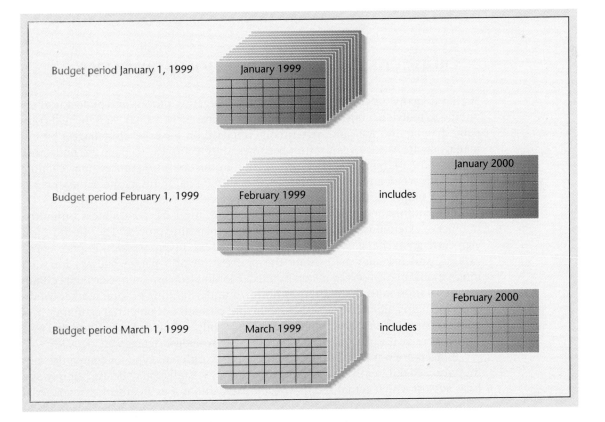

basis for planning, reviewing, and controlling cash flows from and for various activities; this budget is essential to the preparation of a pro forma Statement of Cash Flows." Specific statements regarding the cash budget could include references to minimum desired cash balances and periods of high cash needs. These needs are taken into consideration when the cash budget portion of the master budget is prepared.

Budgetary activities should be listed by job rather than by a person's name because the responsibility for actions should be delegated to whomever is holding each specific job when the manual is implemented. This section should indicate who has the final authority for revising and approving the budget. Budget approval may be delegated to a budget committee or to one or several members of top management.

The *budget calendar* coordinates the budgetary process and should include a timetable for all budgetary activities. The budget timetable is unique to each organization. The larger the organization, the more time will be needed to gather information, coordinate that information, identify weak points in the process or the budget itself, and take corrective action. The calendar should also indicate control points for the upcoming periods, when budget-to-actual comparisons will be made, and when and how feedback will be provided to managers responsible for operations.

Sample forms provide a means for consistent presentation of budget information by all individuals, making summarizations of information easier, quicker, and more effective. The sample forms should be understandable and could include standardized worksheets that allow managers to update historical information to arrive at budgetary figures. This section of the manual may also provide standard cost tables for items on which the organization has specific guidelines or policies. For example, in estimating employee fringe benefit costs, the company rule of thumb may be 30 percent of base salary. Similarly, a company policy may set the daily meal allowance for salespersons at $30; in estimating meal expenses for the future period, the sales manager would simply multiply total estimated travel days by $30.

The last section of the manual includes the *original and revised budgets*. It is helpful for future planning to understand how the revision process works and why changes were made. The final approved budget is composed of many individual budgets, serves as a control document for budget-to-actual comparisons, and is known as the master budget (discussed in a subsequent section of this chapter).

LEARNING OBJECTIVE ❹
What complicates the budgeting process in a multinational environment?

BUDGETING IN AN INTERNATIONAL BUSINESS

Similar to many other business practices, the budgeting process and budget uses are unique to individual businesses. The budgeting process in a small, closely held company may be informal and, potentially, imposed on lower-level managers by top management. As the organization becomes more complex, so does the budgeting process. Lower-level managerial participation in the budgeting process may be more important. When an organization reaches multinational status, participatory budgeting is not simply desired, it becomes necessary for the effort to be effective.

In a multinational environment, an organization faces an almost unlimited number of external variables that can affect the planning process. The effects of foreign currency exchange rates, interest rates, inflation, inventory transfer price implications, and risk may necessitate the preparation of separate budgets for each international market served in addition to a coordinated corporate-wide budget. Budget preparation must incorporate a thorough understanding of local market conditions including all known external forces and estimates of potential economic and market changes. Thus, each foreign operation's budget should also be supported by a comprehensive list of assumptions explaining how budget figures were derived.

Budgets are not only developed differently in different types of companies, but they are used differently. In small organizations, the budget may be used simply as a basis against which actual results are compared and not as a control or managerial

The budgeting process differs between both organizations and cultures. Budgets in Japanese firms are more flexible and short-run oriented than budgets in Western firms. The underlying rationale is that employees can better focus on near-term targets to ascertain that they comply with the organization's highly inflexible vision and strategic plan.

performance evaluation mechanism. As the business expands, the need for budgeting as a control and coordination tool arises because of interactions among multiple departments or organizational units. Managerial and employee performance may then be gauged against the budget and resulting comparisons used in a reward system.

In many circumstances, it is difficult to determine the underlying causes of budget variations because of the effects of noncontrollable factors such as competitive maneuvers, economic conditions, and government regulations. In an international organization, the supporting list of assumptions is critical if the budget is to be used for control and evaluation purposes. Managers and employees should not be faulted for failing to achieve budget targets if the underlying causes reflect unforeseen, noncontrollable factors such as newly introduced governmental policies relating to import or export restrictions, exchange rate fluctuations, or market disturbances created by economic adjustments in a foreign country. Managers should, however, be held accountable for taking advantage of new opportunities created by these same factors.

The News Note on page 292 discusses the differences between the budgeting process and budget usage in the United States and Japan. This excerpt highlights the fact that no single planning process is correct and that not only will differences exist among companies of different sizes, but that multinationals domiciled in different countries will also have different perspectives.

THE MASTER BUDGET

From an accounting standpoint, the budgeting process culminates in the preparation of a **master budget**, which is a comprehensive set of an organization's budgetary schedules and pro forma (projected) financial statements. The master budget is composed of both operating and financial budgets. **Operating budgets** are expressed in both units and dollars. When an operating budget is related to revenues, the units are those expected to be sold, and the dollars reflect selling prices. When an operating budget relates to expense items, the units are those expected to be used and the dollars reflect costs.

Monetary details from the operating budgets are aggregated in **financial budgets**, which reflect the funds to be generated or consumed during the budget period. Financial budgets include the company's cash and capital budgets as well as its

master budget

operating budget

financial budget

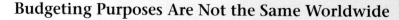

NEWS NOTE

Budgeting Purposes Are Not the Same Worldwide

Japanese planning and budgeting processes are very different from the typical American practice. Japanese companies develop a vision that is relatively permanent. They also develop a strategic plan that, again, is relatively brief and revised infrequently. More important, Japanese companies develop what they call a midterm plan, which really is generated at only a very high level of the organization. It is relatively simple, containing such information as market share, sales, product costs, selling and administrative expenses, financing expenses, and inventory. It is revised periodically but never more than once a year.

The heart of Japanese companies' planning and budgeting is the six-month budget. Some companies tag onto it a rolling set of half-year projections that reach out several additional years. The six-month budget normally is prepared in no more than one month's time and often takes only two or three weeks.

The six-month budget is produced in a fashion similar to U.S. methods, with some top-down guidelines and a bottom-up estimate of achievable results. The finance and accounting staff plays a strong role in facilitation, working with senior management to communicate market realities and with line personnel to revise target costs. Even in the short two- to three-week cycle there may be several iterations of guideline delivery, budget preparation, and presentation.

The final budget is translated into target cost and productivity measures for the various groups. It is fair to say that the purpose to which Japanese companies put their plans and budgets is very different from U.S. companies. The primary purpose is to take a new look at the foreseeable future and to set short-run targets that are communicated clearly to the appropriate levels and groups of management so they can focus their efforts toward achieving them. Japanese companies spend virtually no time each month comparing actual results to budget and, more important, going through a lengthy, drawn-out process of explaining the causes of such variances. Rather, everyone is committed to achieving the targets that have been embodied into the six-month budgets.

Performance measurement and achievement of individual bonuses is another explanation for the different levels of detail generated by U.S. and Japanese companies in preparing annual budgets. In the United States, managers' bonuses and salaries are related directly to how well they achieve their individual plans. Japanese companies, on the other hand, place little emphasis on meeting budget when evaluating individual performance and therefore do not require as detailed a budget or plan.

SOURCE: Robert A. Howell and Michiharu Sakurai, "Management Accounting (and Other) Lessons from the Japanese," *Management Accounting* (December 1992), pp. 32–33. Reprinted from *Management Accounting*, published by the Institute of Management Accountants, Montvale, NJ. Visit our website at www.imanet.org.

LEARNING OBJECTIVE 5
What is the starting point of a master budget and why is this item chosen?

pro forma financial statements. These budgets are the ultimate focal points for the firm's top management.

The master budget is prepared for a specific period and is static rather than flexible. It is static in that it is based on a single, most probable level of output demand. Expressing the budget on a single level of output is necessary to facilitate the many time-consuming financial arrangements that must be made before beginning operations for the budget period. Such arrangements include hiring an adequate number of people, obtaining needed production and/or storage space, obtaining suppliers, confirming prices, delivery schedules, and quality of resources.

The output level of sales or service quantities selected for use in the preparation of the master budget affects all organizational components. It is essential that all the components interact in a coordinated manner. Exhibit 7-7 indicates the budgetary interrelationships among the primary departments of a manufacturing organization. A budget developed by one department is commonly an essential ingredient in developing another department's budget.

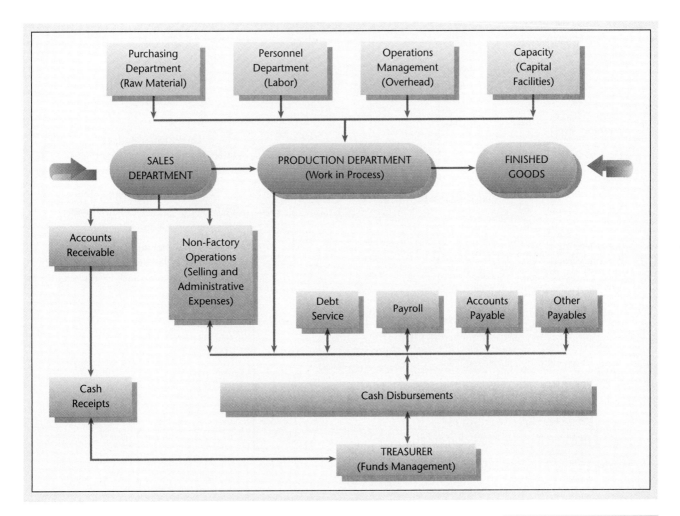

EXHIBIT 7-7

The Budgetary Process in a Manufacturing Organization

Assuming that top management is engaging in participatory budgeting, each department in the budgetary process either prepares its own budget or provides information for inclusion in a budget. As is true at PFG, the budgetary process begins with Sales Department estimates of the types, quantities, and timing of demand for products and services. This information is needed by both Production and Accounts Receivable. Production managers combine sales estimates with information from Purchasing, Personnel, Operations, and Capital Facilities to determine the types, quantities, and timing of products to be produced and transferred to finished goods. Accounts Receivable uses sales estimates, in conjunction with estimated collection patterns, to determine the amounts and timing of cash receipts. Cash receipts information is necessary for the treasurer to properly manage the organization's flow of funds. All areas create cash disbursements that must be matched with cash receipts so that cash is available when it is needed.

In Exhibit 7-7, note that certain information must flow back into the department from which it began. For example, the Sales Department must receive finished goods information to know if goods are in stock (or can be produced to order) before selling products. The treasurer must receive continual input on cash receipts and disbursements as well as provide output to various organizational units on the availability of funds so that proper funds management can be maintained.

Exhibit 7-8 (page 294) presents an overview of the master budget preparation sequence and component budgets, indicates the department responsible for each budget's preparation, and illustrates how the budgets relate to one another. While the flow of information is visible in Exhibit 7-8, the quantitative and monetary implications are not. The remainder of the chapter reflects these implications through the preparation of a master budget.

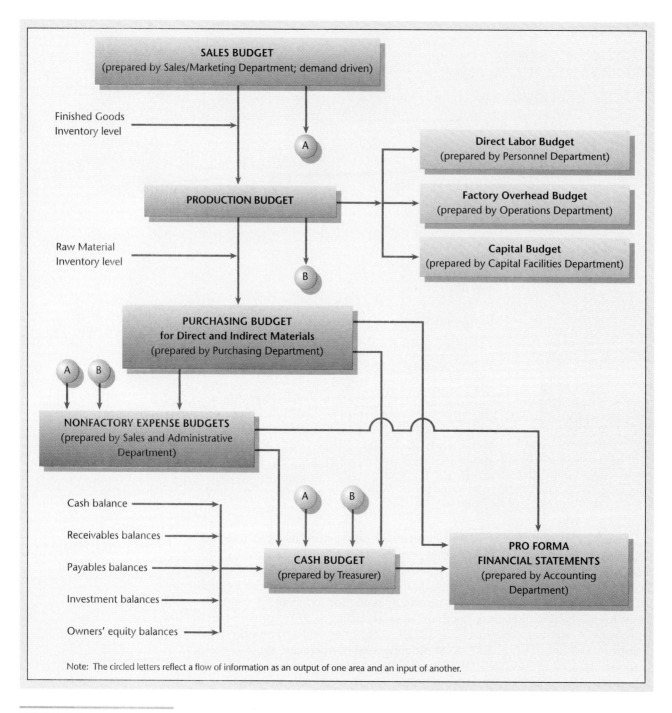

EXHIBIT 7-8

The Master Budget:
An Overview

How are the various master
budget schedules prepared
and how do they relate to one
another?

THE MASTER BUDGET ILLUSTRATED

Precision Inc. is used to illustrate the process of preparing a master budget for 2000.
The company produces metal shut-off valves for use in the natural gas industry. The
master budget is prepared for the entire year and then subdivided into quarterly and
monthly periods. Precision Inc.'s Marketing Division has estimated total sales for the
year at 2,000,000 valves. While annual sales are detailed on a monthly basis, the Precision Inc. illustration focuses only on the first-quarter budgets. The process of developing the master budget is the same regardless of whether the time frame is one year
or one quarter.

  The December 31, 1999, balance sheet presented in Exhibit 7-9 provides account
balances needed to prepare the master budget. The December 31 balances are really

EXHIBIT 7-9

Precision Inc. Balance Sheet (projected) December 31, 1999

ASSETS		
Current Assets		
Cash		$ 5,090
Accounts Receivable	$168,000	
Less Allowance for Uncollectibles	(2,400)	165,600
Inventories		
Direct Material (87,580 ounces)	$ 17,516	
Finished Goods (15,400 units @ $1.26)	19,404	36,920
Total Current Assets		$207,610
Plant Assets		
Property, Plant, and Equipment	$540,000	
Less Accumulated Depreciation	(180,000)	360,000
TOTAL ASSETS		$567,610

LIABILITIES & STOCKHOLDERS' EQUITY		
Current Liabilities		
Accounts Payable	$ 80,000	
Dividends Payable (due 1/15/00)	15,000	
Total Current Liabilities		$ 95,000
Stockholders' Equity		
Common Stock	$300,000	
Retained Earnings	172,610	472,610
TOTAL LIABILITIES AND STOCKHOLDERS' EQUITY		$567,610

projections rather than actual figures because the budget process for 2000 must begin significantly before December 31, 1999. A company's budgetary time schedule depends on many factors, including its size and its degree of forecasting sophistication. Precision Inc. starts its budgeting process in November 1999 when the sales forecast is received by management or the budget committee. The **budget committee** reviews and approves, or makes adjustments to, the master budget and/or the budgets submitted from operational managers. This committee is usually composed of top management and the chief financial officer.

budget committee

Sales Budget

The sales budget is prepared in terms of both units and sales dollars. The selling price set for 2000 is $2.00 per valve, and the price is the same for all sales territories and all customers. Monthly sales demand and revenue for the first five months of 2000 are shown in Exhibit 7-10. Dollar sales figures are computed as sales quantities times product selling price. April and May information is presented because it is needed later to determine production information for the March budget. The "Total for Quarter" column reflects sales only for January, February, and March. A discussion of making comparisons of actual and budgeted revenue once the firm begins to operate under the budget and the related calculations of price and volume variances from budgeted revenue is presented in Appendix 1 to this chapter.

	JANUARY	FEBRUARY	MARCH	TOTAL FOR QUARTER	APRIL	MAY
Sales in units	220,000	205,000	195,000	620,000	180,000	195,000
Sales in dollars	$440,000	$410,000	$390,000	$1,240,000	$360,000	$390,000

Production Budget

The production budget follows naturally from the sales budget and uses information regarding the type, quantity, and timing of units to be sold. Sales information is combined with information on beginning and ending inventories so that managers can schedule the necessary production.

Ending inventory policy (as to quantity of units) is generally specified by company management. Desired ending inventory is normally a function of the quantity and timing of demand in the upcoming period together with the firm's production capacity and speed. Before making a decision about how much inventory to keep on hand, managers should consider the high costs of stockpiling inventory. Management may stipulate that ending inventory be a given percentage of the next period's projected sales. Other alternatives include maintaining a constant amount of inventory, building up inventory levels for future high-demand periods, and keeping inventory levels near zero under a just-in-time system. The decision about ending inventory levels affects whether a firm has constant production with varying inventory levels or variable production with constant inventory levels. And, as indicated in the following quote, the size of the inventory is also directly related to cash flow.

> Mismanagement of your company's inventory can create a financial hemorrhage that may cripple the business for life. Excessive inventory purchases, slow-moving inventory, and the inability to reorder in a timely fashion can all wreak havoc on your cash flow. Remember that inventory is "cash" sitting on your shelves without earning any interest. Actually, it may be one of your firm's larger expenditures, depending on the type of business and industry you are in.[1]

Demand for valves varies throughout the year, and Precision Inc. carries very little inventory. Production time is short, so company management has a policy that Finished Goods Inventory need be only 7 percent of the next month's sales. Based on the ending inventory policy and the sales information from Exhibit 7-10, the production budget shown in Exhibit 7-11 is prepared.

The beginning inventory balance shown for January is the number of units on hand at December 31, 1999. This inventory figure is 15,400 units, which represents 7 percent of January's estimated 220,000 units of sales. March's ending inventory balance is 7 percent of April's estimated 180,000 units of sales. Precision Inc. has no Work in Process Inventory because all units placed into production are fully completed each period.[2]

Purchases Budget

Direct materials are essential to production and must be purchased each period in sufficient quantities to meet production needs and to conform with the company's

EXHIBIT 7-11

Production Budget (for the Three Months and Quarter Ending March 31, 2000)

	JANUARY	FEBRUARY	MARCH	TOTAL
Sales in units (from Exhibit 7-10)	220,000	205,000	195,000	620,000
+ Desired ending inventory	14,350	13,650	12,600	12,600
Total needed	234,350	218,650	207,600	632,600
− Beginning inventory	(15,400)*	(14,350)	(13,650)	(15,400)
Units to be produced	218,950	204,300	193,950	617,200

*From Exhibit 7-9

Note: April's production would be 180,000 + 13,650 - 12,600 = 181,050

[1]Leslie N. Masonson, ed., *Cash Management Performance Report* (Boston: Warren, Gorham & Lamont, January 1991), p. 1.

[2]Most manufacturing entities do not produce only whole units during the period. Normally, partially completed beginning and ending in-process inventories exist. Consideration of partially completed inventories is covered in Chapter 10, on process costing.

Beginning and desired ending inventory quantities of raw material are used in calculating the budgeted amount of purchases. The ease of attainability and crucial nature to production of the raw material will impact the level of inventory a company needs to hold.

ending inventory policies. Precision Inc.'s management has established that direct materials be 10 percent of the following month's production needs. This inventory level is slightly higher than that of the finished goods because the lead time to acquire direct materials is somewhat longer and more uncertain than production time to complete finished goods.

The purchases budget is first stated in whole units of finished products. It is subsequently converted to individual direct material component requirements. Production of each valve requires four ounces of metal alloy. The quantity of material used in the valve gate and its cost are insignificant, so that item is treated as an indirect material. Unit material cost has been estimated by the purchasing agent to be $.20 per ounce. The whole-unit and component purchases budgets for each month of the first quarter of 2000 are shown in Exhibit 7-12. The beginning inventory for January is 10 percent of January production.

Given expected production, the Engineering and Personnel Departments can work together to determine the necessary labor requirements for the factory, sales force, and office staff. Labor requirements are stated in total number of people, and number of specific types of people (skilled laborers, sales people, clerical personnel), as well as production hours required of factory employees. Labor costs are computed based on items such as union labor contracts, minimum wage laws, fringe benefit costs, payroll taxes, and bonus arrangements. The various personnel amounts are shown, as appropriate, in either the direct labor budget, the manufacturing overhead budget, or the selling and administrative costs budget.

	JANUARY	FEBRUARY	MARCH
Units to be produced (from Exhibit 7-11)	218,950	204,300	193,950
+ EI units (10% of next month's production)	20,430	19,395	18,105*
= Total whole unit quantities needed	239,380	223,695	212,055
− Beginning inventory units (10% of current production)	(21,895)†	(20,430)	(19,395)
= Purchases required in whole unit quantities	217,485	203,265	192,660
× Ounces per unit	× 4	× 4	× 4
Total ounces to be purchased	869,940	813,060	770,640
× Price per ounce	× $.20	× $.20	× $.20
Total cost of alloy	$173,988	$162,612	$154,128

*Ten percent of April's production (from Exhibit 7-11)
†Beginning inventory of DM was 87,580 ounces, or enough for 21,895 units.

EXHIBIT 7-12
Purchases Budget (for the Three Months Ending March 31, 2000)

EXHIBIT 7-13

Direct Labor Budget (for the
Three Months and Quarter
Ending March 31, 2000)

	JANUARY	FEBRUARY	MARCH	TOTAL
Units of production	218,950	204,300	193,950	617,200
× Standard hours per unit	× .022	×.022	× .022	× .022
Total hours allowed	4,816.90	4,494.60	4,266.90	13,578.40
× Average wage rate (including fringe benefits)	× $10	× $10	× $10	× $10
Direct labor cost (rounded)	$48,169	$44,946	$42,669	$135,784

Direct Labor Budget

The management of Precision Inc. has reviewed the staffing requirements and has developed the direct labor cost estimates shown in Exhibit 7-13 for the first quarter of 2000. Factory direct labor costs are based on the standard hours of labor needed to produce the number of units shown in the production budget. The average wage rate shown in the exhibit includes both the basic direct labor payroll rate and the payroll taxes and fringe benefits related to direct labor (since these items usually add between 25 and 30 percent to the base labor cost). All compensation is paid in the month in which it is incurred.

Overhead Budget

Overhead is another production cost that must be estimated by management. Exhibit 7-14 presents Precision Inc.'s monthly cost of each overhead item for the first quarter of 2000. The company has determined that machine hours are the best predictor of overhead costs.

In estimating overhead, all costs must be specified and mixed costs must be separated into their fixed (a) and variable (b) elements. Each overhead amount shown is calculated by use of the $y = a + bx$ formula for a mixed cost, in which x is the number of units of activity (in this case, machine hours). For example, February maintenance cost is the fixed amount of $2,600 plus ($5.80 × 200 estimated machine hours), or $2,600 + $1,160 = $3,760. Both total cost and cost net of depreciation are shown in

EXHIBIT 7-14

Manufacturing Overhead
Budget (for the Three
Months and Quarter Ending
March 31, 2000)

			JANUARY	FEBRUARY	MARCH	TOTAL
Estimated Machine Hours (x) (given)			220	200	190	610
		Value of Variable Cost				
	Fixed Cost	per Unit				
Factory Overhead Items:	(a)	(b)				
Non-cash item						
Depreciation	$14,000	$10.00	$16,200	$16,000	$15,900	$ 48,100
Cash items						
Indirect materials	—	$ .10	$ 22	$ 20	$ 19	$ 61
Indirect labor	$ 7,000	.50	7,110	7,100	7,095	21,305
Utilities	3,000	1.60	3,352	3,320	3,304	9,976
Property taxes	5,000	—	5,000	5,000	5,000	15,000
Insurance	6,500	—	6,500	6,500	6,500	19,500
Maintenance	2,600	5.80	3,876	3,760	3,702	11,338
Total cash items	$24,100	$ 8.00	$25,860	$25,700	$25,620	$ 77,180
Total Cost (y)	$38,100	$18.00	$42,060	$41,700	$41,520	$125,280

the budget. The cost net of depreciation is the amount that is expected to be paid in cash during the month and will, therefore, affect the cash budget.

Selling and Administrative (S&A) Budget

Selling, general, and administrative expenses for each month can be predicted in the same manner as overhead costs. Exhibit 7-15 presents the S&A budget. Note that sales figures rather than production levels are used as the measure of activity in preparing this budget. The company's sales force consists of a manager with a monthly salary of $5,000 and four salespeople who receive $500 per month plus a 10 percent commission on sales. Administrative staff salaries total $18,000 per month.

Capital Budget

The budgets included in the master budget focus on the short-term or upcoming fiscal period. Managers, however, must also consider long-term needs in the area of plant and equipment purchases. The process of assessing such needs and budgeting for the expenditures is called **capital budgeting**.[3] The capital budget is prepared separately from the master budget, but since expenditures are involved, capital budgeting does affect the master budgeting process. Sometimes, as in the case of Penn Fuel Gas, the timing of current-year planned capital purchases are dependent on the extent to which actual revenues conform to budgetary revenues. Since a large portion of planned sales of natural gas and propane is dependent upon the weather in the winter months, PFG delays final capital asset purchases planned for the current year until after the winter months.

As shown in Exhibit 7-16 (page 300), Precision Inc. managers have decided that only one capital purchase will be made in the first quarter of 2000. The company is planning to acquire a network of state-of-the-art computers to better control shop-floor activities. This network will cost $240,000 and will be purchased and placed into service at the beginning of January. The company will pay for the acquisition at the end of February. Depreciation on this computer network is included in the overhead calculation in Exhibit 7-14. No equipment will be sold or scrapped when the network is purchased.

capital budgeting

EXHIBIT 7-15

Selling and Administrative Budget (for the Three Months and Quarter Ending March 31, 2000)

	Fixed Cost (a)	Value of Variable Cost per Unit (b)	JANUARY	FEBRUARY	MARCH	TOTAL
Predicted Sales (from Exhibit 7-10)			$440,000	$410,000	$390,000	$1,240,000
S&A Items:						
Non-cash item						
Depreciation	$ 3,800	—	$3,800	$3,800	$3,800	$11,400
Cash items						
Supplies	$ 350	$.02	$9,150	$8,550	$8,150	$25,850
Utilities	200	—	200	200	200	600
Miscellaneous	500	—	500	500	500	1,500
Salaries:						
Sales manager	5,000	—	5,000	5,000	5,000	15,000
Salespeople	2,000	.10	46,000	43,000	41,000	130,000
Administrative	18,000	—	18,000	18,000	18,000	54,000
Total cash items	$26,050	$.12	$78,850	$75,250	$72,850	$226,950
Total Cost (y)	$29,850	$.12	$82,650	$79,050	$76,650	$238,350

---

[3]Chapter 8 covers the concepts and techniques of capital budgeting.

EXHIBIT 7-16
Capital Budget (for the Three Months and Quarter Ending March 31, 2000)

	JANUARY	FEBRUARY	MARCH	TOTAL
Acquisitions:				
Computer network	$240,000	$0	$0	$240,000
Cash payments:				
Computer network	$0	$240,000	$0	$240,000

Cash Budget

LEARNING OBJECTIVE 7
Why is the cash budget so important in the master budgeting process?

After all the preceding budgets have been developed, a cash budget can be constructed. The cash budget may be the most important schedule prepared during the budgeting process because a company cannot survive without cash. "Market growth cannot materialize, expansion will stagnate, capital expansion programs cannot occur, and R&D programs cannot be achieved without adequate cash flow."[4]

The following model can be used to summarize cash receipts and disbursements in a manner that helps managers to devise appropriate financing measures to meet company needs.

CASH BUDGET MODEL

Beginning cash balance
+ Cash receipts from collections
= Cash available for disbursements exclusive of financing
− Cash needed for disbursements
= Cash excess or deficiency (a)
− Minimum desired cash balance
= Cash (needed) or available for investment or repayment

Financing methods:
± Borrow money (repay loans)
± Issue (reacquire) capital stock
± Sell (acquire) investments or plant assets
± Receive (pay) interest or dividends
    Total impact (+ or −) of planned financing (b)
= Ending cash balance (c), where c = a ± b

Budgeting for cash collections at San Francisco's Japanese Tea Garden is less complicated than at many organizations. Ticket revenue is predominantly cash, with two-tiered pricing for adults and children. Thus, there are no cash discounts for prompt payment and no uncollectible accounts.

[4]Cosmo S. Trapani, "Six Critical Areas in the Budgeting Process," *Management Accounting* (November 1982), p. 54.

Cash budgets can be used to predict seasonal variances in any potential cash flow. Such predictions can indicate a need for short-term borrowing and a potential schedule of repayments. The cash budget may also show the possibility of surplus cash, which can be used for funds management, such as for investment. Cash budgets can be used to measure the performance of the accounts receivable and accounts payable departments by comparing actual to scheduled collections, payments, and discounts taken.

Cash Receipts and Accounts Receivable

Once sales revenues have been determined, managers translate that information into expected cash receipts through the use of an expected collection pattern. This pattern considers the actual collection patterns experienced in recent past periods and management's judgment about changes that could disturb current collection patterns. For example, changes that could weaken current collection patterns include recessionary conditions, increases in interest rates, or less strict credit-granting practices.

In specifying collection patterns, managers should recognize that different types of customers pay in different ways. Any sizable, unique category of clientele should be segregated. It is essential for companies to know their customers' payment patterns.

Precision Inc. has two types of customers. Forty percent of the customers pay cash and receive a 2 percent discount. The remaining 60 percent of the customers purchase products on credit and have the following collection pattern: 30 percent in the month of sale and 69 percent in the month following the sale. One percent of credit sales are uncollectible. Precision Inc.'s collection pattern is diagrammed in Exhibit 7-17.

Using the sales budget, information on December 1999 sales, and the collection pattern, management can estimate cash receipts from sales during the first three months of 2000. Management must have December sales information because collections for credit sales extend over two months, meaning that some collections from the $400,000 of December 1999 sales occur in January 2000. Projected monthly collections for the first quarter of 2000 are shown in Exhibit 7-18 (page 302). The individual calculations relate to the alternative collection patterns and corresponding percentages presented in Exhibit 7-17.

The December collection amounts can be reconciled to the December 31, 1999, balance sheet (Exhibit 7-9), which indicated an Accounts Receivable balance of $168,000. This amount appears in the collection schedule as follows:

January collections of December sales	$165,600
January estimate of December bad debts	2,400
December 31, 1999, balance in Accounts Receivable	$168,000

January 2000 sales of $440,000 are used as an example of the collection calculations in Exhibit 7-18. Line A of the diagram in Exhibit 7-17 represents cash sales of 40 percent, or $176,000. These sales will be collected net of the 2 percent discount:

Sales to customers allowed discount (40% × $440,000)	$176,000
Discount taken by customers (2% × $176,000)	(3,520)
Net collections from customers allowed discount	$172,480

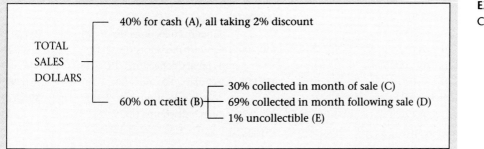

EXHIBIT 7-17
Collection Pattern for Sales

	JANUARY	FEBRUARY	MARCH	TOTAL	DISCOUNT	UNCOLLECTIBLE
From:						
December 1999 Sales:						
$400,000(60%)(69%)	$165,600			$ 165,600		
$400,000(60%)(1%)						$2,400
January 2000 Sales:						
$440,000(40%)*	172,480N			172,480	$3,520	
$440,000(60%)(30%)	79,200			79,200		
$440,000(60%)(69%)		$182,160		182,160		
$440,000(60%)(1%)						2,640
February 2000 Sales:						
$410,000(40%)*		160,720N		160,720	3,280	
$410,000(60%)(30%)		73,800		73,800		
$410,000(60%)(69%)			$169,740	169,740		
$410,000(60%)(1%)						2,460
March 2000 Sales:						
$390,000(40%)*			152,880N	152,880	3,120	
$390,000(60%)(30%)			70,200	70,200		
$390,000(60%)(1%)						2,340
Totals	$417,280	$416,680	$392,820	$1,226,780	$9,920	$9,840

*The result times 98 percent yields the amount collected; the result times 2 percent yields the amount of the discount. "N" stands for "Net of discount." The total amount of cash sales is the sum of the net of discount collection plus the amount shown on the same line in the discount column.

EXHIBIT 7-18

Cash Collections (for the Three Months and Quarter Ending March 31, 2000)

The next three January calculations in Exhibit 7-18 represent customers who buy on credit (60 percent; line B in Exhibit 7-17) and who (1) pay within the month of the sale (line C), (2) pay in the month after the sale (line D), or (3) do not pay (line E):

Sales to customers on credit (60% × $440,000)	$264,000
Collections in month of sale (30% × $264,000)	79,200
Collections in month after sale (69% × $264,000)	182,160
Uncollectible from January credit sales (1% × $264,000)	2,640

The remaining amounts are computed in the same manner. Note that the collection in the month after the sale is 69 percent of the original credit sale, and uncollectibles are 1 percent of the original credit sales, not of the remaining balance.

Once the schedule of cash collections is prepared, the balances of the Accounts Receivable and Allowance for Uncollectibles accounts can be projected. The T-accounts for Precision Inc. are shown next and will be used in preparing pro forma year-end 2000 financial statements. Note that the Allowance account balance indicates that Precision Inc. has not written off any accounts receivable since December 1999. The company may still believe some of these accounts are collectible or may simply choose to write them off after the end of the first quarter of 2000.

ACCOUNTS RECEIVABLE

12/31/99 Balance			
(Ex. 7-9)	168,000	January collections (Ex. 7-18)	417,280
January 2000 Sales		January discounts (Ex. 7-18)	3,520
(Ex. 7-10)	440,000	February collections (Ex. 7-18)	416,680
February 2000 Sales		February discounts (Ex. 7-18)	3,280
(Ex. 7-10)	410,000	March collections (Ex. 7-18)	392,820
March 2000 Sales		March discounts (Ex. 7-18)	3,120
(Ex. 7-10)	390,000		
3/31/00 Balance	171,300		

ALLOWANCE FOR UNCOLLECTIBLES

12/31/99 Balance (Ex. 7-9)	2,400
January estimate (Ex. 7-18)	2,640
February estimate (Ex. 7-18)	2,460
March estimate (Ex. 7-18)	2,340
3/31/00 Balance	9,840

Cash Disbursements and Accounts Payable

Using the purchases information from Exhibit 7-12, management can prepare an estimated cash disbursements schedule for Accounts Payable. All purchases of direct material are made on account by Precision Inc. The company pays for 40 percent of each month's purchases in the month of purchase, taking a 2 percent cash discount. The remaining 60 percent of each month's purchases are paid in the month following the month of purchase; no discount is available for these payments.

Exhibit 7-19 presents the cash disbursements information related to purchases for the first quarter of 2000. The December 31, 1999 Accounts Payable balance of $80,000 reflected in Exhibit 7-9 represents the 60 percent remaining payment required for December purchases. This amount is also shown in Exhibit 7-19 as the first amount paid. All amounts in this exhibit have been rounded to whole dollars.

The Accounts Payable activity is summarized in the following T-account. The March 31 balance represents 60 percent of March purchases that will be paid during April.

ACCOUNTS PAYABLE

		12/31/99 Balance (Ex. 7-9)	80,000
January payments (Ex. 7-19)	148,203	January purchases (Ex. 7-12)	173,988
January discounts taken (Ex. 7-19)	1,392		
February payments (Ex. 7-19)	168,137	February purchases (Ex. 7-12)	162,612
February discounts taken (Ex. 7-19)	1,301		
March payments (Ex. 7-19)	157,985	March purchases (Ex. 7-12)	154,128
March discounts taken (Ex. 7-19)	1,233		
		3/31/00 Balance	92,477

Given the cash receipts and disbursements information for Precision Inc., the company uses the cash budget model to prepare the cash budget shown in Exhibit 7-20 (page 304). The company has established $5,000 as its desired minimum cash

	JANUARY	FEBRUARY	MARCH	DISCOUNT
Payment for purchases of:				
December 1999 (from Exhibit 7-9)	$ 80,000			
January 2000 (from Exhibit 7-12)				
$173,988(40%)(98%)	68,203N			$1,392
$173,988(60%)		$104,393		
February 2000 (from Exhibit 7-12)				
$162,612(40%)(98%)		63,744N		1,301
$162,612(60%)			$ 97,567	
March 2000 (from Exhibit 7-12)				
$154,128(40%)(98%)			60,418N	1,233
Total disbursements for				
Accounts Payable	$148,203	$168,137	$157,985	

Note: "N" stands for "Net of discount." The total amount of gross purchases being paid for in the month of purchase is the sum of the net of discount payment plus the amount shown on the same line in the discount column.

EXHIBIT 7-19
Cash Disbursements—Accounts Payable (for the Three Months Ending March 31, 2000)

EXHIBIT 7-20

Cash Budget (for the Three Months and Quarter Ending March 31, 2000)

	JANUARY	FEBRUARY	MARCH	TOTAL
Beginning cash balance	$ 5,090	$ 5,088	$ 5,002	$ 5,090
Cash collections (Exhibit 7-18)	417,280	416,680	392,820	1,226,780
Cash available exclusive of financing	$ 422,370	$ 421,768	$397,822	$1,231,870
Disbursements:				
Accounts payable (Exhibit 7-19)	$ 148,203	$ 168,137	$157,985	$ 474,325
Direct labor (Exhibit 7-13)	48,169	44,946	42,669	135,784
Overhead (Exhibit 7-14)*	25,860	25,700	25,620	77,180
S&A expenses (Exhibit 7-15)*	78,850	75,250	72,850	226,950
Total planned disbursements	$ 301,082	$ 314,033	$299,124	$ 914,239
Cash excess or (inadequacy)	$ 121,288	$ 107,735	$ 98,698	$ 317,631
Minimum cash balance desired	5,000	5,000	5,000	5,000
Cash available or (needed)	$ 116,288	$ 102,735	$ 93,698	$ 312,631
Financing:				
Borrow (repay)	$ 0	$ 35,800	$ (35,800)	$ 0
Issue (reacquire) stock	0	0	0	0
Liquidate (acquire) investments	(101,200)	101,200	(57,600)	(57,600)
Sell (pay for) plant assets (Exhibit 7-10)	0	(240,000)	0	(240,000)
Receive (pay) interest or dividends‡	(15,000)	267	(239)	(14,972)
Total impact of planned financing	$(116,200)	$(102,733)	$ (93,639)	$(312,572)
Ending cash balance	$5,088	$5,002	$5,059	$5,059

*These amounts are the net of depreciation figures.

‡ Dividends payable on the December 31, 1999 balance sheet were shown as being owed on January 15, 2000. Interest on investments is calculated assuming a 6 percent rate, and interest on borrowings is calculated assuming an 8 percent rate. Borrowings are made at the beginning of the month, and repayments or investments are made at the end of the month. For February, interest owed is $239 ($35,800 × .08 × 1/12) and interest received is $506 ($101,200 × .06 × 1/12). In March, interest owed is $239 ($35,800 × .08 × 1/12).

balance. The primary reason for maintaining a minimum cash balance is the uncertainty associated with the budgeting process. If management had perfect certainty about cash inflows and outflows, there would be no need for this cash "cushion."

All borrowings by Precision Inc. are assumed to take place in increments of $100 at the beginning of a month. All repayments and investments are made in $100 amounts and are assumed to occur at the end of a month. These assumptions are simplistic, since management would not actually borrow until the need for funds arose and would repay as quickly as possible so as to minimize interest expenditures. Interest on any company investments is assumed to be added to the company's bank account at the end of each month.

Exhibit 7-20 indicates that Precision Inc. has $121,288 in excess cash available in January. This excess not only meets the specified $5,000 minimum balance and the dividend payment requirement from the December 1999 balance sheet, but also gives the firm an opportunity to invest $101,200. In February, Precision Inc. expects to have enough cash to meet its desired minimum cash balance but not enough to pay for the computer network purchased in January. The January investment must be liquidated and an additional $35,800 borrowed. Since the machine does not have to be paid for until the end of the month, the investment can continue to draw interest until that time. The borrowing has been assumed, however, to occur at the beginning of the month for consistency with the previously specified plan. Thus, Precision Inc. earns interest on the investment but must pay interest on the borrowings for February. In March, there is enough cash available to meet budgeted disbursements, pay off the February borrowings, and make a $57,600 investment. Interest on borrowings and investments is calculated at the bottom of Exhibit 7-20. Changes in the interest rate will affect any future budget-to-actual comparisons.

Several things should be specially noted involving the total column in Exhibit 7-20. First, the beginning cash balance is not the total of the three months, but is the balance at January 1. Second, the monthly and quarterly minimum cash balance is $5,000, not $15,000. Last, the ending cash balance should be the same as what appears in the final month of the quarter. These figures (beginning, minimum, and ending cash balances), cash available exclusive of financing, cash excess or inadequacy, and cash available or needed are the only ones that are not summed across from the three-month information; all other figures are totals. These figures can be updated monthly; a spreadsheet program is very useful for this function.

Budgeted Financial Statements

The final step in the budgeting process is the development of budgeted or *pro forma* financial statements for the period. These statements reflect the results that will be achieved if the estimates and assumptions used for all previous budgets actually occur. Such statements allow management to determine if the predicted results are acceptable for the period. If the predicted results are not acceptable, management has the opportunity to change and adjust items before beginning the period.

For example, if expected net income is not considered a reasonable amount, management may discuss raising selling prices or finding ways to decrease costs. Any specific changes considered by management may have related effects that must be included in the revised projections. For example, if selling prices are raised, volume may decrease. Alternatively, reductions in costs from using a lesser grade of materials could increase spoilage during production or the lower quality product could cause a decline in demand. Computer spreadsheet programs are used to quickly and easily make the recalculations necessary from such changes in assumptions.

Cost of Goods Manufactured Schedule
Before an income statement can be drafted, management must prepare a schedule of cost of goods manufactured, which is necessary to determine cost of goods sold.[5] Using information from previous budgets, Precision Inc.'s accountant has prepared the budgeted cost of goods manufactured schedule shown in Exhibit 7-21 (page 306). Since there were no beginning or ending work in process inventories, cost of goods manufactured is equal to the manufacturing costs of the period.

Income Statement
The projected income statement for Precision Inc. for the first quarter of 2000 is presented in Exhibit 7-22 (page 306). This statement uses much of the information previously developed in determining the revenues and expenses for the period.

Balance Sheet
Upon completion of the income statement, Precision Inc. accountants can prepare a pro forma March 31, 2000 balance sheet (Exhibit 7-23, page 307). The letters in parentheses after some of the items in Exhibit 7-23 refer to the calculations shown at the bottom of the exhibit.

---

[5]Chapter 4 discusses the cost of goods manufactured schedule.

EXHIBIT 7-21

Pro Forma Cost of Goods Manufactured Schedule for the First Quarter of 2000

Beginning work in process		$ 0
Cost of direct material used:		
Beginning balance of direct material (Exhibit 7-9)	$ 17,516	
Purchases (net of $3,926 of discounts taken)		
(from Accounts Payable, p. 303)	486,802	
Total direct material available	$504,318	
Ending balance of direct material (Note A)	(14,484)	
Cost of direct material used	$489,834	
Direct labor (Exhibit 7-13)	135,784	
Factory overhead (Exhibit 7-14)	125,280	
Total costs to be accounted for		750,898
Ending work in process		(0)
Cost of goods manufactured		$750,898

Note A

Ending balance (Exhibit 7-12) in units	18,105	
Ounces of alloy per unit	× 4	
Total ounces needed	72,420	
Price per ounce	× $.20	
Ending balance	$14,484	

EXHIBIT 7-22

Pro Forma Income Statement for the First Quarter of 2000

Sales (Exhibit 7-10)		$1,240,000
Less: Sales discounts (from Accounts Receivable, p. 302)		(9,920)
Net sales		$1,230,080
Cost of goods sold:		
Finished goods—12/31/99 (Exhibit 7-9)	$ 19,404	
Cost of goods manufactured (Exhibit 7-21)	750,898	
Cost of goods available for sale	$770,302	
Finished goods—3/31/00 (Note A)	(15,876)	(754,426)
Gross margin		$ 475,654
Expenses:		
Bad debts expense (Note B)	$ 7,440	
S&A expenses (Exhibit 7-15)	238,350	
Interest expense/income (net) (Exhibit 7-20)	(28)	(245,762)
Income before income taxes		$ 229,892
Income taxes (assumed rate of 30%)		(68,986)
Net income		$ 160,924

Note A:

Beginning finished goods (Exhibit 7-9)	15,400	
Production (Exhibit 7-11)	617,200	
Units available for sale	632,600	
Sales (Exhibit 7-10)	(620,000)	
Ending finished goods	12,600	
Costs per unit:		
Direct material	$.80	
Conversion (assumed)	.46	× $1.26
Cost of ending inventory		$15,876

Note B:

Total sales	$1,240,000	
× % credit sales	× .60	
= Credit sales	$ 744,000	
× % estimated uncollectible	× .01	
= Estimated bad debts	$ 7,440	

EXHIBIT 7-23
Pro Forma Balance Sheet,
March 31, 2000

ASSETS

Current Assets		
Cash (Exhibit 7-20)		$ 5,059
Investments (Exhibit 7-20)		57,600
Accounts Receivable (p. 302)	$171,300	
Less Allowance for Uncollectibles (p. 303)	(9,840)	161,460
Inventory		
Direct Materials (Exhibit 7-21, Note A)	$ 14,484	
Finished Goods (Exhibit 7-22, Note A)	15,876	30,360
Total Current Assets		$254,479
Plant Assets		
Property, Plant, and Equipment (a)	$780,000	
Less Accumulated Depreciation (b)	(239,500)	540,500
TOTAL ASSETS		$794,979

LIABILITIES AND STOCKHOLDERS' EQUITY

Current Liabilities		
Accounts Payable (p. 303)		$ 92,477
Income Taxes Payable (Exhibit 7-22)		68,968
Total Current Liabilities		$161,445
Stockholders' Equity		
Common Stock	$300,000	
Retained Earnings (c)	333,534	633,534
TOTAL LIABILITIES AND STOCKHOLDERS' EQUITY		$794,979

(a)	Beginning balance (Exhibit 7-9)	$540,000
	Purchased new network computer system	240,000
	Ending balance	$780,000
(b)	Beginning balance (Exhibit 7-9)	$180,000
	Factory depreciation (Exhibit 7-14)	48,100
	S&A depreciation (Exhibit 7-15)	11,400
	Ending balance	$239,500
(c)	Beginning balance (Exhibit 7-9)	$172,610
	Net income (Exhibit 7-22)	160,924
	Ending balance	$333,534

Statement of Cash Flows

The information found on the income statement, balance sheet, and cash budget is used in preparing a statement of cash flows (SCF). This statement is a principal internal, as well as external, report. The SCF explains the change in the cash balance by reflecting the company's sources and uses of cash. Such knowledge is useful in judging the company's ability to handle fixed cash outflow commitments, adapt to adverse changes in business conditions, and undertake new commitments. Further, because the cash flow statement identifies the relationships between net income and net cash flow from operations, it assists managers in judging the quality of the company's earnings.

While the cash budget is essential to current cash management, the budgeted SCF gives managers a more global view of cash flows by rearranging them into three distinct major activities: operating, investing, and financing. Such a rearrangement permits management to judge whether the specific anticipated flows are consistent with the company's strategic plans. In addition, the SCF incorporates a schedule or narrative about significant noncash transactions, such as an exchange of stock for land, that are ignored in the cash budget.

LEARNING OBJECTIVE 8
How does the statement of cash flows relate to the income statement and the cash budget?

EXHIBIT 7-24

Pro Forma Statement of Cash Flows for the First Quarter of 2000

Operating Activities:			
Cash collections:			
From sales		$1,226,780	
From interest		28	$1,226,808
Cash payments:			
For inventory:			
Direct material	$474,325		
Direct labor	135,784		
Overhead	77,180	$ 687,289	
For non-factory costs:			
Salaries	$199,000		
Supplies	25,850		
Other S&A expenses	2,100	226,950	(914,239)
Net cash inflow from operating activities			$ 312,569
Investing Activities:			
Purchase of plant asset		$ (240,000)	
Short-term investment		(57,600)	
Net cash outflow from investing activities			(297,600)
Financing Activities:			
Issuance of short-term note payable		$ 35,800	
Repayment of short-term note payable		(35,800)	
Payment of dividends (owed at 12/31/99)		(15,000)	
Net cash outflow from financing activities			(15,000)
Net decrease in cash			$ (31)
Alternative (Indirect) Basis			
Operating Activities:			
Net income			$ 160,924
+ Depreciation ($48,100 + $11,400)			59,500
+ Decrease in Accounts Receivable ($165,600 − $161,460)		$ 4,140	
+ Decrease in Inventory ($36,920 − $30,360)		6,560	
+ Increase in Accounts Payable ($92,477 − $80,000)		12,477	
+ Increase in Taxes Payable		68,968	92,145
Net cash inflow from operating activities			$ 312,569

It is acceptable for external reporting to present the operating section of the statement of cash flows on either a direct or an indirect basis. The direct basis uses pure cash flow information—cash collections and cash disbursements for operating activities. The indirect basis begins the operating section with net income and makes reconciling adjustments to derive cash flow from operations. Exhibit 7-24 provides a statement of cash flows for Precision Inc. using the information from the cash budget in Exhibit 7-20. Indirect presentation of the operating section uses the information from the income statement in Exhibit 7-22 and the balance sheets in Exhibits 7-9 and 7-23. This method appears at the bottom of Exhibit 7-24.

Both cash flow from operations and net income are necessary for long-run success in business. It appears that Precision Inc. is performing well on both counts.

CONCLUDING COMMENTS

Because of its fundamental importance in the budgeting process, demand must be predicted as accurately and with as many details as possible. Sales forecasts must indicate type and quantity of products to be sold, geographic locations of the sales, types of buyers, and points in time at which the sales are to be made. Such detail is necessary because different products require different production and distribution facilities; different customers have different credit terms and payment schedules; and different seasons or months may necessitate different shipping schedules or methods.

Estimated sales demand has a pervasive impact on the master budget. To arrive at a valid prediction, managers use all the information available and may combine several estimation approaches. Combining prediction methods provides managers with corroboration of estimates, which reduces uncertainty. Some ways of estimating future demand are (1) asking sales personnel for a subjective consensus; (2) making simple extrapolations of past trends; (3) using market research; and (4) employing statistical and other mathematical models.

Sensitivity analysis is one modeling technique that can be used in assessing risk in the budgeting process. It is a means of determining the amount of change that must occur in one variable before a different decision would be made. In preparing the master budget, for example, the variable under consideration might be selling price, advertising expense, grade of materials used in production, machine hours available, or maintenance expenditures. The technique identifies an "error" range for each of the various estimated values over which the budget would still provide a reasonably acceptable forecast. These repetitive computer simulations can be run after one or more factors have been changed so that managers can review expected results under various circumstances.

After the master budget and all of its pro forma financial statements have been developed, they can and should be used for a variety of purposes. One common use of the master budget is to help the organization obtain bank loans. Banks also need to be kept informed after loans have been obtained. Additionally, management can use master budgets to monitor performance by comparing budgeted figures to actual results. Variances, as they occur, should be investigated so that the underlying causes can be determined. Understanding the reasons for not meeting a budget can be useful in controlling future operations within the budget period, evaluating performance, and budgeting more accurately in the future. Finally, management should be aware that forecasted sales and profits may not materialize, and factors beyond the business's control may create problems. In such instances, it is essential that management has made contingency plans, as discussed in the accompanying News Note.

NEWS NOTE

What Happens If . . . ?

The management accountant should take the initiative for making contingency planning an integral part of the planning and budgeting process. An effective response to a business reversal is not mere recognition of the problem. Rather, early warning signals should trigger implementation of a contingency plan that details the predetermined countermeasures required to avoid a crisis while maintaining the firm's financial integrity.

Preparation of a contingency plan starts with an analysis of the company's financial capacity for responding to and weathering various simulated adversities such as a sales decline caused by a general recession or a change in competitive position. These scenarios serve as the backdrop for designing the strategic maneuvers needed to ensure the firm's survival at various levels of financial distress. The principal components of these strategies are:

- An estimate of the uncommitted liquid reserves that would be readily available during a given emergency.
- A program for reducing both controllable cash outflows and the level of investment in current assets and fixed assets.

⊙ A strategic plan that, in the event of a prolonged or irreparable misfortune, outlines the controlled liquidation of plant, equipment, or business units previously identified as expendable.

Developing a contingency plan, through the combined efforts of the management accountant and top-level management, forces the latter to examine the extent to which resources are available, the strong interdependence of planning and control, and the delicate interrelationship between financial reserves and budgeted cash outflows.

SOURCE: Arthur R. DeThomas, William B. Fredenberger, and Monojit Ghosal, "Turnarounds: Lessons for the Management Accountant," *Management Accounting* (July 1994), p. 25. Reprinted from *Management Accounting*, published by the Institute of Management Accountants, Montvale, NJ. Visit our website at www.imanet.org.

SITE ANALYSIS

At Penn Fuel Gas, budgeting brought the desire for better and faster information. PFG uses a minicomputer-based accounting package for general ledger, human resources, and payables. Yet portions of the accounting system still are manual, and monthly closings can take up to three weeks. PFG responded to some of its information needs by installing a new billing system that computerizes cash receipts and provides excellent summary information. PFG also is looking into a computerized tracking system (for its many construction projects) and improving the computerized fixed asset system by adding a budget feature.

Management wanted a one-year business plan prior to year-end as well as monthly updates (for example, budget vs. actual results). In addition, the board of directors wanted a long-range (three-year) plan each year. To meet these needs, the budget director, Amy Snyder, developed packets for the directors and management.

The board of directors wanted the financial and operational data reported by segment—some reports segmented geographically, some by product line, and others by customer type.

PFG decided to prepare its three-year forecast before doing the annual budget because the board wanted information on ROE and cash flow to analyze future earnings potential, for financing requirements, and for general business planning purposes. Once the three-year plan was reviewed, the first year's data were used as a guideline for the current year annual budget's operational and segment detail.

The budget function was formed with planning as its primary mission. In the early stages of its existence, however, it was expected to analyze company and segment performance. Variance analysis can be both interesting and challenging, because no two years are ever the same.

Budgeting also brings behavioral challenges such as lowballing revenues or padding expenses. PFG has experienced minimal budgeting gamesmanship for two reasons: (1) Budgets are developed with management, arriving at agreed-upon, reasonable expectations; and (2) PFG has not used the budget as a "hammer" at year-end for employees or divisions who did not make budget.

Budgeting has improved communication throughout Penn Fuel Gas, Inc., and has improved teamwork toward a common goal. It has helped the board of directors to represent stockholders better and has provided support to management on major decisions. PFG expects even better planning in the future to result in operational improvements, improved management of resources, better cost control, earnings growth, and improved responsibility resulting from managers' active participation in the planning process.

SOURCE: Robert N. West and Amy M. Snyder, "How to Set Up a Budgeting and Planning System," *Management Accounting* (January, 1997), pp. 20, 25, 26. Published by Institute of Management Accountants, Montvale, N.J.

CROSS-FUNCTIONAL APPLICATIONS

TOPIC OF NOTE	DISCIPLINE	CROSS-FUNCTIONAL APPLICATIONS
Operating Budget (OB)	Marketing Research	Usually market research provides the most critical data for an OB. The selling price, expected sales volume, time of sale or seasonality, and selling-related expenses are projected by market researchers. If their data are reasonably accurate then cost of sales and overhead can be accurately predicted or locked in by contractual arrangements. Reciprocally, marketers must be guided in their research by operational constraints such as production limitations, which are communicated to them by the OB process
	Production Management	In a highly competitive, consumer-driven marketplace often characterized by short and flexible production runs, a production manager must have OB information to plan the optimum use of productive resources. In addition to planning, the expectations of cost control are formally communicated to the production manager by the OB. Purchasing policies in both production and merchandising operations are dependent upon OB information.
	Operations Management	Since most administrative overhead costs can usually be well estimated, operating managers depend on OBs to establish responsibilities, performance criteria, and constraints. Any employee who has requested job-related travel expenses will appreciate the constraining capacity of OBs. In terms of strategic management, the OBs are critical in coordinating the efforts of the various strategic business units toward the overall objectives of the firm.
	Financial Management	Accurate OBs are necessary for financial planners to predict cash flows from operating activities, which are often the most important source and use of cash. Financial planners use this information to determine debt loads and repayment schedules for long-term financing as well as cash requirements or liquid investments over the short run. In the bigger strategic picture, OBs are a necessary input into decisions concerning the acquisition of plant, equipment, technology, and information.
Zero-Based Budgeting (ZBB) (Appendix)	Public Administration	ZBB in governmental organizations was a reaction to a popular demand for more efficiency, change, and flexibility. Public planners regularly relied upon fixed estimates of a budget's dynamic margins (most changeable costs/activities) to project future requirements. ZBB processes require planners to justify non-dynamic costs/activities which are relevant to their mandated objectives. While ZBB requires more resources, it enhances efficiency and flexibility by making planners analyze each resource with respect to the changing environment public emergency services.

CROSS-FUNCTIONAL APPLICATIONS

TOPIC OF NOTE	DISCIPLINE	CROSS-FUNCTIONAL APPLICATIONS
Zero-Based Budgeting (ZBB) (Appendix) (continued)	Operations Research	Operational researchers often have the resources to conceptualize a budget assisted by the ZBB processes which are not available to a particular strategic business unit that is the object of the study. Problems and opportunities can be evaluated more objectively by a comparison of the researchers' ZBB budget with the unit's traditional budgetary process. This reconciliation process will reduce ZBB costs by targeting units of greatest concern to management.
	Engineering	ZBB processes are necessary to guide engineers in their selection of new or alternative technologies where little prior experience exists. A new technology incorporated into an older system requires a top-down budgetary evaluation of the overall operation to conserve resources and maximize efficiency.
	Management	ZBB requires documentation of the decisions and attending costs associated with each planning unit in the organization. Top managers responsible for the overall goal congruence of the organization can review the ZBB documentation to establish priorities, discontinue activities, and slash costs. This review process assists managers in coordinating the activities and evaluating the benefits of the various planning units.

CHAPTER SUMMARY

Budgets may be imposed or participatory, but in either case top management is responsible for assuring that the budget is attainable and acceptable. The common budget period is one fiscal year, segmented for quarterly and monthly periods. Continuous budgets may be used to ensure an ongoing one-year planning cycle.

A budget is the primary basis and justification for financial operations in a firm. Implementing and administering a budget are parts of the coordination and control functions. A well-prepared budget provides the following benefits:

1. A detailed path for managers to follow to achieve organizational goals
2. Improved planning and decision making
3. An allocation of resources among departments
4. A better understanding of key business variables
5. A means of employee participation and influence
6. A means to determine troublesome or hard-to-control cost areas
7. A recognition of departmental interrelationships
8. A means of responding more rapidly to changing economic conditions
9. A means by which managerial performance can be judged

Budget manuals may be used to assure that procedures are standardized and understood by all parties involved in the process. When budgets are used for performance evaluation, care should be taken that the budget is achievable and that managers understand the process by which they will be evaluated.

Planning is the process of setting goals and objectives and translating them into activities and resources required for their accomplishment within a specified time horizon. Budgeting is the quantifying of a company's financial plans and activities. Budgets facilitate communication, coordination, and teamwork.

A master budget is a comprehensive set of projections (pro forma financial statements and their supporting schedules) for a specific budget period. It is composed of operating and financial budgets and is usually detailed by quarters and months.

Sales demand is the proper starting point for the master budget. Once sales demand is determined, managers forecast revenues, production, costs, and cash flows for the firm's activities for the upcoming period. These expectations reflect the firm's input and output of resources and are used in preparing the master budget.

When budgeting, managers need to remember that the various organizational departments interact with each other and the budget for one department may form the basis of or have an effect on the budgets in other departments. For example, the production department's production budget is predicated on sales demand provided by the sales department. The production budget then influences the purchasing department's budget as well as the treasurer's budgeting of cash flows and accounts payable management. Sales also affect cash flows and the selling and administrative expense budget.

Pro forma financial statements help managers determine if their plans will provide the desired results, in terms of both net income and cash flow. Inadequate results should cause a reevaluation of the objectives that have been set, and appropriate changes should be made.

APPENDICES

1. SALES PRICE AND SALES VOLUME VARIANCES

LEARNING OBJECTIVE 9
Why does actual revenue from a product differ from budgeted revenue?

When actual-to-budget comparisons are made, managers are held accountable for the revenues (if any) and the costs in the operating areas over which they have authority and responsibility. Actual performance should be compared against budgeted performance to determine variances from expectations. In making such comparisons, however, management needs to be certain that it is considering results from a proper perspective.

For an operating area in which revenues are being generated (for example, sales for Penn Fuel Gas or the Mercury Division of Ford Motor Company), comparisons should first be made on the revenue level to determine how closely projected revenues are being met. Then, revenue variance calculations can and should be made for both the price and volume elements that comprise revenue.

 www.ford.com

Calculating the difference between actual and budgeted selling prices and multiplying this number by the actual number of units sold will provide the **sales price variance**. This variance indicates the portion of the total variance that is related to a change in selling price. A variance is also created by the difference between actual and budgeted sales

sales price variance

sales volume variance

volumes; multiplying this difference by the budgeted selling price yields the **sales volume variance**. The sales variance model is as follows:[6]

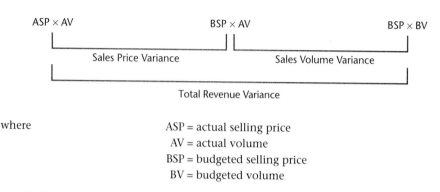

where

ASP = actual selling price
AV = actual volume
BSP = budgeted selling price
BV = budgeted volume

To illustrate these computations, assume that the Maine Lobsters (a fictitious minor-league hockey team) budgets 1999 ticket sales at $70,000 per home game, which represents the sale of an estimated 10,000 tickets at a selling price of $7. At July's first home game, actual gate ticket revenue was $66,000, creating a total unfavorable revenue variance of $4,000. To make a valid comparison, it is necessary to know that the $66,000 was composed of a volume of 12,000 tickets sold at a price of $5.50. Thus, the following variance calculations can be made:

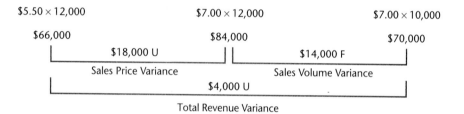

Team management should be pleased with the increased volume but displeased with the reduced selling price. Discussions with managers might indicate that this game was a special promotional game in which everyone received a $1.50 discount for bringing a can of food for charity. If these people enjoyed themselves and will return for future games, the unfavorable revenue variance may be eliminated in the future.

2. ZERO-BASED BUDGETING

Traditional budgeting is often limited in its usefulness as a control tool because poor budgeting techniques are often used. One such technique involves beginning with the prior year's funding levels and treating these as given and essential to operations. Decisions are then made about whether and by what percentage to incrementally raise existing **appropriations**, which represent maximum allowable expenditures. Such an approach has often resulted in what is known as the "creeping commitment syndrome," in which activities are funded without systematic annual regard for priorities or alternative means for accomplishing objectives.

appropriation

To help eliminate the creeping commitment syndrome, **zero-based budgeting (ZBB)** was developed for the government. ZBB is a comprehensive budgeting process that sys-

zero-based budgeting (ZBB)

---

[6]These computations assume the company sells a single product. If the company sells multiple products, another variance will exist called the sales mix variance. This variance explains the change in budgeted revenue caused by selling a mix of products different from the expected. Sales mix is discussed in Chapter 6 on cost-volume-profit analysis, and is further illustrated in Chapter 14. Sales mix variance computations require information on the estimated percentage of total expected sales for each product. For the Penn Fuel Gas, a sales mix variance would be necessary because of offering different types of gas and merchandise.

LEARNING OBJECTIVE ⑩
How does traditional budgeting differ from zero-based budgeting?

tematically considers the priorities and alternatives for current and proposed activities relative to organizational objectives. Annual justification of programs and activities is required so that managers must rethink priorities within the context of agreed-upon objectives. Specifying that each operation be evaluated from a zero-cost base would be unrealistic and extreme, but ZBB does require that managers reevaluate all activities at the start of the budgeting process to make decisions about which activities should be continued, eliminated, or funded at a lower level. Differences between traditional budgeting and zero-based budgeting are shown in Exhibit 7-25.

Zero-based budgeting is applicable in all organizations, especially in the support and service areas, where nonmonetary measures of performance are available. ZBB does not, however, provide measures of efficiency, and it is difficult to implement because of the significant amount of effort necessary to investigate the causes of prior costs and justify the purposes of budgeted costs.

The ZBB process is based on organizational goals and objectives and involves three steps: (1) converting the company activities into decision packages, (2) ranking each decision package, and (3) allocating resources based on priorities. A decision package contains information about the activity: objectives and benefits, consequences of not funding, and necessary costs and staffing requirements. The decision packages are ranked and prioritized on the basis of need, costs, and benefits.

Zero-based budgeting is a rigorous exercise that demands considerable time and effort, as well as wholehearted commitment by the organization's personnel to make it work. An organization lacking the time, effort, and commitment needed should not attempt ZBB. An organization that can supply these three ingredients can use ZBB to become more effective in planning for and controlling costs. One of the major benefits of zero-based budgeting is that, in using it, managers focus on identifying non-value-added activities and working to reduce items that are unnecessary or ineffective expenses.

An organization considering ZBB should assess whether the benefits are worth the costs. Management may consider "zero-basing" certain segments of the company on a rotating basis over a period of years as an alternative to applying the approach to the entire firm annually.

TRADITIONAL BUDGETING	ZERO-BASED BUDGETING
Starts with last year's funding appropriation	Starts with a minimal (or zero) figure for funding
Focuses on money	Focuses on goals and objectives
Does not systematically consider alternatives to current operations	Directly examines alternative approaches to achieving similar results
Produces a single level of appropriation for an activity	Produces alternative levels of funding based on availability of funds and desired results

EXHIBIT 7-25

Differences between Traditional Budgeting and Zero-Based Budgeting

KEY TERMS

Appropriation (p. 314)
Budget (p. 282)
Budget committee (p. 295)
Budget manual (p. 289)
Budget slack (p. 286)
Budgeting (p. 283)
Capital budgeting (p. 299)
Continuous budget (p. 289)

Financial budget (p. 291)
Imposed budget (p. 285)
Master budget (p. 291)
Operating budget (p. 291)
Participatory budget (p. 285)
Sales price variance (p. 313)
Sales volume variance (p. 314)
Zero-based budgeting (ZBB) (p. 314)

SOLUTION STRATEGIES

Budget Manual
Should include:
1. Statements of the budgetary purpose and its desired results
2. A listing of specific budgetary activities to be performed
3. A calendar of scheduled budgetary activities
4. Sample budgetary forms
5. Original, revised, and approved budgets

Sales Budget
    Units of sales
× Selling price per unit
= Dollars of sales

Production Budget
    Units of sales
+ Units desired in ending inventory − Units in beginning inventory
= Units to be produced

Purchases Budget
    Units to be produced
+ EI units
= Total whole unit quantities needed
− BI units
= Purchases required in whole unit quantities
× Appropriate quantity measure of input material
= Quantity of input material needed
× Price per unit measure of input quantity
= Cost of purchases

Direct Labor Budget
    Direct labor hours required for production
× Wages per hour
= Cost of direct labor compensation

Overhead Budget
    Predicted activity base
× VOH rate per unit of activity
= Total variable OH cost
+ Fixed OH cost
= Total OH cost

Selling and Administrative Budget
    Predicted sales dollars (or other variable measure)
× Variable S&A rate per dollar (or other variable measure)
= Total variable S&A cost
+ Fixed S&A cost
= Total S&A cost

Schedule of Cash Collections (for sales on account)
    Dollars of credit sales for month
× Percent collection for month of sale
= Credit to Accounts Receivable for month's sales
− Sales discounts allowed and taken
= Receipts for current month's sales

+ Current month's cash receipts for prior months' sales
= Cash receipts for current month

Schedule of Cash Payments (for purchases on account)

    Total cost of purchases
× Percent payment for current purchases
= Debit to Accounts Payable for month's purchases
− Purchase discounts taken
= Cash payments for current month's purchases
+ Current month's payments for prior months' purchases
= Cash payments for Accounts Payable for current month

Cash Budget

    Beginning cash balance
+ Cash receipts
= Cash available for disbursements
− Cash needed for disbursements:
        Cash payments for Accounts Payable for month
        Cost of compensation
        Total cost of OH less depreciation
        Total SG&A cost less depreciation
= Cash excess or deficiency ⟵
− Minimum desired cash balance
= Cash needed or available for investment or financing

    Cash excess or deficiency ⟵
± Various financing amounts
= Ending cash balance

Revenue Variances

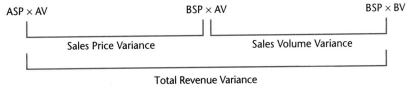

where   ASP = actual selling price
                   AV = actual volume
                BSP = budgeted selling price
                 BV = budgeted volume

DEMONSTRATION PROBLEM

The Brooke's Books Company, April 30, 2000, balance sheet includes the following:

Cash	$ 25,000 debit
Accounts Receivable	100,800 debit
Allowance for Uncollectible Accounts	2,240 credit
Merchandise Inventory	21,000 debit

Company management has designated $25,000 as the firm's monthly minimum cash balance. Other information about the firm follows:

- Revenues of $280,000 and $336,000 are expected for May and June, respectively. All goods are sold on account.
- The collection pattern for Accounts Receivable is 55 percent in the month of sale, 44 percent in the month following the sale, and 1 percent uncollectible.
- Cost of Goods Sold approximates 60 percent of sales revenues.
- Management's desired ending balance of Merchandise Inventory is 10 percent of that month's budgeted sales.
- All Accounts Payable are for inventory and are paid in the month of purchase.
- Other monthly expenses are $37,800, which includes $2,800 of depreciation, but does not include bad debt expense.
- Borrowings or investments can only be made in $5,000 amounts. Interest will be paid at the rate of 10 percent per year; interest will be earned at the rate of 8 percent per year.

Requirements:

a. Forecast the May cash collections.
b. Forecast the May and June cost of purchases.
c. Prepare the cash budget for May including the effects of financing (borrowing or investing).

Solution to Demonstration Problem

a.

	May Collections
From April ($100,800 − $2,240)	$ 98,560
From May ($280,000 × .55)	154,000
Total	$252,560

b.

	May	**June**
Sales	$280,000	$336,000
Cost of goods (60%)	$168,000	$201,600
Add: Desired ending balance	16,800	20,160
Total purchases	$184,800	$221,760
Less: Beginning balance	(21,000)	(16,800)
Cost of purchases	$163,800	$204,960

c.

	May Cash Budget	
Beginning cash balance		$ 25,000
May collections		252,560
Total cash available before financing		$277,560
Disbursements:		
Purchases of merchandise	$163,800	
Other monthly expenses ($37,800 − $2,800)	35,000	
Total disbursements		(198,800)
Cash excess (a)		$ 78,760
Less: Minimum cash balance desired		(25,000) $25,000
Cash available		$53,760
Financing: Acquire investment (b)		(50,000) 3,760
Ending cash balance (c); (c = a − b)		$28,760

END OF CHAPTER MATERIALS

⊙ QUESTIONS

1. Why is budgeting important? Discuss the reasons why it may be more important in some organizations than in others.

2. Briefly describe the basic budgeting process. Which steps do you consider the most critical?

3. Why do most organizations use participatory budgets? Discuss the disadvantages of using such budgets.

4. What is a continuous budget? Why would a company use a continuous budget?

5. List the sections of a budget manual and briefly explain the role of each section.

6. If a given manager fails to achieve his or her budget target, does this necessarily indicate that the manager has performed poorly? Explain.

7. Why is it important to put organizational plans in written form?

8. How are operating and financial budgets different? How are they related?

9. Why is the master budget said to be a static budget? Why is it necessary for the master budget to be static?

10. Why must the beginning of the budget year balance sheet be estimated? Why is it needed in the master budget process?

11. Why is the sales budget the first of the operating budgets prepared?

12. Explain the purposes of the production budget. How is this budget influenced by the firm's inventory policies?

13. What are the primary inputs in the determination of the purchases budget?

14. What source documents would likely be used to compile a direct labor budget?

15. Why is it necessary to separate overhead costs into variable and fixed components to determine the budget for overhead costs?

16. Even though the capital budget is not a component of the master budget, how may it influence the preparation of the master budget?

17. Explain the importance of the cash budget.

18. How are cash collections from sales determined? What part do cash collections play in the budgeting process?

19. How does a firm's credit terms for credit sales affect the pattern for cash collections? Why would a firm give a discount for cash sales?

20. Why would a firm wish to maintain a minimum cash balance?

21. Why are pro forma statements included in the master budget?

22. Since a cash budget is included in the master budget, why is a budgeted statement of cash flows also included?

23. What is the relationship between the budgeted statement of cash flows and the budgeted balance sheet?

24. Give some examples of items included in the financing section of a statement of cash flows and their cash flow effects.

25. Why would it be desirable to prepare the master budget using a spreadsheet program and linking the individual budgets?

26. List the schedules and statements that make up the master budget in the sequence in which they would normally be prepared. If two or more schedules can be prepared simultaneously, so indicate.

27. *(Appendix 1)* What does the sales price variance measure? What does the sales volume variance measure? Collectively, what do the sales price and sales volume variances explain?

28. *(Appendix 2)* What is zero-based budgeting? Why do you think it began in the governmental sector rather than in the business sector?

⊙ **EXERCISES**

29. *(Terminology)* Your dormitory roommate has nearly completed a homework assignment but is having trouble matching the following terms and definitions and has asked for your help. Match the numbered item on the right with the lettered term on the left.

a. Budget committee
b. Sales price variance (appendix)
c. Budgeting
d. Sales volume variance (appendix)
e. Imposed budget
f. Budget
g. Participatory budget
h. Appropriation (appendix)
i. Zero-based budgeting (appendix)

1. Developed through joint decision making by top managers and operating personnel
2. A quantitative expression of commitment to planned activities and resource acquisition and use
3. A difference between actual and budgeted revenues caused by selling a different number of units than budgeted
4. Prepared by top managers with little or no input from operating personnel
5. Reviews, adjusts, and approves the master budget and/or budgets submitted by operational managers
6. A difference between budgeted and actual sales caused by a difference between actual and budgeted sales price
7. Developing a quantitative plan in financial terms to satisfy company goals and objectives
8. Systematically (re)considers current or proposed activities in light of priorities and alternatives for achievement of organizational goals and objectives
9. Maximum allowable expenditure for an item in the budget

30. *(Imposed vs. participatory budgets)* Top management has asked your assistance in trying to determine the advantages of imposed and participatory budgets and has suggested a number of goals they would like to achieve in whatever type of budget they might choose. Indicate whether each of the following is an advantage of an imposed budget (AI), an advantage of a participatory budget (AP), or neither (N).

a. Develop fiscal responsibility and budgetary skills of operating personnel
b. Blend overview of top management with operating details
c. Reduce budgeting to entering data into a computer program
d. Increase chances that strategic plans will be incorporated into planned activities
e. Allow operating managers to completely take over the budgeting process
f. Incorporate top management's knowledge of overall resource availability
g. Produce more realistic budgets
h. Improve morale and motivation
i. Encourage operating managers to establish the long-run company goals
j. Incorporate inputs from persons most familiar with the needs and constraints of organizational units

31. *(Production budget)* McDougal Company has budgeted its third-quarter unit sales for 1999 as follows:

July	8,000
August	10,000
September	11,000

The company desires an ending inventory equal to 8 percent of budgeted sales of the following month. October's sales are expected to be 12,000 units. As manager of production, you have been asked to prepare a third-quarter production budget by month and in total.

32. *(Production budget)* South-Western Electronics has projected quarterly sales of electric motors for the year 2000 as follows:

1st quarter	200,000
2nd quarter	150,000
3rd quarter	250,000
4th quarter	180,000

The firm expects to begin the year 2000 with 80,000 motors. Desired ending balances are to be 40 percent of the subsequent quarter's sales. Sales in the first quarter of 2001 are expected to be 220,000 motors. As production manager, you have been asked to:

a. Prepare a production budget by quarter and in total for the year 2000.

b. Explain how the firm might benefit by reducing the level of finished goods inventories carried.

33. *(Purchases budget)* Flip Flop Flippers expects to sell 15,200 pairs of swim flippers during June. Two pounds of rubber are required to make each pair. The company has a beginning June inventory of 3,300 pairs of flippers and 10,200 pounds of rubber. The company wishes to end June with 7,200 pairs of flippers and 16,000 pounds of rubber. Because flippers can be made very quickly from heated rubber, the firm does not maintain any work in process inventory. The purchasing agent has asked you how much rubber Flip Flop Flippers should budget to buy for June.

34. *(Purchases budget)* Minneapolis Metals expects to sell 74,000 units of its major product in April 2000. Each unit requires two pounds of material A and five pounds of material B. Material A costs $4.80 per pound, and material B costs $2.10 per pound. Expected beginning and ending inventories are as follows:

	APRIL 1	APRIL 30
Finished goods (units)	4,000	6,300
Material A (pounds)	4,000	4,900
Material B (pounds)	6,100	6,000

a. How many pounds of material A does Minneapolis Metals plan to purchase in April? What is the expected cost of those purchases?

b. How many pounds of material B does Minneapolis Metals plan to purchase in April? What is the expected cost of those purchases?

c. Briefly describe how improved raw materials inventory management could reduce the level of raw materials inventories carried.

35. *(Mixed overhead cost budget)* Ander Inc. wants to estimate the cost of manufacturing overhead in the master budget. Overhead is a mixed cost with the following flexible budget formula: $y = \$320,000 + \$14.25X$, where X represents machine hours. The fixed overhead includes $35,000 of depreciation. As a consultant, you have been asked to

a. Calculate the overhead cost assuming Ander Inc. plans to incur 12,000 machine hours for the coming year.

b. Determine how much cash will be spent for overhead if the company incurs the 12,000 machine hours.

36. *(Cash collections)* O'Gwynn Enterprises is experiencing difficulty in estimating cash collections for the second quarter of 1999, and has asked you, its consultant, for help. Inspection of records and documents reveals the following sales information:

the month of sale, 60 percent in the month after the sale, and 15 percent in the second month after the sale. The company has no debt other than what is currently owed for purchases on account.

Frank, who has given you a job every summer you were in college, now needs your help and has requested that you assist him by providing the following:

a. Calculate the July 31 balances for Accounts Receivable and Accounts Payable.

b. Calculate the cash collections expected in August.

c. Calculate the expected total cash disbursements in August.

d. Present a cash budget for August. Assume management wants no more cash on hand at August 31 than the minimum cash balance desired.

e. Prepare an income statement for August. Assume an average gross margin percentage of 40 percent. Ignore income taxes.

f. Explain how and why inventory management must be different for perishable commodities than for nonperishable commodities.

53. *(Pro forma income statement)* The projected January 31, 1999, balance sheet for Lawrence Rubber Co. follows (all dollar amounts are in thousands):

ASSETS

Cash	$ 16,000
Accounts Receivable (net of allowance for uncollectible accounts of $4,000)	76,000
Inventory	32,000
Property, Plant, and Equipment (net)	70,000
Total Assets	$194,000

LIABILITIES AND STOCKHOLDERS' EQUITY

Accounts Payable	$165,000
Common Stock	100,000
Retained Earnings (deficit)	(71,000)
Total Liabilities and Stockholders' Equity	$194,000

Additional information follows:

⊙ Sales are budgeted as follows:

February	$220,000
March	240,000

⊙ Collections are expected to be 60 percent in the month of sale, 38 percent in the next month, and 2 percent uncollectible.

⊙ The company's gross margin is projected at 25 percent of sales. Purchases each month are 75 percent of the next month's projected sales, and these are paid in full in the following month.

⊙ Other expenses for each month, paid in cash, are expected to be $31,000. Monthly depreciation is $10,000.

a. Prepare a pro forma income statement for February.

b. Prepare a pro forma balance sheet for February.

c. Describe any special problems this company may encounter because of its weak balance sheet. As a finance specialist, recommend actions the firm might take to improve the balance sheet.

54. *(Comprehensive)* CareWood makes an environmentally friendly artificial fireplace log. You have been asked to prepare the company's 1999 master budget and have been provided with the following:

a. The 12/31/98 projected balance sheet data follows:

ASSETS

Cash		$ 4,330
Accounts Receivable		6,750
Direct Material Inventory (2,046 pounds)		409
Finished Goods Inventory (1,200 logs)		2,808
Plant and Equipment	$220,000	
Less Accumulated Depreciation	(56,000)	164,000
Total Assets		$178,297

LIABILITIES AND STOCKHOLDERS' EQUITY

Accounts Payable		$ 1,109
Note Payable		20,000
Total Liabilities		$ 21,109
Common Stock	$100,000	
Retained Earnings	57,188	157,188
Total Liabilities and Stockholders' Equity		$178,297

b. Each log requires the following standards for direct material and labor:

⊙ 3.3 pounds of material mix at $.20

   (.3 pound is discarded as waste) $.66

⊙ 2 minutes of labor time; direct labor

   averages $14.40 per hour   .48

   Each finished log requires three minutes of machine time. Variable overhead is applied at the rate of $12 per hour of machine time. Annual fixed production overhead of $42,000 is applied based on an expected annual production capacity of 70,000 logs. The total fixed factory overhead is comprised of the following:

Salaries	$26,000
Insurance	1,800
Fixed portion of utilities	5,300
Depreciation	8,900

   Fixed overhead is incurred evenly throughout the year.

c. Expected sales in units for the first five months of 1999 are:

January	6,000
February	9,000
March	6,500
April	5,900
May	5,100

   CareWood grants no discounts, and all sales are on credit at $6 per log. The company's collection pattern is 80 percent in the month of sale, 15 percent in the month following the sale, and 5 percent in the second month following the sale. The Accounts Receivable balance in the balance sheet data represents amounts remaining due from November sales of $33,000 and December sales of $34,000.

d. CareWood completes all production each day. The desired ending balance of Direct Material Inventory is 10 percent of the amount needed to satisfy the next month's production for finished goods. The desired ending balance in Finished Goods Inventory is 20 percent of the next month's sales.

e. Purchases are paid 70 percent in the month of purchase and 30 percent in the month following the purchase. No discounts are taken. The note payable has a 12 percent interest rate, and the interest is paid at the end of each month. The $20,000 balance of the principal on the note is due on March 31, 1999.

f. CareWood's minimum cash balance desired is $4,000. The firm may borrow at the beginning of a month and repay at the end of the month in $500 increments. Interest on these short-term loans, if any, is payable monthly at a 14% rate. Investments and investment liquidations are made only in $500 amounts at the end of a month. Investments earn 12 percent per year, collected monthly at month's end.

g. Period (S&A) expenses, paid as incurred, run $9,000 per month plus 1 percent of revenue. Direct labor and overhead are paid as incurred.

h. The company accrues income taxes at a 40 percent rate. A quarterly tax installment will be paid on April 15, 1999.

Prepare master budget schedules on a monthly basis for the first quarter of 1999 and pro forma financial statements as of the end of the first quarter. Round all numbers in schedules and pro forma statements to the nearest whole dollar.

55. *(Appendix 1; sales variances)* Mead Industries employs a budgeting system to aid in organizational planning and control. At the end of the period, actual results are compared against budgeted figures. The company's actual and budgeted data for 1999 appear below:

UNIT SALES	BUDGETED	ACTUAL
Product A	24,000	20,000
Product B	16,000	30,000

DOLLAR SALES		
Product A	$96,000	$85,000
Product B	48,000	75,000

COST OF SALES (ALL VARIABLE)		
Product A	$48,000	$50,000
Product B	32,000	60,000

a. Compute the budgeted gross margin for each product.
b. Compute the actual gross margin for each product.
c. Compute the sales variances for each product.
d. Why do the sales volume and price variances not explain the entire difference between budgeted and actual gross margin for both products?

56. *(Appendix 1; sales variances)* MacMillan Sporting Goods manufactures two products: Footballs and Shoulder Pads. For 1999, the firm budgeted the following:

	FOOTBALLS	SHOULDER PADS
Sales	$800,000	$1,200,000
Unit sales price	$40	$30

At the end of 1999, managers were informed of the following:

1. Actual sales of footballs were 21,000 units. The price variance for footballs was $63,000 unfavorable.
2. Actual sales of shoulder pads generated revenue of $1,120,000 and a volume variance of $240,000 unfavorable.

a. Compute the budgeted sales volume for each product.
b. Compute the volume variance for 1999 for footballs.
c. Compute the price variance for 1999 for shoulder pads.
d. Summarize the difference between budgeted and actual sales for 1999.

57. *(Appendix 1; sales variances)* Juan Navarez manages the marketing department at Festive Figurines. He is evaluated based on his ability to meet budgeted revenues. For May 1999, his revenue budget was as follows:

	PRICE PER UNIT	UNIT SALES
Daniel Boone	$240	1,600
Easter Bunny	130	2,150
Pocahontas	160	4,200

The actual sales generated by the marketing department in May were as follows:

	PRICE PER UNIT	TOTAL SALES DOLLARS
Daniel Boone	$230	$391,000
Easter Bunny	140	282,800
Pocahontas	150	622,500

a. For May 1999, compute the sales price variance for Festive Figurines for each product.
b. For May 1999, compute the sales volume variance for Festive Figurines.
c. Assuming that the variances you computed in Parts a and b are controllable by Juan Navarez, discuss what actions he may have taken to cause actual results to deviate from budgeted results.
d. Describe circumstances in which it would be more appropriate to hold the manufacturing manager (rather than the marketing manager) responsible for sales variances.

⊙ **CASES**

58. *(International)* Your Canadian-based consumer electronics firm, CanadaExcel, is in the process of establishing a camcorder assembly plant in Malaysia. The manager of the Malaysian plant is to have responsibility for the following: sourcing materials (about 60 percent of materials will be acquired from outside the company and the other 40 percent will be acquired from internal plants located in Canada and Mexico); hiring, training, and supervising workers; controlling operating costs; meeting a production schedule that is based on projected sales; and maintaining production quality. Completed units will be shipped to internal marketing divisions located in North America.

   Place yourself in the position of controller of CanadaExcel. It is your job to incorporate the operating plans for the Malaysian assembly plant into the company's formal budget. Describe, in general terms, what information you would need to acquire to develop the budget for the Malaysian operation and where you would expect to acquire such information. Further, describe any significant decisions that would be your responsibility to make in compiling the budget.

59. *(Cost budgets)* The Mason Agency, a division of General Service Industries, offers consulting services to clients for a fee. The corporate management at General Service is pleased with the performance of the Mason Agency for the first nine months of the current year and has recommended that the division manager of the Mason Agency, Richard Howell, submit a revised forecast for the remaining quarter, as the division has exceeded the annual plan year-to-date by 20 percent of operating income. An unexpected increase in billed hour volume over the original plan is the main reason for this gain in income. The original operating budget for the first three quarters for the Mason Agency is as follows:

1999–2000 OPERATING BUDGET

	1st Quarter	*2nd Quarter*	*3rd Quarter*	*Total*
Revenue:				
Consulting fees				
Management consulting	$315,000	$315,000	$315,000	$ 945,000
EDP consulting	421,875	421,875	421,875	1,265,625
Total	$736,875	$736,875	$736,875	$2,210,625
Other revenue	10,000	10,000	10,000	30,000
Total	$746,875	$746,875	$746,875	$2,240,625
Expenses:				
Consultant salaries	$386,750	$386,750	$386,750	$1,160,250
Travel and entertainment	45,625	45,625	45,625	136,875
General and administration	100,000	100,000	100,000	300,000
Depreciation	40,000	40,000	40,000	120,000
Corporate allocation	50,000	50,000	50,000	150,000
Total	$622,375	$622,375	$622,375	$1,867,125
Operating income	$124,500	$124,500	$124,500	$ 373,500

   When comparing the actuals for the first three quarters against the original plan, Howell analyzed the variances. His revised forecast for the fourth quarter will reflect the following information:

⊙ The division currently has 25 consultants on staff—10 for management consulting and 15 for EDP consulting, and has hired 3 additional management consultants to start work at the beginning of the fourth quarter in order to meet the increased client demand.

⊙ The hourly billing rate for consulting revenues is acceptable in the market and will remain at $90 per hour for each management consultant and $75 per hour for each EDP consultant. However, owing to the favorable increase in billing hour volume, the hours for each consultant will be increased by 50 hours per quarter.

New employees are as capable as current employees and will be billed at the current rates.

- The budgeted annual salaries and actual annual salaries, paid monthly, are the same at $50,000 for a management consultant and 8 percent less for an EDP consultant. Corporate management has approved a merit increase of 10 percent at the beginning of the fourth quarter for all 25 existing consultants, while the new consultants will be compensated at the planned rate.

- The planned salary expense includes a provision for employee fringe benefits amounting to 30 percent of the annual salaries; however, the improvement of some corporate-wide employee programs will increase the fringe benefit allocation to 40 percent.

- The original plan assumes a fixed hourly rate for travel and other related expenses for each billing hour of consulting. These expenses are not reimbursed by the client, and the previously determined hourly rate has proved to be adequate to cover these costs.

- Other revenues are derived from temporary rentals and interest income and remain unchanged for the fourth quarter.

- Administrative expenses have been favorable at 7 percent below the plan; this 7 percent savings on fourth-quarter expenses will be reflected in the revised plan.

- Depreciation for office equipment and microcomputers will stay constant at the projected straight-line rate.

- Because of the favorable experience for the first three quarters and the division's increased ability to absorb costs, the corporate management at General Service Industries has increased the corporate expense allocation by 50 percent.

a. Prepare a revised operating budget for the fourth quarter for the Mason Agency, which Richard Howell will present to General Service Industries. Be sure to furnish supporting calculations for all revised revenue and expense amounts.

b. Discuss the reasons why an organization would prepare a revised forecast.

(CMA adapted)

60. *(Cash budget)* CrossMan Corporation, a rapidly expanding crossbow distributor to retail outlets, is in the process of formulating plans for 1999. Joan Caldwell, director of marketing, has completed her 1999 forecast and is confident that sales estimates will be met or exceeded. The following sales figures show the growth expected and will provide the planning basis for other corporate departments.

MONTH	FORECASTED SALES	MONTH	FORECASTED SALES
January	$1,800,000	July	$3,000,000
February	2,000,000	August	3,000,000
March	1,800,000	September	3,200,000
April	2,200,000	October	3,200,000
May	2,500,000	November	3,000,000
June	2,800,000	December	3,400,000

George Brownell, assistant controller, has been given the responsibility for formulating the cash flow projection, a critical element during a period of rapid expansion. The following information will be used in preparing the cash analysis:

- CrossMan has experienced an excellent record in accounts receivable collections and expects this trend to continue. The company collects 60 percent of billings in the month after sale and 40 percent in the second month after the sale. Uncollectible accounts are insignificant and should not be considered in the analysis.

- The purchase of crossbows is CrossMan's largest expenditure; the cost of these items equals 50 percent of sales. The company receives 60 percent of the crossbows one month prior to sale and 40 percent during the month of sale.

⊙ Prior experience shows that 80 percent of accounts payable are paid by CrossMan one month after receipt of the purchased crossbows, and the remaining 20 percent are paid the second month after receipt.

⊙ Hourly wages, including fringe benefits, are a function of sales volume and are equal to 20 percent of the current month's sales. These wages are paid in the month incurred.

⊙ Administrative expenses are projected to be $2,640,000 for 1999. All of these expenses are incurred uniformly throughout the year except the property taxes. Property taxes are paid in four equal installments in the last month of each quarter. The composition of the expenses is:

Salaries	$ 480,000
Promotion	660,000
Property taxes	240,000
Insurance	360,000
Utilities	300,000
Depreciation	600,000
Total	$2,640,000

⊙ Income tax payments are made by CrossMan in the first month of each quarter based on income for the prior quarter. CrossMan's income tax rate is 40 percent. CrossMan's net income for the first quarter of 1999 is projected to be $612,000.

⊙ CrossMan has a corporate policy of maintaining an end-of-month cash balance of $100,000. Cash is invested or borrowed monthly, as necessary, to maintain this balance.

⊙ CrossMan uses a calendar year reporting period.

a. Prepare a pro forma schedule of cash receipts and disbursements for CrossMan Corporation, by month, for the second quarter of 1999. Be sure that all receipts, disbursements, and borrowing/investing amounts are presented on a monthly basis. Ignore the interest expense and/or interest income associated with the borrowing/investing activities.

b. Discuss why cash budgeting is particularly important for a rapidly expanding company such as CrossMan Corporation.

c. Do monthly cash budgets ignore the pattern of cash flows within the month? Explain.

(CMA adapted)

61. *(Cash budget)* Collegiate Management Education, Inc. (CME), is a nonprofit organization that sponsors a wide variety of management seminars throughout the Southwest. In addition, it is heavily involved in research into improved methods of teaching and motivating college administrators. The seminar activity is largely supported by fees and the research program by membership dues.

CME operates on a calendar year basis and is in the process of finalizing the budget for 1999. The following information has been taken from approved plans, which are still tentative at this time:

Seminar Program
Revenue—The scheduled number of programs should produce $12,000,000 of revenue for the year. Each program is budgeted to produce the same amount of revenue as the others. The revenue is collected during the month the program is offered. The programs are scheduled during the basic academic year and are not held during June, July, August, and December. Twelve percent of the revenue is generated in each of the first five months of the year, and the remainder is distributed evenly during September, October, and November.

and, of course, this changes the ending inventory estimates. By the way, we make similar adjustments to expenses by adding at least 10 percent to the estimates. I think everyone around here does the same thing."

    a. Marge Atkins and Pete Granger have described the use of budgetary slack.

        1. Explain why Atkins and Granger behave in this manner, and describe the benefits they expect to realize from the use of budgetary slack.

        2. Explain how the use of budgetary slack can adversely affect Atkins and Granger.

    b. As a management accountant, Scott Ford believes that the behavior described by Marge Atkins and Pete Granger may be unethical and that he may have an obligation to not support this behavior. By citing the specific standards of competence, confidentiality, integrity, and/or objectivity from *Statements on Management Accounting*, "Standards of Ethical Conduct for Management Accountants" (Appendix A to text), explain why the use of budgetary slack may be unethical.

(CMA)

67. *Southwest Airlines has been a leader in designing new and more efficient ways of contracting in the air carrier industry. Several years ago it agreed to an unusual 10-year contract with its pilots union that provides no wage increases in the first five years.*

    In lieu of wage increases during the first half of the apparently unprecedented agreement, Southwest's 2,000 pilots were granted options to acquire as many as 1.4 million shares of the Dallas carrier's stock each year during the life of the contract.

    During the second half of the contract, the pilots would receive the options plus three 3 percent wage increases. The pilots also could get additional compensation based on Southwest's profitability.

    And the carrier is unique in the airline industry in that when Southwest employees were promised profit-sharing, they actually received it; the airline had an unbroken string of twenty profitable years.

[Source: Bridget O'Brian, "Southwest Agrees to Pilots Pact Offering No Wage Boost in First Five of 10 Years," *Wall Street Journal*, November 18, 1994, p. A2. Reprinted by permission of *Wall Street Journal*, © 1994 Dow Jones & Company, Inc. All Rights Reserved Worldwide.]

    a. How could the wage agreement with its pilots provide Southwest Airlines with an edge in both competing and planning?

    b. How would the wage agreement likely affect the quality of services provided by Southwest Airlines? (Specifically address the provisions for profit sharing and stock option ownership.)

68. Although this chapter discusses budgeting largely in the context of internal management, budgeting is also important with respect to financial information that is published externally. In short, managers are very concerned with the effect of projected financial results on external investors and financial markets. Consider how one company reacted to large projected increases or decreases in reported earnings:

    In the decade before 1994, GE's earnings rose every year, although net income fell in 1991 and 1993 because of accounting changes related to post-retirement benefits. The gains, ranging between 1.7 percent and 17 percent, had been fairly steady—especially for a company in a lot of cyclical businesses. As a result, GE almost seemed able to override the business cycle.

    How did GE do it? One undeniable explanation was the fundamental growth of its eight industrial businesses and 24 financial-services units. "We're the best company in the world," declares Dennis Dammerman, GE's chief financial officer.

    But another way was "earnings management," the orchestrated timing of gains and losses to smooth out bumps and, especially, avoid a decline. Among big companies, GE was "certainly a relatively aggressive practitioner of earnings management," said Martin Sankey, a CS First Boston Inc. analyst.

    To smooth out fluctuations, GE frequently offset one-time gains from big asset sales with restructuring charges; that kept earnings from rising so high that they couldn't be topped the following year. GE also timed sales of some equity stakes and even acquisitions to produce profit gains when needed.

. . . A look at GE illustrates how analysts say one giant corporation managed earnings. They add that few companies have maneuvered so successfully for so long on so large a scale. GE's size and diversity gave it an unusual array of opportunities, of course. Moreover, Chairman Jack Welch relentlessly monitored GE's profit growth.

[Source: Randall Smith, Steven Lipin, and Amal Kumar Naj, "How General Electric Damps Fluctuations in Its Annual Earnings," *Wall Street Journal,* November 3, 1994, pp. A1, A11. Reprinted by permission of *Wall Street Journal,* © 1994 Dow Jones & Company, Inc. All Rights Reserved Worldwide.]

a. Why would companies want to manage earnings?

b. Is the use of budgeting and forecasting tools to manage earnings an ethical behavior on the part of managers? Explain.

c. How can the management of earnings lead to the long-term loss of profits?

d. Why do larger companies have greater opportunity than smaller companies to engage in earnings management?

Chapter 8 Capital Asset Selection and Capital Budgeting

LEARNING OBJECTIVES

After reading this chapter, you should be able to answer the following questions:

1. **HOW** do managers choose which capital projects to fund?

2. **WHY** do most capital budgeting methods rely on analyses of cash flows?

3. **WHAT** are the differences among payback period, the net present value method, profitability index, and internal rate of return?

4. **HOW** do the underlying assumptions and limitations of each capital project evaluation method affect its use?

5. **HOW** do taxes and depreciation methods affect cash flows?

6. **WHY** are quality management, training, and research and development controlled largely by capital budget analyses?

7. **WHY** do managers occasionally need to quantify qualitative information in making capital budgeting decisions?

8. **WHY** are environmental issues becoming an increasingly important influence on the capital budget?

9. **HOW** and why should management conduct a post-investment audit of a capital project?

10. **WHAT** calculations are necessary to control for the time value of money? (Appendix 1)

11. **HOW** is the accounting rate of return for a project determined? (Appendix 2)

Exxon Corporation

Exxon Corporation is one of the world's giants in the oil industry. The company also has been the industry's most profitable firm. Its five-year average return on investment is 11.1 percent—a level well above the industry average of 9.8 percent. This high rate of return has been driven by massive revenues; in 1996, the firm realized $134 billion in sales. Exxon reported other significant achievements for 1996. For example, in addition to its record earnings of $7.5 billion, the firm increased its dividend paid to shareholders for the 14th consecutive year, recorded record sales of chemical products, achieved its highest performance ever in employee safety, and logged the highest gas sales in 15 years.

Despite all of this success, Exxon management has reason to be concerned. While its competitors have been spending heavily on new investments to achieve future growth, Exxon has used its high level of earnings to pay dividends to shareholders and to repurchase its stock; since 1983, Exxon has repurchased 27 percent of its outstanding common shares. With the cash leaving the company, it is not available to fund growth opportunities. As major competitors, Mobil Corp. and Royal Dutch/Shell Group were investing billions of dollars to develop production and marketing capabilities for liquefied natural gas, Exxon watched. Exxon's chairman, Lee Raymond, saw his company slip from the position of most profitable company in the industry as Royal Dutch/Shell aggressively expanded 1996 output by 18 percent to post profits of $8.3 billion.

Lee Raymond was well aware that the strategies the firm had pursued to make it the industry's most profitable firm were not the strategies that would generate the rate of growth necessary to sustain high profits into the future. Future growth could come only by investing in long-term projects. As Mr. Raymond contemplated new investment strategies, he knew he had several substantial advantages: access to the best technology in the industry, a formidable balance sheet, and an organization that operated with an efficiency that was the envy of the industry.

SOURCES: Exxon 1996 Annual Report; Toni Mack, "The Tiger Is on the Prowl, *Forbes,* April 21, 1997, pp. 42–44.

Mr. Raymond knows that the future of Exxon depends on obtaining and investing capital in projects that will generate cash and profits in the years to come. But all firms, Exxon included, must determine which investment opportunities to pursue from a virtually unlimited list of potential projects. The investment choices ultimately made by Exxon managers will be reflected in the company's capital budget. Making investment decisions is one of the most important tasks managers must undertake. The ultimate success or failure of these decisions will be reflected in profits of future periods.

Investments are made in short-term working capital assets such as inventory, and in long-term capital assets that are used to generate future revenues or cost savings. **Capital assets** provide production, distribution, or service capabilities lasting more than one year. Capital assets may be tangible, such as machinery and buildings, or intangible, such as capital leases and patents. And, as the first News Note in this chapter indicates, expenditures that are not normally treated as capital assets should perhaps be treated as such when making decisions.

The investment in capital assets often coincides with the execution of major strategies such as development of new product lines or acquisitions of other companies. Capital investments are also associated with major management initiatives to improve competitive position such as raising product or service quality through acquisition of new technology. Other capital investments are made to maintain and support existing operations; an example is replacing a worn-out delivery truck with a new van. Capital asset acquisition decisions involve long-term commitments of large amounts of money. Making the most economically beneficial investments within resource constraints is critical to the organization's long-range well-being. Capital budgeting techniques are designed to enhance management's success in making capital investment decisions.

This chapter presents four methods used to analyze capital projects: payback period, net present value, profitability index, and internal rate of return. The role of the capital budget in managing quality, employee training, and research and development is discussed. Also covered in the chapter are some complexities of acquiring automated equipment, control of environmental costs, the need to include qualitative information in decision making, and the desirability of post-investment audits. In Appendix 1 are elementary concepts for measuring the time value of money, and the accounting rate of return measure is presented in Appendix 2.

capital asset

Advertising: Capital or Ordinary Expenditure?

Should advertising be budgeted as an expense or as an investment? Advertising now is accounted for and budgeted as though its benefits were used up immediately, like purchased electricity. Management thinks about advertising as a current expense. The decision as to how much a corporation should spend on persuasion is made by the same criteria as for materials used up in the factory—impact upon the current income. The advertising budget is part of the operating budget.

So far as is known, no corporation puts advertising in its capital budget, but maybe it belongs there. Several parties say so.

- ⊙ The stock market says it belongs there. It says the benefits derived from promotional outlays are just as capitalizable as the tangible assets that the bookkeeper does capitalize.
- ⊙ Corporation presidents say it belongs there, especially when they evoke investments in advertising to justify poor current operating profits.
- ⊙ New entrants into an industry say it belongs there. They say it by including the promotional outlays required to build brand-acceptance as an integral part of the total investment required to break into a business.
- ⊙ Antitrust economists say it belongs there. They say it by viewing brand acceptance, which is built up by promotion, as just as substantial a barrier to entry as the investment required in buildings and machinery.

SOURCE: Joel Dean, "Does Advertising Belong in the Capital Budget?" *Marketing Management* (Vol. 3, No. 2, 1994), pp. 52–56.

THE INVESTMENT DECISION

Capital budgeting is the process of evaluating long-range investment proposals for the purpose of allocating limited resources effectively and efficiently. The future activities, commonly referred to as **projects**, typically include the purchase, installation, and operation of a capital asset. Management must identify the investments that best support the firm as it works to fulfill its goals and objectives. This process requires answers to the following four basic questions:

capital budgeting

project

1. Is the activity worth the investment?
2. Which assets can be used for the activity?
3. Of the suitable assets, which are the best investments?
4. Which of the best investments should the company choose?

Is the Activity Worth the Required Investment?

Companies acquire assets that have value relative to specific organizational activities. For example, oil companies acquire pipelines to economically move their products to large markets. Before making decisions to acquire assets, company management must be certain that the activity for which the assets will be needed is worth the required investment.

Management initially measures an activity's worth by monetary cost–benefit analysis. If an activity's financial benefits exceed its costs, the activity is, to that extent, considered worthwhile. In some cases, however, benefits cannot be measured in terms of money. In other cases, it is known in advance that the financial benefits will

LEARNING OBJECTIVE ❶
How do managers choose which capital projects to fund?

Pipelines are valuable capital assets for oil companies. These snake-like networks wind over water or fields of snow and ice to move oil, gas, and other refined products from drilling sites to processing or distribution points.

not exceed the costs. In either of these situations, an activity meeting either of these criteria may still be judged worthwhile for some qualitative reasons.

For instance, an oil company may invest in advanced systems in its downstream (retail) operations to vend gasoline. Rather than requiring the customer to pay a cashier for gasoline purchases, the customer can simply use the automated equipment to scan a credit or debit card. The result is lower labor costs for the oil company and greater convenience for the customer. Oil company management may not be able to measure the monetary benefits of the automated equipment objectively but may believe it is worth the cost because it provides access to a specific market segment. Another example is a rural hospital that invests in a kidney dialysis machine although there are only a few kidney patients in the area. Hospital administrators may believe the goodwill generated by such an acquisition justifies the cost. If an activity is deemed worthwhile, the question of cost may become secondary.

Which Assets Can Be Used for the Activity?

Selecting the assets for conducting the intended activity is closely related to assessing the activity's worth. As with many managerial decisions, part of the decision process is a comparison of costs and benefits. Management must estimate the cost of the proposed investment to determine if the activity should be pursued. Managers should gather monetary and nonmonetary information about each available and suitable asset. As shown in Exhibit 8-1, this information includes initial cost, estimated life and salvage value, raw material and labor requirements, operating costs (both fixed and variable), output capability, service availability and cost, maintenance expectations, and revenues to be generated (if any).

Of the Suitable Assets, Which Are the Best Investments?

screening decision

In judging the acceptability of capital projects, managers should recognize that there are two types of capital budgeting decisions: screening and preference. A **screening decision** indicates whether a capital project is desirable based on some previously established minimum criterion or criteria. If the project does not meet the minimum standards, it is excluded from further consideration. Once unacceptable projects have

preference decision

been screened out, a **preference decision** is made in which the remaining projects are ranked based on their contributions to the achievement of company objectives.

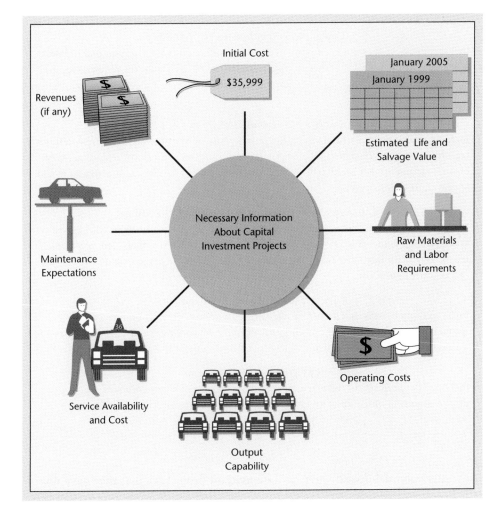

EXHIBIT 8-1
Capital Investment Information

Many companies set up ranking categories such as those shown in Exhibit 8-2 (page 346). Projects are first screened and placed into an appropriate category. Within each category, projects are ranked according to some established criterion or criteria. Resources are then allocated to projects in a top-to-bottom fashion. Management's goal should be to fund those projects that, within budget constraints, will maximize shareholder wealth over the long run.

A company may use one set of techniques to screen projects as to acceptability and another set to rank the projects in order of preference. The method of choosing techniques to be used for screening and ranking varies among companies. Additionally, most large companies have committees to discuss, evaluate, and approve capital projects. In small companies, the owner-managers may simply decide on capital projects.

Which of the Best Investments Should the Company Choose?

Although many worthwhile investments exist, resources at any given time are limited. Therefore, after choosing the best asset for each activity, management must decide which activities and assets to fund. Investment projects may be classified as mutually exclusive, independent, or mutually inclusive.

Mutually exclusive projects are alternative projects that perform the same basic task. When one project is selected from the group, all others will be rejected, as they would provide unneeded or redundant capability. Asset replacement decisions are mutually exclusive projects. If the company keeps the old asset, it will not buy the new one; if the new one is purchased, the old one will be sold.

mutually exclusive project

EXHIBIT 8-2
Ranking Categories for
Capital Projects

Category 1—Required by Legislation

Includes items such as safety equipment and environmental protection equipment. Most companies can ill afford the fines or penalties that can be assessed if the required equipment is not installed; however, these capital acquisitions may not meet the company's minimum return criteria.

Category 2—Essential to Operations

Includes capital assets without which the primary functions of the organization could not continue. This category could include purchases of new capital assets or replacements of broken equipment. For high technology firms, research and development activities would appear in this category.

Category 3—Nonessential But Income Generating

Includes capital assets that would improve organizational operations by providing cost savings or supplements to revenue. Examples include acquisitions of efficient electronic technology to replace labor-intensive technology and investments to expand the variety of a product line.

Category 4—Optional Improvements

Includes capital assets that do not provide any cost savings or additional revenues but would make operations run more smoothly or improve working conditions. Examples include building a break room and a new covered parking lot for employees.

Category 5—Miscellaneous

Includes "pet projects" of managers such as development of a new corporate logo, improvements to offices of corporate managers, and construction of a new executive washroom.

---

independent project

Other potential investments are **independent projects** in that they have no specific bearing on one another. For instance, acquiring a microcomputer system is not related to purchasing an automated teller machine. Each project is analyzed and accepted or rejected on its own merits. While limited resources may preclude the acquisition of all acceptable projects, these projects are not mutually exclusive.

mutually inclusive project

http:// www.exxon.com

Management may be considering certain investments that are all related to a primary project, or are **mutually inclusive**. In this situation, if the primary project is chosen, all related projects are also selected. Alternatively, rejection of the primary project requires rejection of the other related projects. For instance, Exxon decided to expand its development of wells in the North Sea. To handle the increased production of crude oil, the company invested in a new ship to collect, process, and store the oil.

Exhibit 8-3 shows a typical investment decision process. To assure that capital funds are invested in the best projects available, managers must carefully evaluate all projects and decide which ones represent the most effective and efficient uses of resources—a difficult determination. The evaluation process should consider and rank projects based on business activity priorities, project risk, and project cash flows.

CASH FLOWS

LEARNING OBJECTIVE ❷
Why do most capital budgeting methods rely on analyses of cash flows?

An investment is expected to earn some type of return. The amount of the return allows analysts to equate an investment in oil exploration projects, an investment in marketable securities (bonds or stocks), and an investment in an operating asset (refinery). In each case, money is spent and money—in the form of future revenues,

EXHIBIT 8-3
Typical Investment
Decision Process

Activity: Develop in-house system to deliver gasoline and other oil products to retail and commercial operations in North Texas from Houston-area refinery. Distribution presently relies on an independent freight company.

1. Is the activity worth the investment? Yes, the costs of the current product delivery system are causing a decline in profits even as product sales in the North Texas market are growing at a rate of 10 percent per year.
2. Which assets can be used for the activity? *Traditional freight modes:* purchase trucks or railroad tankers. *Other available technology:* lease a pipeline or build a pipeline.
3. Which assets are best investments? Compare all relevant information and choose the best asset candidate from the alternatives. Because the alternatives are mutually exclusive, only one method can be selected. Assume construction of a new pipeline is the preferred alternative.
4. Which investment should the company make? Compare the best asset candidate to the current method of product delivery. This is a mutually exclusive project decision that requires selection of only one delivery mode. Based on an analysis of relevant costs and revenues, either the present delivery contract with the independent freight company will be maintained or the pipeline will be constructed.

Conclusion: Building a new pipeline will result in substantial cost savings over the next fifty years. This alternative is selected.

cash dividends, or cash generated from use—is hopefully returned. Information on the cash generated from asset use is not available from the income statement because it reflects accrual-based revenues and expenses—not all of which may currently be realized as cash. It is the expected cash return on investments that drives individuals and firms to purchase capital assets. Consequently, it is the cash expenditures and cash receipts associated with potential capital assets that are the major focus of investment analysis.

Cash flows are cash receipts and cash disbursements that arise from the purchase, operation, and disposition of capital assets. Cash receipts include project revenues that have been earned and collected, savings generated by reduced project operating costs, and inflows from the asset's sale and release of working capital at the end of the asset's useful life. Cash disbursements include expenditures to acquire the asset, additional working capital investments, and amounts paid for related operating costs.

cash flow

Interest is a cash flow created by the method of financing a project and should not be considered in project evaluation. The funding of projects is a financing, not an investing, decision; and cash flows of the two types of decisions should not be combined. A **financing decision** is a judgment regarding how funds will be raised to make an acquisition. Financing is based on the entity's ability to issue and service debt and equity securities. In contrast, **investing decisions** are judgments about which assets will be acquired by an entity to achieve its stated objectives. Company management must justify the acquisition and use of an asset before justifying the method of financing that asset.

financing decision

investing decision

Cash flows from a capital project are received and paid at different times in a project's life. Within each period, some cash flows occur at the beginning (for example, a payment on a leased asset) and some at the end (for example, a payment on a mortgaged asset). Although many cash flows occur during the period, analysts simplify reality by assuming that flows occur either at the beginning or the end of the period during which they actually occur. Assumed end-of-period cash flows include inflows provided by contribution margins from product sales and outflows for repair expenditures and property taxes on the capital asset.

return of capital
return on capital

A distinction must be made between cash flows representing a return of capital and those representing a return on capital. A **return of capital** is the recovery of the original investment, while a **return on capital** represents income. The return on capital is computed for each period of the investment's life and is equal to the interest included in the receipt or payment. The usual period of analysis is a year. An investment makes a company better off only when, over the life of the investment, it produces cash inflows greater than the investment made plus the cost of the investment capital.

The calculation of cash flows is illustrated by the following example. Big T Oil Company is considering purchasing a fleet of trucks to move jet fuel from the refinery to a pipeline terminal located forty miles from the refinery. Currently the jet fuel is transported by an independent truck freight company. Data relating to the project appear in Exhibit 8-4. This detailed information can be simplified into two basic cash flows: a net negative flow representing the acquisition of the new equipment and a net positive flow representing the net annual cost savings from reduced operating expenses. The savings provided by the new trucks do not represent new cash flows into the company (as would occur with the sale of a product, for example). The savings do, however, represent a decrease in cash outflows—an equally beneficial situation.

Note that depreciation is excluded in these cash flow computations. Depreciation is not a cash flow item; it is important in capital budgeting only to the extent that it reduces the amount of taxable income. Income taxes and the related depreciation effect are important elements in capital budgeting analysis, but add unnecessary complexities at this point. These elements are discussed later in the chapter.

timeline

One helpful tool for analyzing cash flows is a **timeline**, which illustrates the timing of expected cash receipts and payments. On a timeline, cash inflows are shown as positive amounts and cash outflows are shown as negative amounts. The following timeline represents the cash flows from Big T Oil Company's truck fleet purchase. Although individual cash flows can be shown in a timeline, it is easier to use net cash flows. Thus, only two types of cash flows are shown: the net negative flow for the acquisition and the net positive flow produced each year by the cash operating savings.

annuity

The equal annual cash flows are called an **annuity**. The data are shown in thousands of dollars.

Time:	t0	t1	t2	t3	t4	t5	t6
Amount:	−$2,400	+$600	+$600	+$600	+$600	+$600	+$1,300

On a timeline, the acquisition date is time point 0 (t0). Each year thereafter is a period. Periods only serve to separate the times at which flows occur; nothing is presumed to happen during a period. Thus, for example, the net savings provided by the machine each year are shown as occurring at the end of, rather than during, the time period. A less conservative assumption would show the cash flows occurring at the beginning of the period. In period 6, the salvage value of $700,000 is included with the cash operating savings of $600,000 to create a total cash inflow of $1,300,000.

EXHIBIT 8-4

Truck Fleet Acquisition Decision

Purchase price of 20 trucks, trailers, and equipment	$1,800,000
Cost of custom modifications	600,000
Total cash acquisition cost	$2,400,000
Annual cash cost of hiring freight company to move product	$3,200,000
Annual cash operating costs of company-owned fleet	(2,600,000)
Annual cash operating savings	$ 600,000

Expected life of the truck fleet is six years. At the end of the sixth year, the trucks are expected to have a salvage (residual) value of $700,000.

PAYBACK PERIOD

The information on the timing of net cash flows is an input to a simple and often used capital budgeting analysis technique called **payback period**. This method provides a measure of the time it will take a project's cash inflows to equal the original investment. At the end of the payback period, a company has recouped its investment.

In one sense, payback period measures a dimension of project risk by focusing on timing of cash flows. The assumption is that the longer it takes to recover the initial investment, the greater is the project's risk, because cash flows in the more distant future are more uncertain than near-term cash flows. Another reason for concern about long payback periods relates to capital reinvestment. The faster capital is returned from an investment, the more rapidly it can be invested in other projects.

When a project provides an annuity cash inflow, the payback period equals the investment cost divided by the amount of the projected annuity inflow. The payback period for Big T Oil Company's truck fleet is four years ($2,400,000 ÷ $600,000).

To determine the payback period for a project having unequal cash inflows, it is necessary to accumulate the projected cash flows until the original investment is recovered. For instance, consider a project costing $58,000 and providing the following cash flows over its life:

YEAR	AMOUNT
1	$12,000
2	18,000
3	22,000
4	24,000
5	16,000
6	5,000

A yearly cumulative total of the above inflows is prepared:

YEAR	AMOUNT	CUMULATIVE TOTAL
1	$12,000	$12,000
2	18,000	30,000
3	22,000	52,000
4	24,000	76,000
5	16,000	92,000
6	5,000	97,000

At the end of the first three years, $52,000 has been received, and $6,000 more is needed to recover the original $58,000 investment. If the $24,000 inflow in the fourth year is assumed to occur evenly throughout the year, it should take 25 percent ($6,000 ÷ $24,000) of the fourth year to recover the rest of the original investment, giving a payback period for this project of three years and three months.

Company management typically sets a maximum acceptable payback period as part of its evaluation of capital projects. Different categories of capital projects may have different payback criteria. For example, research and development projects may have a required payback of twelve years, but equipment replacement projects may have a required payback of five years. Most companies use payback period as only one of several ways of judging an investment project—usually as a screening technique. Normally, after being found acceptable in terms of payback period, a project is subjected to evaluation by another capital budgeting technique. This second evaluation is performed because the payback period method ignores three important considerations: inflows occurring after the payback period has been reached, the company's desired rate of return, and the time value of money. These issues are incorporated into the decision process by use of discounted future cash flow values.

payback period

LEARNING OBJECTIVE ❸
What are the differences among payback period, the net present value method, profitability index, and internal rate of return?

DISCOUNTED CASH FLOW METHODS

Money has a time value because interest is paid or received on funds.[1] For example, $1,000 received today has greater value than the same sum received one year from today because that money can be invested at an interest rate that will cause it to accumulate to more than $1,000 by the end of one year. This fact encourages the use of discounted cash flow techniques in most capital budgeting situations.

discounting

present value (PV)

Discounting future cash flows means reducing them to their present values by removing the portion representing interest. This imputed interest amount is based on two considerations: the timing of receipts or payments and the assumed interest rate. After discounting, all future values are stated in a common base of current dollars, or **present values (PVs)**. The future value of a cash flow will exceed the present value of the cash flow because the future value includes the interest component. All other factors equal, the future value grows larger as both time and interest rate increase. Using present values of future cash flows occurring at different points in time allows managers to view all project amounts in common terms (present values). Cash flows occurring at the beginning of a project are already stated at their present values and do not need to be discounted.

Because current expenditures such as initial project investment are undiscounted in the capital budgeting process, it is extremely important for managers to obtain the best possible information about these cash flows. Next, the amounts and timing of future cash inflows and outflows must be carefully estimated. Managers need to consider all future cash flows—those that are obvious and those that might be hidden. Companies installing computer systems, for example, find that the highest costs are those that are not readily apparent: supplies, support, training, maintenance, and opportunity costs.

discount rate

cost of capital (COC)

To appropriately discount the future cash flows, managers must estimate the rate of return on capital required by the company. This rate of return is called the **discount rate** and is used to determine the imputed interest portion of future cash receipts and expenditures. The discount rate should equal or exceed the company's **cost of capital (COC)**, which is the weighted average rate for the costs of the various sources of funds (debt and stock) that comprise a firm's capital structure.[2] For example, a company with a COC of 10 percent pays an annual average of 10 percent on each capital dollar to finance investment projects. To determine if a capital project is a worthwhile investment, this company should generally use a minimum rate of 10 percent to discount the project's future cash flows.

Three discounted cash flow techniques are the net present value method, the profitability index, and the internal rate of return. These methods are discussed and illustrated in the following subsections.

Net Present Value Method

net present value method

The **net present value method** uses discounted cash flows to compare the rate of return on a project to the desired rate of return (discount rate). A discount rate may be selected that is unique to categories of projects because different types of projects may be viewed dissimilarly by management; and the discount rate may be adjusted up or down to compensate for unique underlying factors in alternative investment projects.

---

[1]Time value of money and present value computations are reviewed in Appendix 1 of this chapter. These concepts are essential to your understanding of the rest of the chapter; be certain they are clear to you before continuing.

[2]Some managers believe the discount rate should reflect the opportunity cost of capital, which is the highest rate of return that could be earned by using capital for the most attractive alternative project available. Using the opportunity cost of capital to discount project cash flows reflects the benefits that could have been realized from the foregone opportunity. Use of this rate has theoretical merit, but its application is generally not feasible. Therefore, most companies use the overall cost of capital as the discount rate. The computations involved in calculating the cost of capital are covered in finance textbooks and are beyond the scope of this text.

For instance, managers in multinational organizations may use cost of capital as the discount rate for domestic projects but use a higher rate for international investments. The higher rate compensates for the greater risks involved in those projects; greater risks may be associated with factors such as foreign exchange fluctuations and political instability. Managers may also raise or lower the discount rate to compensate for qualitative factors. For instance, an investment in high-technology equipment that would provide a strategic advantage over competitors might be discounted at a rate lower than the COC. This lower rate would provide higher present values for the cash flows and make it easier for such a project to be selected as a viable candidate for funding.

In the net present value method, each cash flow is discounted based on the rate of return specified by the company. A project's **net present value (NPV)** is the difference between the present values of all the project's cash inflows and cash outflows.

net present value (NPV)

The data provided in Exhibit 8-4 are used to illustrate the computation of net present value; the calculations are shown in Exhibit 8-5. First, net present value is computed using a 10 percent rate and then recomputed based on a 14 percent rate.

The truck fleet acquisition project generates a positive net present value regardless of whether the 10 or 14 percent discount rate is used. NPV represents the net cash benefit or cost to a company acquiring and using the investment asset. Applying this criterion, whenever the NPV is zero or greater, the project is acceptable on a quantitative basis. The truck fleet acquisition is acceptable under either the 10 or 14 percent discount rate. If the NPV is zero, the actual rate of return on the project is equal to the desired rate of return. If the NPV is positive, the actual rate is greater than the desired rate. If NPV is negative, the actual rate of return is less than the desired rate of return.

EXHIBIT 8-5

Big T Oil Company's Fleet Acquisition Decision

Cash flow timeline

Time:	t0	t1	t2	t3	t4	t5	t6
Amount:	−$2,400	+$600	+$600	+$600	+$600	+$600	+$1,300

NPV Calculation (assuming a 10% discount rate)

(1)	(2)	(3)	(4)	(5) = (3) × (4)
DESCRIPTION	TIME	CASH FLOW AMOUNT	DISCOUNT FACTOR	PRESENT VALUE
Investment	t0	$(2,400,000)	1.0000[1]	$(2,400,000)
Cash savings	t1−t5	600,000	3.7908[2]	2,274,480
Cash savings & salvage	t6	1,300,000	.5645[3]	733,850
Net present value				$ 608,330

NPV Calculation (assuming a 14% discount rate)

(1)	(2)	(3)	(4)	(5) = (3) × (4)
DESCRIPTION	TIME	CASH FLOW AMOUNT	DISCOUNT FACTOR	PRESENT VALUE
Investment	t0	$(2,400,000)	1.0000[1]	$(2,400,000)
Cash savings	t1−t5	600,000	3.4331[2]	2,059,860
Cash savings & salvage	t6	1,300,000	.4556[3]	592,280
Net present value				$ 252,140

[1] The discount factor of 1.000 indicates that no discounting occurs with respect to cash flows made at the start of a project.
[2] The annual cash savings for years one through five are treated as an annuity because the annual cash flow is identical for these years. In the first example, the discount factor is for a 10 percent rate and in the second example, the discount factor is for a 14 percent discount rate.
[3] The discount factor is for a single cash flow occurring in the sixth period. In the first example, the discount factor is based on a 10 percent rate and in the second example, the discount factor is based on a 14 percent rate.

If all estimates are correct, the truck fleet acquisition being considered by Big T Oil Company will provide a return of over 14 percent. The exact rate of return is not determined by the net present value method unless the NPV happens to be exactly equal to zero.

Exhibit 8-5 demonstrates that when the discount rate is set to 14 percent, a different NPV results than when 10 percent is selected as the discount rate. As the discount rate rises, the NPV decreases; as the discount rate decreases, the NPV rises. Thus, each unique discount rate generates a unique NPV.[3]

The NPV is also sensitive to other assumptions made. Changes in the estimated amounts or timing of cash inflows and outflows affect the net present value of a project. The effects on the NPV of cash flow changes depend on the nature of the changes themselves. For example, decreasing the estimate of cash outflows causes NPV to increase; reducing the stream of the cash inflows causes NPV to decrease. When amounts and timing of cash flows change in conjunction with one another, it is impossible to predict the effects of the changes without calculating the results.

Although the net present value method does not provide the expected rate of return on a project, unless the computed NPV equals zero, it does provide information on how the actual rate compares with the desired rate. This information allows managers to eliminate from consideration any projects on which the rates of return are less than the desired rate.

The NPV method can be used to select the best project when choosing among investments that can perform the same task or achieve the same objective. However, when making investment comparisons, managers must use the same project life span for all projects under consideration. This is necessary because the funds released from a shorter-lived project can be used for another investment, which will generate additional dollars of revenues and create additional dollars of costs.[4]

Further, NPV should not be used to compare independent investment projects that do not have approximately the same original asset cost. Such comparisons favor projects having higher net present values over those with lower net present values without regard to uneven amounts of capital invested in the projects. Logically, companies should invest in projects that produce the highest return per investment dollar.

Profitability Index

profitability index (PI)

Projects with different costs can be compared by use of a variation of the NPV method known as the profitability index (PI). The **profitability index** is a ratio of the present value of all cash flows occurring after time period 0 to the time period 0 net investment. The PI is calculated as follows:

$$PI = \frac{\text{Present value of net future cash flows}}{\text{Net investment}}$$

Using a 10 percent discount rate, the truck fleet acquisition project of Big T Oil Company is approximately 1.25, calculated as $3,008,330 divided by $2,400,000. The present value of the net future cash inflows is equal to the net present value of $608,330 plus the investment cost of $2,400,000.

---

[3]Under some circumstances, a project may have more than one discount rate that will generate the same NPV. However, this rarely occurs and is associated with projects that have large cash outflows at both the beginning and end of the project.

[4]If the alternative projects' lives are not equal, they are treated for computational purposes as if they were. For example, if Big T Oil Company could purchase or lease the truck fleet, but the required lease has a life of three years while the purchase alternative has a six-year life, managers could compare the two alternatives either by using only three years of cash flows on the purchase alternative or by assuming that another lease could be executed at the end of the first lease. For the latter assumption, managers would make appropriate estimates relating to any cash flows that varied from the first and second lease agreements. Computer packages are available to quickly do "what if" (or sensitivity) analysis for such scenarios.

An NPV of $0 is the equivalent of a PI of 1. Accordingly, the general rule for project acceptability when the profitability index is used is that the PI should be equal to or greater than 1.00. Such a PI indicates that the present value of the expected net cash inflows is equal to or greater than the investment cost. Thus, Big T Oil Company would consider the fleet acquisition an acceptable project.

The present value of the net future cash flows represents an output measure of the project's worth. This amount equals the cash benefit provided by the project, or the present value of future cash inflows minus the present value of future cash outflows. The present value of the investment represents an input measure of the project's cost. By relating these two measures, the profitability index gauges the firm's efficiency at using its capital. The higher the index, the more efficient are the firm's capital investments.

In some instances, the NPV and PI methods provide different conclusions as to the relative ranking of projects. For example, the NPV of Project A may be higher than the NPV of Project B, but the PI for Project B may be greater than that for Project A. In such a case, either of the following two conditions must exist for the PI to provide better information than the NPV.

First, the projects must be mutually exclusive. Accepting one project must require rejecting the other. This condition would be met if, for example, Big T Oil Company were considering the purchase of a truck fleet from alternative suppliers such as Peterbilt and Kenworth. Alternatively, the availability of investment funds must be limited. If Big T Oil Company's total capital budget is constrained by the availability of capital, buying the truck fleet might preclude investment in another project such as acquiring new refinery equipment.

Like the net present value method, the profitability index does not indicate an investment's expected rate of return. This measure is provided by the project's internal rate of return.

Internal Rate of Return

A project's **internal rate of return (IRR)** is its expected rate of return. The IRR is the discount rate that causes the NPV of a project to equal zero. This relationship can also be expressed as the discount rate that causes the present value of all cash inflows to equal the present value of all cash outflows. This relationship is shown in the following formula:

internal rate of return (IRR)

$$\text{NPV} = -\text{ Investment} + \text{PV of cash inflows} - \text{PV of other cash outflows}$$
$$0 = -\text{ Investment} + [\text{Cash inflows (Discount factor)}] - [\text{Cash}$$
$$\text{outflows (Discount factor)}]$$

In evaluating a capital project, managers have information about the investment amount, cash inflows, and cash outflows. Thus, the only missing items in the formula are the discount factors that identify the specific discount rate (IRR).

When all cash flows after time period 0 comprise an annuity, the NPV formula can be restated as follows:

$$\text{NPV} = -\text{ Investment} + \text{PV of annuity}$$
$$0 = -\text{ Investment} + (\text{Annuity cash flow} \times \text{Discount factor})$$

Determining the internal rate of return involves substituting known amounts (investment and annuity) into the formula, rearranging terms, and solving for the unknown (the discount factor).

$$\text{NPV} = -\text{ Investment} + (\text{Annuity} \times \text{Discount factor})$$
$$0 = -\text{ Investment} + (\text{Annuity} \times \text{Discount factor})$$
$$\text{Investment} = (\text{Annuity} \times \text{Discount factor})$$
$$\text{Investment} \div \text{Annuity} = \text{Discount factor}$$

The solution yields a discount factor for the number of annuity periods of project life at the internal rate of return. Tracing this factor in an appropriate PV table to its associated interest rate provides the internal rate of return.

To illustrate, consider a possible project that will cost $30,000 (initial investment) and produce annual net cash inflows of $4,600 for eight years. Assume there are no other cash flows. These values are substituted into the NPV equation, which then is solved for the present value factor.

$$
\begin{aligned}
\text{NPV} &= -\text{ Investment} + (\text{Annuity} \times \text{Discount factor}) \\
0 &= -\$30,000 + (\$4,600 \times \text{Discount factor}) \\
\$30,000 &= (\$4,600 \times \text{Discount factor}) \\
\$30,000 \div \$4,600 &= \text{Discount factor} \\
6.5217 &= \text{Discount factor}
\end{aligned}
$$

The table of present values of an ordinary annuity (Table 2, Appendix C) will provide the internal rate of return. In the table, find the row representing the project's life (in this case, eight periods). Look across the row for the 6.5217 discount factor yielded by the equation. The IRR (or its approximation) is the rate at the top of the column containing the factor. The 6.5217 factor on row 8 falls between the discount factors for 4 percent (6.7327) and 5 percent (6.4632). Interpolation, a computer program, or a programmable calculator gives 4.78 percent as the IRR for this project, if all assumed project information holds true.[5]

When a project does not have equal annual cash flows, finding the IRR involves an iterative trial-and-error process. An initial estimate is made of a rate believed to be close to the IRR, and the NPV is computed. If the resulting NPV is negative, a lower rate is estimated, and the NPV is computed again. If the NPV is positive, a higher rate is tried. This process is continued until the net present value equals zero, at which time the internal rate of return has been found.

Exhibit 8-6 uses data given in Exhibit 8-5 for Big T Oil Company to demonstrate this process. The truck fleet acquisition was shown to have an expected rate of return of more than 14 percent (since discounting at that rate resulted in a positive NPV). Exhibit 8-6 indicates a first estimate of 18 percent as the IRR for this project, but the NPV is negative at this discount rate. A second estimate of 17 percent is made, result-

EXHIBIT 8-6

Trial-and-Error Determination of IRR for Big T Oil Company Truck Fleet Investment

Because the NPV was found to be positive using a discount rate of 14%, the next iteration uses a discount rate of 18 percent. Those calculations follow.

$$
\begin{aligned}
\text{NPV} &= -\text{ Investment} + (\text{PV of cash inflows}) - (\text{PV of cash outflows}) \\
\text{NPV} &= -\$2,400,000 + (\$600,000 \times 3.1272) + (\$1,300,000 \times .3704) - \$0 \\
&= -\$2,400,000 + \$1,876,320 + \$481,520 - \$0 \\
&= -\$42,160
\end{aligned}
$$

Because using 18 percent produces a negative NPV, the IRR must be between 18 percent and 14 percent. Because the NPV found using 18 percent as the discount rate is very close to $0, the IRR is much closer to 18 percent than to 14 percent. The next iteration uses 17 percent as the discount rate.

$$
\begin{aligned}
\text{NPV} &= -\$2,400,000 + (\$600,000 \times 3.1994) + (\$1,300,000 \times .3898) - \$0 \\
&= -\$2,400,000 + \$1,919,640 + \$506,740 - \$0 \\
&= \$26,380
\end{aligned}
$$

The IRR is between 17 percent and 18 percent.

---

[5]Interpolation is the process of finding a term between two other terms in a series. The difference in the NPVs at 4 percent and 5 percent is $2,479 [$1,941 − (− $538)]. The interpolation process gives the following computation: Actual rate = 4% + [($1,941 ÷ $2,479)(1.0)] = 4% + (.78)(1.0) = 4.78% (rounded). The 1.0 represents the 1 percent difference between the 4 percent and 5 percent rates.

ing in a positive NPV. Thus, the internal rate of return falls between 17 percent and 18 percent.

Once the IRR on a project is known, it is compared with the company's discount rate or a preestablished **hurdle rate**. A company's hurdle rate is the rate of return deemed by management to be the lowest acceptable return on investment. This rate should be at least equal to the cost of capital. It is typically the discount rate used in computing net present value amounts.

hurdle rate

If a project's IRR is equal to or greater than the hurdle rate, the project is considered an acceptable investment. The higher the internal rate of return, the more financially attractive is the investment proposal. In choosing among alternative investments, however, managers cannot look solely at the internal rates of return on projects. The rate does not reflect the dollars involved. An investor would normally rather have a 10 percent return on $1,000 than a 100 percent return on $10!

ASSUMPTIONS AND LIMITATIONS OF METHODS

Each capital budgeting technique has its own underlying assumptions and limitations; these are summarized in Exhibit 8-7 (page 356). To derive the most success from the capital budgeting process, managers should understand the basic similarities and differences of the various methods and use several techniques to evaluate a project.

All of the methods share two limitations: (1) they do not consider management preferences about the pattern of cash flows, and (2) they use a single, deterministic measure of cash flow amounts rather than ranges of cash flow values based on probabilities. Management can compensate for the first limitation by subjectively favoring projects whose cash flow profiles better suit organizational preferences, assuming other project factors are equal. The second limitation can be overcome by use of probability estimates of cash flows. These estimates can be input into a computer program to determine a distribution of cash flows for each method under various conditions of uncertainty.

The previous examples of capital budgeting analysis have all ignored one major influence—taxation and its effects on cash flows. This topic is covered in the following section.

LEARNING OBJECTIVE 4
How do the underlying assumptions and limitations of each capital project evaluation method affect its use?

THE EFFECTS OF TAXATION ON CASH FLOWS

Income taxes are a significant aspect of the business world. Tax planning is a central part of management planning and overall business profitability. Managers should give thorough consideration to the tax implications of all company decisions. In evaluating capital projects, managers should use after-tax cash flows to determine projects' acceptability. It is only the amount of cash that remains after paying taxes that is available for management's use. Like interest on debt, depreciation on capital assets is deductible in computing taxable income. As taxable income decreases, so do the taxes that must be paid; thus, cash flow is affected.

Continuously profitable businesses generally find it advantageous to claim depreciation deductions as rapidly as permitted by tax law. As noted earlier, depreciation expense is not a cash flow item. Companies neither pay nor receive any funds for depreciation. However, by reducing the amount of taxable income, depreciation expense becomes a **tax shield** for revenues. The amount of the tax shield depends on the asset's cost, life, and the depreciation method chosen. The tax shield produces a **tax benefit** equal to the depreciation amount multiplied by the tax rate. Thus, the tax benefit of depreciation increases with increases in the tax rate and the depreciation amount.

LEARNING OBJECTIVE 5
How do taxes and depreciation methods affect cash flows?

tax shield
tax benefit

EXHIBIT 8-7
Selected Assumptions and Limitations of Capital Budgeting Methods

ASSUMPTIONS	LIMITATIONS
Payback	
■ Speed of investment recovery is the key consideration ■ Timing and size of cash flows are accurately predicted ■ Risk (uncertainty) is lower for a shorter payback project	■ Ignores cash flows after payback ■ Basic method treats cash flows and project life deterministically without explicit consideration of probabilities ■ Ignores time value of money ■ Cash flow pattern preferences are not explicitly recognized
Net Present Value	
■ Discount rate used is valid ■ Timing and size of cash flows are accurately predicted ■ Life of project is accurately predicted ■ If the shorter-lived of two projects is selected, the proceeds of that project will continue to earn the discount rate of return through the theoretical completion of the longer-lived project	■ Basic method treats cash flows and project life deterministically without explicit consideration of probabilities ■ NPV does not measure expected rates of return on projects being compared ■ Cash flow pattern preferences are not explicitly recognized ■ IRR of project is not reflected
Profitability Index	
■ Same as NPV ■ Size of PV of net inflows relative to size of PV of investment measures efficient use of capital	■ Same as NPV ■ Gives a relative answer but does not reflect dollars of NPV
Internal Rate of Return	
■ Hurdle rate used is valid ■ Timing and size of cash flows are accurately predicted ■ Life of project is accurately predicted ■ If the shorter-lived of two projects is selected, the proceeds of that project will continue to earn the IRR through the theoretical completion of the longer-lived project	■ Projects are ranked for funding based on IRR rather than dollar size ■ Does not reflect dollars of NPV ■ Basic method treats cash flows and project life deterministically without explicit consideration of probabilities ■ Cash flow pattern preferences are not explicitly recognized ■ It is possible to calculate multiple rates of return on the same project
Accounting Rate of Return	
(presented in Appendix 2 to this chapter)	
■ Effect on company accounting earnings relative to average investment in a project is a key consideration ■ Size and timing of investment cost, project life, salvage value, and increases in earnings can be accurately predicted	■ Ignores cash flows ■ Ignores time value of money ■ Treats earnings and project life deterministically without explicit consideration of probabilities

The concepts of tax shield and tax benefit are illustrated on the following income statements. The tax rate is assumed to be 40 percent.

NO DEPRECIATION DEDUCTION INCOME STATEMENT		DEPRECIATION DEDUCTION INCOME STATEMENT	
Sales	$2,200,000	Sales	$2,200,000
Cost of goods sold	(900,000)	Cost of goods sold	(900,000)
Gross margin	$1,300,000	Gross margin	$1,300,000
Expenses other than depreciation	(300,000)	Expenses other than depreciation	(300,000)
Depreciation expense	0	Depreciation expense	(400,000)
Income before taxes	$1,000,000	Income before taxes	$ 600,000
Tax expense (40%)	(400,000)	Tax expense (40%)	(240,000)
Net income	$ 600,000	Net income	$ 360,000

The tax shield is the depreciation expense amount of $400,000. The tax benefit is $160,000 ($400,000 × 40%), or the difference between $400,000 of tax expense on the first income statement and $240,000 of tax expense on the second income statement. Because taxes are reduced by $160,000, less cash must be spent, and net cash inflows increase.

Income tax laws regarding depreciation are subject to periodic revision and vary from country to country. In analyzing capital investments, managers need to use the most current depreciation regulations to calculate cash flows from projects. Different depreciation methods may have significantly different impacts on after-tax cash flows. For a continuously profitable company, an accelerated method of depreciation will produce higher tax benefits in the early years of asset life than will the straight-line method. These higher tax benefits will translate into a higher net present value over the life of the investment project.

Even when managers use the most current tax regulations in evaluating a capital project, rules may change again, and the expected depreciation method or rate may not be available by the time the investment is actually made and the asset placed into service. Such changes can dramatically affect the timing of projected after-tax cash flows. However, once purchased and placed into service, an asset can generally be depreciated according to the method allowed at that point, regardless of tax law changes that occur later.

Changes may also occur in the tax rate structure. Rate changes are relatively unpredictable. For example, the maximum U.S. federal corporate tax rate for many years was 46 percent; then the Tax Reform Act of 1986 lowered this rate to 34 percent. A reduction in the tax rate lowers the tax benefit provided by the depreciation tax shield because the cash flow impact is lessened. Tax rate changes can, of course, cause actual outcomes to vary from expected outcomes.

Illustration of After-Tax Cash Flows in Capital Budgeting

Big T Oil Company is considering the purchase of an advanced, computerized system to monitor its pipeline flows. The system would allow an increase in throughput and reduce operating costs and the potential for undetected leaks. Information about this investment is given in Exhibit 8-8 (page 358). Cash flows of the project would represent only a small part of Big T Oil's total cash flows. However, the effect of the project on the company's total tax liability must be estimated and included in the project analysis.

The incremental income tax each year is added to the other cash outflows in a capital budgeting project. The amount of incremental, net after-tax cash flows can be estimated for the project as follows:

EXHIBIT 8-8
Advanced Pipeline Monitoring
System Data

Estimated life	8 years	
Cost	$640,000	
Residual value	$ 60,000	
Estimated additional annual revenue		$ 80,000
Estimated annual operating cost savings		25,000
Net operating cash flow		$105,000
Tax rate for Big T Oil		35%
Discount rate and hurdle rate for IRR		12%
Minimum payback period		5 years

Depreciation deduction for tax purposes (assuming use of straight-line method):
$640,000 ÷ 8 = $80,000

Notes:

1. For tax purposes, no salvage value is recognized in computing depreciation deductions.
2. The actual amount of depreciation allowed for tax purposes is computed based on tax rules that go beyond the scope of this course; thus, straight-line depreciation is assumed.

$$NATCF = t(D) + (1 - t)(NOCF)$$
$$T = t(NOCF - D)$$

where
$NATCF$ = net after-tax cash flows
t = tax rate
D = depreciation for period
$NOCF$ = net operating cash flows
T = income tax for period

The net annual after-tax cash flows from the operation of the computerized monitoring system are as follows:

$$NATCF = .35(\$80,000) + (1-.35)\$105,000$$
$$NATCF = \$28,000 + \$68,250$$
$$NATCF = \$96,250$$

The cash flow from the residual value of the equipment is computed as

$$After\text{-}tax\ residual = Residual\ amount(1-t)$$
$$= \$60,000(1-.35)$$
$$= \$39,000$$

There is logic in the preceding calculation: because the full cost of the asset has been depreciated with no allowance for a salvage value, the entire sales value of the asset is subject to taxation. The net after-tax cash flow timeline is

Time	t0	t1	t2	t3	t4	t5	t6	t7	t8
Investment	−$640,000								
NATCF		$96,250	$96,250	$96,250	$96,250	$96,250	$96,250	$96,250	$96,250
Residual									$39,000

The net present value of the investment is calculated as follows using a discount rate of 12 percent:

DESCRIPTION	TIME	AFTER-TAX CASH FLOW	DISCOUNT FACTOR	PRESENT VALUE
Investment	t0	$(640,000)	1.0000	$(640,000)
NATCF	t1−t8	96,250	4.9676	478,132
Residual	t8	39,000	.4039	15,752
Net Present Value				$(146,116)

Note that the after-tax cash flow for the investment is identical to the pre-tax amount. This is because no tax deduction is allowed for that expenditure; instead that amount is expensed for tax purposes through periodic depreciation.

Since the NPV is negative, the computerized monitoring system will earn a rate lower than the 12 percent discount rate. The project is not acceptable based on the NPV criterion.

The PI for the investment is determined as follows:

PI = Present value of net future cash flows ÷ Present value of investment
  = (NPV + Investment) ÷ Present value of investment
  = ($(146,116) + $640,000) ÷ $640,000
  = $493,884 ÷ $640,000
  = 0.77

This result is less than 1.00; thus, the investment earns less than the 12 percent discount rate.

The internal rate of return for the system must be less than 12 percent because there is a negative NPV based on a 12 percent discount rate. Because the cash flows are not even each year, a trial-and-error approach to determining the IRR must be used. Trial and error attempts show the IRR is about 5.3 percent. This is proven in the NPV calculations that follow which are based on a 5 percent discount rate. The NPV of $8,478 is relatively near $0, the value of the NPV when the IRR is used as the discount rate.

DESCRIPTION	TIME	AFTER-TAX CASH FLOW	DISCOUNT FACTOR	PRESENT VALUE
Investment	t0	$(640,000)	1.0000	$(640,000)
NATCF	t1−t8	96,250	6.4632	622,083
Residual	t8	39,000	.6768	26,395
Net Present Value				$ 8,478

The payback period of the computer is found by dividing the investment cost by the NATCF: $640,000 ÷ $96,250 = 6.65 years. Because the company's maximum acceptable payback period is five years, the payback period on this project is unacceptable.

Based solely on quantitative investment criteria, each of the previous techniques indicates that purchasing the computerized pipeline monitoring system is a not a viable investment for Big T Oil Company. However, the company should consider whether any financial costs or benefits have been omitted before concluding the project is unacceptable. Additionally, any qualitative benefits of this project, such as a reduced likelihood of undetected leaks, should be considered.

The capital budget is a key tool in implementing management's strategies. The capital budget is also a key control tool for managing quality, employee training, and research and development. This is the subject of the next section.

INVESTING TO MANAGE QUALITY COSTS AND INVESTING IN TRAINING AND RESEARCH AND DEVELOPMENT

Many important responsibilities of managers are directly or indirectly achieved by effective management of the capital budget. One such area of responsibility is quality management. In Chapter 3, control of quality was discussed in terms of managing four related costs: internal failure, external failure, appraisal, and prevention. Total quality cost is the sum of costs in these four categories. It is argued that management

LEARNING OBJECTIVE 6

Why are quality management, training, and research and development controlled largely by capital budget analyses?

of quality costs requires analysis of tradeoffs among the categories. Specifically, spending greater amounts for prevention and appraisal are likely to lead to reductions in both failure cost categories.

Prevention and appraisal costs are both partly managed in the capital budget. For example, quality problems can be prevented by acquiring more sophisticated manufacturing technology and by training workers to use manufacturing techniques that reduce errors. Statistical quality controls can be applied to monitor operations and determine when acceptable error tolerances are exceeded.

Quality issues are rarely considered in isolation in capital budgeting decisions. In fact, quality may be a secondary issue in some capital budgeting decisions. To illustrate how quality considerations can be impounded in capital budget analysis, assume that Ace Lighting Company produces several products—one of which is a security light. Data for the security light follow.

Expected sales volume by future budget year:

YEAR		SALES VOLUME
2000	(t1)	25,000
2001	(t2)	40,000
2002	(t3)	50,000
2003	(t4)	20,000

By the end of 2003, the life cycle of the security light will be over. During the remaining life cycle of the product, assuming no changes in production methods are made, the unit production costs are expected to be as follows:

Direct labor	$ 9
Direct material	8
Variable overhead	7
Total variable production costs	$24[6]

Company management is evaluating the possibility of installing automated equipment that would reduce the cost of direct labor from $9 to $5 per unit. The equipment would cause variable overhead to increase by $1 per unit; no other costs or revenues would be affected (ignoring quality costs). Thus, variable cost would decrease by a net amount of $3 per unit. The estimated acquisition cost of the new equipment is $330,000 and would be installed at the start of the year 2000.

The timeline of cash flows for the project follows:

t0	t1	t2	t3	t4
−$330,000	$75,000	$120,000	$150,000	$60,000

Assuming the company's cost of capital is 10 percent, the pre-tax NPV of the project follows:

DESCRIPTION	TIME	CASH FLOW	DISCOUNT FACTOR	PRESENT VALUE
Investment	t0	$(300,000)	1.0000	$(330,000)
Cash savings	t1	75,000	.9091	68,183
Cash savings	t2	120,000	.8265	99,180
Cash savings	t3	150,000	.7513	112,695
Cash savings	t4	60,000	.6830	40,980
Net Present Value				$ (8,962)

Based on the NPV, the project is unacceptable. However, assume that the new technology would generate many fewer defective products than the existing manual conversion process, and the company inspects each light upon completion for defects. To simplify the example, assume any defective light produced is identified in the process of inspection; there are no external defects. Defective lights are scrapped be-

---

[6]Fixed costs are ignored in the example because they are not relevant to the decision.

cause it is not economical to rework them. Under the manual production process, defects are produced at a rate of 2 percent of units sold. With the advanced technology, defects are estimated to be only .25 percent of units sold. The following table shows the potential savings in quality defect costs:

YEAR	COST SAVINGS
2000	$24 \times 25,000 \times (.02 - .0025) = \$10,500$
2001	$24 \times 40,000 \times (.02 - .0025) = \$16,800$
2002	$24 \times 50,000 \times (.02 - .0025) = \$21,000$
2003	$24 \times 20,000 \times (.02 - .0025) = \$ 8,400$

The timeline of revised cash flows for the project follows:

	t0	t1	t2	t3	t4
Investment	−$330,000				
Labor savings		$75,000	$120,000	$150,000	$60,000
Quality cost savings		10,500	16,800	21,000	8,400
Total cash flows	−$330,000	$85,500	$136,800	$171,000	$68,400

Considering the quality cost savings, together with the labor savings, a new NPV can be calculated:

DESCRIPTION	TIME	CASH FLOW	DISCOUNT FACTOR	PRESENT VALUE
Investment	t0	$(300,000)	1.0000	$(330,000)
Cash savings	t1	85,500	.9091	77,728
Cash savings	t2	136,800	.8265	113,065
Cash savings	t3	171,000	.7513	128,472
Cash savings	t4	68,400	.6830	46,717
Net Present Value				$ 35,982

By considering the quality costs, the NPV of the proposed project has been increased dramatically. The project is now acceptable. If this example were expanded, many additional quality costs could be considered in the NPV framework. For example, external failure costs can be considered—costs such as warranty expense, customer returns, and loss of reputation. Savings from reducing inspections could also be considered.

Learning something from a textbook is sometimes no substitute for on-the-job training. Investment in teaching employees how to do their jobs more effectively and efficiently pays off through higher quality products and fewer defects.

Training costs also should be examined in the capital budget using discounted cash flow analysis. Much like investment in new equipment, training costs are incurred in the present to generate future benefits. Because the benefits of training can persist for the entire tenure of an employee, it is proper to regard training benefits as multi-period. Along with acquisition of advanced technology, providing training to employees is a fundamental tool to improve quality.

Like investment in new technology, investment in training results in an increase in prevention costs in the present, to be offset by future decreases in other quality cost categories. Particularly, decreases in external and internal failure costs should result from effective training expenditures.

Although quality is certainly an important dimension of organizational performance that is partly managed by the capital budget, the capital budget may be even more important for managing research and development activities.

Managing Research and Development

Another major area of managerial responsibility that ties directly to capital budgeting is evaluation of research and development projects. Research and development (R&D) activities are necessary to generate the innovative products and services that will provide future revenues. As competition in the global market intensifies, the pressure to effectively manage R&D activities increases.

Because many firms competing in a given market today have developed effective R&D programs, the life cycles of many products have decreased. The reduction in life cycle is caused by one competitor introducing a new product to the market that is soon made obsolete by the new product introduction of a second competitor. Once an innovative product reaches the market, competitors can respond more quickly than ever before with products that meet or exceed the quality and features of the "innovative" product. This fact is highlighted in the following News Note.

In this competitive game whose outcome depends on the pace of introducing new products, the generation of future profits critically depends on effective capital budget analysis. Research and development requires a commitment of cash and other resources in the present to reap cash inflows from sales of products in the future. Like

NEWS NOTE

Just How Important Is Research and Development?

The Product Development & Management Association surveyed its members about the importance of new products in generating new sales.

At the two hundred U.S. companies surveyed by the organization in 1996, new products accounted for 28 percent of total sales in the previous five years, and that figure was expected to increase to 37 percent in the next five years. Similarly, new products were expected to account for 39 percent of total profits in the next five years, up from 25 percent in the previous five.

In the study, new products were defined as applications, major product changes, and new-to-the-world products. Though a time frame was not specified, the study encompassed products introduced into the market in the previous five years, according to the association.

Robert G. Cooper, a professor of marketing and technology management at McMaster University in Hamilton, Ontario, notes that the percentage of sales coming from new products "has been increasing over the past few years—across all industries and sizes of businesses."

Now, Cooper says, it's not unusual for U.S. companies to have 50 percent of sales—and about 40 percent of profits—coming from products five years old or less.

SOURCE: Roberta Maynard, "The Heat Is On," excerpted by permission, *Nation's Business* (October 1997) pp. 14–16, 18, 20, 22, 23. Copyright 1997, U.S. Chamber of Commerce.

all other capital projects, research and development activities should be managed using discounted cash flow techniques that relate the future cash inflows to the current outflows. Furthermore, the analysis must consider the fact that life cycles are likely to get shorter over time, requiring firms to recapture their investments quickly if new products are to be profitable. Although strategy of the firm is the major driver of R&D, capital budget analysis is the major control tool.

In addition to R&D, the acquisition of high tech assets that are related to quality initiatives, product life-cycle management, and new product development has a large role in determining the success of businesses today.

HIGH-TECH INVESTMENTS AND QUALITATIVE CONSIDERATIONS

One area of business investment in which uncertainty is extremely prevalent is that of high-technology equipment. Some of the most pressing investment decisions currently facing American companies are those related to the purchase of automated and robotic equipment.

High-technology equipment generally requires massive monetary investment. Justification of such equipment must include the numerous advantages from these investments, including significantly reduced labor costs, increased quality and quantity of production, shortened processing time, and increased utility and maintenance costs. Thus, significant thought should be given to the investment's tangible benefits (such as increased output) and intangible benefits (such as increased customer satisfaction with the quality of products). The grid shown in Exhibit 8-9 identifies some of the quantifiable and nonquantifiable benefits of high-tech capital equipment and their association with the short-term financial and long-term strategic objectives of the organization. As indicated in the News Note on page 364, many companies find high-tech projects including investments in information technology to be difficult to analyze quantitatively.

EXHIBIT 8-9

Characteristics of High-Technology Capital Projects

	QUANTIFIABLE	NON-QUANTIFIABLE
FINANCIAL (shorter-term)	• Material cost reduction • Labor savings • Inventory reduction • Scrap/waste reduction • Increased capacity	• Setup reduction • Elimination of non-value-added activities (moves; inspections) • Reduced manufacturing leadtime • Reduced administration cycle time • Increased plant safety
STRATEGIC (longer-term)	• Increased flexibility • Improved quality • Increased market share due to new product/innovation • Price premiums due to shorter leadtimes	• Improved employee morale • Improved work environment • Ability to attract better employees • Better skilled employees • Perceived technology leadership by customer • Regulatory requirements met

SOURCE: Chris Koepfer, "To Buy or Not to Buy—A New Look at Justifying Capital Equipment," *Modern Machine Shop* (November 1992), p. 72. Used by permission of *Modern Machine Shop*, Copyright 1992, Gardner Publications Inc., Cincinnati, Ohio USA.

What's Information Worth?

Think back to the last project you were involved in that applied information technology in a business setting. Do you remember what the anticipated costs were? Did you know, in dollar terms, what the expected benefits were? How about the overall business case for the project?

What's that you say? You never knew the return on investment? Perhaps it was a secret, the sort the executive committee keeps to itself. More likely, I suspect, is that the return wasn't calculated in the first place. Now, if you are a member of the group that can describe the costs of information technology in great detail, you are probably muttering that the benefits to be calculated were "soft," and couldn't be measured. Consequently, it wasn't possible to determine the return anyway.

Are we communicating yet? Too often, calculating and measuring the return for an information technology project is set aside because it seems too difficult. But didn't our training as accountants include the capital budgeting process, where we ranked alternative projects based on their relative net present values, or on return on investment? For some time, information technology projects have been among the most significant capital projects businesses undertake. One of the reasons for their failure is that they often are not subject to a capital budget process. A return target is not calculated. But if you don't calculate the return, then your business case is also suspect. The core of any business case is that the projected benefits (return), and estimated costs (investment), are compared.

SOURCE: Deryck Williams, "Foolproof Projects," reproduced with permission from *CA Magazine* (September 1995), pp. 35–36. Published by the Canadian Institute of Chartered Accountants, Toronto, Canada.

Considerations in High-Tech Investment Analysis

Managers making decisions about investments in automated equipment or equipment that enhances product or process quality should make their capital budgeting analyses carefully. First, the discount or hurdle rate used should be chosen very thoughtfully. Although interest rates are fairly low at this time, managers often still set hurdle or discount rates between 12 and 18 percent. Such high rates severely penalize capital investments (such as flexible manufacturing systems) that require high initial investments and may take many years to achieve payback.

LEARNING OBJECTIVE 7
Why do managers occasionally need to quantify qualitative information in making capital budgeting decisions?

Second, both the quantitative and qualitative benefits to be provided by all capital expenditures need to be considered, especially high-tech ones. In making investment decisions, because of the difficulty in determining their worth, management has often assigned a zero dollar value to benefits such as reduced product development time, shortened delivery time, and improved competitive position. Some managers do attempt to quantify these qualitative factors in their analyses. Quantifying every benefit is important because it overcomes the main excuse managers have for making investments without an evaluation.

A third item to consider in regard to high-tech investments is that such projects are not "free-standing." Many high-tech investments are interrelated, integrated parts of a whole and should not be viewed as individual projects. The benefits of the "bundled" project are greater than the benefits that would accrue from the individual elements. Consider that after General Motors made a multibillion-dollar investment in robots in the 1980s, the company failed to reengineer factories so the robots could be used to their full potential to produce "different models and innovative designs by the car lot. [Instead, the company simply] wound up using the robots as an inflexible substitute for labor."[7]

http:// www.gm.com

[7]Rob Norton, "A New Tool to Help Managers," *Fortune*, May 30, 1994, p. 140.

Robotic equipment, such as this welder, can perform tasks much more rapidly and with higher quality than humans often can. Although quantifying some of the benefits of using automated technology may be difficult, to not do so is to ignore a very large part of why the equipment is being considered for purchase—hardly a rational attitude!

Finally, consideration should be given to the opportunity cost of not acquiring automated equipment. The opportunity cost of nonautomation refers to the competitive disadvantage a company will experience when its competitors acquire such equipment and experience the qualitative benefits mentioned earlier.

In making capital budgeting decisions, managers should quantify all benefits and costs that can be quantified with any reasonable degree of accuracy. Managers can also attempt to quantify the qualitative benefits using probabilities. The probabilities can be included in calculations of the investment's net present value or internal rate of return. Alternatively, management can simply make subjective evaluations of nonquantifiable items to make certain that those items are properly weighted in the decision model.

The hottest high-tech investments being made by manufacturers are flexible manufacturing systems (FMSs) that use computer-controlled robots to produce numerous high-quality, customized products at very low per-unit costs. The keys to customization are small lot sizes, rapid setup, and a great deal of information; the ability to be flexible is useful only if a company understands its customers and sales market. Salespeople working for companies that have FMSs will soon be able to ask customers what they want rather than telling them what the company has available. FMSs are not inexpensive, but the investment can pay for itself through increased sales at higher prices as well as lower costs.

Another area of growing importance to firms is the influence of their operations on the environment. The effect of operations on the environment can have substantial impacts on future costs. These effects can be partly controlled by capital budgeting decisions.

INVESTING TO MANAGE ENVIRONMENTAL COSTS

The impact of organizations on the environment is becoming an increasing concern to governments, citizens, investors, and businesses. Accountants are increasingly concerned with both measuring business performance with regard to environmental issues and management of environmental costs. In the future, investors are likely to

LEARNING OBJECTIVE 8
Why are environmental issues becoming an increasingly important influence on the capital budget?

Chapter 9 Introduction to a Standard Cost System

LEARNING OBJECTIVES

After reading this chapter, you should be able to answer the following questions:

1 WHY
are standard cost systems used?

2 HOW
are standards for material and labor set?

3 HOW
are material, labor, and overhead variances calculated?

4 HOW
can variances be used for control and performance evaluation purposes?

5 HOW
do organizational evolution and desired level of attainability affect standard setting?

6 HOW
are standard setting and standard usage changing in modern business?

7 WHAT
journal entries are needed in a standard cost system? (Appendix)

American Apparel

"Made in the U.S.A." is a phrase that is no longer often associated with clothing. But American Apparel, founded in early 1977, is an exception to the rule. This company, located in rural mid-Mississippi, makes garments for some of the great active-wear companies in the business: Nike, Adidas, Reebok, and Puma. Why do these brand name giants use the services of a small, privately held company to produce their knit golf shirts? Although off-shore production facilities may be able to make golf shirts at a slightly lower cost, American Apparel differentiates its products by focusing on providing high levels of product and service quality to its customers. In addition, this quality focus provides the underlying rationale for the company's emphasis on employee training and concern for the local economy.

Shirt manufacturing at American Apparel is a standardized process; each shirt of the same size for the same company's order needs to be identical. Because of the substantial level of competition, price is set by the competition and American Apparel must exercise extreme cost control efforts. Thus, material and labor specifications must be available and adhered to for each product so that the company can meet customer expectations and remain profitable. Standard costing allows company management to understand the quantities and costs that will be incurred in shirt production and, more importantly, what impacts deviations from these standards will have on costs and profits.

SOURCE: Interview with Bill Corhern, President & CEO, American Apparel, 1998.

*T*hree of *American Apparel's* goals are to produce and sell quality products, to deliver outstanding customer service, and to provide financial and personal recognition of employees. To help attain these goals, the company establishes production standards that allow management to determine causes of variations, take corrective action, and monitor and reward performance. Performance can be evaluated by comparing actual results against a predetermined measure or criterion. Thus, standards (or benchmarks) must exist to ensure product quality and consistency. Without such standards, employees cannot know what is expected. Without the actual-to-standard comparison, employees and management cannot know if expectations were met or whether problems exist. Such lack of knowledge makes managerial control impossible.

Almost all organizations develop and use some type of standards. For example, charities set a standard for the amount of annual contributions to be raised, sales managers set standards against which employee business expenses are compared, and hotels have standard times for cleaning a guest room. Because different production methods and information objectives exist in organizations, no single standard cost system is appropriate for all situations. Thus, many forms of standard cost systems are in use. Some systems use standard prices, but not standard quantities; other systems (especially in service entities) use labor, but not material, standards. Traditional standard cost systems require price and quantity standards for both material and labor.

This chapter discusses a traditional standard cost system using standards for the three product cost components: direct material (DM), direct labor (DL), and factory overhead (OH). Chapter examples assume the use of only one material and one labor category in production activities. The chapter provides information on why standard cost systems are used, how material and labor standards are developed, how deviations (or variances) from standard are calculated, and what information can be gained from detailed variance analysis. Innovative trends in the use of standard costing systems are also discussed. Journal entries used in a standard cost system are presented in the chapter appendix.

STANDARD COST SYSTEMS

LEARNING OBJECTIVE ❶
Why are standard cost systems used?

http:// www.americanapparel.com

Standards can be used with either job order or process costing systems to provide important information for managerial planning, controlling, and decision making. In planning, standards are used to coordinate activities more quickly and easily than otherwise would be possible. For example, if American Apparel plans to produce

20,000 shirts for Adidas in June, plant management can project material, labor, and overhead costs by reviewing the standard costs established for each of these cost elements.

Standards can also be used for motivation and control. One requirement for control is that managers be aware of differences between the actual activities and resource consumption and the expected activities and resource consumption. A standard cost system helps companies recognize **variances**—or deviations between actual and standard costs or quantities—and correct problems resulting from excess costs or usage. Actual cost systems do not provide these benefits, and normal cost systems cannot provide them for material and labor.

If the variances are significant, managers can exert influence to correct that which is causing the difference. Suppose American Apparel's actual cost for cotton cloth for the 20,000 shirts was $1,000 less than expected. Management would investigate this difference to determine its cause. Several possibilities exist: the price paid per bolt of cloth was less than expected, or new technology or employee cross-training and team efforts made production more efficient by generating less scrap and, thus, lowering cost.

Note that the explanations of the $1,000 difference suggest that there are two possible underlying causes of the variance. One relates to material cost and the other relates to quantity of material used. These causes can exist separately or together. To properly evaluate performance, managers need to be able to determine which part of the total variance relates to which cause.

The availability of standards speeds up and improves decision making because managers have a predetermined, rigorous set of expectations upon which to base decisions, such as accepting a job at a specified price. Performance evaluation is also improved through comparing actual and standard costs of operations and highlighting significant differences.

DEVELOPMENT OF A STANDARD COST SYSTEM

Although initiated by manufacturing companies, standard cost systems are also applicable to service entities. Regardless of the type of organization in which they are being used, it is critical that the standards development process is handled in a knowledgeable and thorough manner.

The estimated cost to manufacture a *single unit* of product or to perform a *single service* is the **standard cost**. Standards are traditionally established for each component (material, labor, and overhead) of product cost. Developing a standard cost involves judgment and practicality in identifying the types of material and labor to be used and their related quantities and prices. Developing standards for overhead requires that costs have been appropriately classified according to cost behavior, valid allocation bases have been chosen, and a reasonable level of activity has been specified.

A primary objective in manufacturing a product or performing a service is to minimize unit cost while achieving certain quality specifications. Almost all products can be manufactured with a variety of inputs (material, labor, and overhead) that would generate the same basic output. This is true even after output quality has been specified. Input choices ultimately affect the standards that are set.

Once management has established the design and manufacturing process that will produce the desired output quality and has determined which input resources will be used, quantity and price standards can be developed. Standards should be developed by representatives from the following areas: management accounting, product design, industrial engineering, personnel, data processing, purchasing, and production management. It is especially important in the process of standard setting to involve managers and, to some extent, employees whose performance will be

http:// www.adidas.com

variance

standard cost

compared with the standards. Involvement helps assure credibility of the standards and helps motivate personnel to operate as closely as possible to the standards. Information from suppliers can also be useful, especially in the area of setting material price standards.

MATERIAL STANDARDS

LEARNING OBJECTIVE ❷
How are standards for material and labor set?

In developing material standards, the specific direct material components used to manufacture the product or to perform the service must be identified and listed. Three things must be known about the materials: what inputs are needed, what the quality of those inputs must be, and what quantities of inputs of the specified quality are needed.

Determination of what inputs are needed is a design specification. For example, to make a golf shirt, American Apparel must have cloth, findings (thread, buttons, and labels), collars and cuffs, and packaging. Many cost-benefit trade-offs are involved in making quality decisions, so managers should consult material experts, engineers, accountants, and marketing personnel to determine which choices are most appropriate. Generally, as the grade of raw material rises, so does the cost. Decisions about material input components usually attempt to balance the interrelationships of cost, quality, quantity, and selling price.

Given the quality selected for each necessary component, physical quantity estimates can be made in terms of weight, size, volume, or other measures. These estimates can be based on results of engineering tests, opinions of people using the materials, and/or historical data. Information about direct material components, their specifications (including quality), and their quantities are listed on a **bill of materials**. Even companies that do not have formal standard cost systems are likely to develop bills of materials for each of their products simply as a guide for production activity.

Exhibit 9-1 illustrates a bill of materials for a six-button summer crop-top woman's shirt produced by an illustrative company named Kosciusko Clothing (KC). Company management has chosen to view the thread used in production as an indirect material and part of variable overhead. Thus, thread is not shown on the bill of materials.

After the standard quantities of material components have been developed, prices are determined for each component. The purchasing agent is most likely to have the expertise to estimate standard prices. Prices should reflect factors such as desired quality, reliability and physical proximity of the supplier, and quantity and purchase discounts allowed. If purchasing agents are involved in setting reasonable price standards for materials, these individuals are more likely to be able to explain causes of any future variations from the standards.

When all quantity and price information has been gathered, component quantities are multiplied by unit prices to yield the total cost of each component. These totals are summed to determine the total standard material cost of one unit of product. The total standard material cost, along with other total costs, for one summer shirt produced by Kosciusko Clothing is shown later, in Exhibit 9-3.

bill of materials

EXHIBIT 9-1
Bill of Materials

Product: One size fits all, short, button-front shirt		Revision Date: 3/1/00	
Product Number: Stock Keeping Unit (SKU) #312		Standard Job Size: 400	
COMPONENT ID#	QUANTITY REQUIRED	DESCRIPTION OF COMPONENT	COMMENTS
F-4	1.2 square yards	White cotton fabric	Highest quality
B-3	6 buttons	Plastic buttons	Multi-color; imprinted with KC logo
L-1	1 label	Label	Imprinted with KC logo

As with other direct materials, certain specifications need to be made about zippers when they are used in clothing. The bill of materials should indicate zipper color, type (metal or plastic), and length.

LABOR STANDARDS

The procedures for developing labor standards are similar to those used for material standards. Each worker operation, such as bending, reaching, lifting, moving materials, cutting and sewing fabric, attaching sundry items (such as zippers, snaps, and patches), and packaging, should be identified. When operations and movements are specified, activities such as setup must be considered because they are performed during the production process. All unnecessary movements by workers and of materials as well as any rework activities should be disregarded when time standards are set and should be minimized or eliminated as non-value-added activities.

Each production operation must be converted to quantitative information to be a usable standard. Time and motion studies, discussed in the following News Note (page 398), may be performed by the company.[1] Alternatively, times developed from industrial engineering studies or from historical data may be used.[2] Historical data, however, may incorporate past inefficiencies or may not consider recently added technologically advanced machinery or recently received worker training. For example, after American Apparel instituted a modular production system and cross-trained employees, labor time for all efforts was reduced.

After labor tasks have been analyzed, an **operations flow document** can be prepared that lists all necessary activities and the time allowed for each. All activities should be analyzed as to their ability to add value to the product or service. Any non-value-added activities that are included in the operations flow document should be targeted for reduction or elimination. Exhibit 9-2 (page 398) presents a simplified operations flow document that reflects the manufacturing process for a short, six-button shirt at Kosciusko Clothing. This document shows 5.5 minutes of move time that is non-value-added.

Labor rate standards should reflect the wages and fringe benefits paid to employees who perform the various production tasks. All personnel doing the same job in a given department may be paid the same wage rate. Alternatively, if employees within a department performing the same or similar tasks are paid different wage rates, a

LEARNING OBJECTIVE ➋
How are standards for material and labor set?

operations flow document

---

[1]In performing internal time and motion studies, observers need to be aware that employees may engage in slowdown tactics when they are being clocked. The purpose of such tactics is to have a relatively long time set as the standard, so that the employees will appear more efficient when actual results are measured.

[2]An employee time sheet indicates what jobs were worked on and for what period of time. Time sheets can also be prepared for machines by use of machine clocks or counters. Bar coding is another way to track work flow through an organization.

[(27 ÷ 60) × $7]. The fixed overhead rate for these two departments is $6 per machine hour. According to the operations flow document in Exhibit 9-2, the departments have a total of 18 (6 + 4 + 5.5 + 2 +.5) minutes of machine time. Thus, a total of $1.80 [(18 ÷ 60) × $6] of fixed factory overhead will be applied to each shirt in these two departments. The costs associated with the 5.5 minutes of move time are considered part of factory overhead and the overhead costs caused by move time are included in the predetermined factory overhead rates.

After the bill of materials, operations flow document, and standard overhead costs have been developed, a **standard cost card** is prepared. This document (shown in Exhibit 9-3) summarizes all the standard quantities and costs needed to complete one SKU #312 shirt.

Standard costs and quantities are used during the period to assign costs to inventory accounts. In an actual or normal cost system, actual material and labor costs are charged to Work in Process Inventory as production occurs. In most standard cost systems, standard rather than actual costs of production are charged to Work in Process Inventory.[3] Any difference between actual and standard costs is a variance.

standard cost card

EXHIBIT 9-3
Standard Cost Card

Product: One size fits all, short, button-front shirt   **SKU Number: 312**

DIRECT MATERIAL

			Departments		
ID#	Unit Cost	Total Quantity	Cutting Cost	Sewing Cost	Total Cost
F-4	$3.50 per square yard	1.2 sq. yds.	$4.20		$4.20
B-3	$ .15 each	6 per shirt		$.90	.90
L-1	$ .08 each	1 per shirt		.08	.08
DIRECT MATERIAL TOTALS			$4.20	$.98	$5.18

DIRECT LABOR

			Cutting	Sewing	Total
ID#	Average Wage per Minute*	Total Minutes	Cost	Cost	Cost
27	$.16	8.5	$1.36		$1.36
29	.16	6.5	1.04		1.04
33	.20	7.0		$1.40	1.40
35	.24	3.5		.84	.84
37	.14	1.5		.21	.21
DIRECT LABOR TOTALS		27.0	$2.40	$2.45	$4.85

PRODUCTION OVERHEAD

Type of Overhead	Cost Driver	Standard Time Allowed	Standard Departmental Rate	Total Cost
Variable	Direct Labor Time	27 minutes	$7.00 per DLH	$3.15
Fixed	Machine Time	18 minutes	$6.00 per MH	1.80
OVERHEAD TOTAL				$4.95

Total cost = $5.18 + $4.85 + $4.95 = $14.98

*Note: Labor cost per minute equals hourly rates divided by 60.

---

[3]The standard cost of each cost element (direct material, direct labor, variable overhead, and fixed overhead) is said to be applied to the goods produced. This terminology is the same as that used when overhead is applied to inventory based on a predetermined rate.

Because they are common input measures, direct labor hours and machine hours are used and referred to in the models that follow. Alternative cost drivers such as setup time, pounds of material moved, or number of defective units produced may be more appropriately related to cost incurrence. Using these measures does not change the manner in which the calculations are made.

VARIANCE COMPUTATIONS

The most basic variance computation is the total difference between actual cost incurred and standard cost allowed for the period's output. This variance can be diagrammed as follows:

LEARNING OBJECTIVE ❸
How are material, labor, and overhead variances calculated?

Actual Cost of Actual   Standard Cost of Actual
Production Inputs   Production Outputs

Total Variance

A total variance can be computed for each production cost element; however, total variances do not provide useful information for determining why cost differences occurred. To help managers in their control function, total variances for materials and labor are subdivided into price and quantity elements.

A **price variance** reflects the difference between what was paid and what should have been paid for inputs during the period. A **quantity variance** provides a monetary measure of the difference between the quantity of actual inputs and the standard quantity of inputs allowed for the actual output of the period. Quantity variances focus on the efficiency of results—the relationship of inputs to outputs. Quantity can be measured as pounds of material, hours of direct labor time, number of setups, or any other specified and reasonable indicator of output.

price variance
quantity variance

The diagram used to calculate a total variance can be expanded to provide a general model indicating the subvariances:

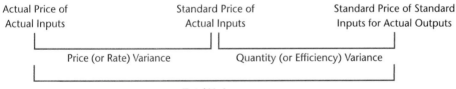

Actual Price of   Standard Price of   Standard Price of Standard
Actual Inputs   Actual Inputs   Inputs for Actual Outputs

Price (or Rate) Variance   Quantity (or Efficiency) Variance

Total Variance

The middle column is a budget column and indicates what costs should have been incurred for actual inputs. The far-right column uses a measure of output known as the **standard quantity allowed**. This quantity measure translates actual output into the standard quantity of input that *should have been used* to achieve the actual level of output. The right-hand measurement is computed as the standard quantity allowed multiplied by the standard price of the input resources.

standard quantity allowed

The diagram can be simplified using the abbreviated notations shown in Exhibit 9-4 (page 402). This model progresses from the *actual* price of *actual* input on the left to the *standard* price of *standard* input allowed on the right. The middle measure of input is a hybrid of *actual* quantity and *standard* price. The price variance portion of the total variance is measured as the actual input quantity multiplied by the difference between the actual and standard prices:

$$\text{Price Variance} = AQ\,(AP - SP)$$

EXHIBIT 9-4
Simplified Variance Model

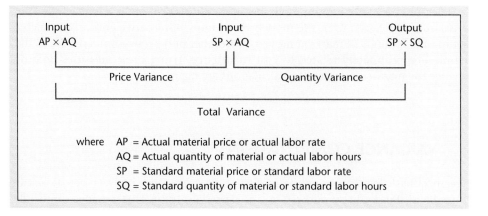

The quantity variance is determined as the standard price multiplied by the difference between the actual quantity used and the standard quantity allowed for the actual output:

$$\text{Quantity Variance} = \text{SP} (\text{AQ} - \text{SQ})$$

Production of Shirt #312 in the Cutting Department of Kosciusko Clothing is used to illustrate variance computations. The standard costs in this department are taken from the standard cost card in Exhibit 9-3 and are repeated at the top of Exhibit 9-5. Also shown in the exhibit are the actual quantity and cost data for the week of June 12–16, 2000. This information is used in computing the material, labor, and overhead variances for the week. Variance computations must indicate whether the variance is favorable (F) or unfavorable (U).

Material Variances

Using the model and inserting information concerning material quantities and prices provides the following computations. (Note that the standard quantity for cloth is taken from the bottom of Exhibit 9-5.)

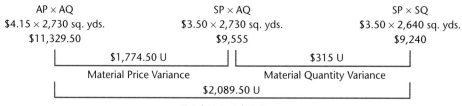

The subvariances for materials are known as the material price and material quantity variances. The **material price variance (MPV)** indicates the amount of money spent below (F for favorable) or above (U for unfavorable) the standard price for the quantity of materials purchased. For Kosciusko Clothing, the actual price paid for cotton fabric was $4.15 per square yard, while the standard price was $3.50, giving an unfavorable material price variance of $1,774.50. This variance can also be calculated as [2,730 ($4.15 − $3.50) = 2,730 ($.65) = $1,774.50]. The sign of the unfavorable variance is positive because the actual price is *more than* the standard price.

material price variance (MPV)

The **material quantity variance (MQV)** indicates the cost saved (F) or expended (U) because of the difference between the actual quantity of material used and the standard quantity of material allowed for the goods produced or services rendered during the period. If the actual quantity used is less than the standard quantity allowed, the company has been more efficient than expected; if a greater quantity has been used than allowed, the company has been less efficient. Kosciusko Clothing

material quantity variance (MQV)

EXHIBIT 9-5

Standard/Actual Cost Data
for Week of June 12–16, 2000
(Cutting Department)

Standards for 1 shirt SKU #312:

1.2 square yards of white cotton fabric at $3.50 per square yard	$4.20
15 minutes of labor at $9.60 per hour ($.16 per minute)	2.40
Applied variable factory overhead (based on 15 minutes of direct labor time at $7 per DLH)	1.75
Applied fixed factory overhead (based on 10 minutes of machine time at $6 per MH)*	1.00
Total standard Cutting Department cost per shirt	$9.35

Actual data for June 12–16, 2000:

Number of shirts produced	2,200
Square yards of cotton fabric used	2,730
Price per square yard of cotton fabric used	$4.15
Direct labor hours incurred	500
Average direct labor wage per hour	$10
Total variable factory overhead cost	$3,360
Machine hours used	350
Total fixed factory overhead	$2,875

Standard Quantities Allowed

DIRECT MATERIAL: Standard quantity allowed for cloth = 2,200 shirts × 1.2 square yards per shirt = 2,640 square yards

DIRECT LABOR: Standard quantity allowed for direct labor hours = 2,200 shirts × 15 minutes per shirt = 33,000 minutes or 550 hours

VARIABLE FACTORY OVERHEAD: Applied on the basis of direct labor hours = 2,200 shirts × 15 minutes per shirt = 33,000 minutes or 550 hours

FIXED FACTORY OVERHEAD: Standard quantity allowed for machine hours = 2,200 shirts × 10 minutes per shirt = 22,000 minutes or 366 2/3 hours

*The $6 rate per machine hour is based on total expected fixed overhead of $124,800 for the year and an expected 20,800 machine hours related to the production of these shirts. This product is expected to be produced evenly at the rate of 2,496 shirts per week for 50 weeks of the year or 124,800 shirts for the year.

used 90 more square yards of cotton fabric than the standard allowed for the production of 2,200 shirts. This inefficient usage resulted in an unfavorable material quantity variance [$3.50 (2,730 − 2,640) = $3.50 (90) = $315].

The total material variance of $2,089.50 U can be calculated by taking the difference between $11,329.50 (the total actual cost of inputs) and $9,240 (the total standard cost of the outputs). The total variance also represents the summation of the individual material price and quantity subvariances: ($1,774.50 U + $315 U = $2,089.50 U).

Point of Purchase Material Variance Model

A total variance for a cost component *generally* equals the sum of the price and quantity subvariances. An exception to this rule occurs when the quantity of material purchased is not the same as the quantity of material placed into production. In such cases, the general model is altered slightly to provide information more rapidly for management control purposes.

Because the material price variance relates to the purchasing (not production) function, the altered model calculates the material price variance at the point of purchase and bases that calculation on the quantity of materials *purchased* rather than the quantity of materials *used*. This variation in the model allows the material price variance to be isolated or pinpointed as close to the variance source and as quickly as possible. The material quantity variance is still computed on the basis of the actual quantity of materials used in production.

Assume that Kosciusko Clothing had purchased 3,000 square yards of cotton fabric for production of SKU #312 shirts but had only used 2,730 during the week of June 12–16, 2000. The point of purchase material price variance is calculated as follows:

This change in the general model is shown below, with subscripts to indicate actual quantity purchased (p) and used (u).

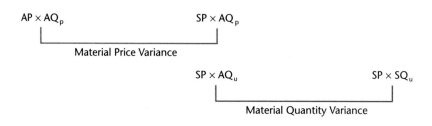

The material quantity variance is still calculated as presented earlier because the actual quantity of cotton fabric used in production is not determined by the amount purchased. Thus, the MQV would remain at $315 U. A point of purchase variance computation results in the material price and quantity variances being computed from different bases. For this reason, these variances should not be summed; thus, no total material variance can be determined.

Labor Variances

The price and usage elements of the total labor variance are called the labor rate and labor efficiency variances. The model for computing these variances and computations for Kosciusko Clothing follow. The standard quantity is taken from the bottom of Exhibit 9-5 for direct labor hours.

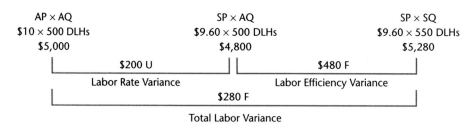

labor rate variance (LRV)

The **labor rate variance (LRV)** shows the difference between the actual rate or actual weighted average rate paid to the direct labor workers for the period and the standard rate for all hours actually worked during the period. The labor rate variance can also be computed as [500 × ($10 − $9.60) = 500 ($.40) = $200 U].

labor efficiency variance (LEV)

The **labor efficiency variance (LEV)** compares the number of actual direct labor hours worked with the standard hours allowed for the actual number of shirts produced. The difference is multiplied by the standard labor rate to establish a dollar value for the efficiency (F) or inefficiency (U) of the direct labor workers. The labor efficiency variance can also be calculated as [$9.60 × (500 − 550) = $9.60 (−50) = −$480 F]. The sign of the favorable variance is negative because the actual number of hours worked is *less than* the standard hours allowed to make the actual number of shirts.

The total labor variance ($280 F) can be determined by subtracting the total standard labor cost for the actual production ($5,280) from the total actual labor cost ($5,000). Alternatively, the total labor variance can be found by adding the labor rate and efficiency variances [$200 U + (−$480 F)].

The accompanying News Note provides a slightly different perspective on efficiency variances. It suggests that the efficiency variance is truly composed of two elements—quality problems and efficiency problems—that should be accounted for separately.

As the News Note points out, a company may achieve reductions in labor time and, thus, have favorable efficiency variances by producing defective or poor-quality units. For example, assume that workers who are earning $15 per hour can produce one unit of product in two hours. During a period, 1,500 units are made in 2,610 hours. The standard quantity of time allowed for production is 3,000 hours. The labor efficiency variance is $15 (2,610 − 3,000), or $5,850 F. However, 80 of the 1,500 units were defective and nonsalable. The favorable efficiency variance of $5,850 fails to include the impact of those nonquality units. A quality variance can be computed as follows: 80 defective units × 2 hours per unit × $15 per hour or $2,400 U. Subtracting this unfavorable quality variance from the $5,850 favorable efficiency variance provides a net true efficiency variance for the production of 1,420 good units, or $3,450 F. This restated efficiency variance can be shown as follows:

1,420 good units × 2 hours per unit = 2,840 standard hours allowed (SHA)
2,840 SHA − 2,610 actual hours = 230 hours less than standard (F)
230 hours × $15 standard cost per hour = $3,450 F efficiency variance

Factory Overhead Variances

The use of separate variable and fixed factory overhead application rates and accounts allows the computation of separate variances for each type of overhead. These separate computations provide managers with the greatest detail as well as the greatest flexibility for control and performance evaluation purposes. Also, because of increased use of nonsimilar bases for various overhead allocations, each different cost pool for variable and fixed factory overhead may require separate price and usage

NEWS NOTE

Separating Quality Problems from Efficiency Problems

Historically, efficiency variances have been computed by multiplying excess inputs by the standard price. In recent years, this approach has been criticized for motivating managers to ignore quality concerns to avoid unfavorable efficiency variances. In other words, there is an incentive to produce a low-quality product by minimizing the amount of material used or the time spent in production.

An approach could be taken that separates the efficiency variance from the quality variance. Inputs consisting of conversion time or material used in defective units would be captured in the quality variance.

Separating the two variances allows production decision makers to evaluate the trade-offs between efficiency and quality. They can minimize production time to gain a favorable efficiency variance but this probably will increase the number of defective units and result in an unfavorable quality variance. Likewise, trying to minimize the number of defective units may result in investing more time and more material and therefore having an unfavorable efficiency variance.

SOURCE: Carole Cheatham, "Updating Standard Cost Systems," *Journal of Accountancy* (December 1990), pp. 59–60. Reprinted with permission from the *Journal of Accountancy*, Copyright 1990 by American Institute of CPAs. Opinions of the authors are their own and do not necessarily reflect policies of the AICPA.

computations. In the Cutting Department of Kosciusko Clothing, variable and fixed factory overhead calculations are based, respectively, on direct labor hours and machine hours.

As with material and labor, total variable and total fixed factory overhead variances can be divided into specific price and quantity subvariances for each type of overhead. The overhead subvariances are referred to as follows:

Variable overhead price element ———▶ Variable overhead spending variance
Variable overhead quantity element ———▶ Variable overhead efficiency variance
Fixed overhead price element ———▶ Fixed overhead spending variance
Fixed overhead quantity element ———▶ Volume variance

Variable Overhead

The total variable overhead (VOH) variance is the difference between actual variable factory overhead costs incurred for the period and standard variable factory overhead cost applied to the period's actual production or service output. The difference at year-end is the total variable factory overhead variance, which is also the amount of underapplied or overapplied variable factory overhead. The following diagram illustrates the computation of the total variable overhead variance.

Actual Variable   Variable Overhead Cost
Overhead Cost   Applied to Production

Total Variable Overhead (VOH) Variance
(Underapplied or Overapplied Variable Overhead)

The following variable factory overhead variance computations use the June 12–16, 2000, data for the Cutting Department of Kosciusko Clothing. The actual variable factory overhead cost for the week was $3,360 for 500 hours of work or $6.72 per direct labor hour. Five hundred fifty standard direct labor hours were allowed for that week's production and each direct labor hour was expected to cost the company $7 in variable factory overhead. The variable overhead variances for the Cutting Department are computed as follows:

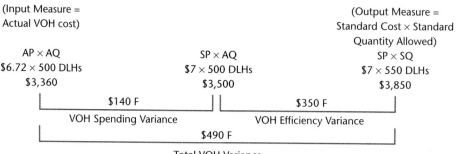

(Input Measure = Actual VOH cost)		(Output Measure = Standard Cost × Standard Quantity Allowed)
AP × AQ	SP × AQ	SP × SQ
$6.72 × 500 DLHs	$7 × 500 DLHs	$7 × 550 DLHs
$3,360	$3,500	$3,850

$140 F $350 F
VOH Spending Variance   VOH Efficiency Variance
$490 F
Total VOH Variance

variable overhead spending variance

variable overhead efficiency variance

The **variable overhead spending** (or budget) **variance** is the difference between actual variable factory overhead and budgeted variable factory overhead based on actual input. The **variable overhead efficiency variance** is the difference between budgeted variable factory overhead at the actual input activity and budgeted variable factory overhead at standard input (such as DLHs) allowed. This variance quantifies the effect of using more or less actual input than the standard allowed. When actual input exceeds standard input allowed, operations appear inefficient. Excess input also means that more variable overhead is needed to support the additional input.

Fixed Overhead

The total fixed overhead (FOH) variance is the difference between actual FOH cost incurred and standard FOH cost applied to the period's actual production. This difference is also the amount of underappplied or overapplied fixed overhead for the period. The following model shows the computation of the total fixed overhead variance.

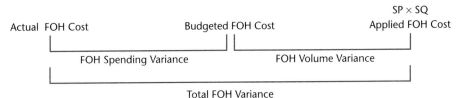

Actual Fixed
Overhead Cost

Fixed Overhead Cost
Applied to Production

Total Fixed Overhead (FOH) Variance
(Underapplied or Overapplied Fixed Overhead)

The total fixed overhead variance is subdivided into its price and quantity elements by the insertion of *budgeted* fixed overhead as a middle column into the model.

Actual FOH Cost

Budgeted FOH Cost

SP × SQ
Applied FOH Cost

FOH Spending Variance

FOH Volume Variance

Total FOH Variance
(Underapplied or Overapplied FOH)

In the model, the left column is simply labeled "actual FOH cost" and is not computed as a price times quantity measure because fixed overhead is generally acquired in lump-sum amounts rather than on a per-unit input basis. The **fixed overhead spending** (or budget) **variance** is the difference between actual and budgeted fixed overhead. The fixed overhead **volume variance** is the difference between budgeted and applied fixed overhead. Budgeted fixed overhead is a constant amount throughout the relevant range; thus, *the middle column is a constant figure regardless of the actual quantity of input or the standard quantity of input allowed.* This concept is a key element in computing FOH variances. The budgeted amount of fixed overhead is equal to the standard FOH rate times the estimated capacity measure used to compute the standard rate.

fixed overhead spending variance

volume variance

The Cutting Department of Kosciusko Clothing had estimated that 2,496 shirts would be produced each week, amounting to a total of 416 hours of machine time (2,496 × 10 minutes = 24,960 minutes; 24,960 minutes ÷ 60 minutes = 416 hours). Since each hour of machine time was expected to cost $6, the weekly fixed factory overhead budget for the department is $2,496 (416 × $6).

Applied fixed overhead equals the FOH application rate times the standard input allowed for the production achieved. In regard to fixed factory overhead, the standard input allowed for the production achieved measures capacity utilization for the period. The standard input for Kosciusko Clothing's Cutting Department is 10 minutes of machine time per shirt; thus, since 2,200 shirts were produced, the standard machine time allowed is 366⅔ hours, as shown at the bottom of Exhibit 9-5.

Inserting the data for the Cutting Department into the model gives the following:

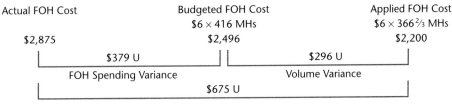

Actual FOH Cost

$2,875

Budgeted FOH Cost
$6 × 416 MHs
$2,496

Applied FOH Cost
$6 × 366⅔ MHs
$2,200

$379 U
FOH Spending Variance

$296 U
Volume Variance

$675 U

Total FOH Variance

The week's actual fixed overhead cost is $2,875, while the budgeted amount is $2,496. The $379 unfavorable difference is the FOH spending variance, which could be related to a variety of causes such as increased rent payments or insurance premiums for machinery and equipment.

The FOH application rate is $6 per machine hour. This rate exists because the company expected a total of $124,800 in fixed overhead costs for the year and chose an expected annual capacity level of 20,800 machine hours. Each shirt requires ten minutes of machine time, so the company can make six shirts in an hour. Therefore, expected capacity of shirts for the year is 124,800 shirts (20,800 hours × 6 shirts per hour) over a fifty-week work-year. Had any capacity level other than 20,800 machine hours been chosen, the fixed overhead rate would have been different, even though the total amount of budgeted fixed overhead ($124,800) would have been the same. *If any level of capacity is experienced other than that which was used in determining the application rate, a volume variance will occur.* For example, if Kosciusko Clothing had chosen 110,000 shirts (or 2,200 shirts per week) as the denominator level of activity for setting the predetermined FOH rate, there would be no volume variance for the week of June 12–16, 2000. If any number of shirts less than 2,200 had been chosen as the denominator level of activity, the volume variance would have been favorable.

The difference between the $2,496 budgeted FOH and the $2,200 applied FOH gives the $296 unfavorable volume variance for the week. This variance is also equal to the difference of 296 shirts (2,496 − 2,200) that the company expected to make but did not produce multiplied by the $1 standard fixed overhead rate per shirt. The variance is unfavorable because fewer shirts were produced this week than budgeted. The $675 unfavorable total fixed factory overhead variance is the underapplied balance in the fixed factory overhead account for the week.

COST CONTROL AND VARIANCE RESPONSIBILITY

LEARNING OBJECTIVE ④
How can variances be used for control and performance evaluation purposes?

variance analysis

Cost control focuses on the variances between actual costs incurred for a period and the standard costs that should have been incurred based on actual output. To exercise any type of effective control, managers first must be provided with detailed information on the various cost components. Second, a well-designed system of cost control and variance analysis should capture variances as early as possible.

Variance analysis is the process of categorizing the nature—favorable or unfavorable—of the differences between standard and actual costs and seeking the reasons for those differences. The cost control and variance analysis system should help managers determine who or what is responsible for the variance and who is best able to explain it. When variances reflect poor performance, an early measurement system may allow operational performance to be improved. The longer the reporting of a variance is delayed, the more difficult it becomes to determine its cause.

Material price and labor rate variances are not as controllable at the production or service level as are material quantity and labor efficiency variances. Price and rate standards are more dependent on outside forces, such as market competition and wage contracts, than are usage standards.

Material Variances

Material price variances are normally determined at the point of purchase. Although not always able to *control* prices, purchasing agents, if given adequate lead time and resources, should be able to *influence* prices. This influence is exerted through knowing what suppliers are available and choosing suppliers that provide the appropriate material in the most reasonable time span at the most reasonable cost. The purchasing agent can also influence material prices by purchasing in quantities that provide price discounts or by engaging in contractual arrangements such as long-term purchase contracts, as American Apparel does with some of its preferred suppliers.

The purchasing agent is usually the person who is best able to explain why a material price variance occurs. Also, as part of the team that originally set the material price standard, the purchasing agent is usually the individual responsible for material price variances.

Material quantity variances can be determined when materials are issued or used. Such variances are considered the responsibility of the person in charge of the job or department. Materials are ordinarily requisitioned based on the number of actual units to be produced times the standard quantity per unit. When additional materials are taken out of inventory, material requisition slips of a different color may be filled out. These color-coded excess requisition slips allow control to occur as work is under way rather than at the end of the period or when production is completed. Monitoring requisition slips for significant excess material withdrawals alerts managers to seek causes for the excesses and, if possible, take timely corrective action.

Some production settings, such as chemical and petroleum processing, involve a continuous flow of material. In these cases, it may not be practical or reasonable to isolate quantity variances when materials are placed into production. The material quantity variance is more feasibly measured when production is complete and the total quantity of production is known. Measuring usage for relatively short time periods and reporting quantity variances after production is complete can still assist management in controlling operations. Labor efficiency variances are also more appropriately measured at the end of production in these types of manufacturing operations.

There are exceptions to the normal assignment of responsibility for material price and quantity variances. Assume that the manager in the Cutting Department at Kosciusko Clothing asks the purchasing agent to acquire, without adequate lead time, additional quantities of cotton fabric. She makes this request because the marketing manager has just told her that the demand for style 312 shirts has unexpectedly increased. Making a spur-of-the-moment acquisition of this kind could result in paying a price higher than standard. Price variances resulting from these types of causes should be assigned to production or marketing/merchandising—for inadequate predictions—not to purchasing.

In contrast, assume the purchasing agent acquires inferior-quality cotton fabric that results in excess consumption and an unfavorable quantity variance. This quantity variance should be assigned to purchasing rather than to production. Such situations are likely to be identified from continuous, rather than end-of-period, reporting.

Labor Variances

Labor rate and labor efficiency variances are commonly identified as part of the payroll process and assigned to the person in charge of the production or service area. This assignment assumes that that manager has the ability to influence the type of labor personnel used. For instance, the Cutting Department manager could use skilled or unskilled workers to align, mark, and cut material. Using highly skilled, highly paid individuals for lower-level jobs could cause an unfavorable labor rate variance, accompanied by a favorable labor efficiency variance. Thus, as with material variances, correlations may exist between labor variances.

Sometimes a common factor may cause multiple variances. For instance, in manufacturing, the purchase of inferior-quality materials could result in a favorable material price variance, an unfavorable material quantity variance, and an unfavorable labor efficiency variance. The efficiency variance could reflect increased production time, since many units were rejected as substandard because of the inferior materials. In another common situation, the use of lower-paid, less-skilled workers results in a favorable rate variance but causes excessive material usage and decreased labor efficiency.

The probability of detecting relationships among variances is improved, but not assured, by timely variance reporting. The accounting and reporting process should highlight interrelationships of variances, and managers should be aware of the possibility of such relationships when reviewing variance reports.

Proprietors of these outdoor markets pace the possibility of significant material price variances. For instance, droughts can raise prices from the standards generally paid for produce and flowers.

Overhead Variances

The difference between actual and applied overhead is the amount of underapplied or overapplied overhead or the total overhead variance that must be explained. Control purposes differ for variable and fixed overhead because of the types of costs that make up the two categories as well as the ability of managers to influence those costs.

Variable Overhead

Variable overhead costs are incurred on a continual basis as work is performed and are directly related to that work. Because of this direct relationship to activity, control of VOH costs is similar to that for material and labor. Companies control variable overhead by (1) keeping actual costs in line with planned costs for the actual level of activity and (2) getting the planned output yield from the overhead resources placed into production.

Variable overhead spending variances are commonly caused by price differences—paying average actual prices that are higher or lower than the standard prices allowed. Such fluctuations often occur because price changes have not been reflected in the standard rate. For instance, average indirect labor wage rates, supply costs, or utility rates may have increased or decreased since the standard VOH rate was computed. In such instances, the standard rate should be adjusted.

If managers have no control over prices charged by external parties, they should not be held accountable for variances arising because of such price changes. In contrast, if managers could influence prices—for example through long-term purchase arrangements—such options should be investigated as to their long-term costs and benefits before a decision is made to change the standard. Waste or spoilage of resources, such as indirect materials, is another possible cause of the VOH spending variance.

The VOH efficiency variance reflects the managerial control implemented or needed in regard to the yield of output as related to input. VOH represents a variety of resources that, like direct material and direct labor, bear a known and measurable relationship to the activity base used to represent production activity. These resources are managed by monitoring and measuring their actual use in conformity with standard usage, promptly investigating any variances, and adjusting resource usage when necessary. Control of the variable overhead resource elements can only be achieved if the variance from standard for each VOH component is analyzed rather than attempting to analyze and control variable overhead in total. The cost and usage of each component of VOH could react independently of one another.

If variable factory overhead is applied on the basis of direct labor hours, the signs (favorable or unfavorable) of the variable overhead and direct labor efficiency variances will be the same, because the actual and standard hours compared in the two calculations are the same. However, when alternative overhead application bases are used, the signs of these two variances may no longer be related to one another. Use of any alternative base, including those provided under activity-based costing, does not affect the implementation of a standard cost system.

Fixed Overhead

Control of fixed factory overhead is distinctly different from control of variable factory overhead because fixed overhead may not be directly related to current activity. Since many types of fixed factory costs must be committed to in lump-sum amounts before current period activity takes place, managers may have only limited ability to control FOH costs in the short run. Once managers commit to a fixed cost, it becomes unchangeable for some period of time *regardless of whether actual work takes place*. Thus, control of many fixed overhead costs must occur at the *time of commitment* rather than at the *time of production activity*.

The FOH spending variance normally represents a variance in the costs of fixed overhead components, although this variance can also reflect mismanagement of resources. Control over the FOH spending variance often must take place on a transaction-by-transaction basis when managers arrange for facilities. Many fixed overhead costs are basically uncontrollable in the short run. For example, depreciation expense is based on the factory's historical cost, salvage value, and expected life. Utility costs, which are partially fixed, are often set by rate commissions and are influenced by the size and type of the physical plant. Even a "turn-off-the-lights" program can reduce utility costs only by a limited amount. Repairs and maintenance, which are also partially fixed, can be controlled to some extent, but are highly affected by the type of operation involved. Salaries are contractual obligations that were set at the time of employment or salary review.

The information provided by a total FOH spending variance amount would not be specific enough to allow management to decide whether corrective action was possible or desirable. Individual cost variances for each component need to be reviewed. Such a review will help managers determine the actual causes of and responsibility for the several components of the total fixed overhead spending variance.

In addition to controlling spending, utilizing capacity is another important aspect of managerial control. Capacity utilization is reflected in the volume variance because that computation is directly affected by the capacity level chosen to calculate the predetermined or standard fixed overhead application rate. Although utilization is controllable to some degree, the volume variance is the variance over which managers have the least influence and control, especially in the short run. But it is important that managers exercise what ability they do have to influence and control capacity utilization.

An unfavorable volume variance indicates less-than-expected utilization of capacity. If available capacity is currently being used at a level below or above that which was anticipated, managers should recognize that condition, investigate the reasons for it, and initiate appropriate action as needed. The degree of capacity utilization should always be viewed in relation to inventory and sales. If capacity is overutilized (a favorable volume variance) and inventory is stockpiling, managers should decrease capacity utilization. A favorable volume variance could, however, be due to increased sales demand with no stockpiling of inventory—in which case no adjustments should be made to reduce utilization.

If capacity is underutilized (an unfavorable volume variance) and sales are back-ordered or going unfilled, managers should try to increase capacity utilization. However, managers must understand that underutilization of capacity is not always undesirable. In a manufacturing company, it is more appropriate for managers not to produce goods that would simply end up in inventory stockpiles. Unneeded inventory production, although it serves to utilize capacity, generates substantially more costs for material, labor, and overhead, including storage and handling costs. The positive impact that such unneeded production will have on the fixed overhead volume variance is outweighed by the unnecessary costs of accumulating excess inventory.

Managers can sometimes influence capacity utilization by modifying work schedules, taking measures to relieve production constraints, eliminating non-value-added activities, and carefully monitoring the movement of resources through the production or service process. Such actions should be taken during the period rather than after the period has ended. Efforts to be made after work is completed may improve next period's operations but will have no impact on current work.

Expected annual capacity—rather than practical or theoretical capacity—is often selected as the denominator level of activity by which to compute the predetermined fixed factory overhead application rate. Use of this base does, however, ignore an important management concern: that of unused capacity. Having, but not using, capacity creates additional non-value-added organizational costs. The only way these costs can be highlighted is through the selection of practical or theoretical capacity to compute the fixed factory overhead application rate.

Rather than using the traditional fixed overhead computations, companies may want to compute fixed overhead variances in a manner that could provide additional information. This innovative process is described in Exhibit 9-6, using Kosciusko Clothing's production of Shirt #312. In this example, the fixed factory overhead rate is computed on the basis of practical capacity rather than expected annual capacity. This computation allows managers to focus on the cost of unused capacity so that it can be accounted for and, therefore, analyzed and controlled.[4]

EXHIBIT 9-6

Calculating a Capacity Utilization Variance

Total fixed factory overhead costs (from Exhibit 9-5)	$124,800
Total practical annual capacity of factory in MHs	25,000
Total expected annual capacity of factory in MHs (from Exhibit 9-5)	20,800

Predetermined fixed factory overhead rate based on practical capacity =
   $124,800 ÷ 25,000 = ≈$4.99 per MH

Practical capacity		25,000 MHs
Expected annual capacity		20,800 MHs
Unused capacity		4,200 MHs
Multiplied by the cost per MH	× $	4.99
Cost of unused capacity		$20,958

If 20,000 MHs are the standard hours allowed for actual production, the company would have a capacity utilization variance of $3,992 U [(20,800 − 20,000) × $4.99].

If 21,000 MHs are the standard hours allowed for actual production, the company would have a capacity utilization variance of $998 F [(20,800 − 21,000) × $4.99].

---

[4]This discussion is based on the work of Robert S. Kaplan in "Flexible Budgeting in an Activity-Based Costing Framework," *Accounting Horizons* (June 1994), p. 104–109.

CONVERSION COST AS AN ELEMENT IN STANDARD COSTING

Conversion cost consists of both direct labor and manufacturing overhead. The traditional view separates the elements of product cost into three categories: direct material, direct labor, and overhead. This practice is appropriate in labor-intensive production settings; however, in more highly automated factories, direct labor cost generally represents an extremely small part of total product cost. In such circumstances, one worker may oversee a large number of machines and may deal more with troubleshooting machine malfunctions than converting raw materials into finished products. These new conditions mean that workers' wages are more closely associated with indirect labor than direct labor.

Many companies have responded to having large overhead costs and small direct labor costs by adapting their standard cost systems to provide for only two elements of product cost: direct material and conversion. In these situations, conversion costs are likely to be separated into their variable and fixed components. Conversion costs are also likely to be separated into direct and indirect categories based on their ability to be traced to a machine rather than to a product. Overhead may be applied by use of a variety of cost drivers, including machine hours, cost of materials, number of production runs, number of machine setups, and throughput time.

Variance analysis for conversion cost in automated plants normally focuses on the following: (1) spending variances for overhead costs, (2) efficiency variances for machinery and production costs rather than labor costs, and (3) the traditional volume variance for production. In an automated system, managers are likely to be able to better control not only the spending and efficiency variances but also the volume variance. For instance, the idea of planned output is essential in a just-in-time system. Variance analysis under a conversion cost approach is illustrated in Exhibit 9-7. Regardless of the method by which they are computed, variances that are significant

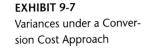

EXHIBIT 9-7

Variances under a Conversion Cost Approach

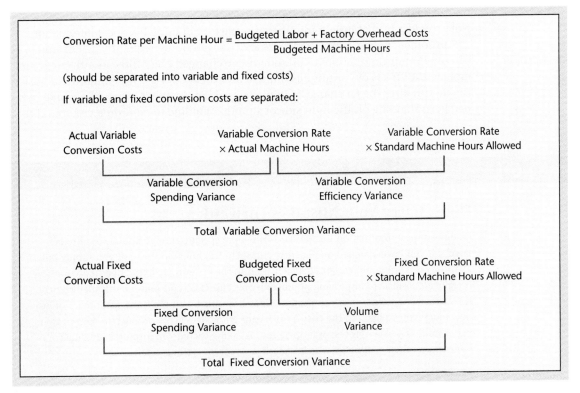

in amount must be analyzed so that they can assist managers in gaining production efficiencies and in controlling costs.

CONSIDERATIONS IN ESTABLISHING STANDARDS

LEARNING OBJECTIVE ⑤
How do organizational evolution and desired level of attainability affect standard setting?

When standards are established, appropriateness and attainability should be considered. Appropriateness, in relation to a standard, refers to the basis on which the standards are developed and how long they are expected to last. Attainability refers to the degree of difficulty or rigor that should be incurred in achieving the standard.

Appropriateness

Although standards are developed from past and current information, they should reflect technical and environmental factors expected for the period in which the standards are to be applied. Factors such as material quality, normal ordering quantities, employee wage rates (including expectations of increases in the minimum wage), degree of plant automation, facility layout, and mix of employee skills should be considered. Management should not think that standards, once set, will remain useful forever. Standards must evolve over an organization's life to reflect its changing methods and processes. Current operating performance cannot be compared against out-of-date standards because to do so would generate variances that would be illogical for planning, controlling, decision making, or evaluating performance.

To illustrate this point, suppose that American Apparel had set labor time standards before initiating the modular, cross-functional teams that caused labor times to decline drastically, in part because of the elimination of many non-value-added labor movements. If these standards were not changed after the factory reorganization, consistently favorable labor efficiency variances would result. Managers should recognize that these efficiency variances would not be relevant to evaluating worker performance, determining inventory valuation, or making product pricing decisions. Rather, the new time reductions would make the standards obsolete and worthless. The following News Note provides further insight into the rationale for not using historical information.

In some Japanese firms, standards are changed quite frequently. For example, at **Citizen Watch Company, Ltd.**, standards are changed every three months to accommodate the effects of continuous improvement (CI) efforts. The standard is adjusted the month after the CI change is implemented. For instance, suppose a worker who had been standing on the right side of a production line to perform a task found that

www.citizenwatch.com

NEWS NOTE

Don't Carry Your Mistakes Forward

Using historical information for standards is seldom specific enough and never provides targets. If you have operated inefficiently and spent too much in the past, you simply build all those costs and problems and deficiencies into the system. That kind of cost accounting is really an obstacle to improving productivity because it accepts and rewards inefficiency. If you are going to improve, you need to know how much you *should* be spending, not just how much you've spent in the past. That means going over every product, looking at every part, examining every process and operation, breaking each down into its individual components and then coming up with standard costs for everything you do.

SOURCE: Jack Stack, *The Great Game of Business* (New York: Currency Doubleday, 1992), p. 101.

he could reduce the time to perform that task by fifteen seconds if he stood on the left side of the line. This change is implemented in March, but the standard would not be adjusted until April. The delay in changing the standard is made so that the worker will have time to get used to the new procedure. By April, company management expects no labor time variance to occur from the new standard.

Citizen measures its success in meeting standards using an "achievement ratio," which is expected to be 100 percent, that is, no variance. If a 1 percent unfavorable variance occurs, a review of the process is triggered. Such a low tolerance for nonconformance is not unusual in Japanese firms and indicates how tightly Japanese production processes are controlled.[5]

Attainability

Standards provide a target level of performance and can be set at various levels of rigor. The level of rigor reflected in the standard affects motivation, and one reason for using standards is to motivate employees. Standards can be classified by their degree of rigor, ranging from easy to difficult. The classifications are similar to the levels of capacity discussed in Chapter 4: expected, practical, and theoretical.

Expected standards are set at a level that reflects what is actually expected to occur in the future period. Such standards anticipate future waste and inefficiencies and allow for them. As such, expected standards are not of significant value for motivation, control, or performance evaluation. Any variances from expected standards should be minimal and managers should take care that expected standards are not set to be too easy to achieve.

Standards that can be reached or slightly exceeded approximately 60 percent to 70 percent of the time with reasonable effort by workers are called **practical standards**. These standards allow for normal, unavoidable time problems or delays such as machine downtime and worker breaks. Practical standards represent an attainable challenge and have traditionally been thought to be the most effective at inducing the best worker performance and at determining how effectively and efficiently workers are performing their tasks. Both favorable and unfavorable variances result from the use of moderately rigorous standards such as these.

Standards that allow for no inefficiencies of *any* type are called **theoretical standards**. Theoretical standards encompass the highest level of rigor and do not allow for normal operating delays or human limitations such as fatigue, boredom, or misunderstanding. Traditionally, theoretical standards were not used because they resulted in discouraged and resentful workers who ultimately ignored the standards. Variances from theoretical standards were always unfavorable and these variances were not considered useful for constructive cost control or performance evaluation. Even in a plant that is entirely automated, there is still the possibility of human or machine failure. This traditional perspective has, however, begun to change, as the section on page 416 explains.

Depending on the type of standard in effect, the acceptable ranges used to apply the management by exception principle differ. **Management by exception** allows managers to set upper and lower limits of tolerance for deviations and investigate only deviations that fall outside those tolerance ranges. This difference is especially notable for deviations on the unfavorable side. If a company uses expected standards, the ranges of acceptable variances should be extremely small, since actual cost should closely conform to the standard. In contrast, a company using theoretical standards would expect variances to fall within very wide ranges of acceptability because of the level of rigor of the standards. The following News Note (page 416) about a study of manufacturing company controllers provides some reasons why managers are using more formalized methods of judging when to investigate variances than those used in the past.

expected standard

practical standard

theoretical standard

management by exception

[5]Robin Cooper, *When Lean Enterprises Collide: Competing through Confrontation* (Boston: Harvard Business School Press, 1995), pp. 247–248.

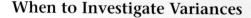

NEWS NOTE

When to Investigate Variances

Variance investigation policies for materials and labor at large companies are moving away from pure judgment and toward the use of structured or formalized exception procedures.

One explanation is that the results are being driven by manufacturing innovations that lead to shorter production runs and shorter product life cycles. In such an environment, monthly variance reports may be so untimely as to be virtually useless. In a flexible manufacturing environment, production runs can be extremely short—only days or perhaps even hours. To provide timely feedback in an environment where the nature of operations and the products being produced change rapidly, more accounts and greater reporting frequency are required.

Another explanation relates to the increasing globalization of markets rather than to the characteristics or individual operating policies of the firm. When competing internationally, companies face more competitors, are less likely to be the lowest-cost producers, and face more uncertainties than in domestic markets. By reducing production cost surprises, intensified management accounting (in the frequency of reports and the details of variance composition) can compensate for these additional uncertainties.

SOURCE: Bruce R. Gaumnitz and Felix P. Kollaritsch, "Manufacturing Variances: Current Practice and Trends," *Journal of Cost Management* (Spring 1991), pp. 63–64. Reprinted with permission from *The Journal of Cost Management*, © 1991, Warren, Gorham & Lamon, 31 St. James Avenue, Boston, Mass. 02116. All rights reserved.

Variances large enough to fall outside the ranges of acceptability generally indicate trouble. The variances themselves, though, do not reveal the cause of the trouble or the person or group responsible. To determine causes of variances, managers must investigate problems through observation, inspection, and inquiry. Such investigations involve the time and effort of people at the operating level as well as accounting personnel. Operations personnel should be alert in spotting variances as they occur and should record the reasons for the variances to the extent that those causes can be determined. For example, operating personnel can readily detect and report causes such as machine downtime or material spoilage.

How well a company determines the causes of variances is often proportional to how much time, effort, and money is spent in gathering information about variances during the period. Managers must be willing and able to accumulate variance information regularly and consistently to evaluate the evidence, isolate the causes, and if possible influence performance to improve the process. If variances are ignored when they occur, it is often impossible or extremely costly to determine the relevant data and to take corrective action at a later time.

CHANGES IN THE USE OF STANDARDS

LEARNING OBJECTIVE 6
How are standard setting and standard usage changing in modern business?

Sometimes, in using variances from standards for control and performance evaluation purposes, accountants (and to a certain extent businesspeople in general) believe that an incorrect measurement is employed. For example, the chapter stated that material standards often include a factor for waste and labor standards are commonly set at the expected level of attainment, even though this level allows for downtime and human error. The practice of using standards that are not aimed at the highest possible theoretical level of attainment is now being questioned in a business environment concerned with world-class operations, especially continuous improvement.

Use of Theoretical Standards for Quality Improvement

Japanese influence on American management philosophy and production techniques has been substantial in the recent past. Just-in-time (JIT) production systems and total quality management (TQM) concepts were both imported to this country as a result of an upsurge in Japanese productivity. These two world-class concepts are notable departures from the traditional view that ideals should not be used in standards development and application. Rather than including waste and inefficiency in the standards and then accepting additional waste and spoilage deviations under a management by exception principle, both JIT and TQM begin from the premises of zero defects, zero inefficiency, and zero downtime. Under such a system, theoretical standards become expected standards, with either no or only a minimal acceptable level of deviation from standards.

Although workers may, at first, resent the introduction of standards set at a "perfection" level, it is in their and management's best long-run interest to have such standards. When a standard permits a deviation from the ideal, managers are allowing for inefficient resource utilization. Setting standards at the tightest possible theoretical level is intended to produce the most useful information for managerial purposes as well as the highest-quality products and services at the lowest possible cost. If no inefficiencies are built into or tolerated in the system, deviations from standards should be minimized and overall organizational performance improved.

If theoretical standards are to be implemented, management must be prepared to go through a four-step "migration" process. First, teams should be established to determine where current problems lie and identify the causes of those problems. Second, if the causes relate to equipment, facility, or workers, management must be ready to invest in plant and equipment items, equipment rearrangements, or worker training so that the standards are amenable to the operations. Training is essential if workers are to perform at the high levels of efficiency demanded by theoretical standards. If the causes are related to external sources, such as poor-quality material, management must be willing to change suppliers or pay higher prices for higher-quality input. Third, because workers have now often been assigned the responsibility for quality, they must also be given the authority to react to problems as discussed in the following News Note (page 418). "The key to quality initiatives is for employees to move beyond their natural resistance-to-change mode to a highly focused, strategic, and empowered mind-set. This shift unlocks employees' energy and creativity, and leads them to ask, 'How can I do my job even better today?' "[6] Fourth, requiring people to work at their maximum potential demands recognition, meaning that management must provide rewards for achievement.

Whether setting standards at the theoretical level will become the norm of American companies cannot be determined at this time. However, the authors believe that the level of attainability for standards will move away from the expected and closer to the ideal. This conclusion reflects the current business environment in which companies most often must meet competitors head-to-head; if a company's competitor uses the highest possible standards as product norms, that company must also use such standards to compete on quality and to meet cost and, thus, profit margin objectives. Higher standards for efficiency automatically mean lower costs because of the elimination of non-value-added activities such as waste, idle time, and rework.

Basing Price Variance on Purchases Rather Than Usage

Traditionally, the material price variance computation has been more commonly based on purchases than on usage. This choice allows management to calculate the variance as near as possible to the time of cost incurrence. Although a point-of-purchase

---

[6]Sara Moulton, Ed Oakley, and Chuck Kremer, "How to Assure Your Quality Initiative Really Pays Off," *Management Accounting* (January 1993), p. 26.

NEWS NOTE

Empowering Employees Is an Ethical Business Practice

Making employees more involved in and responsible for their work activities increases the value of those individuals not only to the organization, but also to themselves and to society as a whole. The organizational benefits gained from empowerment are that employees have a sense of ownership of and work harder toward goals they have set for themselves. Thus, employee involvement automatically promotes a higher degree of effort on the part of the work force. We avoid the basis of the Marxist critique of capitalism: the exploitation and subsequent alienation and rebellion of the worker. Problems will be solved more quickly and, therefore, the cost of errors will be reduced.

Providing training to employees for improving skills and/or decision making results in a person who is a more valuable and productive member of the company and society. Additionally, empowered employees are less likely to become bored and should experience more job satisfaction. Lastly, empowering employees provides a valuable means by which people's "timeless quest to express themselves and establish their individuality be furthered in the face of a world that is becoming more complex and more dependent on technology." The pinnacle of Maslow's hierarchy of needs is achieved as well: self-actualization.

SOURCE: Cecily Raiborn and Dinah Payne, "TQM: Just What the Ethicist Ordered," *Journal of Business Ethics* (Vol. 15, 1996), p. 969. With kind permission from Kluwer Academic Publishers.

calculation allows managers to see the impact of buying decisions more rapidly, such information may not be highly relevant in a just-in-time environment. Buying materials that are not needed currently requires that the materials be stored and moved—both non-value-added activities. Any price savings from such purchases should be measured against the additional costs of such a purchase.

Additionally, a point-of-purchase price variance may reduce a manager's ability to recognize a relationship between a favorable material price variance and an unfavorable material usage variance. If a favorable price variance results from the purchase of lower quality materials, the effects of that purchase are not known until the materials are actually used.

Long-term versus Short-term Standards

Standards have traditionally been set after prices and quantities for the various cost elements were comprehensively investigated. These standards were almost always retained for at least one year and, sometimes, for many years. The current business environment including outsourcing, supplier contractual relationships, technology advancements, competitive niches, and enhanced product design and time-to-market considerations changes so rapidly that a standard may no longer be useful for management control purposes throughout an entire year. Company management needs to consider whether to ignore rapid changes in the environment or to incorporate those changes into the standards during a year in which *significant* changes occur.

Ignoring the changes is a simplistic approach that allows the same type of cost to be recorded at the same amount all year. Thus, for example, any material purchased during the year is recorded at the same standard cost regardless of when the purchase was made. This approach, although simplifying record keeping, eliminates any opportunity to adequately control costs or evaluate performance. Additionally, such an approach could create large differences between standard and actual costs, making standard costs unacceptable for external reporting.

Changing the standards to reflect price or quantity changes makes some aspects of management control and performance evaluation more effective and others more difficult. For instance, financial plans prepared under the original standards must be adjusted before appropriate actual comparisons can be made against them. Changing the standards also creates a problem for record keeping and inventory measurement. At what standard cost should a product be recorded—the standard in effect when that product was made or the standard in effect when the financial statements are prepared? If standards are changed, they are more closely related to actual costs but many of the benefits discussed earlier in the chapter might be compromised.

Management may consider combining these two choices in the accounting system. Plans prepared by use of original and new standards can be compared; any variances reflect changes in the business environment. These variances can be designated as uncontrollable, such as changes in the market price of raw material; internally initiated, such as changes in standard labor time resulting from employee training or equipment rearrangement; or internally controllable, such as excess usage of material or labor time caused by the purchase of inferior materials.

SITE ANALYSIS

American Apparel

It only takes a short conversation with American Apparel's president Bill Corhern to understand the organization's success. He continuously emphasizes his company's dedication to two things: a quality product and an empowered workforce. Without the first, American Apparel could not retain its high-profile clients; without the second, the company could never produce its high quality products. American Apparel's product simply has to be better; it can't compete solely on the basis of cost.

Breaking the traditional manufacturing environment of an in-line sewing operation (in which garment pieces flow from individual to individual, each of whom performs a specialized task) to a modular team concept was a radical step for such a small organization. It required substantial training so that employees could perform multiple tasks—and perform them well. Employee empowerment provided a benefit not originally considered: it took the matter of worker productivity out of the hands of company management and placed it in the work teams. Corhern rarely gets involved in production issues any longer: "The teams are self-disciplining. If a team member is not performing up to par, the other team members either get that person 'on board' or make the comfort level such that that person would prefer not to continue." Thus, labor efficiency variances are negligible.

American Apparel's primary concern these days is not about standard cost variances. Costs are under control; productivity is high; workers are achieving bonuses based on team activity goals; and, best of all, employee morale is high in a work environment typically viewed as tedious. The concern of company management is an ability to remain profitable in the face of potential additional increases to the minimum wage law that will affect American, but not off-shore, clothing manufacturers. American Apparel knows that customers are willing to pay for a quality product and the company has "tightened its belt" to be competitive with foreign producers. But if costs are increased, will American Apparel's customers be willing to pay a premium price for the "Made in the U.S.A." label? Corhern hopes so—for the sake of the workers his company has so carefully trained to be concerned about customer satisfaction through product quality.

SOURCE: Interview with Bill Corhern, president & CEO, American Apparel, 1998.

CROSS-FUNCTIONAL APPLICATIONS

TOPIC OF NOTE	DISCIPLINE	CROSS-FUNCTIONAL APPLICATIONS
Variance Analysis	Management	Entire systems of management—such as management-by-exception, total quality management, and contingency theory—depend upon assigning responsibility to various managers and controlling performance with variance analysis (VA). VA also assists managers in strategic planning and organizational activities.
	Economics	Economic inefficiencies in a firm can be identified by comparing actual operating activities with those expected. This process can improve the measurement of marginal and incremental costs on which managers base their decisions.
	Human Resource Management	VA can identify talented managers and those who may require more training, education, or motivation. Employee training is a strain on the limited human-resources budget. VA permits employee training to be targeted and even prioritized to affect the most critical activities.
	Engineering	VA engineers, to improve their system/process efficiency, need a benchmark for their activities. In an environment where firms are closely linked in a technological sense, a common benchmark for operations is almost a necessity.
		Standard setting is particularly challenging for manufacturing engineers because the production process usually involves modeling people–machine relationships, which are complex in application. Despite the uncertainty, attempts are made to set reliable standards to assist in analyzing and predicting manufacturing process efficiency.
	Purchasing	VA can assist outsourcing decisions and monitor changes in outsourcing competence. As the traditional boundaries between organizations become more dynamic, it is reasonable to require suppliers to operate within the limits of customers' control requirements. JIT inventory and relationship marketing often depend upon a supplier's ability to operate within a customer's strategic standards.
	Service Industries	VA can clarify the often inexact requirements set by public law or union negotiations. When VA is combined with legal standards or union job descriptions, the performance and quality considerations can be evaluated over the long run with the same effectiveness as a production environment.
Standard Setting	Finance	Strategic financial planning depends upon acceptable and attainable standards for return on assets, investment capital, long-run profitability, and equity versus debt structure for an organization. In a rapidly changing capital market environment, financial planners must use the most updated standards to control and predict the course of their organizations in a competitive market as well as for evaluating alternative sources and uses of capital.

CROSS-FUNCTIONAL APPLICATIONS

TOPIC OF NOTE	DISCIPLINE	CROSS-FUNCTIONAL APPLICATIONS
Standard Setting (continued)	Labor and Industrial Relations	Standard setting is often a major point of contention in labor–management negotiations because it involves the labor cost input into a product as well as the working environment and performance evaluation of employees. Although measurements can stray from ideal standards or strategic goals by a wide margin, the important consideration is the cooperation in the process. If high standards are set in an environment of narrow, detached input, low morale and poor output are probable consequences.
	Operations Research	Methods of operational planning—such as optimization roles in decision making, utility-preference modeling, scheduling, and simulation of operating systems—all depend upon reliable standard setting. As a bonus, standards that are generally accepted as reliable can validate the modeling process as well.

CHAPTER SUMMARY

A standard cost is a budget for one unit of product or service output and provides a norm against which actual cost can be compared. In a traditional standard cost system, standards are computed for prices and quantities of each product component (material, labor, variable overhead, and fixed overhead). Standards should be developed by a team composed of professional staff and managers as well as employees whose performance will be evaluated by such standards. A standard cost card is used to accumulate and record specific information about the components, processes, quantities, and costs that form the standard for a product. The material and labor sections of the standard cost card are derived from the bill of materials and the operations flow document, respectively.

In a standard costing system, actual and standard costs are recorded; then, variances are computed and analyzed. Each total variance is separated into subvariances relating to price and quantity or rate and efficiency elements.

Variance analysis provides a basis for management planning, control, and performance evaluation. Using standard costs, managers can forecast what costs should be at various levels of activity and can compare those forecasts with actual results. When large variances are observed, the causes should be determined and, if possible, corrective action taken. For this reason, variances should be recorded as early and often in the production/service process as is feasible.

Standards should be appropriate and attainable. They should reflect current relevant technical and operational expectations. The level of rigor chosen for the standards should be based on realistic expectations and motivational effects on employees. The practical level has typically been thought to have the best motivational impact; however, some Japanese firms use theoretical standards to indicate their goals of minimum cost and zero defects.

Some companies are changing the way standards are set and used. Traditionally, standards have included some level of waste and spoilage and, regarding fixed overhead, have been based on expected activity levels. These standards were commonly held constant for a year or longer. Recently, many firms have discovered that their standards have not been useful in implementing process, quality, or cost improvements. Thus, managers are revising standards to reflect technology advances, process improvements, and global market competitiveness.

APPENDIX

STANDARD COST SYSTEM JOURNAL ENTRIES

LEARNING OBJECTIVE ⑦
What journal entries are needed in a standard cost system?

EXHIBIT 9-8
Journal Entries for Cutting Department, Week of June 12–16, 2000

Journal entries for the information contained in the chapter related to Kosciusko Clothing Cutting Department are given in Exhibit 9-8. The material price variance in this exhibit is accounted for based on the secondary information that 3,000 square yards of cotton fabric were purchased. Note that unfavorable variances have debit balances and favorable variances have credit balances. Unfavorable variances represent excess costs, while

	Raw Material Inventory	10,500	
	Material Price Variance	1,950	
	Accounts Payable		12,450
	To record the purchase of 3,000 square yards of cotton fabric at $4.15 per square yard.		
	Work in Process Inventory—Cutting Dept.	9,240	
	Material Quantity Variance	315	
	Raw Material Inventory		9,555
	To record the issuance and usage of 2,730 square yards of cotton fabric for 2,200 shirts.		
	Work in Process Inventory—Cutting Dept.	5,280	
	Labor Rate Variance	200	
	Labor Efficiency Variance		480
	Wages Payable		5,000
	To record the usage of 500 direct labor hours at a wage rate of $10 per DLH.		
During period:	Variable Overhead—Cutting Dept.	3,360	
	Various accounts		3,360
	To record actual variable overhead costs.		
During period:	Fixed Overhead—Cutting Dept.	2,875	
	Various accounts		2,875
	To record actual fixed overhead costs.		
At end of period (or upon completion of production):	Work in Process Inventory—Cutting Dept.	6,050	
	Variable Overhead—Cutting Dept.		3,850
	Fixed Overhead—Cutting Dept.		2,200
	To apply variable overhead at $7 per DLH and fixed overhead at $6 per MH for actual production of 2,200 shirts.		
At year-end (assuming that the week's variances are the only ones that remain at year-end):	Variable Overhead—Cutting Dept.	490	
	VOH Spending Variance—Cutting Dept.		140
	VOH Efficiency Variance—Cutting Dept.		350
	To close the variable overhead account.		
	FOH Spending Variance—Cutting Dept.	379	
	FOH Volume Variance—Cutting Dept.	296	
	Fixed Overhead—Cutting Dept.		675
	To close the fixed overhead account.		

favorable variances represent cost savings. Since standard costs are shown in Work in Process Inventory (a debit-balanced account), it is reasonable that excess costs are also debits.

Although standard cost systems are useful for internal reporting, such costs are not acceptable for external reporting unless they are *substantially equivalent* to those that would have resulted from using an actual cost system.[7] If standards are achievable and updated periodically, this equivalency should exist. Using standards for financial statements should provide fairly conservative inventory valuations because the effects of excess prices and/or inefficient operations are minimized.

If actual costs are used in financial statements, the standard cost information shown in the accounting records must be adjusted at year-end to approximate actual cost information. The nature of the year-end adjusting entries depends on whether the variance amounts are significant or not.

All manufacturing variances (material, labor, and overhead) are considered together in determining the appropriate year-end disposition. If the combined impact of these variances is considered insignificant, standard costs are approximately the same as actual costs, and the variances are closed to Cost of Goods Sold (or Cost of Services Rendered in a service organization). Unfavorable variances are closed by being credited; favorable variances are closed by being debited. In a manufacturing company, although all production of the period has not yet been sold, this treatment of insignificant variances is justified on the basis of the immateriality of the amounts involved.

In contrast, if the total variance amount is significant, the overhead variances are prorated at year-end to ending inventories and Cost of Goods Sold in proportion to the relative size of those account balances. This proration disposes of the variances and presents the financial statements in a way that approximates the use of actual costing. The disposition of significant variances is similar to the disposition of large amounts of underapplied or overapplied overhead shown in Chapter 4. The material price variance based on purchases is prorated among Raw Material Inventory, Work in Process Inventory, Finished Goods Inventory, and Cost of Goods Sold or Cost of Services Rendered. All other variances occur as part of the conversion process and are prorated only to the Work in Process Inventory, Finished Goods Inventory, and Cost of Goods Sold or Cost of Services Rendered accounts.

KEY TERMS

Bill of materials (p. 396)	**Standard cost** (p. 395)
Expected standard (p. 415)	**Standard cost card** (p. 400)
Fixed overhead spending variance (p. 407)	**Standard quantity allowed** (p. 401)
Labor efficiency variance (LEV) (p. 404)	**Theoretical standard** (p. 415)
Labor rate variance (LRV) (p. 404)	**Variable overhead efficiency variance** (p. 406)
Management by exception (p. 415)	
Material price variance (MPV) (p. 402)	**Variable overhead spending variance** (p. 406)
Material quantity variance (MQV) (p. 402)	
Operations flow document (p. 397)	**Variance** (p. 395)
Practical standard (p. 415)	**Variance analysis** (p. 408)
Price variance (p. 401)	**Volume variance** (407)
Quantity variance (p. 401)	

---

[7]Actual product costs should not include extraordinary charges for such items as waste, spoilage, and inefficiency. Such costs should be written off as period expenses.

SOLUTION STRATEGIES

Variances in Formula Format

Material price variance = AQ (AP − SP)

Material quantity variance = SP (AQ − SQ)

Labor rate variance = AQ (AP − SP)

Labor efficiency variance = SP (AQ − SQ)

Variable overhead spending variance = Actual VOH − (SR × AQ)

Variable overhead efficiency variance = SR (AQ − SQ)

Fixed overhead spending variance = Actual FOH − Budgeted FOH

Fixed overhead volume variance = Budgeted FOH − (SR × SQ)

Variances in Diagram Format

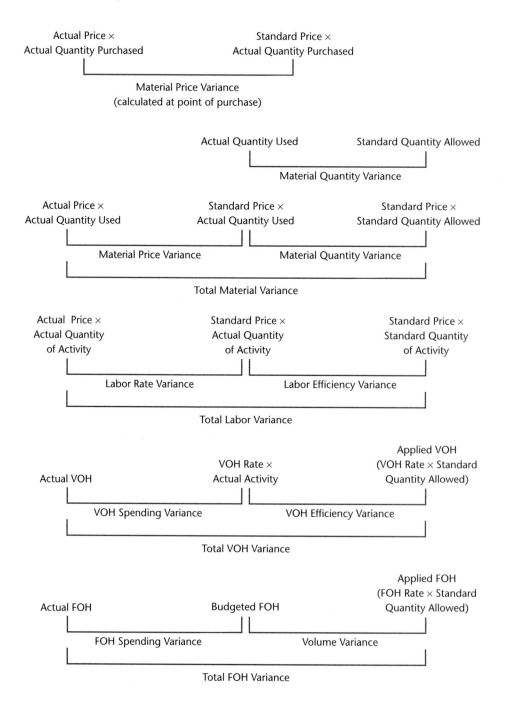

DEMONSTRATION PROBLEM

Squeaky Clean manufactures industrial sponges. The production operation is a simple process requiring only one material and very little labor. Variable factory overhead is applied on a machine hour (MH) basis. Fixed factory overhead is applied on a material weight basis; the predetermined rate was based on a production budget of 105,000 pounds of sponges (or 140,000 sponges) per month. The following standard costs and quantities have been developed for one sponge:

Direct material (12 ounces of man-made sponge)	$ .50 per ounce	$6.000
Direct labor (1.5 minutes)	$7.20 per DLH	.180
Variable factory overhead (2.4 minutes)	$9.60 per MH	.384
Fixed factory overhead ($3.20 per pound)	$ .20 per ounce	2.400
Total cost per sponge		$8.964

For May, company records give the following actual cost and production information:

Purchases of sponge: 95,000 pounds at $8.45 per pound
Usage of sponge: 93,720 pounds
Direct labor: 3,045 hours at $7.25 per hour
Machine time: 5,110 hours
Variable overhead: $48,610
Fixed overhead: $328,000
Production: 125,000 sponges

Required:
Compute all material, labor, and overhead variances.

Solution
Determine appropriate standards for all cost elements.

125,000 sponges × 12 ounces = 1,500,000 ounces; 1,500,000 ÷ 16 = 93,750 pounds of DM

125,000 sponges × 1.5 minutes = 187,500 minutes; 187,500 ÷ 60 = 3,125 hours of DL time

125,000 sponges × 2.4 minutes = 300,000 minutes; 300,000 ÷ 60 = 5,000 hours of machine time

Budgeted FOH = 105,000 pounds of sponges × $3.20 per pound = $336,000

Direct Material:

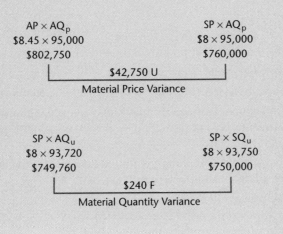

$AP \times AQ_p$		$SP \times AQ_p$
$8.45 × 95,000		$8 × 95,000
$802,750		$760,000
	$42,750 U	
	Material Price Variance	

$SP \times AQ_u$		$SP \times SQ_u$
$8 × 93,720		$8 × 93,750
$749,760		$750,000
	$240 F	
	Material Quantity Variance	

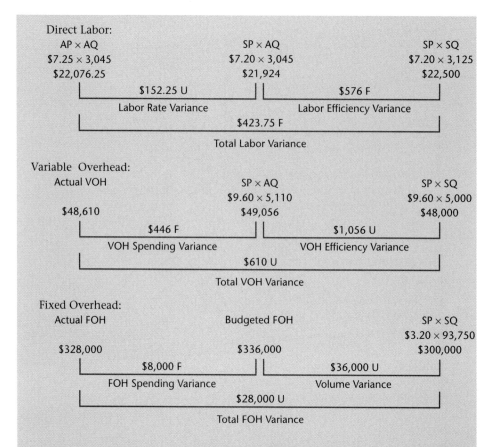

Direct Labor:

AP × AQ	SP × AQ	SP × SQ
$7.25 × 3,045	$7.20 × 3,045	$7.20 × 3,125
$22,076.25	$21,924	$22,500

$152.25 U
Labor Rate Variance

$576 F
Labor Efficiency Variance

$423.75 F
Total Labor Variance

Variable Overhead:

Actual VOH	SP × AQ	SP × SQ
	$9.60 × 5,110	$9.60 × 5,000
$48,610	$49,056	$48,000

$446 F
VOH Spending Variance

$1,056 U
VOH Efficiency Variance

$610 U
Total VOH Variance

Fixed Overhead:

Actual FOH	Budgeted FOH	SP × SQ
		$3.20 × 93,750
$328,000	$336,000	$300,000

$8,000 F
FOH Spending Variance

$36,000 U
Volume Variance

$28,000 U
Total FOH Variance

NOTE: The FOH volume variance is unfavorable because the company planned to make 105,000 pounds of sponges (140,000 sponges), but made only 93,750 pounds of sponges (125,000 sponges). Each unproduced pound of sponge did not bear an allocated FOH cost of $3.20. Thus, the total volume variance is $36,000, or 11,250 pounds of sponges not made times $3.20 per pound. This calculation could also have been made on the basis of sponges: 15,000 sponges not produced times a FOH rate per sponge of $2.40, equaling $36,000.

END OF CHAPTER MATERIALS

⊙ QUESTIONS

1. Why is a standard costing system regarded as both a planning and a control tool?

2. What is a variance and what does it measure?

3. Why are standards necessary for each cost component of a product or service?

4. Describe a situation that illustrates the following statement: "Almost all products can be manufactured with a variety of inputs that would generate the same basic output."

5. Would an actual or a standard product costing system provide the better opportunity to evaluate the control of costs for a period? Explain.

6. Why should individuals other than accountants be involved in the standard setting process? Provide examples of who these additional individuals should be and what important information they might provide.

7. What is a bill of materials and how is it used in a standard cost system?

8. What is an operations flow document? How is it used in a standard cost system?

9. Why is a predetermined overhead rate considered a standard?

10. In a standard cost system, is standard cost or actual cost charged to Work in Process Inventory for direct material and direct labor? Explain. How are actual costs reflected in a standard cost system?

11. "Overhead standards should be set using the most available measurement in the production or service area, such as direct labor hours." Discuss the validity of this statement.

12. What is meant by "standard quantity allowed" when this term is used in relation to direct material? To direct labor? To overhead? Provide an example for each cost element.

13. Why is the computation of the material price variance frequently based on the quantity of material purchased, rather than the quantity used, during the period?

14. If the material price variance is computed on the basis of quantity of material purchased rather than used, can a total material variance be computed? Explain your answer.

15. As the manufacturing vice-president of Turner Controls, you have noticed that one manufacturing plant has experienced several large unfavorable material quantity variances during the prior quarter. Before starting your probe of the matter, list some possible reasons for this type of variance.

16. Your factory operations this period have shown a large favorable labor rate variance. Why might this have occurred? Would you expect your labor efficiency variance to be favorable or unfavorable? Why?

17. You are the supervisor of the Harvey Mail Service. Service quality in the organization is not measured relative to direct labor time. Additionally, there is a consistently large and favorable efficiency variance. Provide one positive and one negative analysis of this variance.

18. Is fixed factory overhead controlled by management on a per-unit basis? Explain your answer.

19. Of what importance is capacity utilization to managers? When managers control utilization, are they always controlling costs? Explain.

20. What is variance analysis and why is it conducted by managers?

21. For the following variances indicate (a) when each variance should be calculated and (b) to whom responsibility for the variance should be assigned and why.
    a. Material price variance
    b. Material quantity variance
    c. Labor rate variance
    d. Labor efficiency variance
    e. Variable overhead spending variance
    f. Volume variance

22. Why is a "conversion cost" category emerging in some companies to replace the traditional cost categories of direct labor and manufacturing overhead?

23. Why is it important for managers to update standards periodically?

24. What is management by exception, and what is its role in a management control system that uses standard costing?

25. *(Appendix)* If the variances incurred in a given period are not significant in amount, how are they typically closed out at the end of the period? Why is this disposition acceptable?

⊙ EXERCISES

26. *(Terminology)* Match each item in the right-hand column with a term in the left-hand column.

a. Operations flow document	1. A standard that allows for no human or mechanical error
b. Practical standard	2. The difference between budgeted and applied fixed overhead
c. Standard	3. A listing of tasks required to make a product
d. Theoretical standard	4. A document specifying the materials required for a product
e. Labor rate variance	5. The process of identifying causes of variances
f. Overhead spending variance	6. A norm for a cost or a quantity
g. Volume variance	7. The difference between the actual and budgeted overhead
h. Standard cost card	8. The standard of performance that has reasonable probability of attainment
i. Variance analysis	9. The difference between standard and actual labor wages
j. Bill of materials	10. The document listing standard cost of all inputs for a product

27. *(Material variances)* You are the purchasing agent for Heyd & Co., which makes statues of endangered animals. Wildlife and environmental groups sell the statues at fund-raisers. In June 2000, you bought 105,600 pounds of material at an average price of $2.40 per pound. That month, 99,400 pounds of material were used to produce 225 statues. The material standard for each statue is 420 pounds of material at a standard cost of $2.25 per pound.
   a. Calculate the material price variance, based on quantity purchased.
   b. Calculate the material quantity variance.
   c. What potential reasons might you have for the unfavorable price variance?

28. *(Material variances)* The Waterworld Store experienced the following costs and quantities related to direct material during August 2000:

Actual quantity purchased	136,500 liters
Actual quantity used	130,500 liters
Standard quantity allowed	132,900 liters
Actual unit price per liter	$14.50
Standard unit price per liter	$13.90

   Mr. Costner, the company president, has requested that you determine the material price and quantity variances.
   a. Compute the material price variance based on (1) quantity purchased and (2) quantity used.
   b. Compute the material quantity variance.
   c. Why can a material price variance be computed on two different bases, but a labor rate variance cannot?

29. *(Material variances)* You have just received the following information related to your company's purchases and usage of paper during October. The company runs high-volume calendar printing jobs.

Sheets of paper purchased in October	1,000,000
Sheets of paper used in October	780,000
Standard quantity allowed for good production	794,000
Actual unit purchase price per sheet	$.037
Standard unit price per sheet	$.039

   a. Calculate the material price variance based on the quantity purchased and the material quantity variance.
   b. You have asked the vice-president of manufacturing to explain the difference between theoretical, practical, and expected standards. How might she explain these differences?
   c. How would using theoretical standards change the variance information calculated in Part a? (No specific numerical calculations are necessary.)

30. *(Material variances)* Constance Corp. manufactures wooden block pencil holders. During the first week of March, the following information was provided to management:

Material quantity variance	$1,600 U
Total material variance	$2,540 U

Each holder requires 3 square inches of wood from boards that are cut to spec for the company. Thirty-nine hundred twenty square feet of wood were purchased and used during the week. The actual price per inch of wood was $.82. The standard quantity of wood allowed was 3,750 square feet.
   a. What was the material price variance?
   b. How many holders were produced during the week?
   c. What was the standard cost per inch of wood?

31. *(Labor variances)* Wilson Automotive uses a standard cost system and experienced the following results related to direct labor in December:

Actual hours worked	41,250
Standard hours allowed for production	40,500
Actual direct labor rate	$7.25
Standard direct labor rate	$6.75

As the cost accountant for the company, calculate the
   a. total actual payroll.
   b. labor rate variance.
   c. labor efficiency variance.

32. *(Labor variances)* Evelyn's Quilts makes a one-design queen-size quilt and uses a standard costing system. During February, the following direct labor hours and costs were incurred:

Standard hours	5,400
Actual hours	5,100
Standard wage rate per hour	$11.75
Actual wage rate per hour	$12.00

   a. You have been asked to determine total actual labor cost, standard labor cost, and the labor rate and efficiency variances.
   b. Given this information, write a memo to Ms. Evelyn about the possible causes of the rate and efficiency variances.

33. *(Labor variances)* Blanchard Cabinets builds 4-by-6-foot bookcases. Each bookcase requires seven direct labor hours and the average standard hourly wage of workers is $9. During October, Blanchard Cabinets built 1,200 bookcases. Direct labor time was 8,000 hours, and gross pay was $74,800. Donald Blanchard has asked you to analyze direct labor costs and labor efficiency for him.
   a. Compute the labor variances.
   b. Provide an explanation of the direct labor variances that is consistent with the results.

34. *(Labor variances)* Jovanovich Insurance's information about direct labor for September is as follows:

Efficiency variance	$17,380 U
Actual direct labor rate per hour	$7.50
Standard direct labor rate per hour	$7.90
Standard hours allowed	20,000

Calculate:
   a. actual hours worked during September.
   b. total payroll.
   c. the labor rate variance.
   d. Given the above information, Peter Jovanovich has asked your human resource firm for some suggestions to better motivate his employees. Prepare a short memo providing him some feedback.

35. *(Variable overhead variances)* Celine Corp. produces engraved wood plaques; each plaque requires fifteen minutes of machine time. During April, 1,800 units were

manufactured. The company's predetermined variable overhead rate per machine hour is $14. In April, $6,200 of variable overhead costs were incurred and machine time was clocked at 410 hours.

a. What is the total applied variable overhead for the month?

b. Calculate the variable overhead variances.

c. This is the sixth month in a row that there has been a significant favorable variable overhead efficiency variance. Provide the company accountant an appropriate explanation as to why so few machine hours are being used relative to the standard.

36. *(Variable overhead variances)* Nadia Co. manufactures three products (tables, chairs, and desks) and uses direct labor hours as its overhead application base. Standard hours allowed for each product follow:

Table	10 DLHs
Chair	3 DLHs
Desk	12 DLHs

The standard variable overhead application rate is $4 per direct labor hour. Production for June was 100 tables, 400 chairs, and 60 desks. Actual direct labor hours incurred were 3,020 and actual variable overhead was $11,900.

a. Determine the total applied variable overhead for June.

b. Calculate the variable overhead spending, efficiency, and total variances.

c. Are direct labor hours a reasonable application base in an automated plant? Why or why not?

37. *(Fixed overhead variances)* Use the information given in Exercise 36 and the following additional information. Nadia's fixed overhead application rate at expected annual capacity is $2 per direct labor hour. Monthly expected capacity is 3,000 direct labor hours. In June, actual fixed overhead was $6,100.

a. What is total monthly budgeted fixed overhead?

b. What is total applied fixed overhead for June?

c. Compute the fixed overhead spending, volume, and total variances.

d. Discuss the meaning of the fixed overhead volume variance.

38. *(Fixed overhead variances)* Wayans Co. produces briefcases. The standard variable and fixed overhead application rates per briefcase are, respectively, $.80 and $.50 per machine hour. Each briefcase takes four machine hours. During May 2000, the company had the following production statistics:

Total fixed overhead applied to production	$225,000
Actual fixed overhead	240,000
Volume variance	5,000 F
Variable overhead spending variance	10,000 F

Calculate the following May information for your supervisor:

a. Standard machine hours allowed.

b. Number of briefcases produced.

c. Budgeted amount of fixed overhead.

d. Expected capacity in machine hours.

e. Fixed overhead spending variance.

39. *(Overhead variances)* Joyner Manufacturing employs a standard costing system. In the company's Georgia plant, factory overhead is applied to production on the basis of machine hours. The following information from the Georgia plant pertains to October:

Standard variable factory overhead rate per machine hour	$12
Standard fixed factory overhead rate per macnine hour	$10
Standard machine hours for month	4,200
Actual machine hours for month	4,400
Total budgeted monthly fixed factory overhead	$40,000
Actual fixed factory overhead	$45,000
Actual variable factory overhead	$47,500

Calculate the:
a. total actual overhead cost.
b. total applied overhead.
c. variable overhead variances.
d. fixed overhead variances.

40. *(Overhead variances)* Coretta Concrete manufactures industrial pipe. The company uses a standard cost system and applies variable factory overhead to production using pounds of product moved. The standard variable factory overhead rate is set at $9 per pound moved. The standard weight per unit is .75 pounds. For the year 2000, budgeted fixed factory overhead is $480,000; fixed factory overhead is applied to production using direct labor hours. The standard time per unit is .5 direct labor hour. Budgeted direct labor hours for the year 2000 were 60,000. The following data pertain to the year 2000:

Number of units produced	82,000
Actual weight of units	62,300
Actual direct labor hours	42,000
Actual variable overhead cost	$582,000
Actual fixed overhead cost	$476,000

a. The company CEO, Loretta Scott, has asked you to determine the amount of total applied overhead, variable overhead variances, and fixed overhead variances.
b. What explanations might you offer Ms. Scott for the variances calculated in Part a?

41. *(Overhead variances)* Titanic Inc. uses a standard costing system. Standard cost data for the company's best-selling product, a large plastic iceberg, follow:

Direct material	$3
Direct labor	6
Variable overhead	4
Fixed overhead (based on 600,000 units expected capacity)	5
Total	$18

Titanic produced 399,000 units in the year 2000. Actual variable overhead was $2,100,000 and actual fixed overhead was $4,500,000. Overhead is applied on a machine hour basis; each iceberg takes 20 minutes of machine time. Actual machine hours used for the year were 130,000.
a. Calculate the variable overhead variances.
b. Calculate the fixed overhead variances.
c. Unfortunately, a downturn in demand occurred, and Titanic Inc. only sold 100,000 units during the year. Is the volume variance a valid reflection of capacity utilization? Provide the rationale for your answer.

42. *(Conversion cost variances)* The Iowa facilities of Spuds Inc. were automated in late 1999. As division manager, you convinced corporate headquarters to allow you to change your standard costing system. The most significant change was to combine direct labor and variable overhead into a single conversion cost pool. In its first year of implementing the new system, the following standards were set:

Variable conversion cost per machine hour	$12
Fixed conversion cost (based on 80,000 budgeted machine hours) per machine hour	$10

Data related to the actual results for the year 2000 are:

Actual machine hours worked	76,000
Standard machine hours allowed	78,000
Variable conversion costs	$904,600
Fixed conversion costs	$784,000

a. Compute the variable conversion cost variances for the year.
b. Compute the fixed conversion cost variances for the year.
c. The Iowa plant of Spuds Inc. produces goods only as they are ordered by customers. Who has the greatest control over the fixed conversion cost volume variance and why? When should control be exercised over fixed overhead costs, and why?

a. Using the previous information, prepare variance computations for management's consideration. (Hint: Under the conventional approach, there will be a direct labor efficiency variance, a direct labor rate variance, and a total direct labor variance. Under a different logical approach, there will be a direct labor efficiency variance, a direct labor rate variance, a direct labor "joint" variance, and a total direct labor variance.)

b. Contrast these two approaches and make some recommendations to management. [SOURCE: Nabil Hassan and Sarah Palmer, "Management Accounting Case Study: Day-Mold," Institute of Management Accountants (IMA), *Management Accounting Campus Report* (Spring 1990). Reprinted with permission from the IMA's Committee on Academic Relations.]

50. *(Overhead variances)* KEEP-M-OUT makes an adjustable window screen. Standard time and costs per screen follow:

Machine time (hours)	.20
VOH rate per machine hour	$8.50
FOH rate per machine hour	$6.50

At the end of May 2000, papers on the desk of the company's accountant were partially ruined by a driving rain blowing through the screened windows. The following May 2000 operating statistics were still legible on the accountant's report to management:

Total fixed overhead applied to production	$715,000
Actual variable overhead	937,400
Actual fixed overhead	709,000
Volume variance	13,000 F
Variable overhead spending variance	10,900 U

The company accountant is on vacation. Because you recently took a management accounting course paid for by KEEP-M-OUT, you have been asked to provide the following information:

a. Standard machine hours allowed
b. Number of screens produced
c. Budgeted fixed overhead
d. Expected annual capacity in machine hours
e. Fixed factory overhead spending variance
f. Fixed factory overhead total variance
g. For variable overhead:
   (1) Total applied variable overhead
   (2) Total variable overhead variance
   (3) Actual machine hours incurred
   (4) Variable overhead efficiency variance
   (5) Actual variable overhead rate per machine hour
h. The president of KEEP-M-OUT is curious about the possible causes of the variable overhead spending variance. Who would you suggest that she call (other than the vacationing accountant) to explain the variance? Defend your answer.

51. *(Overhead variances)* Chavez & Martin LLP is a small law firm. Variable and fixed overhead are applied to cases as follows:

Variable overhead: applied on a basis of per-page of documentation generated during the month at the rate of $.22 per page

Fixed overhead: applied on a basis of monthly billable hours generated at the rate of $15 per hour; this rate was derived with the expectation of 1,600 billable hours per month

During July 2000, the attorneys at Chavez & Martin LLP worked on a variety of cases. The total pages of documentation generated during July was 198,000; total billable hours were 1,450. Actual variable and fixed overhead amounts for July were $48,650 and $25,000, respectively.

a. What is the budgeted annual fixed overhead for Chavez & Martin LLP?
b. Determine the variable and fixed overhead variances.

56. *(All variances*
year 2000 foi
mulching m

DIRECT MATE
Mower blades
Universal ada

DIRECT LABO
Grinding pro
Finishing and

FACTORY OVI
Variable
Fixed
Total cost per
* Based on expected

Actual re
Mower blades
Mower blades
Universal ada
Universal ada
Grinding proc
Finishing and
Actual machir
Actual variable
Actual fixed fa

a. Prepare the
  (1) Purcha
  (2) Issue d
  (3) Accrue
  (4) Incur n
  (5) Apply i
  (6) Close y
  (7) Transfe
  (8) Sell 4,0
b. Close all va
c. If collective
  entry have

⊙ **CASES**

57. *(Material and l.*
frozen desserts
on the basis of
similar produc
tant. John Wal
cost system for
workers on pro
believes that th
and make bette

ColdKing'
in 10-gallon ba
raspberries are
perfections in t
every four quai
for the sorting
ceptable raspbe
utes of direct la

---

c. Why is the variable overhead efficiency variance zero? In a law firm, what bases other than pages of documentation might be more useful to allocate variable overhead? Could a standard ever be set for these bases so that an efficiency variance could be calculated?

52. *(Overhead variances)* Slavik Enterprises uses a standard cost system for planning and control purposes. For August 2000, the firm expected to produce 4,000 units of product. At that level of production, expected factory overhead costs are:

Variable	$ 9,600
Fixed	24,000

At standard, two machine hours are required to produce a single unit of product. Actual results for August follow:

Units produced	4,200
Machine hours worked	8,600
Actual variable factory overhead	$9,460
Actual fixed factory overhead	$24,900

a. Calculate standard hours allowed for actual output.
b. Calculate all overhead variances.
c. For the year 2001, the firm is considering automating a production process that is currently performed manually. In its standard cost system, which standards would likely be affected by such a change? Explain. What individuals would likely be consulted to assist in revising the standards?

53. *(All variances)* Patio Solutions manufactures picnic table kits that are sold in various large discount department stores. The standard cost card indicates the following costs are incurred to produce a single picnic table kit:

60 board feet of pine lumber	$54
2 pipe frame units	18
1 package of fasteners	8
.5 hours of direct labor at $14 per hour	7
Variable factory overhead at $20 per machine hour	4
Fixed factory overhead at $15 per machine hour*	3
Total	$94

*Based on budgeted annual FOH of $30,000 and expected annual capacity of 2,000 hours.

During April 2000, the firm had the following actual data related to the production of 11,000 picnic kits:

PURCHASE AND USAGE OF MATERIAL

Lumber	690,000 board feet at $.85 per board foot
Frame units	22,250 units at $9.10 per unit
Packages of fasteners	11,120 packages at $6.90 per package

DIRECT LABOR USED

5,600 hours at $14.20 per hour

FACTORY OVERHEAD COSTS

Actual machine hours recorded	2,000
Actual variable factory overhead incurred	$38,000
Actual fixed factory overhead incurred	$32,300

a. Calculate material, labor, and overhead variances.
b. Provide a possible explanation for each variance computed.

54. *(All variances)* Mfume Mfg. Company manufactures plastic and aluminum products. During the winter, substantially all production capacity is devoted to lawn sprinklers. Because a variety of products are made throughout the year, factory volume is measured by machine hours rather than units of product.

The company has developed the following standards for the production of a lawn sprinkler:

After blending, the sherbet is packaged in quart containers. Wakefield has gathered the following cost information:

⊙ ColdKing purchases raspberries at a cost of $.80 per quart.
⊙ All other ingredients cost a total of $.45 per gallon.
⊙ Direct labor is paid at the rate of $9 per hour.
⊙ The total cost of material and labor required to package the sherbet is $.38 per quart.

a. Develop the standard cost for each direct cost component and the total cost of a 10-gallon batch of raspberry sherbet. The standard cost should identify the
   (1) standard quantity.
   (2) standard rate.
   (3) standard cost per batch.
b. As part of the implementation of a standard cost system at ColdKing, John Wakefield plans to train those responsible for maintaining the standards on how to use variance analysis. Wakefield is particularly concerned with the causes of unfavorable variances.
   (1) Discuss the possible causes of unfavorable material price variances, and identify the individual(s) who should be held responsible for these variances.
   (2) Discuss the possible causes of unfavorable labor efficiency variances, and identify the individual(s) who should be responsible for these variances.
c. Assume you have just graduated from college with a degree in accounting and you have been hired by ColdKing. Your first assignment is to develop a new standard for the quantity of raspberries used in production. Your supervisor, the controller, has indicated that a new standard is needed because the year-to-year change in the material quantity variance is simply unpredictable and seems to be unrelated to the effectiveness of production controls. One of your friends who also recently graduated from college has a degree in agronomy; another has a degree in meteorology. How might your two friends assist you in developing a flexible quantity standard?

(CMA adapted)

58. *(Material and labor standards)* As part of its cost control program, Tracer Company uses a standard cost system for all manufactured items. The standard cost for each item is established at the beginning of the fiscal year, and the standards are not revised until the beginning of the next fiscal year. Changes in costs, caused during the year by changes in material or labor inputs or by changes in the manufacturing process, are recognized as they occur by the inclusion of planned variances in Tracer's monthly operating budgets.

Following is the labor standard that was established for one of Tracer's products, effective June 1, 2000, the beginning of the fiscal year.

Assembler A labor (5 hours at $10 per hour)	$ 50
Assembler B labor (3 hours at $11 per hour)	33
Machinist labor (2 hours at $15 per hour)	30
Standard cost per 100 units	$113

The standard was based on the assumption that the labor would be performed by a team consisting of five persons with Assembler A skills, three persons with Assembler B skills, and two persons with machinist skills; this team represents the most efficient use of the company's skilled employees. The standard also assumed that the quality of material that had been used in prior years would be available for the coming year.

For the first seven months of the fiscal year, actual manufacturing costs at Tracer have been within the standards established. However, the company has received a significant increase in orders, and there is an insufficient number of skilled workers available to meet the increased production. Therefore, beginning in January, the production teams will consist of eight persons with Assembler A skills, one person with Assembler B skills, and one person with machinist skills. The reorganized teams will work more slowly than the normal teams, and as a result, only eighty units will be produced in the time in which one hundred units would normally be produced. Faulty work has never been a cause for units to be rejected in the final inspection process, and it is not expected to be a cause for rejection with the reorganized teams.

	Budget	Actual	Variance
Units	2,000	2,200	200 F
Variable costs			
Direct material	$180,000	$220,400	$40,400 U
Direct labor	80,000	93,460	13,460 U
Variable overhead	18,000	18,800	800 U
Total variable costs	$278,000	$332,660	$54,660 U

Funtime's top management was surprised by the unfavorable variances. Janice Rath, management accountant, was assigned to identify and report on the reasons for the unfavorable variances as well as the individuals or groups responsible. After review, Rath prepared the following usage report:

Cost Item	Quantity	Actual Cost
Direct material		
Housing units	2,200 units	$ 44,000
Printed circuit boards	4,700 units	75,200
Reading heads	9,200 units	101,200
Direct labor		
Assembly	3,900 hours	31,200
Printed circuit boards	2,400 hours	23,760
Reading heads	3,500 hours	38,500
Variable overhead	9,900 hours	18,800
Total variable cost		$332,660

Rath reported that the PCB and RH groups supported the increased production levels but experienced abnormal machine downtime. This, in turn, caused idle time, which required the use of overtime to keep up with the accelerated demand for parts. The idle time was charged to direct labor. Rath also reported that the production managers of these two groups resorted to parts rejections, as opposed to testing and modification procedures formerly applied. Rath determined that the Assembly Group met management's objectives by increasing production while utilizing lower than standard hours.

a. For May 2000, Funtime's labor rate variance was $5,660 unfavorable, and the labor efficiency variance was $200 favorable. Calculate the following variances:
   (1) Material price variance
   (2) Material quantity variance
   (3) Variable overhead efficiency variance
   (4) Variable overhead spending variance

b. Using all six variances from Part a, prepare an explanation of the $54,660 unfavorable variance between budgeted and actual costs for May 2000.

c. (1) Identify and briefly explain the behavioral factors that may promote friction among the production managers and the maintenance manager.
   (2) Evaluate Janice Rath's analysis of the unfavorable results in terms of its completeness and its effect on the behavior of the production groups.

(CMA adapted)

61. (Standard setting) Mark-Wright, Inc. (MWI), is a specialty frozen food processor located in the midwest. Since its founding in 1982, MWI has enjoyed a loyal local clientele that is willing to pay premium prices for the high quality frozen foods it prepares from specialized recipes. In the last two years, the company has experienced rapid sales growth in its operating region and has had many inquiries about supplying its products on a national basis. To meet this growth, MWI expanded its processing capabilities, which resulted in increased production and distribution costs. Furthermore, MWI has been encountering pricing pressure from competitors outside its normal marketing region.

As MWI desires to continue its expansion, Jim Condon, CEO, has engaged a consulting firm to assist MWI in determining its best course of action. The consulting firm concluded that, while premium pricing is sustainable in some areas, if sales growth is to be achieved, MWI must make some price concessions. Also, in order to maintain profit margins, costs must be reduced and controlled. The consulting firm recommended the institution of a standard cost system to better accommodate the changes in demand that can be expected when serving an expanded market area.

Condon met with his management team and explained the recommendations of the consulting firm. Condon then assigned the task of establishing standard costs to his management team. After discussing the situation with their respective staffs, the management team met to review the matter.

Jane Morgan, purchasing manager, advised at that meeting that expanded production would necessitate obtaining basic food supplies from other than MWI's traditional sources. This would entail increased raw material and shipping costs and may result in lower quality supplies. Consequently, these increased costs would need to be made up by the processing department if current cost levels are to be maintained or reduced.

Stan Walters, processing manager, countered that the need to accelerate processing cycles to increase production, coupled with the possibility of receiving lower grade supplies, can be expected to result in a slip in quality and a greater product rejection rate. Under these circumstances, per-unit labor utilization cannot be maintained or reduced, and forecasting future unit labor content becomes very difficult.

Tom Lopez, production engineer, advised that if the equipment is not properly maintained, and thoroughly cleaned at prescribed daily intervals, it can be anticipated that the quality and unique taste of the frozen food products will be affected. Jack Reid, vice-president of sales, stated that if quality cannot be maintained, MWI cannot expect to increase sales to the levels projected.

When Condon was apprised of the problems encountered by his management team, he advised them that if agreement could not be reached on appropriate standards, he would arrange to have them set by the consulting firm, and everyone would have to live with the results.

a. (1) Describe the major advantages of using a standard cost system.
    (2) Describe disadvantages that can result from using a standard cost system.
b. (1) Identify those who should participate in setting standards and describe the benefits of their participation in the standard-setting process.
    (2) Explain the general features and characteristics associated with the introduction and operation of a standard cost system that make it an effective tool for cost control.
c. What would be the consequences if Jim Condon has the standards set by the outside consulting firm?

(CMA)

62. *(Implementing a standard cost system)* Some executives believe that it is extremely important to manage "by the numbers." This form of management requires that all employees with departmental or divisional responsibilities spend time understanding the company's operations and how they are reflected by the company's performance reports. Managers are then expected to make their employees aware of important signposts that can be detected in performance reports. One of the various numerical measurement systems used by companies is standard costs.
a. Discuss the characteristics that should be present in a standard cost system to encourage positive employee motivation.
b. Discuss how a standard cost system should be implemented to positively motivate employees.
c. The use of variance analysis often results in "management by exception." Discuss the meaning and behavioral implications of "management by exception." Explain how employee behavior could be adversely affected when "actual to standard" comparisons are used as the basis for performance evaluation.

(CMA adapted)

63. *(Benefits of a standard cost system)* Standard cost accounting is a powerful concept that is important in finance and marketing. The marketing application of the concept is to develop and manage a balanced portfolio of products. Market share and market growth can be used to classify products for portfolio purposes, and the product classifications are often extended to the organizational units that make the product. The market share/growth classifications can be depicted in the following manner.

		MARKET SHARE	
		High	Low
MARKET GROWTH RATE	High	Rising Star	Question Mark
	Low	Cash Cow	Dog

Question marks are products that show high growth rates but have relatively small market shares, such as new products that are similar to their competitors'. Rising stars are high-growth, high-market share products that tend to mature into cash cows. Cash cows are slow-growing established products that can be "milked" for cash to help the question marks and introduce new products. The dogs are low-growth, low-market share items that are candidates for elimination or segmentation.

Understanding where a product falls within this market share/growth structure is important when applying a standard cost system.

a. Discuss the major advantages of using a standard cost accounting system.

b. Describe the kinds of information that are useful in setting standards and the conditions that must be present to support the use of standard costing.

c. Discuss the applicability or nonapplicability of using standard costing for a product classified as a

(1) cash cow.

(2) question mark.

(CMA)

⊙ ETHICS AND QUALITY DISCUSSIONS

64. Many manufacturing costs are easily controlled by use of a standard costing system and traditional variance analysis. Other organizational costs have historically been more difficult to control. Foremost among costs in this category are costs associated with legal work—both by inside and outside counsel. Adding to the difficulty of controlling costs are certain practices that have evolved in the legal industry, especially those used to account for how time is spent. [Note: The January 13, 1995, *Wall Street Journal* article "Ten Ways (Some) Lawyers (Sometimes) Fudge Bills" may provide a useful starting point.]

a. What differences between legal costs and costs such as direct material and direct labor make legal costs more difficult to control?

b. How could concepts used in standard costing for products be applied to other costs, including those incurred for legal work?

c. Provide six suggestions as to how firms could help control their legal costs. Discuss any impacts your suggestions might have on product quality/safety, employee productivity, organizational strategy, and loss contingencies. (A loss contingency is a loss that might occur in the future that would result from a current action. For example, if an airline were to stop doing plane maintenance, there is a high probably that some type of expensive failure would occur in the future.)

65. In today's business world, some customers treat suppliers almost like employees. Supplier representatives work in customers' factories, attend production meetings, place orders for parts, and have access to a variety of data, including sales forecasts. This environment is referred to as JIT II, which was developed to instill harmony for and create efficiencies within both customers and suppliers. JIT II's foundation is one of trust.

For example, in applying JIT II in Honeywell's Golden Valley plant in Minnesota, the company reduced inventory levels to those that can be measured in days rather than weeks or months, cut purchasing agents by one-fourth, and has received numerous suggestions as to part standardization so that products can retain their quality levels, but be made for less. (Note: This discussion was adapted from a January 13, 1995, *Wall Street Journal* article entitled "Strange Bedfellows: Some Companies

Let Suppliers Work On Site and Even Place Orders." This article may be useful to read before addressing the following questions.)

a. Discuss risks that customers bear when they allow suppliers to have access to critical inside information.

b. What types of costs would customers expect to save by having representatives of suppliers on-site? Explain.

c. How would responsibility for purchase price variances change when vendors are allowed to submit their own purchase orders?

d. Other than material price variances, how might the implementation of JIT II affect other standard costs or quantities?

e. How might the implementation of JIT II affect product quality?

66. Mera O'Brien was hired a month ago at the Jackson Division of the Denver Manufacturing Company. O'Brien supervises plant production and is paid $6,500 per month. In addition, her contract calls for a percentage bonus based on cost control. The company president has defined cost control as "the ability to obtain favorable cost variances from the standards provided."

After one month, O'Brien realized that the standards that were used at the Jackson Division were outdated. Since the last revision of standards, the Jackson Division had undergone some significant plant layout changes and installed some automated equipment, both of which reduced labor time considerably. However, by the time she realized the errors in the standards, she had received her first month's bonus check of $5,000.

a. Since the setting of the standards and the definition of her bonus arrangement were not her doing, O'Brien does not feel compelled to discuss the errors in the standards with the company president. Besides, O'Brien wants to buy a red turbo Porsche. Discuss the ethics of her not discussing the errors in the standards and/or the problems with the definition of cost control with the company president.

b. Assume instead that O'Brien has an elderly mother who has just been placed in a nursing home. The older O'Brien is quite ill and has no income. The younger O'Brien lives in an efficiency apartment and drives a six-year-old car so that she can send the majority of her earnings to the nursing home to provide for her mother. Discuss the ethics of her not discussing the errors in the standards and/or the problems with the definition of cost control with the company president.

c. Assume again the facts in Part b. Also assume that the company president plans to review and revise, if necessary, all production standards at the Jackson Division next year. Discuss what may occur if O'Brien does not inform the president of the problems with the standards at the current time. Discuss what may occur if O'Brien informs the president of all the facts, both professional and personal. Can you suggest a way in which she may keep a bonus and still have the standards revised? (Consider the fact that standard costs have implications for sales prices.)

67. Flower Mound Corporation needs to hire four factory workers who can run robotic equipment and route products through processing. All factory space is on a single floor. Labor standards have been set for product manufacturing.

At this time, the company has had ten experienced people apply for the available jobs. One of the applicants is David Sima. David is paralyzed and uses a wheelchair. He has several years' experience using the robotic equipment, but for him to use the equipment, the controls must be placed on a special panel and lowered. Willie Roberts, the personnel director, has interviewed David and has decided against hiring him because Willie does not believe David can work "up to the current labor standard."

a. How, if at all, would hiring a person with a physical disability affect labor variances (both rate and hours) if the standards had been set based on workers without physical disabilities? Provide a rationale for your answer.

b. If a supervisor has decided to hire a worker with a physical disability, how (if at all) should that worker's performance evaluations be affected? Provide a rationale for your answer.

c. What are the ethical implications of hiring people with physical disabilities in preference to those without physical disabilities? What are the ethical implications of hiring the people without physical disabilities in preference to those with physical disabilities?

d. Do you believe that the hiring of individuals with physical disabilities could come under the umbrella concept of "workplace diversity?" Why or why not?

e. On what bases should Willie Roberts make his decision to hire or not hire David Sima? Discuss what you believe to be the appropriate decision process. (Hint: Investigate the implications of the Americans with Disabilities Act before answering this question.)

68. **Marriott International Inc.** has one of America's most successful welfare-to-work programs. Even with intensive support (such as picking welfare trainees up for work, buying them clothes, and arranging for day care), "trainees often show up late, work slowly, fight with co-workers, and go AWOL, for reasons as simple as a torn stocking." (Milbank, *Wall Street Journal,* October 31, 1996).

Even so, the hotel and food-services chain indicated that, between July 1997 and December 1998, it will train and place 800 welfare recipients. The company did, however, tighten the program admission policies to reduce the number of "difficult cases" admitted per 16-participant group. (Note: The October 31, 1996, and July 15, 1997, *Wall Street Journal* articles "Hiring Welfare People, Hotel Chain Finds, Is Tough but Rewarding" and "Marriott Tightens Job Program Screening" may provide a useful starting point.)

a. Assume that you are the training director for this program in San Francisco. How would you explain Marriott's dedication to quality to your welfare-to-worker trainees?

b. Assume that you are Marriott's Head of Housekeeping in Boston. How would you develop a time standard for cleaning rooms? Would you have different standards for non-welfare-to-work trainees and welfare-to-work trainees in the program? For non-trainees and trainees? Explain the rationale for your answers in the form of a prepared discussion with your housekeeping employees.

69. An apparel industry code that seeks to eliminate sweatshops provides the following items: (1) a requirement to pay at least the local minimum wage or prevailing industry wage (which may be substantially below the U.S. minimum wage); (2) a limit of a 60-hour work week with at least one day off; (3) an end to child labor (though, in some countries, 14-year-olds could be employed), prison labor, and physical abuse; and (4) an independent monitoring of conditions in overseas factories used by U.S. companies. Manufacturers that conform to the code would receive a "no sweatshop" label for their products. (Note: The April 10, 1997, *Wall Street Journal* article "Sweatshop Pact: Good Fit or Threadbare?" may provide a useful starting point.)

a. Discuss your perceptions of the adequacy of this code of conduct for U.S. manufacturers.

b. If Vietnam's local minimum wage is $.20 per hour, do you believe that this should be the labor rate standard for a sneaker manufacturer operating in that country? Why or why not?

c. In determining labor time standards, should the standards for a 14-year-old worker be set differently from those for a 26-year-old worker? Why or why not?

70. State governments have instituted academic standards in English, history, math, and science. These standards specify what students should learn in what grades—in an attempt to end what is referred to as "social promotion." (Note: The December 15, 1997, *Forbes* article "The Fight for Higher Standards" may provide a useful starting point.)

a. Assume that you have been asked to chair your state's committee to develop the math standard for the sixth grade. What issues would you consider in setting the standard? (This question does not ask you to address the specific items that you believe the students should know, but rather the fundamental concepts that need to be considered before establishing the standard.)

b. Once the standard has been set, what circumstances might cause you to consider changing the standard? Why?

c. Should there be national, rather than state, standards for education? Discuss the rationale for your answer, including potential obstacles and how they might be overcome.

Chapter 10 Process Costing

Crowley Candy Co., Inc.

Crowley Candy is owned by "Bunny Baron" Gary Crowley and his wife, Mary. The 50-year-old New Orleans, Louisiana, company had its start as Merlin Candies, Inc., with the mass production of hollow chocolate Easter rabbits. Merlin's bunnies (chocolate, peanut butter, and white) are colorfully decorated and range in size from 3½ ounces to 2¼ pounds. The distinctive Merlin chocolate recipe is blended by a major producer, then shipped to New Orleans in 10-pound slabs, 20 tons at a time. Starting in November of each year, the plant and nearby warehouse begin filling up with cases and cases of boxed bunnies. During the majority of the year, three full-time production employees can handle the melting, tempering (a raising and lowering of temperature to obtain proper consistency) and molding of the chocolate. However, just before Easter, Crowley Candy becomes a two-shift per day operation that employs more than twenty people.

SOURCE: 1998 interview with Gary Crowley, Crowley Candy Co., Inc.

*T*he mass production of chocolate Easter bunnies is totally unlike the job order production process discussed in Chapters 2 and 4. *Crowley Candy*, like many other food producers, uses **process costing** to determine the product cost of its bunnies. Process costing is also used by manufacturers of bricks, gasoline, steel, paper, automobiles, and appliances. This costing method accumulates and assigns costs to units of production in companies that make large quantities of homogeneous products in a continuous mass production environment.

process costing

This chapter illustrates the two methods of calculating unit cost in a process costing system: the weighted average and FIFO methods. Once unit cost is determined, total costs are assigned to the units transferred out of a department and to that department's ending Work in Process Inventory.

INTRODUCTION TO PROCESS COSTING

LEARNING OBJECTIVE ❶
How does process costing differ from job order product costing?

process costing system

http:// www.bestfoods.com

In some ways, the cost accumulation in a process costing system is similar to job order product costing procedures. In a **process costing system**, as in a job order system, costs are accumulated by cost component in each production department. As units are transferred from one department to the next, unit costs are also transferred, so that a total production cost is accumulated by the end of production. In a job order system, accumulated departmental costs are assigned to specific jobs, which may be single units or batches of units. In contrast, in a process costing system, accumulated departmental costs are assigned to all the units that flowed through that department during the period. As indicated in Chapter 2, the valuation method chosen (actual, normal, or standard) affects which costs are included in the inventory accounts.

The two primary differences between job order and process costing are (1) the quantity of production for which costs are being accumulated at any one time and (2) the cost object to which the costs are assigned. For example, an entrepreneur who bakes cookies at home for specific orders would use a job order product costing system. The costs of the direct material, direct labor, and overhead associated with production of each baking job would be gathered and assigned to the individual jobs. The cost per cookie could be determined if all the cookies baked for the job were similar.

In contrast, bakeries such as *Entenmann's*, which makes over two million cookies a week, would not use a job order system because volume is simply too great and the cookies are reasonably homogeneous. At Entenmann's, direct material, direct labor, and overhead costs could be gathered during the period for each department and each product. Because a variety of cookies are produced in any department during a period, costs must be accumulated by and assigned to each type of cookie worked on during the period. Production does not have to be complete for costs to be assigned in a process costing system.

As shown in Exhibit 10-1, the costs of inventory components are accumulated in the accounts as the inventory flows through the production process. At the end of production, the accumulated costs must be assigned to all the units produced to determine the cost per unit for purposes of inventory measurement and calculation of cost of goods sold.

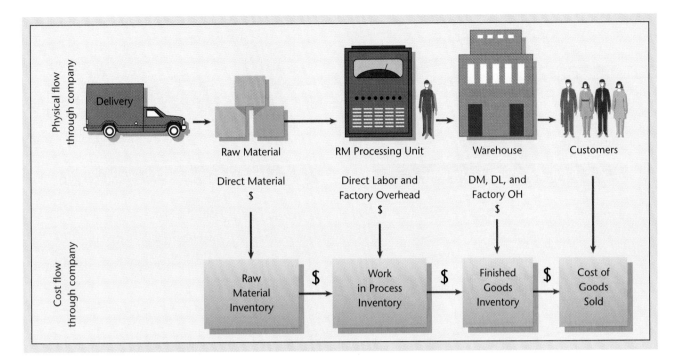

EXHIBIT 10-1
Flow of Costs through
Production

Exhibit 10-2 (page 450) presents the source documents and records used to initially assign costs to production departments during a period. The three products in the exhibit are started in the Mixing Department. Then Products A and B and their related production costs are transferred to the Baking Department. Additional costs in the Baking Department will attach to these products before they are sent to Finished Goods Inventory. Product C, however, does not need to be baked; thus its cost will consist only of material, labor, and overhead costs from the Mixing Department.

As in job order costing, the direct material and direct labor components of product cost present relatively few problems for cost accumulation and assignment. Direct material cost can be measured from the material requisition slips and invoiced prices; direct labor cost can be determined from the employee time sheets and wage rates for the period. These costs are assigned at the end of the period (usually weekly, biweekly, or monthly) from the departments to the units produced. Although direct material and direct labor are easily traced to production, overhead must be allocated to units.

Either an actual overhead amount or a predetermined rate may be used to assign overhead to products. If actual overhead is relatively constant each period and production volume is relatively steady over time, then using actual overhead costs provides a fairly stable production cost. If such conditions do not exist, application of actual overhead will yield fluctuating product costs, and a predetermined overhead rate (or rates) should be used.

Accumulating Costs by Separate Cost Components

Cost assignment in any process costing environment using actual costs is an averaging process. In general, and in the simplest of situations, a product's unit cost results from dividing a period's departmental production costs by that period's departmental quantity of production. However, in most situations, cost components are added at different points in the production process, and thus separate accumulations must be made for each cost component.

For a production operation to begin, some direct material must be introduced. Without any direct material, there would be no need for labor or overhead to be incurred. The material added at the start of production is 100 percent complete

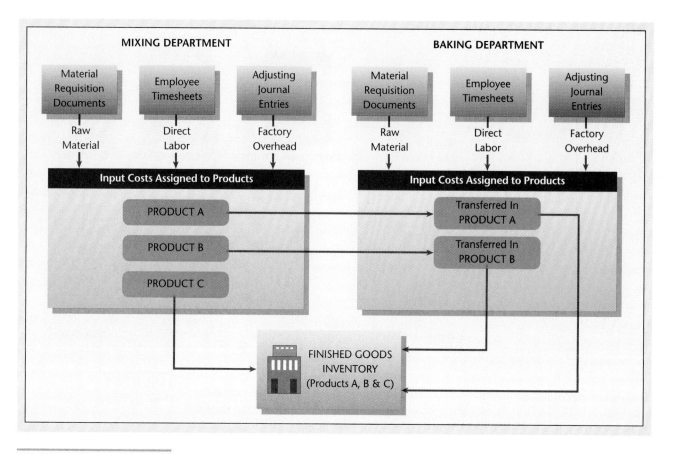

EXHIBIT 10-2

Cost Flows and Cost Assignments

throughout the process regardless of the percentage of completion of labor and overhead. For example, when chocolate rabbits are made, the chocolate must be added in full at the start of production.

Most production processes require more than one direct material. Additional materials may be added at any point or may be added continuously during processing. Materials may even be added at the end of processing. For example, the boxes into which Merlin's rabbits are placed for sale are direct material added at the end of processing. Thus, the rabbit is 0 percent complete as to the box at any point prior to the end of the production process, although other material and some labor and overhead may have been incurred. Exhibit 10-3 provides the production flow for the chocolate rabbit manufacturing process and illustrates the need for separate cost accumulations for each cost component.

As the exhibit shows, the material "chocolate" is 100 percent complete at any point in the rabbit production process after the start of production; no additional chocolate is added later. When labor and overhead reach the 95 percent completion point, a sugar eye and flower as well as a bow are added. Before the 95 percent point, the eyes, flowers, and bows were 0 percent complete; after this point, these materials are 100 percent complete. Last, the rabbits are boxed and are 100 percent complete. Thus, at the end of a period, rabbits could be anywhere in the production process. If, for example, the rabbits were 75 percent complete as to labor and overhead, they would be 100 percent complete as to chocolate, and 0 percent complete as to eyes, flowers, bows, and boxes.

When different components of a product are at different stages of completion, separate cost accumulations are necessary for each cost component. But a single cost accumulation can be made for multiple cost components that are at the same degree of completion. For example, separate cost accumulations would need to be made for the chocolate and the boxes. However, because the sugar eyes, sugar flowers, and bows are added at the same point, these can be viewed as one ingredient (decorations) and a single cost accumulation can be made for it. Additionally, because direct

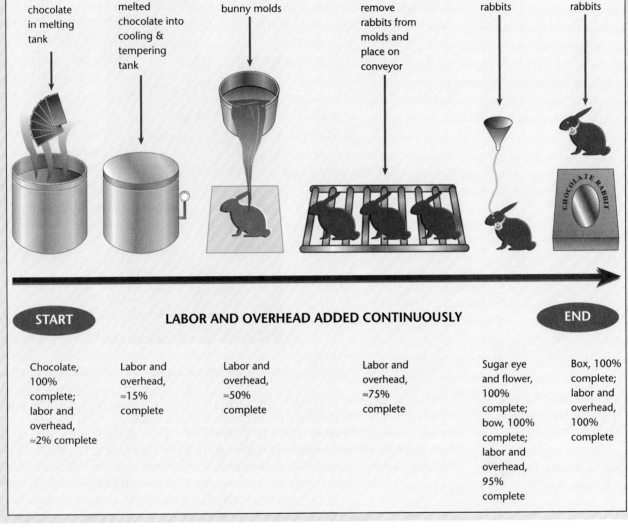

Place chocolate in melting tank

Pump melted chocolate into cooling & tempering tank

Pour into bunny molds

Cool; remove rabbits from molds and place on conveyor

Decorate rabbits

Box rabbits

START

LABOR AND OVERHEAD ADDED CONTINUOUSLY

END

Chocolate, 100% complete; labor and overhead, ≈2% complete

Labor and overhead, ≈15% complete

Labor and overhead, ≈50% complete

Labor and overhead, ≈75% complete

Sugar eye and flower, 100% complete; bow, 100% complete; labor and overhead, 95% complete

Box, 100% complete; labor and overhead, 100% complete

EXHIBIT 10-3

Chocolate Rabbit Manufacturing Process

labor and overhead are incurred at the same rate in the chocolate bunny-making process, these two components may be combined and one cost accumulation can be made for "conversion" as a single category.

In a process-costing environment, costs are accumulated by department and then by cost component for a single time period. Additionally, because most companies manufacture more than one type of product, costs must also be accumulated by product. For example, Crowley Candy would accumulate the costs of producing peanut butter three-ounce rabbits separately from the costs of producing white chocolate one-pound rabbits.

Calculating Equivalent Units of Production

After production costs have been accumulated by department and by cost component, they need to be assigned to the units produced during the period of cost accumulation. If all units were 100 percent complete at the end of each accounting period, units could simply be counted to obtain the denominator for cost assignment. But in most production processes an inventory of partially completed units exists at the end of each period. Any partially completed ending inventory of the current period becomes the partially completed beginning inventory of the next period. Process costing assigns costs to both fully and partially completed units by

Chocolate blocks are put into production at the beginning. At this stage, however, sugar decorations, bows, and boxes are not part of the process. Thus, it is necessary to calculate equivalent units of production for each cost component.

LEARNING OBJECTIVE ❷
Why are equivalent units of production used in process costing?

equivalent units of production (EUP)

converting partially completed units to equivalent whole units or equivalent units of production.

Equivalent units of production (EUP) approximate the number of whole units of output that could have been produced during a period from the actual effort expended during that period. Using EUP is necessary because using only completed units to determine unit cost would not clearly reflect all the work accomplished during a period. For instance, if forty-five partially completed units were determined to be two-thirds complete, these partially completed units would be counted as thirty $(45 \times \frac{2}{3})$ whole units. To calculate equivalent units of production for a period, it is necessary to multiply the number of actual units produced by their percentage of completion at the end of the period.

For example, assume Department One had no beginning inventory. During January, Department One produced 100,000 complete units and 10,000 units that were 20 percent complete. These incomplete units are in ending Work in Process Inventory. The period's equivalent units of production are 102,000 [(100,000 × 100%) + (10,000 × 20%)]. This quantity is used to calculate departmental equivalent unit product costs.

Use of equivalent units of production requires recognition of two factors related to inventory. First, units in beginning Work in Process Inventory were started last period but will be completed during the current period. This two-period production sequence means that some costs related to these units were incurred last period and additional costs will be incurred in the current period. Second, partially completed units in the ending Work in Process Inventory were started in the current period but will not be completed until the next period. Thus, current period production efforts on the ending Work in Process Inventory have caused costs to be incurred in this period and will cause additional costs to be incurred next period.

Qualified production personnel should inspect ending work in process units to determine what proportion of work was completed during the current period. The mathematical complement to this proportion represents the amount of work to be performed next period and is equal to one minus the percentage of work completed in the current period. Physical inspection at the end of last period provided the information about the work to be performed on the beginning inventory in the current period.

INTRODUCING WEIGHTED AVERAGE AND FIFO PROCESS COSTING

A primary purpose of any costing system is to determine product costs for financial statements. When goods are transferred from Work in Process Inventory of one department to another department or to Finished Goods Inventory, a cost must be assigned to those goods. In addition, at the end of any period, a cost amount must be assigned to goods that are only partially complete and still remain in Work in Process Inventory.

There are two primary alternative methods of accounting for cost flows in process costing: the **weighted average method** and the **FIFO** (first-in, first-out) **method**. These methods relate to the way in which physical cost flows are accounted for in the production process. In a very general way, it is helpful to relate these process costing approaches to the cost flow methods used in financial accounting.

In a retail business, the weighted average method is used to determine an average cost per unit of inventory. This cost equals the total cost of goods available divided by total units available. Total cost and total units are the sums of cost and unit information, respectively, for beginning inventory and purchases. Costs and units of the current period are not distinguished in any way from those of the prior period. In contrast, the FIFO method, in retail accounting, separates goods by when they were purchased and what they cost. Unit costs of beginning inventory are the first to be sent to Cost of Goods Sold; units in ending inventory are costed at the most recent purchase prices.

The use of these methods in costing manufactured goods is similar to their use in costing retail sales. The weighted average method computes an average cost per unit of production, while the FIFO method keeps beginning inventory and current period units and costs separated. The denominator used in the unit cost formula differs depending on which method is used. Both methods result in approximately the same unit costs unless a large cost change occurred between periods.

weighted average method

FIFO method

EUP CALCULATIONS AND COST ASSIGNMENT

Exhibit 10-4 (page 454) outlines the six steps necessary to determine the costs assignable to units completed and to units still in process at the end of a period in a process costing system. Each of these steps is discussed briefly, and then a complete example is provided for both weighted average and FIFO costing.

The first step is to calculate the total physical units for which the department is responsible, or the **total units to account for**. This amount is equal to the total number of units worked on in the department during the current period—beginning inventory units plus units started.

Second, determine what happened to the units to account for during the period. This step also requires the use of physical units, which may fit into one of two categories: (1) completed and transferred or (2) partially completed and remaining in Ending Work in Process Inventory.[1]

At this point, verify that the total units for which the department was accountable are equal to the total units that were actually accounted for. If these amounts are not equal, any additional computations will be incorrect.

Third, use either the weighted average or the FIFO method to determine the equivalent units of production for each cost component. If all materials are at the same degree of completion, a single materials computation can be made. If multiple materials are used and are placed into production at different points, multiple EUP

total units to account for

---

[1]Another category, that of spoilage or damaged units, does exist. It is assumed, for purposes of simplicity in this text, that such happenings do not occur.

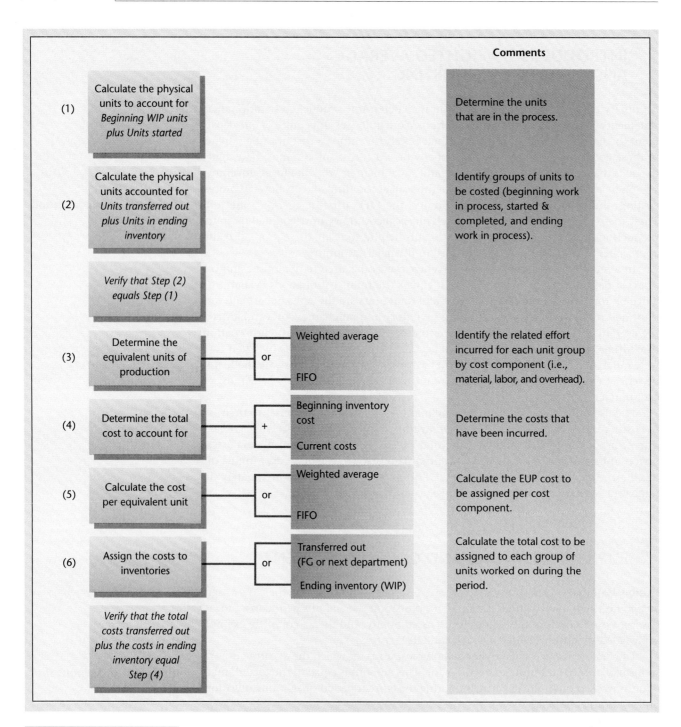

EXHIBIT 10-4

Steps in Process Costing

total cost to account for

calculations may be necessary for materials. If overhead is applied to production using direct labor as a base or if these two factors are always at the same degree of completion, a single EUP calculation can be made for conversion. If neither condition exists, separate EUP calculations must be prepared for labor and overhead.[2]

Fourth, find the **total cost to account for**, which includes the balance in Work in Process Inventory at the beginning of the period plus all current costs for direct material, direct labor, and overhead.

---

[2]As discussed in Chapters 4 and 5, overhead may be applied to products using machine hours or a variety of nontraditional allocation bases (such as number of machine set-ups, pounds of material moved, or number of material requisitions). The number of EUP computations required depends on the number of different cost pools and overhead allocation bases established in a department or company. If there are multiple cost pools and allocation bases, a separate computation will need to be made for each cost pool that is at a different level of completion. Additionally, some highly automated manufacturers may not account for direct labor cost separately (because it is too insignificant); thus, only a single conversion cost category would exist.

Fifth, compute the cost per equivalent unit for each cost component using either the weighted average or the FIFO equivalent units of production calculated in Step 3.

Sixth, use the costs computed in Step 5 to assign costs to the units completed and transferred from the production process and to the units remaining in ending Work in Process Inventory. After this cost assignment is made, verify that the total costs assigned equal the total costs accountable for from Step 4.

Chandra's Chocolates is used to demonstrate the steps involved in the computation of equivalent units of production and cost assignment for both methods of process costing. Chandra's Chocolates uses the same manufacturing process in making solid chocolate greeting cards as Merlin Candies uses in making Easter bunnies. Chandra's views the production process as consisting of two departments, Molding and Boxing. Chocolate is purchased from a vendor and is the only direct material. For purposes of simplicity, any decoration on the cards is minimal and considered part of overhead. Since the chocolate is added at the start of processing, all inventories are 100 percent complete as to material as soon as processing has begun. Labor and overhead are assumed to be added at the same rate throughout the production process. Exhibit 10-5 presents information for June 2000 regarding Chandra's production inventories and costs.

Although quantities are given for both cards transferred out of and cards remaining in ending inventory, it is not essential to provide both of these figures. The number of chocolate greeting cards remaining in process at June 30 can be calculated as the total cards to account for minus the cards completed and transferred during the period. Alternatively, the number of cards transferred out can be computed as the total cards to account for minus the cards in ending Work in Process Inventory.

Weighted Average Method

The weighted average method of computing equivalent units of production adds the units in beginning Work in Process Inventory to the units started during the current period to determine the maximum production for the period. The work performed during the period does not necessarily always result in complete units. The weighted average method is not concerned about what quantity of work was performed in the prior period on the units in beginning inventory. This method focuses only on units that are completed in the current period and units that remain in ending inventory.

STEP 1: Calculate the total units to account for

Units in beginning WIP Inventory	12,000
Units started during current period	115,500
Total units to account for	127,500

STEP 2: Calculate the total units accounted for

Units completed and transferred out	120,700
Units in ending WIP Inventory	6,800
Total units accounted for	127,500

EXHIBIT 10-5

Chandra's Chocolates Production and Cost Information—June 2000

Beginning inventory (30% complete as to conversion)		12,000
Cards started during current period		115,500
Cards completed and transferred to finished goods		120,700
Ending inventory (80% complete as to conversion)		6,800
Cost of beginning inventory:		
Direct material	$ 45,000.00	
Direct labor and overhead	4,678.60	$ 49,678.60
Current period costs:		
Direct material	$334,950.00	
Direct labor and overhead	202,191.00	537,141.00

The units detailed at this point (those transferred out and those in ending inventory) indicate the categories that will be assigned costs in the final step. Notice that the units accounted for in Step 2 equal the units to account for in Step 1.

Completed units are either (1) beginning inventory units that have been completed during the current period or (2) units started and completed during the period. The number of **units started and completed** (S&C) equals the total units completed during the period minus the units in beginning inventory. For Chandra's Chocolates, the number of units started and completed in June is (120,700 − 12,000) or 108,700.

units started and completed

STEP 3: Determine the equivalent units of production

LEARNING OBJECTIVE ❸
How are equivalent units of production computed using the weighted average and FIFO methods of process costing?

At the end of the period, the units in beginning inventory and the units that were started and completed this period are 100 percent complete as to all cost components. The units in ending inventory are 100 percent complete as to direct material, but only 80 percent complete as to labor and overhead. Since labor and overhead are at the same degree of completion, a single EUP conversion calculation can be made for both of these cost components.

The weighted average computations for equivalent units of production are as follows:

	DM EUP	CONVERSION (DL AND OH) EUP
BI (whole units × % complete)	12,000 × 100% = 12,000	12,000 × 100% = 12,000
Units started and completed (whole units × % complete)	108,700 × 100% = 108,700	108,700 × 100% = 108,700
EI (whole units × % complete)	6,800 × 100% = 6,800	6,800 × 80% = 5,440
EUP	127,500	126,140

Note that the first two lines of this schedule (BI and Units started and completed) are equal to the total units completed and transferred out (120,700) given in Step 2.

The weighted average method does not distinguish between units in beginning inventory and units entering production during the period. In this step, the method uses the number of whole units in beginning inventory and the number of units started and completed during the period. By doing so, the weighted average method treats beginning inventory units as though they were started and completed in the current period.

Only when all product components are placed into production at the same time and at the same rate will material, labor, and overhead all be at equal percentages of completion. Generally, the cost components are at different degrees of completion. In such cases, the completion percentage must be separately determined *for each cost component*. If the percentages of completion differ, separate EUP calculations must be made for each cost component.

STEP 4: Determine the total cost to account for

For Chandra's Chocolates, the total cost to account for is $586,819.60.

	DM	CONVERSION	TOTAL
BI cost	$ 45,000.00	$ 4,678.60	$ 49,678.60
Current period costs	334,950.00	202,191.00	537,141.00
Total cost to account for	$379,950.00	$206,869.60	$586,819.60

Total cost will be assigned in Step 6 to the goods transferred out to Finished Goods (or the next department) and to ending Work in Process Inventory in relation to the whole or equivalent whole units contained in each category.

LEARNING OBJECTIVE ❹
How are unit costs and inventory values calculated using the weighted average and FIFO methods of process costing?

STEP 5: Calculate the cost per equivalent unit of production

A cost per equivalent unit of production must be computed for each cost component for which a separate calculation of EUP is made. Because the weighted average method does not distinguish between units in beginning inventory and units started during the period, neither does it differentiate between beginning inventory costs and current period costs. The costs of beginning inventory and of the current period are summed for each cost component and averaged over that component's weighted average equivalent units of production. The calculation of unit cost for each cost component at the end of the period is as follows:

$$\text{Cost per Equivalent Unit} = \frac{\text{Beginning Inventory Cost} + \text{Current Period Cost}}{\text{Weighted Average Equivalent Units of Production}}$$

$$= \frac{\text{Total Cost Incurred}}{\text{Total Weighted Average Equivalent Units}}$$

Under the weighted average method, costs from two different periods are totaled to form the numerator of the unit cost equation, and units from two different periods are used in the denominator. This computation allows total costs to be divided by total units—the common weighted average approach which produces an average component cost per unit. The chocolate company's weighted average calculations for cost per EUP for material and conversion are as follows:

	DM	CONVERSION	TOTAL
Cost to account for (Step 5)	$379,950.00	$206,869.60	$586,819.60
Divided by EUP (Step 3)	÷ 127,500	÷ 126,140	
Cost per EUP	= $2.98	= $1.64	$4.62

The unit costs for the two product cost components are summed to yield the total production cost for all whole units completed during June. For Chandra's Chocolates, this cost is $4.62.

STEP 6: Assign costs to inventories

This step assigns total production costs to units of product. Cost assignment in a department involves determining the cost of (1) goods completed and transferred out during the period and (2) units in ending Work in Process inventory.

The cost of goods transferred out under the weighted average method results from multiplying the total number of units transferred by the total cost per EUP, which combines all component costs. Because this method is based on an averaging technique that combines prior and current period work, the period in which the transferred units were started is not important. All units and all costs have been commingled. The total cost transferred out for Chandra's Chocolates for June is ($4.62 × 120,700) or $557,634.

Ending Work In Process Inventory cost is based on the equivalent units of production for each cost component. The EUP are multiplied by the component cost per unit calculated in Step 5. Cost of ending inventory under the weighted average method is:

Ending Work in Process Inventory:
Direct material (6,800 × 100% × $2.98)	$20,264.00
Conversion (6,800 × 80% × $1.64)	8,921.60
Total cost of ending inventory	$29,185.60

The quantities that result from multiplying whole units by the percentage of completion are equal to the equivalent units of production.

The total costs assigned to transferred-out units and units in ending inventory must equal the total cost to account for. For Chandra's Chocolates, total cost to account for (Step 4) was $586,819.60, which equals transferred-out cost ($557,634) plus ending work in process cost ($29,185.60).

The steps just discussed can be combined into a **cost of production report**. This document details all manufacturing quantities and costs, shows the computation of cost per EUP, and indicates the cost assignment to goods produced during the period. Exhibit 10-6 (page 458) shows the cost of production report for Chandra's Chocolates under the weighted average process costing method.

LEARNING OBJECTIVE ❹
How are unit costs and inventory values calculated using the weighted average and FIFO methods of process costing?

LEARNING OBJECTIVE ❺
How is a cost of production report prepared?

cost of production report

EXHIBIT 10-6
Cost of Production Report
(Weighted Average Method)

PRODUCTION DATA	EQUIVALENT UNITS OF PRODUCTION		
	Whole Units	DM	Conversion
BI	12,000*	12,000	3,600
Units started	115,500		
To account for	127,500		
BI completed	12,000	0	8,400
S&C	108,700	108,700	108,700
Units completed	120,700		
EI	6,800†	6,800	5,440
Accounted for	127,500	127,500	126,140

COST DATA

	Total	DM	Conversion
BI cost	$ 49,678.60	$ 45,000.00	$ 4,678.60
Current period costs	537,141.00	334,950.00	202,191.00
Total cost to account for	$586,819.60	$379,950.00	$206,869.60
Divided by EUP		÷127,500	÷126,140
Cost per EUP	$4.62	$2.98	$1.64

COST ASSIGNMENT

Transferred out (120,700 × $4.62)		$557,634.00
Ending inventory:		
Direct material (6,800 × $2.98)	$ 20,264.00	
Conversion (5,440 × $1.64)	8,921.60	29,185.60
Total cost accounted for		$586,819.60

*Fully complete as to direct material; 30% as to conversion.
†Fully complete as to direct material; 80% as to conversion.

FIFO Method

As mentioned previously, the FIFO method of determining EUP more realistically reflects the way in which most goods actually physically flow through the production system. The FIFO method does not commingle units and costs of different periods, allowing this method to focus specifically on the work performed during the current period. Equivalent units and costs of beginning inventory are withheld from the computation of average current period cost.

Steps 1 and 2 are the same for the FIFO method as for the weighted average method because these two steps involve the use of physical units. Therefore, based on the data from Exhibit 10-5, the total units to account for and accounted for are 127,500.

STEP 3: Determine the equivalent units of production

LEARNING OBJECTIVE ③
How are equivalent units of production computed using the weighted average and FIFO methods of process costing?

Under FIFO, as mentioned, the work performed last period is not commingled with work of the current period. The EUP schedule for FIFO is as follows:

	DM EUP		CONVERSION (DL AND OH) EUP	
BI (whole units × % *not* completed in prior period)	12,000 × 0% =	0	12,000 × 70% =	8,400
Units started and completed (whole units × % complete)	108,700 × 100% =	108,700	108,700 × 100% =	108,700
EI (whole units × % complete)	6,800 × 100% =	6,800	6,800 × 80% =	5,440
EUP		115,500		122,540

Under FIFO, only the work performed on the beginning inventory *during the current period* is shown in the EUP schedule. This work equals the whole units in beginning inventory multiplied by a percentage equal to (1 − the percentage of work done in the prior period). In the Chandra's Chocolates example, no additional direct material is needed in June to complete the 120 units in the beginning inventory. Because beginning inventory was only 30 percent complete as to conversion, the company needs to complete the other 70 percent more conversion on the 12,000 beginning inventory cards during June—or the equivalent of 8,400 units.

The remaining figures in the FIFO EUP schedule are the same as those for the weighted average method. The *only* difference between the weighted average and FIFO EUP computations is that the work performed in the prior period on beginning inventory is not included in current period EUP. This difference is equal to the number of units in beginning inventory multiplied by the percentage of work performed in the prior period. A reconciliation of EUPs determined by the two methods follows.

	DM	CONVERSION
FIFO EUP	115,500	122,540
Plus the EUP in BI (work completed in the prior period:		
DM, 100%; Conversion, 30%)	12,000	3,600
Weighted Average EUP	127,500	126,140

STEP 4: Determine the total cost to account for

This step is the same as under the weighted average method. The total cost to account for is $586,819.60.

STEP 5: Calculate the cost per equivalent unit of production

Because cost determination is made on the basis of equivalent units of production, results under FIFO differ from those obtained under the weighted average method. The calculations for cost per equivalent unit reflect the difference between the quantities that the methods use for beginning inventory. The EUP calculation for FIFO ignores work performed on beginning inventory during the prior period; correspondingly, the FIFO cost per EUP computation also ignores prior period costs and uses only costs incurred in the current period. The FIFO cost per EUP calculation is as follows:

LEARNING OBJECTIVE ❹
How are unit costs and inventory values calculated using the weighted average and FIFO methods of process costing?

$$\text{Cost Per Equivalent Unit} = \frac{\text{Current Period Cost}}{\text{FIFO Equivalent Units of Production}}$$

Calculations for Chandra's Chocolates are:

	DM	CONVERSION	TOTAL
Current period costs	$334,950.00	$202,191.00	$537,141.00
Divided by EUP (Step 3)	÷115,500	÷122,540	
Cost per EUP	$2.90	$1.65	$4.55

The production cost for each whole unit produced during June under the FIFO method is $4.55.

It is useful to recognize the difference between the two total cost computations. The weighted average total cost of $4.62 is the average total cost of each unit completed during June, *regardless of when production was begun*. The FIFO total cost of $4.55 is the total cost of each unit that was *both started and completed* during the current period. The $.07 difference results from the difference in treatment of beginning Work in Process Inventory costs.

STEP 6: Assign costs to inventories

The FIFO method assumes that the units in beginning inventory are completed first during the current period, and thus are the first units transferred out. The remaining units transferred out during the period were both started and completed in the current

LEARNING OBJECTIVE ❹
How are unit costs and inventory values calculated using the weighted average and FIFO methods of process costing?

period. As shown in the cost of production report in Exhibit 10-7, the two-step computation needed to determine the cost of goods transferred out distinctly presents this FIFO logic.

The first part of the cost assignment for units transferred out relates to the beginning inventory units. These units had material and some conversion costs attached to them at the start of the period. These prior period costs were not included in the cost-per-EUP calculations in Step 5. Finishing these units required current period work, and therefore current period costs. To determine the total cost of finished units in beginning inventory, the costs associated with the beginning inventory are added to the current period costs needed to complete those units.

The second part of the cost assignment for units transferred out relates to the units that were started and completed in the current period. The cost of these units is based on current period costs.

This two-step transferred-out cost assignment process is shown below using the Chandra's Chocolates information. The company had 12,000 units in the beginning June inventory and transferred out a total of 120,700 units during the month.

EXHIBIT 10-7

Cost of Production Report (FIFO Method)

PRODUCTION DATA	EQUIVALENT UNITS OF PRODUCTION		
	Whole Units	*DM*	*Conversion*
BI	12,000*	12,000	3,600
Units started	115,500		
To account for	127,500		
BI completed	12,000	0	8,400
S&C	108,700	108,700	108,700
Units completed	120,700		
EI	6,800†	6,800	5,440
Accounted for	127,500	115,500	122,540

COST DATA			
	Total	*DM*	*Conversion*
BI cost	$ 49,678.60		
Current period costs	537,141.00	$334,950.00	$202,191.00
Total cost to account for	$586,819.60		
Divided by EUP		÷115,500	÷122,540
Cost per EUP	$4.55	$2.90	$1.65

COST ASSIGNMENT		
Transferred out		
Beginning inventory costs	$ 49,678.60	
Cost to complete:		
Conversion (8,400 × $1.65)	13,860.00	
Total cost of BI transferred	$ 63,538.60	
Started & completed (108,700 × $4.55)	494,585.00	$558,123.60
Ending inventory:		
Direct material (6,800 × $2.90)	$ 19,720.00	
Conversion (5,440 × $1.65)	8,976.00	28,696.00
Total cost accounted for		$586,819.60

*Fully complete as to direct material, 30% as to conversion. The quantities under EUP for this line are not included in the final EUP summation.
†Fully complete as to direct material, 80% as to conversion.

Transferred out:

(1) Beginning inventory (prior period costs)	$ 49,678.60
Completion of beginning inventory:	
Direct material (12,000 × 0% × $2.90)	0.00
Conversion (12,000 × 70% × $1.65)	13,860.00
Total cost of beginning inventory transferred	$ 63,538.60
(2) Units started and completed (108,700 × $4.55)	494,585.00
Total cost of units transferred out	$558,123.60

Because the chocolate greeting cards in beginning inventory were 100 percent complete as to direct material, no additional material was added during the month. At the start of the month, units were only 30 percent complete as to conversion, so 70 percent of the conversion work is performed during June at current period costs. The units started and completed are costed at the total current period FIFO cost of $4.55 because all work on these units was performed during the current period.

The method of calculating the cost of ending Work in Process Inventory is the same under both the FIFO and weighted average methods. Although the number of equivalent units is the same under both methods, cost per unit differs. Ending work in process cost under FIFO is as follows:

Ending inventory:	
Direct material (6,800 × 100% × $2.90)	$19,720.00
Conversion (6,800 × 80% × $1.65)	8,976.00
Total cost of ending inventory	$28,696.00

The total cost of the units transferred ($558,123.60) plus the cost of the ending inventory units ($28,696.00) equals the total cost to be accounted for ($586,819.60).

Cost assignment is easier for the weighted average method than for the FIFO method. However, simplicity is not the only consideration in choosing a cost flow method. The FIFO method reflects the actual physical flow of goods through production. Furthermore, when period costs do fluctuate, the FIFO method gives managers better information with which to control costs and on which to base decisions because it does not combine costs of different periods. In addition, the FIFO method focuses on current period costs, and managerial performance is usually evaluated on the basis of costs incurred only in the current period.

PROCESS COSTING WITH STANDARD COSTS

All examples in the chapter use actual historical costs to assign values to products under either the weighted average method or FIFO method. Companies may prefer to use standard rather than actual costs for inventory measurement purposes. The use of standard costs simplifies process costing and allows variances to be measured during the period. Actual costing requires that a new production cost be computed each production period. Standard costing eliminates such recomputations, although standards do need to be reviewed (and possibly revised) at least once a year to keep the amounts current. The News Note on page 462 illustrates a food processing business in which labor standards would be quite useful.

Calculations of equivalent units of production for standard process costing are identical to those for FIFO process costing. Unlike the weighted average method, both standard costing and FIFO emphasize the measurement and control of current production and current period costs. The commingling of units and costs that occurs when the weighted average method is used reduces the emphasis on current effort that standard costing is intended to represent and measure.

In a standard cost process costing system, actual costs of the current period are recorded and are compared with the standard costs of the equivalent units of

LEARNING OBJECTIVE 6
What use do standard costs have in a process costing system?

You Can Do *How Many* of Those in an Hour?

The business of Motivatit is seafood. In the company's processing plant in Houma, Louisiana, workers wear thick rubber aprons as they face metal tables piled with fresh, salty-smelling oysters. These professional shuckers pick up an oyster and, hammer in hand, crack the hinge holding the shells together; then the shuckers pry the oysters open, scoop out the meat with a small knife, and toss the meat and shells into separate buckets.

This hands-on approach is unusual in the food processing industry, in which most plants are highly automated. In these environments, workers appear to spend their hours monitoring and assisting fast-moving, computerized machines.

But at Motivatit Seafood, removing the shells and meats from oysters, crabs, and crawfish is too gentle and dexterous for machines to handle completely. Although half-shelled oysters move down an assembly line, human hands seem to do the real work. And at what pace? The best shuckers can repeat the rhythmic hammering, prying, and tossing motion at the rate of almost 500 oysters per hour . . . thereby setting a high standard against which to measure actual production activity.

SOURCE: Bruce Brumberg and Karen Alexrod, "Tastes of Louisiana," New Orleans *Times-Picayune*, September 1, 1996, pp. E-1, E-5.

production. If actual costs are less than standard, there is a favorable variance; unfavorable variances arise if actual costs are greater than the standard. Units are transferred out of a department at the standard cost of each production element.[3]

PROCESS COSTING IN A MULTI-DEPARTMENTAL SETTING

LEARNING OBJECTIVE 7
What is the effect of multi-departmental processing on the computation of equivalent units of production?

Most companies have multiple, rather than single, department processing facilities. In a multi-departmental processing environment, goods are transferred from a predecessor department to a successor department. For example, the production of chocolate greeting cards at Chandra's Chocolates was said to occur in two departments: Molding and Boxing.

As illustrated in Exhibit 10-1, manufacturing costs always follow the physical flow of goods. Therefore, the costs of completed units of predecessor departments are treated as input material costs in successor departments. Such a sequential treatment requires the use of an additional cost component element called "transferred in" or "prior department cost." This element always has a percentage of completion factor of 100 percent, since the goods would not have been transferred out of the predecessor department if they had not been fully complete. The transferred-in element is handled the same as any other cost element in the calculations of EUP and cost per EUP.

A successor department may add additional raw material to the units that have been transferred in or may simply provide additional labor, with the corresponding incurrence of overhead. Anything added in the successor department requires its own cost element column for calculating equivalent units of production and cost per equivalent unit (unless the additional elements have the same degree of completion, in which case they can be combined).

[3]Standard costing and variances are discussed in depth in Chapter 9.

As goods flow through the production process, so do their related costs. Decorating and boxing often occur in a separate department of a multi-departmental plant.

Occasionally, successor departments may change the unit of measure used in predecessor departments. For example, when Chandra's Chocolates produces ½-ounce chocolate Easter eggs, the measure in the Molding Department might be number of eggs; the Packaging Department, however, might use bags of eggs as the measure. Assume that the Molding Department transferred 60,000 chocolate eggs to the next department. If the Packaging Department measures production in 25-count bags of eggs, that department would need to record the receipt as 2,400 bags (60,000 ÷ 25) transferred in.

Exhibit 10-8 (page 464) provides a cost of production report for the Boxing Department at Chandra's Chocolates. Weighted average unit costs from Exhibit 10-6 are used for the units transferred in from the previous department. In this department, chocolate greeting cards are placed in cellophane-fronted cardboard boxes and sealed for customer delivery. The beginning inventory is assumed to be 100 percent complete as to transferred-in units and cost, zero percent complete as to packaging, and 90 percent complete as to conversion. The ending inventory is assumed to be 100 percent complete as to transferred-in units and cost, zero percent complete as to packaging, and 75 percent complete as to conversion. The Boxing Department uses the weighted average process costing method.

LEARNING OBJECTIVE ⑤
How is a cost of production report prepared?

REDUCING SPOILAGE BY IMPLEMENTING QUALITY PROCESSES

This chapter has assumed that there is no nonconforming production; but in reality, most businesses do produce some spoiled or defective units. While accounting for

EXHIBIT 10-8

Multi-Departmental Setting—
Boxing Department
(Weighted Average Method)

PRODUCTION DATA		EQUIVALENT UNITS OF PRODUCTION		
	Whole Units	*Transferred in*	*DM*	*Conversion*
BI	9,300*	9,300	0	8,370
Units transferred in	120,700			
To account for	130,000			
BI completed	9,300	0	9,300	930
S&C	113,100	113,100	113,100	113,100
Units completed	122,400			
EI	7,600†	7,600	0	5,700
Accounted for	130,000	130,000	122,400	128,100

COST DATA				
	Total	*Transferred in*	*DM*	*Conversion*
BI cost	$ 44,930.30	$ 41,666	$ 0	$ 3,264.30
Current period costs	642,329.70	557,634	36,720	47,975.70
Total cost to account for	$687,260.00	$599,300	$ 36,720	$51,240.00
Divided by EUP		÷130,000	÷122,400	÷128,100
Cost per EUP	$5.31	$4.61	$.30	$.40

COST ASSIGNMENT		
Transferred out (122,400 × $5.31)		$649,944
Ending inventory:		
Transferred in (7,600 × $4.61)	$35,036	
Conversion (5,700 × $.40)	2,280	37,316
Total cost accounted for		$687,260

*Fully complete as to transferred-in; 0% as to direct material; 90% as to conversion.
†Fully complete as to transferred-in; 0% as to direct material; 75% as to conversion.

spoilage is beyond the scope of this text,[4] managers should always be alert for ways to minimize spoilage in a production process. The control aspect of quality implementation requires knowledge of the answers to three specific questions:

LEARNING OBJECTIVE 8
How can quality control minimize spoilage?

1. What does the spoilage actually cost?
2. Why does the spoilage occur?
3. How can the spoilage be controlled?

Many companies find it difficult, if not impossible, to answer the question of what spoilage (or lack of quality) costs. One cause of this difficulty is a traditional method of handling spoilage in process costing situations. Under a technique called the **method of neglect**, spoiled units are simply excluded from the equivalent units of production schedule. The total cost of producing both good and spoiled units is assigned solely to the good units, raising the cost of those units. Because the spoiled units are excluded from the extensions in the equivalent units schedule, the costs of those units are effectively buried and hidden in magnitude from managers. In a job order costing environment, an estimate of spoilage cost is often added to total budgeted overhead when the predetermined overhead rate is calculated. When this occurs, spoilage cost is again hidden and ignored.

method of neglect

In service organizations, the cost of spoilage may be even more difficult to determine because spoilage, from a customer's viewpoint, is poor service; the customer simply may not do business with the organization again. Such a cost is not processed by the accounting system. Thus, in all instances, a potentially significant dollar amount

---

[4]Accounting for spoilage can be found in any cost accounting text.

Quality control is extremely important in any food processing company. Even with the best equipment, breakage occurs, but in producing chocolate, such errors can be recycled by remelting.

of loss from nonconformance to requirements is unavailable for investigation as to its planning, controlling, and decision-making ramifications.

As to the second question, managers may be able to pinpoint the reasons for spoilage or poor service but those managers may have a mindset that condones lack of control. First, the managers may believe that a particular cause creates only a minimal amount of spoilage; because of this attitude, they settle for an accepted quality level with some tolerance for error. These error tolerances are built into the system and they become justifications for problems. Production is graded on a curve that allows for a less-than-perfect result.

Incorporating error tolerances into the production system and combining such tolerances with the use of the method of neglect results in a situation in which managers do not have the information necessary to determine how much spoilage is costing the company. Therefore, although they believe that the quantity and cost of spoiled goods are minimal, the managers do not have historical or even estimated accounting amounts on which to base such a conclusion. If managers were aware of the spoilage cost, they could make more informed decisions about whether to ignore the problem causing the spoilage or try to correct its causes.

In other instances, managers may believe that spoilage is uncontrollable. In some cases, this belief is accurate. For example, when a printing press converts from one job to the next, some pages are consistently misprinted. The number is not large, and process analysis has proved that the cost of attempting to correct this production defect would be significantly greater than the savings resulting from the correction. But in most production situations and almost every service situation, the cause of spoiled goods or poor service is controllable. It is only necessary to determine the cause and institute corrective action.

Spoilage has often been controlled through a process of inspecting goods or, in the case of service organizations, surveying customers. Now, companies are deciding that if quality is *built into* a process to prevent defects, there will be less need for inspections or surveys, because spoilage and poor service will be minimized. The goal is, then, to maintain quality through process *control* rather than output *inspection and observation*. Exhibit 10-9 (page 466) contrasts the traditional and total quality management viewpoints on quality.

Many companies are now implementing quality programs to minimize defects or poor service. These companies often employ **statistical process control (SPC)** techniques to analyze their processes for situations that are out of control and creating

statistical process control (SPC)

EXHIBIT 10-9
Contrasting Quality Paradigms

TRADITIONAL PARADIGM	TQM PARADIGM
Responsibility for Quality	
Worker is responsible for poor quality	Everyone is responsible for poor quality
Quality problems start in operations	Majority of the quality problems start long before the operations stage
Inspect quality in	Build quality in
After-the-fact inspection	Quality at the source
Quality inspectors are the gatekeepers of quality	Operators are responsible for quality reliability
Quality control department has large staff	Quality control department has small staff
The focus of the quality control department is to reject poor quality output	The focus of the quality control department is to monitor and facilitate the process
Managers and engineers have the expertise; workers serve their needs	Workers have the expertise; managers and engineers serve their needs
Linkages with Suppliers	
Procure from multiple suppliers	Procure from a single supplier
Acceptance sampling of inputs at point of receipt	Certify suppliers who can deliver the right quantity, right quality, and on time; no incoming inspection
New Product/Service Development	
Separate designers from operations	Use teams with operations, marketing, and designers
Design for performance (with more parts, more features—not to facilitate operations)	Design for performance and ease of processing
Overall Quality Goal	
Zero defects is not practical	Zero defects is the goal
Mistakes are inevitable and have to be inspected out	Mistakes are opportunities to learn and become perfect
It costs too much to make defect-free products	Quality is free
A "reasonable" tradeoff is the key	Perfection is the key; perfection is a journey, not a destination

SOURCE: John K. Shank and Vijay Govindarajan, "Measuring the 'Cost of Quality': A Strategic Cost Management Perspective," *Journal of Cost Management* (Summer 1994), p. 10. Reprinted with permission from *The Journal of Cost Management*, © 1994, Warren, Gorham & Lamont, 31 St. James Avenue, Boston, Mass. 02116. All rights reserved.

spoilage. SPC techniques are based on the theory that a process varies naturally over time from normal, random causes but that some variations occur that fall outside the limits of the natural variations. These uncommon or special-cause variations are typically the points at which the process produces errors, which may be defective goods or poor service. Often, these variations can be—and have been—eliminated by the installation of computer-integrated manufacturing systems, which have internal controls to evaluate tolerances and sense production problems. The control charts discussed in Chapter 3 are one of many SPC techniques used to analyze process results relative to a benchmark, or standard, and in relation to the amount of variation expected in a stable (controlled) process.

SPC requires that persons involved in a problem area select a relevant measure of performance and track that performance measurement over time. The measures selected to prepare control charts for manufacturing companies are nonfinancial ones, such as number of defective products, nonconformances in tolerance levels, and unexpected work slowdowns or stoppages. In service organizations, quality measures used to prepare SPC charts often reflect key indicators of good performance as indicated in the accompanying News Note.

SPC allows the individuals involved in a process to become the quality control monitors and helps to eliminate the need for quality inspections. Thus, the accepted quality level can be raised and the defects reduced significantly. For instance, the *six sigma* defects goal (no more than 3.4 defects per million—or 99.9997% perfect) has been met by several world-class companies that are now attempting to reduce that level to defects per billion. Such a goal is not unusual for companies competing in global, world-class environments.

The development, implementation, and interpretation of an SPC system requires a firm grasp of statistics and is well beyond the scope of this text. However, it is essential for managers and accountants to recognize the usefulness of such a tool in determining why problems occur. The important managerial concern regarding spoilage is to *control* it; properly *accounting for* spoilage costs is a first step in helping managers determine how spoilage can be controlled. Quality control programs can be implemented to develop ideas on redesigning products for higher quality, determine where quality control problems exist, measure the costs associated with those problems, and make a more informed cost-benefit analysis of problem correction.

NEWS NOTE

What Will Be Measured in a Service Company?

Service organizations all share common features that differ from manufacturing. These features include direct contact with the customer, large volumes of transactions and processing, and often large amounts of paperwork. It is easy to see that the sources of error are considerable in recording transactions and in processing. It is not unusual to see a newspaper report of a large error in billing that amounts to thousands or hundreds of thousands of dollars.

Although control charts were first developed and used in a manufacturing context, they are easily applied to service organizations. The major difference is the quality characteristic that is controlled. Many of the standards used in service industries form the basis for quality control charts. Listed below are just a few of the many potential applications of control charts for services.

Organization	Quality Measure
Hospital	lab test accuracy
	on-time delivery of meals and medication
Bank	check-processing accuracy
Insurance company	claims-processing accuracy
	billing accuracy
Post office	sorting accuracy
	time of delivery
	percent express mail delivered on time
Ambulance	response time
Police department	incidence of crime in a precinct
	number of traffic citations
Hotel	proportion of rooms satisfactorily cleaned
	number of complaints received
Transportation	proportion of freight cars correctly routed
Auto service	percent of time work completed as promised
	number of parts out of stock

SOURCE: James R. Evans and William M. Lindsay, *The Management and Control of Quality* (St. Paul: West Publishing Company, 1993), pp. 565–66.

SITE ANALYSIS

Crowley Candy Co., Inc.

Originally, production operations at Crowley Candy were fairly simple: mass production of chocolate Easter rabbits with setups required only to change the size or flavor. Production costs were accumulated by "bunny batch" and were well-known, with the majority of cost attributable to the cost of chocolate and boxes. Labor costs were predominantly at the minimum wage.

But limiting production to Easter bunnies also significantly limited Crowley's ability to generate cash flow—after all, there is not a large demand for chocolate rabbits in November. So Gary Crowley decided to expand his product variety to include chocolate Christmas wreaths, boxed Mardi Gras chocolate comedy/tragedy masks, chocolate greeting cards, and sugar-free chocolate bars. In addition, companies can order logo-imprinted chocolate cards to give to their suppliers, customers, or employees for special occasions.

This diversity in product line has helped the company in several ways. First, cash flow is much more stable throughout the year. Second, the special recipe chocolate made by a Pennsylvania supplier can be ordered in more consistent quantities to ensure a steady supply of the type and quality of chocolate necessary for production. Third, plant capacity is used more effectively throughout the year rather than sitting idle between Easter and early July as was previously the case. Fourth, because the cost system is so well developed, the cost of the new products can be traced to the independent batches of goods produced. Fifth, the quality measures that have worked so well with the original products have been extended to the new product lines. There is little room for waste in a business that relies on a specially made direct material. Last, and very importantly, there are now year-round alternatives to having hidden stocks of Easter bunnies in the house for people who love Crowley's chocolate!

SOURCE: 1998 interview with Gary Crowley, Crowley Candy Co., Inc.

CROSS-FUNCTIONAL APPLICATIONS

TOPIC OF NOTE	DISCIPLINE	CROSS-FUNCTIONAL APPLICATIONS
Cost of Production Report (CPR)	Production Management	The CPR provides a basis for evaluating the performance of a department or a process. Production managers can compare the quantity and cost data in the CPR with predetermined goals to ascertain if operations are proceeding as planned. Actual variations from the plan often suggest problems or opportunities that can benefit the firm if they are identified early.
	Operations Research and Quality Control	When statistical process controls are combined with process costing, the CPR can be used to control and improve a manufacturing process. Often, small or nondestructive sampling can predict acceptable product defects. When variation from expected operating limits occurs, researchers must study the situation to bring the process back into control. A machine in a state of disrepair could spoil excessive material and drive process costs up. This problem could be detected on a detailed CPR and corrected.

CROSS-FUNCTIONAL APPLICATIONS

TOPIC OF NOTE	DISCIPLINE	CROSS-FUNCTIONAL APPLICATIONS
Cost of Production Report (CPR) (continued)	Economics	Economists use CPRs to validate their models of cost structure. The report will assist them in determining whether unit costs, marginal costs, and total costs are reasonable. Because economic cost models proceed from different assumptions and methods than accountants employ, the two approaches can validate one another.
	Market Research	Because cost is a key determinant in the formation of an acceptable selling price, marketers must be aware of CPR data to justify profitability per unit of sale. In addition, pricing policies are frequently related to quantity sold. For example, a small order may be priced on such CPR considerations as excessive units in ending inventory or idle plant capacity. Market share may pivot, in part, on production capacity. Marketers can use the CPR to obtain facts in both capacity and pricing decisions.
	Service Firms	Service firms, such as larger, well-established law firms, use their legal time management system (LTM) to produce cost of production reports. Attorneys are assigned an hourly billing rate related to their competency and level of responsibility. Disbursements (such as supplies or payroll of non-legal staff) can be assigned to a materials or overhead account. Ultimately, billing hours, supplies, and overhead can be allocated to a functional department (such as litigation or legal research). A CPR can focus a service firm manager's attention on inefficiencies, savings, and profitability.
	Financial Accounting	CPR data can support the cost of goods sold information and yield a better understanding of gross margins. This, in turn, provides decision makers more accurate information concerning cash flows related to operating activities.
Statistical Process Control (SPC)	Purchasing	When a firm's product quality depends upon a supplier's materials or subassemblies, it often insists on specific quality standards. A supplier's dependability for quality, service, and delivery time may qualify it as the firm's certified supplier. In addition, the two firms may share technical support as a means of preventing defects. These efforts can be reflected in the customer firm's SPC charts.
	Quality Control Engineers	Quality assurance is significantly increased when SPC is combined with computer-integrated manufacturing systems. Errors and defects are minimized by monitoring the process to prevent their occurrence. Corrections can be made to faulty processes, although not all errors are correctable. Pilots in the airline industry use a variation of SPC in their flight management system to warn them of a questionable flight decision or in-flight hazard before it is too late to correct. Testing and inspection are still necessary to verify the quality conformance; however, the frequency and cost should be reduced.
	Human Resource Management	HR managers benefit from SPC by focusing their resources for training, motivation, and evaluation where it is most critically needed. While rewards and evaluations are often left up to particular department managers in larger organizations, employee training is usually an important function of HR. SPC charts, which are often expressed in nonfinancial

CROSS-FUNCTIONAL APPLICATIONS

TOPIC OF NOTE	DISCIPLINE	CROSS-FUNCTIONAL APPLICATIONS
Statistical Process Control (SPC) *(continued)*	Human Resource Management *(continued)*	measurements, can be used to evaluate employee compliance with quality standards. A "quality team" of employees and a quality chart of desirable performance can help HR to motivate employees, especially when job evaluations and rewards are tied in.
	Design and Manufacturing Engineers	Design engineers are pressed to modify their products from many sides, especially from marketers and production managers. The SPC chart communicates a quality or safety conformity to designers. Bad designs are frequently the basis of product liability litigation. Also, the design and manufacturing engineers must review SPC charts, often adjusting them to reflect changes, such as more convenient processing methods or new technology installations.
	Marketing	Marketers, especially in high technology markets, can use SPC charts as a promotional strategy. This could give a firm access to quality-conscious customers, perhaps even those who certify their suppliers. With the globalization of industry and mega-mergers at hand, firms are pressured to share the technical support systems, and SPC charts can coordinate that arrangement.

CHAPTER SUMMARY

Process costing is used in manufacturing companies producing large quantities of homogeneous products. It is an averaging method used to assign manufacturing costs to units of production for purposes of planning, controlling, decision making, and preparing financial statements.

Either the weighted average or the FIFO method can be used to compute equivalent units of production and assign costs in a process costing system. The difference between the two methods lies solely in the way work performed in the prior period on the beginning Work in Process Inventory is treated. Under the weighted average method, work on beginning inventory is combined with current period work, and the total costs are averaged over all units. Under the FIFO method, work performed in the last period on beginning Work in Process Inventory is not commingled with current period work, nor are costs of beginning Work in Process Inventory added to current period costs to derive unit production cost. With FIFO, current period costs are divided by current period production to generate a unit production cost related entirely to work performed in the current period.

The six basic steps necessary to derive and assign product cost under a process costing system are listed in Exhibit 10-4. Equivalent units of production must be calculated for each cost component. In multi-departmental process environments, costs must be tracked as the goods move through departments and from one department to the next. The tracking takes place through the use of a transferred-in cost component for EUP and cost per EUP computations. Other cost components include direct material, direct labor, and overhead. If different materials have different degrees of completion, each material is considered a separate cost component. If overhead is applied on a direct labor basis or is incurred at the same rate as direct labor, labor and overhead may be combined as a single cost component and referred to as *conversion cost*.

Managers who are aware of spoilage costs can make better decisions as to whether to ignore the causes of spoilage or try to correct them. Impediments to such awareness include using the method of neglect and burying the cost of spoilage in predetermined overhead rates rather than accounting for the spoilage separately. Managers may rationalize the existence of these impediments because they believe that a particular cause only creates an insignificant amount of spoilage; thus, tolerances for error are built into the system. Also, managers may erroneously believe that spoilage is uncontrollable.

Many companies now build quality into their processes, which reduces the need for quality control inspections. Often, these companies use statistical process control (SPC) to reduce spoilage. SPC relies on the idea that natural variations occur in a process over time due to random factors and are to be expected. Out-of-control variations also occur, and these commonly produce defects. Control charts are used by workers to record selected nonfinancial performance measures so that process variations can be analyzed.

APPENDIX

JOURNAL ENTRIES RELATED TO CHANDRA'S CHOCOLATES

Summary journal entries and T-accounts for the Molding and Boxing Departments of the Chandra's Chocolates example given in the chapter (Exhibits 10-5, 10-6, and 10-8) follow. For these entries, the following four assumptions are made: sales for June were 121,000 chocolate greeting cards; all sales were on account for $10 per unit; a perpetual weighted average inventory system is used; and Chandra's Chocolates began June with no Finished Goods Inventory.

LEARNING OBJECTIVE ❾
How are journal entries prepared for a process costing system?

1. Work in Process Inventory—Molding	334,950.00	
Raw Material Inventory		334,950.00
To record issuance of direct material		
(chocolate) to production		
2. Work in Process Inventory—Molding	202,191.00	
Various accounts		202,191.00
To record actual labor and overhead		
costs into production		
3. Work in Process Inventory—Boxing	557,634.00	
Work in Process Inventory—Molding		557,634.00
To transfer completed greeting cards		
to Boxing Department		
4. Work in Process Inventory—Boxing	36,720.00	
Raw Material Inventory		36,720.00
To record issuance of direct material		
(boxes) to production		
5. Work in Process Inventory—Boxing	47,975.70	
Various accounts		47,975.70
To record actual labor and overhead		
costs into production		
6. Finished Goods Inventory	649,944.00	
Work in Process Inventory—Boxing		649,944.00
To transfer cost of completed units to		
finished goods		

7. Cost of Goods Sold   642,510.00

     Finished Goods Inventory   642,510.00

     To transfer cost of goods sold from finished

     goods to cost of goods sold (121,000 × $5.31)

8. Accounts Receivable   1,210,000.00

     Sales   1,210,000.00

     To record June sales on account

     (121,000 × $10)

CHANDRA'S CHOCOLATES T-ACCOUNTS
(Numbers in parentheses indicate the related journal entry.)

WORK IN PROCESS INVENTORY—MOLDING

Beginning balance	49,678.60	Transferred out (3)	557,634.00
DM (1)	334,950.00		
Conversion (2)	202,191.00		
Ending balance	29,185.60		

WORK IN PROCESS INVENTORY—BOXING

Beginning balance	44,930.30	CGM (6)	649,944.00
Transferred in (3)	557,634.00		
DM (4)	36,720.00		
Conversion (5)	47,975.70		
Ending balance	37,316.00		

FINISHED GOODS INVENTORY

Beginning balance	0	CGM (7)	642,510.00
CGM (6)	649,944.00		
Ending balance	7,434.00		

COST OF GOODS SOLD

June CGS (7)	642,510.00		

KEY TERMS

Cost of production report (p. 457)

Equivalent units of production (EUP) (p. 452)

FIFO method (p. 453)

Method of neglect (p. 464)

Process costing (p. 448)

Process costing system (p. 448)

Statistical process control (SPC) (p. 465)

Total cost to account for (p. 454)

Total units to account for (p. 453)

Units started and completed (p. 456)

Weighted average method (p. 453)

SOLUTION STRATEGIES

1. Compute physical units to account for:

     Beginning inventory in whole units

     + Units started (or transferred in) during period

2. Compute physical units accounted for:

     Units completed and transferred out

     + Ending inventory in whole units

3. Compute equivalent units of production per cost component:
   a. Weighted average
      Beginning inventory in whole units
      + Units started and completed*
      + (Ending inventory × Percentage complete)
   b. FIFO
      (Beginning inventory × Percentage *not* complete at start of period)
      + Units started and completed*
      + (Ending inventory × Percentage complete)

4. Compute total cost to account for:
      Cost in beginning inventory
   + Cost of current period

5. Compute cost per equivalent unit per cost component:
   a. Weighted average
      Cost of component in beginning inventory
      + Cost of component for current period
      = Total cost
      ÷ EUP for component
   b. FIFO
      Cost of component for current period
      ÷ EUP for component

6. Assign costs to inventories:
   a. Weighted average
      1. Transferred out
         Whole units transferred × (Total cost per EUP for all components)
      2. Ending inventory
         Sum of EUP for each component × Cost per EUP for each component
   b. FIFO
      1. Transferred out:
         Beginning inventory cost
      + (Beginning inventory × Percentage *not* complete at beginning of period for each component × Cost per EUP for each component)
      + (Units started and completed × Total cost per EUP for all components)
      2. Ending inventory:
         Sum of (EUP for each component × Cost per EUP for each component)

---

*Units started and completed = Units transferred out − Units in beginning inventory

DEMONSTRATION PROBLEM

Schorg Inc., located near Seattle, Washington, manufactures several smoked food items, including smoked salmon. The firm has two departments: the Smoking Department is highly labor-intensive and the Packaging Department is highly automated. Salmon production occurs during four months of the year. Costs in the Smoking Department are accumulated in three cost pools: direct material, direct labor, and overhead. The following production and cost data relate to the November 2000 production of smoked salmon.

Production Data:
Beginning Work in Process Inventory   15,000 pounds
   This inventory is 100% complete as to material,
   60% complete as to direct labor, and 35%
   complete as to overhead.

Started this period	250,000 pounds
Ending Work in Process Inventory	8,000 pounds

    This inventory is 100% complete as to material,
70% complete as to direct labor, and 40%
complete as to overhead.

Cost Data:

	Material	Direct Labor	Overhead
Beginning inventory	$ 34,000	$ 7,274	$ 7,327
Costs incurred in November	787,500	278,960	229,455

Requirements:

a. Use the weighted average method to determine the cost of the smoked salmon transferred to WIP Inventory—Packaging and the cost of the packages of smoked salmon in ending Smoking WIP for November 2000.

b. Repeat Part a, but use the FIFO method.

Solution to Demonstration Problem

a. Weighted average method:

Step 1: Calculate total units to account for:

Beginning inventory	15,000
Units started during current period	250,000
Units to account for	265,000

Step 2: Calculate the total units accounted for:

Units completed and transferred out	257,000
Units in ending WIP inventory	8,000
Units accounted for	265,000

Step 3: Determine the equivalent units of production:

	Material	Direct Labor	Overhead
BI (whole units)	15,000	15,000	15,000
Units started and completed	242,000	242,000	242,000
EI (whole units × % complete)	8,000	5,600	3,200
EUP	265,000	262,600	260,200

Step 4: Determine the total cost to account for:

	Material	Direct Labor	Overhead
BI cost	$ 34,000	$ 7,274	$ 7,327
Current period cost	787,500	278,960	229,455
Total cost to account for	$821,500	$286,234	$236,782

    Total all cost pools = $821,500 + $286,234 + $236,782 = $1,344,516

Step 5: Calculate the cost per equivalent unit of production:

	Material	Direct Labor	Overhead
Total cost	$821,500	$286,234	$236,782
Divided by EUP	÷265,000	÷262,600	÷260,200
Cost per EUP	$3.10	$1.09	$.91

    Total cost per EUP = $3.10 + $1.09 + $.91 = $5.10

Step 6: Assign costs to inventories and goods transferred out:

Cost of goods transferred (257,000 × $5.10)		$1,310,700
Cost of ending inventory:		
Material (8,000 × $3.10)	$24,800	
Direct labor (5,600 × $1.09)	6,104	
Overhead (3,200 × $.91)	2,912	33,816
Total cost accounted for		$1,344,516

b. FIFO method:

Step 1: Calculate total units to account for:

Beginning inventory	15,000
Units started during current period	250,000
Units to account for	265,000

Step 2: Calculate the total units accounted for:

Units completed and transferred out	257,000
Units in ending WIP inventory	8,000
Units accounted for	265,000

Step 3: Determine the equivalent units of production:

	Material	Direct Labor	Overhead
BI (EUP not completed in October)	0	6,000	9,750
Units started and completed	242,000	242,000	242,000
EI (whole units × % complete)	8,000	5,600	3,200
EUP	250,000	253,600	254,950

Step 4: Determine the total cost to account for:

	Material	Direct Labor	Overhead
BI cost	$ 34,000	$ 7,274	$ 7,327
Current period cost	787,500	278,960	229,455
Total cost to account for	$821,500	$286,234	$236,782

Total all cost pools = $821,500 + $286,234 + $236,782 = $1,344,516

Step 5: Calculate the cost per equivalent unit of production:

	Material	Direct Labor	Overhead
Current period cost	$787,500	$278,960	$229,455
Divided by EUP	÷250,000	÷253,600	÷254,950
Cost per EUP	$3.15	$1.10	$.90

Total cost per EUP = $3.15 + $1.10 + $.90 = $5.15

Step 6: Assign costs to inventories and goods transferred out:

Cost of goods transferred:		
Beginning inventory cost ($34,000 + $7,274 + $7,327)		$ 48,601
Costs to complete beginning WIP:		
Material (0 × $3.15)		0
Direct labor (6,000 × $1.10)		6,600
Overhead (9,750 × $.90)		8,775
Total cost of beginning inventory		$ 63,976
Started and completed (242,000 × $5.15)		1,246,300
Total cost of goods transferred		$1,310,276
Cost of ending inventory:		
Material (8,000 × $3.15)	$25,200	
Direct labor (5,600 × $1.10)	6,160	
Overhead (3,200 × $.90)	2,880	34,240
Total cost accounted for		$1,344,516

END OF CHAPTER MATERIALS

⊙ QUESTIONS

1. Describe the characteristics of a production environment in which process costing would likely be found.

2. How are job order and process costing similar? How do they differ?

3. Can a company use both job order costing and process costing for its production activities? If so, give an example. If not, explain why it would not be possible.

4. What source documents are used to provide information on raw material and direct labor usage in a process costing system? Are these different from the source documents used in job order costing? Why or why not?

5. Under what conditions is it appropriate to apply actual overhead to products in a process costing environment?

6. Why is the assignment of costs to products essentially an averaging process?

7. Is one equivalent unit computation sufficient for all of the cost categories (direct material, direct labor, and overhead)? Explain.

8. What is meant by the term *equivalent units of production* (EUP)? Why are EUP needed in process costing, but not in job order costing?

9. What are the two methods used in process costing to assign an average cost to products? How are these methods similar and how do they differ?

10. What are the six steps involved in assigning product costs in a process costing environment? In your answer, indicate in which steps physical units are used and in which steps equivalent units are used.

11. At the end of a period, a department's total production costs are assigned to two groups of products. What are the two groups and where do their costs appear on the financial statements?

12. How are units "started and completed" calculated? Is this figure used in both weighted average and FIFO cost assignment? Why or why not?

13. What is meant by the term *transferred out cost*? Why does the transferred out cost under the weighted average method include only one computation but the FIFO method includes multiple computations?

14. What is the purpose of a cost of production report? Discuss the information provided to managers by this document.

15. Arrange the following terms in an equation so that each side contains two terms and the two sides are equal:

    | Cost of the beginning inventory | (BI) |
    | Costs transferred out | (TO) |
    | Cost of the ending inventory | (EI) |
    | Costs incurred this period | (TP) |

16. Arrange the following terms in an equation so that the two sides are equal with one side representing total units to account for and the other side representing total units accounted for:

    | Units in the beginning inventory | (BI) |
    | Units in the ending inventory | (EI) |
    | Units started and completed | (S&C) |
    | Units started but not completed | (SNC) |
    | Units transferred out | (TO) |

17. Does the weighted average or FIFO method provide the better picture of the actual amount of work accomplished in a period? Explain.

18. In a firm that uses a process costing system as both a tool to evaluate periodic cost control and to assign costs to products, would weighted average or FIFO more likely be used? Explain.

19. In an inflationary environment (in which costs are rising from period to period), would the weighted average or FIFO method assign the higher cost to the ending Work in Process Inventory in a department? (Assume production is stable from period to period.) Explain.

20. Why are the EUP calculations for standard process costing the same as the EUP calculations for FIFO process costing?

21. Under what circumstances will a department have a cost component called *transferred-in*? What degree of completion will the units in this component have?

22. A company has two sequential processing departments. On the cost of production reports, will the cost per unit transferred out of the first department always be equal to the cost per unit transferred into the second department? Why or why not?

23. Why should companies design process accounting systems to capture costs of spoilage?

24. What is meant by the method of neglect? How does the use of this method affect the cost of good production?

25. Why is the cost of "spoilage" so difficult to determine in a service provider?

26. How are statistical process control techniques used by companies to control quality-related costs?

27. *(Appendix)* A food processor transfers $56,000 of products from the Cleaning Department to the Cutting Department. What would the journal entry be for this transfer?

28. *(Appendix)* In a company that uses a process costing system and is made up of three sequential processing departments (Cutting, Stitching, and Finishing, respectively), what journal entry would identify the cost of goods manufactured?

⊙ EXERCISES

29. *(Total units; WA EUP)* La Jolla Corp. uses a weighted average process costing system. All material is added at the start of the process; labor and overhead costs are incurred evenly throughout the production process. The company's records for September contained the following information:

Beginning inventory   32,000 pounds
Started during September   800,000 pounds
Transferred to finished goods   808,000 pounds

As of September 1, the beginning inventory was 60 percent complete as to labor and overhead. On September 30, the ending inventory was 35 percent complete as to labor and overhead.
   a. Determine the total number of pounds to account for.
   b. Determine the equivalent units of production for direct material.
   c. Determine the equivalent units of production for conversion.

30. *(Total units; WA EUP)* Chadwick Ltd. produces a chemical compound in which all material is added at the beginning of the production cycle. At May 1, there were 36,000 gallons in beginning inventory. During May 2000, the company started 920,000 gallons of raw material into production and completed 945,000 gallons.

The beginning inventory was 60 percent complete as to labor and 25 percent complete as to overhead. The ending inventory was 30 percent complete as to labor and 5 percent complete as to overhead.
   a. Determine the total number of gallons to account for.
   b. Determine the equivalent units of production for direct material.
   c. Determine the equivalent units of production for labor.
   d. Determine the equivalent units of production for conversion.

31. *(Total units; FIFO EUP)* Answer Parts a, b, and c to Exercise 29 assuming that La Jolla Corp. uses the FIFO method of process costing.

32. *(Total units; FIFO EUP)* Answer Parts a, b, c, and d to Exercise 30 assuming that Chadwick Ltd. uses the FIFO method of process costing.

33. *(WA EUP)* For each of the following situations, determine the equivalent units of production using the weighted average method:

   a. Units started in production   280,000
      Units transferred out   200,000
      Beginning inventory (60% complete)   40,000
      Ending inventory (75% complete)   120,000

   c. equivalent units of production for overhead.
   d. cost of the units transferred out.
   e. cost of the goods in ending inventory.

43. *(Multi-departmental production; WA method)* Du Charm Inc. produces calendars in a two-process, two-department operation. In the Printing Department, materials are printed and cut. In the Assembly Department, the materials received from Printing are assembled into individual calendars and bound. Each department maintains its own Work in Process Inventory account, and costs are assigned using a weighted average process costing basis. In Assembly, conversion costs are incurred evenly throughout the process; direct material is added at the end of the process. For November 2000, the following production and cost information was available:

   Beginning inventory: 20,000 calendars (30% complete as to conversion); transferred in cost, $25,000; conversion cost, $1,114
   Transferred in during November: 80,000 calendars
   Current period costs: transferred in, $80,000; direct material, $10,500; conversion, $14,960
   Ending inventory: 30,000 calendars (80% complete as to conversion)

       For the Assembly Department, compute the
   a. equivalent units of production for each cost component.
   b. cost per equivalent unit for each cost component.
   c. cost transferred to Finished Goods Inventory.
   d. cost of Ending WIP inventory.

44. *(Missing numbers; multi-departmental production; WA method)* Sip-N-Smak produces fruit drinks in a three-department (Steaming, Mixing, and Packaging) production process. Limited information on the inventory accounts for March follows:

WIP INVENTORY—STEAMING

Beg.	90,000	
DM	270,000	
DL	60,000	?
OH	75,000	
Ending	54,000	

WIP INVENTORY—MIXING

Beg.	300,000	
Trans. In	?	
DM	?	600,000
DL	?	
OH	?	
Ending	210,000	

WIP INVENTORY—PACKAGING

Beg.	270,000	
Trans. In	?	
DM	300,000	
DL	600,000	?
OH	180,000	
Ending	330,000	

FINISHED GOODS INVENTORY

Beg.	495,000	
CGM	?	1,440,000
Ending	?	

   a. What was the cost of goods transferred from the Steaming Department to the Mixing Department in March?
   b. What was the sum of direct material, direct labor, and overhead costs in the Mixing Department for March?
   c. What was the cost of goods manufactured for March?

45. *(Multi-departmental production; FIFO method)* Answer Parts a, b, c, and d to Exercise 43, assuming that Du Charm Inc. uses the FIFO method of process costing.

46. *(Statistical process controls)* Your bicycle is in perfect working order. Assume that the pedals, wheels, chain, and gears on it are the equivalent of a manufacturing process. Keeping the bicycle in the same gear, you have counted the number of revolutions of the pedals that are necessary to move the bicycle a distance of one hundred yards (one production run). You have repeated this process many times (trials), so you have information about multiple production runs.

a. Even though the bicycle is in perfect working order, why will the number of revolutions required to move the bicycle a distance of one hundred yards be expected to vary somewhat from one trial to the next?

b. Suppose the bicycle is in perfect working order and you conduct one hundred trials in which you pedal the bicycle a distance of one hundred yards. How could the resulting information be used as a statistical guide in future tests of whether the bicycle is "in control"?

47. *(Appendix)* The Mulder Pellet Company manufactures alfalfa pellets used as animal feed. Alfalfa is processed in a two-department sequential process. The first process, dehydration, removes moisture from raw alfalfa; the second process, pelletizing, compresses the alfalfa into pellets. The following transactions occurred at Mulder Pellet in January 2000. Journalize each transaction.

a. Alfalfa costing $200,000 was removed from Raw Material Inventory and entered processing in the Dehydration Department.

b. Dehydration paid labor costs of $240,000; of this amount, $160,000 was considered direct. Mulder uses predetermined overhead rates.

c. Other overhead costs amounting to $140,000 were incurred in the Dehydration Department. (Note: credit Accounts Payable.)

d. Goods costing $660,000 were transferred from the Dehydration Department to the Pelletizing Department.

e. Labor costs of $162,000 were incurred in the Pelletizing Department; $124,000 of this amount was considered direct.

f. Other overhead costs incurred in the Pelletizing Department amounted to $226,000. (Note: credit Accounts Payable.)

g. Goods costing $980,000 were transferred from the Pelletizing Department to Finished Goods Inventory.

h. Goods costing $900,000 were sold for $1,460,000 cash.

48. *(Appendix)* Scully Corp. produces a plastic spacecraft. The production process introduces plastic into the Molding Department where it is melted and formed; the crafts then are transferred to the Painting Department where a variety of colors and decorations are added. The Painting Department is highly automated and uses a conversion cost category for labor and overhead. This is the first month of operations for the company.

a. Journalize the following May 2000 transactions for Scully Corp., assuming an actual process costing system.

(1) Five thousand pounds of plastic costing $.55 per pound were purchased on account.

(2) The Molding Department requisitioned 4,960 pounds of plastic from inventory.

(3) The Molding Department accrued direct labor wages of $17,000.

(4) The Molding Department incurred $22,000 in overhead costs. (Credit "various accounts.")

(5) The Molding Department transferred $41,600 of costs for 65,000 spacecraft to the Painting Department.

(6) The Painting Department incurred material cost of $3,250. This material was purchased on a just-in-time basis from the supplier on account.

(7) The Painting Department incurred conversion costs of $9,016. (Credit "various accounts.")

b. What is the cost per spacecraft transferred from Molding to Painting?

c. Assume that Scully uses a weighted average process costing system and that the remaining units in Painting's inventory were 100 percent complete as to transferred in and material costs and 80 percent complete as to conversion. What is the cost per equivalent unit for transferred in, material, and conversion?

d. Prepare the journal entry for the transfer of 62,000 spacecraft from the Painting Department to Finished Goods Inventory.

e. What is the cost of ending inventory in the Painting Department?

d. You have just been informed by your quality control inspectors that 6,000 gallons of the ice cream manufactured this month are not up to the company's quality standards. Thus, you recalculate the cost per equivalent unit by using the "method of neglect"—that is, you assume that a total of only 91,000 gallons of ice cream were completed this month. What are the new costs per equivalent unit (round to the nearest penny)? How much was the cost of spoilage?

56. *(WA EUP; cost distribution; spoilage)* Ellicon Company produces a preservative used for canned food products. The company employs a weighted average process costing system. All material is introduced at the start of the process. Labor and overhead are at the same degree of completion throughout the process. The following information pertains to the company's October operations.

UNIT DATA

Beginning work in process (70% complete)	12,000 gallons
Started this period	24,000 gallons
Ending work in process (40% complete)	17,000 gallons

Cost Data	Direct Material	Conversion
Beginning work in process	$ 9,500	$14,700
Incurred this period	35,600	73,080

a. Determine the total number of units to account for.
b. Compute the equivalent units of production for each cost pool.
c. Compute the total cost to account for and total cost for each cost pool.
d. Compute the cost per equivalent unit for each cost pool.
e. Compute the cost assigned to the goods transferred to Finished Goods Inventory and the cost of ending Work in Process Inventory.
f. The preservative mixture is put through a quality control inspection at the end of the process. You have just been informed that 3,000 gallons that were started this period failed the quality inspection. To hide this production failure, your supervisor had reduced the number of units shown as started this period from 27,000 to 24,000. Compute the actual cost per equivalent unit for each cost component for the period. How would these costs have changed the cost transferred out and the cost of ending inventory?

57. *(WA; multi-departmental cost of production report)* Wisconsin Automotive manufactures car bumpers in a continuous two-department process. For August, company records indicate the following production results in the Machining and Finishing departments:

	MACHINING	FINISHING
Units in beginning inventory	500	350
Units started or transferred in	40,000	?
Units in ending inventory	2,000	600

All materials are added at the beginning of production in Machining and at the end of production in Finishing. The company is highly automated and there is no separate labor category in either department. The conversion rates of completion for units in process at August 1 and 31 follow:

Machining: August 1 (40 percent); August 31 (80 percent)
Finishing: August 1 (30 percent); August 31 (60 percent)
Cost records indicate the following for the month:

	MACHINING		FINISHING	
	Beginning	Current	Beginning	Current
Transferred in	n/a	n/a	$11,235	$?
Material	$11,140	$794,000	0	133,875
Conversion	5,105	618,450	4,533	246,432

Prepare a cost of production report for each department for August assuming that both departments use the weighted average method.

58. *(WA; two materials)* Creative Cake Bakery produces sheet cakes in mass quantities and uses a process costing system to account for its costs. The bakery production line is set up in one department. Batter is mixed first, with all necessary ingredients added at the start of production. The batter is poured into pans, baked, and cooled. Then the cake is iced with a mixture of confectionary sugar and water. The last step in the process is to let the icing harden and move the cake into a display case. Icing is added when the cakes are at the 85 percent stage of completion.

   Production and cost data for April 2000 follow. Beginning inventory consisted of 20 cakes, which were 80 percent complete as to labor and production overhead. The batter associated with beginning inventory had a cost of $66.10, and related conversion costs totaled $40.66. A total of 430 cakes were started during April, and 440 were completed. The ending inventory was 90 percent complete as to labor and production overhead. Costs for the month were: batter, $1,324.40; icing, $166.50; and conversion cost, $857.34.

   a. Determine the equivalent units of production for each cost component for April for Creative Cake Bakery using the weighted average method.

   b. Calculate the cost per unit for each cost component for the bakery for April using the weighted average method.

   c. Determine the appropriate valuation for April's ending Work in Process Inventory and the units transferred to the display case for sale.

   d. The bakery sells its cakes for $12.50 each. During April, 427 cakes were sold. What was the total gross profit margin on the sale of the cakes?

59. *(FIFO; multi-departmental cost of production report)* Use the information in Problem 57 to prepare a cost of production report assuming that Wisconsin Automotive uses a FIFO process costing system. Regardless of the amount calculated as the cost transferred out of Machining, assume that $1,364,055 was the amount transferred into Finishing for the period.

60. *(FIFO; two materials)* Assume that Creative Cake Bakery in Problem 58 uses a FIFO process costing system.

   a. Prepare a cost of production report for the bakery.

   b. Determine the gross margin for the month if 427 cakes were sold for $12.50 each.

   c. Provide some reasons that the bakery would need such a large gross margin per cake.

61. *(WA and FIFO; cost of production report)* In a single-process production system, the Spookum Corporation produces wax lips for Halloween. For September 2000, the company's accounting records reflected the following:

Beginning Work in Process Inventory	
(100% complete as to Material A; 0% complete	
as to Material B; 40% complete as to direct	
labor; 60% complete as to overhead)	10,000 units
Started during the month	80,000 units
Ending Work in Process Inventory	
(100% complete as to Material A; 0% complete	
as to Material B; 30% complete as to direct	
labor; 40% complete as to overhead)	15,000 units

COST DATA	BEGINNING INVENTORY	SEPTEMBER
Material A	$1,900	$ 8,000
Material B	0	37,500
Direct labor	1,195	7,550
Factory overhead	1,530	9,000

   a. For September, prepare a cost of production report, assuming the company uses the weighted average method.

   b. Prepare a cost of production report for September, assuming the company uses the FIFO method.

c. Explain to your plant manager how the weighted average method helps disguise the apparently poor cost control in August.

62. *(WA and FIFO)* Safe-T-Light, Inc., manufactures outdoor patio lights that are sold to major department stores under private labels. At the beginning of March 2000, the company had 4,000 lights in beginning Work in Process Inventory, which were 90 percent complete as to material and 75 percent complete as to conversion. During the month, 22,000 units were started; at the end of March, 5,000 remained in process. The ending Work in Process Inventory was 60 percent complete as to material and 40 percent complete as to conversion.

Actual cost data for the month were as follows:

	MATERIAL	CONVERSION	TOTAL
Beginning inventory	$ 82,200	$ 31,000	$113,200
Current costs	397,800	245,000	642,800
Total costs	$480,000	$276,000	$756,000

a. Prepare EUP schedules under the weighted average and FIFO methods.
b. Prepare cost of production reports under the weighted average and FIFO methods.
c. Discuss the differences in the two reports prepared for Part b. Which would provide better information to departmental managers, and why?

63. *(WA and FIFO EUP; two departments; appendix)* In a two-process operation, Shady Times Inc. manufactures beach umbrellas. Information for a recent period follows:

	DEPARTMENT	
Units	*Assembly*	*Finishing*
Beginning inventory	10,000	12,000
Units started	20,000	
Units transferred	26,000	
Ending inventory	4,000	10,000
Current Costs		
Materials	$22,000	$14,000
Labor	8,136	9,000

Other information: Beginning Work in Process Inventory in the Assembly Department was one-half complete with respect to conversion costs. Material is added at the start of production. Beginning inventory includes $11,300 for material costs and $2,000 for direct labor. Factory overhead is applied at the rate of 50 percent of direct labor cost. Ending inventory is 40 percent complete as to conversion.

Beginning Work in Process Inventory in the Finishing Department was 75 percent complete with respect to conversion costs. Material is added at the end of the process. Beginning inventory includes $17,560 for transferred-in costs and $3,200 for direct labor. Factory overhead is applied at the rate of 100 percent of direct labor cost. Ending inventory was estimated to be 25 percent complete as to conversion.

a. Calculate the cost of goods transferred from each department and the cost of ending work in process inventories. Use the FIFO method for Assembly and the weighted average method for Finishing.
b. Record the journal entries necessary to recognize the activity in each department. Assume the following additional facts:
(1) All units completed during the period were sold for 200 percent of cost.
(2) There was no beginning Finished Goods Inventory.
(3) Applied overhead was equal to actual overhead in each department.

⊙ CASES

64. *(WA; two departments; appendix)* One Deep Well is a small business that provides water to approximately two hundred rural households in western Wyoming. The company

    c. In your opinion, is subcontracting the actual brewing of the beer an ethical practice in light of the fact that the practice is not disclosed to the consumer? Explain.

73. Empowering workers has been an increasingly popular idea to reduce costs and raise productivity; an effort to "white-collarize" factories has been adopted by about 40 percent of United States manufacturers. In a process environment, workers are empowered to stop production lines if defects or variations are noticed. Direct labor costs are reduced and overhead costs rise. But are all workers ready for empowerment? Apparently not—some workers find it extremely stressful. (Note: The September 8, 1997, *Wall Street Journal* article "Not All Workers Find the Idea of Empowerment as Neat as It Sounds" may provide a useful starting point.)

    a. As an employee, would you want to be empowered, and thus responsible for activities such as multi-tasking (being able to operate a variety of equipment), machine maintenance, quality, and team member discipline? Why or why not?

    b. As a manager, would you want your employees to be empowered? Why or why not?

    c. What impacts might employee empowerment have on a process environment?

74. Read the September–October 1996 *Harvard Business Review* article "Breaking the Functional Mind-Set in Process Operations." Prepare a short summary of that article, identifying the quality issues involved in reengineering a process operation. Also include your perception of the ethics of the business process reengineering attempts discussed in this article.

75. FulRange, Inc., produces complex printed circuits for stereo amplifiers. The circuits are sold primarily to major component manufacturers, and any production overruns are sold to small manufacturers at a substantial discount. The small manufacturer segment appears very profitable because the basic operating budget assigns all fixed expenses to units made for the major manufacturers, the only predictable market.

    A common product defect that occurs in production is a "drift," caused by failure to maintain precise heat levels during the production process. Rejects from the 100 percent testing program can be reworked to acceptable levels if the defect is drift. However, in a recent analysis of customer complaints, George Wilson, the cost accountant, and the quality control engineer have ascertained that normal rework does not bring the circuits up to standard. Sampling shows that about one-half of the reworked circuits will fail after extended, high-volume amplifier operation. The incidence of failure in the reworked circuits is projected to be about 10 percent over one to five years' operation.

    Unfortunately, there is no way to determine which reworked circuits will fail, because testing will not detect this problem. The rework process could be changed to correct the problem, but the cost/benefit analysis for the suggested change in the rework process indicates that it is not practical. FulRange's marketing analyst has indicated that this problem will have a significant impact on the company's reputation and customer satisfaction if it is not corrected. Consequently, the board of directors would interpret this problem as having serious negative implications on the company's profitability.

    Wilson has included the circuit failure and rework problem in his report for the upcoming quarterly meeting of the board of directors. Due to the potentially adverse economic impact, Wilson has followed a long-standing practice of highlighting this information.

    After reviewing the reports to be presented, the plant manager and her staff were upset and indicated to the controller that he should control his people better. "We can't upset the board with this kind of material. Tell Wilson to tone that down. Maybe we can get it by this meeting and have some time to work on it. People who buy those cheap systems and play them that loud shouldn't expect them to last forever."

    The controller called Wilson into his office and said, "George, you'll have to bury this one. The probable failure of reworks can be referred to briefly in the oral presentation, but it should not be mentioned or highlighted in the advance material mailed to the board."

Wilson feels strongly that the board will be misinformed on a potentially serious loss of income if he follows the controller's orders. Wilson discussed the problem with the quality control engineer, who simply remarked, "That's your problem, George."

a. Discuss the ethical considerations that George Wilson should recognize in deciding how to proceed in this matter.

b. Explain what ethical responsibilities should be accepted in this situation by
   (1) The controller.
   (2) The quality control engineer.
   (3) The plant manager and her staff.

c. What should George Wilson do in this situation? Explain your answer.

(CMA)

PART 5

Using Managerial Accounting Information for Control

Chapter 11 Controlling Inventory and Production Costs

LEARNING OBJECTIVES

After reading this chapter, you should be able to answer the following questions:

1 WHY
do managers use ABC inventory control systems?

2 HOW
does a company determine from whom, how much, and when to order?

3 WHAT
are the differences between the economic order quantity model and materials requirements planning?

4 WHAT
is the JIT philosophy and how does it affect production?

5 WHAT
is the impact of flexible manufacturing systems on production and on satisfying customers?

6 HOW
would the traditional accounting system change if a JIT inventory system were adopted? (Appendices 1 and 2)

7 HOW
does the product life cycle influence sales and costs? (Appendix 3)

Werthan Packaging, Inc.

Werthan Packaging, Inc. (WPI) of Nashville, Tennessee, is a $50 million multi-wall bag manufacturing firm that has been around since the 1800s. It makes paper bags with multiple-layered "walls" that are used to package products such as dry pet food, cat litter, animal feed, sugar, and bird seed. To survive and prosper in the paper industry's complex and competitive environment, WPI upgraded from 1960s technology to the technology of the 1990s and also changed the way it managed and monitored its performance.

Problems with information systems were numerous. None of these systems reported results that were consistent. None of them shared information. None of them contained accurate data. All of the old systems were creating waste and excessive overhead dollars to operate. To make matters worse, these separate systems inhibited cross-functional communication and cooperation within WPI and discouraged teamwork.

WPI personnel realized that to achieve superior service goals, they would have to begin to work as a team. The "throwing of work over walls" would have to stop, and the sharing of ideas and information to improve the company's ability to service customers would need to start. Company employees agreed to strive to anticipate customer needs, make effective use of integrated systems, reduce lead time and inventory levels, and provide excellent delivery performance.

In 1992, the corporate decision came down—CHANGE. The information-system upgrade objectives were to improve customer service, improve internal communications, and provide tools to be used in obtaining world-class manufacturing status for the company. Various department leaders were interviewed to see what they expected from a new system. All wanted new budgeting, forecasting, and modeling tools.

The Manufacturing and Inventory Control Department wanted integrated capacity requirements planning (CRP) and materials requirements planning (MRP), online update and inquiry capability, production performance tracking tools, inventory control history, accurate and timely shop packet instructions, and a shop floor manpower planning tool that facilitated the process of staffing the plant floor to meet customer demand (sales and operations planning).

SOURCE: Chris McCarthy, "Using Technology as a Competitive Tool," *Management Accounting* (January 1998), pp. 29–30. Reprinted from *Management Accounting*, published by the Institute of Management Accountants, Montvale, N.J. Visit our website at www.imanet.org.

*F*or *Werthan Packaging, Inc.*, the decision to change was not only appropriate but also courageous. WPI had to find new production, marketing, distribution, and inventory management techniques and tools to allow it to successfully compete in what has become a global economy. The choice was courageous because WPI had to extensively revamp its approaches to operations and to invest large sums of money in technology and training.

Like WPI, many companies around the world have begun concentrating on ways to improve productivity, use available technology, and increase efficiency. These efforts are often directed at reducing the costs of producing and carrying inventory.

Aside from the amount spent on plant assets, the amount spent on inventory can be the largest investment made by a company, especially in a retail environment. Unfortunately, until inventory is sold, it provides no monetary benefit to the organization. This chapter deals with several techniques that minimize organizational investment in inventory: economic order quantity (EOQ), order point, and safety stock; materials requirements planning (MRP); just-in-time (JIT) systems; and flexible manufacturing systems (FMS) and computer-integrated manufacturing (CIM).

MANAGING INVENTORY

LEARNING OBJECTIVE ❶
Why do managers use ABC inventory control systems?

ABC analysis

Management needs to control its significant investment in inventory in a way that maximizes attention to the most important inventory items and minimizes attention to the least important items. Unit cost is commonly a factor in the degree of control that is maintained over an inventory item. As the unit cost increases, internal controls, such as access to inventory, are typically tightened, and a perpetual inventory system is more often used. Recognition of the appropriate cost–benefit relationships may result in an **ABC analysis** of inventory, which separates inventory into three groups based on annual cost-to-volume usage.[1] The ABC analysis model is actually an application of Pareto analysis, presented in Chapter 3. As discussed in that chapter, Pareto analysis is a tool used to separate the "vital few from the trivial many."

Items having the highest dollar volume are referred to as A items, while C items represent the lowest dollar volume. All other inventory items are designated as B items. Exhibit 11-1 provides the results of a typical ABC inventory analysis: 20 percent of the inventory items account for 80 percent of the total inventory cost; an additional 30 percent of the items, taken together with the first 20 percent, account for 90 percent of the cost; and the remaining 50 percent of the items account for the remaining 10 percent of the cost.

Once inventory items are categorized as A, B, or C, management can determine the best inventory control method for the items within each category. A-type inventory should require a perpetual inventory system. Such items are likely candidates for purchasing techniques that minimize the funds tied up in inventory investment. The

---

[1]ABC inventory analysis should not be confused with activity-based costing (also ABC), which is covered in Chapter 5.

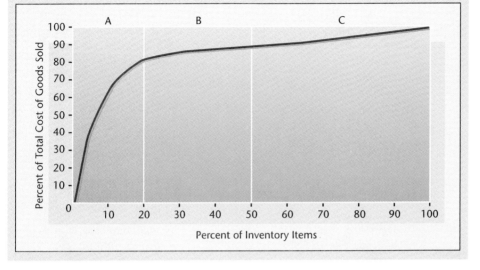

EXHIBIT 11-1
ABC Inventory Analysis

highest-level control procedures should be assigned to these items. Such a treatment reflects the financial accounting concept of materiality.

Controls on C-type inventory items are normally minimal because of the immateriality of the inventory cost. C-category items may justify only periodic inventory procedures and may use either a two-bin or a red-line system. Under a **two-bin system**, two containers (or stacks) of inventory are available for production needs. When it is necessary to begin using materials from the second bin, a purchase order is placed to refill the first bin. Having the additional container or stack of inventory on hand is considered reasonable because the dollar amount of investment for C-category items is insignificant. In a **red-line system**, a red line is painted on the inventory container at a designated reorder point. Both the two-bin and red-line systems require that estimates of production needs and receipt times from suppliers be fairly accurate.

two-bin system

red-line system

For B-type items, the inventory system (perpetual or periodic) and the level of internal control depend on management judgment. Such judgment will be based on how crucial the item is to the production process, how quickly suppliers respond to orders, and whether the estimated benefits of increased controls are greater than the costs. Advances in technology, such as computers and bar coding, have made it easier and more cost beneficial to institute additional controls over inventory.

COSTS ASSOCIATED WITH INVENTORY

Most organizations engaging in a conversion process use both intangible and tangible inputs. For example, direct labor and other types of services are nonphysical and are supplied and consumed simultaneously. In contrast, raw materials are tangible and may be stockpiled for later use. Similarly, outputs of a manufacturing process may be stored until sold. The potential for physical items to be placed in or withdrawn from storage creates opportunities for managers to improve organizational effectiveness and efficiency relative to the quantities in which such items are purchased, produced, and stored.

Good inventory management relies largely on cost-minimizing strategies. As indicated in Exhibit 11-2 (page 498), there are three basic costs associated with inventory: (1) purchasing or production, (2) ordering or setup, and (3) carrying or not carrying goods in stock.

The **purchasing cost** of inventory is the quoted purchase price, minus any discounts allowed, plus shipping cost and insurance charges while the items are in

purchasing cost

....BIT 11-2
Categories of Inventory Costs

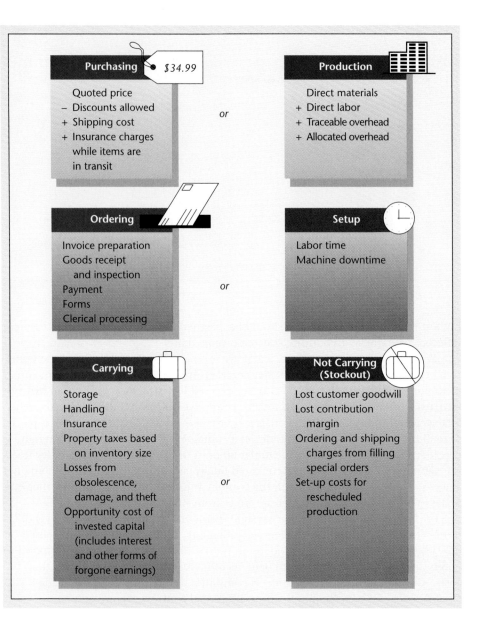

production cost

transit. In a manufacturing company, **production cost** includes costs associated with buying direct materials, paying for direct labor, incurring traceable overhead, and absorbing allocated fixed overhead. Purchasing or production cost is recorded in Merchandise Inventory, Raw Materials Inventory, Work in Process Inventory, or Finished Goods Inventory.

ordering cost

The incremental, variable costs associated with preparing, receiving, and paying for an order are **ordering costs**. These costs include the cost of forms and a variety of clerical costs. Ordering costs are traditionally expensed as incurred. Under an activity-based costing system, however, these costs can be traced to the items ordered as an additional direct cost. Retailers incur ordering costs for all their merchandise inventory. Manufacturers incur ordering costs for raw material purchases. If a manufacturer produces rather than orders a part, direct and indirect **setup costs** (rather than ordering costs) are incurred as equipment is readied for each new production run.

setup cost

carrying cost

Inventory **carrying costs** consist of storage, handling, insurance charges, and property taxes based on inventory size. Because inventory is one of many organizational investments, it should be expected to earn a rate of return similar to other investments.[2] Thus, carrying cost should include an opportunity cost for the amount

---

[2]The rate of return expected should be the weighted average cost of capital, which is discussed in Chapter 8.

invested in inventory. One additional opportunity cost that is often ignored is any possible loss that might result from inventory obsolescence or damage. Carrying costs can be estimated by use of information from various budgets, special studies, or other analytical techniques. One estimate of annual carrying cost is between 20 and 30 percent of inventory value.[3]

While excess inventory generates costs, so can a fully depleted inventory. When a company does not have inventory available upon customer request, a **stockout** occurs. Stockout cost is not easily determinable or recordable. It is an opportunity cost that includes lost customer goodwill, lost contribution margin from not being able to fill a sale, and the ordering and shipping charges incurred from filling special orders.

All of the costs associated with inventory should be considered when purchasing decisions are made—and purchases should be made in reasonable quantities. The economic order quantity model is one technique that is often used to determine reasonable quantity. It is discussed later in this chapter.

stockout

SUPPLIERS AND QUANTITIES

When buying inventory, a purchasing manager needs to make essentially three decisions—from whom, how much, and when. Each of these decisions depends in part on the relationship an organization has with its suppliers. In the past, the buyer–supplier relationship was generally viewed as adversarial; however, many companies are now viewing this relationship as a more cooperative, integrated partnership.

LEARNING OBJECTIVE ②
How does a company determine from whom, how much, and when to order?

What Supplier?

Traditionally, deciding from whom to buy was based primarily on price. A company found several firms that could provide the desired item and chose the firm offering the lowest price. However, the lowest-cost supplier in the short run is not necessarily the best supplier for the long run. The partnership approach views purchase cost in relation to quality and reliability, while taking a long-run perspective on the management of relationships with suppliers. Thus, purchases are made from suppliers offering the most appropriate quality at the best overall price—and delivering in the most reliable manner—to prevent the necessity of having to return unfit goods, the creation of non-value-added paperwork, production delays, or the need to seek alternative suppliers.

Moving from the adversarial to the partnership view of buyer–supplier relations takes time, effort, and trust on the part of both entities. To accommodate such a partnership, changes must be made relative to contract agreements, quality, delivery, and ability to openly communicate information.

The optimal approach to establishing these partnerships provides for a single vendor for each purchased item. Having single suppliers, however, does create the risk of not having alternative sources, especially for critical products or materials, in the event of vendor production strikes, unfair pricing, or shipment delays. Thus, it is often more practical to reduce the number of vendors to a limited group. Vendors are selected on a combination of quality, reliability, and price factors. Interacting with fewer vendors on a long-term basis provides a foundation from which to develop better communications, assure quality and service (including delivery), obtain quantity discounts, and reduce operating costs.

Multiple suppliers may be a necessity for companies manufacturing goods internationally. Such companies may be either required by law or impelled by the need to reduce costs (especially tariffs) to use some proportion of products and components

---

[3]Leslie N. Masonson, ed., "The Inventory Cardiogram: Unlocking an Overlooked Cash Flow Generator," *Cash Management Performance Report* (January 1991), p. 1.

made by local suppliers. Quality and reliability should be as important in choosing international suppliers as in choosing domestic ones.

Long-term contracts that specify exclusive purchasing arrangements for a fixed period of time and under specified conditions—usually associated with quality and reliability—are often signed with the chosen suppliers. An agreed-upon purchase price is set, but should allow for some flexibility in the event of cost or efficiency changes. For example, if the cost of input ingredients for a product increases for all purchasers, upward adjustments might be made to the negotiated price. Alternatively, companies may expect suppliers to become more efficient so that costs will decrease as experience is gained.

In adversarial buyer–supplier relationships, quality control efforts are essential. Karoru Ishikawa, president of Musashi Institute of Technology and professor emeritus at Tokyo University, says there are three stages relative to quality in these relationships:

> In the first stage, the manufacturer checks the entire lot that is brought in
> by the supplier. In the second stage, the manufacturer only sample-checks.
> In the final stage, the manufacturer accepts everything without checking
> the quality. Only in the third stage may it be said that a truly worthwhile
> relationship has been established.[4]

To achieve that third stage, companies have begun certifying vendors as to quality. People from various organizational areas must decide on the factors by which the vendor will be rated and must then weigh these factors as to relative importance. Evaluations should be discussed with the vendors so they will understand their strong and weak points and how they compare with their competitors. Vendors should be monitored after selection to assure continued compliance. Once vendors have been certified, buyers can spend less time performing inspections to find defective products and more time on assuring quality in their own processes and improving their service to customers.

In the traditional system, buyers would order large quantities of goods to obtain quantity discounts or to maximize usage of truck or other shipping container volumes. In contrast, in buyer–supplier partnership arrangements, order size is often considerably reduced and frequency of delivery increased. Long-term supplier contracts are negotiated, and then delivery reliability is monitored. Generally, suppliers missing a certain number of scheduled deliveries by more than a specified number of hours are dismissed. Ford, for example, has some deliveries made every two hours![5] To comply with the need for frequent deliveries, it is desirable for vendors to be located close to the company, which helps to minimize both delivery time and shipping cost. Alternatively, overnight delivery services can be used. These services have recognized the critical nature of prompt delivery and have risen in importance in the business world. Managers of both buying and supplying companies are becoming well-versed in analyzing the cost–benefit relationship involved in using such services.

For a buyer–supplier partnership to be beneficial to both parties, there must be an open exchange of information. Each party must understand the other's processes. The parties normally do this through site visits and discussion. In addition, suppliers are often asked for cost and profit information that would, under the traditional adversarial relationship, be considered "privileged." For example, Scott Paper required its suppliers to open their accounting records and explain their cost structures: what costs represent materials, labor, marketing, and so on. By doing this, Scott justified the elimination of certain cost categories, such as marketing, since the partnership arrangement makes them unnecessary.[6] Suppliers whose processes are inefficient or who are pursuing excessive profit margins create additional costs for the purchasing company, and thus make that company less competitive.

---

[4]Masaaki Imai, *Kaizen* (New York: McGraw-Hill, 1986), p. 213.

[5]David N. Burt, "Managing Suppliers Up to Speed," *Harvard Business Review* (July–August 1989), p. 128.

[6]Myron Magnet, "The New Golden Rule of Business," *Fortune* (February 21, 1994), p. 62.

To build truly productive relationships, purchasing firms should help suppliers improve their processes to achieve reduced costs, as indicated in the next News Note. Purchasing firms should also solicit information from suppliers about cost reduction possibilities related to new or existing products. Such an interchange of information and ideas requires that the partnership be built on a foundation of trust.

What Quantity?

After the supplier is selected, the firm must decide how many units to buy at a time. The objective is to buy in the most economical quantity possible, which requires consideration of the ordering and carrying costs of inventory. One tool used in this decision process is the **economic order quantity (EOQ)** model. The EOQ model provides an estimate of the number of units per order that would achieve the optimal balance between ordering and carrying costs. The EOQ formula is

economic order quantity (EOQ)

$$EOQ = \sqrt{\frac{2QO}{C}}$$

where EOQ = economic order quantity in units
Q = estimated quantity in units used per year
O = estimated cost of placing *one* order
C = estimated cost to carry *one* unit in stock for one year

The EOQ formula does not include purchasing cost, since that amount relates to "from whom to buy" rather than "how many to buy." Purchasing cost does not affect ordering and carrying costs, except to the extent that opportunity cost is calculated on the basis of cost.

NEWS NOTE

Just Returning the Favor

In the early 1930s, Henry Ford opened his factories to the Toyodas, then in the spinning and weaving business, and showed them the secrets of mass production, the assembly line, and interchangeable parts. In late 1991, Shoichiro Toyoda, the aging Toyota chairman, announced it was time for the Japanese to return the favor.

 www.toyota.com

Here's how the supplier counseling works: Toyota assigns a team of engineers to a supplier factory and shows management and workers how to smooth process flows, shrink lead times, and whittle down inventory. Toyota staffers push and monitor them for as long as it takes.

In the case of Garden State Tanning, an automotive leather supplier, for example, Toyota consultants were on site for nearly two years. The results speak for themselves. In January 1992, when Toyota first arrived, Garden State had 140 days of inventory stockpiled. Today, it has just 9. In early 1990 one cut hide in a hundred was defective; today it's one in two thousand.

Toyota has a very clear reason for aiding Garden State. In late 1991, demand for the Lexus exploded. Garden State, the supplier of leather for Lexus seats and consoles, couldn't cope. Rather than just dropping them as a supplier, Toyota stuck with them, demanding change. As a result, Garden State has maintained its near-total hold on Lexus leather.

The true finesse of Toyota's consulting is that it allows the supplier to remain in control of the changes. Says Garden State Chairman Sean Traynor: "Toyota didn't ask us to level our 100-year-old tanning plant and replace it with some robotic, postmodern, glistening gem. They just helped us figure out how to make the production process more efficient inside these old walls."

SOURCE: James Bamford, "Driving America to Tiers," *Financial World* (November 8, 1994), pp. 24–25.

economic production run (EPR)

In a manufacturing company, managers are concerned with "how many units to produce" in addition to "how many units (of a raw material) to buy." The EOQ formula can be modified to yield the appropriate number of units to manufacture in an **economic production run (EPR)**. The EPR quantity minimizes the total costs of setting up a production run and carrying a unit in stock for one year. In the EPR formula, the terms of the EOQ equation are defined as manufacturing costs rather than purchasing costs:

$$EPR = \sqrt{\frac{2QS}{C}}$$

where   EPR = economic production run
          Q = estimated quantity in units produced per year
          S = estimated cost of setting up a production run
          C = estimated cost of carrying one unit in stock for one year

Assume that WPI purchases pulp wood for its production. The purchasing manager has found several suppliers who can continuously provide tons of the proper quality of pulp wood at a cost of $400 per ton. Exhibit 11-3 provides information for use in calculating economic order quantity. The exhibit uses a flexible budget to show the total costs of purchasing 4,200 tons per year in various order sizes.

The EOQ model assumes that orders are filled exactly when needed, so when the order arrives, the inventory on hand is zero units. Thus, the average inventory size is half of the order size. The frequency with which orders must be placed depends on how many units are ordered each time. The total number of orders equals the total annual quantity of units needed divided by the size of the order.

Based on total costs, Exhibit 11-3 indicates that WPI's most economical order size is between 150 and 200 tons. The formula yields a value of 159 tons for the economic order quantity:

$$EOQ = \sqrt{\frac{2QO}{C}} = \sqrt{\frac{2(4,200)(\$30)}{\$10}} = 159 \text{ tons (rounded)}$$

The total annual cost to place and carry orders of 159 tons is $1,587, calculated as follows:

Number of orders (4,200 ÷ 159)	26.4 (rounded)
Average inventory (159 ÷ 2)	79.5
Cost of ordering (26.4 × $30)	$ 792
Cost of carrying (79.5 × $10)	795 (rounded)
Total cost	$1,587

Note again that this total cost does not include the $400 purchase cost per ton.

EXHIBIT 11-3

Yearly Purchasing Cost for Tons of Pulpwood

Quantity needed per year (Q) = 4,200 tons
Cost of ordering (O)   = $30 per order
Cost of carrying (C)   = $10 per ton

Size of order (tons)	50	100	150	200	300
Number of orders	84	42	28	21	14
Average inventory (tons)	25	50	75	100	150
Annual ordering cost	$2,520	$1,260	$ 840	$ 630	$ 420
Annual carrying cost	250	500	750	1,000	1,500
Total annual cost	$2,770	$1,760	$1,590	$1,630	$1,920

The EOQ formula contains estimated values and may produce answers that are unrealistic. For example, it is not feasible to place an order that includes fractions of a ton. And, WPI's supplier may only sell pulpwood in 10-ton quantities. In that case, WPI will need to order 150 or 160 tons at a time. In most instances, small errors in estimating costs or rounding results do not create major impacts on total cost. If the cost of ordering quantities close to the EOQ level is not significantly different from the cost of ordering at the EOQ level, some leeway is available in choosing the order size. Other factors, such as cash availability and storage space constraints, should also be considered.

As order size increases, the number of orders and the total annual ordering costs decline. At the same time, the total annual cost of carrying inventory increases because more units are being held in stock at any given point. Conversely, smaller orders reduce carrying costs but increase annual ordering costs.

Companies are currently decreasing their order costs dramatically by using techniques such as electronic data interchange and **open purchase ordering.** A single purchase order, which expires at a set or determinable future date, is prepared to authorize a supplier to provide a large quantity of one or more specified items. The goods will then be requisitioned in smaller quantities as needed by the buyer over the extended future period. For example, R. J. Reynolds Tobacco Co. estimates that, because of open purchase ordering, "purchase orders that previously cost between $75 and $125 to process now cost 93 cents."[7]

open purchase ordering

http:// www.rjrt.com

Another development in this area involves carrying costs, which are increasing. Companies are using higher estimates of these costs in part because of a greater awareness of the high cost of non-value-added activities, such as move time and storage time for units that were purchased but unneeded. As carrying costs rise, the economic order quantity falls. For example, if WPI's ordering and carrying costs were reversed and estimated at $10 and $30, respectively, the EOQ would be 53 tons of pulpwood.

When to Order?

While the EOQ model indicates how many units to order, managers are also concerned with the **order point**—the inventory level that triggers the placement of an order. Order point is based on usage, the amount of inventory used or sold each day; **lead time,** the time from order placement to order arrival; and **safety stock,** a quantity of inventory carried for protection against stockouts. The size of the safety stock for a particular item should be based on how crucial the item is to the business, the item's purchase cost, and the amount of uncertainty related to both usage and lead time. The optimal safety stock is the quantity that balances the cost of carrying with the cost of not carrying safety stock units.

order point

lead time
safety stock

When companies can project a constant figure for both usage and lead time, the order point is calculated as follows:

$$\text{Order Point} = (\text{Daily Usage} \times \text{Lead Time}) + \text{Safety Stock}$$

Assume that WPI uses 15 tons of pulp wood per day and the company's supplier can deliver pulp wood in three days. If no safety stock is carried, pulp wood should be reordered when 45 tons (15×3) are in inventory, and the order should arrive precisely when the inventory reaches zero.

However, companies often experience excess usage or excess lead time. In such cases, safety stock provides an inventory cushion. Although WPI's average daily usage is 15 tons of pulp wood, the company occasionally uses a greater quantity, but never more than 19 tons in one day. A simple way to estimate safety stock is as follows:

---

[7]Andy Kessler, "Fire Your Purchasing Managers," *Forbes ASAP* (October 10, 1994), p. 33.

$$\text{Safety Stock} = (\text{Maximum Usage} - \text{Normal Usage}) \times \text{Lead Time}$$
$$= (19 - 15) \times 3$$
$$= 12 \text{ tons}$$

Using this estimate, WPI would reorder wood pulp when 57 tons (45 original order point + 12 safety stock) were on hand.

Problems with the EOQ Model

Mathematical determination of economic order quantity and optimal quantity of safety stock will help a company control its investment in inventory. However, such models are only as valid as the estimates used in the formulas. For example, projecting costs such as lost customer goodwill may be extremely difficult. In some cases, the degree of inaccuracy may not be important; in other cases, however, it may be crucial.

The basic EOQ model determines what quantity of inventory to order. But there are at least three major problems associated with this model. First, identifying all the relevant inventory costs, especially carrying costs, is very difficult. Second, the model does not provide any direction for managers attempting to control the individual types of ordering and carrying costs. By considering only trade-offs between total ordering and total carrying costs, the EOQ model fails to lead managers to consider inventory management alternatives that might simultaneously reduce cost in both categories. Third, relationships among inventory items are ignored. For example, WPI might require eight tons of pulp wood for each standard production run. If the EOQs for tons of pulp wood and the chemicals needed for each production run are computed independently, this interrelationship could be overlooked. WPI might find that at a time when 96 tons of pulpwood are on hand, enough for 12 production runs, there are only enough chemicals on hand for three production runs. Computer techniques known as MRP and MRP II overcome this deficiency in the EOQ model by integrating interrelationships of units into the ordering process.

MATERIALS REQUIREMENTS PLANNING

LEARNING OBJECTIVE ❸
What are the differences between the economic order quantity model and materials requirements planning?

materials requirements planning (MRP)

bottleneck

manufacturing resource planning (MRP II)

MRP, or **materials requirements planning**, is a computer simulation system that was developed to answer the questions what, how many, and when items are needed. MRP coordinates the future production output requirements with individual future production input needs using a master production schedule (MPS).

The MPS is developed from budgeted sales information and is essentially equivalent to the production budget shown in Chapter 7, although the MPS has significantly more detail regarding time horizons. Once projected sales and production for a product have been estimated, the MRP computer model accesses the product's bill of materials to determine all production components. Quantities needed are compared with current inventory balances. If purchases are necessary, the estimated lead time for each purchase is obtained from supplier information contained in an internal data base. The model then generates a time-sequenced schedule for purchases and production component needs.

The MPS is integrated with the operations flow documents to project the work load for each work center that would result from the master schedule. The work load is compared with the work center's capacity to determine whether meeting the master schedule is feasible. Potential **bottlenecks**, or resource constraints, are identified so that changes in input factors, such as the quantity of a particular component, can be made. Then the MRP program is run again. This process is repeated until the schedule compensates for all potential bottlenecks in the production system.

A variation of the MRP system is known as **MRP II** or **manufacturing resource planning**. This fully integrated system plans production jobs using the usual MRP method and also calculates resource needs such as labor and machine hours. MRP II involves manufacturing, marketing, and finance in determining the master production schedule. While manufacturing is primarily responsible for carrying out the master schedule, it is essential that appropriate levels of resource and sales support be available to make the plan work.

The MRP models extend, rather than eliminate, the economic order quantity concept. EOQ indicates the most economical quantity to order at one time, and MRP indicates which items of inventory to order at what points in time. The EOQ and MRP models are considered **push systems** of production control because they may cause inventory that is not currently needed to be purchased or produced. Such inventory must be stored—that is, *pushed* into storage—until needed by a work center. Exhibit 11-4 depicts the relationship of inventory to production processes in a traditional push production environment.

push system

Many firms like WPI have achieved such significant benefits as reduced inventories, improved labor and space utilization, improved communications, and streamlined scheduling by using MRP and MRP II. In addition, companies report better customer service because of the elimination of erratic production and back orders. In contrast to the push system technology tools of EOQ, EPR, MRP and MRP II, just-in-time systems are based on a more recently emerging approach known as pull system technology.

JUST-IN-TIME SYSTEMS

Just-in-time (JIT) is a philosophy about when to do something. The *when* is "as needed" and the *something* is a production, purchasing, or delivery activity. The basic elements of the JIT philosophy are outlined in Exhibit 11-5 (page 506). Regardless of the type of organization (retail, service, or manufacturing) in which it exists, a just-in-time system has three primary goals:

LEARNING OBJECTIVE ❹
What is the JIT philosophy and how does it affect production?

just-in-time (JIT)

- ◉ Eliminating any production process or operation that does not add value to the product/service
- ◉ Continuously improving production/performance efficiency
- ◉ Reducing the total cost of production/performance while increasing quality

For example, a company using a **JIT manufacturing system** attempts to acquire components and produce inventory units only as they are needed, minimize product defects, and reduce lead/setup times for acquisition and production.

JIT manufacturing system

EXHIBIT 11-4
Push System of
Production Control

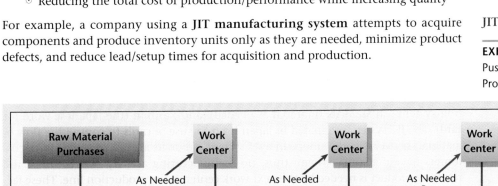

Purchases and production are constantly *pushed down* into storage locations until need arises.

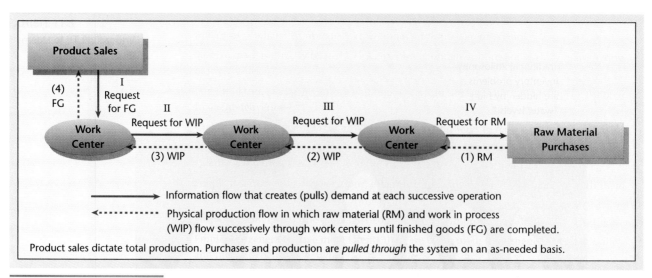

EXHIBIT 11-7

Pull System of
Production Control

http:// www.oregonchain.com

been operational for five to ten years. Exhibit 11-8 details some of the improvements experienced over a four-year period by Oregon Cutting Systems after implementing a JIT program when such programs were beginning to gain popularity.

Any company that aims to achieve the JIT goals must change the majority of its organizational functions. Companies must investigate the partnership-type purchasing arrangements discussed earlier in the chapter. Manufacturers must address product design, product processing, plant layout considerations, and employee empowerment. Product design is discussed in Appendix 3 of the chapter in the presentation of the development stage of the product life cycle; each of the remaining JIT topics are discussed in the following sections.

Product Processing

In making processing improvements, one primary JIT consideration is to reduce machine setup time. Reducing setup time allows processing to shift more rapidly among different types of units, and thus makes the manufacturing process more flexible. A company may need to incur some costs to reduce setup time—for example, for new

NEWS NOTE

You Get What You Want When You Want It

http:// www.mot.com

At the Boynton Beach, Florida, plant where Motorola makes pagers, orders for the pocket-size gizmos stream in from resellers and Motorola salesmen, typically via an 800 line or e-mail. As the salesman spells out what the customer wants—"one Sizzling Yellow pager that goes ding-dong, five in Bimini Blue that beep, ten in Vibra Pink that play a little arpeggio," and so on—the data are digitized and flow to the assembly line. So-called pick-and-place robots select the proper components, but humans assemble the pagers. Often the order is complete within eighty minutes, and depending on where the customer lives, he can have his pagers that same day or the day after.

Motorola thinks of the process not as manufacturing but as rapidly translating data from customers into products; its aim is to do so even faster. Says Sherita Ceasar, director of manufacturing: "Our vision is simultaneous manufacturing, to make the pager even as the customer talks. We're getting close."

SOURCE: Gene Bylinsky, "The Digital Factory," pp. 93, 94. Reprinted from the November 14, 1994, issue of *Fortune* by special permission; © 1994, Time Inc.

EXHIBIT 11-8
Productivity Increases from JIT
at Oregon Cutting Systems

> ⊙ Cut die change time from 6.5 hours to 1 minute and 40 seconds
> ⊙ Cut space requirements 40%
> ⊙ Cut lead times from 21 days to 3 days
> ⊙ Reduced floor space required for manufacturing between 30% and 40%
> ⊙ Reduced setup time for a punch press from 3 hours to 4.5 minutes
> ⊙ Reduced defects 80% with no increases in quality costs
> ⊙ Reduced scrap, sort, and rework 50%
> ⊙ Reduced work in process 85%
> ⊙ Reduced manufacturing costs 35%
> ⊙ Improved shipping productivity 90%
> ⊙ Improved order turnaround time 10–14 days with a 75% order fill rate to 1–2 days with a 97% order fill rate
> ⊙ Reduced product flow distance 94%
> ⊙ Reduced lot sizes between 75% and 90%
>
> SOURCE: Jack C. Bailes and Ilene K. Kleinsorge, "Cutting Waste with JIT," *Management Accounting* (May 1992), p. 29. Reprinted from *Management Accounting*, published by the Institute of Management Accountants, Montvale, N.J. Visit our website at www.imanet.org.

equipment or training. Such increased costs have been found to be more than recovered by the savings derived from reducing downtime, work in process inventory, and materials handling, as well as increasing safety and ease of operation.

Another essential part of JIT product processing is implementing the highest quality standards and focusing on a goal of zero defects. High quality is essential because inferior quality causes additional costs for downtime, rework, scrap, warranty work, and lost customer goodwill. Under JIT systems, quality is determined on a continual basis rather than at quality control checkpoints. Companies using JIT systems achieve continuous quality first by ensuring vendor product quality and then by ensuring quality in the conversion processes.

Quality in manufacturing can be partially obtained through the use of modern production equipment, which often relies on computerized technology to schedule, control, and monitor production processes. Some elements of the production system may be designed to be self-checking—such as the *poka-yoke* techniques discussed in Chapter 3. In the most integrated systems, sophisticated computer programs monitor each process in the production stream and develop statistical data on the reliability of both components and processes. The data are then available for use in programs that design new products and processes, and in evaluating the reliability of components obtained from each internal and external supplier. In the event that defective products are made, they should be promptly discovered and the problem that created them identified and corrected.

Often, the traditional cost accounting system buries quality control costs and costs of scrap in the standard cost of production. For instance, adding excess materials or labor time into the standard quantities creates a "buried" cost of quality. Such costs are often 10 to 30 percent of total production cost. Consider a company making a $10 product that has quality inspection and scrap costs of 10 percent, or $1 per unit. If that company's annual cost of goods sold is $10,000,000, its quality inspection and scrap costs are $1,000,000! When quality is controlled on an ongoing basis, costs of obtaining high quality may be significantly reduced. It is less costly in many manufacturing situations to avoid mistakes than to correct them. The News Note (page 510) demonstrates the point.

Plant Layout

In an effective JIT system, the physical plant is arranged in a way that is conducive to the flow of goods and the organization of workers. Equipment is placed in a rational arrangement based on the materials flow. Such a layout reduces materials-handling

Revealed at Last: The Secret of Jack Welch's Success

http:// www.ge.com

http:// www.alliedsignal.com

General Electric's Jack Welch is now maniacal about hitting his goal of reducing defects to the point where errors would be almost nonexistent: 3.4 defects per million, or 6 sigma. "This is not about sloganeering or bureaucracy or filling out forms," Welch says. "It finally gives us a route to get to the control function, the hardest thing to do in a corporation."

In implementing Six Sigma, Welch borrowed a page from Motorola—whose engineers first embraced the concept in the early 1990s—and from Allied Signal, which followed Motorola's lead.

It took Motorola eight years to get to 6 sigma from about 3 sigma. Welch said he wanted to get there faster and, like Motorola, apply the Six Sigma program to all the company's businesses. Five years, he said, not eight.

That was in 1995. By 1997 GE had reduced its defect rate to more than 3.5 sigma. Welch demanded that the defect reduction program apply not just to goods rolling off all the manufacturing lines but to performance during the product's lifetime as well.

The money for the Six Sigma program has been well spent. Savings at GE's Medical Systems Division alone hit $40 million in 1997. Also in 1997 GE raised its companywide savings estimate for the defect program twice, from between $400 million and $500 million to $600 million, then $650 million.

SOURCE: Michelle Conlin, "Revealed at Last: The Secret of Jack Welch's Success," *Forbes*, January 26, 1998, p.44.

Having workers in linear groups means that there is less opportunity for backlogs to accumulate. Additionally, components or partially completed units do not have to be gathered in batches and moved to distant work stations within the plant.

cost and the lead time required to get work in process from one point to another. Streamlined design allows people to see problems—such as excess inventory, product defects, equipment malfunctions, and out-of-place tools—more easily.

One way to minimize cycle time through the plant is to establish linear or U-shaped groupings of workers or machines, commonly referred to as **manufacturing cells**. A U-shaped manufacturing cell is depicted in Exhibit 11-9. These cells improve materials handling and flow, increase machine utilization rates, maximize communication among workers, and result in better quality control.

A 1994 study by the National Association of Manufacturers in Washington estimates that almost 40 percent of plants with fewer than 100 employees and 74 percent of larger plants use some sort of cell manufacturing.[8] These percentages are substantially higher now. The News Note (page 512) discusses the use of cell manufacturing at an industrial packaging equipment plant in Louisville, Kentucky.

Manufacturing cells create an opportunity for workers to be cross-trained and thereby broaden their skills and deepen their workplace involvement. Training workers to be multiskilled is valid even in nonmanufacturing companies. For instance, USAA—a San Antonio, Texas, insurance and financial services company—consolidated its departments and trained its salespeople to handle every aspect of processing insurance policies after installing a huge network of automated equipment. The cost of training in such situations can be substantial, and workers often resent change. In the long run, however, employers have a more viable workforce, and workers seem to be more satisfied with their jobs. Additionally, companies may find that workers, when they know more about the process as a whole, are better able to provide helpful suggestions about process improvement.

manufacturing cell

Employee Empowerment

An underlying feature of a just-in-time system and its emphasis on cross training is the concept of employee empowerment. Employees can only be empowered if they have the abilities, tools, and training to perform tasks well, are involved in organizational planning, and can trust and be trusted by management. Given these factors, employees will be able to commit themselves to the pursuit of organizational goals and objectives. But before any employee empowerment can take place, the organization must be willing to invest resources in people and training activities.

EXHIBIT 11-9
Depiction of a Manufacturing Cell

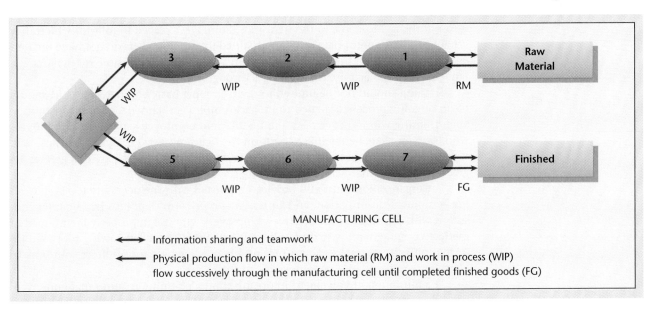

MANUFACTURING CELL

⟷ Information sharing and teamwork

⟵ Physical production flow in which raw material (RM) and work in process (WIP) flow successively through the manufacturing cell until completed finished goods (FG)

[8]Stephanie N. Mehta, "Cell Manufacturing Gains Acceptance at Smaller Plants," *Wall Street Journal*, September 15, 1994, p. B2.

http:// www.lantechinc.com

Keeping It Simple

For 20 years, as the founder and chairman of Lantech Inc., a manufacturer of industrial packaging equipment, Pat Lancaster roared down the same fast lanes as most American industrialists, acquiring ever-bigger mainframes and ever-speedier machines while hiring battalions of programmers, process engineers, and consultants to keep things up and running.

But that was then. These days, the Lantech plant is running on technology that could have been installed 40 years ago. And instead of a mainframe crunching algorithms to maintain process control, Lancaster's managers use simple visual aids like cue cards (to signal when to order new supplies) and strips of tape (to indicate the direction of the production flow).

It's enough to make an automation guru blanch, but there's no arguing with the results. Lantech's productivity is up almost 100 percent since the company scuttled its old high-tech system in 1992. The firm reorganized production from a hurry-up-and-wait pattern, in which inventory was moved in batches from one sector of the factory to another, into a system that consists of several microlines, or production cells. Each of those cells would be responsible for all the processes—sawing, welding, electrical wiring—once spread throughout the whole factory. The reorganization, in turn, would increase the attention given to each step, both because more people would be involved and because the smaller line configuration would make it easier for each person to see what the others were doing. Inventory, on *kanban* cards, were placed on the bottoms of storage bins; when a card became visible, it was picked up and an order faxed to the supplier. With the new system, Lantech makes one set of parts at a time, fabricating them as dictated by actual orders rather than by spreadsheet projections.

Sums up Lancaster: "We were just automating chaos, buying expensive machines to do wasteful things at higher and higher rates of speed." Certainly the absence of towering piles of inventory makes a dramatic impression on anyone visiting the Lantech plant. There's so much space and light, the factory floor feels like a convention center.

SOURCE: Fred Hapgood, "Keeping It Simple," *Inc. Technology*, (1996, No. 1), pp. 66–72.

Any business should recognize that the first condition of hiring and placement is to put the right people in the right jobs. Employees placed in jobs for which they do not have the appropriate skills are destined to fail. If workers do not have the necessary abilities when they are hired, the organization is responsible for making certain that they can acquire these abilities through training.

Training should not be limited to giving people basic competencies but should be an ongoing process designed to increase employees' knowledge and capabilities. Such training will improve both job quality and employee self-esteem. Employees who learn more are better able to perform their current tasks, analyze those tasks and suggest methods of improvement, acquire new skills, and participate to a greater degree in organizational planning.

The organization must also provide employees with the necessary tools—including equipment, information, and authority—to perform their jobs in a manner consistent with organizational objectives. Employees who use improperly maintained or ineffective equipment, who do not have the necessary problem-solving tools and information to investigate and correct problems, or who cannot effect solutions to identified problems are not empowered in their jobs.

At a minimum, involvement in organizational planning requires that employees be told of, and agree with, the business's basic strategy. However, true empowerment means that the company has flattened the organizational structure and pushed decision-making authority and responsibility down to the lowest reasonable level. Flatter structures are more flexible, allowing decisions to be made rapidly in response to need. When such structures exist, feedback must be provided to employees about their involvement and the impact of their decisions.

For empowerment to work effectively in an organization, there must be an atmosphere of trust among all employees at all levels. This element of empowerment is crucial and often difficult to obtain, because many American organizations currently operate in an atmosphere of mistrust between managers and subordinates.[9] This mistrust creates a wide variety of fears: fear of making mistakes, fear of retaliation (including job loss), fear of being viewed as a troublemaker, fear of risk taking, fear of speaking out, and, very importantly, fear of change. Employees' fears can be eliminated only through development of mutual trust, which will allow the fears and their underlying causes to be confronted, analyzed, and resolved.

Overall, the just-in-time philosophy is more than a cost-cutting endeavor. It requires good human resource management and a dedication to teamwork. Exhibit 11-10 provides an action plan for implementing a JIT system.

It is important to note that just-in-time systems may not be appropriate for all types of companies. Companies whose raw materials or components are crucial to processing activities may be unable to afford the potential stockout cost of maintaining minimal inventories.

Finally, when there are unexpected occurrences, such as a rail strike, companies using a just-in-time system may face business closure or limited production for some time—even if they have arranged for alternative means of transport.

THE THREE MOST IMPORTANT RELATIONSHIPS

Every company has a set of upstream suppliers and a set of downstream customers. In a one-on-one context, these parties can be depicted in the following model:

It is at the interfaces of these relationships that real opportunities for improvements exist. By building improved cooperation, communication and integration, these entities can treat each other as extensions of themselves. In so doing, they can enjoy gains in quality, output, and cost efficiency. Non-value-added activities can be reduced or eliminated and performance of value-added activities can be enhanced. Shared expertise and problem solving can be very beneficial. Products and services

1. Determine how well products, materials, or services are delivered now.
2. Determine how customers define superior service, and set priorities accordingly.
3. Establish specific priorities for distribution (and possibly purchasing) functions to meet customer needs.
4. Collaborate with and educate managers and employees to refine objectives and to prepare for implementation of JIT.
5. Execute a pilot implementation project and evaluate its results.
6. Refine the JIT delivery program and execute it companywide.
7. Monitor progress, adjust objectives over time, and always strive for excellence.

SOURCE: Gene R. Tyndall, "Just-in-Time Logistics: Added Value for Manufacturing Cost Management," *Journal of Cost Management* (Spring 1989), pp. 57–59.

EXHIBIT 11-10

Seven Steps to Implement a JIT System

[9]Jack Hagan, *Management of Quality* (Milwaukee: ASQC Quality Press and Business One Irwin, 1994), p. 72.

can be provided faster and with fewer defects, and activities can be performed more effectively and reliably with fewer deficiencies and less redundancy.

Consider the following opportunities for improvement between entities:

⊙ Improved communication of requirements and specifications
⊙ Greater clarity in requests for products or services
⊙ Improved feedback regarding unsatisfactory products or services
⊙ Improvements in planning, controlling, and problem solving
⊙ Shared managerial and technical expertise, supervision, and training

All of the above can also be said for individuals and groups within an organization. Within the company, each employee or work center of employees has both an upstream supplier and a downstream customer who form the context within which work is accomplished. When employees see their internal suppliers and customers as extensions of themselves and work to exploit the opportunities just discussed, teamwork is significantly enhanced.

FLEXIBLE MANUFACTURING SYSTEMS AND COMPUTER INTEGRATED MANUFACTURING

Automated equipment and cellular plant layout, coupled with computer hardware and software technology and new manufacturing systems and philosophies such as JIT and activity-based management, have allowed many manufacturers to change their basic manufacturing philosophy. Traditionally, most manufacturing firms employed long production runs to make thousands of identical models of the same products; this process was encouraged by the idea of economies of scale. After each run, the machines would be stopped, and a slow and expensive setup would be made for the next massive production run. Now an entirely new generation of manufacturing, known as the flexible manufacturing systems (FMS), has been developed. Exhibit 11-11 contrasts a traditional manufacturing system with an FMS.

LEARNING OBJECTIVE ⑤
What is the impact of flexible manufacturing systems on production and on satisfying customers?

computer integrated manufacturing (CIM)

As discussed in Chapter 3, an FMS is a network of robots and material conveyance devices monitored and controlled by computers. The system is characterized by rapid production and prompt responsiveness to changes in production needs. Two or more FMSs connected by a host computer and an information networking system are generally referred to as **computer integrated manufacturing (CIM)**. An FMS is typically associated with short-volume production runs; CIMs are typically used for high-volume lines.

Companies using an FMS or a CIM are able to quickly and inexpensively stop producing one item and start producing another. This ability combined with being able to operate at very high speeds permits a company to manufacture a large assortment of products. Thus, customers are offered a wide variety of high-quality products while the company minimizes its product costs. The system can operate in a "lights-out" (or fully automated) environment and never tire. The News Note on the next page discusses Toshiba's flexible manufacturing system at a plant in Ome, Japan.

http:// www.toshiba.com

The FMS works so fast that moving products along and out of the way of other products is sometimes a problem. Japan's Nissan Motor Company's FMS facility on Kyushu Island has replaced the time-honored conveyor belt with a convoy of little yellow intelligent motor-driven dollies that "tote cars at variable speeds down the assembly line sending out a stream of computer-controlled signals to coach both robots and workers along the way."[10]

The need for direct labor is diminished in such a technology-intensive environment. The workers who remain in a company employing an FMS must be more

[10]Clay Chandler and Joseph B. White, "It's Hello Dollies at Nissan's New 'Dream Factory,'" *Wall Street Journal*, July 6, 1992, p. 1.

FACTOR	TRADITIONAL MANUFACTURING	FMS
Information requirements	Batch-based	On-line, real-time
Product variety	Low	Practically unlimited
Response time to market needs	Slow	Rapid
Worker tasks	Specialized	Diverse
Production runs	Long	Short
Lot sizes	Massive	Small
Basis of performance rewards	Individual	Team
Setups	Slow and expensive	Fast and inexpensive
Product life cycle expectations	Long	Short
Work area control	Centralized	Decentralized
Technology	Labor-intensive	Technology-intensive
Worker knowledge of technology	Low to medium	Highly trained

EXHIBIT 11-11
Comparison of Traditional Manufacturing and an FMS

highly trained than workers in traditional systems and will find themselves handling a greater variety of tasks than the narrowly specialized workers of earlier manufacturing eras. The manufacturing cells are managed by empowered employees who have greater authority and responsibility than in the past. This increase in control is necessary because production and production scheduling changes happen so rapidly on the shop floor. An FMS relies on immediate decisions by persons who "live there" and have a grasp of the underlying facts and conditions.

NEWS NOTE

Flexible Systems Mean Frequent Changes

Flexibility is an explicit goal at Toshiba, whose sales come from products as diverse as appliances and computers, light bulbs and power plants. Okay, so the slogan "Synchronize production in proportion to customer demand" probably made few hearts leap when Toshiba workers first heard it in 1985. The idea was to push Toshiba's factories to adapt faster to market demand. Said Sato: "Customers wanted choices. They wanted a washing machine or a TV set that was precisely right for their needs. We needed variety, not mass production."

Sato hammered home his theme in an almost nonstop series of factory visits. The key to variety: finding ways to make money from ever shorter production runs. Sato urged managers to reduce setup times, shrink lead time, and learn to make more products with the same equipment and people. He said: "Every time I go to a plant I tell the people, 'Smaller lot!'"

Toshiba's computer factory in Ome could be called an "intelligent works" because a snazzy computer network links office, engineering, and factory operations, providing just-in-time information as well as just-in-time parts. Ome workers assemble a variety of word processors on the same line and, on an adjacent one, many varieties of laptop computers. The factory usually made a batch of twenty before changing models, but Toshiba could afford lot sizes as small as ten.

Workers were trained to make each model but didn't need to rely on memory. A laptop at every post displayed a drawing and instructions, which changed when the model did. Product life-cycles for low-end computers are measured in months, so the flexible lines allowed the company to guard against running short of a hot model or overproducing one whose sales have slowed.

SOURCE: Thomas A. Stewart, "Brace for Japan's Hot New Strategy," pp. 64, 74. Reprinted from the September 21, 1992, issue of *Fortune* by special permission; © 1992, Time Inc.

SITE ANALYSIS

Werthan Packaging, Inc.

Clear financial objectives were expected from the Werthan Packaging, Inc. (WPI) upgrade in 1994:

- Achieve 99 percent delivery performance by 1995
- Improve inventory turns by 10 days by 1996
- Reduce old age receivables by $500M by 1997
- Reduce the cost of materials by $1,451M by 1996
- Provide a tool to project capacity requirements
- Provide a tool to support world-class MRPII concepts

The technology upgrade resulted in numerous benefits at WPI that include the following: In operations, WPI's scheduling system is linked to the materials requirements and capacity planning modules and provides consistent data for planning and successful execution of the manufacturing schedule. Lead times and safety stocks are reduced. Delivery performance has improved by 30 percent since changing to the new system.

WPI can now model, in real time, the impact of product changes on pricing. In its shop order entry system, WPI has improved quality, reduced waste, and significantly decreased the number of errors in instruction communications since 1994.

WPI has also improved its financial position since implementing the new system in 1994. Some examples are as follows:

- Material cost has been reduced by two times the original plan goal
- Inventory turns have improved by 20 percent
- Long overdue receivables have been reduced by the original goal amount
- Total liabilities are down by 36 percent
- The liabilities-to-equity ratio has improved from 2.48 to 1.3.

Company personnel are proud of their accomplishments and look forward to the next change around the corner.

SOURCE: Chris McCarthy, "Using Technology as a Competitive Tool," *Management Accounting* (January 1998), pp. 29–30. Published by the Institute of Management Accountants, Montvale, N.J. Visit our website at www.imanet.org.

CROSS-FUNCTIONAL APPLICATIONS

TOPIC OF NOTE	DISCIPLINE	CROSS-FUNCTIONAL APPLICATIONS
Economic Order Quantity (EOQ)	Purchasing	Most firms employ some variation of centralized purchasing to benefit from the savings of large-scale ordering. When technical specifications are beyond the purchasing manager's competence, the EOQ provides a basis to approach the requisitioning department for alternatives by making department personnel aware of the cost constraints. Some firms have established a policy limiting the access of technical sales people to company engineers in an attempt to avoid requisitions that can only be filled by one source. This widespread practice undermines the EOQ cost considerations for which a purchasing manager is responsible.

CROSS-FUNCTIONAL APPLICATIONS

TOPIC OF NOTE	DISCIPLINE	CROSS-FUNCTIONAL APPLICATIONS
Economic Order Quantity (EOQ) *(continued)*	Marketing Research	Marketers often project trends in customer purchasing behavior to concentrate their sales and promotional efforts on the customer's reorder point. Information concerning fluctuations in customer EOQ may signal marketers to change their pricing policy or terms of trade. Intermittently, in-house marketing researchers may influence the EOQ of the company's production department by identifying a shift in product demand.
	Production	The space requirements of an excessive inventory or a prolonged holding period obscure problems such as defective units, deterioration, or obsolescence that may be identified too late to minimize losses or to take corrective action. This situation can result in inefficient production runs, excessive quality costs, and inflexibility in retooling (production changeovers). EOQ's emphasis on cost factors assists production managers, in a cooperative effort with centralized purchasing, to maintain inventories that support flexible decision making and minimize losses of all forms of inventory shrinkage.
Just-in-Time Inventory Management (JIT)	Software Design	The efficient use of JIT systems depends on a close working relationship between customers and their suppliers. Cooperation must be supported by an understanding of both the technical and commercial needs of all involved. Software designers use JIT models to establish technical specifications, usage rates, and delivery times in a common database that is sufficiently flexible to accommodate the requirements of everyone involved. This information-sharing arrangement between organizations is usually a monumental task for software designers.
	Taxation	Many states and some foreign nations charge a tax on inventories that is usually levied only on finished goods. JIT systems can minimize this tax burden by reducing inventories or delaying them in a subassembly status (work in process). Some governments have considered taxing inventories as value is added during processing (ad valorum tax). This form of taxation involves expensive administrative costs; however, if it is used, the JIT systems can provide a greater tax savings for tax managers.
	Quality Assurance/ Quality Control (QA/QC)	QA/QC and safety engineers can discover waste, spoilage, and defective products in a much shorter time, which permits managers to take corrective action or at least minimize loss and liability related to inventory problems. Quality- and safety-conscious firms can experience a reduction in quality costs by adopting or improving the JIT system.
	Industrial Law Enforcement	Law enforcement agencies responsible for industrial espionage, pirating, and theft of inventory are more effective in reducing criminal activity when a JIT system is used. JIT systems usually have well-defined sourcing, product specifications, and handling conditions, which establish responsibility and reduce investigative costs. Criminal conspirators tend to avoid an efficient JIT system, in part because responsible employees at all levels are more aware of their activity in a lean inventory.

CROSS-FUNCTIONAL APPLICATIONS

TOPIC OF NOTE	DISCIPLINE	CROSS-FUNCTIONAL APPLICATIONS
Just-in-Time Inventory Management (JIT) *(continued)*	Environmental and Regulatory Law	Firms that produce toxic or regulated substances, such as chemical manufacturers, have a mandated responsibility to control their products, from inputs to ultimate disposal. JIT systems assist both governmental regulators and a firm's compliance officers with identifying, reporting, and correcting any serious violations with minimal efforts.
	Financial Accounting	Recent Security and Exchange Commission proposals concerning income reporting and comprehensive income may abolish the practice of "income smoothing" by some firms with large inventories. Financial reporting for firms with a reliable JIT system can yield more accurate income and asset-evaluation information. In a lean inventory, cost flows are more predictable, which supports superior matching of cost of goods sold with sales. In addition, financial accounting guidelines usually overstate the value of inventory by understating the carrying costs. Financial management decisions involving cash flows will be enhanced by more accurate income and carrying cost information.

CHAPTER SUMMARY

Classifying inventory into ABC categories allows management to establish controls over inventory items that are related to the cost and volume of inventory items. A-category items require good inventory controls and usually are accounted for using a perpetual inventory system. Two-bin and red-line systems are acceptable for C-category inventory items because of the limited financial investment they involve.

Costs associated with inventory can be significant for any company, and sound business practices seek to limit the amount of those costs. Inventory costs include the costs of purchasing, ordering, carrying, and not carrying inventory. The economic order quantity (EOQ) model determines the purchase order size that minimizes, in total, the costs of ordering and carrying inventory. (This model can also be adapted to find the most economical production run.)

The EOQ model ignores relationships among product components. To overcome this shortcoming, materials requirements planning (MRP) can be used to generate master production and time-sequenced purchasing schedules. Manufacturing resource planning (MRP II) implements MRP on a companywide basis and includes top management input. Both MRP models reflect a push system of production control dictated by delivery lead times and EOQ (or EPR) requirements. Purchased and produced goods must be stored until needed.

In contrast, a pull system of production control, such as just-in-time manufacturing, involves the purchase or production of inventory only as needs arise. Storage is eliminated except for a minimal level of safety stock.

The JIT philosophy can be applied to some extent in any company having inventories. JIT requires that purchases be made in small quantities and that deliveries be frequent. Production lot sizes are minimized so that many different products can be made on a daily basis. Products are designed for quality, and component parts are standardized to the extent possible. Machine setup time is reduced so that production runs can be easily shifted between products. To eliminate the need for or buildup of buffer inventories between operations, plant layout emphasizes manufacturing cells, and the operating capabilities of all factory equipment are considered.

A special type of just-in-time company is one that engages in flexible manufacturing. Flexible manufacturing systems are so fast and versatile that products can be tailored to customer requests in most instances with only an insignificant delay in production time.

APPENDICES

1. ACCOUNTING IMPLICATIONS OF JIT

There are significant accounting implications for companies adopting a just-in-time inventory system. A primary accounting impact occurs in the area of variance analysis. Because a traditional standard cost accounting system is primarily historical in nature, its main goal is variance reporting. Once reported, variances can be analyzed and similar problems can be avoided in the future.

LEARNING OBJECTIVE 6
How would the traditional accounting system change if a JIT inventory system were adopted?

Variance reporting and analysis essentially disappear in JIT systems. Because most variances are first recognizable by a *physical* (rather than financial) occurrence, JIT mandates that variances be brought to an appropiate person's attention immediately so that causes can be ascertained and, if possible, promptly removed. JIT workers are trained and expected to monitor quality and efficiency continually *while production occurs* rather than only at the end of production. Therefore, the number and monetary significance of end-of-period variances that have not already been addressed should be limited.

Under a JIT system, long-term price agreements have been made with vendors, so material price variances should be minimal. The JIT accounting system should be designed so that no one can prepare a purchase order for an amount greater than the designated price without management approval.[11] In this way, the variance amount and its cause are known in advance, providing an opportunity to eliminate the excess expenditure before it occurs. Calls can be made to the vendor to negotiate the price or other vendors can be contacted for quotes.

The ongoing use of specified vendors also gives a company the ability to control material quality. Because raw material quality is expected to be better controlled, material quantity variances caused by substandard material should be rare. If quantity standards are accurate, there should be virtually no favorable material quantity variance during production. Unfavorable usage of material should be promptly detected because of ongoing machine or human observation of processing. When an unfavorable variance occurs, the JIT system is stopped and the problem causing the unfavorable material usage is corrected.

One type of quantity variance is caused not by errors but by engineering changes (ENCs) in the product specifications. A JIT system has two comparison standards, an annual standard and a current standard. Design modifications change the current standard, but not the annual one. If the current, but not the annual standard is changed, the cost effects of making engineering changes after a product has been put into production can be determined. A material quantity variance caused by an ENC is illustrated in Exhibit 11-12 (page 520). In the illustration, the portion of the total quantity variance

---

[11]This procedure can be implemented under a traditional standard cost system as well as under JIT. It is, however, less common in the traditional standard cost system; it is a requirement under JIT.

EXHIBIT 11-12

Material Variances Under a
JIT System

Annual standard:	12 pounds of material A @ $4.40	$52.80
	6 pounds of material B @ $5.20	31.20
		$84.00
Current standard:	10 pounds of material A @ $4.40	$44.00
	8 pounds of material B @ $5.20	41.60
		$85.60

Production during month: 12,000 units

Usage during month:	121,000 pounds of material A @ $4.40	$ 532,400
	95,600 pounds of material B @ $5.20	497,120
	Total cost of material used [TCMU]	$1,029,520

Material quantity variance:

12,000 × 10 × $4.40	$ 528,000
12,000 × 8 × $5.20	499,200
Total cost of material at current standard [TCMCS]	$1,027,200
Total cost of material used [TCMU]	(1,029,520)
Material quantity variance [MQV]	$ 2,320 U

In equation form: MQV = TCMCS − TCMU

Engineering change variance for material:

12,000 × 12 × $4.40	$ 633,600
12,000 × 6 × $5.20	374,400
Total cost of material at annual standard [TCMAS]	$1,008,000
Total cost of material at current standard [TCMCS]	(1,027,200)
Material ENC variance [MENCV]	$ 19,200 U

In equation form: MENCV = TCMAS − TCMCS

caused by the engineering change ($19,200 U) is shown separately from the portion created by inefficiency ($2,320 U). It is also possible to have ENC variances for the labor and overhead or conversion cost categories.

If standard rates and times have been set appropriately in a just-in-time system, labor variances should be minimal. Labor time standards should be carefully evaluated after the implementation of a JIT production system. If the plant is not entirely automated, redesigning the physical layout and minimizing any non-value-added labor activities should decrease the direct labor time component. If the plant is entirely automated, all workers will be classified as indirect labor and, thus, there could be no direct labor variances.

Another accounting change that may occur in a JIT system is the use of a conversion category, rather than separate labor and overhead categories, for purposes of cost control. This category becomes more useful as factories automate and reduce direct labor cost. A standard departmental or manufacturing cell conversion cost per unit of product (or per hour of production time per department) may be calculated rather than separate standards for labor and overhead. The denominator for the cost per unit is practical capacity in either hours or units.[12] For example, if time were used as the base, the conversion cost for a day's production would be equal to the number of units produced multiplied by the standard number of production hours allowed multiplied by the standard cost per hour. Variances would be determined by comparing actual cost with the designated standard.

A JIT system can have a major impact on inventory accounting as well as on variances. Companies employing JIT production processes no longer need a separate inventory account for raw material, because material is acquired only as production occurs. Instead, a Raw and In Process (RIP) Inventory account is used.

---

[12]Practical capacity is the appropriate measure of activity because the goal of JIT is virtually continuous processing. In a highly automated plant, practical capacity is set closer to theoretical capacity than in a traditional plant. However, it may still be unreasonable to set the denominator at the theoretical level because even under a JIT system work stoppages occur for a variety of reasons.

2. BACKFLUSH COSTING

Accounting in a JIT system focuses on the plant's output to the customer.[13] Because each area depends on the previous area, any problems will quickly stop the production process. Daily accounting for the individual costs of production is no longer necessary; all costs should be at standard, since variations are observed and corrected almost immediately.

Further, since costs are more easily traced to their related output in a JIT system, fewer costs are arbitrarily allocated to products. Costs are incurred in specified cells on a per-hour or per-unit basis. Energy costs are direct to production in a comprehensive JIT system because there should be a minimum of downtime by machines or unplanned idle time for workers. Virtually the only costs still being allocated are costs associated with the structure (building depreciation, rent, taxes, and insurance) and machinery depreciation. By comparison, activity-based-costing attempts to allocate manufacturing overhead costs to products more accurately than under traditional cost accounting systems by using multiple cost drivers rather than by using departmental overhead application rates.

Backflush costing is a streamlined cost accounting method that speeds up, simplifies, and reduces accounting effort in an environment that minimizes inventory balances, requires few allocations, uses standard costs, and has minimal variances from standard. During the period, this costing method records purchases of raw material and accumulates actual conversion costs. Then, either at completion of production or upon the sale of goods, an entry is made to allocate the total costs incurred to Cost of Goods Sold and to Finished Goods Inventory, using standard production costs.

backflush costing

Implementation of a just-in-time system can result in significant cost reductions and productivity improvements. But even within a single company, not all inventories need to be managed according to a just-in-time philosophy. The costs and benefits of any inventory control system must be evaluated before management installs the system.

Exhibit 11-13 (page 522) provides information on a product of the Bernard Company. This information is used to illustrate the journal entries for backflush costing. The company has a long-term contract with its supplier for raw material at $75 per unit, so there is no material price variance. Bernard's JIT inventory system has minimum inventories that remain constant from period to period. Beginning inventories for June are assumed to be zero.

Three alternatives are possible to the entries in Exhibit 11-13. First, if Bernard's production time were extremely short, the company might not journalize raw material purchases until completion of production. In that case, entries (1) and (3) from Exhibit 11-13 could be combined as follows:

Raw and In Process Inventory	30,000	
Finished Goods	5,180,000	
Accounts Payable		1,530,000
Conversion Costs		3,680,000

If goods were immediately shipped to customers on completion, Bernard could use a second alternative, in which entries (3) and (4)(a) from Exhibit 11-13 could be combined in the following manner to complete and sell the goods:

Finished Goods	51,800	
Cost of Goods Sold	5,128,200	
Raw and In Process Inventory		1,500,000
Conversion Costs		3,680,000

---

[13]A company may wish to measure the output of each manufacturing cell or work center rather than total output. Although this practice may reveal problems in a given area, it does not correlate with the JIT philosophy, which emphasizes a team approach, plantwide attitude, and total cost picture.

EXHIBIT 11-13

Backflush Costing

Bernard Company's standard production cost per unit:

Raw material	$ 75
Conversion	184
Total cost	$259

No beginning inventories exist.

(1) Purchased $1,530,000 of raw material in June:

Raw and In Process Inventory	1,530,000	
Accounts Payable		1,530,000
Purchased material at standard cost under a		
long-term agreement with supplier.		

(2) Incurred $3,687,000 of conversion costs in June:

Conversion Costs	3,687,000	
Various accounts		3,687,000
Record conversion costs. Various accounts include		
wages payable for direct and indirect labor, accumulated		
depreciation, supplies, etc.		

(3) Completed 20,000 units of production in June:

Finished Goods (20,000 × $259)	5,180,000	
Raw and In Process Inventory (20,000 × $75)		1,500,000
Conversion Costs (20,000 × $184)		3,680,000

(4) Sold 19,800 units on account in June for $420:

(a) Cost of Goods Sold (19,800 × $259)	5,128,200	
Finished Goods		5,128,200
(b) Accounts Receivable (19,800 × $420)	8,316,000	
Sales		8,316,000

Ending Inventories:

Raw and In Process ($1,530,000–$1,500,000)	$30,000
Finished Goods ($5,180,000–$5,128,200)	51,800

In addition, there are underapplied conversion costs of $7,000 ($3,687,000–$3,680,000).

The third alternative reflects the ultimate JIT system, in which only one entry is made to replace entries (1), (3), and (4)(a) in Exhibit 11-13. For Bernard, this entry would be:

Raw and In Process Inventory (minimal overpurchases)	30,000	
Finished Goods (minimal overproduction)	51,800	
Cost of Goods Sold	5,128,200	
Accounts Payable		1,530,000
Conversion Costs		3,680,000

Note that in all cases, entry (2) is not affected. All conversion costs must be recorded as incurred, or accrued at the end of a period, because of their effect on a variety of accounts.

3. PRODUCT LIFE CYCLE AND COST CONTROL ISSUES

LEARNING OBJECTIVE ❼

How does the product life cycle influence sales and costs?

The product life cycle stage is a significant consideration in executing a firm's planning and control functions regarding product costs and other costs. The stage a product has reached in its life cycle significantly affects sales volume, price, and unit production cost. Both revenues and costs for a given product change as the product advances through development, introduction, growth, maturity, and harvest stages.

Total revenues are nonexistent during the development stage and commence during introduction. They typically rise during growth, level off in maturity, and decline during

Fashion trends seem to run through the product life cycle over and over again. However, changes do occur relative to colors, patterns, and fabric usage.

harvest. In contrast, costs are characteristically high during development and introduction and tend to stabilize as production becomes routine. Rigorous product development and design efforts are usually worthwhile because 80 to 90 percent of a product's life cycle cost is determined by decisions made before production begins.

Products and services, like people, go through a series of life cycle stages. It is not easy to determine how old a product must be before it moves from one stage to another. Some products, such as the hula hoop, come and go fairly quickly; others, such as Barbie and Ken dolls, have changed minimally and managed to remain popular products. Still other products, such as bell-bottoms and miniskirts, have been revitalized and have come back from the dead with renewed vigor. Services, too, change over time. For instance, twenty years ago personal financial planning and home health-care services were in their infancy, and long-distance bus service was beginning to decline in importance. Today, long-term-care insurance is making its debut. It is difficult, if not impossible, to predict what services will be available in 2015.

The stages of the product life cycle are development, introduction, growth, maturity, and harvest; relative sales levels for these stages are shown in Exhibit 11-14 (page 524). Companies must be aware of the life cycle stage at which each of their products have arrived, because the stage may have a tremendous impact on costs, sales, and pricing strategies.

⊙ DEVELOPMENT STAGE

If products are designed properly, they should require only a minimal number of engineering changes after being released to production. Each time an engineering change is made, one or more of the following problems occurs, creating additional costs: The operations flow document must be reprinted, workers must relearn tasks, machine dies or set-ups must be changed, and parts currently ordered or in stock may be made obsolete. As indicated in Exhibit 11-15 (page 524), if cost and time to market are not to be affected significantly, any design changes must be made early in the process.

EXHIBIT 11-14
Product Life Cycle

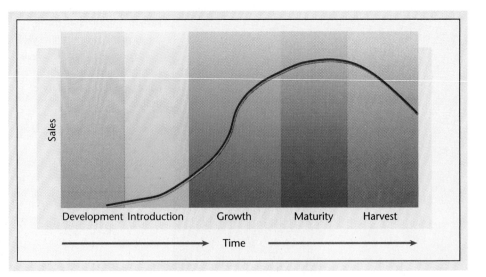

Products need to be designed to use the fewest number of parts, and parts should be standardized to the greatest extent possible. Consumers may appreciate some degree of variety, but a company can end up with too much of a good thing; for example, "at one point, Nissan had 300 different ashtrays in its cars."[14] Changes can be made after original design, but any cost savings generated by such changes will be substantially less than if the changes had been made early in the design/development process.

Decisions made during the development stage are particularly important. They can affect product sales, design, production costs, and quality for the remainder of the product's life cycle.

EXHIBIT 11-15

Design Change Effects on Cost and Time to Market

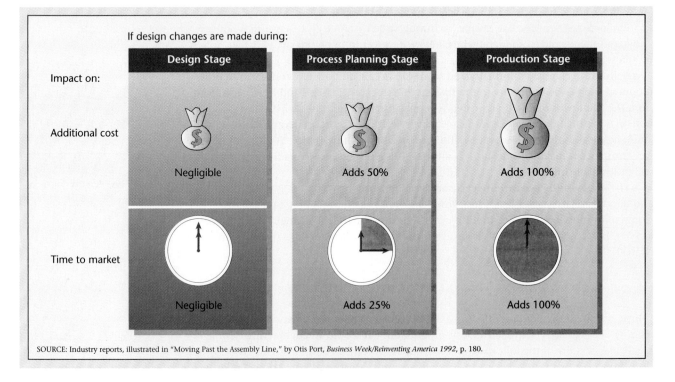

SOURCE: Industry reports, illustrated in "Moving Past the Assembly Line," by Otis Port, *Business Week/Reinventing America 1992*, p. 180.

---

[14]Jacob M. Schlesinger, Michael Williams, and Craig Forman, "Japan Inc., Wracked by Recession, Takes Stock of Its Methods," *Wall Street Journal*, September 29, 1993, p. A4.

⊙ INTRODUCTION STAGE

Product introduction is essentially a start-up phase. Sales are usually quite low, and selling prices often are set according to the market price of similar substitute goods or services, if such goods or services are available. Costs, however, can be quite substantial in the introduction phase. Costs incurred during this phase are typically related to product design, market research, advertising, and promotion.

⊙ GROWTH, MATURITY, AND HARVEST STAGES

The growth stage begins when the product first breaks even. During the growth stage, the product has been accepted by the market, and profits begin to rise. Product quality also may improve during this stage because competitors may have improved on original production designs. Prices are fairly stable during this period because many substitutes exist or because consumers have become attached to the product and are willing to pay a particular price for it rather than buy a substitute.

In the maturity stage, sales begin to stabilize or slowly decline, and firms often compete on the basis of selling price. Costs are often at their lowest level during this period, so profits may be high. Some products, like Kool-Aid, seem to remain at this stage forever.

The harvest (decline) stage reflects waning sales. During the harvest stage, prices are often cut dramatically to stimulate business. As the name implies, management usually attempts to generate as much short-term profits and cash flow as possible at this stage.

⊙ COST AND PRICE CHANGES OVER LIFE

Customers are concerned with obtaining a high-quality product or service for a price they perceive to be reasonable. Product prices change, however, over the product life cycle. Producers of goods and providers of service should be concerned with maximizing profits over a product's or service's life cycle because, to be profitable, the product or service must generate revenues in excess of its total (not single period-by-period) costs.

Because each stage of the product life cycle influences sales and costs differently, each requires its own budgetary focus. Then, as activity takes place and plans are implemented, a monitoring system needs to be in place to capture sales and costs and compare them to an appropriately prepared budget for each particular life cycle stage. Such a comparison provides feedback so that managers will have the information by which to direct activities to achieve desired results throughout each stage of the product life cycle.

KEY TERMS

are unhappy about downtime caused by shortages of raw material. Holster believes the company may be losing as much as $220,000 in revenue as a result of these problems.

ProCorp manufactures only one product: boomerangs (trademarked "Boomers"). The single raw material used in making Boomers is plastic, with each Boomer requiring 8 ounces of red plastic. ProCorp expects to manufacture 300,000 Boomers this year with a steady demand through the entire year. The ordering costs for clerical processing are $30 per order of plastic. There is a three-day delay between placement of an order and receipt of the inventory. The carrying costs for storage, handling, insurance, and interest are $.72 per Boomer unit per year.

a. Discuss the general benefits of a well-managed inventory policy.

b. By using the economic order quantity formula, ProCorp, Inc., determined that the optimal economic order quantity is 2,500 pounds of plastic, which will produce 5,000 units.
   1. Discuss how an increase in each of the following components will affect the economic order quantity: annual sales demand; ordering costs; and carrying costs for storage, handling, insurance, and interest.
   2. Determine the number of times ProCorp will order plastic during the year.

c. ProCorp, Inc., while reviewing its safety stock policy, has determined that an appropriate safety stock is 1,250 pounds of plastic, which will produce 2,500 units.
   1. Describe the factors that affect an appropriate safety stock level.
   2. List the effects of maintaining an appropriate safety stock level on ProCorp's short-term and long-term profitability.
   3. Identify the effect that a well-implemented just-in-time inventory procedure will have on safety stock level, and explain why it will have this effect.

(CMA adapted)

43. *(Objectives of JIT)* The management at Megafilters, Inc., has been discussing the possible implementation of a just-in-time (JIT) production system at its Illinois plant, where oil filters and air filters for heavy construction equipment and large, off-the-road vehicles are manufactured. The Metal Stamping Department at the Illinois plant has already instituted a JIT system for controlling raw materials inventory, but the remainder of the plant is still discussing how to proceed with the implementation of this concept. Some of the other department managers have grown increasingly cautious about the JIT process after hearing about the problems that have arisen in the Metal Stamping Department.

Robert Goertz, manager of the Illinois plant, is a strong proponent of the JIT production system and recently made the following statement at a meeting of all departmental managers. "Just-in-time is often referred to as a management philosophy of doing business rather than a technique for improving efficiency on the plant floor. We will all have to make many changes in the way we think about our employees, our suppliers, and our customers if we are going to be successful in using just-in-time procedures. Rather than dwelling on some of the negative things you have heard from the Metal Stamping Department, I want each of you to prepare a list of things we can do to make a smooth transition to the just-in-time philosophy of management for the rest of the plant."

a. The just-in-time management philosophy emphasizes objectives for the general improvement of a production system. Describe several important objectives of this philosophy.

b. Discuss several actions that Megafilters, Inc., can take to ease the transition to a just-in-time production system at the Illinois plant.

c. For the JIT production system to be successful, Megafilters, Inc., must establish appropriate relationships with its vendors, employees, and customers. Describe each of these three relationships.

(CMA adapted)

44. *(Implementing JIT) Successfully implementing JIT requires certain conditions be met. Consider the case of Allen-Edmonds Shoe Corp., a 71-year-old maker of expensive shoes. In*

1990, the Port Washington, Wis., company tried just-in-time methods to speed production, boost customer satisfaction, and save money. The result? "It really flopped miserably," says John Stollenwerk, the company's president and biggest shareholder. The manufacturer lost $1 million on the project—and in 1991, resumed doing some things the old way.

"It's somewhat difficult for a small company to achieve some of the just-in-time gains of large companies," said Thomas W. Bruett, a partner at Ernst & Young *who advised Allen-Edmonds on production techniques.*

Like owners of other small, old-line manufacturing firms, Mr. Stollenwerk also had difficulty persuading some of his 325 production workers to accept change. At the outset, Mr. Stollenwerk thought just-in-time concepts could stem his firm's loss of business from retailers unwilling to wait as many as eight weeks for their shoe orders. He sought to slice overall production time by as much as 87 percent, to five days.

However, problems plagued the company from the start. To achieve the teamwork and quality focus that JIT demanded, the company dropped its piecework pay plan and adopted an hourly pay plan. But the culture wasn't ripe for such a change: as productivity plummeted, Allen-Edmonds workers complained about co-workers slacking off. One employee who made $9 to $10 an hour, stitching wingtips and other pieces, says she observed "more breaks, more laughing, more giggling." A stitcher must pay attention, she insisted, because "you see the same shoe all day long in a nine-hour day, and your eyes can eventually cross."

Finally, after the company lost $1 million in 1990, it reinstated piecework.

Also, it wasn't easy to get suppliers to go along with the just-in-time strategy of matching delivery to need. Suppliers of leather soles did agree to make deliveries weekly, rather than monthly, to Allen-Edmonds.

But European tanneries supplying calf-skin hides refused to cooperate. They stuck with their practice of processing huge quantities of hides at once and wouldn't handle small batches to meet the weekly needs of a small customer.

[SOURCE: Barbara Marsh, "Allen-Edmonds Shoe Tries 'Just-in-Time' Production," *Wall Street Journal*, March 4, 1994, p. B2. Reprinted by permission of *Wall Street Journal*, © 1994 Dow Jones & Company, Inc. All Rights Reserved.]

a. Why might the implementation of JIT be more difficult in a small firm than in a large firm?

b. How does the "culture" of a firm influence its potential to successfully implement JIT?

c. Describe any recommendations for changes that you might have made to Allen-Edmonds in advance of the company's attempt to implement JIT.

45. *(JIT, special orders)* Systrack Systems produces a private brand of compact disc player. The company makes only one type of player. It is sold through various distribution organizations, which resell the players under their own brand names. The quality of Systrack Systems' product is high, equal to that of nationally branded competitors.

The compact disc industry is highly concentrated, with three major players holding the lion's share of the market. A half-dozen other suppliers, such as Systrack Systems, hold small and about equal market shares. All three of the major suppliers have high-quality products. Consumers are aware of this, leading to a tendency for them to see all brands, including private brands, as about the same. As a result, price competition is intense; and the introduction of new technology as soon as possible is a very important element of marketing strategy.

Systrack Systems has significant experience in the production of compact disc players, having produced an average of 500,000 units per year over the past three years. During manufacturing, compact disc players go through three major processes: cutting, assembly, and finishing. Historically, the manufacturing costs of producing one compact disc player are as follows:

Direct material	$ 40
Direct labor	30
Variable overhead	20
Fixed overhead	10
Total manufacturing costs	$100

At present, Systrack Systems operates at 80 percent of production capacity. The product is sold at $150 in the market.

Andrea Chicoine, president of Systrack Systems, is very interested in converting the company's conventional accounting system to an activity-based costing system and also introducing just-in-time measures into her manufacturing system. Chicoine has asked her controller, John Russ, to submit a comparison of the manufacturing costs under the present system and under a just-in-time system to meet a 100,000-unit special order at a price of $110 per unit. The company has the capacity to meet the special order at no increase in fixed costs. According to Russ's report, if a JIT system is implemented, the following manufacturing costs will be incurred, and manufacturing overhead will be allocated based on an activity-based costing system:

Direct material	$40
Direct labor	35
Variable overhead	15
Fixed overhead	5
Total manufacturing costs	$95

A JIT manufacturing system requires the establishment of manufacturing cells in the plant. The company has to adopt the philosophy of total quality control (TQC). No scrap or waste is allowed. Inventory levels should be zero, because JIT is a demand pull approach. Workers in each cell are trained to perform various tasks within the cell. Therefore, idle time is not permissible. Finally, each cell is considered a separate unit.

Under an activity-based costing system, manufacturing overhead costs are applied to products based on cost drivers and not on departmental overhead rates. Plant layout should be changed, and manufacturing cells should be developed. Many costs that are considered indirect costs under the current system will be considered direct costs that are easy to trace to the final product and are measured precisely. A JIT system considers direct labor costs as fixed costs, not variable costs, as under conventional accounting systems. This is legitimate because workers are trained to perform various jobs within a given work cell. Chicoine is convinced that a JIT manufacturing system would allow the company to more accurately determine product costs.

[Source: Adapted from Nabil Hassan, Herbert E. Brown, and Paula M. Saunders, "Management Accounting Case Study: Systrack Systems," *Management Accounting Campus Report* (Spring 1991).]

a. Should the special order be accepted or rejected under the conventional system? Under the JIT system? Show computations.

b. If the cost activities described in the case will result in different cost estimates and different contribution margins, which cost accounting system is preferable for pricing this special order? Explain.

46. *(Benefits of adopting JIT)* AgriCorp is a manufacturer of farm equipment that is sold by a network of distributors throughout the United States. A majority of the distributors are also repair centers for AgriCorp equipment and depend on AgriCorp's Service Division to provide a timely supply of spare parts.

In an effort to reduce the inventory costs incurred by the Service Division, Richard Bachman, division manager, implemented a just-in-time inventory program on June 1, 2000, the beginning of the company's fiscal year. Because JIT has been in place for a year, Bachman has asked the division controller, Janice Grady, to determine the effect the program has had on the Service Division's financial performance. Grady has been able to document the following results of JIT implementation:

⊙ The Service Division's average inventory declined from $550,000 to $150,000.

⊙ Projected annual insurance costs of $80,000 declined 60 percent because of the lower average inventory.

⊙ A leased 8,000 square foot warehouse, previously used for raw material storage, was not used at all during the year. The division paid $11,200 annual rent for the warehouse and was able to sublet three-quarters of the building to several tenants at $2.50 per square foot, while the balance of the space remained idle.

⊙ Two warehouse employees whose services were no longer needed were transferred on June 1, 2000, to the Purchasing Department to assist in the coordination of the JIT program. The annual salary expense for these two employees totaled $38,000 and continued to be charged to the indirect labor portion of fixed overhead.

⊙ Despite the use of overtime to manufacture 7,500 spare parts, lost sales caused by stockouts totaled 3,800 spare parts. The overtime premium incurred amounted to $5.60 per part manufactured. The use of overtime to fill spare parts orders was immaterial prior to June 1, 2000.

Prior to the decision to implement the JIT inventory program, AgriCorp's Service Division had completed its 2000–2001 fiscal budget. The division's pro forma income statement, without any adjustments for JIT inventory, is presented next. AgriCorp's borrowing rate related to inventory is 9 percent after income taxes. All AgriCorp budgets are prepared using an effective tax rate of 40 percent.

AGRICORP SERVICE DIVISION
PRO FORMA INCOME STATEMENT
FOR THE YEAR ENDING MAY 31, 2001

Sales (280,000 spare parts)		$6,160,000
Cost of goods sold		
Variable	$2,660,000	
Fixed	1,120,000	(3,780,000)
Gross profit		$2,380,000
Selling and administrative expense		
Variable	$ 700,000	
Fixed	555,000	(1,255,000)
Operating income		$1,125,000
Other income		75,000
Income before interest and taxes		$1,200,000
Interest expense		(150,000)
Income before income taxes		$1,050,000
Income taxes		(420,000)
Net income		$ 630,000

a. Calculate the after-tax cash savings (loss) for AgriCorp's Service Division that resulted during the 2000–2001 fiscal year from the adoption of the JIT program.

b. Identify and explain the factors, other than financial, that should be considered before a company implements a JIT program.

(CMA)

⊙ ETHICS AND QUALITY DISCUSSION

47. A plant manager and her controller were discussing the plant's inventory control policies one day. The controller suggested that the plant's ordering policies needed revising. The controller argued that the revision was needed because of new technology that had been put in place in the plant's purchasing department. Among the changes were: (1) installation of computerized inventory tracking; (2) installation of electronic data interchange capabilities, which would allow communications with the plant's major suppliers; and (3) installation of in-house facilities for electronic fund transfers.

a. As technology changes, why should managers update ordering policies for inventory?

b. What would be the likely impact of the changes in this plant on the EOQ of material inputs?

c. What experts should be invited to provide input into designing new policies for ordering materials?

48. In 1994 *Ford Motor Co. halted production at its Kansas City, Mo., assembly plant of one line of compact sedans for one week because of a fuel-leakage problem with 28,500 of the cars.*

Ford wanted to rush replacement fuel-tank assemblies to dealers and customers. Of the 28,500 affected cars, nearly 8,000 had been delivered to U.S. and Canadian customers. The shutdown was expected to cost Ford production of 6,400 cars. Ford hoped to recoup its lost production through additional overtime shifts at the Kansas City plant.

This problem stemmed from a tricky weld near the fuel tank's filler pipe, Ford said. When the weld is improperly made, fuel can leak from the reinforcement on the fuel tank. Ford said it learned of the problem from its customers.

[SOURCE: Oscar Suris, "Ford Is Halting The Production Of a New Line," *Wall Street Journal*, October 18, 1994, p. A4. Reprinted by permission of *Wall Street Journal*, © 1994 Dow Jones & Company, Inc. All Rights Reserved.]

   a. This story indicates one reason for making engineering changes. What are some other possible reasons for such changes?

   b. Why would Ford elect to shut down assembly operations to correct the production flaw?

   c. In what ways might a firm learn of the existence of production flaws? Why would a firm prefer to learn of such flaws from some source other than customers?

49. *Although federal law allows food to contain small traces of bugs, molds and other substances, officials acknowledge that the shard of glass found in a jar of baby food, the maggot in a bag of frozen green beans, or the caustic cleaner in chicken broth should be taken seriously.*

While soda companies in June 1993 were busy assuring the public about the safety precautions in their processing plants, authorities received three legitimate reports of foreign objects in soda cans and bottles.

In Connecticut, a metal and plastic piece from a filling machine was found in a can of caffeine-free Coca-Cola. In Florida, a screw was found in a can of Diet Pepsi. And in Massachusetts, Coca-Cola initiated a recall after it discovered a defect that caused the plastic bottlecap liners to fall into bottles during production, posing a choking hazard.

[SOURCE: Anthony Giorgianni, "Objects in Food More Common Than Syringes in Soda," *(New Orleans) Times-Picayune*, August 18, 1993, p. E6.]

   a. What do the preceding examples of food contamination suggest about the importance of suppliers, such as those that supply containers or production machinery, to product quality?

   b. In the food industry, which in your opinion is more important to the financial prospects of a firm—actual quality of the product as measured by some objective scale, or quality as subjectively perceived by the consumer? Explain.

   c. What are the ethical considerations in determining the quality of products offered by the food industry?

50. Laura Applegate is the production manager for the DeRigeur Company, located in a small town in Mississippi. DeRigeur is the only major employer in the county, which has substantial unemployment.

Laura is in the process of trying to introduce manufacturing cells in the company. Of the 150 employees at DeRigeur, approximately 80 percent have little formal education and have worked for the company for 15 years or more. Some—but not all—of these employees are close to retirement.

In talking with the employees, Laura determines that most would require substantial training before they would be able to change from performing their current single-task production jobs to handling multifunctional tasks.

A neighboring county has a vocational-technical school that is educating many young people in the use of the new types of multitask equipment that could be used at DeRigeur. Laura has discussed the company's plans with the head of the vo-tech school, who has indicated that the school could easily provide a cadre of 150 well-trained employees within the next 10 months—approximately the time it will take the equipment to arrive and be installed.

Laura is excited to hear this, because DeRigeur would not have to pay for training and would be able to hire new graduates at a slightly lower hourly wage because of their lack of experience. Her only difficulty is trying to determine how to remove the older workforce from the plant. She decides to institute a rigorous training program that would be intolerable for most of the less-educated employees.

a. Discuss the business sense of hiring graduates with the necessary skills rather than paying for on-location training.

b. Discuss the ethics of the plan to remove the current workforce.

c. Why should Laura and DeRigeur be concerned about the welfare of the current workforce if it makes good business sense to hire the graduates of the vo-tech school?

51. Two potential impediments to the implementation of JIT and other quality-oriented production systems that require employee participation are union contracts and labor relations laws such as the National Labor Relations Act. In the case of labor unions, union officials are often suspicious of management actions taken in the name of quality improvement because employers have frequently used such quality initiatives as excuses to fire employees. This historical context of quality improvement has caused present-day mistrust between employees and managers. Implementation of genuine quality-enhancing programs is often met with suspicion by employees.

Even so, labor and management are trying to cooperate in some firms for the sake of their mutual survival. For example, in 1994 Levi Strauss worked out an agreement with its labor union that allowed the union to sign up an additional 10,000 of the company's employees. In exchange the union agreed to certain changes to make the company more efficient. For example, in its Harlingen, Texas, plant, the company restructured the production line of 320 people into teams of approximately 15 workers.

Some employees felt that the new agreement began a new age of trust and cooperation between their union and their employer; other workers were more suspicious of the new, cozy relationship between management and the union.
[SOURCE: Adapted from Josh Lemieux, "Hopes Set on Levi Strauss, Union Pact," *Bryan-College Station [Texas] Eagle*, October 16, 1994, p. C3.]

a. Why might unionization constrain the successful implementation of quality-oriented programs in U.S. manufacturing plants?

b. What are the ethical obligations of management to workers in implementing quality programs?

c. What ethical obligations do employees bear in implementing new programs devised by managers?

Chapter 12 Controlling Noninventory Costs

Alaska Airlines

Alaska Air is relatively small. Flying only north-south routes in the West, it carried just short of 12 million passengers in 1996; though up 16.4 percent from 1995, that total accounted for only 2.1 percent of U.S. domestic traffic. Its routes stretch from five cities in the Russian Far East, south to four in Mexico. And while it intends to add new cities from one end of that strip to the other, it doesn't plan to branch out. The company says its narrow range insulates it from major airlines whose systems are built around huge hubs connecting east-west traffic.

When low-cost carriers invaded the Pacific Northwest, Alaska Airlines looked vulnerable. It had some of the industry's highest fares and costs, and little experience defending its skies.

But five years later, the arrival of Southwest Airlines and its no-frills imitators seems to have benefited the Alaska Air Group Inc. unit. How the nation's 10th largest airline turned to its own advantage the coming of low-fare rivals is simpler to explain than it was to accomplish: Alaska generally retained its top-notch service while slashing its fares. When the dust settled, it was the only full-service carrier left on many of its routes, making it the obvious choice for anyone wanting a reserved seat, a nonstop flight, or more than peanuts for a meal. Its revenues and profits are fatter than ever, its traffic is up sharply and its share of the fast-growing West Coast market is at a record level.

SOURCE: Susan Carey, "How Alaska Airlines Beat Back Challenges from Bigger Rivals," *Wall Street Journal,* May 19, 1997, p. A1. Reprinted by permission of *Wall Street Journal,* © 1997 Dow Jones & Company, Inc. All Rights Reserved Worldwide.

*A*ny business wanting to succeed must not only generate reasonable levels of revenues but also control the costs that are matched against those revenues. For airlines, there is often limited control over fares—a competitor's price on a given route must usually be matched or the company can lose market share. *Alaska Air,* for example, was once forced to match competitors' $25 fares in California even though the company did not have the cost control to afford such fares. Its costs were over ten cents a mile compared to the seven or eight cents a mile cost for the competition. It was imperative for the company's survival to determine ways to get a handle on costs. Company management quickly recognized the interaction among cost control, efficiency, and profitability.

cost control system

Previous chapters presented various ways to control costs. For example, control of direct material and direct labor costs are typically linked to the development and implementation of a standard cost system. Additionally, just-in-time inventory techniques can significantly reduce the costs of warehousing and purchasing. This chapter focuses on three topics related to cost control. First, the **cost control system**, which covers all the formal and informal activities related to controlling costs, is discussed. This system is used to analyze and evaluate how well expenditures were managed during a period. Second, costs that are set by management at specific levels each period are considered. Often, these costs are difficult to control because their benefits are harder to measure than those provided by costs that are fixed by long-term commitments. Third, the use of flexible, rather than static, budgets to control costs is reviewed. The chapter appendix considers an alternative budgeting method (program budgeting) used in governmental and not-for-profit entities because of the unique nature of their output.

COST CONTROL SYSTEMS

The cost control system is an integral part of the overall organizational decision support system. This system should provide information for planning and for determining the efficiency of activities. As indicated in Exhibit 12-1, an effective control system must perform at three points: before, during, and after an event. An event could be a period of time, the manufacture of a product, or the performance of a service.

LEARNING OBJECTIVE ❶
Why is cost consciousness of great importance to all members of an organization?

cost consciousness

Managers alone cannot control costs. An organization is composed of a group of individuals whose attitudes and efforts should be considered in determining how an organization's costs may be controlled. Cost control is a continual process that requires the support of *all* employees at *all* times. Thus, a good control system encompasses not only the functions shown in Exhibit 12-1 but also the ideas about cost consciousness shown in Exhibit 12-2. **Cost consciousness** refers to a companywide

CONTROL POINT	REASON	COST CONTROL METHODS
Before an event	Preventive; reflects planning	Budgets; standards; policies concerning approval for deviations; expressions of quantitative and qualitative objectives
During an event	Corrective; ensures that the event is being pursued according to plans; allows managers to correct problems as they occur	Periodic monitoring of ongoing activities; comparison of activities and costs against budgets and standards; avoidance of excessive expenditures
After an event	Diagnostic; guides future actions	Feedback; variance analysis; responsibility reports (discussed in Chapter 14)

EXHIBIT 12-1
Functions of an Effective Cost Control System

employee attitude toward the topics of cost understanding, cost containment, cost avoidance, and cost reduction. Each of these topics is important at a different stage of the control system.

Cost Understanding

Control requires that a set of expectations exist. Thus, cost control is first exercised when a budget is prepared. Budgets can be properly prepared only when the reasons for periodic cost changes are understood. Budgets allow expected costs to be compared with actuals. Knowing that variations occurred is important, but cost control can be achieved only if managers understand why costs differed from the budgeted amounts.

Cost Differences Related to Cost Behavior

Costs may change from previous periods or differ from budget expectations for many reasons. Some costs change because of their underlying behavior. A total variable or mixed cost increases or decreases with increases or decreases in activity level. If the current period's activity level differs from a prior period's activity level or from the budgeted activity level, total actual variable or mixed cost will differ from that of the prior period or that in the budget. For example,  Alaska Airlines' food costs (on

EXHIBIT 12-2
Cost Control System

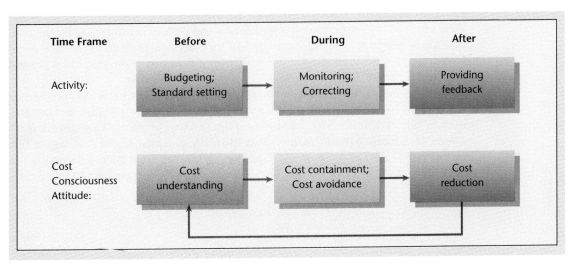

meal-hour flights) will vary almost in direct proportion to the number of passengers. A flexible budget can compensate for differences by providing expected variable costs at any actual activity level. Managers can then make valid budget-to-actual cost comparisons to determine if total variable costs were properly controlled.

In addition to the reactions of variable costs to changes in activity levels, the following three factors can cause costs to differ from those of prior periods or from the budget. In considering these factors, remember that an external *price* becomes an internal *cost* when a good or service is acquired.

Cost Differences Related to Quantity Purchased

A simple reason for an actual per-unit cost differing from that shown in the budget is that the quantity purchased was different from what was expected. Firms are normally given quantity discounts, up to some maximum level, when bulk purchases are made. Therefore, a cost per unit may change when quantities are purchased in lot sizes different from those of previous periods or those projected. Involvement in group purchasing arrangements can make quantity discounts easier to obtain. For example, if Alaska Airlines joined with other soft drink purchasers (even competing airlines) in negotiating the cost of soft drinks, the per unit cost might be reduced significantly. Consider that, in spring 1993, seventeen institutions in the Virginia Council of Independent Colleges jointly negotiated long-distance telephone services. A bid from MCI dropped service from $.21 to about $.07 per minute, with an expected total savings of $5+ million over the three-year life of the contract.[1]

Cost Differences Related to Inflation/Deflation

Fluctuations in the value of money are called general price-level changes. When the general price level changes, the prices of goods and services also change. General price-level changes affect almost all prices approximately equally and in the same direction, if all other factors are constant. Thus, a budgeted cost of $150,000 might become an actual cost of $154,500 with an annual inflation rate of three percent.

Some companies include price-escalation clauses in sales contracts to cover the inflation occurring from order to delivery. Such escalators are especially prevalent in industries having production activities that require substantial time. For instance, the airplane manufacturing industry uses escalation clauses that averaged over 3 percent per year from 1989 to 1995.[2]

Cost Differences Related to Supply/Supplier Cost Adjustments

The relationship of the availability of a good or service to the demand for that item affects its selling price. If supply of an item is low but demand is high, the selling price of the item increases. The higher price often stimulates greater production, which, in turn, increases supply. In contrast, if demand falls but supply remains constant, the price falls. This lowered price should motivate lower production, which lowers supply. Therefore, price is consistently and circularly influenced by the relationship of supply to demand. Price changes for independent items are specific price-level changes, and these may move in the same or opposite direction as a general price-level change.

To illustrate, gasoline prices soared in early 1996 because of two supply-related factors. First was a harsh winter that caused refineries to reduce gasoline, and increase heating oil production. Second, several refineries had problems that caused shutdowns, which also reduced supply.[3] This situation increased Alaska Airlines' jet fuel expense from 1995 to 1996 by $37.7 million.[4] However, since then, production has been up and the price of jet fuel has dropped to about 39 cents a gallon by early

---

[1]Julie L. Nicklin, "Cost-Cutting Consortia," *Chronicle of Higher Education* (April 6, 1994), p. A52.

[2]Howard Banks, "Moment of Truth," *Forbes*, May 22, 1995, p. 56.

[3]"They're Back: High Gas Costs Fuel Carpools," (New Orleans) *Times-Picayune*, April 26, 1996, p. C3.

[4]Alaska Airlines, *1996 Annual Report*; www.alaskaairlines.com; accessed April 26, 1998.

1998. A mere one-cent drop in the price of jet fuel means the following increases in annual operating profits: UAL Corp. (United Airlines), $30 million; Continental Airlines, $15 million; and Trans World Airlines, $7 million.[5] Because of the size of Alaska Airlines, its profit increase would be less than TWA's—but still a hefty amount.

Specific price-level changes may also be caused by advances in technology. As a general rule, as suppliers advance the technology of producing a good or performing a service, its cost to producing firms declines. Assuming competitive market conditions, such cost declines are often passed along to consumers of that product or service in the form of lower selling prices. To demonstrate the basic interaction of increasing technology and decreasing selling prices and costs, consider the greeting cards that play songs when they are opened. Those cards contain more computer processing power than existed in the entire world before 1950.[6]

Of course, when suppliers incur additional production or performance costs, they typically pass such increases on to their customers as part of specific price-level changes. Such costs may be within or outside the company's control. A cost factor that is within an organization's control is the necessity to upgrade computer systems to account for the "millennium bug" or Year 2000 problem. Exhibit 12-3 shows the ten largest cost amounts that have been incurred by U.S. companies as of early 1998. The News Note on page 546 indicates that, internationally, many companies may not be incurring costs related to this problem—which may be good in the short run because there are no costs to pass along to customers—but could create serious problems in the near future.

Sometimes, cost increases are caused by increases in taxes or regulatory requirements. For instance, a 1998 recommendation from the National Transportation Safety Board urged the Federal Aviation Administration to immediately order inspections, and possible rerouting, of airplane center fuel tank wires. Such an action could easily cost the industry hundreds of millions of dollars, so there is a question of "balancing airline economic and operating needs with safety concerns."[7] Exhibit 12-4 (page 547) indicates the results of a survey about how a company absorbs federal regulation costs.

The quantity of suppliers of a product or service can also affect selling prices. As the number of suppliers increases in a competitive environment, prices tend to fall. Likewise, a reduction in the number of suppliers will, all else remaining equal, cause prices to increase. A change in the number of *suppliers* is not the same as a change in the quantity of *supply*. If the supply of an item is large, one normally expects a low price; however, if there is only one supplier (or one primary supplier), the price can

 www.ual.com

http:// www.flycontinental.com

http:// www.twa.com

COMPANY	SPENDING
Citicorp	$600 million
General Motors	$410–$540 million
BankAmerica	$380 million
AT&T	$350 million
GTE	$350 million
Chase Manhattan	$300 million
Bell Atlantic	$200–$300 million
J.P. Morgan	$250 million
Bankers Trust	$180–$230 million
Owens Corning	$179 million

SOURCE: Corporate SEC filings, as shown in Lee Gomes, "Companies Estimate 'Year 2000' Computer Costs," *Wall Street Journal*, April 9, 1998, p. B8. Reprinted by permission of *Wall Street Journal*, © 1998 Dow Jones & Company, Inc. All Rights Reserved.

EXHIBIT 12-3

Year 2000 Computer Costs Spending to Date

---

[5]Susan Warren, "Airlines Pocket Huge Savings on Fuel Costs," *Wall Street Journal* March 20, 1998, p. B1.

[6]John Huey, "Waking Up to the New Economy," *Fortune*, June 27, 1994, p. 37.

[7]David Field and Gary Stoller, "Inspections of 747s Could Cost Bundle," *USA Today*, April 9, 1998, p. 1B.

NEWS NOTE

Millennium Bug? We'll Just Spray, Thank You

Many European businesses are not tackling the computer software flaw called the "millennium bug." So, on January 1, 2000, many computers worldwide will think it's January 1, 1900.

Although the United Kingdom, the Netherlands, and Scandinavia are upgrading; Belgium, France, Germany, Austria and Switzerland constitute a "danger zone." Examples:

- In Germany, only 8 percent of the companies have a formal program, compared with 80 percent of large U.S. companies.
- A 1997 study indicated that 20 percent of French companies haven't started overhauling information systems.
- Even though Central and Eastern European countries are less computer dependent than their western neighbors, the scarce local talent who could help eradicate the bug are being lured to higher-wage nations.
- European governments, preoccupied with creating a single currency, are budgeting woefully inadequate amounts to upgrade their computers, threatening commerce with breakdowns in public services.

Alternatively, some Asian companies have their own solution to this computer conundrum: They don't believe there is a millennium, because their computers are programmed to recognize traditional cultural calendars rather than the Western one. Examples:

- At many Thai businesses and government offices, the Western year 1998 is the year 2541. The Thai calendar originates with the birth of Buddha. Hence, no problem until 2600.
- In Taiwan, the Western year 1998 is 1987. There, the twentieth century didn't get started until 1911, when the last Chinese imperial dynasty was toppled and a republic established.
- Even in technologically sophisticated Japan, a handful of businesses may use a calendar that starts anew with each emperor's reign. In those companies, 1998 is the year Heisei 10, dating from when Emperor Akihito took the throne.

Unfortunately, traditional calendars offer no protection from the millennium bug because the underlying operating system and other software in virtually all computers recognize the Western calendar.

The probability of a huge disaster on January 1, 2000, may not be high, but some companies will have difficulties processing transactions, bank accounts will be frozen, and loans won't go through. And, even if all U.S. systems are fixed, there will be little protection from problems if confused computers paralyze their European and Asian customers and suppliers: the global networked economy is actually quite fragile.

SOURCES: David J. Lynch, "In Europe: Denial, Inaction Threaten USA," and James Cox, "In Asia: Already Hard-Hit Region Virtually Unprepared," *USA Today,* April 13, 1998, p. 3B.

http://www.delta-air.com

remain high because of supplier control. For example, in a Delta-dominated market in 1993, a round-trip New Orleans–Atlanta plane ticket cost about $283. In 1994, because of the start of operation from discount airline ValuJet, the price dropped to $98.[8] When ValuJet stopped flying in 1996, airfares to and from cities served by that airline increased rapidly. Fares dropped again when ValuJet was re-created as AirTran, and reinstituted discount flight service to selected cities.

http://www.airtran.com

Another example relates to medications. When pharmaceuticals are first introduced under patent, the supply may be readily available, but the selling price is high,

[8]Diego Buneul and Sheila Grissett, "Travelers Express Doubts as ValuJet Shuts Down in N.O.," (New Orleans) *Times-Picayune,* June 18, 1996, p. A1.

EXHIBIT 12-4
Dealing with Regulation Costs

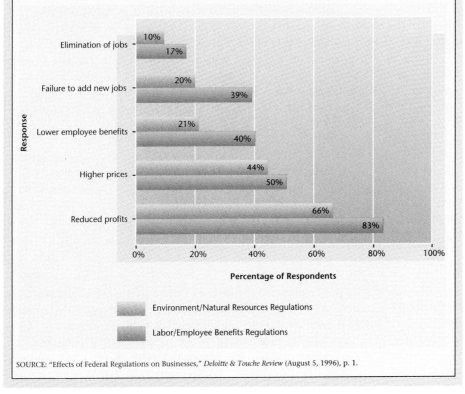

Most businesses pass the cost of complying with federal regulations on to others, through reduced profits for the company's owners/stockholders, increased prices for consumers, and/or decreased benefits for employees. Although 1 in 6 respondents (in an 800-response survey) laid off workers to deal with the cost of labor/employee benefits regulations, such costs are more likely to cause companies to avoid hiring new people.

SOURCE: "Effects of Federal Regulations on Businesses," *Deloitte & Touche Review* (August 5, 1996), p. 1.

since there is only a single source. As patents expire and generics become available, selling prices decline because more suppliers can produce the item. For example, when the patents on Syntex Corp.'s antiarthritis drugs Naprosyn and Anaprox expired in December 1993, two-thirds of the prescriptions filled within a month were filled with generic versions and the price plummeted more than 80 percent.[9]

In some cases, all other factors are not equal, and the quantity of suppliers may not affect the selling price of a good or service. Firms may unethically conspire to engage in **price fixing** or setting an item's price at a specified level. Buyers must purchase the good or service at the specified price because no suppliers are offering the item at a lower price. Price fixing may be vertical or horizontal.

price fixing

Vertical price fixing (also known as resale price maintenance) involves agreements by businesses and their distributors to control the prices at which products may be sold to consumers. All vertical price fixing is illegal. Companies may set suggested retail selling prices for items, but any attempts to prohibit retailers from selling below those prices are considered antitrust activities. The News Note on page 548 discusses a recent price-fixing settlement between Reebok and the Federal Trade Commission (FTC).

vertical price fixing

 www.reebok.com

In **horizontal price fixing**, competitors attempt to regulate prices by agreeing on either a selling price or the quantity of goods that may be produced or offered for sale. Airlines, oil and credit card companies, the NCAA, and universities have all been accused of horizontal price fixing. In 1998, a record $110 million fine resulted from a FTC price fixing charge against Ucar International Inc.[10] The company conspired

horizontal price fixing

 www.ucar.com

---

[9]Elyse Tanouye, "Price Wars, Patent Expirations Promise Cheaper Drugs," *Wall Street Journal*, March 24, 1994, p. B1.

[10]Gordon Fairclough, "Ucar to Pay Record $110 Million in Federal Probe of Price Fixing," *Wall Street Journal*, April 8, 1998, p. B8.

Discounted Footwear? Not Reeboks

In May 1995, the FTC and all 50 state attorneys general announced an agreement with Reebok International Ltd. settling charges that Reebok and its Rockport Co. subsidiary tried to fix footwear prices with retailers. Reebok was charged with coercing retailers into agreeing to keep prices above certain levels. Some retailers increased prices up to 30 percent to abide by a specified minimum retail price in fear that Reebok would no longer fill orders.

Athletic-footwear producers often pressure retailers to sell their shoes at suggested retail prices. But an athletics editor for *Footwear News* said that Reebok actually put that policy in writing. In late 1992, Reebok insisted that retailers keep prices inflated during certain peak shopping periods causing several disgruntled retailers to approach federal regulators about the practice.

Although not admitting guilt, Reebok and Rockport agreed not to attempt to set or control retail prices for their shoes nor to threaten retailers with suspension or termination if suggested prices are not maintained. The companies also agreed to pay $9.5 million, of which about $1.5 million covered litigation costs. The remainder was distributed among the states to improve public and nonprofit athletic facilities and services.

SOURCE: Adapted from Viveca Novak and Joseph Pereira, "Reebok and FTC Settle Price-Fixing Charges," *Wall Street Journal*, May 5, 1995, p. B1. Reprinted by permission of *Wall Street Journal*, © 1995 Dow Jones & Company, Inc. All Rights Reserved Worldwide.

with other companies to fix prices and reduce competition in the international market for graphite electrodes, an essential component in electric-arc furnaces used to make steel. Under U.S. law, injured parties can sue for treble damages if price fixing can be shown; thus, Ucar showed a $310 million charge to cover all potential liabilities.

Price fixing is also frowned upon in the European Union. In 1994, the European Union Commission fined 19 carton-board manufacturers $164.9 million for price fixing. The cartel operated from 1986 to 1991 and engaged in biannual price increases of 6 percent to 10 percent. The companies agreed among themselves which would be the first to announce the new higher price.[11]

Although the preceding reasons indicate why costs change, they do not indicate what managers can do to contain the costs. Minimizing the upward trends means controlling costs. The next section discusses some concepts of cost containment.

Cost Containment

cost containment

To the extent possible, managers should attempt to practice **cost containment** through minimizing period-by-period increases in per-unit variable and total fixed costs. Cost containment is generally not possible for increases resulting from inflation, tax and regulatory changes, and supply and demand adjustments because these forces occur outside the organizational structure.

However, costs that rise because of reduced competition, seasonality, and quantities purchased are subject to cost containment activities. A company should look for ways to cap upward changes in these costs. For example, purchasing agents should be aware of alternative suppliers for needed goods and services and determine which of those suppliers can provide needed items in the quantity, quality, and time desired. Comparing costs and finding new sources of supply can increase buying power and contain or reduce costs.

If bids are used to select suppliers, the purchasing agent should remember that a bid is merely the first step in negotiating. Although a low bid may eliminate some competition from consideration, additional negotiations between the purchasing

[11]Charles Goldsmith, "EU Fines 19 Carton-Board Companies Record $164.9 Million for Price Fixing," *Wall Street Journal*, July 14, 1994, p. A6.

Major airlines are acutely aware of the need to control meal costs of domestic flights. Some companies have reduced costs by eliminating "presentation frills," such as lettuce leaves under vegetables; others serve sandwiches rather than hot meals. Less likely to be reduced are the costs of food and beverages in first-class cabins.

agent and the remaining suppliers may result in a purchase cost lower than the bid amount, or concessions such as faster and more reliable delivery may be obtained. Purchasing agents must remember that the supplier offering the lowest bid amount is not necessarily the best supplier to choose, as indicated in the accompanying News Note. Additionally, reduced costs can often be obtained when long-term or single-source contracts are signed with suppliers.

NEWS NOTE

Price Isn't Everything

All too often companies fail to operate their purchasing function in strategically consistent ways. They go after transaction price reduction instead of purchasing for maximum value or minimum total cost.

A recent example of this price mentality creating an undesirable situation was with a large multinational organization. In this case, the organization was relying heavily on the support of a technologically capable supplier to help develop a new product. The supplier invested months in this development effort—at no cost to the multinational. However, when the product moved into production and the purchasing department finally became involved in the process, the key raw materials were sent out for bid. The supplier who had helped with the development quoted a reasonable price, but it was not the lowest. As a result of purchasing's focus on price, the supplier lost the contract. The multinational obtained a lower price for the raw materials, but lost part of the technical capabilities needed for future product development. Furthermore, once into production, the alternative supplier's product fell short of the manufacturing yield expectations set during the development phase.

SOURCE: Steven Mehltretter, "Strategic Sourcing Means Just That—Sourcing Strategically," *CMA Magazine* (February 1996), p. 6. Reprinted with permission of The Society of Management Accountants of Canada.

Companies should be aware of the suppliers available for needed goods and services. New suppliers should be investigated to determine whether they can provide needed items in the quantity, quality, and time desired. Comparing costs and finding new sources of supply can increase buying power and reduce costs. Buying in bulk is not a new or unique idea, but it is often not applied on an extended basis for related companies or enterprises. In a corporation, one division can take the responsibility for obtaining a supplier contract for items (such as computer disks) that are necessary to all divisions. The savings resulting from buying a combined quantity appropriate for all divisions could offset the additional costs of shipping the disks to the divisions.

A company may circumvent seasonal cost changes by postponing or advancing purchases of goods and services. However, such purchasing changes should not mean buying irresponsibly or incurring excessive carrying costs. As discussed in the previous chapter, the concepts of economic order quantities, safety stock levels, materials requirements planning, and the JIT philosophy should be considered in making purchases.

Cost Avoidance and Reduction

cost avoidance

Cost containment can prove very effective if it can be implemented. In some instances, cost containment may not be possible but cost avoidance may be. **Cost avoidance** means finding acceptable alternatives to high-cost items and not spending money for unnecessary goods or services. Avoiding one cost may require that an alternative, lower cost be incurred. For example, Alaska Airlines replaced its $15 all-wool blankets with $2 wool-blend blankets. Additionally, after determining that first-class passengers rarely ate lunch desserts, Alaska substituted chocolate mints.

cost reduction

Closely related to cost avoidance, **cost reduction** means lowering current costs. Management at many companies believes that cost reduction automatically means labor reduction. But the following quote provides a more appropriate viewpoint:

> Cutting staffs to cut costs is putting the cart before the horse. The only way to bring costs down is to restructure the work. This will then result in reducing the number of people needed to do the job, and far more drastically than even the most radical staff cutbacks could possibly do. Indeed, a cost crunch should always be used as an opportunity to re-think and to re-design operations.[12]

Sometimes cutting costs by cutting people merely creates other problems. The people who are cut may have been performing a value-added activity, and by eliminating them, a company may reduce its ability to do necessary and important tasks. This point is illustrated in the following example: After a 1994 downsizing of about

http:// www.delta-air.com

3,000 workers, Delta Air Lines decided in early 1996 to rehire over 650 baggage handlers, fuelers, gate agents and ticket counter employees in response to customer complaints about service levels.[13] Thus, the cost reduction was not proportionate to the potential for revenue reduction from dissatisfied flyers.

strategic staffing

Companies are beginning to view their personnel needs from a **strategic staffing** perspective. This outlook requires departments to analyze their personnel needs by considering long-term objectives and determining a specific combination of permanent and temporary or highly skilled and less-skilled employees that offers the best opportunity to meet those needs. If an organization's workload fluctuates substantially, temporaries (temps) can be hired for peak periods. Temps are also being hired to work on special projects, provide expertise in a specific area, or fill in until the right full-time employee can be found for a particular position. Temps may cost more per hour than full time workers, but total cost may be reduced because companies do not have to pay payroll taxes, fringe benefits, or Social Security for temps. Using temporary workers provides a flexible staffing "cushion" that helps insulate the jobs of permanent, core employees.

---

[12]Peter Drucker, "Permanent Cost Cutting," *Wall Street Journal,* January 11, 1991, p. A8.

[13]Associated Press, "Customers' Gripes Force Delta to Rehire Workers," (New Orleans) *Times-Picayune,* February 2, 1996, p. C6.

A starting point for determining appropriate cost reduction practices is to focus on the activities that are creating costs. As discussed in Chapter 5 on activity-based management, reducing or eliminating non-value-added activities will cause the associated costs to be reduced or eliminated. Carrier Corporation, the world's largest producer of air conditioning and heating products, has instituted an effective activity-based costing and management (ABCM) system that is used, in part, to highlight areas that increase product costs and areas where costs need to be cut. Carrier uses ABCM to "quantify the benefits of redesigning plant layouts, using common parts, outsourcing, strengthening supplier and customer relationships, and developing alternative product designs."[14]

http:// www.carrier.com

Companies may also reduce costs by outsourcing specific activities or services rather than maintaining internal departments. Data processing, internal audit, legal, travel, and accounting are all prime candidates for outsourcing. As indicated in Chapter 1, however, companies must make certain that they are not outsourcing core competencies or competitive advantage activities. As the accompanying News Note describes, both cost savings and higher quality can be advantages of outsourcing.

Two often overlooked important sources of cost reduction ideas are employees and suppliers. After an Alaska Airlines manager noticed that baggage handlers did not use the disposable gloves stocked by the company, they were eliminated at an annual cost savings of $10,000. At Chrysler, the SCORE (Supplier Cost Reduction Effort) program initiated in 1989 encourages cost-cutting ideas from suppliers; by mid-1997, over 25,000 ideas had been submitted that were expected to save $3.7 billion once they were all implemented.[15]

http:// www.chrysler.com

Benchmarking is especially important in the cost reduction area so that companies can become aware of costs that are unnecessary. Exhibit 12-5 (page 552) compares the airline industry benchmark of cost per available seat mile among Alaska,

---

NEWS NOTE

Do It Better Elsewhere!

Stimson Lane Vineyards and Estates markets and sells wine. "We want to spend our time on our core business," says Dave Fitzpatrick, director of accounting and information systems. "That's why we elected to outsource our travel and expense services."

Outsourcing to the Gelco Information Network has allowed Stimson to track double the number of corporate travelers in a quarter of the time it previously took. Aside from the time savings, Stimson can upgrade the accounting personnel's work level so they are doing value-added analysis instead of spending time on the minutiae. The Gelco system allows Stimson travelers to log travel-related expenses by phone, using the keypad to type in codes and expense amounts. Gelco's central processing system checks expenses against Stimson corporate guidelines and flags inconsistent data for review. Approved expenses are consolidated into an electronic feed to Stimson's general ledger, eliminating the time and potential mistakes inherent in manual keying of expense data. The system also allows Stimson to track travel expenses by brand and region.

http:// www.gelconet.com

Fitzpatrick believes outsourcing the travel and expense system was a good move at the right time. "We plan to expand our services with Gelco soon. Our way is to partner with our vendors and let them know what we need down the road and work together to make sure we get the new features and benefits we need," Fitzpatrick says.

SOURCE: Shimon Avish, "Stimson Vineyards Tracks Wine Sellers," reprinted from *Management Accounting* (September 1997), p. 46. Published by the Institute of Management Accountants, Montvale, N.J. Visit our website at www.imanet.org.

---

[14]Dan W. Swenson, "Managing Costs through Complexity Reduction at Carrier Corporation," *Management Accounting* (April 1998), pp. 20–21.[15]Nichole M. Christian, "Chrysler Suppliers' Cost-Savings Ideas Likely to Add $325 Million to Its '97 Net," *Wall Street Journal,* June 5, 1997, p. A6.

[15]Nichole M. Christian, "Chrysler Suppliers' Cost-Savings Ideas Likely to Add $325 Million to Its '97 Net," *Wall Street Journal,* June 5, 1997, p. A6.

EXHIBIT 12-5
Cost per Available Seat Mile

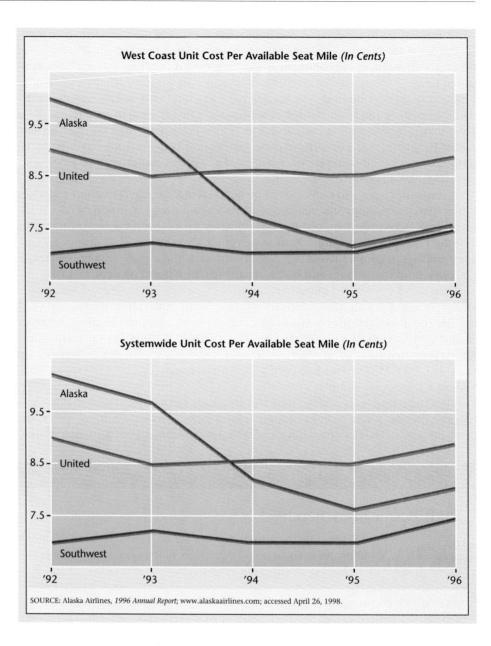

SOURCE: Alaska Airlines, *1996 Annual Report*; www.alaskaairlines.com; accessed April 26, 1998.

United (a major carrier with hub locations, different service classes, and nonlocalized flights), and Southwest (a low-fare airline known for its cost control). Exhibit 12-6 provides a more focused view of benchmarking by providing the average and world-class labor costs for certain processes—indicating substantial cost reduction opportunities for most companies.

EXHIBIT 12-6
Labor Costs for
Selected Processes

PROCESS	MEASURE	AVERAGE	WORLD-CLASS
Payables	Invoice	$2.90	$0.71
Receivables	Remittance	$0.71	$0.01
Travel and expense	Expense report	$7.60	$1.29
Fixed assets	Asset tracked	$5.90	$0.16
Payroll	Paycheck	$3.00	$0.95

SOURCE: Christine A. Gattenio, "How to Benchmark the Performance of Your Finance Function," *CMA Magazine* (April 1996), p. 23. Reprinted with permission of The Society of Management Accountants of Canada.

IMPLEMENTING A COST CONTROL SYSTEM

Managers may adopt the five-step method of implementing a cost control system shown in Exhibit 12-7. First, the type of costs incurred by an organization must be understood. Are the costs under consideration fixed or variable, product or period? What cost drivers affect those costs? Has management committed to incurring the costs for the long term or short term? Second, the need for cost consciousness must be communicated to all employees for the control process to be effective. Employees must be aware of which costs need to be better controlled and why cost control is important to both the company and to the employees themselves. Third, employees must be educated in cost control techniques, encouraged to provide ideas on how to control costs, and motivated by some type of incentives to embrace the concepts. The incentives may range from simple verbal recognition to monetary rewards to time off with pay. Managers must also be flexible enough to allow for changes from the current method of operation. Fourth, reports must be generated indicating actual results, budget-to-actual comparisons, and variances. These reports must be evaluated by management as to why costs were or were not controlled in the past. Such analysis may provide insightful information about cost drivers so that the activities causing costs may be better controlled in the future. And last, the cost control system should be viewed as a long-run process, not a short-run solution. "To be successful, organizations must avoid the illusion of short-term, highly simplified cost-cutting procedures. Instead, they must carefully evaluate proposed solutions to ensure that these are practical, workable, and measure changes based on realities, not illusions."[16]

Following these five steps will provide an atmosphere conducive to controlling costs to the fullest extent possible as well as deriving the most benefit from the costs that are incurred. Expected future costs should be compared to expected benefits before cost incurrence takes place. The costs should also have been incorporated into the budgeting system because costs cannot be controlled *after* they have been incurred. Alternatively, future costs may be controlled based on information learned about past costs. Cost control should not cease at the end of a fiscal period or because

EXHIBIT 12-7

Implementing a Cost Control System

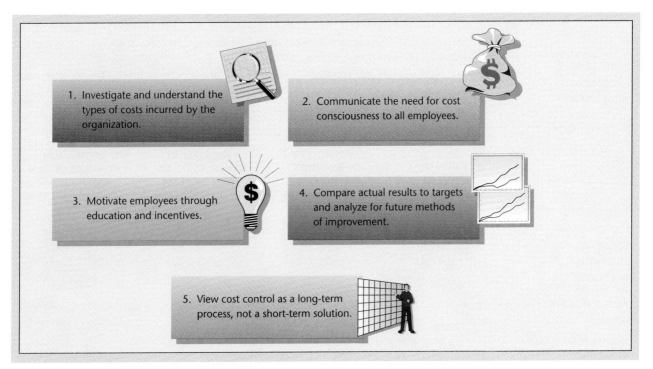

1. Investigate and understand the types of costs incurred by the organization.

2. Communicate the need for cost consciousness to all employees.

3. Motivate employees through education and incentives.

4. Compare actual results to targets and analyze for future methods of improvement.

5. View cost control as a long-term process, not a short-term solution.

---

[16]Mark D. Lutchen, "Cost-Cutting Illusions," *Today's CPA* (May/June 1989), p. 46.

costs were reduced or controlled during the current period. However, distinct differ-ences exist in the cost control system between committed and discretionary costs.

COMMITTED COSTS

Managers are charged with planning and controlling the types and amounts of costs needed to conduct business activities. All activities and the costs created by them can be categorized as either committed or discretionary. The primary difference between the two categories is the time period for which management binds itself to the activ-ity and the cost.

LEARNING OBJECTIVE 2
How are committed and discre-tionary costs differentiated?

committed cost

Costs associated with the plant assets and personnel structure that an organization must have to operate are known as **committed costs**. The amount of committed costs is normally dictated by long-run management decisions involving the desired level of operations and reflects organizational capacity. Committed costs include depreciation, lease rentals, property taxes, and salaries of upper-level management. Such costs can-not easily be reduced even during periods of temporarily diminished activity. For an air-line, committed costs relate to items such as airplane and headquarters depreciation, pilot and senior flight attendants' salaries, and airport gate leases. Quality costs incurred for prevention activities that involve technology investments are also committed costs.

One method of controlling committed costs involves comparing the expected benefits of having plant assets or human resources with the expected costs of such in-vestments. Managers must decide what activities are needed to attain company objec-tives and what capacity is needed to support those activities. After the facilities and core personnel assets are acquired or hired to provide the designated capacity, man-agement is generally committed to both the activities and their related costs for the long run. However, before acquisition, management should calculate how changes in committed fixed costs can affect income in the event of changes in operating activity.

The managers of Independent Airlines are considering an investment of $1,000,000 in automated ticketing equipment. Depreciation on the equipment will be $200,000 per year. The company's cost relationships indicate that variable costs are 45 percent of revenues, giving a contribution margin of 55 percent. Exhibit 12-8 illustrates the potential effects of this long-term commitment on net income under three conditions: maintenance of current revenues, a 20 percent increase in revenues, and a 20 percent decrease in revenues.

EXHIBIT 12-8
Risk Related to Committed Costs

Note that the $200,000 increase in depreciation expense affects the income state-ment more significantly when sales decline than when sales increase. This effect is

	CURRENT LEVEL OF OPERATIONS	(A) CURRENT LEVEL OF REVENUES AND INCREASE IN DEPRECIATION	(B) INCREASE IN REVENUES OF 20% AND INCREASE IN DEPRECIATION	(C) DECREASE IN REVENUES OF 20% AND INCREASE IN DEPRECIATION
Revenues	$5,000,000	$5,000,000	$6,000,000	$4,000,000
Variable costs	(2,250,000)	(2,250,000)	(2,700,000)	(1,800,000)
Contribution margin	$2,750,000	$2,750,000	$3,300,000	$2,200,000
Fixed costs	(2,400,000)	(2,600,000)	(2,600,000)	(2,600,000)
Net income	$ 350,000	$ 150,000	$ 700,000	$ (400,000)

Each change from the original income level to the new income level is explained as the change in the contribution margin minus the increase in fixed costs:

Change to (a) = Increase in CM − Increase in FC = $0 − $200,000 = $(200,000)
Change to (b) = Increase in CM − Increase in FC = $550,000 − $200,000 = +$350,000
Change to (c) = Decrease in CM − Increase in FC = $(550,000) − $200,000 = $(750,000)

To make filling up cars easier for customers, Shell is committing massive amounts of money to redesign and reequip its gas stations. Such investments in capital assets can impact a firm's operating leverage and ability to withstand downturns in demand.

caused by the relationship between a company's variable and fixed costs or **operating leverage**. Typically, highly labor-intensive organizations, such as McDonald's or Domino's Pizza, have high variable costs and low fixed costs and, thus, have low operating leverage. These companies can show a profit even when they experience wide swings in volume levels. Conversely, organizations that are highly capital-intensive, such as Alaska Airlines and Caterpillar, have a high operating leverage or a cost structure that includes low variable and high fixed costs. These companies must have fairly high sales volumes to cover fixed costs, but sales above the breakeven point produce large profits.

Companies that have fairly high contribution margins (that is, revenues minus total variable costs) can withstand large fixed costs increases as long as revenues increase. However, these same companies are affected more strongly when revenues decrease because the margin available to cover fixed costs erodes so rapidly. As the magnitude of committed fixed costs increases, so does the risk of incurring an operating loss in the event of a downturn in demand. Therefore, managers must be extremely careful about the level of fixed costs to which they commit the organization.

Committed costs may also be controlled by making the available capacity more productive. Sometimes increased productivity may result from bottleneck reductions or from new ideas for utilization. In other cases, it may result from new flexibility. For instance, in 1995, Alaska Airlines negotiated new union contracts that allowed three hours more of flight time than the eight hours flown per day in 1993. The increased flying hours gave the company the equivalent of 28 additional planes at virtually no cost, allowing new routes and more daily round trips.

A third method of controlling committed costs involves comparing actual and expected results from plant asset investments. Making these comparisons help managers review and evaluate the accuracy of their cost and revenue predictions relative to capital investments.[17] Deviations from projections should be investigated and, if possible, actions taken to eliminate the causes of lower-than-expected performance.

operating leverage

http:// www.mcdonalds.com

http:// www.dominos.com

http:// www.alaskair.com

http:// www.cat.com

---

[17]This comparison is called a post-investment audit and is discussed in Chapter 8.

An organization cannot operate without some basic level of plant and human assets. Considerable control can be exercised over the process of determining how management wishes to define *basic* and what funds will be committed to those levels. However, management needs to regularly review its capacity decisions and compare the benefits from capacity commitments with their related costs. Excess capacity may be expensive and inefficient as discussed in the accompanying News Note.

DISCRETIONARY COSTS

LEARNING OBJECTIVE ❷
How are committed and discretionary costs differentiated?

discretionary cost

In contrast to a committed cost, a **discretionary cost** is one "that a decision maker must periodically review to determine that it continues to be in accord with ongoing policies."[18] A discretionary fixed cost reflects a management decision to fund an activity *at a specified amount for a specified time*. Discretionary costs relate to company activities that are viewed as important but optional. Discretionary cost activities are usually service-oriented and include employee travel, repairs and maintenance, advertising, research and development, and employee training and development. There is no correct amount at which to set funding for discretionary costs, and there are no specific activities whose costs are always considered discretionary in all organizations. In the event of cash flow shortages or forecasted operating losses, discretionary costs may be more easily reduced than committed costs.

Discretionary costs, then, are generated by relatively unstructured activities that vary in type and magnitude from day to day and whose benefits are often not measurable in monetary terms. For example, in 1998, Anheuser-Busch decided to pay a record $2 million per 30-second commercial during the 1999 Super Bowl.[19] How does

---

NEWS NOTE

Making Rational Capacity Decisions

The cost of capacity in most companies is substantial and continues to grow. Unused or under-utilized capacity involves waste and foregone profits.

The prevalence, at any given time and in any given area, of excess capacity is not the issue. Capacity resources, whether people or equipment, often are committed in amounts that turn out to be incongruous with actual amounts needed at any given time. Justifications for this include cyclical or seasonal business, a desire to get out in front of competitors, industry-wide overcapacity, demand/mix volatility, ongoing improvements in productivity, and anticipated sales growth.

Awareness of the magnitude of the cost of capacity resources, used and unused, will direct greater attention to managing capacity and will provide more accurate information for decisions including pricing, downsizing, and redeployment. There is also a greater chance that future conditions of excess or unused capacity will be reduced by emphasizing the cost of current capacity, reviewing past decisions through post-implementation audits, articulating policies and assigning clear responsibility for capacity management, and seeking greater capacity flexibility.

Refusing to identify the cost of excess resources allows competitors who are better informed about their costs to enjoy a significant competitive advantage and misses opportunities to be more profitable.

SOURCE: John M Brausch and Thomas C. Taylor, "Who Is Accounting for the Cost of Capacity?" Reprinted from *Management Accounting* (Feburary 1997), p. 50. Published by the Institute of Management Accountants, Montvale, N.J. Visit our website at www.imanet.org.

---

[18]Institute of Management Accountants (formerly National Association of Accountants), *Statements on Management Accounting Number 2: Management Accounting Terminology* (Montvale, N.J.: National Association of Accountants, June 1, 1983), p. 35.

[19]Melanie Wells, "Busch Buys $2M Super Bowl Ad," *USA Today*, April 14, 1998, p. 4B.

the company know that this advertising campaign will be cost-beneficial and create product demand? Expenditures of this magnitude require that management have some idea of the benefits that are expected, but measuring results is often difficult. With regard to advertising and other promotional tools, management can employ market research to ascertain effectiveness. But could Alaska have spent less than $67.4 million in 1997 on maintenance and still had the same clean flight record and been in compliance with aircraft maintenance regulations? There is no safe way to determine the answer to that question.

Thus, discretionary costs are not usually susceptible to the precise measures available to plan and control variable production costs or the reasonably estimable cost/benefit evaluation techniques available to control committed costs. Because the benefits of discretionary cost activities cannot be assessed definitively, these activities are often among the first to be cut when profits are lagging. Thus, proper planning for discretionary activities and costs may be more important than subsequent control measures. Control after the planning stage is often restricted to monitoring expenditures to assure conformity with budget classifications and preventing managers from overspending their budgeted amounts.

Budgeting Discretionary Costs

Budgets are described in Chapter 7 as both planning and controlling devices. Budgets serve to officially communicate a manager's authority to spend up to a maximum amount (appropriation) or rate for each budget item. Budget appropriations serve as a basis for comparison with actual costs. Accumulated expenditures in each budgetary category are periodically compared with appropriated amounts to determine whether funds have been underexpended or overexpended.

Before top management can budget amounts for discretionary cost activities, goals must be translated into specific objectives and policies that will lead to organizational success. Management should decide which discretionary activities will help accomplish the chosen objectives and to what degree. Funding levels should be set only after discretionary cost activities have been prioritized and cash flow and income expectations for the coming period have been reviewed. Management tends to be more generous in making discretionary cost appropriations when the organization is facing a strong economic outlook rather than a weak one.

Because the optimal amount for a discretionary cost activity is not known, discretionary cost appropriations are generally based on three factors: the activity's perceived significance to the achievement of goals and objectives; the upcoming period's expected operating level; and managerial negotiations in the budgetary process. For some discretionary costs, managers are expected to spend the full amount of their appropriations within the specified time frame. For others, the "less is better" adage is appropriate.

Consider, for example, the difference between machine maintenance and executive travel and entertainment. Top management would probably not consider foregoing preventive maintenance to be a positive measure of cost control. In fact, spending (with supervisory approval) more than originally appropriated in this area might be necessary or even commendable—assuming that positive results are indicated. However, spending less than budgeted on travel and entertainment (while simultaneously achieving the desired results) would probably be considered positive performance.

Managers often view discretionary activities and costs as though they were committed. A discretionary expenditure such as employee training may be budgeted on an annual basis as a function of planned volume of company sales. After this appropriation has been justified, management may decide that that year's appropriation will not be reduced regardless of the level of actual sales. Such an occurrence is likely in regard to employee training costs when management is committed to total quality. A manager who states that a particular activity's cost will not be reduced during a period has chosen to view that activity and cost as committed. But this viewpoint does not change the underlying discretionary nature of the item. In such circumstances, top management must have a high degree of faith in the ability of lower-level management to perform the specified tasks in an efficient manner.

Part of the difference in management attitude between committed and discretionary costs has to do with the ability to measure the benefits provided by those costs. Whereas benefits of committed fixed costs can be measured on a before-and-after basis through the capital budgeting and post-investment audit processes, the benefits from discretionary costs are often not distinctly measurable in monetary terms.

Measuring Benefits from Discretionary Costs

LEARNING OBJECTIVE ❸
How can the benefits from discretionary cost expenditures be measured?

Because benefits from some activities traditionally classified as discretionary cannot be adequately measured, companies often assume that the benefits—and, thus, the activities—are unimportant. However, many discretionary activities such as repairs, maintenance, research and development, and employee training are critical to a company's position in a world-class environment. These activities, in the long run, produce quality products and services; therefore, before reducing or eliminating expenditures in these areas, managers should attempt to more appropriately recognize and measure the benefits of activities through the use of surrogate or substitute nonmonetary measures.

http:// www.motorola.com

Devising such surrogate measures often requires substantial time and creativity. Exhibit 12-9 presents examples of some surrogate measures for determining the effectiveness of various discretionary costs. Some of these measures are verifiable and can be gathered quickly and easily; others are abstract and require a longer time horizon before they can be obtained. The News Note on the next page about Motorola indicates why the measure of a discretionary cost must often be stated as a nonmonetary, rather than a monetary one.

The money spent on a discretionary activity is the input to a process that should provide some desired output. Unfortunately, as mentioned, the outputs produced by most discretionary cost activities are difficult to value on a monetary basis. Nevertheless, managers compare input costs and output results to assess whether there is a reasonable cost/benefit relationship between the two. Managers use this cost/benefit relationship to judge how efficiently costs were used and how effectively they achieved their purposes. These relationships can be seen in the following model:

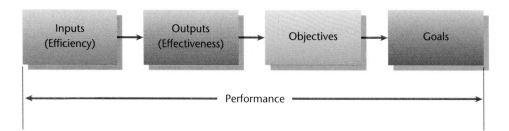

efficiency

The degree to which comparing outputs to inputs reveals a satisfactory relationship reflects the **efficiency** of an activity. Thus, efficiency is a yield concept and is usually measured by a ratio of output to input. For instance, one measure of automobile efficiency is the number of miles the car travels per gallon of gas consumed. The higher the number of miles per gallon, the greater the efficiency. In contrast, comparing actual output results for a particular period to desired output results indicates the **effectiveness** of an activity. Effectiveness measures how well the firm's objectives and goals were achieved.

effectiveness

DISCRETIONARY COST ACTIVITY	SURROGATE MEASURE OF RESULTS
Preventive maintenance	Reduction in number of equipment failures Reduction in unplanned downtime Reduction in frequency of production interruptions caused by preventable maintenance activities
Advertising	Increase in unit sales in the two weeks after an advertising effort relative to the sales two weeks prior to the effort Number of customers alluding to the ad Number of coupons clipped from the ad and redeemed
University admissions recruiting trip	Number of students met who requested an application Number of students from area visited who requested to have ACT/SAT scores sent to the university Number of admissions that year from that area
Prevention and quality-appraisal activities	Reduction in number of customer complaints Reduction in number of warranty claims Reduction in number of product defects discovered by customers
Staffing law school clinic for indigents	Number of clients served Number of cases effectively resolved Number of cases won
Executive retreat	Proportion of participants still there at end of retreat Number of useful suggestions made Values tabulated from an exit survey

EXHIBIT 12-9

Nonmonetary Surrogate Output Measures from Discretionary Costs

NEWS NOTE

The Money Spent Is Not the Proper Measure

The first step to increasing white-collar productivity may be figuring out how to measure it. At one time, Motorola charted the productivity of its communications-sector employee recruiting department by the amount of money the recruiters spent to sign up each new hire. The goal was to spend less per hire each year. Productivity went up steadily, but without regard to the quality of the people who were joining the company. Noted a Motorola quality manager and VP: "If you hired an idiot for 39 cents you would meet your goal."

Motorola completely revamped the way it calculated the effectiveness of its employees to emphasize quality. Measurement of the recruiting department was determined by how well the recruits subsequently did at the company. Did they turn out to be well qualified for the job or did they need a lot of remedial training? Were they hired at the right salary or did they leave six months later for a higher-paying job at another company? Judged by such standards, the department decided to increase its spending per new hire.

SOURCE: Ronald Henkoff, "Make Your Office More Productive," *Fortune,* February 25, 1991, p. 76.

Determination of both efficiency and effectiveness requires a valid measure of output. When such a measure is available, efficiency and effectiveness can be measured and assessed as follows:

	Actual Result	*compared with*	**Desired Result**
Efficiency $=$	$\dfrac{\text{Actual Output}}{\text{Actual Input}}$		$\dfrac{\text{Planned Output}}{\text{Planned Input}}$
or			
Efficiency $=$	$\dfrac{\text{Actual Input}}{\text{Actual Output}}$		$\dfrac{\text{Planned Input}}{\text{Planned Output}}$
Effectiveness $=$	$\dfrac{\text{Actual Output}}{\text{Planned Output}}$		Preestablished Standard

A reasonable measure of efficiency can exist only when inputs and outputs can be matched in the same period and when there is a credible causal relationship between them. These two requirements make measuring the efficiency of discretionary costs very difficult. First, several years may pass before output occurs from some discretionary cost expenditures. Consider, for example, the length of time between making expenditures for research and development or a drug rehabilitation program and the time at which results of these types of expenditures are visible. Second, there is frequently a dubious cause–effect relationship between discretionary cost inputs and resulting outputs. For instance, assume that you clip out and use a cents-off coupon for Crest toothpaste from the Sunday paper. Can Procter & Gamble be certain that it was the advertising coupon that caused you to buy the product, or might you have purchased the toothpaste anyway?

Effectiveness, on the other hand, is determined for a particular period by comparing the results achieved with the results desired. Determination of an activity's effectiveness is unaffected by whether the designated output measure is stated in monetary or nonmonetary terms. But management can only subjectively attribute some or all of the effectiveness of the cost incurrence to the results. Subjectivity is required because the comparison of actual output to planned output is not indicative of a perfect causal relationship between activities and output results. *Measurement of effectiveness does not require the consideration of inputs, but measurement of efficiency does.*

Assume that last month Independent Airlines increased its expenditures on customer service and, during that period, customer service complaints dropped by 12 percent. The planned decrease in complaints was 15 percent. Although management was 80 percent effective $(.12 \div .15)$ in achieving its goal of decreased customer dissatisfaction, that result was not necessarily related to the customer service program expenditures. It is possible that the decline in complaints was caused partially or entirely by other factors, such as use of better equipment, improved communications of flight information, or better weather that allowed flights to depart and arrive on schedule. Management, therefore, does not know for certain whether the customer service program was the most cost-efficient way in which to decrease customer complaints.

The efficiency relationship between discretionary costs and their desired results is inconclusive at best, and the effectiveness of such costs can only be inferred from the relationship of actual to desired output. Because many discretionary costs result in benefits that must be measured on a nondefinitive and nonmonetary basis, it is difficult to exercise control of these costs during activities or after they have begun. Therefore, planning for discretionary costs may be more important than subsequent control measures. Control after the planning stage is often relegated to monitoring discretionary expenditures to ensure conformity with budget classifications and preventing managers from overspending their budgeted amounts.

http:// www.proctergamble.com

Employee suggestions provide an inexpensive way to improve process efficiency and effectiveness. Additionally, their implementation raises employee morale—a benefit that money can't buy.

Controlling Discretionary Costs Using a Budget

Control of discretionary costs is often limited to a monitoring function. Management compares actual discretionary expenditures with budgeted amounts to determine variances in attempts to understand the cause and effect relationships of discretionary activities. Variances can often be explained with reference to the various cost consciousness attitudes.

LEARNING OBJECTIVE 4
How does a budget help in controlling discretionary costs?

Need for Flexible Budgets

Before comparing budget and actual costs, management must be certain that the comparisons are appropriate. Because total variable costs change in direct proportion to changes in a related activity level, the original budget may not provide the best comparison base. For example, assume that the original budget had been calculated on 100,000 units of sales and that 125,000 units were actually sold. It would be incorrect to compare the variable costs budgeted for 100,000 units with variable costs for 125,000 units. Thus, the budget would need to be revised to use in the comparison by recomputing the appropriations using the actual cost driver level. This process would use cost formulas, discussed in Chapter 4, that indicate the variable and fixed cost behaviors.

Exhibit 12-10 provides a flexible budget for the quarterly expenses of Airline Bag Handlers Inc. (ABH), which performs contract baggage handling for Independent Airlines and other small carriers. The company is located on the airport grounds and

	VARIABLE COST PER BAG HANDLED	BAGS HANDLED		
		225,000	250,000	285,000
Discretionary costs				
Employee training	$.05	$ 11,250	$ 12,500	$ 14,250
Maintenance	.10	22,500	25,000	28,500
Advertising	.02	4,500	5,000	5,700
Committed costs				
Wages and fringe benefits	.38	85,500	95,000	108,300
Committed fixed costs				
Utilities		1,092	1,092	1,092
Salaries and fringe benefits		48,000	48,000	48,000
Depreciation		30,000	30,000	30,000
Total expenses		$202,842	$216,592	$235,842

EXHIBIT 12-10
ABH Flexible Budget

provides its own operating equipment. ABH's management funds employee training and maintenance to improve the quality of service provided to customers. Advertising is considered a discretionary cost and is budgeted at two cents for each bag handled. Wages are for workers and security personnel, who are paid on an hourly basis. Although these workers are essential to operating activities, the committed cost is partially tied to workload. Utility cost is budgeted as fixed because the firm operates twelve hours per day, seven days per week, and thirteen weeks in the quarter. Should operating hours need to be extended, additional utility cost is expected at the rate of $1 per hour. Salaries and fringe benefits are for management level personnel and, like depreciation and property taxes, are fixed amounts.

Comprehensive Example

Ms. Carolyn Williams, the controller for ABH, budgeted operating activity for the first quarter of 2001 at 250,000 pieces of luggage. The airlines pay ABH $1 per bag handled. Thus, the budgeted income statement for the quarter would show a pretax operating income of $33,408. This amount is the difference between $250,000 budgeted handling fee revenue and total budgeted expenses of $216,592 (shown in the middle column of Exhibit 12-10).

Ms. Williams collected the revenue and expense data shown in Exhibit 12-11 during the first quarter of 2001. Because of the late arrival of some flights, ABH complied with requests to stay open two extra hours on ten different nights. New contracts were responsible for the majority of the increase in bags handled.

After reviewing the actual results, ABH's board of directors requested a budget-to-actual comparison from Ms. Williams and explanations for the cost variances. Because every cost was higher than originally budgeted, the board was of the opinion that costs had not been properly controlled. Ms. Williams prepared the comparison presented in Exhibit 12-12 on the next page and provided the following explanations for the variances. Each explanation is preceded by the related budget item number. Note that the variances are based on comparisons between a revised budget that uses actual bags handled as the cost driver. Comparisons between the original budget and actual results for the variable cost items are not useful for control purposes because variable costs automatically rise with increases in cost driver activity.

Explanations:

1. The $280 favorable revenue variance resulted from a renegotiation of one of ABH's contracts. Independent Airlines agreed to pay four cents above the standard $1 handling charge per bag because of ABH's high-quality service and reputation for not damaging customer luggage. After the contract renegotiation, ABH handled 7,000 pieces of baggage for Independent during the quarter. *Comment: Independent Airlines can view this cost as a type of cost*

EXHIBIT 12-11

ABH Actual Results—
First Quarter 2001

Revenue:		
Handling fees (285,000 bags)		$285,280
Expenses:		
Employee training	$ 13,640	
Maintenance	27,400	
Advertising	5,800	
Wages and fringe benefits	108,900	
Utilities	1,235	
Salaries and fringe benefits	49,200	
Depreciation	32,000	(238,175)
Pretax operating income		$ 47,105

BUDGET ITEM #1		ORIGINAL BUDGET	BUDGET BASED ON ACTUAL RESULTS	ACTUAL RESULTS	VARIANCES
Revenue:					
Handling fees	(1)	$250,000	$285,000	$285,280	$ 280 F
Expenses:					
Employee training	(2)	$ 12,500	$ 14,250	$ 13,640	$ 610 F
Maintenance	(3)	25,000	28,500	27,400	1,100 F
Advertising	(4)	5,000	5,700	5,800	100 U
Wages and fringe benefits	(5)	95,000	108,636*	108,900	264 U
Utilities	(6)	1,092	1,112*	1,235	123 U
Salaries and fringe benefits	(7)	48,000	48,000	49,200	1,200 U
Depreciation	(8)	30,000	30,000	32,000	2,000 U
Total expenses	(9)	$216,592	$236,198	$238,175	$1,977 U
Pretax operating income		$ 33,408	$ 48,802	$ 47,105	$1,697 U

*Because ABH Inc. needed to remain open an additional twenty hours during the budget period, these amounts have been adjusted from the flexible budget shown in Exhibit 12-10. The extra wages per hour were $16.80 (three people at $5.60 per hour each), resulting in an increase of $336 above the original $108,300. Utility cost for the extra twenty hours was $1 per hour which, when added to the original budgeted figure of $1,092, gave a budgeted cost of $1,112.

EXHIBIT 12-12
ABH Budget-to-Actual Comparison—First Quarter 2001

avoidance—avoiding significantly higher costs of customer complaints regarding baggage handling.

2. The discretionary training costs were lower than expected because ABH experienced little turnover during the period and, thus, the company was able to avoid some expected training costs. Comment: This explanation reflects ABH's understanding of the long-run quality considerations of having well-trained employees.

3. Maintenance cost was less than that budgeted because ABH signed a new long-term contract with Schorg Services to provide necessary and preventive maintenance for all baggage handling equipment. Comment: ABH has practiced cost reduction while simultaneously retaining maintenance quality.

4. ABH's advertising cost was greater than expected because the print shop used by the company had increased the price of brochures. Comment: The printer explained to ABH that paper prices had increased because of inflation and downturn in supply.

5. The original budget shown in Exhibit 12-10 showed wages as a variable cost per piece of luggage handled. Given its normal operating hours, ABH can handle up to 300,000 pieces of luggage. Comment: This cost category increase was not related to the quantity of baggage handled, but rather to the additional hours of work and, potentially, to changes such as an increase in the minimum wage. Thus, this cost change could reflect the nature of variable costs or a higher cost arising from new government regulations.

6. The utility cost variance was influenced by two factors: the additional twenty hours of operation and an increase in local utility rates. Comment: The first explanation reflects an understanding of the nature of variable costs: additional hours worked caused additional costs to be incurred. The second explanation reflects an understanding of the nature of specific price level adjustments. The increase in utility rates could possibly have been caused by inflation, an increase in demand with no corresponding increase in supply, or additional utility regulatory costs being passed along to the utility's customers.

7. A new scheduler was hired at the beginning of the quarter at $4,800 more per year than the one who was replaced. Comment: Increases in salaries are typically caused either by inflation or supply and demand relationships for professional staff.

8. The depreciation increase was related to the purchase of several new pieces of baggage handling equipment. This equipment purchase had been included in the capital budget for the end of 2001, not during the first quarter. However, the purchase was made with board approval when a competitor went bankrupt during the quarter and had a distress liquidation sale. *Comment: Acquiring the baggage handling equipment is a good example of cost containment. ABH wanted to buy the equipment and had an opportunity to buy it at a substantial savings, although earlier than anticipated. This purchase created an unfavorable first quarter cost variance for depreciation, but it shows an instance of planning, foresight, and flexibility. The long-run benefits of this purchase are twofold. First, a favorable variance will be shown in the capital budget when the equipment's actual and expected costs are compared. Second, in future periods, the budgeted committed cost for depreciation will be less than it would have been had the purchase not been made at this time.*

SITE ANALYSIS

Alaska Airlines

In the early 1990s, two low-cost carriers entered the Pacific Northwest with fares as much as 70% less than Alaska's. Fearful of losing market share, Alaska matched the upstarts' low fares. This decision resulted in a loss of $116 million in two years—after 19 consecutive years of profit.

So the airline went on a diet. It got rid of its inefficient 727s, reducing its fleet to just two types of planes and gaining big savings in maintenance, training and parts inventories. It canceled aircraft orders, renegotiated aircraft leases, refinanced debt and shelved plans for a new maintenance base. It dropped marginal routes. One fewer flight attendant was assigned to each plane, increasing the cabin crew's workload.

"We looked at every expense in the company," said Harry Leyr, senior vice-president of finance. "We got down to examining things in the hundreds of dollars. We're still small enough so we could get into it in depth. But it took months." He and his team took steps as minor as cutting newspaper subscriptions at headquarters and removing a spoon on first-class meal trays. In all, he figures the company reduced its expenses about 10 percent, or $110 million, a year.

When it came to passenger amenities, however, the company took a considered approach. Alaska refused to buy frozen coach-class hot entrees from outside vendors and still cooks all its food from scratch—even though it is more expensive.

Even as it was cutting costs, Alaska invested in labor-saving technology. It says it was the first U.S. carrier to sell tickets on the Internet, and it was early to offer electronic ticketing, which saves about $500,000 a year in distribution costs. Many of its airport check-in counters are equipped with easy-to-use computer terminals on which passengers can select their seats, receive boarding passes and even get bar-coded destination tags for their checked luggage. This system reduced the number of check-in clerks needed to process Alaska's growing traffic.

After three years of cost-cutting and recasting its amenities, Alaska got its costs down to levels approaching its low-fare competitors, which now also include Reno Air and America West Airlines. Alaska says its costs were 8.1 cents a mile in 1996. Excluding the higher expenses of flying in Alaska, it claims it nearly matched Southwest's 7.5 cents a mile.

According to Merrill Lynch, Alaska is No. 1 in market share in twenty-one of its top twenty-five routes and has higher yields—the average a passenger pays to fly a mile—than its competitors on twenty-two of its top twenty-five routes.

SOURCE: Susan Carey, "How Alaska Airlines Beat Back Challenges from Bigger Rivals," *Wall Street Journal*, May 19, 1997, p. A1. Reprinted by permission of *Wall Street Journal*, © 1997 Dow Jones & Company, Inc. All Rights Reserved Worldwide.

CROSS-FUNCTIONAL APPLICATIONS

TOPIC OF NOTE	DISCIPLINE	CROSS-FUNCTIONAL APPLICATIONS
Committed versus Discretionary Costs	Legal Services	Common contractual negotiations and legal review follow-ups for sales/purchase agreements, leases, acquisitions, and outsourcing should provide the principal with the greatest flexibility to change his or her decision in relation to an ever-changing environment. Attorneys must be aware of which committed costs are most constraining to management decision making in each situation. For instance, an operating lease on a retail outlet for the introduction of a new product may be a greater long-run risk in terms of committed cost than the same terms in a contract that adds one outlet to a well-established product line.
	Marketing and Sales Management	Sales personnel, often eager to close a contract, may ignore profitability in terms of other marketing objectives, such as new business recruitment or increased territorial share of the market. They must be made aware that certain committed costs, such as distribution costs in a sparsely populated region, could reduce profitability. Marketing departments are frequently evaluated for performance as revenue centers. However, their budgets should guide them in distinguishing between the constraints of committed costs, such as media advertisement, as opposed to more discretionary promotional costs like coupons, rebates, or discounts.
	Engineering	The specifications for manufacturing resources such as materials or parts are frequently selected by research, design, or manufacturing engineers who surrender requisitions to a centralized purchasing department. Engineers are courted by sales representatives who focus on technical specifications that may be appropriate to the buyer's product line. Since discretion is a critical point in the procurement of technical resources, engineers must be guided by the concept of cost flexibility when they select among alternative resources.
	Organizational Theory	When organizations merge, the discretionary costs of support services such as accounting or human resources are often reduced by centralization—which accounts for employee lay-off announcements that usually follow a merger. However, committed costs are outside the reach of managerial decisions, and frequently the efficiencies of scale in centralization are offset by the "sunk" nature of committed costs. In a merger, buyout, or acquisition decision, committed costs are a key determinant.
	Pension Funding	Nationally, organizations have sought to reduce their committed costs and the risk of sharp increases for benefits such as health care. Pension planners have minimized the risk of future pension liabilities to their organizations and reduced the current minimum accrual required in financial accounting by shifting the terms of pension agreement away from committed cost. In a corporation, this shift would improve both the stockholders' equity and debt-related measurements.

CROSS-FUNCTIONAL APPLICATIONS

TOPIC OF NOTE	DISCIPLINE	CROSS-FUNCTIONAL APPLICATIONS
Program Budgeting	Legislative Processes	Elected representatives, oversight committees, and regulatory agencies use the program budgets of publicly funded organizations to determine if social goals have been achieved in a reasonably cost-effective manner. Organizations are established to provide programs that carry out the mandated objectives. Legislative oversight committees monitor the results of program operations for effectiveness and program budgets coordinate the decisions and activities of these three groups.
	Public Administration	Public administrators, as well as not-for-profit managers, use program budgets to focus attention on the delivery of results in a service area. The program budget is used to help control discretionary costs, to communicate expectations, and to assist management in decision-making and strategic planning.
	Fund Raising/ Promotion	Program budgets are often used for promotional purposes for two reasons. First, a more aware and cost-conscious public wants reassurances that their contributions are being spent effectively. Charitable organizations now have rigorous public disclosure requirements following some national scandals. Second, the ability of a program budget to show a plight, such as hungry children, and the related program results such as feeding a child for one day in relation to a small cost such as $.75 per day, create very effective fund-raising tools.
	Business Management	Program budgets are used by businesses that have certain activities mandated under regulatory law, such as accommodations for the disabled or toxic waste disposal. Government regulators may establish targeted results; however, they usually do not prescribe the methods. A manager can use a program budget to communicate the efforts expended to achieve the targeted results, especially when a firm must report itself as out of compliance with targeted results.

CHAPTER SUMMARY

Cost control is essential to an organization's long-run success. An effective cost control system encompasses efforts before, during, and after a cost is incurred. Regardless of the type of cost involved, managers and other employees must exercise attitudes of cost consciousness to provide the best means of cost control. Cost consciousness reflects employees' predisposition toward cost understanding, cost containment, cost avoidance, and cost reduction.

Two types of costs are committed and discretionary costs. Committed costs are the long-run costs of establishing and maintaining the fundamental plant assets and permanent organizational personnel required to operate at a level desired by top management. Careful consideration must be given to the selection of that activity level because the choice binds the company to a specified level of fixed costs for the long run. Most discretionary costs are appropriated annually for the conduct of service-type activities that managers may consider optional in the short run. The outputs of discretionary activities are often nonmonetary and qualitative in nature. Discretionary activities should be planned to achieve results that fit within an overall management philosophy.

People and organizations engage in activities to produce results, and those activities create costs. Comparing actual outputs with actual inputs reflects efficiency, while comparing actual outputs with desired results reflects effectiveness. Efficiency plus effectiveness reflects desirable performance. Measuring the outputs generated by cost inputs, however, is not always easy. Surrogate measures of output can be useful in estimating the success of discretionary activities and costs.

Budgeting is a primary tool in planning and controlling discretionary activities and costs. Budget appropriations provide both authorization for spending and the bases against which actual costs are compared. Care must be taken that appropriate levels of activity are used for budget-to-actual comparisons, so that cost control can be effective. Adjustments prior to comparisons are most important for variable costs.

APPENDIX

PROGRAM BUDGETING

The problem of controlling discretionary costs has been particularly acute in governmental and other not-for-profit entities. In addition, activities performed by these organizations produce results that often are difficult to measure in monetary terms or may take several years to be measurable, though the related activities must be funded annually. Traditional budgeting often uses the current year's spending levels in setting the budget for the next year. Additions to the budget each year may lead to nonprioritized and ever-increasing spending levels (the creeping commitment syndrome). **Program budgeting** is useful for cost control because it allows resource inputs to be related to service outputs so that managers can focus on the relevant cost–benefit relationships.

Program budgeting starts by defining objectives in terms of output results rather than quantity of input activities. For instance, an input measure of an executive development program might be a statement of the target number of courses each person must complete by year-end. An output measure might state the objective in terms of expected improvement rates on executive annual performance evaluations. Once output results have been defined in some measurable terms, effectiveness can be measured. Program budgeting involves a thorough analysis of alternative activities for achieving a firm's objectives. This analysis includes projecting both quantitative and qualitative costs and benefits for each alternative and selecting those alternatives that, in the judgment of top management, yield the most satisfactory result at the most reasonable cost. These choices are then translated into budget appropriations to be acted on by the managers responsible for the related programs.

Program budgeting requires the use of detailed surrogate measures of output. These measures call for answers to the following questions:

1. When should results be measured? Since many not-for-profit programs are effective only after some time has passed, it may be necessary to employ different measures at different times to determine effectiveness. When should these measurements initially be made, and how often should they be made thereafter?

2. What results should be chosen as output measures? Many not-for-profit programs have multiple results. For example, reading programs for the adult illiterate can affect employment rates, overall crime reduction statistics, welfare

LEARNING OBJECTIVE ⑤
How is program budgeting used for cost control in not-for-profit entities?

program budgeting

dollar reductions, and so on. Should these results be ranked in importance, or should all results be given equal weight?

3. What actually caused the result? Is there really a cause-and-effect relationship between the observed result and the not-for-profit program? For example, did an adult literacy program cause a decrease in unemployment statistics, or did that decrease result from an unrelated job placement program?

4. Did the program actually affect the target population? An adult literacy program may have been aimed at the unemployed. If most of the persons who attended the program already had jobs, the program did not affect the target group. However, it could still be considered effective if the participants increased their job skills and employment levels.

Program budgeting is useful not only in government and not-for-profit organizations but also in service departments of for-profit businesses. Program budgeting can help managers evaluate and control discretionary activities and costs, avoid excessive cost expenditures, and assure that expenditures are used for programs and activities that generate the most beneficial results.

KEY TERMS

Committed cost (p. 554)
Cost avoidance (p. 550)
Cost consciousness (p. 542)
Cost containment (p. 548)
Cost control system (p. 542)
Cost reduction (p. 550)
Discretionary cost (p.556)
Effectiveness (p. 558)

Efficiency (p. 558)
Horizontal price fixing (p. 547)
Operating leverage (p. 555)
Price fixing (p. 547)
Program budgeting (p. 567)
Strategic staffing (p. 550)
Vertical price fixing (p. 547)

SOLUTION STRATEGIES

Efficiency (relationship of inputs and outputs):
    Actual yield ratio = Actual output ÷ Actual input
                        or
                        Actual input ÷ Actual output
    Desired yield ratio = Planned output ÷ Planned input
                        or
                        Planned input ÷ Planned output
Effectiveness (actual output compared with desired output)
Efficiency + Effectiveness = Performance
Cost variances
Comparison of actual costs with budgeted costs—allows management to compare discrepancies from the original plan
Comparison of actual costs with budgeted costs at actual activity level—allows management to determine how well costs were controlled; uses a flexible budget

DEMONSTRATION PROBLEM

Petunia Press just purchased a color printer that was advertised as being able to print 600 copies an hour, while only using 4.8 ounces of ink per running hour. During the first week, the printer ran continuously for 30 hours. Thus, planned input is 144 ounces of ink, and planned output is 18,000 copies. Management wants to know the printer's efficiency and effectiveness and has provided you with the following statistics:

Actual copies printed	18,720
Actual ounces of ink used	170

Requirements:
a. Calculate the planned output for 30 operating hours.
b. Calculate the degree of effectiveness of the printer in its first week.
c. Calculate planned efficiency for the printer.
d. Calculate the actual efficiency of the printer in its first week.
e. Comment on the printer's performance.

Solution to Demonstration Problem
a. Planned output: 30 hours × 600 copies = 18,000 copies
b. Degree of effectiveness: Actual output ÷ Planned output = 18,720 ÷ 18,000 = 104 percent
c. Planned efficiency: Planned input ÷ Planned output = 144 ounces ÷ 18,000 copies = .008 ounces per copy
d. Actual efficiency: Actual input ÷ Actual output = 170 ounces ÷ 18,720 = ≈.009 ounces per copy
e. Assuming that all the copies were good, the effectiveness of the printer is better than expected. The efficiency of the printer is less than expected. The latter, however, might be corrected after the printer is broken in.

END OF CHAPTER MATERIALS

⊙ QUESTIONS

1. In a cost control system, at what points in time can control over an activity be exerted? Why are these points of cost control important?
2. Explain the meaning and significance of cost consciousness.
3. Why is on-the-job training an important component in the process of instilling cost consciousness within an organization?
4. What factors may cause costs to change from one period to another? Which of these are subject to cost containment and which are not? What creates the difference in controllability?
5. What options does a company have when its costs change because of higher prices from suppliers or from increased costs of complying with government regulations?
6. Compare and contrast general and specific price-level changes.
7. Does a change in the quantity of supply cause costs to change in the same manner as a change in the quantity of suppliers? Why or why not?
8. Compare and contrast horizontal and vertical price fixing. Why are such practices not only illegal, but also unethical?
9. Comment on the following statement: "The quickest way to reduce costs in most organizations is to eliminate employee positions."
10. What are some reasons to use temporaries in what were previously full-time labor positions? What are some reasons against such usage?
11. Why should activity-based management be considered an integral part of cost control?
12. Comment on the following statement: "My company is extremely cost conscious. Everything is outsourced except order-taking."
13. How might members of the supply chain be helpful in an organization's quest for cost containment?

14. What are the five steps that can be used to implement a cost control system? Why is each of these important?

15. Since committed costs are in place for the long run, how can they be controlled?

16. How do committed and discretionary costs differ? Does management's attitude toward a cost affect whether it is classified as discretionary or committed? If so, how? If not, why not?

17. Is an investment in expensive, automated technology wise in an industry characterized by wide variations in demand? What if that industry were highly competitive? Provide underlying reasons for your answers.

18. Why should excess capacity be of extreme concern to an organization's managers?

19. What issues does management need to consider when setting the budget appropriations for discretionary costs?

20. Why is it difficult to measure the output of activities funded by discretionary costs?

21. If a manager having responsibility for a discretionary cost spends less than is budgeted for that cost, should that manager be praised? Discuss the rationale for your answer.

22. What are surrogate output measures? Explain their use in connection with discretionary costs.

23. Define *efficiency* and *effectiveness* and distinguish one from the other.

24. Management performance is evaluated by how efficiently and effectively the company's goals are achieved. Describe the links from inputs to goals by which management performance can be described and measured.

25. Why is measuring the efficiency of discretionary costs often difficult? How can discretionary cost effectiveness be measured?

26. Of what importance is budgeting in the control of discretionary costs?

27. Why is the budget that is used for planning purposes not necessarily the best budget to use for evaluating cost control?

28. Is a budget-to-actual comparison essential in the control of discretionary costs? Provide the rationale for your answer.

29. *(Appendix)* What is program budgeting? How does it differ from traditional budgeting?

30. *(Appendix)* What problems might be encountered in using program budgeting? Why might such problems arise?

⊙ **EXERCISES**

31. *(Terminology)* Match each item in the right-hand column with a term in the left-hand column.

    a. Discretionary cost
    b. Committed cost
    c. Operating leverage
    d. Cost containment
    e. Cost consciousness
    f. Efficiency
    g. Effectiveness
    h. Cost avoidance
    i. Cost reduction
    j. Cost control system

    1. A reflection of an organization's variable and fixed cost structure
    2. An attitude regarding cost understanding, cost containment, and cost reduction
    3. A measure of input-output yield
    4. An optional cost incurred to fund an activity for a specified period
    5. The process of holding unit variable costs and total fixed costs at prior-period levels
    6. A cost incurred to provide physical or organizational capacity
    7. A logical structure of activities designed to analyze and evaluate how well expenditures were managed during a period
    8. The process of finding acceptable alternatives for high priced items and not buying unnecessary goods or services
    9. A process of lowering current costs
    10. An assessment of how well a firm's goals and objectives were achieved

32. *(Cost consciousness)* As the manager of a local accounting firm, you hire temporary staff to work on small audit engagements and tax work. These employees are paid $25 per hour with no fringe benefits. However, temporary employees who work more than 1,600 hours in a year are given a 10 percent bonus above normal compensation for all hours over 1,600. Each permanent staff member receives $36,000 annually, to which fringe benefits of 24 percent are added.
    a. Explain whether the practice of hiring part-time staff is an example of cost containment, cost avoidance, or cost reduction.
    b. At what level of hours of work should you hire permanent staff rather than part-time employees?

33. *(Cost consciousness)* Below are various actions taken by management teams to control costs. For each item listed, indicate whether the action indicates an application of cost understanding, cost containment, cost avoidance, or cost reduction.
    a. A company canceled its contract with an external firm that it used for training in computerized manufacturing methods. At the same time, the firm created an in-house training department. Even though the in-house training will be more expensive, management believes the extra cost is justified because of the flexibility in scheduling training sessions.
    b. A municipality, faced with a 13 percent increase in health insurance premiums, raised the deductible on its coverage, and was able to keep health insurance costs at the prior year's level.
    c. Anticipating a rise in raw material prices, a manufacturing firm used forward contracts to acquire a year's supply of materials at the current prices.
    d. Because beef by-product costs had been rising over the past year, a dog food manufacturer increased the proportion of pork by-products relative to the content of beef by-products in the mix of its dog food.
    e. Because a small foreign country offered a 10-year income tax holiday for new businesses, a U.S. leather-goods manufacturer relocated its production facilities to that country.
    f. Because it had suffered large losses caused by currency fluctuations, a U.S. importer instituted a practice of hedging its currency translation risk.
    g. After the new union contract was signed, wage rates for highly skilled workers rose by 18 percent. As a result, a tool-and-die maker elected to automate three of its higher-volume production processes. This decision resulted in a cost savings of $1,400,000 over a period of 5 years.

34. *(Cost control activities)* You have just been appointed as the new director of Youth Hot Line, a not-for-profit organization that operates a phone bank for individuals experiencing emotional difficulties. The phones are staffed by qualified social workers and psychologists who are paid on an hourly basis. In your first week at Youth Hot-Line, you took the following actions:
    a. Increased the budget appropriation for advertising of the Hot Line.
    b. Exchanged the more expensive pushbutton, cream-colored designer telephones for regular, pushbutton desk telephones.
    c. Eliminated the call-forwarding feature installed on all telephones since Youth Hot Line will now be staffed 24 hours a day.
    d. Eliminated two paid clerical positions and replaced these individuals with volunteers.
    e. Ordered blank notepads for the counselors to keep by their phones; the old notepads (stock now depleted) had the Youth Hot Line logo and address printed on them.
    f. Negotiated a new contract with the telephone company; Youth Hot Line will now pay a flat rate of $100 per month, regardless of the number of telephones installed by the Hot Line. The previous contract charged the organization $10 for every telephone. At the time that contract was signed, Youth Hot Line only had ten telephones. However, with the increased staff, you plan to install at least five additional telephones.

Indicate whether each of the actions represents cost understanding, cost containment, cost avoidance, or cost reduction. Some actions may have more than one implication; if they do, indicate the reason.

35. *(Committed versus discretionary costs)* Indicate whether each of the following sentences best relates to committed (C) costs or discretionary (D) costs. Explain the rationale for your choice.
    a. Temporary reductions in this cost can usually be made without impairing the firm's long-range capacity or profitability.
    b. Control is first provided over this cost during the capital budgeting process.
    c. This cost is primarily affected by long-range decisions regarding desired capacity levels.
    d. Examples of this cost include property taxes, depreciation, and lease rentals.
    e. This cost often provides benefits that are not monetarily measurable.
    f. Examples of this cost include research and development, quality control, and advertising.
    g. This cost cannot be easily reduced, even during temporary slowdowns in activity.
    h. Outcomes often cannot be demonstrated to be closely correlated with this cost.
    i. This cost usually relates to service activities.
    j. No correct amount at which to set funding levels usually exists for this cost.

36. *(Committed versus discretionary costs)* Following is a list of specific discretionary and committed costs.
    ⊙ Advertising
    ⊙ Charitable contributions
    ⊙ Employee safety training
    ⊙ Equipment depreciation
    ⊙ Executive training
    ⊙ Insurance on equipment
    ⊙ Interest expense
    ⊙ Legal staff salaries
    ⊙ Marketing research
    ⊙ Preventive maintenance
    ⊙ Property taxes
    ⊙ Quality control
    ⊙ Research and development
    ⊙ Secretarial pool wages

    Answer the following questions about each of the preceding items.
    a. Is each cost ordinarily classified as committed (C) or discretionary (D)?
    b. What is a monetary or nonmonetary surrogate measure of output for any item you designated as discretionary?
    c. Which costs could be classified as either committed or discretionary, depending on management attitude?

37. *(Effectiveness measures)* As the chief executive officer of Eatontown General Hospital, you must report to the board of directors about how funds were spent during the year. Some of the funding activities for the current year follow.
    a. Placed a full-page advertisement in the local Yellow Pages.
    b. Acquired new software to track patient charges and prepare itemized billings.
    c. Sent two upper-level managers to seminars entitled "Strategic Planning in a Health Maintenance Organization World."
    d. Redecorated the main lobby.
    e. Redecorated the patient rooms on the maternity floor.
    f. Installed a kidney dialysis machine.
    g. Built an attached parking garage for the hospital.

    Provide nonmonetary, surrogate measures that would help evaluate the effectiveness of the money spent.

38. *(Surrogate measures of output)* The Coast Casino and Hotel has established performance objectives for each major operational area for the budget year. Following are some of the major objectives that were established for the budget year 2000. For each objective, identify a surrogate measure of performance.

    a. Increase volume of customer traffic at the gaming tables.

    b. Decrease the labor content per beverage served to customers.

    c. Increase the length of stay per hotel guest.

    d. Attract more out-of-state visitors and reduce the number of in-state visitors.

    e. Increase convention business.

    f. Increase the quality of room-cleaning services.

    g. Increase the relative amount of gaming revenue generated by the slot machines.

39. *(Effectiveness and efficiency measures)* At the beginning of 2000, you were hired as the head of a new department by Sonoma College. Your department's objective for 2000 was to recruit 300 top out-of-state students, given a budget of $400,000. By year-end 2000, the department had been credited with recruiting 325 new students and used $460,000 in its recruiting efforts.

    a. How effective was your department? Show calculations.

    b. How efficient was your department? Show calculations.

    c. What other factors should be determined in evaluating your department's effectiveness and efficiency?

40. *(Efficiency vs. effectiveness)* You own a fleet of deep-sea fishing excursion boats operating out of Newport. You want to put the more efficient of two available diesel engines into one of your older boats. In previous years, the two engines were used on boats similar to the one in which the installation will be made. Records show that engine A ran 22,500 miles and consumed 2,500 gallons of fuel, and engine B ran 19,950 miles and consumed 2,100 gallons of fuel. Diesel fuel is expected to cost $1.40 per gallon next year. The refitted boat is expected to run 2,980 miles next year.

    a. Which engine has demonstrated more efficiency?

    b. How much will be spent next year on diesel fuel if engine A is installed?

    c. How much will be spent next year on diesel fuel if engine B is installed?

    d. How much savings will there be if the more efficient engine is installed?

41. *(Efficiency vs. effectiveness)* As the manager of Lucinda's Secretarial Services, you conclude that the number of original letters typed is a good measure of your typing staff's output. The 2000 budget for this part of your organization is $114,000 and you have estimated that 40,000 pages would be typed for clients during the year.

    Review of the actual results showed that 29,400 pages were typed. The payroll for the typing staff was $109,760. Another 2,500 pages were sent to an external agency at an additional cost of $2,875.

    a. What were the typing department's planned and actual degrees of efficiency? What was the external degree of efficiency in having letters processed?

    b. What was the typing area's degree of effectiveness?

    c. What reasons can you give for the external cost per letter being so much less than the internal cost per letter?

    d. Discuss the pros and cons of large organizations outsourcing all typing work.

42. *(Effectiveness and efficiency)* Hargrave PLC is instituting a quality control program. You have estimated that each quality control inspector should make an average of five inspections per hour. Of every 100 units produced, three should be inspected. An average hourly rate of $15 has been established for these inspectors. In the first month of the program, 190,000 units were produced and 5,130 inspections were made. The inspectors were paid $15,834 for 1,015 hours of work.

    a. How effective were the inspectors?

    b. How efficient were the inspectors?

c. If Hargrave planned on producing 190,000 units per month and could hire three full-time inspectors, each to work 200 hours monthly at a salary of $2,400 per month and use $15-per-hour part-time inspectors for the needed extra inspections, how much better or worse off would the company be than with the current system, assuming that the standard hourly rate was paid to the part-timers?

43. *(Flexible budget)* As the marketing manager for KJ Enterprises, you have determined the following cost formulas for your department:

Management salaries	$19,500 per month
Worker wages	$15.00 per hour
Utilities	$3,700 plus $.45 per hour
Maintenance	$1,000 plus $.70 per hour
Supplies	$7,500 plus $9.40 per hour
Equipment depreciation	$6,750 per month

a. Prepare your department's budget for April 2000, assuming that 1,050 hours will be worked during the month.
b. Are the figures presented in Part a correct for comparative purposes if 1,120 hours were actually worked during the month? If not, what would the appropriate figures be?

44. *(Controlling quality costs)* Gaubert Drapes produces a wide variety of window coverings to customer specifications. Quality costs incurred in the Draperies Division for 2000 follow:

Prevention	$ 400,000
Appraisal	100,000
Internal failure costs	300,000
External failure costs	200,000
Total	$1,000,000

a. Would a committed or discretionary cost occur if the company spent $300,000 on a new computer-controlled machine to lay out and cut material, replacing a manual cutting system? Which categories of failure costs would be affected by such a decision? Explain.
b. You are trying to quantify the benefits and costs associated with the acquisition of the machine referred to in Part a. What could each of the following experts add to your understanding of benefits and costs associated with the machine?
   (1) Electrical engineer
   (2) Mechanical engineer
   (3) Production supervisor
   (4) Marketing director
   (5) Cost accountant
c. You have determined that projected external failure costs for 2001 could be halved from their 2000 levels by either spending $80,000 more on appraisal or spending $120,000 more on prevention. Why might you opt to spend the $120,000 on prevention rather than the $80,000 on appraisal?

45. *(Benchmarking quality costs)* For a benchmark, assume that the typical firm incurs quality costs in the following proportions:

Prevention	25%
Appraisal	25%
Internal failure	25%
External failure	25%
Total costs	100%

Explain why each of the following types of firms might have a spending pattern for quality costs that differs from the benchmark.

a. Architectural firm
b. Hair salon
c. Heavy equipment manufacturer
d. Health maintenance organization

⊙ PROBLEMS

46. *(Cost consciousness)* Temporary or part-time employees are sometimes hired to
    a. Draw house plans for construction companies.
    b. Make desserts for restaurants.
    c. Perform legal research for law firms.
    d. Prepare tax returns for CPA firms.
    e. Sell clothing in department stores during the Christmas season.
    f. Serve as security guards.
    g. Tailor men's suits for department stores.
    h. Teach evening courses at universities.
    i. Work as medical doctors in the emergency rooms of hospitals.
    j. Write articles for monthly magazines.
    For each job listed, suggest potential advantages and disadvantages of using temporary or part-time employees from the perspective of both the employer and the end user of the product or service.

47. *(Cost consciousness)* Elyssa and Bob Schultz are preparing their December household financial budget. They plan on adjusting their November budget to reflect differences between November and December activities. The Schultzes are expecting out-of-town guests for two weeks over the holiday season. The following items detail contemplated budgetary changes from November to December for the Schultz family:
    a. Increase the grocery budget by $135.
    b. Decrease the commuter transportation budget by $50 to reflect the days off from work.
    c. Change food budget to reflect serving pizza rather than steak or lobster each weekend.
    d. Budget an extra $70 for utilities.
    e. Reduce household maintenance budget by $60 to reflect the fact that outside maid services will not be used over the holiday period.
    f. Buy generic breakfast cereal rather than name-brand due to the quantity the guests will consume.
    g. Buy paper plates rather than run the dishwasher.
    h. Buy the institutional-size packages of napkins rather than smaller-size packages.
    i. Budget the long-distance phone bill at $50 less because there will be no need to call the relatives who will be visiting.
    j. Budget movie rentals for $3 per tape rather than spend $7 per person to go to the movies.
    k. Postpone purchasing needed work clothes until January.
    l. Budget funds to repair the car. Elyssa plans to use part of her vacation time to make the repairs herself rather than take the car to a garage in January.
    Indicate whether each of the above items is indicative of cost understanding (CU), cost containment (CC), cost avoidance (CA), or cost reduction (CR). Some items may have more than one answer.

48. *(Committed versus discretionary cost)* Logan Sports is concerned about proper staffing in its expanded purchasing department. Historically, it has taken an average of 30 minutes to prepare each purchase order. As department manager, you believe that the predicted number of purchase orders is highly correlated with the predicted sales for any future year. The average revenue for each of the last three years has been $12,000,000, with an average of 40,000 purchase orders in each of those years. A full-time purchasing agent is paid $32,000 annually. Part-time purchasing staff can be hired at $14 per hour.

Full-time employees work 8 hours per day, 5 days per week, 50 weeks annually. Budgeted revenue for the year 2000 is $12,600,000.

  a. How many purchase orders are predicted for 2000?
  b. If only part-timers were used, what would it cost to staff the department for 2000?
  c. If only full-timers were used, what would it cost to staff the department for 2000?
  d. You want to have eight full-time employees (other than yourself) and to staff the remaining hours needed with part-timers. What would your staff costs be (excluding your salary)?

49. *(Cost control) Recently, the California State University system placed a purchase order (PO) for a book published by a small New Canaan, Conn., company, The Information Economics Press. The following is a copy of the letter the press sent back to the California procurement officer:*

  We have your eight page PO#940809 for one copy of our book "The Politics of Information Management." We are unable to fill your $49 order for the following reasons:

  ⊙ *In the Purchase Order Terms and Conditions you wish us to waive any infringement of our copyrighted materials by officers, agents and employees of the California State University. We cannot agree to make available a valuable copyright for the price of a book.*

  ⊙ *You will withhold all payments or make a 38% withholding in order to file a year-end 1099 form. We are unable to handle the paperwork of a separate 1099 for every book we sell. That would double our paperwork.*

  ⊙ *You are requiring us to file a Vendor Data Record (form 204) which is largely identical with your Vendor Information form. Filing both forms takes excessive amounts of time.*

  ⊙ *We are a small business, and therefore you require that we submit a copy of the OSMB Small Business Certification. We do not have an OSMB Certification and we do not know where to get one.*

  ⊙ *Your attachment to form 204 specifies that I obtain a determination with regard to my being classified either as resident or non-resident subject to California tax withholdings, to be reclaimed by filing at year-end California tax returns. We do not plan to make any tax filings in California.*

  ⊙ *Your contract rider contains a Privacy Statement on unspecified disclosures that makes us liable for penalties of up to $20,000.*

  ⊙ *As a condition of our filling out the order you are asking us to post statements notifying all employees of compliance with Code Section 8355 and certifying as to our adopting a four point Drug-Free Awareness program that complies with California law. Deviations are punishable as perjury under the laws of the State of California. Please note our firm has only two employees, who do not take even an aspirin.*

  ⊙ *Your Minority/Women Business Enterprise Self Certification Form 962 requires detailed statistics on ethnic characteristics of our firm, defining each ethnic group according to their stated geographic origins. To assist in making such distinctions you provide a check list of ethnic identity of the owners of this firm, leaving us by default with only one open choice, Caucasian, which you do not define. My husband and I do not know of any ancestors who may have ever been in the proximity of the Caucasian mountains, and therefore we are unable to comply with your requirement to identify our ethnic origin according to your geographic rules.*

  We therefore suggest that you purchase our book at a bookstore.

  [Source: Mona Frankel, "Just Go to the Bookstore and Buy One," *Wall Street Journal*, October 18, 1994, p. A20. Reprinted by permission of *Wall Street Journal*, © 1994 Dow Jones & Company Inc. All Rights Reserved Worldwide.]

  a. What cost control strategy was the author of the preceding letter employing in her decision to reject the book order? Explain.
  b. What appears to be the source of most of the complexity associated with the purchase order? Explain.
  c. What does the letter suggest about the opportunity for improved cost control in the California State University purchasing system? Explain.

50. *(Cost control and financial records)* Turbo Propulsion is a medium-sized manufacturing plant in a capital-intensive industry. The corporation's profitability is very low at the

moment. As a result, investment funds are limited and hiring is restricted. These consequences of the corporation's problems have placed a strain on the plant's repair and maintenance program. The result has been a reduction in work efficiency and cost control effectiveness in the repair and maintenance area.

The assistant controller proposes the installation of a maintenance work order system to overcome these problems. This system would require a work order to be prepared for each repair request and for each regular maintenance activity. The maintenance superintendent would record the estimated time to complete a job and send one copy of the work order to the department in which the work was to be done. The work order would also serve as a cost sheet for a job. The actual cost of the parts and supplies used on the job as well as the actual labor costs incurred in completing the job would be recorded directly on the work order. A copy of the completed work order would be the basis of the charge to the department in which the repair or maintenance activity occurred.

The maintenance superintendent opposes the program on the grounds that the added paperwork will be costly and nonproductive. The superintendent states that the departmental clerk who now schedules repairs and maintenance activities is doing a good job without all the extra forms the new system would require. The real problem, in the superintendent's opinion, is that the department is understaffed.

a. Discuss how such a maintenance work order system would aid in cost control.

b. Explain how a maintenance work order system might assist the maintenance superintendent in getting authorization to hire more mechanics.

(CMA)

51. *(Efficiency versus effectiveness)* The health care industry has recently found itself in a new era that is characterized by cost competition. As a result of the new emphasis on cost management, many existing practices are being revised or dropped. Following are changes that have been made by specific health care providers. For each change mentioned, indicate whether the change is intended to control cost through increased efficiency or increased effectiveness. Also indicate whether the change represents cost understanding, cost containment, cost avoidance, or cost reduction. Discuss your justification for each answer.

a. Before entering the hospital for chemotherapy, a patient's health care provider required her to drink more than two quarts of water at home. By doing so, a day's stay in the hospital for hydration was avoided.

b. By administering an antibiotic within two hours of each operation, a hospital reduced the post-operation infection rate from 1.8 percent of patients to .4 percent of patients.

c. Some surgeons have started removing the drainage tubes from heart-bypass patients 24 hours after the operation rather than 48 hours after the operation. The change reduces the length of the typical hospital stay.

d. Doctors at a major hospital tightened scheduling requirements for blood analysis so that results were obtained on the same day that the blood was drawn. The change allowed many patients to be dismissed immediately.

e. A hospital began a practice of paying about $130 per average dose of a new antinausea drug to be administered to chemotherapy patients. The drug allowed vomiting to be controlled much faster and the patient to be more comfortable and dismissed a day earlier.

[Facts based on Ron Winslow, "Health-Care Providers Try Industrial Tactics to Reduce Their Costs," *Wall Street Journal*, November 3, 1993, pp. A1, A5. Reprinted by permission of *Wall Street Journal*, © 1993 Dow Jones & Company, Inc. All Rights Reserved Worldwide.]

52. *(Efficiency versus effectiveness)* Leonardo Construction Co. budgeted $280,000 for its bid department to make bids on potential bridge-building contracts in 2000. The company expected to issue 400 bids in 1998. When 2000 activity was analyzed in early 2001, the following statistics were ascertained:

Actual bids prepared	440
Actual bid expenses	$292,600

a. Was the bid department effective? Present calculations.

b. Was the bid department efficient? Present calculations.

c. Did the bid department stay within its budget? If not, discuss what bid department personnel might have done before overspending the budget.

53. *(Efficiency standards)* You have been asked to monitor the efficiency and effectiveness of a newly installed machine. The machine's guarantee states that it can produce 7,800 gaskets per kilowatt hour (kwh). The production defect rate is estimated at 1.5 percent. The machine is equipped with a device to measure the number of kwhs used. During the first month of use, the machine produced 1,390,000 gaskets, of which 14,000 were flawed, and it used 175 kwhs.

a. What is the efficiency standard for flawless output?

b. Calculate the achieved efficiency and effectiveness for the first month and briefly comment on them.

c. Assume that the company was charged $1.60 per kwh during the first month this machine was in service. Estimate the company's savings or loss in power costs because of the machine's efficiency level in the first month of operations.

d. What amount of quality control do you think a major automobile manufacturer buying this company's gaskets would want the company to have and why?

54. *(Cost control)* As the finance officer for Ridenour Electronics, you have observed that the EDP department was justifying ever larger budget requests on the basis of ever larger usage by the company's various departments. User departments are not charged for EDP services and state that EDP personnel are always helpful in recommending ways the department can be of greater service.

Operating statistics for the EDP department for 2000 follow:

⊙ Budget—$107,500 based on 2,150 hours of run time; of this amount, $75,250 relates to fixed costs

⊙ Actual—$43,700 variable cost (incurred for 2,300 hours of run time); $75,250 fixed cost

a. Did the EDP department operate within its approved budget? Present calculations.

b. Calculate the department's effectiveness and comment.

c. Was the department efficient in using its variable costs? Fixed costs?

d. Devise an hourly rate scheme to charge EDP users for the cost of operating the EDP department. Do you think charging for EDP services will slow expansion of the EDP department budget? Explain.

55. *(Budget/actual comparison)* Management at Muir Wood Products evaluates performance in part through the use of flexible budgets. Selling expense budgets at three activity levels within the relevant range are shown below.

Activity measures:

Unit sales volume	15,000	17,500	20,000
Dollar sales volume	$15,000,000	$17,500,000	$20,000,000
# of orders processed	1,500	1,750	2,000
# of salespersons	100	100	100

Monthly expenses:

Advertising and promotion	$1,500,000	$1,500,000	$1,500,000
Administrative salaries	75,000	75,000	75,000
Sales salaries	90,000	90,000	90,000
Sales commissions	450,000	525,000	600,000
Salesperson travel	200,000	225,000	250,000
Sales office	445,000	452,500	460,000
Shipping	650,000	675,000	700,000
Total	$3,410,000	$3,542,500	$3,675,000

The following assumptions were used to develop the selling expense flexible budgets:

- ⊙ The average size of the company's sales force during the year was planned to be 100 people.
- ⊙ Salespersons are paid a monthly salary plus commission on total sales dollar.
- ⊙ Travel costs are mixed. The fixed portion is related to the number of salespersons; the variable portion fluctuates with sales dollars.
- ⊙ Sales office expense is a mixed cost, with the variable portion related to the number of orders processed.
- ⊙ Shipping expense is a mixed cost, with the variable portion related to the number of units sold.

A 90-person sales force generated 1,600 orders during November, resulting in a sales volume of 16,000 units. Total sales amounted to $14.9 million. November selling expenses were

Advertising and promotion	$1,450,000
Administrative salaries	80,000
Sales salaries	92,000
Sales commissions	460,000
Salesperson travel	185,000
Sales office	500,000
Shipping	640,000
Total	$3,407,000

- a. Explain why one of the original selling expense flexible budgets would not be appropriate for evaluating the company's November selling expense, and indicate how the flexible budget would have to be revised.
- b. Determine the company's budgeted variable cost per salesperson and variable cost per sales order.
- c. Prepare a selling expense report for November that can be used to evaluate its control over selling expenses. The report should include the appropriate budgeted amount, actual expense, and dollar variation for each selling expense item.
- d. Determine the company's actual variable cost per salesperson and variable cost per sales order processed.
- e. Comment on the effectiveness and efficiency of the salespersons during November.

(CMA adapted)

56. *(Appendix)* Indicate whether each item in the following list describes traditional budgeting (T) or program budgeting (P). After identifying the appropriate type of budgeting, discuss how the other budgeting method differs.
- a. It is especially useful in government and not-for-profit entities and for service activities in for-profit firms.
- b. It begins with amounts budgeted in prior year and builds on those numbers based on expansion of resources to fund greater input activity.
- c. It begins by defining objectives in terms of output results rather than quantity of input activities.
- d. It is concerned with alternative approaches to achieving similar results.
- e. It treats the prior year's funding levels as given and essential to operations.
- f. It requires the use of surrogate measures of output.
- g. It focuses on budgeted monetary levels rather than on goals, objectives, and outputs.
- h. It is particularly well suited to budgeting for discretionary cost expenditures.
- i. It requires an analysis of alternative activities for achieving a firm's objectives.
- j. It is concerned with choosing the particular results that should be used as output measures.

⊙ CASES

57. *(Cost control)* The following graph indicates where each part of the dollar that a student pays for a new college textbook goes.

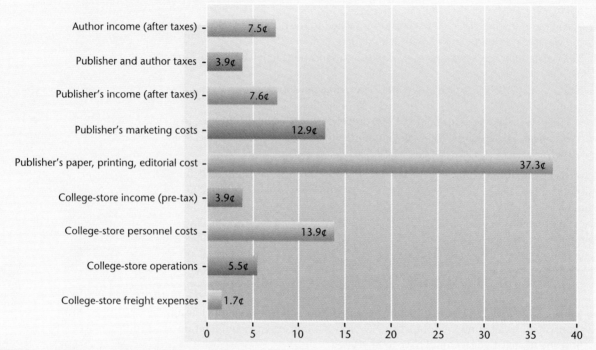

SOURCE: Association of American Publishers and National Association of College Stores, "Where Does the Textbook Dollar Go?" *The Chronicle of Higher Education* (September 22, 1995), p. A51.

Students are frustrated with the cost of their textbooks, but most publishers would say that the selling prices have merely kept pace with inflation. Buying used books is an option, but publishers say that used books simply drive up the cost of future texts: if the publisher cannot sell as many of the new edition as are printed, the price is raised "to compensate for decreased sales volume, and the cycle starts again." Publishers also must cover the costs of many non-salable supplements that are requested by faculty such as instructor manuals, solutions manuals, transparency acetates, videos, and test banks (hard copy and electronic). Additionally, as the books become more elaborate with multiple colors, photographs, and periodical cites, costs also increase. Write a paper that does the following:

a. Provides suggestions for ways the college/university bookstore could control costs.

b. Provides suggestions for ways the publisher could control costs.

c. Provides suggestions for ways students can legally control textbook expenditures (i.e., substantial reproduction of the text is illegal).

d. Discusses why college textbooks today are so different from college textbooks of 20 years ago. Are these differences cost-beneficial from your perspective?

58. *(Governmental cost control)* According to an article ("GAO Report: Pentagon Keeps Buying Unneeded Supplies") by Steven Komarrow in the February 28, 1997, issue of *USA Today*, the Pentagon appears to engage in less-than-effective cost control. The estimate is that about 1.5 million out of 3.3 million stocked items are in excess supply or no longer needed.

a. Assume that you are in charge of the Department of Defense's supply system. Defend the acquisition and retention of what have been designated as unneeded items.

b. Assume that you are the head of the General Accounting Office. Discuss your reply to Part a.

c. What type of cost consciousness ideas would you suggest to the Pentagon, and how would these ideas help? What would be the deterrents to implementation?

59. *(Analyzing cost control)* The financial results for the Continuing Education Department of BusEd Corporation for November 2000 are presented in the schedule at the end of the case. Mary Ross, president of BusEd, is pleased with the final results but has observed that the revenue and most of the costs and expenses of this department exceeded the budgeted amounts. Barry Stein, vice-president of the Continuing Education Department, has been requested to provide an explanation of any amount that exceeded the budget by 5 percent or more.

Stein has accumulated the following facts to assist in his analysis of the November results:

◉ The budget for calendar year 2000 was finalized in December 1999, and at that time, a full program of continuing education courses was scheduled to be held in Chicago during the first week of November 2000. The courses were scheduled so that eight courses would be run on each of the five days during the week. The budget assumed that there would be 425 participants in the program and 1,000 participant days for the week.

◉ BusEd charges a flat fee of $150 per day of course instruction, so the fee for a three-day course would be $450. BusEd grants a 10 percent discount to persons who subscribe to its publications. The 10 percent discount is also granted to second and subsequent registrants for the same course from the same organization. However, only one discount per registration is allowed. Historically, 70 percent of the participant day registrations are at the full fee of $150 per day, and 30 percent of the participant day registrations receive the discounted fee of $135 per day. These percentages were used in developing the November 2000 budgeted revenue.

◉ The following estimates were used to develop the budgeted figures for course-related expenses.

Food charges per participant day (lunch/coffee breaks)	$ 27
Course materials per participant	8
Instructor fee per day	1,000

◉ A total of 530 individuals participated in the Chicago courses in November 2000, accounting for 1,280 participant days. This number included 20 persons who took a new, two-day course on pension accounting that was not on the original schedule; thus, on two of the days, nine courses were offered, and an additional instructor was hired to cover the new course. The breakdown of the course registration was as follows:

Full fee registrations	704
Discounted fees	
Current periodical subscribers	128
New periodical subscribers	128
Second registrations from the same organization	320
Total participant day registrations	1,280

◉ A combined promotional mailing was used to advertise the Chicago program and a program in Cincinnati that was scheduled for December 2000. The incremental costs of the combined promotional price were $5,000, but none of the promotional expenses ($20,000) budgeted for the Cincinnati program in December will have to be incurred. This earlier-than-normal promotion for the Cincinnati program has resulted in early registration fees collected in November as follows (in terms of participant days):

Full fee registrations	140
Discounted registrations	60
Total participant day registrations	200

◉ BusEd continually updates and adds new courses, and includes $2,000 in each monthly budget for this purpose. The additional amount spent on course development during November was for an unscheduled course that will be offered in February for the first time.

Barry Stein has prepared the following quantitative analysis of the November 2000 variances:

BUS ED CORPORATION
STATEMENT OF OPERATIONS
CONTINUING EDUCATION DEPARTMENT

	Budget	Actual	Favorable/ (Unfavorable) Dollars	Favorable/ (Unfavorable) Percent
Revenue				
Course fees	$145,500	$212,460	$ 66,960	46.0
Expenses				
Food charges	$ 27,000	$ 32,000	$ (5,000)	(18.5)
Course materials	3,400	4,770	(1,370)	(40.3)
Instructor fees	40,000	42,000	(2,000)	(5.0)
Instructor travel	9,600	9,885	(285)	(3.0)
Staff salaries & benefits	12,000	12,250	(250)	(2.1)
Staff travel	2,500	2,400	100	4.0
Promotion	20,000	25,000	(5,000)	(25.0)
Course development	2,000	5,000	(3,000)	(150.0)
Total expenses	$116,500	$133,305	$(16,805)	(14.4)
Revenue over expenses	$ 29,000	$ 79,155	$ 50,155	172.9

BUS ED CORPORATION
ANALYSIS OF NOVEMBER 2000 VARIANCES

Budgeted revenue		$145,500
Variances:		
Quantity variance [(1,280 − 1,000) × $145.50]	$40,740 F	
Mix variance [($143.25 − $145.50) × 1,280]	2,880 U	
Timing difference ($145.50 × 200)	29,100 F	66,960 F
Actual revenue		$212,460
Budgeted expenses		$116,500
Quantity variances		
Food charges [(1,000 − 1,280) × $27]	$ 7,560 U	
Course materials [(425 − 530) × $8]	840 U	
Instructor fees (2 × $1,000)	2,000 U	10,400 U
Price variances		
Food charges [($27 − $25) × 1,280]	$ 2,560 F	
Course materials [($8 − $9) × 530]	530 U	2,030 F
Timing differences		
Promotion	$ 5,000 U	
Course development	3,000 U	8,000 U
Variances not analyzed (5% or less)		
Instructor travel	$ 285 U	
Staff salaries and benefits	250 U	
Staff travel	100 F	435 U
Actual expenses		$133,305

After reviewing Barry Stein's quantitative analysis of the November variances, prepare a memorandum addressed to Mary Ross explaining the following:

a. The cause of the revenue mix variance.

b. The implication of the revenue mix variance.

c. The cause of the revenue timing difference.

d. The significance of the revenue timing difference.

CROSS-FUNCTIONAL APPLICATIONS

TOPIC OF NOTE	DISCIPLINE	CROSS-FUNCTIONAL APPLICATIONS
Program Budgeting	Legislative Processes	Elected representatives, oversight committees, and regulatory agencies use the program budgets of publicly funded organizations to determine if social goals have been achieved in a reasonably cost-effective manner. Organizations are established to provide programs that carry out the mandated objectives. Legislative oversight committees monitor the results of program operations for effectiveness and program budgets coordinate the decisions and activities of these three groups.
	Public Administration	Public administrators, as well as not-for-profit managers, use program budgets to focus attention on the delivery of results in a service area. The program budget is used to help control discretionary costs, to communicate expectations, and to assist management in decision-making and strategic planning.
	Fund Raising/ Promotion	Program budgets are often used for promotional purposes for two reasons. First, a more aware and cost-conscious public wants reassurances that their contributions are being spent effectively. Charitable organizations now have rigorous public disclosure requirements following some national scandals. Second, the ability of a program budget to show a plight, such as hungry children, and the related program results such as feeding a child for one day in relation to a small cost such as $.75 per day, create very effective fund-raising tools.
	Business Management	Program budgets are used by businesses that have certain activities mandated under regulatory law, such as accommodations for the disabled or toxic waste disposal. Government regulators may establish targeted results; however, they usually do not prescribe the methods. A manager can use a program budget to communicate the efforts expended to achieve the targeted results, especially when a firm must report itself as out of compliance with targeted results.

CHAPTER SUMMARY

Cost control is essential to an organization's long-run success. An effective cost control system encompasses efforts before, during, and after a cost is incurred. Regardless of the type of cost involved, managers and other employees must exercise attitudes of cost consciousness to provide the best means of cost control. Cost consciousness reflects employees' predisposition toward cost understanding, cost containment, cost avoidance, and cost reduction.

Two types of costs are committed and discretionary costs. Committed costs are the long-run costs of establishing and maintaining the fundamental plant assets and permanent organizational personnel required to operate at a level desired by top management. Careful consideration must be given to the selection of that activity level because the choice binds the company to a specified level of fixed costs for the long run. Most discretionary costs are appropriated annually for the conduct of service-type activities that managers may consider optional in the short run. The outputs of

CROSS-FUNCTIONAL APPLICATIONS

TOPIC OF NOTE	DISCIPLINE	CROSS-FUNCTIONAL APPLICATIONS
Committed versus Discretionary Costs	Legal Services	Common contractual negotiations and legal review follow-ups for sales/purchase agreements, leases, acquisitions, and outsourcing should provide the principal with the greatest flexibility to change his or her decision in relation to an ever-changing environment. Attorneys must be aware of which committed costs are most constraining to management decision making in each situation. For instance, an operating lease on a retail outlet for the introduction of a new product may be a greater long-run risk in terms of committed cost than the same terms in a contract that adds one outlet to a well-established product line.
	Marketing and Sales Management	Sales personnel, often eager to close a contract, may ignore profitability in terms of other marketing objectives, such as new business recruitment or increased territorial share of the market. They must be made aware that certain committed costs, such as distribution costs in a sparsely populated region, could reduce profitability. Marketing departments are frequently evaluated for performance as revenue centers. However, their budgets should guide them in distinguishing between the constraints of committed costs, such as media advertisement, as opposed to more discretionary promotional costs like coupons, rebates, or discounts.
	Engineering	The specifications for manufacturing resources such as materials or parts are frequently selected by research, design, or manufacturing engineers who surrender requisitions to a centralized purchasing department. Engineers are courted by sales representatives who focus on technical specifications that may be appropriate to the buyer's product line. Since discretion is a critical point in the procurement of technical resources, engineers must be guided by the concept of cost flexibility when they select among alternative resources.
	Organizational Theory	When organizations merge, the discretionary costs of support services such as accounting or human resources are often reduced by centralization—which accounts for employee lay-off announcements that usually follow a merger. However, committed costs are outside the reach of managerial decisions, and frequently the efficiencies of scale in centralization are offset by the "sunk" nature of committed costs. In a merger, buyout, or acquisition decision, committed costs are a key determinant.
	Pension Funding	Nationally, organizations have sought to reduce their committed costs and the risk of sharp increases for benefits such as health care. Pension planners have minimized the risk of future pension liabilities to their organizations and reduced the current minimum accrual required in financial accounting by shifting the terms of pension agreement away from committed cost. In a corporation, this shift would improve both the stockholders' equity and debt-related measurements.

An organization cannot operate without some basic level of plant and human assets. Considerable control can be exercised over the process of determining how management wishes to define *basic* and what funds will be committed to those levels. However, management needs to regularly review its capacity decisions and compare the benefits from capacity commitments with their related costs. Excess capacity may be expensive and inefficient as discussed in the accompanying News Note.

DISCRETIONARY COSTS

LEARNING OBJECTIVE ❷
How are committed and discretionary costs differentiated?

discretionary cost

In contrast to a committed cost, a **discretionary cost** is one "that a decision maker must periodically review to determine that it continues to be in accord with ongoing policies."[18] A discretionary fixed cost reflects a management decision to fund an activity *at a specified amount for a specified time*. Discretionary costs relate to company activities that are viewed as important but optional. Discretionary cost activities are usually service-oriented and include employee travel, repairs and maintenance, advertising, research and development, and employee training and development. There is no correct amount at which to set funding for discretionary costs, and there are no specific activities whose costs are always considered discretionary in all organizations. In the event of cash flow shortages or forecasted operating losses, discretionary costs may be more easily reduced than committed costs.

Discretionary costs, then, are generated by relatively unstructured activities that vary in type and magnitude from day to day and whose benefits are often not measurable in monetary terms. For example, in 1998, Anheuser-Busch decided to pay a record $2 million per 30-second commercial during the 1999 Super Bowl.[19] How does

---

NEWS NOTE

Making Rational Capacity Decisions

The cost of capacity in most companies is substantial and continues to grow. Unused or under-utilized capacity involves waste and foregone profits.

The prevalence, at any given time and in any given area, of excess capacity is not the issue. Capacity resources, whether people or equipment, often are committed in amounts that turn out to be incongruous with actual amounts needed at any given time. Justifications for this include cyclical or seasonal business, a desire to get out in front of competitors, industry-wide overcapacity, demand/mix volatility, ongoing improvements in productivity, and anticipated sales growth.

Awareness of the magnitude of the cost of capacity resources, used and unused, will direct greater attention to managing capacity and will provide more accurate information for decisions including pricing, downsizing, and redeployment. There is also a greater chance that future conditions of excess or unused capacity will be reduced by emphasizing the cost of current capacity, reviewing past decisions through post-implementation audits, articulating policies and assigning clear responsibility for capacity management, and seeking greater capacity flexibility.

Refusing to identify the cost of excess resources allows competitors who are better informed about their costs to enjoy a significant competitive advantage and misses opportunities to be more profitable.

SOURCE: John M Brausch and Thomas C. Taylor, "Who Is Accounting for the Cost of Capacity?" Reprinted from *Management Accounting* (Feburary 1997), p. 50. Published by the Institute of Management Accountants, Montvale, N.J. Visit our website at www.imanet.org.

---

[18]Institute of Management Accountants (formerly National Association of Accountants), *Statements on Management Accounting Number 2: Management Accounting Terminology* (Montvale, N.J.: National Association of Accountants, June 1, 1983), p. 35.

[19]Melanie Wells, "Busch Buys $2M Super Bowl Ad," *USA Today*, April 14, 1998, p. 4B.

To make filling up cars easier for customers, Shell is committing massive amounts of money to redesign and reequip its gas stations. Such investments in capital assets can impact a firm's operating leverage and ability to withstand downturns in demand.

caused by the relationship between a company's variable and fixed costs or **operating leverage**. Typically, highly labor-intensive organizations, such as McDonald's or Domino's Pizza, have high variable costs and low fixed costs and, thus, have low operating leverage. These companies can show a profit even when they experience wide swings in volume levels. Conversely, organizations that are highly capital-intensive, such as Alaska Airlines and Caterpillar, have a high operating leverage or a cost structure that includes low variable and high fixed costs. These companies must have fairly high sales volumes to cover fixed costs, but sales above the breakeven point produce large profits.

operating leverage

http:// www.mcdonalds.com

http:// www.dominos.com

http:// www.alaskair.com

http:// www.cat.com

Companies that have fairly high contribution margins (that is, revenues minus total variable costs) can withstand large fixed costs increases as long as revenues increase. However, these same companies are affected more strongly when revenues decrease because the margin available to cover fixed costs erodes so rapidly. As the magnitude of committed fixed costs increases, so does the risk of incurring an operating loss in the event of a downturn in demand. Therefore, managers must be extremely careful about the level of fixed costs to which they commit the organization.

Committed costs may also be controlled by making the available capacity more productive. Sometimes increased productivity may result from bottleneck reductions or from new ideas for utilization. In other cases, it may result from new flexibility. For instance, in 1995, Alaska Airlines negotiated new union contracts that allowed three hours more of flight time than the eight hours flown per day in 1993. The increased flying hours gave the company the equivalent of 28 additional planes at virtually no cost, allowing new routes and more daily round trips.

A third method of controlling committed costs involves comparing actual and expected results from plant asset investments. Making these comparisons help managers review and evaluate the accuracy of their cost and revenue predictions relative to capital investments.[17] Deviations from projections should be investigated and, if possible, actions taken to eliminate the causes of lower-than-expected performance.

---

[17]This comparison is called a post-investment audit and is discussed in Chapter 8.

e. The primary cause of the unfavorable total expense variance.

f. How the favorable food price variance was determined.

g. The impact of the promotion timing difference on future revenues and expenses.

h. Whether the course development variance has an unfavorable impact on the company.

(CMA)

⊙ ETHICS AND QUALITY DISCUSSIONS

60. The most popular United States air traffic route in the east may be the 14-mile flight between the Pentagon and Andrews Air Force Base. According to the *Washington Post*, top military officials made this flight 238 times in 1993 and the average cost per flight is between $1,000 and $3,000. By car, the trip takes about 25 minutes which, using taxi rates, amounts to $22. Using these estimates, if all trips were made by taxi, the total cost of the trips would have been approximately $5,236 for 1993.

A secretary of a former Secretary of Defense indicated that the flights were an issue of efficiency because of potential extensive ground congestion.

a. Evaluate the argument that air transportation is used in the name of efficiency.

b. Could the use of air transportation be better justified on the grounds of effectiveness? Explain.

c. Could the use of air transportation be defended on the basis of quality considerations? Explain.

61. Assume that you are in charge of a social service agency that provides counseling services to welfare families. The agency's costs have been increasing with no corresponding increase in funding. In an effort to reduce some costs, you implement the following ideas:

⊙ Counselors are empowered to make their own decisions about the legitimacy of all welfare claims.

⊙ To emphasize the concept of doing it right the first time, counselors are told not to review processed claims at a later date.

⊙ To discourage out-of-control conditions, an upper and lower control limit of 5 minutes is set on a standard 15-minute time for consultations.

Discuss the ethics as well as the positive and negative effects of each of the ideas listed.

62. *For Caesar O'Neal, a nausea-free day is priceless. But for the hospital treating the 6-foot-8-inch University of Florida football player for liver cancer, the price of delivering that relief is becoming troublesome.*

Mr. O'Neal has been getting massive chemotherapy, including a round last fall that left him vomiting so much that he nearly quit treatment. After that crisis, doctors gave him Zofran, a powerful antinausea drug. Now chemotherapy isn't so frightening, Mr. O'Neal says as he sits on his bed sipping Gatorade. Instead of suffering anguish after each treatment, he can enjoy small pleasures such as video games, big meals or chats with relatives.

But Zofran is one of the most expensive drugs around—and a hot issue as hospitals and drug makers clash over the cost of medications. A standard 32-milligram dose of Zofran—less than a single teardrop—costs hospitals $143. Factor in expenses for stocking it and having nurses administer it intravenously, and each use of Zofran can turn into a $300 patient charge. By weight, gem-quality diamonds are cheaper.

Many doctors and nurses, however, think they can slash Zofran costs without making patients feel worse. "We may be overusing the drug," says Robert Benjamin, an oncologist who treats Mr. O'Neal at the University of Texas M.D. Anderson Cancer Center in Houston. He and other doctors around the U.S. think Glaxo's official package inserts, though approved by the Food and Drug Administration, overstate the Zofran dose that many patients need.

M.D. Anderson is seeking to trim its spending on costly antinausea drugs such as Zofran by 10 percent this year. Other teaching hospitals, in Boston, New York and Chicago, are looking for cuts of 25 percent to 50 percent—mostly by drafting new treatment standards that lean on doctors to shrink dosages or try less costly substitutes.

[Source: George Anders, "Costly Medicine Meets Its Match: Hospitals Just Use Lower Doses," *Wall Street Journal*, August 1, 1994, pp. A1, A6. Reprinted by permission of *Wall Street Journal*, © 1994 Dow Jones & Company, Inc. All Rights Reserved Worldwide.]

   a. What cost control strategy are health administrators attempting to employ for Zofran?

   b. What are the ethical considerations in reducing drug costs by cutting doses and switching to less costly substitutes?

   c. What is the ethical responsibility of the pharmaceutical manufacturer in setting the prescribed doses for medicines it develops?

63. Procedures such as cataract surgery, partial mastectomies, gall-bladder removals, and heart catheterizations are being performed in hospitals without an overnight stay. Doctors explain that new surgical techniques using laser technology and advances in anesthesia make some operations faster and less drastic than in the past. Besides, quick turnarounds provide one important way for hospitals to hold down costs.

    Advances in technology have dramatically affected cost control efforts in the medical field. Select another industry and conduct a library search on how technology has affected costs and cost control strategies. Write a report on your findings including ethics and quality issues.

64. *Kirsh Guilory pumped out Cajun music, vendors hawked Creole crafts, but the crawfish delicacies dished out along food row at the New Orleans Jazz and Heritage Festival were not from the bayous and backwaters of Louisiana. The Chinese have taken over the crawfish pies, etouffee, filé gumbo, and most other crawfish dishes served at the festival. Captured, cooked, peeled and processed with low-cost labor in China, the crawfish from overseas are too cheap to pass up, say the merchants who sell food at the fest.*

    "I had to go to the Chinese tails," said Clark Hoffpauer, whose festival specialty is crawfish etouffee. "They're at least $2 a pound cheaper, and when you talk 1,700 pounds, that's quite a bit of change. I'd rather use Louisiana crawfish. After all, this is about Louisiana heritage, but business is business."

    [SOURCE: Mary Foster, "China Syndrome," (New Orleans) *Times-Picayune*, May 3, 1996, p. C-1.]

    a. Is "business is business" a true statement? Discuss the concept of this statement relative to costs, employment, and tradition.

    b. Provide some examples in which you would believe that the quality of a product and/or the ethics of a company would be enhanced if management considered all of the stakeholders in an organization in addition to costs when making a "business is business" decision.

65. Obtain a copy of "Can the Savoy Cut Costs and Be the Savoy?" by Janet Guyon (*Wall Street Journal*, October 25, 1994, p. B1). After reading of the services offered by that hotel, answer in detail the question asked in the title of the article. Can you think of other similar situations in regard to cost-cutting abilities?

66. Canada is considering requiring immigrants to speak either English or French. Why? A government report states that this will reduce language-training costs and help ensure that the people will integrate into Canadian life. Many Canadians as well as immigrants want the proposal scrapped. (Note: The April 1, 1998, *Wall Street Journal* article "Canadians Clash over Cost of Diversity" may provide a useful starting point.)

    a. What are the costs and benefits of diversity—within an organization or within a country?

    b. Who pays when immigrants do not speak the language of the country to which they are immigrating? How is payment made? Can you think of a methodology in which the costs in Part a could be passed to the immigrants?

    c. Why might such a language requirement be beneficial to immigrants?

67. In early 1998, Warner Bros. announced that it would cancel or postpone several high-profile movies. Warner Bros. management indicates that the company will begin making only about 20 movies per year rather than 30. Cost containment is the phrase of the moment, after some films' costs escalated dramatically. (Note: The April 23, 1998, *Wall Street Journal* article "Warner Bros. Cancels Films, Cuts Budgets" may provide a useful starting point.)

  a. Discuss the relationship between movie cost and movie quality.
  b. Provide some reasons that film costs are almost consistently over budget.
  c. If you were part of the management team at Warner Bros., what cost containment techniques would you implement? Why?

Chapter 13 Controlling Costs in the Changing Workplace

LEARNING OBJECTIVES

After reading this chapter, you should be able to answer the following questions:

1 WHAT is open-book management and why does its adoption require changes in accounting methods and practices?

2 WHY are games often used as the basis to teach and motivate open-book management concepts?

3 WHY is implementing open-book management more difficult in large organizations than in small organizations?

4 WHY does business process reengineering cause radical changes in how firms execute processes?

5 WHY is throughput an important performance measure for organizations that apply the theory of constraints?

6 HOW does throughput accounting differ from variable cost accounting?

7 HOW does value chain cost analysis create opportunities to achieve competitive advantages using concepts of interorganizational cost management?

8 WHAT factors are driving the increased reliance on outsourcing; and what are the financial considerations of the outsourcing decision?

9 WHY are joint ventures and strategic alliances increasingly used by firms to exploit new market opportunities?

10 HOW are target costing and value engineering used to manage costs? In which life cycle stage are these tools used?

11 WHAT are the competitive forces that are driving decisions to downsize and restructure operations?

12 WHY are operations of many firms becoming more diverse and how does the increasing diversity affect the roles of the firms' accounting systems?

Springfield Remanufacturing Corporation

The 1980s were not kind to firms serving the farm sector of the U.S. economy. Crop prices were depressed, inflation increased operating costs, and consequently, farmers had no capital to purchase equipment. International Harvester, one of the giants of the farm equipment industry, was forced to pare down its operations to get cash for survival.

When Jack Stack acquired Springfield Remanufacturing from International Harvester in 1983, it was on the brink of collapse. Crippled by a highly leveraged buyout, the company faced an 89:1 debt-to-equity ratio, a first-year operating loss of $60,488, and 119 employees who needed paychecks. All the signs indicated a rapid demise. But, within a few years, Stack had returned the business to profitability—a company with a healthy balance sheet and a promising future.

One key to Stack's successful turnaround of the Springfield, Missouri-based company stems from the way he reconceptualized the business. Instead of seeing the company's mission as reconditioning engines of worn-out bulldozers, tractors, and eighteen-wheelers, he saw it as educating workers in how business works. He persuaded employees to view running the business as a game they could learn to play—and win.

*I*n solving the business problems of *Springfield Remanufacturing*, Jack Stack created a new management model for involving workers in organizational decision making. This model required revolutionary changes in the manner accountants generated and disseminated information in his firm. In this chapter, we examine recent changes, and future trends, in business practices. Many of these changes and trends will have profound effects on the accounting systems of organizations. These effects are emphasized in the discussion.

OPEN-BOOK MANAGEMENT

open-book management

Open-book management is a philosophy about increasing a firm's performance by involving all workers, and by assuring that all workers have access to operational and financial information necessary to achieving performance improvements. The application of this philosophy is appropriate in decentralized organizations that have empowered employees to make decisions. Proponents of open-book management argue that the open-book approach helps employees understand how their work activities affect the costs and revenues of the firm. With this understanding, employees can adopt or change work practices to either increase revenues or decrease costs.

However, merely opening the financial records to a firm's employees won't necessarily solve any problems or improve anyone's performance. Most employees, particularly nonmanagerial workers, have no developed skills in interpreting business financial information nor any understanding of accounting concepts and methods. Even many functional specialists who are highly educated have little knowledge of how profits are generated and performance is measured in financial terms. For example, the CFO of Planning Systems Inc. described a recent experience in his firm with implementing open-book management and employee empowerment.[1]

> Eight months ago, one of our newly "empowered" cost-center managers, who happens to also be an engineer, informed me he was leasing a new color copier for three years and he'd pay for it by charging internal users for every copy made. He envisioned selling the service to outside users and had even made revenue projections. "Does the government have any rules against making too much money?" he asked me with a big grin.
> . . . [W]e haven't hit a single projection [on the color copier] and the financing costs are putting the cost center in the red. When I asked Mr. Empowerment about his plans, he said all startups lose money and muttered something like, "Nothing ventured, nothing gained." He also said he'd never take on another project like this without listening to the advice of someone who knows the financial side well, and I promise never to tell him how to blow up a submarine.

LEARNING OBJECTIVE ❶
What is open-book management and why does its adoption require changes in accounting methods and practices?

If financial information is to be the basis of employee decision making, the information must be structured with the level of sophistication of the decision maker in mind. Providing such information requires accountants to become much more creative in the methods used to compile and present financial data. Some common principles of open-book management are provided in Exhibit 13-1. Effective open-

---

[1]Robert R. Falconi, "Too Many Cooks Spoil the Books," *Financial Executive* (November/December 1995) pp. 15–16. Reprinted with permission © 1995 by Financial Executives Institute, 10 Madison Avenue, PO Box 1938, Morristown, NJ 07962-1938. (973) 898-4600.

1. Turn the management of a business into a game that employees can win.
2. Open the books and share financial and operating information with employees.
3. Teach the employees to understand the company's financial statements.
4. Show employees how their work influences financial results.
5. Link nonfinancial measures to financial results.
6. Target priority areas and empower employees to make improvements.
7. Review results together and keep employees accountable. Regularly hold performance review meetings.
8. Post results and celebrate successes.
9. Distribute bonus awards based on employee contributions to financial outcomes.
10. Share the ownership of the company with employees. Employee stock ownership plans (ESOPs) are routinely established in firms that practice open-book management.

SOURCE: Tim Davis, "Open-Book Management: Its Promises and Pitfalls," *Organizational Dynamics* (Winter 1997), pp. 6–20. Reprinted by permission of the publisher, © 1997. American Management Association, New York. http://www.amanet.org. All rights reserved.

EXHIBIT 13-1
Ten Common Principles of Open-Book Management

book management requires sharing accounting and financial information with employees who have little knowledge of accounting concepts. Games can be used to teach these concepts to financially unsophisticated employees.

Games People Play

Games make learning both fun and competitive while allowing for complex financial practices to be simplified. To illustrate how games can be used in open-book management, assume that Halifax Building Systems, a manufacturer of steel doors and frames, has decided to implement open-book management concepts. One of its key departments is Assembly.

Assembly is responsible for combining components of various models of doors and frames into finished products. Most of the components that are required for assembly are manufactured in other departments of the company.

Assembly employees consist of one manager and ten workers. All workers are highly skilled in the technical aspects of assembling door and frame components; however, none of the workers know anything about financial management or accounting techniques. For these workers, the game must begin with very simple

LEARNING OBJECTIVE ❷
Why are games often used as the basis to teach and motivate open-book management concepts?

Everyone likes to play games, and open-book management links playing with learning. The best outcome is always a win-win situation.

accounting principles. The outcomes of the game, as determined by financial and nonfinancial performance measurements, must be easy to comprehend and must be easily related to the motivation for establishing the game—maximizing firm profit, customer satisfaction, and shareholder value.

The data in Exhibit 13-2 pertain to one product, an economy garage door, that passes through Assembly. These data have been provided by the controller of Halifax and have been gathered from production and accounting records for the most recent month.

In designing a system to provide information to the Assembly Department employees, the starting point is to determine the objectives of the system. Reasonable initial design objectives include

⊙ causing Assembly Department employees to understand how their work affects achievement of corporate objectives;
⊙ making Assembly Department workers understand how their work affects upstream and downstream departments; and
⊙ generating demand from the employees for information and training that leads to improvements in performance in the Assembly Department.

Because overhead is a more difficult cost to comprehend, relative to direct materials and direct labor, information on overhead costs may be excluded from the initial system that is developed for assembly employees. Direct materials and direct labor will be the information focus. Further, because employees can exert no control over the price of materials purchased or the labor rate paid per hour, these data might be presented at budgeted or standard, rather than actual, cost. If presented at actual cost, variations in purchase prices occurring throughout the year might disguise from the financially unsophisticated workers other more important information (e.g., quantities of materials consumed). If desirable, a more sophisticated system can be developed once the workers fully understand the initial system.

One of the motivations for providing information to the assembly workers is to cause the workers to understand how their actions affect achievement of the overall corporate objectives. To initiate this understanding, management can establish a sales price for the output of the Assembly Department. Assume the initial price for the assembled economy door is set at $150; it is not necessary that the established sales price represent actual market value. It is important that a sales price be established so that a measure of the department's contribution to corporate profits can be established. For the assembly workers, the per-unit profit calculation is as follows:

Sales price	$150.00
Direct costs (from Exhibit 13-2)	(137.48)
Profit	$ 12.52

EXHIBIT 13-2
Economy Garage Door
Assembly Department
Cost Data

	ITEM	QUANTITY	UNIT COST	TOTAL COST
Materials				
	Door Panels	6	$ 5.00	$ 30.00
	Door Frame			
	Top	1	7.00	7.00
	Bottom	1	8.00	8.00
	Sides	2	4.00	8.00
	Panel Connectors	24	2.00	48.00
	Bolts	96	0.10	9.60
	Nylon bushings	96	0.03	2.88
Direct Labor		2 hours	12.00	24.00
				$137.48

Total profits equal per unit profit multiplied by the number of units produced. Workers will soon realize as they analyze this simple profit calculation that they can increase profits by decreasing costs or by increasing the number of units made. However, because the information contains no quality effects, some elementary quality information could be added. For example, quality defect costs could be charged to the Assembly Department. An income statement for the Assembly Department for a period would then appear as follows:

Sales	$XXXXXX
Direct costs	(XXXXXX)
Margin	$ XXXXX
Rework and defects	(XXXX)
Profit	$ XXXX

With this profit calculation, workers will comprehend that profit maximization requires maximization of output, minimization of direct costs, and minimization of quality defects.

One Japanese company, Higashimaru Shoyu, a maker of soy sauce, has gone so far as to create its own internal bank and currency.[2] Each department purchases its required inputs from other departments using the currency and established transfer prices. In turn, each department is paid in currency for its outputs. The flow of currency reinforces the profit calculations applying to each department.

 www.higashimaru.co.jp

To exploit the financial information they are given, workers should be educated about ways to improve profits. The "game" of trying to increase profits serves as motivation for workers to learn about cost and operational management methods. By relating the training to the game, its relevance is immediately obvious to the workers and they will seek training to help them both understand how to read and comprehend a simple income statement, and to identify approaches that can be used to improve results.

Motivating Employees

It cannot be assumed that the assembly workers are internally motivated to play the game well. Instead, the game should be motivated by upper management. The obvious way to motivate workers to use the information that they receive to improve profit is to link their compensation to profits. For example, workers in the Assembly Department can be paid bonuses if profits are above a target level. Alternatively, the workers can be paid a bonus that is a percentage of profits. In either case, the linkage of compensation to profits is a necessary step to motivate workers to have an interest in the game and to improve their performance. The positive effects of a good bonus program are described by Jack Stack, CEO of Springfield Remanufacturing:

http:// www.srcreman.com

> Its whole purpose is to make the company stronger, more competitive, able to survive and prosper in the months and years ahead. Earning a profit is just part of it. What really determines a company's success, after all, is its ability to generate cash and make smart decisions about how to use it.
>
> A good bonus program draws people into that process. It drives the value of the company by educating people, not with formal training programs but through the work they do every day on the job. It gives them the tools they need to make and understand decisions. It provides them with business knowledge they can use to enhance their own standard of living and job security as they're making a measurable difference to the company as a whole.
>
> . . . And, when the bonus comes, they know they've earned it. They know they're getting the reward because they took responsibility, because they increased the economic value of the company and strengthened the community. It's not a gift, and it's not an entitlement. It's payment for a job well done.[3]

---

[2]Robin Cooper, *When Lean Enterprises Collide (Competing through Confrontation)* (Boston: Harvard Business School Press, 1995).

[3]Jack Stack, "The Problem with Profit Sharing," *Inc.* (November 1996), p. 67.

Without interorganizational sharing of information, Larson would provide the new motor to Westcott for $48 and pocket the cost savings. However, such a strategy would not aid the value chain's competitive position because the final price of the product to the consumer would not be affected. By sharing information about the cost savings generated by the R&D effort with Westcott, the price agreement between Larson and Westcott can be modified based on the lower production cost.

By sharing at least some of the cost savings with Westcott, Larson will help Westcott lower its price and improve its competitive position in the marketplace. The rewards for the value chain will be increased market share and increased profits. Larson's reward will be an increase in its volume of business, increased profits, and the likelihood of more business from Westcott for components on new or existing products.

One other area in which information sharing can benefit firms in a value chain is quality management. Because quality is one of the factors that is considered by consumers in determining the value of a product, quality level is a variable that can be manipulated within the value chain to increase profits. For example, assume that Larson produces three quality grades of electric motors. The costs to produce each grade are, respectively, $25, $35, and $45. The major quality distinction in the three motors is life expectancy. In the original draft of product specifications for a new high-end washing machine, Westcott's managers included the highest quality motor as a component. However, after discussing the differences in quality of the three motors with Larson engineers, Westcott managers were able to determine that the price and overall quality of the washing machine would be virtually unaffected by switching motors because the life expectancy of other major components of the washing machine were less than the expected life of the $35 motor. By using the $35 motor instead of the $45 motor, Westcott was able to offer a lower price and gain greater market share in the top end of the market.

The higher levels of efficiency and effectiveness firms achieve through applying the methods discussed in this chapter have created new problems for firms. For example, as efficiency increases, fewer employees are required to accomplish the work of the organization. Accordingly, as efficiency increases without substantial growth in operations, firms must determine ways to deal with workers who are no longer needed. This is the subject of the following section.

DOWNSIZING AND RESTRUCTURING

LEARNING OBJECTIVE ⑪
What are the competitive forces that are driving decisions to downsize and restructure operations?

Global competition is a fact of life in many industries today. Survival in these industries requires firms to continually improve their abilities to provide quality products at competitive prices. Many of the methods discussed in this chapter have proven useful in improving efficiency and quality. Quality and efficiency have also been improved by availability of automated technology to replace manual technologies, particularly in manufacturing. However, as efficiency improvements are realized, firms create additional problems they must solve. Foremost among these problems is what to do with excess personnel.

One of the grim realities of ever-improving efficiency is that, to achieve a given level of output, ever fewer workers are required. Because of evolving business management practices such as process reengineering, firms are constantly restructuring operations to maintain or gain competitive advantages. Each successful restructuring leverages the work of employees into more output. At higher levels of efficiency, fewer workers are needed and a reduction in work force is required.

However, not all firms are able to adapt and survive under the pressures of global competition. Just as global competition has driven firms to higher and higher levels of quality and efficiency, competitive pressures drive some businesses out of competition altogether. In this competitive environment, firms are forced to evaluate which businesses they want to defend and which they are willing to sacrifice to the competition.

No, aliens aren't taking away workers by the millions—but downsizing and restructuring are causing many jobs to be eliminated. Ethical manager behavior would reposition and retrain employees so they may continue as viable parts of the workforce.

Both the businesses that are striving to remain viable and those that are retreating from the competition are forced into restructuring operations and reducing employment. **Downsizing** is the common term used for management actions that reduce employment and restructure operations as a response to competitive pressures. The following News Note describes a typical downsizing and restructuring decision.

downsizing

NEWS NOTE

Just Another Restructuring and Downsizing

http:// www.championpaper.com/homepage.html

Champion International Corp. said it plans to sell noncore businesses providing 24 percent of its revenue, cut a third of its workforce over the next two years, and take a $553 million charge, in a bid to strengthen its main coated-paper operations.

The moves, which analysts said were long overdue at the Stamford, Conn., paper maker, follow an industry trend toward focusing on smaller, more strategic groups of businesses and shedding noncore operations. Champion had previously disposed of far-flung operations, such as furniture and carpet making, but had resisted more substantial changes until yesterday's announcement (10/08/97).

Under the plan, Champion said the $553 million charge would reduce earnings by $5.77 a share, most of which is to be recorded in the fourth quarter. In the year-ago quarter, the company earned $10.1 million, or 11 cents a share, on sales of $1.4 billion.

The company said the restructuring is expected to boost pretax profit by a total of $400 million over the next three years. The revamping includes the sale of operations that contributed $1.4 billion in revenue last year and the cutting of about 6,250 workers, most of whom are with operations to be sold. The company also expects to trim an additional 2,000 jobs from its current 24,400 work force.

Much of the $553 million charge represents the planned write-down of the operations to be sold because, as analysts said, the businesses are expected to sell for less than their book value.

SOURCE: Jonathan Welsh, "Champion International to Sell Businesses," *Wall Street Journal*, Oct. 9, 1997, p. A3. Reprinted by permission of *Wall Street Journal*, © 1997 Dow Jones & Company, Inc. All Rights Reserved Worldwide.

The events at Champion are typical of downsizing: workforce reduction, restructuring of jobs and processes, and spin-offs or sales of noncore businesses. The recent Laborforce 2000 Survey of more than four hundred American-based businesses provides insight into how downsizing relates to competitive pressures facing businesses. When asked what strategic issues were of greatest concern to their companies, managers indicated the following three areas:[12]

- global competitiveness,
- economic concerns, such as a need to cut costs and improve profitability, and
- quality, productivity, and customer service.

The most common response to these strategic issues has been downsizing. In fact, 64 percent of the survey respondents downsized plants and facilities, and slightly over half of the firms sold off some business units. Furthermore, over 70 percent of the manufacturing and financial services respondents expected to continue downsizing throughout the 1990s. The biggest single reason cited for downsizing was the need to reduce costs and improve profits. Most firms in the survey (75 percent) also made substantial investments in advanced technology in conjunction with downsizing. Another study estimates that downsizing has eliminated over three million jobs in the United States alone since 1990.[13]

The risks and dangers of downsizing as a response to competitive pressures are many. First, firms may find that through rounds of layoffs they have depleted their talent pool. The collective knowledge of the workforce may be reduced to the point that the ability to creatively solve problems and generate innovative ideas for growth is greatly diminished. Second, to survive in the presence of global competition, trust and effective communication must exist between workers and managers. Following successive rounds of layoffs, morale diminishes, the trust of workers in managers wanes, and workers stop communicating and sharing information with managers. The workers fear that sharing information leads to managerial insights about how to further increase productivity and reduce costs by eliminating more of the workforce. Many of the new management methods discussed in this chapter depend heavily on cooperation among all of a firm's employees. Third, downsizing can destroy corporate cultures in which lifetime employment has been one of the key factors in attracting new employees. Furthermore, with the reduction in jobs, many firms have eliminated positions that once served as feeder pools for future top management talent.

Downsizing is an accounting issue because of its implications for financial reporting and its role in cost management. The financial reporting consequences of downsizing are significant. Because downsizing and restructuring often occur together, the firm often reports large, one-time losses for the year in which these changes are instituted. The losses are associated with sales of unprofitable assets and severance costs connected with layoffs of employees.

From a cost management perspective, accountants must understand the full consequences, costs and otherwise, of downsizing. Before recommending downsizing to improve organizational efficiency, accountants should examine the likely impact on customer service, employee morale and loyalty, and future growth opportunities. Further, careful cost analysis should be conducted. In Exhibit 13-12 is a framework for analyzing downsizing decisions. The exhibit demonstrates that strategic decisions affect the manner in which inputs—i.e., labor, capital, purchased materials, and services—are converted into outputs for customers. Downsizing involves a change in the mix of inputs used to produce outputs. Downsizing puts more emphasis on technologically based conversion processes and reduces the level of manual conversion processes, thus reducing the requirement for labor. The two-directional arrows in Exhibit 13-12 show the potential increased outsourcing from suppliers and increased dependence on technology, as substitutes for labor.

[12]Philip H. Mirvis, "Human Resource Management: Leaders, Laggards, and Followers," *Academy of Management Executive* (May 1997) pp. 43–56.

[13]Tomasz Mroczkowski and Masao Hanaoka, "Effective Rightsizing Strategies in Japan and America: Is There a Convergence of Employment Practices?" *Academy of Management Executive* (May 1997) pp. 57–67.

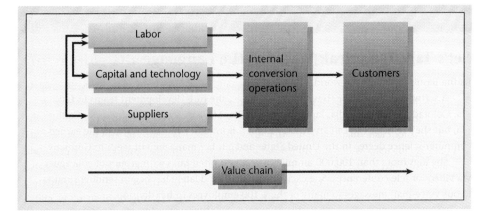

EXHIBIT 13-12
Cost Management Framework

The financial analysis of the downsizing decision is complex. The decision relies on comparing cost savings generated in the future from reduced labor costs to the current outlay for restructuring and acquiring additional technology. Capital budgeting methods discussed in Chapter 8 should be applied to this decision. If the downsizing decision involves a sale of assets, the financial analysis must include a comparison of the cash to be realized from the sale to the annual net revenues or net cash flows that will not be realized in the future because of the reduction in assets. Again, capital budgeting methods should be used in this comparison. The capital budgeting tools provide managers with information about how downsizing is likely to affect profitability and the return on invested capital.

WORKFORCE DIVERSITY

Under the pressure of global competition, many firms have expanded operations geographically. By sourcing and marketing globally, firms are able to develop new markets, reduce costs of inputs, and manage the effects of troughs and peaks in local economies. The globalization of operations presents managers with new opportunities and challenges.

With manufacturing and other operations distributed around the world, companies are discovering that their employees have very divergent religions, races, values, work habits, cultures, political ideologies, and education levels. As the next News Note (page 614) indicates, coordinating a diverse workforce can be challenging.

Corporate policies and information systems must adapt to the changing workforce and greater diversity of operations. For the accounting function, this often results in a larger role in managing operations. Although different languages and cultures can impede unambiguous communication within globally dispersed operations, accounting information can be a powerful coordinating mechanism. The interpretation of accounting information is not contingent on culture, language, or other variables that change from country to country. In fact, internal accounting measurements can be defined without dependence on cultural interpretation. Thus, accounting is an ideal international technical language.

Managing a global business, relative to a business that operates only in one country, involves many considerations in addition to coordinating employees. Global businesses must consider country differences in currency values; labor practices; political risks; tax rates; infrastructure such as ports, airports and highways; and commercial laws. These additional considerations require development of new systems and controls to manage risks and exploit opportunities.

The trend to increase diversity can be problematic in light of other business practices discussed in this chapter. For example, business process reengineering and

LEARNING OBJECTIVE ⑫
Why are operations of many firms becoming more diverse and how does the increasing diversity affect the roles of the firms' accounting systems?

expectations, achieved performance, cost management, coordination of operations, and other operational dimensions.

KEY TERMS

Cost table (p. 607)
Cross-functional team (p. 614)
Downsizing (p. 611)
Open-book management (p. 588)
Strategic alliance (p. 606)
Target costing (p. 607)

Theory of constraints (p. 595)
Throughput (p. 595)
Throughput accounting (p. 598)
Value chain (p. 600)
Value engineering (p. 608)
Vertical integration (p. 600)

END OF CHAPTER MATERIALS

⊙ QUESTIONS

1. Why do proponents of open-book management argue that employees can improve organizational performance if they have access to financial information of the firm?

2. Why does the use of open-book management require a strong emphasis on financial training?

3. How can games be used to implement open-book management practices?

4. If games are used in the practice of open-book management, should employee compensation be linked to the outcomes of the games? Explain.

5. When open-book management practices are adopted, what adjustments must be made in the accounting function of the adopting organization?

6. Business process reengineering and open-book management can both be used to improve organizational performance. What are the major similarities and differences between these two methods?

7. What are the major competitive forces that are driving the increased use of business process reengineering?

8. Exhibit 13-3 provides a list of steps to follow in implementing business process reengineering. How can an organization determine if its reengineering efforts are successful after following these steps?

9. What is the theory of constraints? What are the foundation beliefs of the theory?

10. What is the objective firms strive for in managing by the theory of constraints? Discuss.

11. In the theory of constraints, how are performance measures used to improve the management of constrained resources?

12. What is throughput accounting? How does throughput accounting differ from variable costing and absorption costing?

13. Why does successful competition in the global market rely on effective interorganizational, as well as intraorganizational, management of costs?

14. *Outsourcing* is a term often heard in business today. Discuss the factors that are driving increased reliance on outsourcing and the types of activities that are frequently outsourced.

15. What are the major risks associated with outsourcing and what types of activities should never be considered for outsourcing?

16. Strategic alliances are popular today for exploiting new market opportunities. What are strategic alliances and why are managers using this organizational structure so frequently today?

17. How do target costing and value engineering facilitate the exchange of information between firms in the same value chain?

18. How does the exchange of information by firms in a value chain increase the opportunities for the value chain to become more competitive?

19. Headlines about downsizing are seen daily in the financial press in the late 1990s. What is downsizing and what are the market forces that drive downsizing?

20. When downsizing is pursued too aggressively by a firm, certain business risks are increased. Discuss these risks.

21. Why is diversity of workforce a fact of life for most global businesses? How does increasing diversity affect the demands placed on the accounting system?

22. As a decision-making structure, cross-functional teams are used extensively in business today. What advantages might be gained by organizing a cross-functional team to design a new product rather than delegating the entire design responsibility to the in-house engineering department?

23. How does the use of cross-functional teams change the role of the accounting function in an organization?

⊙ EXERCISES

24. *(Open-book management) Monopoly*, a board game of Parker Brothers, has been popular for many years. Assume that you have just been hired by a company in the steel industry. The company manufactures a variety of products from stock steel components. Management of your new employer is examining the potential use of open-book management techniques. Prepare a written report for the top managers in your company discussing your recommendations for implementing open-book management. In your report, discuss how you would use *Monopoly* as a training tool for workers who have little knowledge of financial management.

25. *(Open-book management)* You have been hired as a consultant by a company that manufactures toys from plastic stocks and resins. The company management is presently wrestling with ways to improve the quality of its products. Evidence of quality problems is everywhere: high rates of product defects, many customer returns, poor rate of customer retention, and high warranty costs. Top management has traced virtually all quality-related problems to the production department.

   Production workers in the company are paid based on a flat hourly rate. No bonuses are paid based on corporate profits or departmental performance measures. As the outside consultant prepare an oral report to present to the top management of your client discussing how open-book management could be applied to address the quality problems. At a minimum, include in your report the following: how quality information would be conveyed to workers, how workers would be trained to understand the information, and how incentives would be established for improved quality performance.

26. *(Insource/Outsource)* The UR Advantage Company manufactures various types of shoes for sports and recreational use. Several types of shoes require a built-in air pump. Presently, the company makes all of the air pumps it requires for production. However, management is evaluating an offer from Bounce Supply Company to provide air pumps at a cost of $8 each. UR Advantage's management has estimated that the variable production costs of the air pump amount to $6 per unit. The firm also estimates that it could avoid $50,000 per year in fixed costs if it purchased rather than produced the air pumps.

And while the No. 3 automaker has been mum about its bargaining position, signals emerging from Chrysler indicate that the UAW couldn't make a better choice of companies for obtaining some of its chief objectives. Chrysler, of course, is expected to push hard for union concessions on work rules and wage issues.

But individuals close to the situation say that Chrysler, eager to win a settlement without a strike, isn't likely to force a walkout over the union's demands to add jobs or at least farm out less work to independent suppliers. Clearly, Chrysler is in a much better position than Ford Motor Co., which will open talks first on Monday, or General Motors Corp., which will open talks Wednesday, to promise more assembly and parts-plant jobs.

But GM has sent strong signals that it may not be able to live with terms set at Chrysler. In particular, because GM manufactures far more of its own parts than its Detroit rivals, terms in the current national UAW contract put its huge parts-making unit at a competitive disadvantage, and GM wants to farm out more work—not less—to lower-cost suppliers.

[SOURCE: Angelo B. Henderson and Gabriella Stern, "Economy: Chrysler May Be Pliable Partner for UAW; but GM Might Not Accept Terms, and the Result Could Be Confrontation," *Wall Street Journal*, June 7, 1996, p. A2. Reprinted by permission of *Wall Street Journal*, © 1996 Dow Jones & Company, Inc. All Rights Reserved Worldwide.]

   a. From the perspective of price-based competition, why would GM want the flexibility to outsource more of its parts and components?
   b. From the perspective of managing quality, how could outsourcing positively or negatively affect GM's ability to manage quality relative to its competitor Chrysler?
   c. What ethical responsibility does GM bear to the union in seeking to outsource more of its parts manufacturing?

38. Strategic alliances and joint ventures are being used with increasing frequency to exploit market opportunities. For example, according to Coopers & Lybrand, 55 percent of the nation's fastest-growing companies are involved in an average of three alliances.
   a. From the perspective of controlling the quality of production, discuss how a strategic alliance is significantly different from a typical vendor/customer relationship.
   b. How can the accounting function contribute to the management of quality for joint ventures?

39. *General Motors Corp. is delaying plans to open a major assembly plant in Thailand while it rethinks what car to build there, said John F. Smith Jr., GM's chairman, president, and chief executive officer.*

Specifically, Mr. Smith said that because of the Thai economic crisis, the market in the country probably won't support production of the European-designed Opel Astra.

At one time, GM was counting on its Thai assembly plant to serve as a keystone to its strategy for building market share in the region. But now, say people close to the situation, the originally planned investment of $750 million in the Thai plant has been reduced to around $450 million.

"My judgment is that the debacle in Asia will require that we do a lower-cost car in Asia," Mr. Smith said in an interview. "With the crash in the currency, the Opel Astra is too expensive a vehicle to expect to sell in high volumes in Asia."

Mr. Smith didn't suggest a price level for the Thai car. But he said that because of the change in plans and the need to design the car, the Thai plant's opening would be delayed beyond the original 1999 target. However, he didn't say when GM now hopes to start production.

In discussing the need for a less expensive car for Asia, Mr. Smith disclosed an expansion of the No. 1 automaker's low-cost car plans. Previously, GM had said it planned to build what it hopes will be the world's lowest-cost car at a new plant in Brazil. The project, code-named "Blue Macaw" within GM, has been aiming to build a car that GM can sell in

Brazil for about $7,000, partly by more intimately involving suppliers in the car's assembly. The cheapest car made in Brazil today is Fiat SpA's $10,000 Uno.

[SOURCE: Rebecca Blumenstein, "GM Delays Plans to Open Big Thai Plant," *Wall Street Journal*, Jan. 6, 1998, p. A2. Reprinted by permission of *Wall Street Journal*, © 1998 Dow Jones & Company, Inc. All Rights Reserved Worldwide.]

a. This news article indicates that the automobile market varies greatly around the globe. Discuss how global pricing considerations would affect global management of quality.

b. What ethical issues must GM consider in its global management of quality and prices?

Chapter 14 Responsibility Accounting and Transfer Pricing in Decentralized Operations

LEARNING OBJECTIVES

After reading this chapter, you should be able to answer the following questions:

1. **WHEN**
   are decentralized operations appropriate?

2. **HOW**
   does responsibility accounting relate to decentralization?

3. **WHAT**
   are the differences among the four types of responsibility centers?

4. **WHAT**
   is suboptimization and what are its effects?

5. **HOW**
   and why are transfer prices for products used in organizations?

6. **WHAT**
   are the differences among the various definitions of product cost?

7. **HOW**
   and why are transfer prices for services used in organizations?

Teva Pharmaceutical Industries Ltd.

In the mid-1980s, Teva Pharmaceutical Industries Ltd. decided to enter the generic drug market. Already a successful worldwide manufacturer of proprietary drugs, the Israel-based company wanted to vie globally in this competitive new market, particularly in the United States. The move has proved lucrative so far, as sales have been increasing at an annual rate of nearly 20 percent. In 1996, Teva's worldwide sales were $954 million and its after-tax net income, $73 million.

As part of its new strategy, Teva reorganized its pharmaceutical operations into decentralized cost and profit centers consisting of one operations division and three marketing divisions. The operations division is made up of four manufacturing plants in Israel, which are organized as cost centers because plant managers have no control over product mix or pricing. The plants produce to the orders placed by the marketing divisions, and plant managers are responsible for operational efficiency, quality, cost performance, and capacity management.

The marketing divisions are organized into the U.S. market (through Teva's Lemmon subsidiary), the local market (Israel), and the rest of the world. All three have substantially different sales characteristics. The Lemmon USA division handles about 30 products, each sold in large quantities. The Israeli division handles 1,200 products in different packages and dosage forms, with many being sold in quite small quantities. The division handling sales to the rest of the world works on the basis of specific orders and tenders (a request from a customer for a price/bid to deliver a specified product or service), some of which are for relatively small quantities. All three divisions order and acquire most of their products from the operations division, although occasionally they turn to local suppliers. The marketing divisions are responsible for decisions about sales, product mix, pricing, and customer relationships.

Teva's managers decided to introduce a transfer pricing system, which they hoped would enhance profit consciousness and improve coordination between operations and marketing. They were concerned with excessive proliferation of the product line, acceptance of many low-volume orders, and associated large consumption of production capacity for changeovers.

Teva bases its transfer price system on a prospective activity-based costing (ABC) calculation. Prices are set for the coming year based on budgeted data. The company calculates standard activity cost driver rates for each activity. During the year, these costs get charged to products based on the actual quantity of activities demanded during the year. The use of standard activity cost driver rates enables product costs to be calculated in a predictable manner throughout the year. It also eliminates monthly or quarterly fluctuations in product costs caused by variations in actual spending, resource usage, and activity levels.

SOURCE: Robert S. Kaplan, Dan Weiss, and Eyal Desheh, "Transfer Pricing with ABC," Reprinted from *Management Accounting* (May, 1997), pp. 20–21. Published by the Institute of Management Accountants, Montvale, N.J. Visit our website at www.imanet.org.

*M*any large companies expand over the years until their corporate structures are so cumbersome that they hinder, rather than help, achievement of organizational goals and objectives. In such cases, top managers often decide to change those structures so the companies can more effectively use their resources and their employees' talents.

Each organization's structure evolves as its goals, technology, and employees change. For many companies, the progression goes from highly centralized to highly decentralized. The degree of centralization reflects a chain of command, authority and responsibility relationships, and decision-making capabilities. This chapter discusses the extent to which top managers delegate authority to subordinate managers and the reporting systems that can be used to communicate managerial responsibility. In addition, since many decentralized organizations exchange goods and services internally, the concept of transfer pricing among organizational units is discussed.

DECENTRALIZATION

The degree to which authority is retained by top management (centralization) or released from top management and passed to lower managerial levels (decentralization) can be viewed in terms of a continuum. In a completely centralized firm, a single individual, usually the company owner or president, performs all decision making and retains full authority and responsibility for that organization's activities. In contrast, a purely decentralized organization has virtually no central authority, and each subunit acts as a totally independent entity. Either of these extremes represents a clearly undesirable arrangement. In the totally centralized company, the single individual may not have enough expertise or information to make decisions in all areas. In the totally decentralized firm, subunits may act in ways that are not consistent with the goals of the total organization. Factors associated with pure centralization and pure decentralization are presented in Exhibit 14-1. Most businesses —regardless of national domicile—fall somewhere between the extremes at a point dictated by practical necessity or, as with Teva, by management design.

While almost every organization is decentralized to some degree, quantifying the extent of decentralization may not be possible. Some subunits may have more autonomy than others. In addition to top management philosophy, decentralization depends on the type of organizational units. For example, a unit, segment, or division that operates in a turbulent environment and must respond quickly to new and unanticipated problems is likely to be a prime candidate for decentralization.

As indicated in the accompanying News Note, top management must also consider the subunit managers' personalities and perceived abilities. Managers in decentralized environments must be goal-oriented, assertive, decisive, and creative. While these employee traits are always desirable, they are essential for decentralized company managers. Managers in decentralized companies must also be willing to accept the authority delegated by top management and to be judged based on the outcomes of the decisions that they make. Some subunit managers may be either reluctant or unable to accept this authority or responsibility. Therefore, a company may allow

FACTOR	CONTINUUM		
	Pure Centralization ———————>		Pure Decentralization
Age of firm	Young	———————>	Mature
Size of firm	Small	———————>	Large
Stage of product development	Stable	———————>	Growing
Growth rate of firm	Slow	———————>	Rapid
Expected impact of incorrect decisions on profits	High	———————>	Low
Top management's confidence in subordinates	Low	———————>	High
Historical degree of control in firm	Tight	———————>	Moderate or loose
Use of technology	Low	———————>	High
Rate of change in the firm's market	Slow	———————>	Rapid

EXHIBIT 14-1

Continuum of Authority in Organizational Structures

some units to be highly decentralized, while others are only minimally decentralized. Since managerial behaviors change and managers are replaced, supervisors should periodically reassess their decisions about a unit's extent of decentralization.

Decentralization does not necessarily mean that a unit manager has the authority to make all decisions concerning that unit. Top management selectively determines what types of authority to delegate and what types to withhold. For example,

NEWS NOTE

Style Relates to Both Who You Are and Where You're From

When Stig Eriksson and Peter Williams report that most people are delighted to be given greater responsibility and power, with more independence from their boss, they might seem to be stating the obvious. But the two European managers of 3M, the diversified US multinational, have also found that others "are uncomfortable, and need to be coached," as Williams puts it.

The type of response depends partly on the person's character and experience, but also often on their nationality, adds Eriksson. People from relatively authoritarian cultures such as Germany, France, and Italy, tend to be unsettled by being allowed considerable autonomy and can take longer to get used to it.

Eriksson and Williams, who are at the heart of a radical reorganisation of the 21,000-person European operations of 3M, have experienced both types of reaction from their staff this year. The reorganisation has transferred most business responsibility from separate country subsidiaries to a network of 19 pan-European divisions—what 3M calls "European Business Centres."

SOURCE: Christopher Lorenz, "Facing Up to Responsibility," London *Financial Times*, December 15, 1993, p. 11.

As companies such as Daewoo become more global, top management must learn to relinquish some level of authority and responsibility to divisional managers. Decentralization creates many advantages, especially relative to the ability to react to local conditions rapidly . . . but there are also disadvantages if an integrated system of communication among all divisions and corporate headquarters does not exist.

many large, diversified companies want decentralization with centralized reporting and control. They achieve this goal in part by establishing coordinated accounting methods and by retaining certain functions at headquarters. Treasury and legal work are often provided by headquarters, sometimes through freestanding service centers whose output is charged to the various decentralized companies. In addition, purchasing is frequently consolidated for efficiency, effectiveness, and coordination.

Like any management technique, decentralization has advantages and disadvantages. These pros and cons are summarized in Exhibit 14-2 and discussed in the following sections.

EXHIBIT 14-2
Advantages and Disadvantages of Decentralization

Advantages
- ⊙ Helps top management recognize and develop managerial talent
- ⊙ Allows managerial performance to be comparatively evaluated
- ⊙ Often leads to greater job satisfaction
- ⊙ Makes the accomplishment of organizational goals and objectives easier
- ⊙ Allows the use of management by exception

Disadvantages
- ⊙ May result in a lack of goal congruence or suboptimization
- ⊙ Requires more effective communication abilities
- ⊙ May create personnel difficulties upon introduction
- ⊙ Can be extremely expensive
- ⊙ Requires accepting inappropriate decisions as it is a training ground

Advantages of Decentralization

LEARNING OBJECTIVE ❶
When are decentralized operations appropriate?

Decentralization has many personnel advantages. Managers have both the need and the opportunity to develop their leadership qualities, creative problem-solving abilities, and decision-making skills. Decentralized units provide excellent settings for training personnel and for screening aspiring managers for promotion. Managers can be judged on job performance and on the results of their units relative to units headed by other managers; such comparisons can encourage a healthy level of organizational competition. Decentralization also often leads to greater job satisfaction for managers because it provides for job enrichment and gives a feeling of increased importance to the organization. Employees are given more challenging and responsible work that provides greater opportunities for advancement.

In addition to the personnel benefits, decentralization is generally more effective than centralization in accomplishing organizational goals and objectives. The decentralized unit manager has more knowledge of the local operating environment than top management, which means (1) reduction in decision-making time, (2) minimization of difficulties resulting from attempts to communicate problems and instructions through an organizational chain of command, and (3) quicker perceptions of environmental changes. Thus, the manager of a decentralized unit not only is in closest contact with daily operations but also is charged with making decisions about those operations.

A decentralized structure also allows implementation of the management by exception principle. Top management, when reviewing divisional reports, can address issues that are out of the ordinary rather than dealing with operations that are proceeding according to plans.

An alternative to either centralization or decentralization is outsourcing. Outsourcing is discussed in the accompanying News Note.

NEWS NOTE

Reimbursing Time Inc. Journalists

Time Inc.'s worldwide network of journalists routinely overcomes all sorts of hurdles to report on newsworthy events for *People, Fortune, Sports Illustrated*, and the company's flagship magazine, *Time*, along with many other well-known Time Inc. publications. But when it came time to log travel and expenses, those very same journalists faced hurdles of a more frustrating nature.

Time Inc. always had a review and audit process for T & E (travel and entertainment) but it was decentralized. Each publication kept its own records, adding another layer of frustration to the process. Time Inc.'s reporters accessed a petty cash window to get their travel expenses up front. This solution offered little incentive for staff to file reports after their travel, making the reconciliation process a challenge.

Time, Inc. learned from benchmarking studies that its cost of tracking travel and expenses was above the average. "We knew we had to consolidate the T & E reporting structure and eliminate travel advances, and we were investigating 'best practices' for all of finance and accounting," Donna Stuermer says. "It quickly became obvious that we could streamline the T & E part of the process by outsourcing the work."

Now, Time Inc. uses Gelco Information Network's outsource expense management solution that allows travelers to report expenses immediately and gives three-day turnaround on expenses, directly depositing expense reimbursements into staff's personal accounts. Gelco also pays the corporate card expenses automatically. "Our people are happy now because they get their money quickly. And we're pleased that the cost of managing T & E and reimbursing travelers dropped by more than 50% since implementation," Stuermer says.

http:// www.time.com

http:// www.gelco.net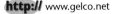

SOURCE: Shimon Avish, "T & E Expense: To Outsource or Not?" Reprinted from *Management Accounting* (September 1997), p. 47. Published by the Institute of Management Accountants, Montvale, N.J. Visit our website at www.imanet.org.

Disadvantages of Decentralization

goal congruence

Not all aspects of a decentralized structure are positive. For instance, authority and responsibility for making decisions may be divided among too many individuals, which can result in a lack of goal congruence among the organizational units. (**Goal congruence** exists when the personal and organizational goals of decision makers throughout a firm are consistent and mutually supportive.) In a decentralized company, unit managers are essentially competing with one another since the results of unit activities are compared. Unit managers may make decisions that positively affect their own units but are detrimental to other organizational units or to the whole company. This process results in suboptimization, which is discussed later in the chapter.

A decentralized organization requires more effective methods of communicating plans, activities, and achievements because decision making is removed from the central office. Top management has delegated the authority to make decisions to unit managers but still retains the ultimate responsibility to corporate ownership for the effects of those decisions. Thus, to determine if operations are progressing toward established goals, top management must be continuously aware of events occurring at lower levels. If decentralization gets totally out of control, top management must be willing to step in and take action. To illustrate, operating control at the various Daewoo companies in Korea was given to individual company presidents. But Chairman Kim Woo-Choong took over Daewoo Shipbuilding after labor costs had risen tenfold in ten years and employees had been receiving free haircuts that cost the company $60 a month (including lost time) for every employee. One of the chairman's first acts in making the near-bankrupt company profitable again was to remove the barbershops, which saved $8 million per year.[1]

http://www.daewoo.com

Some employees may be disturbed when top management attempts to introduce decentralization policies. Employees may be asked to do too much too soon or without enough training. Furthermore, some top managers have difficulty relinquishing control or are unwilling or unable to delegate effectively.

A final disadvantage of decentralization is that it may be extremely expensive. In a large company, it is unlikely that all subordinate managers have equally good decision-making skills. Thus, the first cost is for training lower-level managers to make better decisions. Second, there is the potential cost of poor decisions. Decentralization implies the willingness of top management to let subordinates make some mistakes, but says Asea Brown Boveri's Percy Barnevik, "You have to accept a fair share of mistakes. I tell my people that if we make 100 decisions and 70 turn out to be right, that's good enough. I'd rather be roughly right and fast than exactly right and slow."[2] This philosophy is reiterated in the following quote:

> Decentralization of authority in itself has ethical consequences. It absolutely requires trust and latitude for error. The inability to monitor the performance—especially when measurement of results is the only surveillance—of executives assigned to tasks their superiors cannot know in detail results inexorably in delegation. The leaders of a corporation are accustomed to reliance upon the business acumen of . . . managers, whose results they watch with a practiced eye. Those concerned with the maintenance of the ethical standards of the corporation are dependent just as much on the ethical judgment and moral character of the managers to whom authority is delegated. Beyond keeping our fingers crossed, what do we do?[3]

Decentralization can also create a duplication of activities that can be quite expensive in terms of both time and money. An example of this can be seen in the accompanying News Note in which a decentralized network of banks found it necessary to recentralize, in part to unify its resources for greater efficiency and effectiveness.

---

[1]Laxmi Nakarmi, "At Daewoo, a 'Revolution' at the Top," *Business Week*, February 18, 1991, pp. 68–69.

[2]William Taylor, "The Logic of Global Business: An Interview with ABB's Percy Barnevik," *Harvard Business Review* (March–April 1991), p. 101.

[3]Kenneth R. Andrews, ed., *Ethics in Practice: Managing the Moral Corporation* (Boston: Harvard Business School Press, 1989), p. 7.

After Long Overhaul, Banc One Now Faces Pressure to Perform

Until a few years ago, Mr. John B. McCoy was considered a boy wonder of banking. After succeeding his father and grandfather at the helm of Banc One Corp. at age 40, he charmed Wall Street investors and Main Street customers with a self-assured but easygoing sense of entitlement and a simple formula: Buy one small bank after another, tack up "Banc One" signs, and let the local chairman run the show. Using that friendly approach, Mr. Mc-Coy bought more than a hundred banks and built Banc One into the nation's seventh-largest bank, stretching from Ohio to Texas and Arizona.

But in late 1994, Banc One tripped over its troubled portfolio of derivatives. . . . Mr. McCoy spent that Christmas sunk in self-doubt, and then he did something uncharacteristic: He issued an executive order. He scrapped most of Banc One's guiding tenets, many of which had been formulated by his father, John G. McCoy. He stripped his eighty or so bank chiefs of much of their power and told them to expect more directives from headquarters. He showed some old-timers the door and brought in outsiders who had expertise that, he conceded, he himself lacked.

By 1994, some bank officers, including Richard J. Lehmann, were complaining about the rising cost of maintaining so many separate systems and banks. For example, Banc One had twenty-three different telephone banking centers, too many to operate one common 800 number for all its customers. It maintained thirty-two offices to analyze commercial customers' accounts. Customers from Ohio couldn't use the Banc One branches they visited while vacationing in Arizona. Big, nonbank competitors such as FMR Corp.'s Fidelity Investments and Merrill Lynch & Co. were peeling away Banc One's best customers.

In addition, in its reorganization Banc One slashed expenses in earnest. It trimmed its telephone-banking centers to two and the data-analysis offices to one. It cut its computer-operating systems from four to one. From nintey-two offices where checks were cleared, Banc One went to seventeen, with plans to cut further. . . . For customers, the makeover is supposed to provide seamlessness: uniform products, spread across all branches, in all states, linked by one computer network, so that Banc One branches are as alike as McDonald's restaurants. The company promises that many loan decisions still will be made locally.

SOURCE: Matt Murray, "After Long Overhaul, Banc One Now Faces Pressure to Perform," *Wall Street Journal*, March 10, 1998, pp. A1, A10. Reprinted by permission of *Wall Street Journal*, © 1998 Dow Jones & Company, Inc. All Rights Reserved Worldwide.

http:// www.bankone.com

http:// www.fidelity.com

http:// www.merrilllynch.com

Another cost of decentralization relates to developing and operating a more sophisticated planning and reporting system. Since top management delegates decision-making authority but retains ultimate responsibility for decision outcomes, a reporting system must be implemented that will provide top management with the ability to measure the overall accountability of the subunits. This reporting system is known as a responsibility accounting system.

RESPONSIBILITY ACCOUNTING SYSTEMS

Responsibility accounting refers to an accounting system that provides information to top management about the performance of an organizational unit. As decentralization became more prevalent in the business environment, responsibility accounting systems evolved from the increased need to communicate operating results through the managerial hierarchy.

A responsibility accounting system produces **responsibility reports** to assist each successively higher level of management in evaluating the performances of its

responsibility accounting

LEARNING OBJECTIVE ❷
How does responsibility accounting relate to decentralization?

responsibility report

subordinate managers and their respective organizational units. These reports reflect the revenues and/or costs under the control of a specific unit manager. Any revenues or costs that are not under the control of a specific unit manager should not be shown on his or her responsibility reports. For example, a portion of straight-line depreciation on the company headquarters building may be allocated to the Sales Department. Because the manager of the Sales Department has no control over this cost, it should not be included on the responsibility report of the Sales Department manager. Much of the information communicated on these reports is monetary, although other data may be included. Examples include proportion of deliveries made on-time, number of defects generated by production for the month, and tons of waste produced during the month.

The number of responsibility reports routinely issued for a decentralized unit depends on how much influence that unit's manager has on the unit's day-to-day operations and costs. If a manager strongly influences all operations and costs of a unit, one report will suffice for both the manager and the unit. Normally, however, some costs are not controlled, or are only partially or indirectly controlled, by the unit manager. In such instances, the responsibility report takes one of two forms. First, a single report can be issued that shows all costs incurred in the unit, separately classified as either controllable or uncontrollable by the manager. Alternatively, separate reports can be prepared for the manager and the unit. The manager's report includes only costs under his or her control, while the unit's report includes all costs.

A responsibility accounting system is the lynch pin in making decentralization work effectively. The responsibility reports about unit performance are primarily tailored to fit the planning, controlling, and decision-making needs of subordinate managers. Top managers review these reports to evaluate the efficiency and effectiveness of each unit and each manager.

One purpose of a responsibility accounting system is to "secure control at the point where costs are incurred instead of assigning them all to products and processes remote from the point of incurrence."[4] This purpose agrees with the concepts of standard costing and activity-based costing. In standard costing, variances are traced to the person (or machine) responsible for the variance; for example, the material purchase price variance can generally be traced to the purchasing agent. Activity-based costing attempts to trace as many costs as possible to the activities that caused the costs rather than using highly aggregated allocation techniques.

Control procedures are implemented for the following three reasons:

⊙ Managers attempt to cause actual operating results to conform to planned results. This conformity is known as effectiveness.
⊙ Managers attempt to cause, at a minimum, the standard output to be produced from the actual input costs incurred. This conformity is known as efficiency.
⊙ Managers need to ensure, to the extent possible, a reasonable utilization of plant and equipment. Utilization is primarily affected by product or service demand. At higher volumes of activity or utilization, fixed capacity costs can be spread over more units, resulting in a lower unit cost. However, demand for the product or service must first be generated before the benefits of spreading the overhead can be realized. Otherwise output is produced that creates holding costs that burden the company.

Responsibility accounting implies that subordinate managers accept the authority given to them by top management and helps them in conducting the five basic control functions shown in Exhibit 14-3. Budgets are used to officially communicate output expectations (sales, production, and so forth) and, through budget appropriations, to delegate the authority to spend. Ideally, subunit managers negotiate budgets

---

[4]W. W. Cooper and Yuri Ijiri, eds., *Kohler's Dictionary for Accountants* (Englewood Cliffs, N.J.: Prentice-Hall, 1983), p. 435.

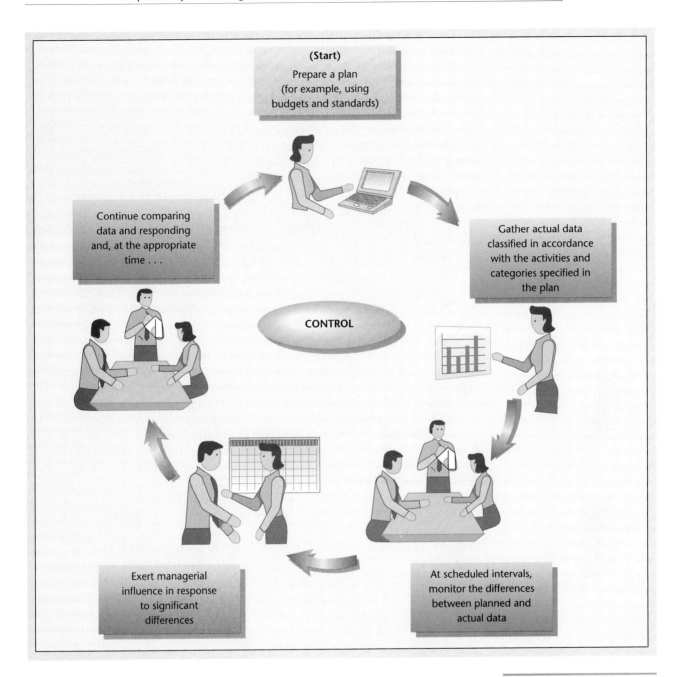

and standards for their units with top management for the coming year. Involvement in the budgeting process is essential for motivating those whose performance will be evaluated on budget-to-actual comparisons.

The responsibility accounting system should be designed so that actual data are captured in conformity with budgetary accounts. During the year, the accounting system records and summarizes data for each organizational unit. Operating reports comparing actual account balances with budgeted, standard, or target amounts are prepared periodically and issued to managers. Because of day-to-day contact with operations, managers should be aware of any significant variances before they are reported, identify variance causes, and attempt to correct causes of the problems. Top managers, on the other hand, may not know about operational variances until they receive responsibility reports. By the time top management receives the reports, problems causing the variances should have been corrected, or subordinate managers should be able to explain why the problems were not or could not have been resolved.

The responsibility reports received by top management may compare actual performance against the master budget. Such a comparison can be viewed as yielding an overall performance evaluation, since the master budget reflects management's expectations about sales prices, volume, and mix, as well as costs. However, using the budget for comparison may be inappropriate in some cases. For example, if the budget has an allowance for scrap built into the materials usage estimate, comparing results with the budget figure fails to support a focus on total quality. In such a case, a positive variance relative to the budget should not be judged as favorable performance if significant scrap still is being produced. Establishing a target goal of zero scrap would mean that any variance would be identified as unfavorable.

Perhaps a more appropriate form of responsibility report is that associated with the flexible budget. This report form compares actual information about controllable items (revenues and/or costs) both with the master budget and with amounts based on the achieved activity level. This secondary comparison is more useful for control purposes, since both operating results and budget figures are based on the same level of activity.

Regardless of the comparisons provided, responsibility reports reflect the upward flow of information from operational units to top management. These reports indicate the broadening scope of managerial responsibility. Managers receive detailed information on the performance of their immediate areas of control and summary information on all other organizational units for which they are responsible. Summarizing results causes a pyramiding of information. Reports for the lowest-level units are highly detailed, while reports are less specific at the top of the organization. Upper-level managers desiring information more specific than that provided in summary reports can review the responsibility reports prepared for their subordinates.

Exhibit 14-4 illustrates the March set of performance reports for the Generics Division of Heinrick Chemicals, a fictional Dutch conglomerate. All information is shown in the home office currency of Dutch Guilders (Hfl). The Mixing and Preparing Department's actual costs are compared with those in the flexible budget. Data for Mixing and Preparing are then aggregated with data of other departments under the control of the production vice-president. These combined data are shown in the middle section of Exhibit 14-4. In a like manner, the total costs of the production vice-president's area of responsibility are combined with other costs for which the company president is responsible and are shown in the top section of Exhibit 14-4.

Variances should be individually itemized in lower-level performance reports so that the manager under whose supervision those variances occurred has the detail needed to take appropriate corrective action. Under the management by exception principle, major deviations from expectations are highlighted in the subordinate manager's reporting section to assist upper-level managers in making decisions about when to become involved in the subordinate's operations. If no significant deviations exist, top management is free to devote its attention to other matters. In addition, such detailed variance analysis alerts operating managers to items they may need to explain to superiors.

In addition to the monetary information shown in Exhibit 14-4, many responsibility accounting systems are now providing information on critical nonmonetary measures of the period's activity. Some examples are shown in Exhibit 14-5. Many of these measures are equally useful for manufacturing and service organizations and can be used along with basic financial measurements in judging performance.

The performance reports of each management layer are reviewed and evaluated by all successive layers of management. Managers are likely to be more careful and alert in controlling operations knowing that the reports generated by the responsibility accounting system reveal financial accomplishments and problems. Thus, in addition to providing a means for control, responsibility reports can motivate managers to influence operations in ways that will reflect positive performance.

The focus of responsibility accounting is people. The people emphasized are the managers responsible for an organizational unit such as a department, division, or geographic region. The subunit under the control of a manager is called a **responsibility center.**

responsibility center

PRESIDENT'S PERFORMANCE REPORT

	Actual Results	Flexible Budget	Variance Over(Under)
Administrative Office—President	Hfl 267,200	Hfl 264,000	Hfl 3,200
Financial Vice-President	313,200	316,600	(3,400)
Production Vice-President	1,105,200	1,103,800	1,400
Sales Vice-President	368,800	366,000	2,800
Totals	Hfl 2,054,400	Hfl 2,050,400	Hfl 4,000

PRODUCTION VICE-PRESIDENT'S PERFORMANCE REPORT

	Actual Results	Flexible Budget	Variance Over(Under)
Administrative Office—VP	Hfl 243,000	Hfl 240,000	Hfl 3,000
Inspect, Polish and Package	112,600	113,400	(800)
Finishing	168,000	169,600	(1,600)
Mixing and Preparing	581,600	580,800	800
Totals	Hfl 1,105,200	Hfl 1,103,800	Hfl 1,400

MIXING AND PREPARING MANAGER'S PERFORMANCE REPORT

	Actual Results	Flexible Budget	Variance Over(Under)
Direct Material	Hfl 163,400	Hfl 166,400	Hfl (3,000)
Direct Labor	255,200	253,000	2,200
Supplies	24,600	23,400	1,200
Indirect Labor	59,600	58,600	1,000
Power	50,200	52,200	(2,000)
Repairs and Maintenance	17,200	16,200	1,000
Other	11,400	11,000	400
Totals	Hfl 581,600	Hfl 580,800	Hfl 800

EXHIBIT 14-4

Generics Division March 2000 Performance Reports

EXHIBIT 14-5

Nonmonetary Information for Responsibility Reports

- ⊙ Departmental/divisional throughput
- ⊙ Number of defects (by product, product line, supplier)
- ⊙ Number of orders backlogged (by date, quantity, cost, and selling price)
- ⊙ Number of customer complaints (by type and product); method of complaint resolution
- ⊙ Percentage of orders delivered on time
- ⊙ Manufacturing (or service) cycle efficiency
- ⊙ Percentage of reduction of non-value-added time from previous reporting period (broken down by idle time, storage time, quality control time)
- ⊙ Number of employee suggestions considered significant and practical
- ⊙ Number of employee suggestions implemented
- ⊙ Number of unplanned production interruptions
- ⊙ Number of schedule changes
- ⊙ Number of engineering change orders; percentage change from previous period
- ⊙ Number of safety violations; percentage change from previous period
- ⊙ Number of days of employee absences; percentage change from previous period

TYPES OF RESPONSIBILITY CENTERS

LEARNING OBJECTIVE ❸
What are the differences among the four types of responsibility centers?

Responsibility accounting systems identify, measure, and report on the performance of people who control the activities of responsibility centers. There are four classifications of responsibility centers, based on the manager's scope of authority and type of financial responsibility: cost, revenue, profit, and investment. They are illustrated in Exhibit 14-6 and discussed in the following sections.

Cost Centers

cost center

In a **cost center**, the manager has the authority only to incur costs and is specifically evaluated on the basis of how well costs are controlled. In many cost centers, no revenues are generated because the unit does not engage in any revenue-producing activity. For example, the placement center in a university may be a cost center, since it does not charge for the use of its services but does incur costs.

In other instances, revenues may be associated with a particular subunit, but they either are not under the manager's control or are not effectively measurable. The first type of situation exists in a governmental agency that is provided a specific proration of sales tax dollars but has no authority to levy or collect the related taxes. The second situation could exist in discretionary cost centers, such as a marketing research or a research and development department, in which the outputs (revenues or benefits generated from the cost inputs) are not easily measured.[5] In these situations, revenues should not be included in the manager's responsibility accounting report. As discussed in the accompanying News Note, a person's performance should be judged only in relation to his or her specific duties and responsibilities.

In the traditional manufacturing environment, a standard costing system is generally used, and variances are reported and analyzed. In such an environment, the highest priority in a cost center is often the minimization of unfavorable cost vari-

EXHIBIT 14-6
Types of Responsibility Centers

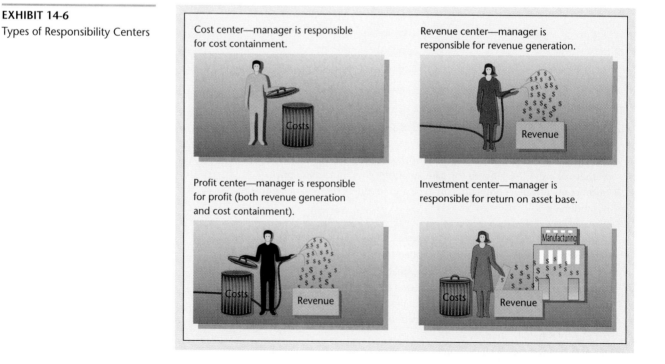

---

[5]Discretionary costs are discussed in Chapter 12.

NEWS NOTE

Performance Measurements Must Correlate with Jobs

Measuring individual processes with overall gross indicators is analogous to measuring a professional baseball player on his team's overall performance. It isn't fair to say that a player is no good because his team has a losing record. It is fair, however, to measure that player on RBIs, batting average, or on-base percentage because he can influence those measures directly. In the manufacturing process, it is not fair to measure a line foreman on cost of production as a percentage of sales because he cannot control sales price, sales volume, or many elements of cost. It is fair to measure that foreman on utility usage, cycle time, and schedule attainment, which he can control and influence directly.

SOURCE: Mark E. Beischel and K. Richard Smith, "Linking the Shop Floor to the Top Floor," Reprinted from *Management Accounting* (October 1991), p. 26. Published by the Institute of Management Accountants, Montvale, N.J. Visit our website at www.imanet.org.

ances. Top management may often concentrate only on the unfavorable variances occurring in a cost center and ignore the efficient performance indicated by favorable variances. For example, referring back to Exhibit 14-4, the production vice-president of the Generics Division of Heinrick Chemicals might focus only on the unfavorable material and power variances for the Mixing and Preparing Department while disregarding the favorable variances for the other costs of production. Significant favorable variances should not be ignored if the management by exception principle is to be applied appropriately. Using this principle, all variances—both favorable and unfavorable—that fall outside the preestablished limits for normal deviations should be investigated.

In the Heinrick Chemicals example, Gottfried Menchen, the manager of the Mixing and Preparing Department, should have determined the causes of the variances before filing the report. For instance, it is possible that substandard material was purchased and caused excessive usage. If this is the case, the purchasing agent, not Mr. Menchen, should be held accountable for the variance. Other possible causes for the unfavorable material variance include increased material prices, excess waste, or some combination of all these causes. Only additional inquiry or investigation can determine whether that variance could have been controlled by Menchen. Similarly, the power variance may have resulted from an increase in utility costs.

The favorable direct labor variance should also be analyzed. Mr. Menchen may have used inexperienced personnel who were being paid lower rates. Such a situation might explain both the favorable direct labor variance and, to some extent, the unfavorable direct material variance (because the workers were less skilled and may have overused material). Alternatively, the people working in the Mixing and Preparing Department could simply have been very efficient this period. In this case, Menchen would compliment and reward the efficient employees and might also consider incorporating the improvement as a revised time standard.

Revenue Centers

A **revenue center** is strictly defined as an organizational unit whose manager is accountable only for the generation of revenues and has no control over setting selling prices or budgeting costs. In many retail stores, the individual sales departments are considered independent units and managers are evaluated based on the total revenues generated by their departments. Departmental managers, though, may not be given the authority to change selling prices to affect volume, and they often do not participate in the budgeting process. Thus, the departmental managers may have no impact on costs. In general, however, few pure revenue centers exist.

revenue center

Individual departments in a large retail store may be treated as cost or revenue centers by the store manager, while the store itself may be treated as a profit or investment center by corporate headquarters. Such designations reflect the degree of control a manager has over selling prices, costs, and plant assets.

Managers of revenue centers are typically responsible for revenues and also are involved in planning and control related to some, but not necessarily all, of the center's costs. Thus, a more appropriate term for this organizational unit is a "revenue and limited cost center." For example, a sales manager who is responsible for the sales revenues generated in her territory may additionally be accountable for controlling the mileage and other travel-related expenses of her sales staff. She may not, however, be able to influence the types of cars her sales staff obtain, because cars are acquired on a fleetwide basis by top management.

Salaries, if directly traceable, are often a cost responsibility of a revenue center manager. This situation reflects the traditional retail environment in which each sales clerk is assigned to a specific department and is only allowed to check out customers who want to purchase that department's merchandise. Most stores have found such a checkout situation detrimental to business, because customers are forced to wait for the appropriate clerk. Clerks in many stores are now allowed to assist all customers with all types of merchandise. Such a change in policy converts what was a traceable departmental cost into an indirect cost. Stores carrying high-cost, high-selling-price merchandise normally retain the traditional system. Managers of such departments are thus able to trace sales salaries as a direct departmental cost.

In analyzing variances from budget, managers in a revenue center need to consider three possible causes: sales price differences, sales mix differences, and volume differences. The effects of sales price differences and volume differences were discussed in the appendix to Chapter 7. The model presented in that chapter is expanded below to illustrate the effect of a difference in product sales mix from that which was budgeted.

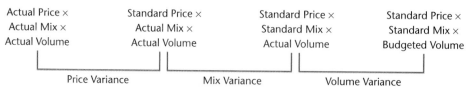

Actual Price ×	Standard Price ×	Standard Price ×	Standard Price ×
Actual Mix ×	Actual Mix ×	Standard Mix ×	Standard Mix ×
Actual Volume	Actual Volume	Actual Volume	Budgeted Volume
	Price Variance	Mix Variance	Volume Variance

Exhibit 14-7 presents the revenue statistics and variance computations for the Canadian Sales Division of Heinrick Chemicals for June 1999. The Canadian Sales Division is a wholesaler that sells to retailer chains in lot sizes of 1,000 units each. Inspection of the results reveals that (1) prices increased (except for Hunger sup-

BUDGET	LOTS	LOT PRICE	REVENUE	STANDARD MIX FOR BUDGETED VOLUME	
Vitamins (V)	3,000	C$1,400	C$4,200,000	3,000 ÷ 6,000 =	50.0%
Hunger suppressant (H)	2,000	1,600	3,200,000	2,000 ÷ 6,000 =	33.3%
Facial cream (F)	1,000	1,100	1,100,000	1,000 ÷ 6,000 =	16.7%
Totals	6,000		C$8,500,000		100.0%

Actual Mix for Actual Volume

Vitamins	3,200	C$1,500	C$4,800,000	
Hunger suppressant	1,800	1,600	2,880,000	
Facial cream	1,100	1,200	1,320,000	
Totals	6,100		C$9,000,000	

Standard Mix for Actual Volume

Vitamins	(6,100 × .500) = 3,050
Hunger suppressant	(6,100 × .333) = 2,031
Facial cream	(6,100 × .167) = 1,019

	Actual Price × *Actual Mix* × *Actual Volume*	*Standard Price* × *Actual Mix* × *Actual Volume*	*Standard Price* × *Standard Mix* × *Actual Volume*	*Standard Price* × *Standard Mix* × *Budgeted Volume*
V	C$1,500(3,200) = C$4,800,000	C$1,400(3,200) = C$4,480,000	C$1,400(3,050) = C$4,270,000	C$1,400(3,000) = C$4,200,000
H	C$1,600(1,800) = 2,880,000	C$1,600(1,800) = 2,880,000	C$1,600(2,031) = 3,249,600	C$1,600(2,000) = 3,200,000
F	C$1,200(1,100) = 1,320,000	C$1,100(1,100) = 1,210,000	C$1,100(1,019) = 1,120,900	C$1,100(1,000) = 1,100,000
Totals	C$9,000,000	C$8,570,000	C$8,640,500	C$8,500,000

C$430,000 F	C$70,500 U	C$140,500 F
Price Variance	Mix Variance	Volume Variance

C$500,000 F
Total Revenue Variance

EXHIBIT 14-7
Variances for a Revenue Center

pressants), causing an overall favorable price variance; (2) the actual mix included more of the lower-priced products (vitamins and facial cream) than the standard mix, causing an overall unfavorable mix variance; and (3) the number of lots sold (6,100) was greater than the number of lots budgeted (6,000), causing a favorable volume variance. The Canadian Sales Division's manager is to be commended for good performance.

Profit Centers

In **profit centers**, managers are responsible for generating revenues and for planning and controlling all expenses. A profit center manager's goal is to maximize the center's net income. Profit centers should be independent organizational units whose managers have the authority to obtain resources at the most economical prices and to sell products at prices that will maximize revenue. If managers do not have complete authority to buy and sell at objectively determined costs and prices, it is difficult to make a meaningful evaluation of the profit center. The News Note (page 646) discusses one company's reasons for establishing profit centers.

profit center

Profit centers are not always manufacturing divisions or branches of retail stores. A dental clinic may view each department (Cleaning, X-Ray, Teeth and Gum Restoration, and Crown Fabriction) as a profit center, and a university may view certain educational divisions as profit centers (undergraduate education, non-degree-seeking night school, and graduate divisions).

To illustrate the variance computations for a profit center, assume that Heinrick Chemicals uses 18-wheelers to deliver products throughout western Europe and

Changing Performance Measures at Caterpillar

To remain competitive, companies need to institute a balanced set of financial and nonfinancial performance measures that relate directly to the organization's mission, objectives, strategies, and critical success factors such as customer delivery, quality, flexibility, productivity, and financial performance. Without them, companies won't have an accurate picture of how they are performing, in which areas they are achieving success, and in which areas they need to make changes.

http:// www.cat.com

At Caterpillar's Wheel Loaders and Excavators Division (WLED) in Aurora, Ill., significant revisions have been made in both organizational structure and performance measures. The revisions came about largely because Caterpillar changed its overall corporate structure from a "functional bureaucratic" organization to a "profit center" organization and instituted performance measures appropriate to the new structure. Since then, the division has achieved outstanding success and continuous improvement. During the process, participants discovered some performance principles that other companies can apply, regardless of size.

One goal of the reorganization and new performance measurement system was to increase responsiveness, flexibility, and customer focus, so Caterpillar created minibusinesses within the company that concentrate on each customer's product needs. This decentralized approach allows each division to focus on product design, manufacturing, pricing, and parts and service for each customer.

For example, under the previous structure, a customer who wanted to buy a hydraulic excavator would contact a dealer who would work with the massive Caterpillar organization. Today the same customer still would contact the Caterpillar dealer—whose role is unchanged—but the customer's needs would be addressed by the Hydraulic Excavator Product Group within the WLED.

Another goal of the reorganization and new performance measurement system was to drive authority, responsibility, and decision making downward in the organization—empowering employees and holding them accountable for results. By doing so, Caterpillar believed it would develop more broadly-based businesspeople throughout the organization and allow them to make better use of their experience and innovativeness within their areas of expertise.

SOURCE: James Hendricks, David Defreitas, and Delores Walker, "Changing Performance Measures at Caterpillar." Reprinted from *Management Accounting* (December 1996), pp. 18–19. Published by the Institute of Management Accountants, Montvale, N.J. Visit our website at www.imanet.org.

each truck is considered a profit center. The budgeted and actual revenues and expenses for "Tour de France," a truck for which Claudette Harfleur is responsible, are shown in Exhibit 14-8. The profit center should be judged on the F67,250 of profit center income (in Franch francs—F), but Harfleur should be judged on the controllable margin of F96,500. Harfleur should point out that her delivery revenues were greater than budgeted because she drove more miles than budgeted. Thus, using the master budget as a basis for comparison, it is natural that unfavorable variances would exist for all of the variable costs.

The comparison of actual results to a flexible budget at the actual activity level shown in Exhibit 14-9 provides better information for assessing cost control within the profit center. Harfleur did a good job controlling the costs of her profit center; the problem area is related to the noncontrollable fixed overhead. She should investigate the causes for the F2,250 unfavorable variance. Then she and her manager can discuss any ideas she may have for addressing those causes. It is also possible that the budgeted figure for the noncontrollable fixed overhead is inappropriate because of cost increases for some or all of the items composing that fixed overhead pool.

	MASTER BUDGET	ACTUAL	VARIANCE
Delivery revenues	F180,000	F186,000	F6,000 F
Variable costs:			
Direct labor	F 4,500	F 4,600	F 100 U
Gas and oil	37,800	39,050	1,250 U
Variable overhead	7,740	7,850	110 U
Total	F 50,040	F 51,500	F1,460 U
Contribution margin	F129,960	F134,500	F4,540 F
Fixed overhead—controllable	(38,400)	(38,000)	400 F
Segment margin—controllable	F 91,560	F 96,500	F4,940 F
Fixed overhead—not controllable			
by profit center manager	(27,000)	(29,250)	(2,250)U
Profit center income	F 64,560	F 67,250	F2,690 F

EXHIBIT 14-8
Profit Center Master Budget
Comparisons for August 2000

	FLEXIBLE BUDGET	ACTUAL	VARIANCE
Delivery revenues	F186,000	F186,000	F 0
Variable costs:			
Direct labor	F 4,650	F 4,600	F 50 F
Gas and oil	39,060	39,050	10 F
Variable overhead	7,998	7,850	148 F
Total	F 51,708	F 51,500	F 208 F
Contribution margin	F134,292	F134,500	F 208 F
Fixed overhead—controllable	(38,400)	(38,000)	400 F
Segment margin—controllable	F 95,892	F 96,500	F 608 F
Fixed overhead—not controllable			
by profit center manager	(27,000)	(29,250)	(2,250) U
Profit center income	F 68,892	F 67,250	F1,642 U

EXHIBIT 14-9
Profit Center Flexible Budget
Comparisons for August 2000

Investment Centers

An **investment center** is an organizational unit in which the manager is responsible for generating revenues, planning and controlling costs, and acquiring, using, and disposing of plant assets. The manager performs each of these activities with the aim of earning the highest feasible rate of return on the investment base. Many investment centers are independent, freestanding divisions or subsidiaries of a firm. This independence allows investment center managers the opportunity to make decisions about all matters affecting their organizational units and to be judged on the outcomes of those decisions.

investment center

Assume that Walker Pharmaceuticals (a subsidiary of Heinrick Chemicals) is an investment center headed by Henri LeBaron. The 2000 income statement for the company (in Swiss francs–Fr) is as follows:

Sales	Fr1,613,200
Variable expenses	900,000
Contribution margin	Fr 713,200
Fixed expenses	490,000
Net income	Fr 223,200

LeBaron has the authority to set selling prices, incur costs, and acquire and dispose of plant assets. The plant has an asset base of Fr2,480,000; and thus, the rate of return on assets for the year was 9 percent (Fr223,200 ÷ 2,480,000). In evaluating the performance of Walker Pharmaceuticals, top management would compare this rate of return with the rates desired by Heinrick Chemicals' management and with the rates of other investment centers in the company. Rate of return and other performance measures for responsibility centers are treated in greater depth in Chapter 15.

SUBOPTIMIZATION

Because of their closeness to daily divisional activities, responsibility center managers should have more current and detailed knowledge about sales prices, costs, and other market information than does top management. Managers of profit and investment centers are encouraged, to the extent possible, to operate those subunits as separate economic entities while making certain that they exist to achieve goals consistent with those of the larger organization of which they are part.

Regardless of size, type of ownership, or product or service being sold, one basic goal for any business is to generate profits. For other organizations, such as charities and governmental entities, the ultimate financial goal may be to break even. The ultimate goal will be achieved through the satisfaction of organizational **critical success factors**—those items that are so important that, without them, the organization would cease to exist. Most organizations would consider quality, customer service, efficiency, cost control, and responsiveness to change as five critical success factors. If all of these factors are managed properly, the organization should be financially successful. If they are not, sooner or later the organization will fail. All members of the organization—especially managers—should work toward the same basic objectives if the critical success factors are to be satisfied. Losing sight of the overall organizational goals while working to achieve a separate responsibility center's conflicting goal will result in suboptimization.

Suboptimization exists when individual managers pursue goals and objectives that are in their own and/or their segments' particular interests rather than in the company's best interest. Because managers of profit and investment centers have great flexibility in regard to financial decisions, these managers must remember that their operations are integral parts of the entire corporate structure. Thus, actions of these organizational units should be in the best long-run interest of both the unit and its parent organization. Unit managers should be aware of and accept the need for goal congruence throughout the organization.

For suboptimization to be limited or minimized, top management must be aware of it and must develop ways to avoid it. One way managers can limit suboptimization is by communicating corporate goals to all organizational units. Exhibit 14-10 depicts other ways of limiting suboptimization as stairsteps to the achievement of corporate goals. These steps are in no hierarchical order. If any steps are missing, however, the climb toward corporate goals and objectives becomes more difficult for divisional managers.

Companies may define their organizational units in various ways based on management accountability for one or more income-producing factors—costs, revenues, and/or assets. To properly evaluate the accomplishments of segments and their managers, a company, such as Teva Pharmaceutical Industries, will often set a price at which to transfer goods or services between segments. Such prices can help measure a selling segment's revenue and a buying segment's costs.

TRANSFER PRICING

Responsibility centers often provide goods or services to other company segments. These transfers require that a **transfer price** (or charge-back system) be established to account for the flow of these goods or services within the company. A transfer price

Sidebar notes:

critical success factor

LEARNING OBJECTIVE 4
What is suboptimization and what are its effects?

suboptimization

transfer price

LEARNING OBJECTIVE 5
How and why are transfer prices for products used in organizations?

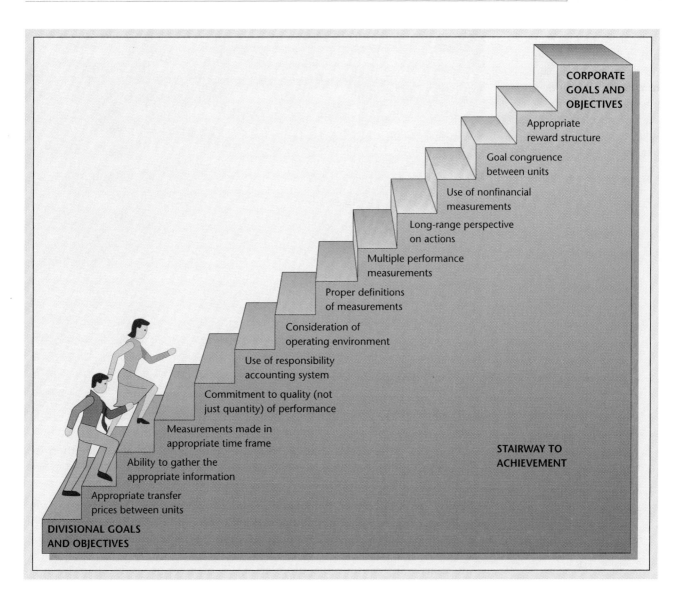

EXHIBIT 14-10
Performance Measures to Limit Suboptimization

is an *internal* charge established for the exchange of goods or services between organizational units of the same company. Internal company transfers should be presented on external financial statements at the producing segment's costs. Thus, if transfers are sold at an amount other than cost, the intersegment profit, expense, and/or revenue must be removed from the accounts for external financial reporting.

Intracompany transfers should be made only if they are in the best interest of the whole organization. If both the buying and selling managers have the authority to negotiate the transfer price, the following general rules create the limits of the transfer pricing model:[6]

- The maximum transfer price should be no greater than the lowest market price at which the buying segment can acquire the goods or services externally.

- The minimum transfer price should be no less than the sum of the selling segment's incremental production costs plus the opportunity cost of the facilities used. Incremental cost refers to the additional cost of producing a contemplated quantity of output, which generally means variable costs of production. Examples of opportunity cost include forgone contribution margin on

[6]These rules are more difficult to implement when the selling division is in a captive relationship and is not able to sell its products outside the corporate entity. In such situations, opportunity cost must be estimated to give the selling division an incentive to transfer products.

Companies often sell components between divisions using transfer prices. Determination of a transfer price for these engine blocks can be made on the basis of unit cost or market value, or it could result from negotiation between divisional managers.

alternative products not made and rent on the facilities that would otherwise be available if the company were not making the product which is the subject of the transfer price analysis.

The difference between this model's upper and lower limits is the corporate profit (or savings) generated by producing internally rather than buying externally. The transfer price acts to "divide the corporate profit" between the buying and selling segments. From the company's perspective, any transfer price set between these two limits is generally considered appropriate. If the market price is less than the internal incremental cost, it may be concluded that the competition is significantly more efficient than the firm at making a specific product. In this case, management should consider either discontinuing production of that product or finding ways to make it more efficiently and competitively.

To illustrate use of this model, assume that product K is made by Division A of Heinrick Chemicals Company. Product K has per unit incremental production and opportunity costs of $8 and $5, respectively. The $5 opportunity cost represents the forgone unit contribution margin on a similar product the company would otherwise make. If Division A were to sell product K to Division B, the minimum transfer price would be $13. The same product is available from external suppliers for $11. Heinrick Chemicals' management has two choices. First, it can have Division A stop making product K and, instead, have Division B buy it from the external suppliers. This decision is reasonable since, compared with those suppliers, Division A does not appear to be cost efficient in its production activities. Stopping production would release the facilities for other, more profitable purposes. Or management could insist that Division A improve its efficiency and reduce the cost of making product K. Either choice would benefit the company as a whole.

After the transfer price range limits have been determined, management may consider understandability in choosing a price within the range. Managers should be able to comprehend how a transfer price was set and how it will affect their divisions' profits. Most transfer prices are cost-based, market-based, or arrived at through a process of negotiation.

Assume that the Sussex Division (managed by Mr. Henry Higgins) of Heinrick Chemicals manufactures the basic compounds needed to formulate its antioxidant pill for the Montbatton Pharmaceutical Sales Territory (managed by Ms. Julie Pickering). The managers are attempting to establish a transfer price for each lot-size of 1,000 bottles. Sussex Division data (shown in Exhibit 14-11) are used to illustrate various transfer pricing approaches. Note that Sussex Division is capable of supplying all external and internal production needs.

Cost-Based Transfer Prices

Because of its emphasis on cost, the cost-based method of establishing a transfer price would seem to be logical and appropriate. There are, however, numerous ways to compute cost. Product cost is defined in Chapter 4 as including direct material, direct labor, variable production overhead, and fixed production overhead. This definition reflects the concept of absorption, or full, costing. In contrast, variable costing includes only those cost components that change in relationship to volume (direct material, direct labor, and variable production overhead) in product cost. Variable costing treats fixed production overhead as a period expense. If cost is to be used as the basis for setting a transfer price, a definition of the term *cost* must first be agreed on by the managers engaging in the intracompany transfer.

The absorption cost for a 1,000-bottle lot is $358 ($160 DM + $48 DL + $72-VOH + $78 FOH). A transfer price equal to absorption cost provides a contribution toward covering the selling division's fixed production overhead. Such a transfer price does not produce the same amount of income that would be generated if the transferring division sold the goods externally, but it does provide for coverage of all production costs.

A transfer price for a lot size of bottles of antioxidant pills based on variable cost is either $280 or $288. The difference depends on whether variable cost is defined as variable production cost or total variable cost. Using either of these costs as the transfer price will not give Mr. Higgins much incentive to transfer the antioxidant pills internally. Fixed costs of Sussex Division would not be reduced by selling internally and no contribution margin would be generated by the transfers to help cover these fixed expenses.

One final difficulty with using a cost-based transfer price is whether an actual or standard cost should be used. If actual costs are used, inefficiencies in production may not be corrected, since their cost will simply be covered by the buying division.

LEARNING OBJECTIVE **6**
What are the differences among the various definitions of product cost?

EXHIBIT 14-11

Standard Cost and Other Information about Antioxidant Pills

Standard production cost per lot:		
Direct material (DM)	$160	
Direct labor (DL)	48	
Variable overhead (VOH)	72	
Variable selling and administrative	8	
Total variable costs		$288
Fixed overhead (FOH)*	$ 78	
Fixed selling and administrative*	10	88
Total costs		$376
Normal mark-up on variable cost (50%)		144
List selling price		$520

Estimated annual production: 400,000 lots

Estimated sales to outside entities: 150,000 lots

Estimated intracompany transfers: 250,000 lots

*Fixed costs are allocated to all lots produced based on estimated annual production.

But, if standard costs are used, and savings are effected over standard costs, the buying division will be "paying" more than actual cost for the goods.

Market-Based Transfer Prices

To avoid the problems involved in defining *cost*, some companies simply use a market price approach to setting transfer prices. Market price is believed to be an objective measure of value and simulates the selling price that would exist if the segments were independent companies. If a selling division is operating efficiently relative to its competition, it should ordinarily be able to show a profit when transferring products or services at market prices. An efficiently operating buying division should not be troubled by a market-based transfer price. After all, that is what would have to be paid for the goods or services if the alternative of buying internally did not exist.

Still, several problems may exist with using market prices for intracompany transfers. The first problem is that transfers may involve products that have no exact counterpart in the external market. Second, market price may not be entirely appropriate because of internal cost savings arising from reductions in bad debts, packaging, advertising, and delivery expenditures. Third, difficulties can arise in setting a transfer price when the market is depressed because of a temporary reduction in demand for the product. Should the current depressed price be used as the transfer price, or should the expected long-run market price be used? Last, a question exists as to what is the "right" market price to use. Different prices are quoted and different discounts and credit terms are allowed to different buyers. Thus, it may not be possible to determine the most appropriate market price to charge.

Negotiated Transfer Prices

negotiated transfer price

Because of the problems associated with both cost-based and market-based prices, **negotiated transfer prices** are often set through a process of bargaining between the selling and purchasing unit managers. Such prices are normally below the external sales price of the selling unit, above that unit's incremental costs plus opportunity cost, and below the market purchase price for the buying unit. A negotiated price meeting these specifications falls within the range limits of the transfer pricing model.

A negotiated transfer price for the Sussex Division of Heinrick Chemicals would be less than the $520 list selling price or the Montbatton Pharmaceutical Sales Division's buying price, if lower. The price would also be set greater than the $288 incremental (variable) costs. If some of the variable selling costs could be eliminated, the incremental cost would even be less. If Sussex Division could not sell any additional lots of antioxidant pills externally or downsize its facilities, there would be no opportunity cost involved. If neither of these conditions exist, an opportunity cost would have to be determined. This could increase total costs to as much as the $520 list selling price, if all lots could be sold externally.

Authority to negotiate a transfer price implies that division managers have the autonomy to sell or buy products externally if internal negotiations fail. To encourage cooperation between the transferring divisions, top management may consider allowing each party to set a different transfer price.

Dual Pricing

dual pricing arrangement

Since a transfer price is used to satisfy internal managerial objectives, **dual pricing arrangements** can be used that allow different transfer prices for the selling and the buying segments. The selling division records the transfer of goods or services at a market or negotiated market price, which provides a profit for that division. The buying division records the transfer at a cost-based amount, which provides a minimal cost for that division. Dual transfer pricing gives managers the most relevant information for decision making and performance evaluation.

Choosing the Appropriate Transfer Price

The final determination of which transfer pricing system to use should reflect the circumstances of the organizational units, as well as corporate goals. No one method of setting a transfer price is best in all instances. Exhibit 14-12 provides the results of a transfer pricing survey of 143 large industrial companies and indicates that multiple definitions of transfer prices are employed at individual firms. Also, transfer prices are not permanent; they are frequently revised in relation to changes in costs, supply, demand, competitive forces, and other factors. Such cost adjustments can encourage efficient use of divisional resources by stimulating internal consumption during downturns in demand and rationing consumption during peak demand times.

Regardless of what method is used, a thoughtfully set transfer price will provide the following advantages:

- ◉ A means of encouraging what is best for the organization as a whole.
- ◉ An appropriate basis for the calculation and evaluation of segment performance.
- ◉ The rational acquisition or use of goods and services between corporate divisions.
- ◉ The flexibility to respond to changes in demand or market conditions.
- ◉ A means of motivating managers in decentralized operations.

Setting a reasonable transfer price is not an easy task. Everyone involved in the process must be aware of the positive and negative aspects of each type of transfer price and be responsive to suggestions of change if the need is indicated.

Pricing Methods	DOMESTIC TRANSFERS		INTERNATIONAL TRANSFERS	
	# of Firms	% of Total	# of Firms	% of Total
Cost-based methods:				
Actual or standard variable production cost	8	3.6	2	1.2
Actual full production cost	20	9.0	6	3.8
Standard full production cost	34	15.2	11	7.0
Actual variable production plus a lump-sum subsidy	2	0.9	2	1.3
Full production cost (actual or standard) plus a markup	37	16.6	42	26.8
Other	2	0.9	2	1.3
Subtotal for cost-based	103	46.2	65	41.4
Market-based methods:				
Market price	56	25.1	41	26.1
Market price less selling expenses	17	7.6	19	12.1
Other	9	4.0	12	7.7
Subtotal for market-based	82	36.7	72	45.9
Negotiated price	37	16.6	20	12.7
Other methods	1	0.5	0	0.0
Total—all methods	223*	100.0	157*	100.0

*Many firms use more than one domestic or international transfer price.
SOURCE: Roger W. Tang, "Transfer Pricing in the 1990s." Reprinted from *Management Accounting* (February 1992), p. 24. Published by the Institute of Management Accountants, Montvale, N.J. Visit our website at www.imanet.org.

EXHIBIT 14-12
Survey of Transfer Pricing Methods

TRANSFER PRICES FOR SERVICE DEPARTMENTS

LEARNING OBJECTIVE ❼
How and why are transfer prices for services used in organizations?

Setting transfer prices for products moving between one organizational unit and another is a well-established practice. Instituting transfer prices for services is a less common technique but an effective one for some types of service departments. Examples of services for which transfer prices may be used include computer services, secretarial services, legal services, and maintenance services. If management is considering setting a transfer price for a service department, the questions in Exhibit 14-13 should first be answered. The exhibit also presents some suggestions as to how the transfer price should be set. All the questions should be considered simultaneously and the suggestions combined to form a reasonable transfer price.

A department planning to use transfer prices for services must decide on a capacity level for use in price development. This decision is equivalent to that made in setting a predetermined overhead rate. For example, a service department may use expected annual capacity or practical capacity. If expected annual capacity is chosen, the transfer price per unit of service will be higher than if practical capacity is chosen. If the service department uses expected annual capacity and performs more services than expected, a favorable volume variance will arise.[7] Users, though, will not

EXHIBIT 14-13

Setting a Transfer Price
for Services

	IF RESPONSE IS:	
Questions	*Yes*	*No*
Is the service department to be considered a "money maker"?	Set transfer price using market-based, negotiated, or dual pricing.	Set transfer price using cost-based prices.
Does a user department have significant control over the quantity and quality of service used?	Use a base that reflects total quantity of activity of service department.	Transfer prices are not particularly useful.
Do opportunities exist to use external services rather than internal services?	Use a base that reflects the typical manner in which external purchases are made.	Set transfer price by negotiation or upper level management; use a base that reflects quantity of activity of service department
Is there a reasonable alternative (or surrogate) measure of service benefits provided to users?	Use a base representing total volume of alternative measures produced by service department.	Transfer prices are not particularly useful.
Are the services provided of a recurring nature?	Use a fixed price for each service used.	Use a price that reflects degree of use, constrained by whether user can bear the cost.
Are all services provided of a similar nature?	Use a fixed price based on a single factor of use.	Use a price that reflects degree of use, constrained by whether user can bear the cost.
Are the services performed typically expensive?	Use market-based or negotiated prices, constrained by whether user can bear the cost. The base may be more complex than typical.	Use cost-based or negotiated prices. The base should be easy to understand and to compute.

[7]Volume variances are covered in Chapter 9, on standard costing.

necessarily benefit from reduced charges because the transfer price is not normally changed. Use of practical capacity will, on the other hand, create a lower price. It might also encourage more internal services use and generate ideas as to how to use the additional capacity to fill outside needs. In addition, if the practical capacity level is not achieved, an unfavorable volume variance is noted, and the opportunity cost of underutilization is clearly identifiable.

In developing transfer prices for services, general costs must be allocated to the various departments equitably, and the underlying reason for cost incurrence must be determined. Transfer prices are useful when service departments provide distinct, measurable benefits to other areas or provide services having a specific cause-and-effect relationship. Transfer prices in these circumstances can provide certain advantages (see Exhibit 14-14) to the organization in both the revenue-producing and service departments.

First, transfer prices can encourage more involvement between the user and service departments. Users are more likely to suggest ways for the service department to improve its performance, since improved performance could result in lower transfer prices. Service departments are more likely to interact with users to find out the specific types of services that are needed and to eliminate or reduce those that are not cost beneficial.

Second, use of a transfer price for services should cause managers to be more cost conscious. Managers of user departments should attempt to eliminate waste. For example, if an MIS Department charged recipients in other departments for the number of reports received, managers would be less likely to request reports simply to be "on the receiving list," as sometimes occurs. For managers of the service departments, cost consciousness is directed at monitoring the cost to provide services. If excessive costs are incurred, a reasonable transfer price may not cover costs or a high transfer price may not be justifiable to users.

Last, transfer prices can provide information useful in evaluating managerial performance. Responsibility reports for user departments show a service department cost related to the quantity of actual services used. User department managers should be able to justify what services were used during the period. Transfer prices allow service departments to be treated as money-making operations rather than simply cost-generating operations. Responsibility reports of these departments indicate the transfer prices charged and the costs of providing services. Thus, these managers can be

EXHIBIT 14-14
Advantages of Transfer Prices for Services

	USER DEPARTMENTS	PROVIDER DEPARTMENTS
User involvement	Because they are being charged for services, user departments may suggest ways in which provider departments can improve services.	Because they are charging for the services they are providing, provider departments may become more aware of the needs of their users and seek to develop services that are more beneficial to user departments.
Cost consciousness	Because they are being charged for services, user departments may restrict usage to those services that are necessary and cost beneficial.	Because they are charging for the services they are providing, provider departments must be able to justify the prices charged and, thus, may maintain more control over costs.
Performance evaluations	Because control over amount of services used exists, user departments can include costs in performance evaluations.	Because transfer prices can generate "revenues" for their departments, provider department managers have more ways to evaluate departmental performance.

held accountable for cost control and profitability. The cost effectiveness of the provider department can then be determined and compared with the cost of outsourcing.

Although transfer prices for services can be effective tools, they do have certain disadvantages. First, there can be, and often is, disagreement among unit managers as to how the transfer price should be set. Second, implementing transfer prices in the accounting system requires additional organizational costs and employee time. Third, transfer prices may not work equally well for all types of service departments. Service departments that do not provide measurable benefits or cannot show a distinct cause-and-effect relationship between cost incurrence and service use by other departments should not use transfer prices. Finally, depending on how the transfer price is set, a transfer price may cause dysfunctional behavior among the organizational units; for example, certain services may be underutilized or overutilized. A company should weigh the advantages and disadvantages of using transfer prices before deciding whether a transfer pricing system would enhance or detract from organizational effectiveness and efficiency.

TRANSFER PRICING IN MULTINATIONAL SETTINGS

Because of the differences in tax systems, customs duties, freight and insurance costs, import/export regulations, and foreign exchange controls, setting transfer prices for products and services becomes extremely difficult when the company is engaged in multinational operations. In addition, as shown in Exhibit 14-15, the internal and external objectives of transfer pricing in multinational enterprises (MNEs) differ.

Because of these differences, there is no simple way to determine transfer prices in MNEs. Multinational companies may use one transfer price when a product is sent to or received from one country and a totally different transfer price for the same product when it is sent to or received from another. However, some guidelines as to transfer pricing should be set by the company and followed on a consistent basis. For example, a company should not price transfers to nondomestic subsidiaries in a way that would send the majority of costs to a subsidiary in the country with the highest tax rate *unless that pricing method was reasonable and equitable to all subsidiaries.* The general test of reasonableness is that transfer prices should reflect unbiased, or "arm's length," transactions.

As indicated in the accompanying News Note, multinational entity transfer prices are now being carefully scrutinized by tax authorities in both the home and host countries because such prices determine which country taxes the income from the transfer. The United States Congress is concerned about both U.S. multinationals operating in low-tax countries and foreign companies operating in the United States.

EXHIBIT 14-15
Multinational Company
Transfer Pricing Objectives

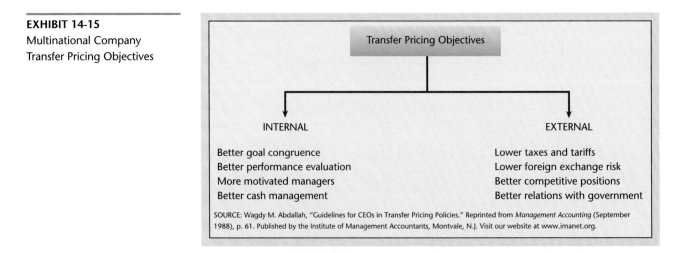

SOURCE: Wagdy M. Abdallah, "Guidelines for CEOs in Transfer Pricing Policies." Reprinted from *Management Accounting* (September 1988), p. 61. Published by the Institute of Management Accountants, Montvale, N.J. Visit our website at www.imanet.org.

The United States Isn't Alone in Concerns with Transfer Pricing

International tax planning may be complicated, but its rewards can be significant. Consider the case of Wind River Systems, a developer in Alameda, Calif., whose success was significantly based on the way the company managed its international tax liabilities.

With operations around the world—three wholly owned subsidiaries in Europe, majority ownership in a joint venture in Japan, and distribution agreements with independent contractors in other nations—Wind River faced corporate tax rates that can be much higher than those for companies that operate only in the United States. So it has devised a "transfer-pricing" strategy that minimized its global tax rates, bringing them to an average of less than 35%, compared with a worst-case scenario of almost 50%.

The goal of transfer pricing is to set international prices so that more profits are realized in those countries that have lower tax rates. So does it make sense to *lose* money on all ventures based overseas and declare all profits in the States, thus paying the lowest possible overall tax bill? Don't even think of it. Just as the IRS pays strict attention to the profits that foreign companies with U.S. operations declare for U.S. tax purposes, foreign governments closely examine the tax statements of U.S. businesses and their overseas subsidiaries. Companies that appear to transfer price too aggressively run the risk of costly audits.

Another caveat: while your transfer-pricing strategy needn't be set in stone for eternity, you cannot be tweaking it constantly to accommodate recent financial results. "If one of our foreign subsidiaries had a particularly good year," explained Wind River's chief financial officer, "I couldn't charge that subsidiary more for our software products so that it would recognize less profit, thus minimizing its taxes. That country's tax authority would come down on us in a second." Many nations in Western Europe are very aggressive about auditing foreign companies' transfer-pricing policies.

SOURCE: Reprinted with permission of *Inc.* magazine, Goldhirsh Group, Inc., 38 Commercial Wharf, Boston, MA 02110. "Controlling Global Taxes," Jill Andresky Fraser, (August 1993), p. 35 (http://www.inc.com). Reproduced by permission of the publisher via Copyright Clearinghouse Center, Inc.

Congress believes that, in both situations, companies could avoid paying U.S. corporate income taxes by using misleading or inaccurate transfer pricing. Thus, the Internal Revenue Service (IRS) may be quick to investigate U.S. subsidiaries that operate in low-tax countries or areas and suddenly show unusually high profits. If foreign companies charge their U.S. subsidiaries higher prices than what they would charge subsidiaries in their home country, U.S. taxable income (and thus the tax base) will decline—which may also bring about an IRS review.

The IRS will discuss and preapprove some transfer pricing agreements, which should help MNEs to set "reasonable" transfer prices. An advance determination ruling is valid for three years, assuming that the term is appropriate for the industry, product, or transaction involved. The fee is based on the taxpayer's gross income and, for the original determination, ranges from $5,000 to $25,000. Routine renewals are priced from $5,000 to $7,500. But the cost may be worthwhile, considering the quantity of documentation required to justify transfer prices and potential penalties for lack of documentation. The IRS can assess penalties of 20 percent or 40 percent for, respectively, "substantial" or "gross" valuation misstatements of income.[8]

As mentioned in Chapter 1, transfers among nations are becoming easier because of trade arrangements such as the European Union, the North American Free Trade

---

[8]Revenue Procedure 96-53, 1996-2 C.B. 375, amending and superseding Revenue Procedure 91-22.

Zone, and the General Agreement on Tariffs and Trade and its World Trade Organization. These arrangements should help reduce the significance of transfer price manipulations through the harmonization of tax structures and reductions in import/export fees, tariffs, and capital movement restrictions.

Multinational companies must be able to determine the effectiveness of their transfer pricing policies.

> [In this determination,] two criteria can be used: (a) does the system achieve economic decisions that positively affect MNE performance, including international capital investment decisions, output level decisions for both intermediate and final products, and product pricing decisions for external customers? and (b) do subsidiary managers feel that they are being fairly evaluated and rewarded for their divisional contributions to the MNE as a whole?[9]

If the answers to both of these questions are yes, then the company appears to have a transfer pricing system that appropriately coordinates underlying considerations, minimizes internal and external goal conflicts, and balances short- and long-range perspectives of the multinational company.

SITE ANALYSIS

Teva Pharmaceutical Industries Ltd.

With Teva's continued growth, requests for investments in new production capacity arise continually. ABC's highlighting of unused capacity often reveals where production can be expanded without spending additional money. A second source is the capacity released by ceasing production of unprofitable products — when feasible without disrupting customer relations.

The transfer pricing system also motivates cost reduction and production efficiencies in the manufacturing plants. Managers in the different divisions now work together to identify ways to reduce unit and batch-level expenses. Manufacturing, purchasing, and marketing employees conduct common searches for lower-cost, more reliable, and higher-quality suppliers to reduce variable materials costs. Marketing managers compare Teva's production costs with those of alternative suppliers around the world. They share this information with manufacturing managers who learn where process improvements are required and may concur with a decision to outsource products where the external suppliers' costs are lower than Teva could achieve in the foreseeable future. These actions contribute to increasing Teva's long-term profitability.

The activity-based cost information also helps managers determine which manufacturing facility is appropriate for different types of products. Thus, ABC information also is being used to determine operating strategy.

Perhaps most important, the introduction of ABC-based transfer prices has led to a dramatic reduction in the conflicts among marketing and manufacturing managers. The managers now have confidence in the production cost economics reported by the transfer price system. Manufacturing managers who "sell" the product concur with the reasonableness of the calculated transfer price. Teva's senior executives interpret the sharp reduction in intraorganizational conflicts as one of the most important signs that the use of activity-based transfer prices is succeeding.

SOURCE: Robert S. Kaplan, Dan Weiss, and Eyal Desheh, "Transfer Pricing with ABC," *Management Accounting* (May 1997), pp. 26–28.

---

[9]Wagdy M. Abdallah, "Guidelines for CEOs in Transfer Pricing Policies," *Management Accounting* (September 1988), p. 61.

CROSS-FUNCTIONAL APPLICATIONS

TOPIC OF NOTE	DISCIPLINE	CROSS-FUNCTIONAL APPLICATIONS
Transfer Pricing	Marketing	A strategic business unit may have an option to sell its output without further processing to an outside customer or to another unit within the firm. In the absence of top management guidelines for internal purchasing, the producing unit must consider the transfer price in relation to the current market value when making both production and sales decisions. If the marketing department of the producing unit is evaluated as a revenue center, then its motive would be selling price optimization. Consider the same unit as an investment center, and the producing unit could be more flexible in its pricing policy. Transfer pricing often has other non-financial objectives to a marketer, such as the predictability of future business, order size, price stability, and convenience.
	Taxation	The sales tax on producer goods accrues at the point of consumption. Transfer pricing guides firms involved in international business operations in minimizing the sales tax in broadly diversified organizations. In addition, fluctuating foreign currency exchange rates and taxation policies must be factored into transfer pricing. In any particular business environment, income taxes may be minimized by a high transfer price and sales/consumption taxes can be maximized. A tax manager must influence transfer pricing decisions.
	Organization Theory	The top management of vertically integrated organizations must consider the impact of transfer pricing on the performance evaluation of their various divisions. A blanket policy such as variable cost-based transfer pricing could minimize the segment margin of the producing division and perhaps exaggerate the contribution of the consumer unit in overall financial performance. Even at full costing or market price costing, a distortion of true performance can occur because frequently in-house transactions have a lower administrative cost than outsourcing.
	Operations Research	Researchers often use transfer pricing as a "shadow price" in mathematical models and computer simulations of optimum performance in productive capacity, sales, and profitability. Suboptimization models can be designed to compensate an autonomous division for accepting less profitability, based upon transfer pricing imposed on it by strategic planning.
	Engineering	Shared information and technological resources usually reduce design, manufacturing, and packaging costs. The formation of transfer pricing is heavily influenced by such synergies as engineering specifications and standards, as well as the ultimate use for the product. This synergy is often extended to vital customers; however, the overall costs are usually less in-house. Transfer pricing policies set a guideline for engineers in both the design of a product and the convenience of manufacturing it.

CROSS-FUNCTIONAL APPLICATIONS

TOPIC OF NOTE	DISCIPLINE	CROSS-FUNCTIONAL APPLICATIONS
Transfer Pricing *(continued)*	Legal Services	Contract negotiators and legal service reviewers must consider transfer pricing when they involve their divisions in sales/purchase agreements. In practice a transfer price is negotiated with contingent terms, such as price or quantity fluctuations, continued relationships, and services to the buyer. Negotiators and attorneys must be aware of the contingencies that influence any particular transfer price to design an agreement that gives a manager maximum flexibility for future decisions in an ever-changing business environment.
Responsibility Reporting	Marketing Management	A product or product line is frequently a strategic business unit (SBU) within the larger marketing department; or, occasionally, a firm is organized around product divisions. Responsibility reporting communicates the operating results of product SBUs and their management upward in the organization. Upper-level management can focus its attention on extraordinary performance evaluations, which often suggest a strength, weakness, opportunity, or threat for a particular SBU. A surge or slide in the expected sales performance of a product could be the result of an internal strength/weakness or some external opportunity/threat. The responsible product manager must prepare a report for his superiors describing the nature of the sales variance.
	Production Management	Complex engineering projects are often organized along a matrix management system. A project manager is responsible for moving a particular product through functional departments for processing. Disagreement frequently occurs between project and departmental managers because their objectives may conflict. Responsibility reporting assists top managers in resolving the friction inherent in matrix management by subordinating the performance of various projects or units to the strategic plan. A department manager may be called upon to use highly specialized employees in a lower technical capacity or at overtime rates because a project's performance could have strategic priority over containment of departmental cost. In this situation, the responsibility reports are a tool to implement strategic planning.
	Contract Law	Large government projects, such as weapon systems for the defense department, frequently use cost-plus contracting arrangements to assure suppliers of a profit margin in the uncertainty of high research and development investments. After decades of profiteering on unrestrained cost, defense contractors have been constrained by performance-measuring guidelines established by the Department of Defense termed *cost accounting standards*. This situation is unique in that responsibility reporting is made to a consumer entity above top management for approval. For example, extraordinary material costs or unusual handling by a contractor's purchasing department could invoke D.O.D. auditors to reduce the cost basis of the responsible department.
	Human Services Administration	Both public and private support for human services are often linked to the responsibility reports of individual administrators. Responsibility reporting in human services is usually linked to the behavioral results of the recipients as opposed to the predominately financial performance measurement used in commerce. Social welfare administrators may be funded on job placements for welfare recipients. In an attempt to shoulder the burden of social responsibility, many businesses have adopted similar responsibility reporting criteria, such as the recruitment, hiring, and job training of the socially dependent.

CHAPTER SUMMARY

Centralization refers to a concentration of management control at high organizational levels, while decentralization refers to the downward delegation of decision-making authority to subunit managers. Thus, a decentralized organization is composed of operational units led by managers who have some autonomy in decision making. The degree to which a company is decentralized depends on top management philosophy and the unit managers' abilities to perform independently. Decentralization provides the opportunity for managers to develop leadership qualities, creative problem-solving abilities, and decision-making skills. It also lets the individual most closely in tune with the operational unit and its immediate environment make the decisions for that unit and reduces the time spent in communicating and making decisions.

In a decentralized structure, subunit managers are evaluated in part by use of responsibility reports. Responsibility reports reflect the upward flow of information from each decentralized unit to the top of the organization. Managers receive information regarding the activities under their immediate control and under the control of their direct subordinates. The information is successively aggregated, and the reports allow the application of the management by exception principle.

Responsibility centers are classified as cost, revenue, profit, or investment centers. Each classification reflects the degree of authority managers have for financial items within their subunits. The type of responsibility center also affects the kind of performance measurements that can be used for the center and its manager.

Transfer prices are intracompany charges for goods or services exchanged between segments of a company. Product transfer prices are typically cost-based, market-based, or negotiated. A dual pricing system that assigns different transfer prices to the buying and selling units may also be used. Management should promote a transfer pricing system that is in the best interest of the whole company, motivates managers to strive for segment effectiveness and efficiency, and is practical.

Setting transfer prices in multinational enterprises is a complex process because of the differences that exist in tax structures, import/export regulations, customs duties, and other factors associated with international subsidiaries and divisions. A valid transfer price for a multinational firm is one that achieves economic benefit for the entire company and generates support from the domestic and international managers utilizing the system.

KEY TERMS

Cost center (p. 642)
Critical success factor (p. 648)
Dual pricing arrangement (p. 652)
Goal congruence (p. 636)
Investment center (p. 647)
Negotiated transfer price (p. 652)
Profit center (p. 645)

Responsibility accounting (p. 637)
Responsibility center (p. 640)
Responsibility report (p. 637)
Revenue center (p. 643)
Suboptimization (p. 648)
Transfer price (p. 648)

SOLUTION STRATEGIES

Transfer Prices (Cost-based, market-based, negotiated, dual)
Assuming both managers have the authority to negotiate transfer price:

Upper Limit: Lowest price available from external suppliers

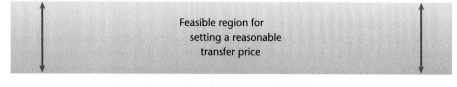

Feasible region for
setting a reasonable
transfer price

Lower Limit: Incremental costs of producing and selling the
transferred goods or services plus the opportunity
cost for the facilities used

DEMONSTRATION PROBLEM

Jorgensen Company of Sweden makes duck callers. The firm's annual revenue is SKr14,000,000. (SKr is the symbol for the krona, the currency unit in Sweden.) Johan Ericsen, the firm's controller, devised a new budgetary system. Annual budget figures are divided into 12 equal monthly amounts for monthly performance evaluations. Greta Thommasen, vice-president of production, was distressed when she reviewed the following responsibility report for the Forming and Polishing Department for March 2000:

FORMING AND POLISHING DEPARTMENT—RESPONSIBILITY REPORT
FOR THE MONTH ENDED MARCH 31, 2000

	Actual	Budget	Variance Over (Under)
Volume in units	**3,822**	**3,600**	**222**
Variable production costs:			
Direct material	SKr119,250	SKr115,200	SKr 4,050
Direct labor	140,650	133,200	7,450
Variable overhead	168,170	159,840	8,330
Total	SKr428,070	SKr408,240	SKr19,830
Fixed production costs:			
Depreciation	SKr 7,200	SKr 7,200	Skr 0
Indirect labor	15,840	16,000	(160)
Insurance	1,150	1,150	0
Taxes	1,440	1,440	0
Other	4,930	4,460	470
Total	SKr 30,560	SKr 30,250	SKr 310
Corporate costs:			
Quality assurance staff	SKr 17,890	SKr 11,520	SKr 6,370
Selling and general	19,560	17,280	2,280
Total	SKr 37,450	SKr 28,800	SKr 8,650
Total costs	SKr496,080	SKr467,290	SKr28,790

Requirements:
a. Discuss the weaknesses in the report.
b. Revise the report to reduce or eliminate the weaknesses.
c. Variances greater than 10 percent of budget are considered to be significant enough to be investigated. Identify these.

(CMA adapted)

Solution to Demonstration Problem

a. There are two major deficiencies in the report:
1. Responsibility reports for a cost center should compare actual costs with flexible budget costs. The report presented compares actual costs with static budget costs (which were estimated for 3,600 units, while actual production was 3,822 units). Costs measured at two different activity levels are not comparable for control or evaluation purposes.
2. The report presented includes corporate costs that are not within the control of the Forming and Polishing Department manager. Some of the fixed production costs probably also are not controllable by the manager of this cost center, although the problem does not provide enough information to address this concern.

b.

FORMING AND POLISHING DEPARTMENT—RESPONSIBILITY REPORT
FOR THE MONTH ENDED MARCH 31, 2000

Volume in units	Actual (3,822)		Budget (3,822)		Variance Over (Under)
	Per unit	Total	Per unit	Total	
Variable production costs:					
Direct material	SKr 31.20	SKr119,250	SKr 32.00	SKr122,304	SKr(3,054)
Direct labor	36.80	140,650	37.00	141,414	(764)
Variable overhead	44.00	168,170	44.40	169,697	(1,527)
Total	SKr112.00	SKr428,070	SKr113.40	SKr433,415	SKr(5,345)
Fixed production costs:					
Depreciation		SKr 7,200		SKr 7,200	SKr 0
Indirect labor		15,840		16,000	(160)
Insurance		1,150		1,150	0
Taxes		1,440		1,440	0
Other		4,930		4,460	470
Total		SKr 30,560		SKr 30,250	SKr 310
Total production costs		SKr458,630		SKr463,665	SKr(5,035)

c. Only the "other" cost category reflects a variance exceeding 10 percent of budget. Note that the revised report provides a more realistic and a more favorable view of performance than does the original report.

END OF CHAPTER MATERIALS

⊙ QUESTIONS

1. Differentiate decision-making authority between centrally organized and decentralized companies.

2. Would a very young company or a large mature company be more likely to employ decentralized management? Explain.

3. Why do the personality traits of subunit managers affect the success of efforts to decentralize decision making?

4. Some organizational activities are more likely to be decentralized than others. What activities are most likely to be decentralized? Least likely? Why?

5. Top managers at Worldwide Manufacturing Company are pondering the possibility of decentralizing control of all foreign operating divisions. The firm has traditionally maintained very tight central control over these operations. What major costs of decentralization should Worldwide's top managers consider in making their decision?

6. What is a responsibility accounting system? What is its role in a decentralized firm?

7. Why is a segment manager's performance evaluated separately from the segment's performance?

8. Describe the four types of responsibility centers. For each type, how can performance be measured?

9. How are variances used by managers in controlling the organization?

10. How is the philosophy of management by exception employed in responsibility accounting systems?

11. Describe how suboptimization is related to the performance measures that are used to evaluate segment managers and segment performance.

12. Is managerial performance always evaluated solely on financial measures? Explain.

13. What is a transfer price? What role does a transfer price play in a decentralized company?

14. What are the high and low limits of transfer prices, and why do these limits exist?

15. A company is considering use of a cost-based transfer price. What argument favors the use of standard, rather than actual, cost?

16. What practical problems may interfere with the use of a market-based transfer price?

17. What is dual pricing? What is the intended effect of dual pricing on the reported performance of each division affected by the dual price?

18. How can service departments use transfer prices and what advantages do transfer prices have over cost allocation methods?

19. Explain why determining transfer prices may be more complex in a multinational setting than in a domestic setting.

20. Why do state, federal, and foreign taxing authorities scrutinize transfer price determination in multinational companies?

⊙ EXERCISES

21. *(Terminology)* Your college dorm roommate has asked you to help him/her to match each of the lettered items on the left with the number of the appropriate item on the right.

a. Suboptimization
b. Dual pricing arrangement
c. Centralized organization
d. Goal congruence
e. Profit center
f. Decentralized organization
g. Cost center
h. Investment center
i. Responsibility center
j. Revenue center

1. Decisions in this type of company are made by division managers
2. Manager is primarily responsible for generating revenues, controlling costs, and managing assets
3. Manager is primarily responsible for controlling operating costs
4. The process of making decisions that may not be in the best interest of the entire firm
5. Price charged to buying division differs from price paid to selling division
6. Organizational and personal goals are consistent
7. Manager is responsible for revenue generation and operating cost control
8. Manager is primarily responsible for revenue generation
9. The organizational cost object under the control of a manager
10. Decisions in this type of company are generally made by top management

22. *(Centralized versus decentralized control)* Each of the following independent descriptions characterizes some trait of an organization. You have become involved in the formation of a new company and are considering how to structure it. For each de-

scription below, you have been asked by your investor group to indicate whether the firm would be more likely to adopt a centralized (C) or decentralized (D) control structure.

a. The firm has just been established.
b. A bad decision would have disastrous consequences for the company.
c. The firm is growing very rapidly.
d. The entrepreneurial CEO is the firm's founder and wants to maintain involvement in all aspects of the business.
e. The firm's operations span the globe. Many of the foreign divisions have operations that are very sensitive to volatility in local economic conditions.
f. Top management expresses sincere doubts about the capability of lower-level managers to make sound economic decisions.

23. *(Decentralization advantages and disadvantages)* The local chapter of the Chamber of Commerce has invited you to give an after-dinner speech on selecting an appropriate organizational structure. A friend of yours has suggested a number of issues that might be considered in choosing between a centralized organization and a decentralized one. However, before he could discuss these issues with you, he became lost in cyberspace and refuses to be disturbed. Since your talk is tonight, you need to decide whether each of the following might be a potential advantage (A) of decentralization, a disadvantage (D) of decentralization, or neither (N).

a. Promotion of goal congruence
b. Support of training in decision making
c. Development of leadership qualities
d. Complication of communication process
e. Cost of developing planning and reporting systems
f. Placement of decision maker closer (in time and place) to problem
g. Speed of decisions
h. Use of management by exception principle by top management
i. Greater job satisfaction
j. Delegation of ultimate responsibility

24. *(Cost variances)* The Tool and Die Department of Metro Manufacturing is structured as a cost center. Below are selected budget and actual costs of the department for 1999:

	PLANNING BUDGET	ACTUAL	FLEXIBLE BUDGET
Professional labor	$900,000	$925,000	$1,000,317
Supplies	14,000	15,200	16,200
Materials	114,000	119,350	117,200
Energy	26,000	29,300	32,100
Quality control	172,600	172,000	195,100
Depreciation	250,000	250,000	250,000
Software amortization	90,000	103,000	90,000

Metro has a policy of investigating any variance that differs from the expected amount for the actual level of operations by 5 percent or more. The company accountant has become ill and the CEO has enlisted you to address the following:

a. Which budget amount, planning or flexible, reflects the expected level of cost occurrence for the actual level of operations?
b. Based on your answer in Part a, compute variances for each cost category.
c. Which variances should be further investigated?
d. Which favorable variances, if any, might be of great concern to management? Explain.

25. *(Revenue variances)* Namer Industries produces and sells a stainless steel surgical knife. The Marketing Department is evaluated based on a comparison of achieved revenues with budgeted revenues. For 2000, the company projected sales to be 410,000 units at an average price of $42. The company actually sold 425,000 knives at an average

price of $39.50. The Marketing Department manager is upset and has enlisted your help in trying to understand the revenue shortfall.

a. Compute the revenue price and volume variances for 2000.

b. The president of Namer is curious as to why you didn't compute a sales mix variance. Write a brief memo to her explaining why a sales mix variance is inappropriate for her company.

c. Based on your computations in Part a, can you determine whether profits were above or below the budget level? Explain.

26. *(Revenue variances)* The Sales Department of the Aqua Store is responsible for sales of two principal products: flippers and masks. For August 2000, the Sales Department's actual and budgeted sales were as follows:

	FLIPPERS		MASKS	
	Dollars	*Units*	*Dollars*	*Units*
Budgeted sales	$20,000	4,000	$80,000	4,000
Actual sales	18,000	3,000	69,000	3,000

The sales manager for the Aqua Store is your friend and has asked you to help her with the following.

a. For August 2000, compute the price variance for the Sales Department of the Aqua Store.

b. Compute the volume variance for the Sales Department for August 2000.

c. Compute the sales mix variance for the Sales Department for August 2000.

d. Explain why you would expect a relatively minor sales mix variance for this company even when substantial variances may arise for sales volume and price.

27. *(Revenue variances)* Fine Leather Products Inc. manufactures two products: women's shoes and baseball gloves. For 2000, the firm budgeted the following:

	SHOES	BASEBALL GLOVES
Sales	$800,000	$1,800,000
Unit sales price	$40	$30

At the end of 2000, managers were informed that total actual sales amounted to 70,000 units and totaled $2,700,000. Shoe sales for the year amounted to 30,000 units at an average price of $35.

a. Compute the total revenue variance for 2000.

b. Compute the price variance for 2000.

c. Compute the sales mix variance for 2000.

d. Compute the sales volume variance for 2000.

28. *(Profit center variances)* Cascade Inns evaluates its inns and innkeepers based on a comparison of actual profit with budgeted profit. A budgeted 2000 income statement for the Cascade Inn in Buffalo follows:

Revenues		$2,650,000
Cost of services provided:		
Direct labor	$265,000	
Supplies	53,000	
Variable overhead	318,000	(636,000)
Contribution margin		$2,014,000
Fixed overhead—controllable		(320,000)
Controllable segment margin		$1,694,000
Fixed overhead—not controllable		
by segment manager		(1,220,000)
Profit center income		$ 474,000

For 2000, actual revenues generated were $2,900,000. Actual variable costs were: direct labor, 12 percent of revenues; supplies, 3 percent of revenues; variable overhead, 14 percent of revenues. Controllable fixed costs amounted to $330,000 and other fixed overhead costs amounted to $1,425,000.

a. Prepare an actual income statement for 2000.

b. Compute revenue and cost variances for 2000.

c. Evaluate the performance of the manager of the Buffalo inn for 2000.

d. Evaluate the performance of the Buffalo inn for 2000.

29. *(Transfer pricing)* The Accessory Division, an autonomous segment (profit center) of All-American Motors, is considering what price to charge for transfers of water pumps to the Large Truck Division of the company. The following data on production cost per water pump have been gathered:

Direct materials	$20.40
Direct labor	4.20
Variable overhead	12.60
Fixed overhead	10.80
Total	$48.00

The Accessory Division sells the water pumps to external buyers for $63. Managers of the Large Truck Division have received external offers to provide comparable water pumps ranging from $55 at one company to $73 at another. Top management has engaged you for help in developing a transfer price for these water pumps.

a. Determine the upper and lower limits for the transfer price between the Accessory Division and the Large Truck Division.

b. What is the transfer price if it is equal to full production cost?

c. What is the transfer price if it is equal to variable production cost?

d. Why would the Accessory Division be reluctant to transfer goods at a price equal to variable cost?

30. *(Transfer pricing)* Bridgeport Corporation has several operating divisions. The Motor Division manufactures motors for ceiling fans and other appliances. The Fan Division manufactures ceiling fans and several other products that require a motor similar to the one produced by the Motor Division. The Motor Division sells 90 percent of its output externally and transfers the other 10 percent to the Fan Division. Bridgeport Corporation makes all internal transfers at market price. The Motor Division's cost and revenue structure follows:

Sales price per motor	$75
Variable manufacturing costs	37
Fixed manufacturing costs	14
Variable selling and administration	2
Fixed selling and administration	5

Both per-unit fixed cost computations are based on an expected capacity of 200,000 units. As a student intern assigned to Bridgeport's finance office, you have been assigned to address the following items.

a. From the perspective of Bridgeport Corporation, what is the variable cost of producing and selling a fan motor?

b. What is the variable cost of a fan motor from the perspective of the Fan Division?

c. Under what circumstances would it be desirable for the Fan Division to know the true variable cost of an electric fan motor?

31. *(Transfer pricing)* Among other products, the Office Supplies Division of Upscale Artifacts Company produces small plastic cases. Forty percent of its output is sold to the Garden Division of Upscale Artifacts Company. All other output is sold to external parties. All internal transfers occur at a fixed price of $1.25. Office Supplies Division's expected results for 2000 are shown below.

	INTERNAL	EXTERNAL
Sales (150,000 units)	$75,000	$135,000
Costs:		
Variable	(30,000)	(45,000)
Fixed	(36,000)	(54,000)
Gross profit	$ 9,000	$ 36,000

Office Supplies Division has received an external offer that would enable it to sell, at $1.40 per unit, all the units now scheduled to be sold internally. To accommodate this sale, Garden Division would have to purchase its units externally for $1.70 per unit. The two division managers have come to you, the firm's chief accountant, with the following questions.

a. By what amount will Office Supplies Division's gross profit change if it accepts the offer from the external party?

b. By what amount will Garden Division's gross profit change if Home Products Division accepts the offer from the external party?

c. Assume Office Supplies Division negotiates a transfer price with Garden Division of $1.40 per unit. However, the additional gross profit (relative to the normal internal sales price) generated for Home Products Division by this transfer price will be split between Home Products Division and Garden Division. What will be the actual transfer price for each unit after this sharing of profit takes place?

d. How could a dual pricing system be used to provide incentive for an internal transfer in this situation?

32. *(Transfer pricing)* Accessories Division produces a speaker set that is sold to Stereo Division at the market price of $90. Accessories Division does not sell any speakers externally. Annual production and sales are 40,000 sets. The cost of production for a speaker set is shown below:

Variable production costs	$55
General fixed overhead ($12 per hour;	
1 hour for production time)	12
Direct fixed overhead ($320,000 ÷ 40,000)	8
Unit cost	$75
Variable shipping expenses	4
Total unit cost	$79

General fixed overhead is composed of some allocated production costs relating to the building and the production activities. Discontinuation of speaker production would save Accessories Division $40,000 in annual direct fixed overhead. Accessories Division's management has asked you to address the following items.

a. Determine the incremental cost of producing one speaker set.

b. Assume Accessories Division is operating at full capacity. What is the appropriate unit cost to be used to set a minimum transfer price for selling speaker sets to Stereo Division? Why is this cost most appropriate?

33. *(Transfer pricing for services)* A friend of yours has suggested some issues to consider in deciding whether each of the following might be a potential advantage of using transfer prices for service department costs, a potential disadvantage of using transfer prices for service department costs, or neither. Indicate whether each of the following conditions constitutes a potential advantage (A), a potential disadvantage (D), or neither (N).

a. Can make a service department into a profit center

b. May reduce goal congruence

c. Can make users and providers more cost conscious

d. Can increase disagreements about how transfer prices should be set

e. Can put all service departments on an equal footing

f. Can cause certain services to be underutilized or overutilized

g. Can improve ability to evaluate performance

h. Can increase communication about what additional services are needed and which can be reduced or eliminated

i. Requires additional cost and employee time commitment

34. *(Transfer pricing for services)* The computer operation of Brown Legal Services is in the process of developing a transfer price for its services. Capacity is defined by the computer operation in minutes of computer time. Expected annual capacity for next year

(2000) is 600,000 minutes, and full capacity is 800,000 minutes. Costs of the computer area for 2000 are expected to total $720,000.

a. What is the transfer price if it is based on expected annual capacity?

b. What is the transfer price if it is based on full capacity?

c. Assume the actual cost of operating the computer area in 2000 is $745,000. What is the total variance of that department? What are some possible causes of that variance?

⊙ PROBLEMS

35. *(Responsibility reports)* Metropolitan Engineering Associates was suffering from a decline in profit because of competitive pressures. One of its responses to declining profitability was to establish a responsibility accounting system. One of the responsibility centers established was the Electrical Engineering Division. This division is treated as a cost center for control purposes. In the first year (2000) after responsibility accounting was put in place, the responsibility report for the Electrical Engineering Division contained the following comparisons:

	BUDGETED	ACTUAL	VARIANCE
Variable costs:			
Professional labor	$1,000,000	$ 940,000	$60,000 F
Travel	50,000	40,000	10,000 F
Supplies	100,000	90,000	10,000 F
Fixed costs:			
Professional labor	400,000	405,000	(5,000) U
Facilities cost	250,000	265,000	(15,000) U
Insurance	80,000	78,000	2,000 F
Totals	$1,880,000	$1,818,000	$62,000 F

For 2000, the Electrical Engineering Division projected it would generate $2,000,000 of revenues; it actually generated $1,800,000. The company has consulted with you to help them understand what is happening. You decide to address the items that follow.

a. What are the major weaknesses in the responsibility report above?

b. Recast the responsibility report in a more meaningful format for cost control evaluation.

c. Metropolitan Engineering Associates utilizes a management by exception philosophy. Using the report prepared in Part b, which costs are likely to receive additional evaluation? Explain.

d. In most organizations, who would you expect to be involved in establishing policies on which variances should be investigated? Explain.

36. *(Performance report)* On January 1, 2000, Tom Clark was promoted to the position of production manager in Seattle Seafood Company. The firm purchases raw fish, cooks and processes the fish, and then cans the fish in single-portion containers. The canned fish is sold to several wholesalers that specialize in providing food to school lunch programs in the Northwest region of the United States and certain areas in Canada. All processing is conducted in the firm's highly automated plant in Seattle, Washington. Performance of the production manager is evaluated on the basis of a comparison of actual costs with standard costs. Only costs that are controllable by the production manager are included in the comparison (all are variable). The cost of fish is noncontrollable. Standard costs per pound of canned fish for 2000 were set as follows:

Direct labor	$.50
Repairs	.10
Maintenance	.60
Indirect labor	.10
Power	.20

For 2000, the company purchased 2,500,000 pounds of fish and canned 1,500,000 pounds. There were no beginning or ending inventories of raw, in-process, or canned fish. Actual 2000 costs were:

Direct labor	$600,000
Repairs	160,000
Maintenance	650,000
Indirect labor	155,000
Power	315,000

As the chief managerial accountant for the company, you have been asked to address the following.

a. Prepare a performance report for Tom Clark for 2000.

b. Evaluate Tom Clark's performance based on your report.

c. Tom feels that his 2000 performance is so good that he should be considered for immediate promotion to the position of vice-president of operations. Do you agree? Defend your answer.

d. Should additional performance measures (other than standard cost variances) be added to evaluate the production manager's performance? If so, identify the measures you would recommend.

37. *(Cost center performance)* Nancy Padgett is a production supervisor at the West Virginia plant of Appalachian Steelworks. As plant production supervisor, Ms. Padgett is evaluated based on her ability to meet standard production costs. At the West Virginia plant, the firm manufactures steel bridge guards. The standard costs to produce a one-foot section of bridge guard are given below:

Metal		$12.00
Galvanizing ($10 per gallon)		2.00
Direct labor ($15 per hour)		3.00
Overhead		
Welding supplies	$ .90	
Utilities	1.10	
Indirect labor	.80	
Machine maintenance/repairs	.40	
Equipment depreciation	2.20	
Miscellaneous	.80	6.20
Total		$23.20

In October 2000, the West Virginia plant produced 35,000 feet of bridge guards. During October, the plant incurred the following costs:

Metal		$507,500
Galvanizing ($9.40 per gallon)		65,800
Direct labor ($14.90 per hour)		104,300
Overhead		
Welding supplies	$34,900	
Utilities	38,300	
Indirect labor	25,500	
Machine maintenance and repairs	21,200	
Equipment depreciation	77,000	
Miscellaneous	29,500	226,400
Total		$904,000

a. For October 2000, management has requested that you compute the variance for each production cost category in the West Virginia plant.

b. Based on the variances computed in Part a, management has asked you to evaluate the performance of Nancy Padgett. Which variances might deserve closer scrutiny by top management? Explain.

38. *(Revenue center performance)* David Leno manages the Sales Department at Arizona Electric Supply. He is evaluated based on his ability to meet budgeted revenues. He

has asked your help in several ways listed below. For May 2000, Mr. Leno's revenue budget was as follows:

	PRICE PER UNIT	UNIT SALES
Floor lamps	$107	960
Hanging lamps	55	2,800
Ceiling fixtures	75	4,240

The actual sales generated by Mr. Leno's department in May were as follows:

	PRICE PER UNIT	TOTAL SALES IN DOLLARS
Floor lamps	$115	$ 93,150
Hanging lamps	50	207,000
Ceiling fixtures	78	315,900

a. For May 2000, compute the revenue price variance in the Sales Department at Arizona Electric Supply.

b. For May 2000, compute the revenue mix variance in the Sales Department at Arizona Electric Supply.

c. For May 2000, compute the revenue volume variance in the Sales Department at Arizona Electric Supply.

d. Based on your answers to Parts a, b, and c, evaluate the performance of Mr. Leno.

e. Assume you are Mr. Leno's supervisor. Why might you want to consider giving Mr. Leno the authority to set the salary and commission structure for the salespersons?

39. *(Profit center performance)* Beth Jackson, the head of the accounting department at Red River State University, has felt increasing pressure to raise external monies to compensate for dwindling state financial support. Accordingly, in early January 2000, she conceived the idea of offering a three-day accounting workshop in income taxation for local CPAs. She asked Jim Thomas, a tenured tax professor, to supervise the planning for the seminar which was to be held in late March 2000. In early February, Professor Thomas presented Jackson with the following budgetary plan:

Revenues ($800 per participant)		$80,000
Expenses:		
Speakers ($1,000 each)	$10,000	
Rent on facilities	7,200	
Advertising	4,200	
Meals and lodging	36,000	
Departmental overhead allocation	7,000	(64,400)
Profit		$15,600

Explanation of budget items: The facilities rent of $7,200 is a fixed rental which is to be paid to a local hotel for use of its meeting rooms. The advertising is also a fixed budgeted cost. Meals expense is budgeted at $10 per person per meal (a total of nine meals are to be provided for each participant); lodging is budgeted at the rate of $90 per participant per night. The departmental overhead includes a specific charge for supplies costing $20 for each participant as well as a general allocation of $5,000 for use of departmental secretarial resources. After reviewing the budget, Jackson gave Thomas approval to proceed with the seminar.

As Dr. Jackson's assistant, you have been asked to address several issues presented below.

a. Recast the income statement above in a segment income statement format.

b. Assume the actual financial results of the seminar were as follows:

Revenues (120 participants)		$77,000
Expenses:		
Speakers ($1,550 each)	$ 1,550	
Rent on facilities	8,400	
Advertising	5,800	
Meals and lodging	43,200	
Departmental overhead allocation	7,400	(80,300)
Loss		$ (3,300)

Explanation of actual results: Because signups were running below expectations, the seminar fee was reduced from $800 to $600 for late enrollees, and advertising expense was increased. These changes caused the number of participants to be larger than expected, so a larger meeting room had to be rented from the local hotel. In budgeting for the speakers, Professor Thomas neglected to include airfare, which averaged $500 per speaker.

Recast the actual results in a segment income format.

c. Compute variances between the budgeted segment income statement and the actual segment income statement. Identify and discuss the factors that are primarily responsible for the difference between the budgeted profit and the actual loss on the tax seminar.

d. Evaluate Professor Thomas's management of the tax seminar.

40. *(Transfer prices)* Better Homes Products' American operations are organized into two divisions: West and East. West Division sells a component that could be used by East Division in making one of the company's principal products. East Division has obtained three price quotations from external suppliers for the component: $154, $138, and $143. Examination of West Division's accounting records pertaining to the production of the component reveals the following costs: direct materials, $56; direct labor, $44; variable overhead, $18; and fixed overhead, $25. As the chief accountant, you have been directed by the CEO to determine the following.

a. What savings (or profits) would be available to Better Homes Products if East Division bought the component internally rather than externally?

b. What would the transfer price be if the two divisions agreed to split the total company savings evenly between them?

c. Assuming dual transfer pricing is used, set the maximum realistic price for West Division and the minimum realistic price for East Division.

41. *(Transfer pricing)* Two of the divisions of Heavy-Duty Equipment Company are the Motor Division and the Dragline Division. The Motor Division produces motors that are used by both the Dragline Division and a variety of external industrial customers.

For external sales, sales orders are generally produced in 100-unit lots. Based on this typical lot size, the cost per motor is as follows:

Variable production costs	$2,100
Fixed manufacturing overhead	900
Variable selling expenses	300
Fixed selling expenses	420
Fixed general and administrative expenses	640
Total unit cost	$4,360

Motor Division normally has earned a profit margin of 20 percent on internal sales but has set the external selling price at $5,400. Because a significant number of sales are being made internally, Motor Division managers have now decided that $5,400 is the appropriate price to use for all future transfers to the Dragline Division. Previous transfers have been based on full cost plus the stipulated per-unit profit.

When the managers in Dragline Division hear of this change in the transfer price, they become very upset since the change will have a major negative impact on Dragline's net income. Because of competition, corporate management has asked Motor Division to lower its sales prices, and consider reducing the transfer price. At the same time, Dragline Division management has asked to be allowed to buy motors externally. Bill Bird, Dragline's president, has gathered the following price information in order to help the two divisional managers negotiate an equitable transfer price:

Current external sales price	$5,400
Total variable production cost plus 20% profit margin ($2,100 × 1.2)	2,520
Total production cost plus 20% profit margin ($3,000 × 1.2)	3,600
Unit bid price from external supplier (if motors are purchased in 100-unit lots)	4,800

Mr. Bird is a former college classmate of yours and has asked you to help him analyze the following matters.

a. Discuss advantages and disadvantages of each of the above transfer prices to the selling and buying divisions and to Heavy-Duty Equipment Company. Explain what circumstances would make each of the alternative prices the most appropriate choice.

b. If Motor Division can sell all of its production externally at $5,400 each, what is the appropriate transfer price and why?

42. *(Transfer pricing)* The Accessories Division of Johnson Power Sources manufactures a starter with the following standard costs:

Direct materials	$ 10
Direct labor	60
Overhead	30
Total unit cost	$100

The standard direct labor rate is $30 per hour, and overhead is assigned at 50 percent of the direct labor rate. Normal direct labor hours are 20,000, and the overhead rate is $5 variable and $10 fixed per direct labor hour.

The starters sell for $150, and the Accessories Division is currently operating at a level of about 16,000 direct labor hours for the year. Transfers in Johnson Power Sources are normally made at market price, although the divisional managers are permitted to negotiate a mutually agreed upon transfer price.

The Motor Division currently purchases 2,000 starters annually from the Accessories Division at the market price. The divisional manager of the Motor Division indicates that she can purchase the starters from a foreign supplier for $140. Since she is free to select a supplier, she has indicated that she would like to negotiate a new transfer price with the Accessories Division. The manager of the Accessories Division indicates that he believes that the foreign supplier is attempting to "buy in" by selling the starters at what he considers an excessively low price. As Vice-President of Finance for Johnson Power Sources, your expertise has been requested in the following matters.

a. From the viewpoint of the firm, should the Motor Division purchase the starters internally or externally? Show calculations and explain.

b. From the viewpoint of the Motor Division, should the starters be purchased internally or externally? Show calculations and explain.

c. Assume that the Accessories Division is presently operating at capacity and could sell the starters that it now sells to the Motor Division to external buyers at its usual price. From the viewpoint of the firm, should the Motor Division purchase the starters internally or externally? Show calculations and explain.

d. If you were the marketing manager of the Motor Division, what concerns might you have regarding the decision to buy internally or externally?

43. *(Calculate income using transfer pricing)* Irresistible Scents Ltd. manufactures a line of perfume. The manufacturing process is basically a series of mixing operations involving the addition of certain aromatic and coloring ingredients. The finished products are packaged in company-produced glass bottles and packed in cases containing six bottles.

Management feels that the sale of its product is heavily influenced by the appearance of the bottle and has, therefore, devoted considerable managerial effort to the bottle production process. This has resulted in the development of certain unique processes in which management takes considerable pride.

The two areas (perfume production and bottle manufacturing) have evolved almost independently over the years; in fact, rivalry has developed between management personnel about which division is more important to Irresistible Scents. This attitude was probably intensified when the bottle manufacturing plant was purchased intact 10 years ago. No real interchange of management personnel or ideas (except at the top corporate level) has taken place.

Since the Bottle Division was acquired, its entire production has been absorbed by the Perfume Division. Each area is considered a separate profit center and evaluated as such. As the new corporate controller, you are responsible for the definition of a proper transfer price to use between the bottle production profit center and the packaging profit center. At your request, the general manager of the Bottle Division has asked certain other bottle manufacturers to quote a price for the quantity and sizes demanded by the Perfume Division. These competitive prices for cases of six bottles each are as follows:

VOLUME	TOTAL PRICE	PRICE PER CASE
2,000,000 cases	$ 8,000,000	$4.00
4,000,000 cases	14,000,000	3.50
6,000,000 cases	20,000,000	3.33

A cost analysis of the internal bottle plant indicates that it can produce bottles at these costs:

VOLUME	TOTAL PRICE	PRICE PER CASE
2,000,000 cases	$ 6,400,000	$3.20
4,000,000 cases	10,400,000	2.60
6,000,000 cases	14,400,000	2.40

The above analysis represents fixed costs of $2,400,000 and variable costs of $2 per case.

These figures have given rise to considerable corporate discussion about the proper value to use in the transfer of bottles to the Perfume Division. This interest is heightened because a significant portion of a division manager's income is an incentive bonus based on profit center results.

The Perfume Division has the following costs in addition to the bottle costs:

VOLUME	TOTAL COST	COST PER CASE
2,000,000 cases	$32,800,000	$16.40
4,000,000 cases	64,800,000	16.20
6,000,000 cases	96,780,000	16.13

Market Research has furnished you with the following price-demand relationships for the finished product:

SALES VOLUME	TOTAL SALES REVENUE	SALES PRICE PER CASE
2,000,000 cases	$ 51,000,000	$25.50
4,000,000 cases	91,200,000	22.80
6,000,000 cases	127,800,000	21.30

a. Irresistible Scents has used market-based transfer prices in the past. Using the current market prices and costs, and assuming a volume of 6,000,000 cases, calculate the income for the Bottle Division, the Perfume Division, and Irresistible Scents Ltd.

b. The 6,000,000-case production and sales level is the most profitable volume for which of the following: the Bottle Division, the Perfume Division, or Irresistible Scents Ltd.? Explain your answer.

c. As the corporate controller, answer the following question posed by the president of Irresistible Scents Ltd.: "Why have we structured the bottle operation as a separate division?"

(CMA adapted)

44. *(Evaluating transfer pricing policy)* Madison Decorative Floors operates with 10 profit centers. Company policy requires all transfers between corporate units to be made at fair market price. Tile Division has been asked to produce 10,000 standard tiles for Consumer Products Division. Tile Division is operating at full capacity and could otherwise sell any output it produces externally. This order represents 10 percent of the division's capacity, stated in terms of machine hours. Tile Division has quoted a $3.50 price per unit, but Consumer Products Division has found an external com-

pany that will make the tiles for $2.80. Since corporate policy states that external market prices must be used, Tile Division will be required to sell the units at $2.80. Tile Division's total variable cost for this specific type of tile is $2.20.

You have just graduated with a business degree, and your dad owns Madison Decorative Floors. He has asked you to help him with the following matters.

a. What amount of contribution margin will Tile Division earn at the originally quoted price? At the externally quoted price?

b. What effect does the use of the externally quoted purchase price of $2.80 have on Madison Decorative Floors' net income?

c. Some of the time that would be required to produce Consumer Products Division's order could be used instead to produce a special order for an outside company. Discuss how Tile Division management should make the choice between producing the order for Consumer Products Division and producing the outside company's order. What factors should be considered?

d. Should market price always be used to set a transfer price between organizational units? If so, discuss why. If not, discuss why not and when it is appropriate.

45. *(Transfer prices)* Industrial Solutions Inc. has several regional divisions, which often purchase from each other. The company is fully decentralized, with divisions buying from and selling to each other or in outside markets. Conveyor Systems Division purchases most of its needs for hydraulic pumps from Hydraulic Division. The managers of these two divisions are currently negotiating a transfer price for the hydraulic pumps for next year. Hydraulic Division prepared the following financial information for negotiating purposes:

Costs of hydraulic pumps as manufactured by Hydraulic Division:

Direct material costs	$120
Direct labor costs	40
Variable overhead costs	30
Fixed overhead costs	50
Fixed selling expenses	30
Fixed administrative expenses	20
Total	$290

Hydraulic Division is currently operating at 70 percent of its capacity. It is the policy of the division to target a net income to sales ratio of 20 percent.

The current market price for hydraulic pumps is $260 each. Recently, there has been a drop in price for such products because of industry advances in production technology.

Answer each of the following questions independently.

a. If Hydraulic Division desires to achieve its goal of a net income to sales ratio of 20 percent, what should the transfer price of pumps be?

b. If Hydraulic Division wants to maximize its income, what transfer price would you recommend it offer to the Conveyor Systems Division?

c. What is the price that you believe should be charged by Hydraulic Division if overall company profit is to be maximized?

(CMA adapted)

46. *(Transfer pricing)* AmerElectric is a decentralized company with divisions throughout the United States. Each division has its own sales force and production facilities and is operated autonomously as either a profit or an investment center. Switch Division has just been awarded a contract for a product that uses a component manufactured by Wire Division as well as by outside suppliers. Switch Division uses a cost figure of $3.80 for the component in preparing the bid for the new product. This cost figure was supplied by Wire Division in response to Switch Division's request for the average variable cost of the component.

Wire Division has an active sales force that is continually soliciting new customers. Its regular selling price for the component needed by Switch Division for the new product is $6.50. Sales of the component are expected to increase. Wire Division management has the following costs associated with the component:

Standard variable manufacturing cost	$3.20
Standard variable selling and distribution expenses	.60
Standard fixed manufacturing cost	1.20
Total	$5.00

The two divisions have been unable to agree on a transfer price for the component. Corporate management has never established a transfer price because no interdivisional transactions have ever occurred. The following suggestions have been made for the transfer price.

- Regular selling price
- Regular selling price less variable selling and distribution expenses
- Standard manufacturing cost plus 15 percent
- Standard variable manufacturing cost plus 20 percent

a. Compute each of the suggested transfer prices.
b. Discuss the effect each of the transfer prices might have on Wire Division management's attitude toward intracompany business.
c. Is the negotiation of a price between Switch Division and Wire Division a satisfactory method for solving the transfer price problem? Explain your answer.
d. Should the corporate management of AmerElectric become involved in this transfer controversy? Explain your answer.

(CMA adapted)

⊙ CASES

47. *(Responsibility accounting)* Family Resorts, Inc., is a holding company for several vacation hotels in the northeast and mid-Atlantic states. The firm originally purchased several old inns, restored the buildings, and upgraded the recreational facilities. The inns have been well received by vacationing families, as many services are provided that accommodate children and afford parents time for themselves. Since the completion of the restorations 10 years ago, the company has been profitable.

Family Resorts has just concluded its annual meeting of regional and district managers. This meeting is held each November to review the results of the previous season and to help the managers prepare for the upcoming year. Prior to the meeting, the managers have submitted proposed budgets for their districts or regions as appropriate. These budgets have been reviewed and consolidated into an annual operating budget for the entire company. The 2000 budget has been presented at the meeting and accepted by the managers.

To evaluate the performance of its managers, Family Resorts uses responsibility accounting. Therefore, the preparation of the budget is given close attention at headquarters. If major changes need to be made to the budgets submitted by the managers, all affected parties are consulted before the changes are incorporated. The following are two pages from the budget booklet that all managers received at the meeting.

FAMILY RESORTS, INC.
RESPONSIBILITY SUMMARY
($000 OMITTED)

Reporting Unit: Family Resorts	
Responsible Person: President	
Mid-Atlantic Region	$605
New England Region	365
Unallocated costs	(160)
Income before taxes	$810

Reporting Unit: New England Region
Responsible Person: Regional Manager

Vermont	$200
New Hampshire	140
Maine	105
Unallocated costs	(80)
Total contribution	$365

Reporting Unit: Maine District
Responsible Person: District Manager

Harbor Inn	$ 80
Camden Country Inn	60
Unallocated costs	(35)
Total contribution	$105

Reporting Unit: Harbor Inn
Responsible Person: Innkeeper

Revenue	$600
Controllable costs	(455)
Allocated costs	(65)
Total contribution	$ 80

The budget for Family Resorts, Inc., follows.

FAMILY RESORTS, INC.
CONDENSED OPERATING BUDGET—MAINE DISTRICT
FOR THE YEAR ENDING DECEMBER 31, 2000
($000 OMITTED)

	Family Resorts	Mid-Atlantic	New England	Unallo-cated[1]	Vermont	New Hamp.	Maine	Unallo-cated[2]	Harbor	Camden Country
Net sales	$ 7,900	$4,200	$3,700		$1,400	$1,200	$1,100		$600	$500
Cost of sales	(4,530)	(2,310)	(2,220)		(840)	(720)	(660)		(360)	(300)
Gross margin	$ 3,370	$1,890	$1,480		$ 560	$ 480	$ 440		$240	$200
Controllable expenses										
Supervisory expenses	$ 240	$ 130	$ 110		$ 35	$ 30	$ 45	$ 10	$ 20	$ 15
Training expenses	160	80	80		30	25	25		15	10
Advertising expenses	500	280	220	$ 50	55	60	55	15	20	20
Repairs and maintenance	480	225	255		90	85	80		40	40
Total controllable expenses	$(1,380)	$ (715)	$ (665)	$(50)	$ (210)	$ (200)	$ (205)	$(25)	$ (95)	$ (85)
Controllable contribution	$ 1,990	$1,175	$ 815	$(50)	$ 350	$ 280	$ 235	$(25)	$145	$115
Expenses controlled by others										
Depreciation	$ 520	$ 300	$ 220	$ 30	$ 70	$ 60	$ 60	$ 10	$ 30	$ 20
Property taxes	200	120	80		30	30	20		10	10
Insurance	300	150	150		50	50	50		25	25
Total expenses controlled by others	$(1,020)	$ (570)	$ (450)	$(30)	$ (150)	$ (140)	$ (130)	$(10)	$ (65)	$ (55)
Total contribution	$ 970	$ 605	$ 365	$(80)	$ 200	$ 140	$ 105	$(35)	$ 80	$ 60
Unallocated costs[3]	(160)									
Income before taxes	$ 810									

[1]Unallocated expenses include a regional advertising campaign and equipment used by the regional manager.

[2]Unallocated expenses include a portion of the district manager's salary, district promotion costs, and district manager's car.

[3]Unallocated costs include taxes on undeveloped real estate, headquarters expense, legal, and audit fees.

a. Responsibility accounting has been used effectively by many companies, both large and small.

    1. Define responsibility accounting.

    2. Discuss the benefits that accrue to a company using responsibility accounting.

    3. Describe the advantages of responsibility accounting for the managers of a firm.

b. The budget of Family Resorts, Inc. was accepted by the regional and district managers. Based on the facts presented, evaluate the budget process employed by Family Resorts by addressing the following:

    1. What features of the budget preparation process are likely to result in the managers' adopting and supporting the budget process?

    2. What recommendations, if any, could be made to the budget preparers to improve the budget process? Explain your answer.

(CMA)

48. *(Responsibility accounting and segment reporting)* Pittsburgh-Walsh Company (PWC) is a manufacturing company whose product line consists of lighting fixtures and electronic timing devices. The Lighting Fixtures Division assembles units for the upscale and midrange markets. The Electronic Timing Devices Division manufactures instrument panels that allow electronic systems to be activated and deactivated at scheduled times for both efficiency and safety purposes. Both divisions operate in the same manufacturing facility and share production equipment.

PWC's budget for the year ending December 31, 2000, was prepared on a business segment basis under the following guidelines:

⊙ Variable expenses are directly assigned to the incurring division.

⊙ Fixed overhead expenses are directly assigned to the incurring division.

⊙ Common fixed expenses are allocated to the divisions on the basis of units produced, which bear a close relationship to direct labor. Included in common fixed expenses are costs of the corporate staff, legal expenses, taxes, staff marketing, and advertising.

⊙ The production plan is for 8,000 upscale fixtures, 22,000 midrange fixtures, and 20,000 electronic timing devices.

PITTSBURGH-WALSH COMPANY
BUDGET FOR THE YEAR ENDING DECEMBER 31, 2000
(AMOUNTS IN THOUSANDS)

	Lighting Fixtures		Electronic Timing Devices	Totals
	Upscale	Midrange		
Sales	$1,440	$770	$800	$3,010
Variable expenses				
Cost of goods sold	(720)	(439)	(320)	(1,479)
Selling and administrative	(170)	(60)	(60)	(290)
Contribution margin	$ 550	$271	$420	$1,241
Fixed overhead expenses	(140)	(80)	(80)	(300)
Segment margin	$ 410	$191	$340	$ 941
Common fixed expenses				
Overhead	(48)	(132)	(120)	(300)
Selling and administrative	(11)	(31)	(28)	(70)
Net income (loss)	$ 351	$ 28	$192	$ 571

PWC established a bonus plan for division management that requires meeting the budget's planned net income by product line, with a bonus increment if the division exceeds the planned product line net income by 10 percent or more.

Shortly before the year began, the CEO, Jack Parkow, suffered a heart attack and retired. After reviewing the 2000 budget, the new CEO, Joe Kelly, decided to close the lighting fixtures midrange product line by the end of the first quarter and use the available production capacity to increase the remaining two product lines. The marketing staff advised that electronic timing devices could grow by 40 percent with increased direct sales support. Increases above that level and increasing sales of upscale lighting fixtures would require expanded advertising expenditures to increase consumer awareness of PWC as an electronics and upscale lighting fixture company. Kelly approved the increased sales support and advertising expenditures to achieve the revised plan. Kelly advised the divisions that for bonus purposes, the original product line net income objectives must be met, but he did allow the Lighting Fixtures Division to combine the net income objectives for both product lines for bonus purposes.

Prior to the close of the fiscal year, the division controllers were furnished with preliminary actual data for review and adjustment, as appropriate. These following preliminary year-end data reflect the revised units of production amounting to 12,000 upscale fixtures, 4,000 midrange fixtures, and 30,000 electronic timing devices.

PITTSBURGH-WALSH COMPANY
PRELIMINARY ACTUALS FOR THE YEAR
ENDING DECEMBER 31, 2000
(AMOUNTS IN THOUSANDS)

| | Lighting Fixtures | | Electronic Timing | |
	Upscale	Midrange	Devices	Totals
Sales	$2,160	$140	$1,200	$3,500
Variable expenses				
Cost of goods sold	(1,080)	(80)	(480)	(1,640)
Selling and administrative	(260)	(11)	(96)	(367)
Contribution margin	$ 820	$ 49	$ 624	$1,493
Fixed overhead expenses	(140)	(14)	(80)	(234)
Segment margin	$ 680	$ 35	$ 544	$1,259
Common fixed expenses				
Overhead	(78)	(27)	(195)	(300)
Selling and administrative	(60)	(20)	(150)	(230)
Net income (loss)	$ 542	$ (12)	$ 199	$ 729

The controller of the Lighting Fixtures Division, anticipating a similar bonus plan for 2001, is contemplating postponing the recognition of some revenues until next year because the sales are not yet final and advancing into the current year some expenditures that will be applicable to the first quarter of 2001. The corporation would meet its annual plan, and the division would exceed the 10 percent incremental bonus plateau in the year 2000 despite the postponed revenues and advanced expenses contemplated.

a. 1. Outline the benefits that an organization realizes from segment reporting.
   2. Evaluate segment reporting on a variable cost basis versus an absorption cost basis.
b. 1. Segment reporting can be developed based on different criteria. What criteria must be present for division management to accept being evaluated on a segment basis?
   2. Why would the managers of the Electronic Timing Devices Division be unhappy with the current reporting, and how should the reporting be revised to gain their acceptance?
c. Are the adjustments contemplated by the controller of the Lighting Fixtures Division unethical? Explain.

(CMA)

49. *(Performance report)* Golf course maintenance at the Westlake Country Club is managed by the greenskeeper and treated as a cost center. Performance measurement

is based on a comparison of the budgeted amounts with the actual expenses for the year. The following statement has been prepared by the bookkeeper of the club.

WESTLAKE COUNTRY CLUB
GOLF COURSE EXPENSES
FOR THE YEAR ENDED
DECEMBER 31, 2000

	Budgeted amount	Actual expense	Variance
Payroll and payroll taxes	$54,000	$54,500	$ (500)
Sand and gravel	300	500	(200)
Topsoil	1,000	800	200
Fertilizer	5,000	8,500	(3,500)
Fungicide	1,000	1,400	(400)
Grass seed	800	300	500
Parts	2,500	1,800	700
Petroleum products	1,800	3,100	(1,300)
Golf equipment	500	100	400
Uniforms	300	0	300
Training	300	0	300
Equipment rental	2,500	250	2,250
Utilities	3,000	5,100	(2,100)
Depreciation	5,000	5,000	0
Total	$78,000	$81,350	$(3,350)

The budget for the golf course is prepared by the greens committee and Mr. Jim Wallace, the greenskeeper. The budget is approved by the board of directors of the club and is used in evaluating the performance of Mr. Wallace at the end of the year. As a part of this evaluation, the following conversation takes place between Mr. Driver, the president of the club, and Mr. Wallace:

Mr. Driver: Jim, you should realize that the golf course budget represents the best judgments of the greens committee and the board of directors as to how resources should be used on the golf course. It is my opinion that differences between each budgeted amount and the expense incurred should be minor if you operate the course as directed by the committee with the approval of the board. The only items on this report where I view the differences as insignificant are payroll and depreciation. In many areas, such as fertilizer, petroleum products, and utilities, you significantly exceeded the budgeted amounts. To cover up these excesses, you failed to carry out our wishes concerning golf equipment and uniforms, and I can't explain the problem with equipment rental. I have received several complaints from our members about the condition of our markers and ball washers and the appearance of the help on the course. I now see how this is reflected in this report. Besides that, we have had many complaints as to the condition of the course.

Mr. Wallace: My understanding has been that I am to run the golf course and try to remain within the total budget. I can explain all of the differences that show up on this report. The cost of fertilizer, fungicide, petroleum products, and utilities went up significantly this year. Because of this, we only put out a minimum of fertilizer. It was either this or incur a significant budget overrun. The late summer was very dry, which required excessive pumping, and this added to the increased utility cost.

Mr. Driver: Jim, you're telling me that the budget did not allow for any price increases, but I know this is not the case.

Mr. Wallace: I know price increases were built into the budget, but they in no way covered the actual increases for the year. No one could have anticipated the short supply of fertilizer and fungicide that existed this year.

Mr. Driver: You should have limited your expenditures for these items to the amounts in the budget, and you should have bought the new uniforms and golf equipment and started some of the reseeding that was included in your budget.

Mr. Wallace: In my opinion, I did the best job possible to maintain the course, given the economic and weather conditions during the year. These things cannot be anticipated in preparing a budget. I must use my professional judgment in some of these matters. In addition, concerning the depreciation, I have nothing to do with it! It just shows up at the end of each year.

Mr. Driver: I am not sure that helps the situation.

a. Explain how Mr. Driver and Mr. Wallace differ in the way that they interpret the budget and in the way they believe Mr. Wallace's performance is to be evaluated.

b. Prepare a report suggesting how the differences you identified in Part a can be reconciled.

c. Do you see any problems with the treatment of depreciation in the budget? Explain.

d. Who should evaluate Mr. Wallace's performance: the greens committee or the board of directors? Explain.

50. *(Cost center performance)* The Advertising Department of Ace Wholesale Sporting Goods is evaluated as a cost center. The fiscal year for the company ends on July 30, and divisional managers are evaluated on their ability to operate within their budgets. For the last several years, the Advertising Department has run out of office supplies in June, and the advertising manager has made a vigorous attempt to control the volume of mail leaving the department.

During these year-end periods, office equipment is not repaired, photo supplies run short, the signing of advertising and printing contracts is postponed, and all travel is eliminated. Because of these shortages, sales personnel and manufacturers' representatives frequently complain of inadequate service during these year-end periods. Several employees in the Advertising Department have observed that this condition is being encountered earlier each year. Some employees have been known to stockpile office supplies during the year so that they can function at the year's end.

a. Describe the probable causes of the problems in the Advertising Department.

b. Write a memo to the Advertising Department manager suggesting several means by which some of these problems can be corrected.

c. How could advice from an expert in human behavior be used to deal with the games that are being played with the budget?

⊙ ETHICS AND QUALITY DISCUSSIONS

51. The New England Division is one of several divisions of North American Products. The divisional manager has a high degree of autonomy in operating the division. New England Division's management staff consists of a division controller, a division sales manager, and a division production manager, all reporting to the division manager. The division manager reports to the executive vice-president at corporate headquarters, while the division controller has a functional reporting relationship to the corporate controller.

The members of the management staff of the New England Division have developed good working relationships with each other over the past several years. Regularly scheduled staff meetings are held, and most of the management process is carried out through daily contact among the members of the staff.

An important staff meeting is held each September. At the meeting, management makes decisions required to finalize the annual budget to be submitted to corporate headquarters for the coming calendar year. The fourth-quarter plans are finalized, and the current year's forecasted results are reviewed prior to completion of the budget for the coming year.

For the first time in recent years, the budgeted amounts of the New England Division for the coming year (2000) show no growth and lower profits than the forecast for the current year. A review of the coming year's plans has not uncovered any alternatives that could improve the sales and profits. This unusual situation is of concern to the division manager because he has developed the reputation for producing growing profits. In addition, growth and profits affect the division manager's performance evaluation and annual bonus.

During the meeting in September 1999, the division manager stated that he would like to see some of the profits shifted from 1999 to 2000. He has heard that another company shifted profits. He believes the following actions were used to accomplish this objective:

- Shipments made to customers in the last two weeks of December were not billed until January
- The sales force was instructed to encourage customers to specify January delivery rather than December wherever possible
- Abnormally generous amounts were used to establish accruals for warranties, bad debts, and other expenses
- Raw materials for which title had passed and that were in transit at the end of December were recorded as purchased in December; however, the raw materials were not included in the year-end inventory
- Sales on account for the last day of December were not recorded until the first business day of January
- The cleaning and painting of the exterior of the plant was rescheduled to be completed in the current year rather than in the coming year as planned

The dollar amounts involved in these actions were material and would be material for the New England Division if similar actions were taken. The division manager asks the division controller if profits would be shifted from 1999 to 2000 if actions similar to these were carried out at the New England Division.

a. For each of the enumerated items, indicate whether there would be a shift of profit from 1999 to 2000.

b. How could the described manipulations of the responsibility accounting system adversely affect the quality of work performed in the division?

c. Comment on the ethics of accelerating or delaying transactions in order to manipulate the level of reported profit by a division.

52. A large American corporation participates in a highly competitive industry. To meet this competition and achieve profit goals, the company has chosen the decentralized form of organization. Each manager of a decentralized profit center is measured on the basis of profit contribution, market penetration, and return on investment. Failure to meet the objectives established by corporate management for these measures is unacceptable and usually results in demotion or dismissal of a profit center manager.

An anonymous survey of managers in the company has revealed that the managers feel pressure to compromise their personal ethical standards to achieve corporate objectives. For example, at certain plant locations there is pressure to reduce quality control to a level that cannot assure that all unsafe products will be rejected. Also, sales personnel are encouraged to use questionable sales tactics to obtain orders, including gifts and other incentives to purchasing agents.

The chief executive officer is disturbed by the survey findings. In his opinion, such behavior cannot be condoned by the company. He concludes that the company should do something about this problem.

a. Discuss what might be causing the ethical problems described.

b. Outline a program that could be instituted by the company to help reduce the pressures on managers to compromise personal ethical standards in their work.

(CMA)

53. Egret and Swan are partners in an accounting firm. Egret runs the tax practice and is both a CPA and a CMA. Swan is in charge of the management consulting area; his background is in information systems and statistics. Egret and Swan used to be good friends; but since his divorce, Egret believes that everyone is out to take him for everything possible. In addition to their salaries, Egret and Swan receive (1) a bonus based on the profits of their respective practice areas and (2) a share of total profits after expenses. The tax practice has consistently shown higher profits than the consulting area, although consulting revenues are growing and costs are remaining fairly constant.

    Recently, Swan asked for some help regarding several of his client engagements in tax matters. Egret also needed some computer assistance from Swan's area. Therefore, they agreed to establish a transfer price for such assistance. The transfer price was to be the cost of service provided. At the end of the year, the tax area showed a very large profit while the consulting area's increase was not so substantial, even though several new clients had been acquired. Egret spent his bonus on a trip to the island of St. Thomas and felt much better when he returned after three weeks. He hoped the following year would be even more profitable, since he was using absorption (full) cost as the basis for transferring his assistance to consulting and Swan was using variable cost as the basis for transferring his assistance to tax.

    a. Do you think it is necessary to inform the uninformed about the differences in how things can be defined in accounting? You do not need to limit this discussion to cost-based transfer prices.

    b. Is Egret being unethical in the distribution of profits with Swan? Discuss.

    c. Is Egret being illegal in the distribution of profits with Swan? Discuss.

    d. The assistance being rendered between the two areas is similar to a product, since both areas produce revenues. Suggest an equitable way to determine a transfer price for the firm, and discuss how your transfer price would affect the bonuses earned by Egret and Swan.

54. The Robinson Company has several plants, one of which produces military equipment for the federal government. Many of the contracts are negotiated by use of cost plus a specified markup. Some of the other plants have been only marginally profitable, and the home office has engaged a consultant, Mr. Slick, to meet with top management. At the meeting, Slick observes that the company isn't using some of the more "creative" accounting techniques to shift costs toward the plant serving the federal government and away from the marginally profitable plants. He notes that "transfer pricing and service department allocations involve a lot of subjectivity, and there is plenty of room to stack the deck and let the taxpayer foot the bill. Taxpayers will never know, and even if the government suspects, it can't prove motive if we document the procedures with contrived business jargon." One of the staff states that "this would be a way to get back some of those exorbitant income taxes we have had to pay all these years." The company president ends the meeting and asks for some time to consider the matter.

    a. What is the purpose of setting transfer prices and making service department allocations?

    b. Can or should transfer prices and service department allocations be used to shift income from one plant to another? If so, under what conditions?

    c. Do you think that what the consultant is suggesting is legal? Ethical? Ever been done? Discuss your reasoning for each answer.

55. Klein Corp. is a diversified manufacturing company with corporate headquarters in Kansas City. The three operating divisions are the Aerospace Division, the Ceramic Products Division, and the Glass Products Division. Much of the manufacturing activity of the Aerospace Division is related to work performed for the government space program under negotiated contracts.

Klein Corp. headquarters provides general administrative support and computer services to each of the three operating divisions. The computer services are provided through a computer time-sharing arrangement whereby the central processing unit (CPU) is located in Kansas City and the divisions have remote terminals that are connected to the CPU by telephone lines. One standard from the Cost Accounting Standards Board provides that the cost of general administration may be allocated to negotiated defense contracts. Further, the standards provide that, in situations in which computer services are provided by corporate headquarters, the actual costs (fixed and variable) of operating the computer department may be allocated to another division based on a reasonable measure of computer usage.

The general managers of the three divisions are evaluated based on the before-tax performance of the divisions. The November 1997 performance evaluation reports (in millions of dollars) for each division are presented on the facing page.

	AEROSPACE DIVISION	CERAMIC PRODUCTS DIVISION	GLASS PRODUCTS DIVISION
Sales	$ 23.0	$ 15.0	$ 55.0
Cost of goods sold	(13.0)	(7.0)	(38.0)
Gross profit	$ 10.0	$ 8.0	$ 17.0
Selling and administrative:			
Division selling and			
administration costs	$ 5.0	$ 5.0	$ 8.0
Corporate general			
administration costs	1.0	—	—
Corporate computing	1.0	—	—
Total	$ (7.0)	$ (5.0)	$ (8.0)
Profit before taxes	$ 3.0	$ 3.0	$ 9.0

If they are not charged for computing services, the operating divisions may not make the most cost-effective use of the resources of the Computer Systems Department of Klein Corp.

Outline and discuss a method for charging the operating divisions for use of computer services that would promote cost consciousness on the part of the operating divisions and operating efficiency by the Computer Systems Department.

(CMA adapted)

Chapter 15 Measuring and Rewarding Performance

Harnischfeger Industries

Harnischfeger Industries is a leader in providing heavy equipment to the mining and paper industries. This Fortune 500 firm, headquartered in Milwaukee, employs 17,500 and generated over $3 billion of sales in 1997. Recently, the firm has been setting records in generating sales, bookings and order backlogs—all signs of a healthy future. However, as recently as 1993 the firm was struggling financially. Corporate management attributes the change in the company's fortunes to a change in the way the firm defines success. The pulse of the firm is now measured by "economic value added," or EVA. EVA is a performance measure that relates a firm's profits to its level of investment.

Fran Corby, executive vice president, Finance & Administration, notes that before Harnischfeger Industries adopted the EVA concept in 1993, the company was income statement driven. "We were focused on bookings and we thought sales and earnings would follow. We didn't take into account the cost of capital to get bookings. Ignoring the cost of capital can produce uneconomic growth."

Another inhibitor to Harnischfeger's success was capital management. Instead of being used for long-term strategic decision-making, capital expenditures were seen as short-term fixes to the annual budget. Capital just kept going up, to the point where return on equity was a lot lower than the cost of capital.

"Clearly, we needed a mechanism to evaluate decisions. . . to get people focused on a complete decision," says Corby. "We needed to create value for shareholders. . . to build value in the company." EVA has been the answer. "It gives everyone a common formula for evaluating decisions," he says. "It guides the business decisions that both employees and managers make, day in and day out. We can apply this simple concept to a decision, a business, a purchase and a strategic acquisition."

SOURCE: http://www.harnischfeger.com; accessed July 6, 1998.

A t Harnischfeger Industries, top management and the board of directors determined that EVA was the performance measure by which all managers' performances would be judged. Accordingly, 100 percent of management's incentive pay has been linked to EVA performance.[1] *The result has been a tremendous improvement in organizational performance. By linking managers' incentives to EVA, and because EVA is believed by the board of directors to be highly correlated with stock price, the pay and performance evaluation of Harnischfeger's management has been directly linked to the performance measure of greatest interest to stockholders—stock price.*

Although EVA is the key performance measure at Harnischfeger, two of the other performance dimensions that are carefully monitored include international market leadership and technological leadership.[2] *Most firms recognize that multiple performance measures better capture more of the important dimensions of organizational performance than does a single performance measure. For example, if quality, cost, and market growth are all important dimensions of performance, it is unlikely that any single performance measure will capture performance in each dimension. The current trend in performance measurement is to use both short-term and long-term measures as well as financial and nonfinancial measures.*

This chapter covers two related sets of topics. First, performance measurement is discussed in the context of conventional monetary indicators such as cash flows, return on investment, and residual income. The more innovative nonmonetary and monetary performance measures that are needed by world-class, customer-driven companies such as Harnischfeger Industries are also addressed. Second, a variety of employee rewards that might be used by a company seeking to balance short-run and long-run interests are presented.

MEASURING ORGANIZATIONAL AND EMPLOYEE PERFORMANCE

As indicated in previous chapters, people must have benchmarks against which to compare their accomplishments in order to evaluate performance. A benchmark can be monetary, such as a target level of EVA, or nonmonetary, such as product defect rate or market share. Whatever measures are used, the following four general rules for performance measurement are appropriate:

---

[1] Carl Quintanilla, "Corporate Focus: Harnischfeger Seeks Additional Part to Become Whole; Bid for Giddings Is One Facet of Long-Term Effort to Shore Up Units," *Wall Street Journal*, May 2, 1997, p. B3.

[2] http://www.harnischfeger.com; accessed July 6, 1998.

1. Measures that assess progress toward organizational goals and objectives should be established.
2. Persons being evaluated should have had some input in developing the performance measurements and should be aware of them.
3. Persons being evaluated should have the appropriate skills and be provided the necessary equipment, information, and authority to be successful under the measurement system.
4. Feedback relative to performance should be provided in a timely and useful manner.

Objectives of Organizational Subunits

In selecting performance measures, missions of specific subunits must be considered. For example, objectives established for newly formed divisions are likely described in terms of sales growth, market share, research and development success, or rate of new product introductions. For these divisions, the use of profit measures to assess performance is inappropriate. Performance should be measured in ways that capture achievement of the objectives. For example, growth in market share would be one suitable measure. Alternatively, objectives for mature divisions can be couched in terms of profits and cash flows; hence, profit measures are appropriate for evaluating the relative success of mature divisions.

Need for Multiple Measures

Because organizations have a variety of goals and objectives, some of which are related to product life cycle issues, it is unlikely that a single measure or even several measures of the same type will effectively assess organizational progress toward all of those goals and objectives. A primary goal is, by necessity, to be financially solvent. Because solvency is determined by the relationship between cash inflows and cash outflows, cash flow is often used as a performance measure. If the organization is profit oriented, a goal of the firm is to provide a satisfactory return to shareholders. This requirement is satisfied by generating a net income considered by the owners to be sufficient, relative to the assets (capital) invested. Accordingly, some measurement of income is used by virtually all businesses to assess performance.

Although financial measures provide necessary indications of performance, they do not address some of the new issues of competitive reality essential to business survival in a global economy. Many companies have established goals relative to

LEARNING OBJECTIVE ❶
Why should organizations use multiple performance measures to assess performance?

Multiple performance measures can be used to evaluate the success of any activity—even Mardi Gras holiday in New Orleans. The city evaluates the success of this festivity by measures that include visitor spending, hotel occupancy rates, and tons of garbage cleaned up.

customer satisfaction rates, product defect rates, lead time to market, and environmental social responsibility. Such goals are not measured directly by income. Companies producing inferior goods, delivering late, abusing the environment, or, in general, making customers dissatisfied will lose market share and eventually will be forced out of business. Nonfinancial performance measures can be developed that indicate progress (or lack thereof) toward achievement of the important, long-run critical success factors of world-class companies. As the following quote indicates, selecting performance measures is a crucial organizational decision because the performance measures will determine how, and on what bases managers and other employees focus their time and attention.

> Performance measures are usually used to track progress towards [a] target.
> Often the measures become a surrogate for the target itself. When we turn
> our attention to what gets measured, and only what gets measured, we may
> overlook avenues of investigation that offer far greater opportunities to
> achieve [the target].[3]

Nonfinancial indicators are, in effect, surrogate measures of financial performance. The accompanying News Note indicates how nonfinancial performance measures can be used to create an incentive for managers to achieve organizational diversity goals.

Financial and nonfinancial performance measures can be combined to provide a comprehensive portrayal of organizational and managerial performance. Exhibit 15-1 illustrates a balanced scorecard that ultimately links all aspects of performance to the company's strategies. The balanced scorecard provides a set of financial and nonfinancial measures that encompass both internal and external perspectives.

Think of the balanced scorecard as the dials and indicators in an airplane cockpit. For the complex task of navigating and flying an airplane, pilots need detailed information about many aspects of the flight. They need information on fuel, air

---

NEWS NOTE

http:// www.tenneco.com

http:// www.hcc.com

http:// www.marriott.com

Want More Diversity? Then, Just Pay for It!

Ilene S. Gordon, a 14-year veteran of Tenneco Inc., has enjoyed mentoring colleagues. But when it comes to hiring and promoting women and minorities, she has an incentive besides personal satisfaction. Part of her pay depends on it.

Ten years ago, Tenneco introduced financial incentives for so-called diversity goals—in other words, a portion of managers' bonuses is tied to how many women and minorities they hire and move up the corporate ladder. In that time, says Stephen J. Smith, human resources vice president, the Houston-based oil company has doubled the number of professional women and minorities throughout the company.

Tenneco is one of a handful of corporations using pay incentives to integrate their workforce. Such companies, including Hoechst Celanese Corp. and Marriott International Inc., say executives place greater emphasis on diversity when it becomes a paid performance measurement. Critics on both sides of the diversity debate have complaints about these programs, but many managers say they are the most practical to change the composition of the workplace.

"What the boss measures is what people work on," says Ms. Gordon. "You have to have specific goals. That's how the organization gets the message."

SOURCE: Stephanie N. Mehta, "Executive Pay (A Special Report); Diversity Pays: Some Companies Link Managers' Pay to Minority Hiring," *Wall Street Journal*, April 11, 1996, p. R12. Reprinted by permission of *Wall Street Journal*, © 1996 Dow Jones & Company, Inc. All Rights Reserved Worldwide.

---

[3]Gay Gooderham and Jennifer La Trobe, "Measures Must Motivate," *Cost and Measurement* (October 1997) p. 52.

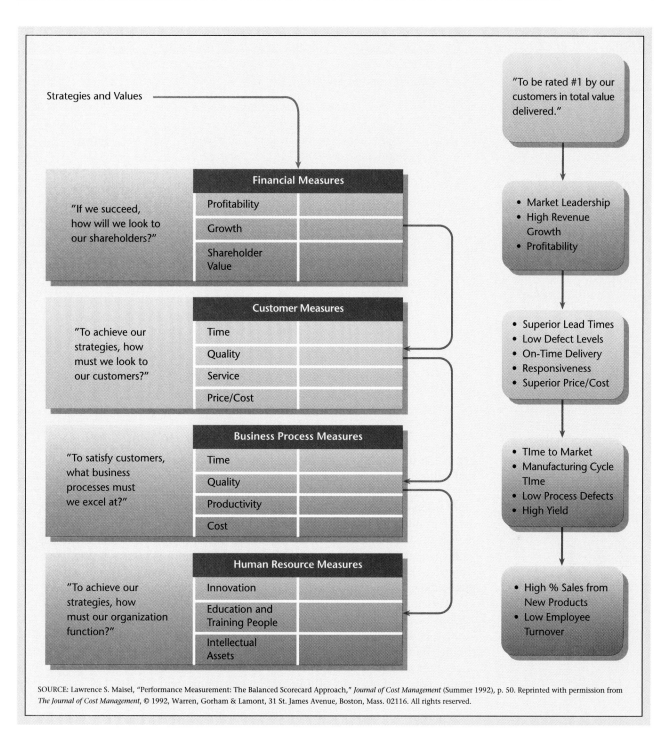

EXHIBIT 15-1

Performance Measurement "Balanced Scorecard"

speed, altitude, bearing, destination, and other indicators that summarize the current and predicted environment. Reliance on one instrument can be fatal. Similarly, the complexity of managing an organization today requires that managers be able to view performance in several areas simultaneously.[4]

The News Note "Why Measures Matter" considers the motivations for using a balanced scorecard to measure performance and why the balanced scorecard includes more than financial measurements.

[4]Robert S. Kaplan and David P. Norton, "The Balanced Scorecard—Measures that Drive Performance," *Harvard Business Review* (January–February 1992), p. 72.

Why Measures Matter

Research on more than 3,000 companies in North America has shown that the strongest drivers of competitive achievement are the intangibles, especially intellectual property, innovation, and quality. If these factors are important, then they should be measured, because "What gets measured gets done."

Some of the most important intangible assets a company can have are relationships, with customers and with employees. Employee loyalty and customer loyalty are closely linked, and retaining both is essential for success. Both are stakeholders; and there is no conflict between satisfying stakeholders and shareholders. You cannot do one without the other.

The quality of important relationships must therefore be reflected in a performance measurement framework, often called a scorecard, because of the sporting analogy. Remember, "If you aren't keeping score, then you're only practicing."

A rich performance framework does not mean just picking a few nonfinancial measures to stand alongside the financial measures. Measures not only reflect strategy, they are also used for process control, so naturally they must be based on an analysis of the company's processes, as well as an understanding of how these processes are supported by knowledge and relationships.

Source: Thomas G. McWeeney, "Linking Resources to Planning and Performance Measurement," *Public Manager* (Fall 1997) pp. 35–36.

Awareness of and Participation in Performance Measures

Regardless of which performance measures are selected, they must be set at levels that will encourage employees to do their best. Such a notion obviously means that individuals who will be evaluated by those measures must know about them. Communication of information is essential in any performance measurement process. Individuals must know and understand the performance measures to be used so that they can make a conscious choice to perform or not perform in a manner consistent with the measurement system. Withholding information about measures will keep employees from performing at their highest level of potential, will be frustrating for them, and will not support feelings of mutual respect and cooperation.

Participation in devising performance measures captures the attention of those persons being evaluated and results in a social contract between participants and evaluators. Individuals demonstrate a mutual respect for each other's ability to contribute effectively to the development process. Employee involvement in a performance measurement system is critical because "management attempts to bolster productivity will plateau without employee support, which is the key to achieving maximum productivity."[5]

Performance measures should also promote harmonious operations among organizational units. The effects of suboptimization can then be minimized because all employees will be working toward the same goals.

Appropriate Tools for Performance

Managers must place individuals in appropriate jobs, because employees who are put in jobs for which they are unsuited are destined to fail. Assuming employees possess basic competencies, they must be given the appropriate tools—including equipment, information, authority, training, and support—to perform their jobs in a manner consistent with the measurement process. Competent individuals or teams of work-

---

[5]Dan J. Seidner and Glenn Kieckhaefer, "Using Performance Measurement Systems to Create Gainsharing Programs," (Grant Thornton) *Manufacturing Issues* (Summer 1990), p. 8.

ers having the necessary job tools can be held responsible for their performance. If these tools are unavailable, people cannot be expected to accomplish their tasks.

Employee performance should be monitored and feedback provided on a continuous basis. Positive feedback encourages employees to continue favorable behaviors, while negative feedback creates awareness of problems so that employees can respond with different behaviors.

Performance measurement and evaluation, on the other hand, should take place at one or more specified and known points in time. Waiting until some future measurement point to provide feedback allows employees no opportunity for early adjustment. Performance measurement typically relies on information generated during the management control process. A wide variety of nonfinancial performance measures can be used at all organizational levels: market share, schedule attainment percentage, level of machine downtime, number of defects, or proportion of personnel retained during a period. For lower-level employees, financial measurement often focuses on aspects such as achievement of budget objectives and/or variances from budget or standard. For managerial-level employees, financial performance measurement is affected by their levels of authority and responsibility.

FINANCIAL PERFORMANCE MEASUREMENTS FOR MANAGERS

Attempts to use financial measures to evaluate higher-level managerial performance must consider the type of responsibility center over which the manager has control. If a manager is responsible for only one monetary item (such as in a cost or revenue center), performance measurements are limited to those relevant to that single monetary measure. Alternatively, profit and investment center managers are responsible for their centers' revenues and expenses. Given this greater accountability, a greater number of financial measures can be used to evaluate performance.

Divisional Profits

The segment margin of a profit center or income of an investment center is a frequently used measure of divisional performance.[6] This amount is compared with the center's budgeted segment margin or income, as well as the associated revenue and expense amounts to determine where objectives were exceeded or were not achieved. However, as with any other accounting income–based amounts, the individual components used to derive the segment margin are subject to manipulations such as the following:

- Sales transactions can be shifted between periods.
- If a cost flow method other than FIFO is being used, inventory purchases can be accelerated or deferred at the end of a period to change Cost of Goods Sold.
- If actual overhead is allocated to Inventory, an increase in production will cause cost per unit to decline because of the nature of fixed costs.
- Replacement of workers who have resigned or been terminated can be deferred to minimize salary expense for the period.
- Routine maintenance, advertising, or other discretionary costs can be delayed or eliminated to reduce expenses.
- Depreciation methods may be changed.

Any of these adjustments can cause reported segment margin to conform to budget expectations, but such tactics normally are not in the center's long-run best interest.

---

[6]The term "segment margin" is defined as segment sales minus (direct variable expenses plus avoidable fixed expenses). Thus, the margin would include neither unavoidable fixed costs nor allocated common costs.

Divisional segment margin or income is a short-term measure. Most reward systems (promotion, pay raises, bonuses, and so on) are based on annual performance. However, a year may be too short an interval for evaluating the quality of a manager's decisions. A periodic income measure should be used as a key performance measure only if a short-term focus is appropriate.

Cash Flow

Use of accrual-based segment margin or income as a performance measure may divert management's attention from two critical issues—the size and the direction of cash flows. Profit and investment center managers know that continuous liquidity is essential for their entities to succeed. Thus, another important performance measure is cash flow. The statement of cash flows (SCF) highlights the cash impacts of the three primary categories of business activities: operating, investing, and financing. A cash-based portrayal of operations helps managers to judge an entity's ability to meet current, fixed cash outflow commitments, undertake new commitments, and adapt to adverse changes in business conditions. Also, by identifying relationships between segment margin (or net income) and net cash flow from operations, the cash flow statement assists managers in judging the quality of the entity's earnings.

Like segment margin and income, cash flow can be manipulated and relates to the short run rather than the long run. But, as pointed out earlier, adequate cash flow is essential to business success. Inadequate cash flow may indicate poor judgment and decision making on the part of the entity's manager. A variety of financial ratios that include cash flow information, such as the current ratio, acid test ratio, and number of days' collections in accounts receivable, can help managers conduct their functions efficiently and effectively.

Return on Investment

return on investment (ROI)

Because they are responsible for generating revenues, controlling costs, and acquiring, using, and disposing of assets, investment center managers can be evaluated using return on investment. **Return on investment (ROI)** is a ratio that relates income generated by an entity to the resources (or the asset base) used to produce that income. The return on investment formula is:

$$\text{ROI} = \text{Income} \div \text{Assets Invested}$$

LEARNING OBJECTIVE ❷
How are return on investment (ROI) and residual income (RI) similar and different?

Before the ROI formula can be used effectively, the numerator and denominator must be specifically defined. In Exhibit 15-2 are questions relative to these definitions—and the answers to and rationale for each, assuming that the entity being measured is an investment center. The answers would be different if ROI were being calculated for an entire company. The ROI formula can be used to evaluate individual investment centers, as well as to make intracompany, intercompany, and industry comparisons, if managers making these comparisons are aware of and allow for any differences in the entities' characteristics and accounting methods.

Exhibit 15-3 (page 696) uses data for the Bellingham Machine Company to illustrate ROI computations. The company has three product-line divisions: Machinery, Materials Handling, and Tools. All of the divisions are operated as separate investment centers.

profit margin
asset turnover

To provide useful information about individual factors that compose the rate of return, the ROI formula can be restated in terms of profit margin and asset turnover. **Profit margin** is the ratio of income to sales; it indicates what proportion of each sales dollar is *not* used for expenses and so becomes profit. **Asset turnover**, which is calculated as sales divided by assets, shows the sales dollars generated by each dollar of assets and measures asset productivity. The ROI formula restated in terms of profit margin and asset turnover is called the **Du Pont model**:

Du Pont model

EXHIBIT 15-2
ROI Definitional Questions
and Answers

QUESTION	PREFERABLE ANSWER	RATIONALE
Is income defined as segment margin or operating income?	Segment margin	This amount includes only elements controllable by the investment center manager.
Is income defined on a before-tax or after-tax basis?	Before-tax basis	Investment centers are not taxed separately; if they were, the tax would probably be a different amount.
Is income defined on a before-interest or after-interest basis?	Before-interest basis	Interest rates are generally negotiated based on the company's (not the investment center's) credit-worthiness; if the center had to borrow funds as an independent entity, the rate might be different.
Should assets be defined as ⊙ total assets utilized, ⊙ total assets available for use, or ⊙ net assets (equity)?	Total assets available for use	The investment center manager is responsible for *all* assets, even idle ones.
Should plant assets be included in the asset denominator at ⊙ original costs, ⊙ depreciated book values, or ⊙ current values?	Current values	These values measure the opportunity cost of using the assets.
Should beginning, ending, or average assets be used?	Average assets	Periodic income relates to assets used during the entire period.

$$\text{ROI} = \text{Profit Margin} \times \text{Asset Turnover}$$

$$= \frac{\text{Income}}{\text{Sales}} \times \frac{\text{Sales}}{\text{Assets}}$$

As with the original ROI formula, terms must be specifically defined before the formula can be used for comparative or evaluative purposes. This model provides refined information about organizational improvement opportunities. Profit margin can be used to indicate management's efficiency as shown in the relation between sales and expenses. Asset turnover can be used to judge the effectiveness of asset use relative to revenue production. Calculations based on the Bellingham Machine Company information are given in Exhibit 15-4 (page 696). Income and asset base are defined as segment margin and total historical cost. Thus, these computations provide the same answers as those given in Exhibit 15-3.

With the profit margin and asset turnover ratios computed for each division, the division's performance can be evaluated relative to benchmark ratios. The benchmark ratios could be expectations of performance for each division, industry performance levels, or similar ratios for specific competitors. Because the three divisions compete in different industries, it would not be appropriate to compare one internal division relative to the performance of the others.

ROI is affected by management decisions involving sales prices, volume and mix of products sold, expenses, and capital asset acquisitions and dispositions. Return

EXHIBIT 15-3

Bellingham Machine
Company Divisional ROI
Computation

	MACHINERY	MATERIALS HANDLING	TOOLS	TOTAL
Revenues	$ 6,000,000	$ 967,400	$1,771,000	$8,738,400
Direct costs:				
Variable	(2,100,000)	(387,000)	(815,500)	(3,302,500)
Fixed (avoidable)	(1,100,000)	(120,000)	(302,000)	(1,522,000)
Segment margin	$ 2,800,000	$ 460,400	$ 653,500	$3,913,900
Unavoidable fixed				
and allocated costs	(725,000)	(92,400)	(153,000)	(970,400)
Operating income	$ 2,075,000	$ 368,000	$ 500,500	$2,943,500
Taxes (34%)	(705,500)	(125,120)	(170,170)	(1,000,790)
Net income	$ 1,369,500	$ 242,880	$ 330,330	$1,942,710
Current assets	$ 110,000	$ 42,000	$ 90,000	
Plant assets	11,422,000	995,000	8,825,000	
Total asset cost	$11,532,000	$1,037,000	$8,915,000	
Accumulated depreciation	(1,750,000)	(123,000)	(4,568,000)	
Asset book value	$ 9,782,000	$ 914,000	$4,347,000	
Liabilities	(4,205,000)	(117,000)	(927,000)	
Net assets	$ 5,577,000	$ 797,000	$3,420,000	
ROI: Segment margin	$ 2,800,000	$ 460,400	$ 653,500	
÷ Assets invested*	÷$11,532,000	÷$1,037,000	÷$8,915,000	
= Return on investment	24.3%	44.4%	7.3%	

*While use of current values would have been preferable, Bellingham Machine Company found these values difficult to obtain and had more confidence in the original cost of the assets used.

on investment may be increased through various management actions, including: (1) raising sales prices, if demand will not be impaired; (2) decreasing expenses; and (3) decreasing dollars invested in assets, especially if those assets are no longer productive. Thus, actions to improve performance should be taken only after all the interrelationships that determine ROI have been considered. A change in one of the component elements can affect many of the others. For instance, a selling price increase can reduce sales volume if demand is elastic with respect to price.

Assessments of whether profit margin, asset turnover, and return on investment are favorable or unfavorable can be made only by comparison of actual results for each component. Valid bases of comparison include expected results, prior results, and results of similar entities. Many companies establish target rates of return either for the company or for each division. These rates are based on the nature of the in-

EXHIBIT 15-4

Bellingham Machine Company DuPont Model ROI Computations

ROI = Profit Margin × Asset Turnover
    = (Income ÷ Sales) × (Sales ÷ Assets)

MACHINERY:

ROI = ($2,800,000 ÷ $6,000,000) × ($6,000,000 ÷ $11,532,000)
    = .467 × .520 = 24.3%

MATERIALS HANDLING:

ROI = ($460,400 ÷ $967,400) × ($967,400 ÷ $1,037,000)
    = .476 × .933 = 44.4%

TOOLS:

ROI = ($653,500 ÷ $1,771,000) × ($1,771,000 ÷ $8,915,000)
    = .369 × .199 = 7.3%

dustry or market in which the company or division operates. Favorable results should mean rewards for investment center managers.

Unfavorable rates of return should be viewed as managerial opportunities for improvement. Factors used in the computation should be analyzed for more detailed information. For example, if asset turnover is low, additional analyses can be made of inventory turnover, accounts receivable turnover, machine capacity level experienced, and other rate-of-utilization measures. Such efforts should help indicate the causes of the problems so that adjustments can be made. Another measure related to return on investment is the residual income of an investment center.

Residual Income

Residual income (RI) is the profit earned that exceeds an amount "charged" for funds committed to an investment center. The amount charged for funds is equal to a management-specified target rate of return multiplied by the assets used by the division. The rate can be changed periodically to reflect market rate fluctuations or to compensate for risk. The residual income computation is:

residual income (RI)

LEARNING OBJECTIVE ❷
How are return on investment (ROI) and residual income (RI) similar and different?

$$\text{Residual Income} = \text{Income} - (\text{Target Rate} \times \text{Asset Base})$$

Perhaps the most significant advantage of residual income over return on investment is that residual income provides a dollar figure of performance rather than a percentage. It is always to a company's advantage to obtain new assets if they will earn an amount greater than the cost of the additional investment. Expansion, or additional investments in assets, can occur in an investment center as long as positive residual income is expected on the additional investment.

Residual income can be calculated for each investment center of Bellingham Machine Company. The company has established 12 percent as the target rate of return on total historical cost of assets invested and continues to define income as segment margin. Calculations are shown in Exhibit 15-5. The residual income measures provide a clear indication of the relative contributions of the three divisions to the profit of the company. Although the Machinery and Materials Handling divisions are contributing substantial profits to the company, the profit of the Tools Division is insufficient to cover the required return on capital.

Limitations of Return on Investment and Residual Income

When used to measure investment center performance, return on investment and residual income have certain limitations (see Exhibit 15-6, page 698) that must be considered by managers.

Item 1 problems are common to most accounting-based measurements. However, use of ROI or RI in the new global environment can lead to significant problems listed in Item 2. For example, intangible assets such as patents are significant keys to

---

Residual Income = Income − (Target Rate × Asset Base)

MACHINERY:
RI = $2,800,000 − [.12 ($11,532,000)] = $2,800,000 − $1,383,840 = $1,416,160

MATERIALS HANDLING:
RI = $460,400 − [.12 ($1,037,000)] = $460,400 − $124,440 = $335,960

TOOLS:
RI = $653,500 − [.12 ($8,915,000)] = $653,500 − $1,069,800 = $(416,300)

EXHIBIT 15-5
Bellingham Machine Company Residual Income Calculations

EXHIBIT 15-6
Limitations of ROI and RI

1. Problems related to income
   - Income can be manipulated on a short-run basis by accelerating or delaying the recognition of income and expenses.
   - Because income depends on accounting methods selected, all investment centers must use the same methods if comparisons are to be made.
   - Accrual-based income reflects neither the cash flow patterns nor the time value of money, and these performance dimensions are generally important.
2. Problems related to the asset base
   - Some asset investment values are difficult to measure or assign to investment centers, while some other values, such as research and development, are not capitalized.
   - Current managers may be evaluated on decisions over which they had no control, such as decisions by previous managers to acquire some of the assets included in the division's investment base.
   - Inflation causes investment book values to be understated unless they are price-level adjusted.
3. ROI and RI reflect investment center performance without regard to company-wide objectives, which can result in suboptimization.

successfully competing today. The market values of such assets may differ very substantially from the assets' book values. Furthermore, some intangible assets may simply be ignored by traditional accounting methods, and therefore will be ignored by the analysis. A reputation for high-quality output and a high level of customer loyalty are examples of such assets.

Additionally, ROI and RI are short-term performance measures; consequently, they are better measures of performance for mature divisions than for high-growth divisions. For divisions that have opportunities for high rates of growth, the ROI and RI measures punish managers who currently invest in assets that do not generate returns until future periods.

Economic Value Added

Perhaps the most popular trend in performance measurement is the development of measures intended to more directly align the interests of common shareholders and managers. Leading this trend is corporate adoption of the measure known as **economic value added (EVA)**, which is the primary performance measure used at Harnischfeger Industries. Conceptually similar to RI, EVA is a measure of the income produced above the cost of capital. The major distinction between RI and EVA is that the target rate of return for EVA is applied to the capital invested in the division or firm as opposed to the market value or book value of book assets, which is the measure used for RI. Furthermore, because only after-tax profits are available to stockholders, EVA is calculated based on after-tax income:

$$\text{EVA} = \text{After-tax Income} - (\text{Cost of Capital \%} \times \text{Capital Invested}).$$

Capital Invested is defined as the market value of total equity and interest-bearing debt. Cost of capital is the weighted-average cost of capital, introduced in Chapter 8. For reasons mentioned earlier, the market value of invested capital can differ considerably from the book or market value of booked assets. As this difference increases, so do the relative benefits of using EVA rather than RI as a performance measure.

It is not uncommon today for the market value of a firm to be as high as five or six times the book value of the firm. Accordingly, RI, which is based on a target rate of return applied to the book value of assets, is likely to indicate much better performance than EVA. This point is demonstrated in Exhibit 15-7. Because the invested

economic value added (EVA)

http:// www.harnischfeger.com

LEARNING OBJECTIVE ❸
Why has economic value added (EVA) become a popular performance measure?

EXHIBIT 15-7
Comparison of RI and EVA for
Bellingham Machine Company

Invested capital	$45,000,000
Book value of assets	26,484,000*
Required return	12%
Net income (sum of divisions' net incomes from Exhibit 15-3)	$1,942,710

RI = Income − (Target Rate × Asset Base)

   = $1,942,710 − (.12 × $26,484,000) = $\underline{\$(1,235,370)}$

EVA = After-tax Income − (Cost of Capital % × Capital Invested)

   = $1,942,710 − (.12 × $45,000,000) = $\underline{\$(3,457,290)}$

*Book value of assets is equal to the sum of asset costs for each of the company's three divisions, as given in Exhibit 15-3 ($11,532,000 + $1,037,000 + $8,915,000) plus an assumed amount of $5,000,000 of corporate assets that are not associated with any of the three divisions.

capital of Bellingham Machine Company far exceeds its book value of assets, the firm's performance measured by EVA is well below the performance measured by RI. The accompanying News Note highlights the popularity of the EVA measure.

Despite the growing popularity of the EVA measure, it cannot measure all dimensions of performance, and it is a short-term measure of performance. Accordingly, the EVA measure can discourage investment in long-term projects because such investments drive up the amount of invested capital immediately but increase after-tax profits only at some point in the future. The result is a near-term decrease in EVA.

NEWS NOTE

EVA, the Hottest Performance Measure Today

"Virtually every major company in North America is in some stage of investigating, designing, or implementing a shareholder-value-based incentive plan," says Mark Ubelhart, practice leader for corporate finance and compensation at Hewitt Associates in Lincolnshire, Ill. "There's incredible momentum."

One reason is that some influential institutional investors and analysts are pressing executives to adopt value-based pay plans to ensure that managers won't get rich unless shareholders do. CS First Boston Corp., in particular, has championed value-based systems: The bank holds annual conferences to bring together executives of companies that use value-based measurements and pay systems and institutional-fund managers.

John B. Blystone, chief executive officer of SPX Corp., got a hefty bonus for 1996. But not because the auto-part supplier's stock more than doubled in value or because net income is back in the black. Instead, Mr. Blystone's bonus—about $920,000 in cash and another $1.05 million credited to a "bonus bank" for possible payout later—depends on a calculation called *economic value added*, or EVA. Here's how to figure it: Take one year's net operating profit after taxes and subtract a theoretical charge for the cost of capital used in the business. The final figure is supposed to reflect what kind of return investors can expect on their money. As of January 1, some 4,700 SPX employees had some piece of their annual pay linked to this measure, under a compensation system designed by New York consulting firm Stern Stewart & Co.

Mr. Blystone, hired from General Electric Co. in late 1995, says EVA is an important part of his turnaround strategy. When linked to compensation, he says, "EVA is a change accelerator."

http:// www.hewitt.com

http:// www.csfb.com

http:// www.spx.com

http:// www.sternstewart.com

http:// www.ge.com

SOURCE: Joseph B. White, "Executive Pay (A Special Report)—The "In" Thing: Value-Based Pay Systems Are the Fad of the Moment in Compensation Circles," *Wall Street Journal*, April 10, 1997, p. R10. Reprinted by permission of *Wall Street Journal*, © 1997 Dow Jones & Company, Inc. All Rights Reserved Worldwide.

Thus, EVA should be supplemented with longer-term financial performance measures, and with nonfinancial performance measures, especially for growth-oriented organizational subunits.

NONFINANCIAL PERFORMANCE MEASURES

Customarily, performance evaluations have been conducted based almost solely on financial results. But top management, in maintaining such a narrow focus, is similar to a baseball player who, in hopes of playing well, concentrates solely on the scoreboard. Both the financial measures and game score reflect the results of past decisions. Success also requires that considerable attention be placed on the individual actions for effective competitiveness, not just the summary performance measure, the score. A baseball player must focus on hitting, fielding, and pitching. A company must focus on performing well in activities such as customer service, product development, manufacturing, marketing, and delivery. For a company to improve, its performance measurements must specifically track the causes and occurrences of these activities.

nonfinancial performance measure (NFPM)

Thus, a progressively designed performance measurement system should encompass both financial and nonfinancial measures, especially those that track factors necessary for world-class status. **Nonfinancial performance measures (NFPMs)** include statistics for activities such as on-time delivery, manufacturing cycle time, set-up time, defect rate, number of unplanned production interruptions, and customer returns. NFPMs have two distinct advantages over financial performance measures:

LEARNING OBJECTIVE ➍
Why are nonfinancial measures important to evaluating performance?

- Nonfinancial indicators directly measure an entity's performance in the activities that create shareholder wealth, such as manufacturing and delivering quality goods and services and providing service for the customer.
- Because they measure productive activity directly, nonfinancial measures may better predict the direction of future cash flows. For example, the long-term financial viability of some industries rests largely on their ability to keep promises of improved product quality at a competitive price.

The performance pyramid depicted in Exhibit 15-8 indicates some financial and nonfinancial measures needed at various organizational levels and for various purposes. Also included are measures that can help in assessing both short-term and long-term organizational considerations.

Selection of Nonfinancial Measures

The set of nonfinancial performance measures that can be used is quite large because it is limited only by the imaginations of the persons establishing the system. Before establishing the measurement system, though, management should strive to identify the firm's critical success factors. A company's critical success factors may include quality, customer satisfaction, manufacturing efficiency and effectiveness, technical excellence, and rapid response to market demands.

For each success factor chosen, management should target a few attributes of each relevant NFPM for continuous improvement. These attributes should include both short-run and long-run measures to properly steer organizational activities. For instance, a short-range success measure for quality is the number of customer complaints in the current period. A long-range success measure for quality is the number of patents obtained to improve the quality of the company's products.

The nonfinancial measures selected for the performance evaluation system can be qualitative or quantitative. Qualitative measures are often subjective; for example, simple low-to-high rankings may be assigned for job skills, such as knowledge, quality of work, and need for supervision. Although such measures provide useful information, performance should also be compared against a quantifiable standard.

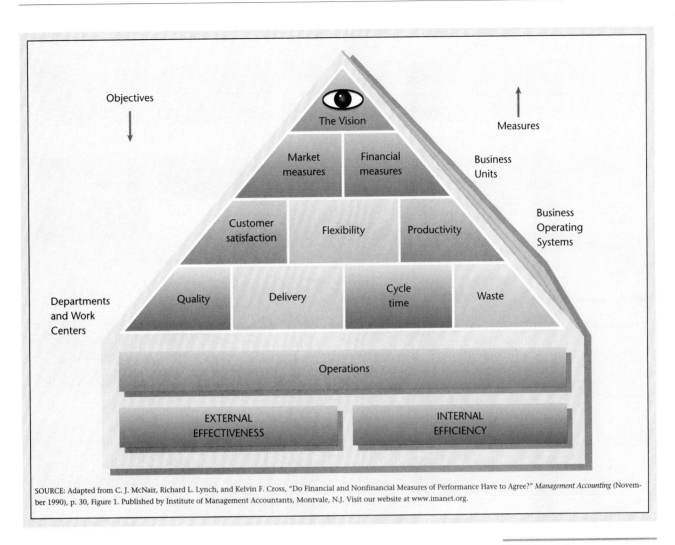

SOURCE: Adapted from C. J. McNair, Richard L. Lynch, and Kelvin F. Cross, "Do Financial and Nonfinancial Measures of Performance Have to Agree?" *Management Accounting* (November 1990), p. 30, Figure 1. Published by Institute of Management Accountants, Montvale, N.J. Visit our website at www.imanet.org.

EXHIBIT 15-8
The Performance Pyramid

Quantitative performance measures are more effective in creating employee receptiveness and compliance, because such measures provide a defined target at which to aim. These measures must be systematically captured and compared with predetermined standards to assess performance.

Establishment of Comparison Bases

After performance measures have been chosen, managers should establish acceptable performance levels by providing bases against which actual measurement data can be compared. These benchmarks can be developed internally (for example, based on a high-performing division) or can be determined from external sources, such as other companies, regardless of whether they are within the company's industry.

In each area in which a performance measurement is to be made, an employee must agree (1) to accept specific responsibility for performance and (2) to be evaluated. A system for monitoring and reporting comparative performance levels should be established at appropriate intervals, as shown in Exhibit 15-9 (page 702). The exhibit reflects a responsibility hierarchy of performance standards, with the broader issues addressed by higher levels of management and the more immediate issues addressed by lower-level employees. Note also that the lower-level measures are monitored more frequently—continuously, daily, or weekly—while the upper-level measures are investigated less frequently—monthly, quarterly, and annually. Measures addressed by middle-level employees (in Exhibit 15-9, the plant manager)

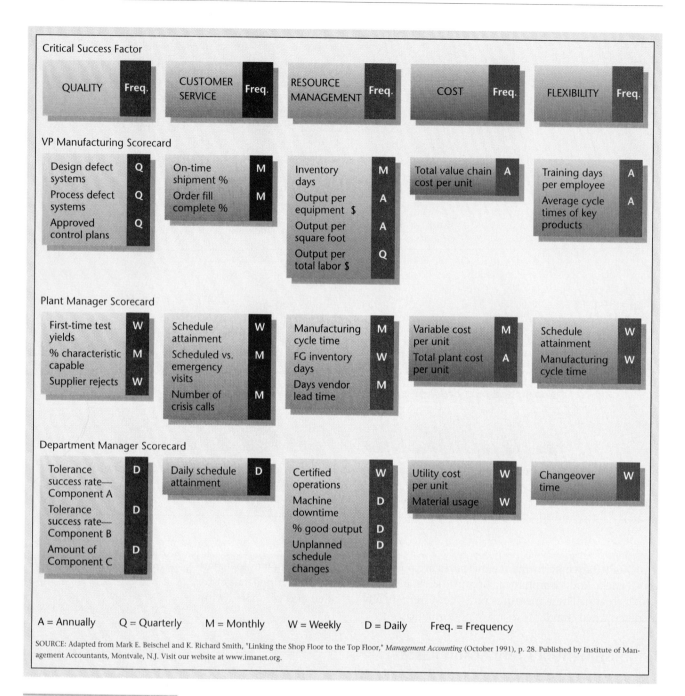

EXHIBIT 15-9

Performance Measurement
Factors and Timetables

are intermediate linkages between the lower-level and upper-level performance measures and require monitoring at intermediate points in time—weekly, monthly, and annually.

A general model for measuring the relative success of an activity compares a numerator representing number of successes with a logical and valid denominator representing total activity volume. For example, market share can be measured as follows:

$$\text{Market Share} = \frac{\text{Number of Units Sold by Specific Firm}}{\text{Total Units Sold in the Industry}}$$

Assume an internal division sold 9,000 units during a period, in which 48,000 units were sold by all the participants in the industry. The division's market share is 18.75 percent (9,000 ÷ 48,000). If a competitive benchmark for market share has been set at 20 percent, success will be evaluated as close to, but slightly below, the mark.

Throughput

All endeavors undertaken to help an organization achieve its goals are considered to be **synchronous management** techniques. "Synchronous management's strategic objective is to simultaneously increase throughput, while reducing inventory and operating expenses."[7] Throughput is a valuable indicator of performance that is gaining wide acceptability. This concept was first introduced in Chapter 13. Throughput can be measured in either financial or nonfinancial terms. Defined in nonfinancial terms, throughput refers to the number of good units produced and sold by an organization within a time period. An important aspect of this definition is that the company must sell the units and not simply produce them for inventory stockpiles. A primary goal of a profit-oriented organization is to make money, and inventory must be sold for profits to be achieved. Throughput can also refer to the number of services requested, performed, and delivered in a period.

synchronous management

One useful way to measure performance is to determine the extent to which the company is meeting its goal of making money by having rapid and high-quality throughput. Throughput, as mentioned, simply reflects how many good units are produced and sold for each available processing hour. Throughput can also be viewed as a set of component elements, as the Du Pont model, presented earlier, includes components of return on investment. Components of throughput include manufacturing cycle efficiency, process productivity, and process quality yield.[8]

$$\text{Throughput} = \frac{\text{Manufacturing}}{\text{Cycle Efficiency}} \times \frac{\text{Process}}{\text{Productivity}} \times \frac{\text{Process}}{\text{Quality Yield}}$$

or

$$\frac{\text{Good Units}}{\text{Total Time}} = \frac{\text{Value-Added Processing Time}}{\text{Total Time}} \times \frac{\text{Total Units}}{\text{Value-Added Processing Time}} \times \frac{\text{Good Units}}{\text{Total Time}}$$

The manufacturing cycle efficiency (as defined in Chapter 5) is the proportion of total processing time from beginning of production to completion, or service performance that is value-added. This time relates to activities that increase the product's worth to the customer. For instance, assume that the Machinery Division of Bellingham Machine Company worked a total of 15,000 hours last month making Product L007. Of these hours, only 6,000 were considered value-added; thus, the division had a manufacturing cycle efficiency of 40 percent.

Total units started, completed, and sold during the period are divided by the value-added processing time to determine **process productivity**. Assume the Machinery Division produced 30,000 units in the 6,000 hours of value-added processing time and all units were sold. Thus, the division had a process productivity rate of 5.0, meaning that 5.0 units were produced in each value-added processing hour.

process productivity

But not all units started, completed, and sold during the period are necessarily good units—some may be defective. The proportion of good units produced is the **process quality yield**. Thus, if only 27,000 of the 30,000 units produced by the Machinery Division last month were good units, the division had a 90 percent process quality yield for the period. This measure reflects the quality of the production process.

process quality yield

The total Product L007 throughput for Machinery Division last month was 1.80 (.40 × 5.0 × .90); that is, the division produced and sold only 1.80 good units for every hour of total actual processing time—quite a difference from the 5.0 units indicated as process productivity! The division could increase throughput by decreasing

---

[7]Victor Lippa, "Measuring Performance with Synchronous Management," *Management Accounting* (February 1990), p. 54.

[8]This expanded throughput formula has been adapted from an article by Carole Cheatham, "Measuring and Improving Throughput," *Journal of Accountancy* (March 1990), pp. 89–91. One assumption that must be made in regard to this model is that the quantity labeled "throughput" is sold. Another assumption is that units started are always completed before the end of the measurement period.

non-value-added activities, increasing total production and sales of units, decreasing the per-unit processing time, or increasing process quality yield.

Quality Indicators

A world-class company that is seeking growth and profitability will do well to systematically measure quality and assess its organizational cost of quality (COQ). Such measures should focus on and be related to actions that add value to products and services for the customer. Exhibit 15-10 presents several examples of quality indicators for each of the four quality classifications, as well as their cost drivers and value-added status.

The only value-added COQ category presented in Exhibit 15-10 is prevention. Because quality cannot be inspected into products, appraisal costs add no customer value. Internal and external failures add no value for anyone; they simply create unnecessary correction costs that make total costs higher for both the company and the customer. These failure costs are the result of poor quality.

A firm can drive down the costs of appraisal, internal failure, and external failure by investing in prevention. Many prevention measures involve one-time costs that improve quality now and long into the future. Some prevention measures are fairly inexpensive. Such measures are often suggested by the employees engaged in the process. Suggestion programs can be effective in pointing out opportunities for continuous improvement that will benefit employees, customers, and the firm and its owners.

ACTIVITY-BASED COSTING AND PERFORMANCE MEASUREMENT

LEARNING OBJECTIVE ⑥
How are activity-based costing concepts related to performance measurement?

Choosing appropriate nonfinancial performance measures can significantly help a company focus on activities that create costs. By controlling these activities, the company can more effectively control costs and improve processes.

EXHIBIT 15-10
Cost of Quality Measurements

COQ CLASSIFICATIONS	MEASURE	OPERATIONAL COST DRIVERS	VA OR NVA
⊙ Prevention	$\dfrac{\text{Prevention cost*}}{\text{Total COQ}}$	Investment in reducing overall COQ operations	VA
⊙ Appraisal	Number of inspections	Set-up frequency Tight tolerance operations Complex design	NVA
⊙ Internal failure	Number of pieces rejected	Machine reliability Tooling age or condition Design error Operator error	NVA
⊙ External failure	Number of customer complaints	Order entry errors Incorrect assembly instructions Product failure Operator error	NVA

*Ideally, the formula should equal 1. Prevention costs are, by definition, all value-added costs. As non-value-added costs included in the denominator are eliminated, total COQ is composed of only value-added costs. Therefore, the formula ideally ends up equaling 1 (value-added costs ÷ value-added costs), which is the target measurement.

SOURCE: Michael R. Ostrenga, "Return on Investment through the Cost of Quality," *Journal of Cost Management* (Summer 1991), p. 43. Reprinted with permission from *The Journal of Cost Management*, © 1991, Warren, Gorham & Lamont, 31 St. James Avenue, Boston, Mass. 02116. All Rights Reserved.

Activity-based costing is concerned with reducing non-value-added activities to increase throughput. Traditional performance measurements in accounting are filled with factors that contribute to non-value-added activities. Material and labor standards often include factors for waste and idle time. Predetermined overhead rates are based on estimates of expected capacity usage rather than full capacity usage. Inventories are produced to meet budget expectations rather than sales demand. Detailed explanations of how to treat spoiled and defective unit costs are provided in organizational accounting procedures. Exhibit 15-11 provides some traditional performance indicators and some potential suboptimizing results they may encourage.

If companies are to move toward world-class operations, non-value-added activities must be removed from performance evaluation measurements and value-added activities must be substituted. For example, when a performance measurement is the cost of defective units produced during a period, the original assumption is that management is expecting defects to occur and will accept some stated or implied defect cost. Instead, when the performance benchmark is zero defects, the assumption is that no defects will occur. It seems reasonable that managers would strive harder to eliminate defects under the second measurement than under the first.

Because activity-based costing focuses on actions that add value from a customer's viewpoint, this accounting method stresses external performance measurements. Customers define good performance as that which equals or exceeds their expectations as to quality, cost, and delivery. Companies that cannot measure up will find themselves without customers and without a need for financial measures of performance. In this regard, nonfinancial measures are more effective because they can be designed to monitor the characteristics desired by external parties rather than internal financial goals.

MEASUREMENT	ACTION	RESULT
Purchase price variance	Purchasing increases order quantity to get lower price and ignores quality and speed of delivery	Excess inventory; increased carrying cost; suppliers with the best quality and delivery are overlooked
	Purchasing acquires inferior quality materials to generate positive price variances	Production quality suffers and customers receive inferior goods
Machine utilization percentage	Supervisor requires employees to produce more than daily unit requirements to maximize machine utilization percentage	Excess inventory; wrong inventory
Scrap built into standard cost	Supervisor takes no action if there is no variance (from the lax standard)	Inflated standard; scrap threshold built in
Overhead rate based on expected capacity	Supervisor overproduces WIP or FG to have a favorable fixed overhead volume variance	Excess inventory
Responsibility center reporting	Management focus is on responsibility centers instead of activities	Missed cost reduction opportunities because common activities among responsibility centers are overlooked

EXHIBIT 15-11
Traditional Performance
Measurements and Results

EXHIBIT 15-12

Plan-Performance-Reward Model

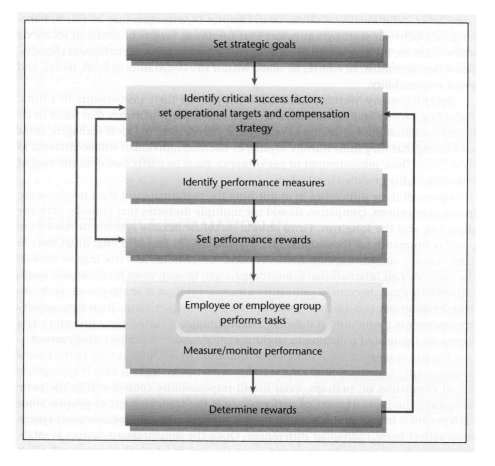

Pay-for-Performance Plans

Recall that what gets measured gets employees' attention—especially when compensation is involved. Therefore, in structuring a pay-for-performance plan, it is crucial that the defined performance measures be highly correlated with the organization's operational targets. Otherwise, suboptimization may occur and workers can earn incentive pay even though broader organizational objectives are not achieved.

Tying an organization's pay-for-performance plan to goals established in the strategic planning phase is the first step to motivating employees to focus on productivity improvement. The entire package of decisions regarding performance measurements can be referred to as a performance management system, depicted in Exhibit 15-13. When employees meet improvement objectives, rewards follow, and corporate results such as growth in market share, faster throughput, and greater profits can be expected. Reevaluating the performance measurement linkages with the satisfaction of corporate goals completes the cycle.

Traditionally, performance measures have focused on short-run profits without giving adequate attention to long-run performance. Pay-for-performance criteria should encourage employees to adopt a long-run perspective. To encourage a long-range perspective, many top executives receive a significant portion of their compensation in the form of stock or stock options. This pattern is clearly shown in Exhibit 15-14, which shows the total pay and stock-based pay for the eight most highly paid U.S. executives for 1997.

Because many companies have shifted from evaluating workers by observing their inputs to evaluating them based on their outputs, new problems have been created in the pay-for-performance relationship for workers as well as managers. Earlier chapters have stressed the importance of evaluating managers and workers only on

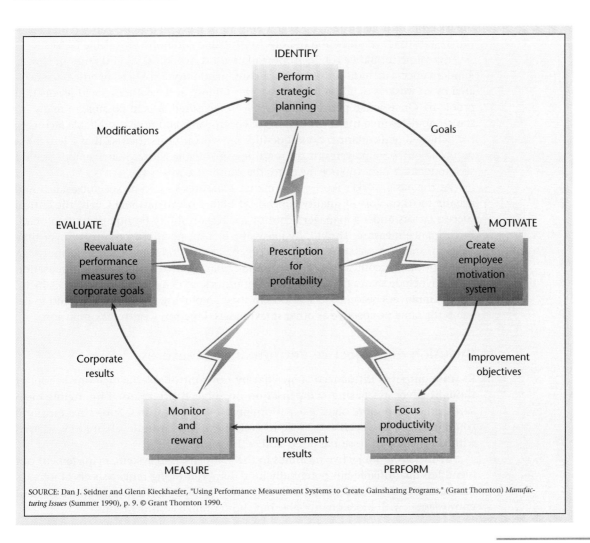

SOURCE: Dan J. Seidner and Glenn Kieckhaefer, "Using Performance Measurement Systems to Create Gainsharing Programs," (Grant Thornton) *Manufacturing Issues* (Summer 1990), p. 9. © Grant Thornton 1990.

EXHIBIT 15-13
Performance Management System

EXHIBIT 15-14
Who Made the Biggest Bucks

NAME	COMPANY	1997 COMPENSATION	
		TOTAL	STOCK OR OPTIONS
Sanford I. Weill	Travelers Group Inc.	$230,500,000	$220,200,000
Philip J. Purcell	Morgan Stanley Dean Witter & Co.	50,000,000	36,400,000
Robert B. Shapiro	Monsanto Co.	49,300,000	46,700,000
John F. Welch Jr.	General Electric Co.	39,800,000	31,800,000
Harvey Golub	American Express Co.	33,200,000	27,100,000
Charles A. Heimbold Jr.	Bristol-Myers Squibb Co.	29,200,000	25,300,000
Lawrence A. Bossidy	Allied Signal Inc.	28,200,000	23,100,000
William C. Steere Jr.	Pfizer Inc.	28,100,000	15,400,000

SOURCE: Anonmous, "Executive Pay (A Special Report); Who Made the Biggest Bucks," *Wall Street Journal*, April 9, 1998, p. R1. Reprinted by permission of *Wall Street Journal*, © 1998 Dow Jones & Company, Inc. All Rights Reserved Worldwide.

the basis of controllable factors. Regrettably, most performance measures tend to capture results that are a function of both controllable and noncontrollable factors.

Actual performance results from worker effort, worker skill, and random effects. Random effects include performance measurement error, problems or efficiencies created by co-workers or adjacent work stations, illness, and weather-related production problems. Once actual performance has been measured, it is impossible in many instances to determine the contributions of controllable and noncontrollable factors to the achieved performance. Consequently, the worker bears the risk that a less-than-desirable outcome may result from an uncontrollable cause. Management should seek to identify performance measures that minimize this risk.

At the basic worker level, performance measures should be specific and should usually focus on cost or quality control. At higher organizational levels, the critical success factors under a manager's control and responsibility become more important. Performance measures should, by necessity, be less specific, focus on a longer time horizon, and be more concerned with organizational longevity than with short-run cost control or income. This type of thinking has resulted in shifts in compensation plans to include shares of corporate common stock, as demonstrated in Exhibit 15-14. When employees become stockholders in their employing company, they tend to develop the same perspective as other stockholders: long-run wealth maximization.

Inclusion of Subjective Performance Measures

Because output is influenced somewhat by noncontrollable factors, one school of thought advocates basing compensation on subjectively-assessed intangible measures rather than more objective, performance-related measures. Subjective measures could include items such as leadership skills, flexibility, attitude, ability to work well with colleagues, professional pride, and enthusiasm.

By including subjective measures in the compensation system, management can blend less quantifiable but potentially more important long-range aspects of job performance—such as leadership, responsiveness, pride in work, cooperativeness, and enthusiasm—with more quantifiable but shorter-range considerations.

Compensation Packages

Conventionally, the compensation system has been based primarily on current monetary incentives. Middle managers are paid salaries with the opportunity for raises based on some measure of performance, usually accounting-related, such as segment income, divisional return on investment, or residual income. Lower-level workers are compensated through wages, usually specified by union contract or tied to the minimum wage law, based on the number of hours worked or production level achieved; current or year-end bonuses may be given when performance is above some specified quantitative measure. If provided, worker performance bonuses usually amount to a fairly small sum or percentage of wages. Significant incentive pay is usually limited to top management, and possibly the sales force, regardless of the levels of employees who may have contributed to increased profits. This type of traditional compensation system provides little motivation to improve organizational performance for employees who are not top managers.

As with performance measures, an employee's organizational level and current compensation should affect the types of rewards chosen. Individuals at different levels of employment typically view monetary rewards differently because of the relationship of pay to standard of living. Using relative pay scales is essential to recognizing the value of this difference. At lower employee levels, more incentives should be monetary and short term; at higher levels, more incentives should be nonmonetary and long term. The system should, though, include some nonmonetary and long-term incentives for lower-level employees and some monetary and short-term incentives for top management. Such a two-faceted compensation system provides lower-paid people with tangible rewards that directly enhance their lifestyles—more money—but also provides rewards (such as stock options) that cause them to take a long-run "ownership" view of the organization. In turn, top managers, who are well paid by most standards, would receive more rewards (stock and stock options) that should cause them to be more concerned about the organization's long-term well-being rather than short-term personal gains.

Another consideration in designing compensation packages is to balance the incentives provided for both groups, or teams, and individuals. In automated production systems, workers function more by indirectly monitoring and controlling machinery and are, therefore, less directly involved in hands-on production. Additionally, evolving organizational and managerial philosophies, such as total quality management and implementation of quality circles, have stressed group performance and the performance of work in teams.

Incentive plans for small groups and individuals are often virtually interchangeable. As the group grows larger, incentives must be in place for both the group and the individual. Group incentives are necessary to encourage cooperation among workers. However, if only group incentives are offered, the incentive compensation system may be ineffective because the reward for individual effort goes to the group. The larger the group size, the smaller the individual's share of the group reward becomes. Eventually, individual workers will be encouraged to free-ride on the group. This situation occurs when individuals perceive their proportional shares of the group reward as insufficient to compensate for their efforts.

A recent study found that two-thirds of surveyed companies use quantifiable measures of team effectiveness in addition to measures of individual effectiveness.[10] The study also found that subjective, qualitative measures are frequently used to assess the performance of individuals in teams, such as level of cooperation and level of participation in teams.

In addition to various forms of monetary compensation, workers may be motivated by nonfinancial factors. Although all employees value and require money to satisfy basic human needs, other human needs are not necessarily fulfilled with monetary wealth. Employees generally desire some compensation that is not monetary in nature but that satisfies the higher-order social needs of humans. For example, workers and managers are typically more productive in environments in which they

Rewards for performance do not always have to be monetary. Sometimes, tokens of appreciation convey an equally satisfying acknowledgment for a job performed well.

[10]Jac Fitz-Enz, "Measuring Team Effectiveness," *HR Focus* (August 1997), p. 55.

believe their efforts are appreciated. Simple gestures such as compliments and small awards can be used by superiors to formally recognize contributions of subordinates. Allowing subordinates to participate in decisions affecting their own welfare and the welfare of the firm also contributes to making employment socially fulfilling. Such efforts provide assurance to employees that they are serving a productive role in the firm and that superiors are attentive to and appreciative of employee contributions.

The following News Note indicates that Chinese managers are often motivated by factors that differ from their Western counterparts. The News Note illustrates well the concept that the greatest benefit is created when the form of pay motivates employees to perform.

Compensation Differentials

A debate in the financial press involves perceptions that the disparity between the pay of ordinary workers and the pay of top managers is too large. Plato argued that no one should earn more than five times the pay earned by the lowest-paid worker. In the early 1900s, J. P. Morgan took the position that the differential should be no more than twenty times. In general, neither Plato's nor Morgan's compensation relationships have held true in the United States, where CEOs' compensation relative to that of lower-level employees has well exceeded those limits. The News Note "Who Says What's Fair?" indicates that the debate is alive today.

Salary differentials between workers and CEOs are often created by a self-fulfilling prophecy on the part of the board of directors. It is a common practice for a company's board of directors to survey a group of similar organizations to determine the average compensation for an executive. If the company's executive appears to be underpaid, the board will increase his or her compensation. Thus, the next time the survey is performed, the average will be increased—regardless of managerial performance. Such indiscreet consumption of organizational resources can cause common stock prices to decline and can undermine the stockholder-value maximization goal.

NEWS NOTE

Keep the Cash; Just Give Me a Home

By most measures Liang Yong is doing well. He joined a Chinese joint-venture affiliate of Hoechst AG in 1983, shortly after graduating from Beijing Normal University, and worked his way up to head of the German chemical company's animal-health division in China. Now 46 years old, he is Hoechst's most senior local manager in the country. He has a car, a mobile phone, and five weeks of vacation.

Still, things could be better. Mr. Liang, his wife, and teenage son squeeze into a small rented apartment in Beijing. He would love to buy his own home, but Beijing housing costs are steep. A new 1,000-square-foot apartment could easily cost the equivalent of $90,000 to $100,000, and mortgage loans are hard to obtain in a banking system designed to finance state-owned factories rather than consumer dreams. "I'm really thinking day and night of buying an apartment," sighs Mr. Liang.

Hoechst, it turns out, is working on a plan to help him and other prized managers do just that, says Jurgen Bauerle, chairman of the company's China division.

Like many other multinationals operating in China, Hoechst sees generous compensation packages, including housing benefits, as essential for attracting and retaining executives.

SOURCE: Bob Hagerty, "Executive Pay (A Special Report); Asian Scramble: Multinationals in China Hope Lucrative Compensation Packages Can Attract the Local Executives They Desperately Need," *Wall Street Journal*, April 10, 1997, p. R12. Reprinted by permission of *Wall Street Journal*, © 1997 Dow Jones & Company, Inc. All Rights Reserved Worldwide.

NEWS NOTE

Who Says What's Fair?

General Electric Co. Chairman John F. Welch fended off criticisms of his compensation at the company's annual meeting here and emphasized how a massive and widely publicized quality program at GE is getting results.

A few stockholders, including some representing unions, argued that Mr. Welch's pay is too high in relation to that of "front-line union workers," who they estimated make about $33,000 annually. Last year Mr. Welch's salary and bonus were $6.3 million. The executive also received a $15.1 million payment under a three-year performance compensation plan.

"Sure, I'm one of the fat cats," Mr. Welch said. "In fact, I'm the fattest cat [at GE], because I'm lucky enough to have this job." But he said GE has broadened its stock-option plan to cover far more employees than in the past.

"It isn't a question of ratios" between the highest and lowest paid, Mr. Welch argued at the meeting. "It's a question of the market. If an executive is offered more by another company, he may leave GE."

SOURCE: William M. Carley, "GE Chairman Defends Pay, Stresses Quality; 'I'm One of Fat Cats,' Welch Says at Meeting; Stock Split Approved," *Wall Street Journal*, April 24, 1997, p. A4. Reprinted by permission of *Wall Street Journal*, © 1997 Dow Jones & Company, Inc. All Rights Reserved Worldwide.

http:// www.ge.com

Care must also be taken that a company's compensation strategy does not result in suppressing creativity, innovation, risk taking, and proactive assumption and conduct of job responsibilities. If monetary rewards can be withheld when failure occurs, employees who are otherwise industrious and cooperative might avoid taking actions or making proposals that could fail. Fear of failure can be reduced if management creates an atmosphere of employee empowerment in which failure is accepted as part of the progression toward continuous improvement.

Organizational compensation packages must be developed that blend organizational goals with monetary and nonmonetary employee rewards. Only if there is a perception of equity across the contributions and entitlements of labor, management, and capital will the organization be capable of achieving the efficiency to compete in global markets.

GLOBAL COMPENSATION

With international operations increasing, plans that compensate expatriate employees and managers on a fair and equitable basis must be developed. **Expatriates** are parent-company and third-country nationals assigned to a foreign subsidiary or foreign nationals assigned to the parent company. Placing employees in foreign countries requires careful consideration of compensation. What is thought to be a fair and reasonable compensation package in one setting may not be fair and reasonable in another.

Expatriates' compensation packages must reflect labor market factors, cost-of-living considerations, and currency fluctuations, as well as tax consequences. Since expatriates have a variety of financial requirements, these individuals may be paid in the currency of the country where they have been relocated, or in their home currency, or a combination of both. An expatriate's base salary and fringe benefits should typically reflect what he or she would have been paid domestically. This base should then be adjusted for reasonable cost-of-living factors. These factors may be

expatriate

LEARNING OBJECTIVE ⑧
How do expatriate reward systems differ from those for domestic operations?

When employees go to other countries to live and work, their compensation needs to reflect life-style differences. For instance, the street vendors and outdoor cafes in Switzerland are moderately priced alternatives to the stores and restaurants in metropolitan U.S. cities.

http:// www.towersperrin.com

obvious, such as needs similar to those that would have been obtained in the home country (transportation, shelter, clothing, and food), or the need to be compensated for a spouse's loss of employment; or they may be less apparent, such as a need to hire someone in the home country to care for young children or to manage an investment portfolio.

Price-level adjustment clauses are often included in the compensation arrangement to mitigate any local currency inflation or deflation. Regardless of the currency makeup of the pay package, the fringe benefit portion related to retirement must be tied to the home country and should be paid in that currency. These adjustments can be very expensive. For example, Douglas R. Stanton, a Hong Kong–based partner for the consulting firm Towers Perrin Inc., says he knows of one company whose expatriate general manager collects compensation equal to a quarter of the firm's revenue in China.[11]

Income taxes are important in expatriates' compensation packages because such individuals may be required to pay taxes in the local country, the home country, or both. Some countries, such as the United States and Great Britain, exempt expatriates from taxation on a specified amount of income earned in a foreign country. If a tax treaty exists and local taxes are paid on the balance of the nonexempt income of an expatriate, those taxes may be credited against the expatriate's home-nation income taxes.

In conclusion, tying the compensation system to performance measurement is essential because everyone in business recognizes that what gets measured and rewarded is what gets accomplished. Businesses must focus their reward structures to motivate employees to succeed at all activities that will create shareholder and personal value. In this highly competitive age, the new paradigm of success is to provide high-quality products and services at a reasonable price while generating a reasonable profit margin.

---

[11]Bob Hagerty, "Executive Pay (A Special Report); Asian Scramble: Multinationals in China Hope Lucrative Compensation Packages Can Attract the Local Executives They Desperately Need," *Wall Street Journal*, April 10, 1997, p. R12.

SITE ANALYSIS

Harnischfeger Industries

Harnischfeger Industries has succeeded in harnessing the energy of its employees through its new focus on EVA. The company's recent success is impressive. The ultimate investor performance measure, stock price, has increased from about $14 in 1993 to around $40 in 1997. The stock price increase has been driven by EVA performance, which increased from $(126) million in 1993 to $49 million in 1997. At Harnischfeger, after-tax profits in excess of 12 percent of capital generate positive economic value for shareholders.

Harnischfeger was one of the first U.S. companies to adopt the EVA performance measure. Leading the charge in 1993 was the company's new chairman, Jeffery Grade. In taking the reins of the company, Mr. Grade worked diligently to develop a higher level of financial discipline in corporate management. The introduction of EVA played a large role in establishing greater discipline in managing capital. At the time EVA was introduced in 1993, a five-year plan was established to generate positive EVA by 1998. However, the company turnaround was so swift that positive EVA was generated by 1996—two years ahead of schedule.

Now, Harnischfeger uses EVA to evaluate all acquisitions. It helps answer questions such as: What level of profitability does this provide? What synergy does this give us? What is the cost of capital? When the answers don't suggest positive EVA, the acquisitions have not been made.

Most employees aren't involved on a daily basis with assessing the possibility of an acquisition. They do, however, have the ability to identify better, quicker, or more cost-effective ways to perform their work and create positive EVA. With employees focused on performance, the good results lead to good rewards. For the company's U.S. employees, the EVA profit-sharing program has produced cash bonuses.

EVA puts the shareholders' interest in the front. By managing toward positive EVA, the company has improved margins, better managed assets, and grown its businesses. And, as EVA improves, greater shareholder value at the company is created, as indicated by close correlation between the two: as EVA improves, stock value tends to increase.

When asked whether Harnischfeger could be successful without EVA, Fran Corbin, vice president of Finance and Administration, responded, "Yes, but it would be much, much harder."

SOURCE: http://www.harnischfeger.com; accessed July 6, 1998.

CROSS-FUNCTIONAL APPLICATIONS

TOPIC OF NOTE	DISCIPLINE	CROSS-FUNCTIONAL APPLICATIONS
Financial Performance Measurements (FPMs)	Financial Management	FPMs such as return on investment (ROI), return on assets (ROA), residual income (RI), and economic value added (EVA) establish performance expectations and guide investment decisions. Creditors and investors evaluate firms in terms of stock prices, income generation, cash flows, and dividend payouts. FPMs give financial managers a relatively standardized benchmark to compare alternative investment opportunities and to examine such opportunities from the perspective of creditors and investors.

CROSS-FUNCTIONAL APPLICATIONS

TOPIC OF NOTE	DISCIPLINE	CROSS-FUNCTIONAL APPLICATIONS
Financial Performance Measurements (FPMs) *(continued)*	Management	Senior level managers use FPMs to measure performance of investment centers. The performance of operating managers, and the rewards provided to them, are linked to FPMs such as ROI, RI, and EVA. Increasingly, the use of FPMs is complemented by selected nonfinancial performance measures to assess other dimensions of performance such as quality, customer service, and safety.
	Labor and Industrial Relations	In some large multinational firms, union leaders hold positions on boards of directors. Union leaders want to be assured that union members receive an appropriate share of the financial benefits that are generated by corporate operations. Many unionized firms have negotiated labor agreements with unions to tie pension fund contributions or profit-sharing provisions to FPMs.
	Financial Analysis	Financial analysts, inside and outside the firm, can provide valuable insights about the financial health of a company by comparing the FPMs of a firm to those of firms in the same industry or to industrial averages. These comparisons may expose problems and opportunities that require further research by management. Sometimes firms use different accounting methods, and these differences can make comparisons more difficult for analysts.
	Research and Development (R&D)	The evaluation of R&D managers must be based on FPMs that are long-term oriented. For example, net present value (NPV) and internal rate of return (IRR) are appropriate measures because they are capable of capturing the multiple-period costs and benefits of R&D projects.
Nonfinancial Performance Measurements (NFPMs)	Sales Management	NFPMs provide sales managers with standards and objectives necessary to coordinate their contributions to the overall corporate strategic plan. Exceptional salespeople are often defined in terms of narrow departmental objectives such as recruitment of new business or achievement of sales quotas. Rewards are provided to salespeople based on the achieved level of performance.
	Production/Operations Management	Production managers' decisions concerning quality, delivery time, machine usage, inventory holdings, and scrap and waste management are often guided by NFPMs.
	Economics	Economists regularly incorporate NFPMs in both macro- and microeconomic modeling. For example, in 1997 a blue ribbon advisory commission appointed by President Clinton recommended a downward adjustment to the consumer price index (CPI) because of the improved quality, durability, and multi-functionality of new products available to the consumer. This recommendation resulted in a reduction in the cost of living adjustment in pension contracts and transfer payments.

CROSS-FUNCTIONAL APPLICATIONS

TOPIC OF NOTE	DISCIPLINE	CROSS-FUNCTIONAL APPLICATIONS
Nonfinancial Performance Measurements (NFPMs) (continued)	Human Resource Management (HR)	HR managers are guided by NFPMs in decisions concerning the training, evaluation, and motivation of employees. While individual departments set technical standards for employment decisions, HR is responsible for meeting external legal standards and internal ethical standards in such decisions.
		There are many demographic dimensions to diversity: age, gender, race, geographic location, educational level, and income level. Each of these demographic factors can affect the demand for existing and potential products. Having a diverse employee base allows a firm to develop better strategies for marketing consumer products to markets with a specific demographic profile by using such approaches as market segmentation, product differentiation, custom packaging, and targeted promotion.
		Recently, legal issues and social responsibilities have dominated use of HR resources for other purposes, such as screening and promotion decisions. For example, maintaining compliance with affirmative action rules and other nondiscrimination provisions has been a heavy burden for HR departments.
	Service Operations	NFPMs enhance financial performance measurements in applying concepts of responsibility accounting. To illustrate the use of NFPMs in a service organization, consider their use in a typical university. NFPMs for faculty include new program development, contributions to research and teaching, and service to the community.
	Labor and Industrial Relations	Management's negotiations with labor unions often pivot on nonfinancial performance dimensions such as a ratio of employees to machines, safety, and quality of employee performance. In a manufacturing setting, machine output may be dictated by a labor agreement rather than the technical capacity of the machine.
	Management	Programs of state and federal governments to increase diversity in employment throughout the economy have led to new considerations in managers' hiring decisions. For example, welfare reforms and targeted job tax credits have created a financial incentive for managers to hire from minority groups.

CHAPTER SUMMARY

Performance measures should assess progress toward goals and objectives and should be accepted by those being evaluated. Using multiple measures of the firm's critical success factors is more effective than using a single performance measure. Divisional profits and cash flow are frequently used financial performance measures.

Two other significant financial measures of performance are return on investment and residual income. Return on investment is computed as segment margin, or net income, divided by invested assets. Residual income is the amount of segment margin, or net income, in excess of an amount calculated by use of a preestablished "interest charge" on the asset base. Both ROI and RI provide important information about the efficiency and effectiveness of managers. Neither should be used alone, however, and their inherent limitations, including the fact that they can be manipulated because of their basis in accounting, should be considered.

One of the most popular, evolving performance measures is economic value added (EVA). EVA is superior to other short-term financial performance measures because of its close linkage to stockholders' interests. EVA is measured as the difference between net income for a period and the dollar cost of invested capital for a period.

Financial measures can be effectively coupled with nonfinancial measures to provide a more complete and useful picture of performance. One useful nonfinancial measure is throughput—the nondefective goods or services started, finished, and sold by an organization during a period. When throughput is increased, the company goal of making money is enhanced. Various quality measures have also gained prominence as companies begin to compete more heavily in the global marketplace. These measures focus on activities that add value for the customer.

Performance measures may be more difficult to establish for multinational units than for domestic units because of differences in taxes, tariffs, currency exchange rates, and transfer restrictions. Because of such differences, top management may wish to consider extending the use of qualitative performance measures.

Customarily, compensation systems have often been based solely on individual performance and short-run financial results. Because of operational changes and shifts in managerial philosophies, performance measurements and their related rewards now encompass group success, nonfinancial performance attributes, and long-run considerations. Companies also need to recognize that some top managers' compensation grossly exceeds pay to ordinary workers. Such excesses can be counterproductive, causing a demoralizing effect within the firm, and ultimately, failure to maximize long-term stockholder wealth. Thus, it is important that the compensation strategy and system are in harmony with the performance measurement system and that together they serve to assure fairness, effectiveness, and efficiency in an organization.

KEY TERMS

Asset turnover (p. 694)
Compensation strategy (p. 707)
Du Pont model (p. 694)
Economic value added (EVA) (p. 698)
Expatriate (p. 713)
Nonfinancial performance measure (NFPM) (p. 700)

Process productivity (p. 703)
Process quality yield (p. 703)
Profit margin (p. 694)
Residual income (RI) (p. 697)
Return on investment (ROI) (p. 694)
Synchronous management (p. 703)

SOLUTION STRATEGIES

Performance Measurements for Responsibility Centers
- ⊙ Profit Center

    Budgeted divisional profits
- − Actual divisional profits
- = Variances (consider materiality)

Cash inflows
− Cash outflows
= Net cash flow (adequate for operations?)
⊙ Investment Center
Budgeted investment center profits
− Actual investment center profits
= Variances (consider materiality)

Cash inflows
− Cash outflows
= Net cash flow (adequate for operations?)

Return on Investment = Income ÷ Assets Invested (high enough rate?)

Du Pont model:
ROI = Profit Margin × Asset Turnover
    = (Income ÷ Sales) × (Sales ÷ Assets)
        (high enough rate?)

RI = Income − (Target Rate × Asset Base)

or

RI = Asset Base × (ROI − Target Rate)
    (positive or negative? high enough amount?)

EVA = After-tax Income − (Cost of Capital % × Capital Invested)
    (positive or negative? high enough amount?)

Measuring Throughput

$$\text{Throughput} = \frac{\text{Manufacturing}}{\text{Cycle Efficiency}} \times \frac{\text{Process}}{\text{Productivity}} \times \frac{\text{Process}}{\text{Quality Yield}}$$

or

$$\frac{\text{Good Units}}{\text{Total Time}} = \frac{\text{Value-Added Processing Time}}{\text{Total Time}} \times \frac{\text{Total Units}}{\text{Value-Added Processing Time}} \times \frac{\text{Good Units}}{\text{Total Units}}$$

Designing a Reward System

It is impossible to design a generic incentive model that would be effective across a variety of firms. However, affirmative answers to the following questions provide guidance as to the applicability of a proposed incentive and reward plan for a particular organization.

1. Will the organizational and subunit objectives be achieved if the proposed compensation structure is implemented?

2. Is the proposed structure consistent with the organizational design, culture, and management philosophy?

3. Are there reasonable and objective performance measures that are good surrogates for the organizational objectives?

4. Are factors beyond employee/group control minimized under the performance measures of the proposed compensation structure?

5. Are there minimal opportunities for employees to manipulate the performance measurements tied to the proposed compensation structure?

6. In light of the interests of managers, workers, and stockholders, is the proposed reward structure fair and does it encourage and promote ethical behavior?

7. Is the proposed reward structure arranged to take advantage of potential employee/employer tax benefits?

8. Does the proposed reward structure promote harmony between employee groups?

9. Is there an adequate balance between group and individual incentives?

DEMONSTRATION PROBLEM

Meltzer Wholesaling sells a broad line of clothing goods to specialty retail and department stores. For last year, the company's Canadian Division had the following performance targets:

Asset turnover	1.8
Profit margin	8%
Target rate of return on investments for EVA, RI	10%
Income tax rate	25%

Actual information concerning the performance of the Canadian Division for last year follows:

Total assets at beginning of year	$ 4,800,000
Total assets at end of year	7,200,000
Total invested capital (annual average)	11,000,000
Sales	12,000,000
Variable operating costs	5,000,000
Direct fixed costs	6,280,000
Allocated common costs	800,000

Requirements:

1. For the Canadian Division of Meltzer Wholesaling, compute the segment margin and average assets for the year.
2. Based on segment income and average assets, compute the actual profit margin, asset turnover, and ROI.
3. Evaluate the ROI performance of the Canadian Division.
4. Using your answers from question 2, compute Canadian Division's residual income using segment margin.
5. Compute the EVA of the Canadian Division using net income. Why are EVA and RI levels different?
6. Based on the data given in the problem, discuss why ROI, EVA and RI may be inappropriate measures of performance for Canadian Division.

Solution to Demonstration Problem

1.

Sales	$12,000,000
Variable costs	(5,000,000)
Direct fixed costs	(6,280,000)
Segment margin	$ 720,000

Average assets = ($4,800,000 + $7,200,000) ÷ 2 = $ 6,000,000

2. Profit margin = $\dfrac{\$\ 720,000}{\$12,000,000}$ = 6%

   Asset turnover = $\dfrac{\$12,000,000}{\$\ 6,000,000}$ = 2

   ROI = 6% × 2 = 12%

3. The target ROI for the division was 8% × 1.8 = 14.4%. The division generated a ROI of only 12 percent. Thus, the division did not achieve its target rate of return. The poor performance resulted from the division's failure to achieve the target profit margin. Even though the asset turnover target was exceeded, the ROI fell below the target level because the profit margin was 2% below its target level.

4. RI = $720,000 - (.10 \times \$6,000,000)$
   = $720,000 - \$600,000 = \underline{\$120,000}$

5. After-tax income = Segment margin − taxes
   = $720,000 - (\$720,000 \times .25) = \$540,000$

   EVA = $540,000 - (.10 \times \$11,000,000) = \underline{\$(560,000)}$

   EVA and RI differ for two reasons. First, RI is based on segment margin, rather than after-tax, income; second, RI is based on the book value of investment while EVA is based on the market value of investment.

6. As discussed in the chapter, ROI, RI, and EVA are measures of short-term performance. These measures may be particularly inappropriate for divisions that have long-term missions, such as growth. In this case, the relatively large growth in assets of Canadian Division from the beginning to the end of the period may indicate that this division is oriented to growth. If so, the ROI and RI measures will provide an incentive contrary to the growth mission.

END-OF-CHAPTER MATERIALS

⊙ QUESTIONS

1. What basic rules should be observed in selecting benchmarks for evaluating managers' performance?

2. Should performance measures be financial, nonfinancial, or both? Justify your answer.

3. What is the message conveyed by the phrase "managers devote their attention to activities that get measured"?

4. How can feedback, both positive and negative, be used to improve managerial performance?

5. Why must the process of designing performance measures take into account the possibility of manipulation?

6. What are the two primary financial requirements for the success of a profit or investment center? Why are these important?

7. What is the major difference between a profit center and an investment center? How does this difference create a need for different financial performance measures in these two types of centers?

8. Discuss the most appropriate definition of the term "assets invested" in computing return on investment.

9. What is the Du Pont model? What are its component ratios and how are they calculated?

10. What is residual income and how is it used to measure divisional performance? How is it similar to and different from the return on investment measure?

11. Describe the circumstances in which use of ROI would likely create a suboptimization problem. Under what circumstances would use of this measure be less likely to create a suboptimization problem?

12. How is economic value added computed? Why is the measure potentially superior to residual income?

13. Modular Office Systems manufactures movable partitions for commercial offices. Recently, the company has become much more concerned about reducing the number of flaws in its completed products. Identify some performance measures that the company could use to monitor the effectiveness of its efforts to improve product quality.

14. What is captured by a throughput measure? Why is throughput defined on the basis of goods sold rather than goods produced?

15. Why is prevention the only value-added cost of quality category?

16. How can activity-based costing concepts be used in designing performance measures?

17. Why is the design of performance measures a more complex task in multinational companies than in single-country operations?

18. To be effective, why must firms link the compensation system to the performance measurement structure?

19. Why is it desirable to have chief executives (as well as other managers) own stock in their companies?

20. What special considerations bear on designing pay plans for expatriates?

⊙ EXERCISES

21. *(Terminology)* Match the definitions on the right with the terms on the left. Definitions may be used more than once or not at all.

    a. Throughput
    b. Economic value added
    c. Synchronous management
    d. Residual income
    e. Compensation strategy
    f. Expatriate
    g. Du Pont model
    h. Asset turnover
    i. Profit margin
    j. Process quality yield

    1. A parent-company worker in a foreign subsidiary
    2. A measure of asset productivity
    3. A method of computing ROI as the product of two separate ratios
    4. All endeavors that help an organization achieve its goal
    5. After-tax profits minus a charge for cost of invested capital
    6. Profits that exceed a normal return on assets
    7. A ratio of income to sales
    8. A ratio of good units to total units
    9. A plan for determining the role of compensation in an organization
    10. The total good output completed and sold within an operating period

22. *(ROI)* Johnson Wholesale Supply is comprised of three autonomous divisions. Data for each division for the year 1999 follow:

DIVISION	1	2	3
Segment income	$20,000	$ 225,000	$ 150,000
Asset investment	80,000	1,500,000	1,500,000

Compute the return on investment in each division.

23. *(ROI)* The managers of Hong Kong Industries are evaluating use of ROI to measure performance. The managers have gathered the following information for their most recent operating period.

Average assets invested	$ 3,600,000
Revenues	14,400,000
Expenses	13,004,000

    a. Calculate profit margin.
    b. Calculate asset turnover.
    c. Calculate return on investment using your answers to Parts a and b.

24. *(ROI)* For the most recent fiscal year, the Pullman Division of Modern Luggage generated an asset turnover ratio of 5 and a profit margin (as measured by the segment margin) ratio of 4 percent on sales of $4,000,000. Compute:
   a. Average assets employed by Pullman Division
   b. Segment margin
   c. ROI

25. *(ROI)* Your managerial accounting class has been assigned a case, but the teacher has provided only partial information. You have been told that a division of a company has an ROI of 12.5 percent, average total assets of $3,400,000, and total direct expenses of $1,275,000. You have been asked to do the following:
   a. Determine segment income.
   b. Determine total revenues.
   c. Determine asset turnover.
   d. Determine profit margin.
   e. Prove that ROI is 12.5 percent from the amounts calculated in Parts a to d.

26. *(ROI, RI)* East L.A. Law, Inc., has a target rate of return of 14 percent for its Criminal Law Division. For 1998, the Criminal Law Division generated gross fees of $10,000,000 on average assets of $5,000,000. The Criminal Law Division's variable costs were 35 percent of sales and fixed costs were $3,750,000. For 1998, compute the Division's
   a. Residual income
   b. Profit margin
   c. Asset turnover
   d. Return on investment

27. *(RI)* North and South Divisions of Western Financial Corp. reported the following data for 1999 (in thousands):

	NORTH DIVISION	SOUTH DIVISION
Segment income	$ 30,000	$ 68,000
Investment	180,000	290,000

   a. Assuming the firm charges each division 12 percent of the capital invested, determine the residual income for each division.
   b. Based on the preceding information, which division is more successful? Explain.

28. *(RI)* Tennessee Chemical is comprised of two divisions. Following is some financial information about each of these divisions.

	INDUSTRIAL PRODUCTS	CONSUMER PRODUCTS
Sales	$4,800,000	$ 8,400,000
Total variable cost	1,200,000	5,460,000
Total fixed cost	2,800,000	1,250,000
Average assets invested	4,000,000	10,000,000

   a. What is each division's residual income if the company has established a 14 percent target rate of return on invested assets?
   b. Which division is more successful? Explain.
   c. What would be each division's residual income if its sales increased by 10 percent and no other changes occurred? Which division would be more successful if such a sales change occurred? Explain.
   d. Explain why the answers to Parts b and c differed or did not differ.

29. *(EVA)* Chancellor Environmental Services Co. relies on the EVA measure to evaluate the performance of certain segment managers. The target rate of return on invested capital for all segments is 16 percent. One subsidiary, Water Systems, generated after-tax income of $1,800,000 for the year just ended. For the same period, the invested capital in the subsidiary was $12,000,000. Compute the EVA of Water Systems.

30. *(EVA)* Stealth Technology Corporation has a required rate of return of 12 percent on invested capital. The firm's Laser Division generated an EVA of $4,000,000 last year. The amount of capital invested in Laser Division is $38,000,000.
   a. How much after-tax income was generated by Laser Division last year?
   b. As the controller of Stealth Technology Corporation, how could you determine the level of capital investment for a particular division?

31. *(EVA; suboptimization; nonfinancial performance evaluation)* Mary Jenks is a division manager of Carolina Pneumatic. She is presently evaluating a potential new investment that has the following characteristics:

Capital investment required	$8,000,000
Net annual increase in after-tax divisional income:	
Year 1	800,000
Year 2	800,000
Year 3	1,160,000
Year 4	2,900,000
Year 5	2,700,000

Ms. Jenks is evaluated and compensated based on the amount of EVA her division generates. More precisely, she receives an annual salary of $350,000 plus a bonus equal to 12 percent of divisional EVA. Carolina Pneumatic has a required rate of return of 13 percent.
   a. Compute the effect of the new investment on the level of divisional EVA for years 1 through 5.
   b. Determine the effect of the new project on Ms. Jenks's compensation for each of the five years.
   c. Based on your computations in Part b, will Ms. Jenks want to invest in the new project? Explain.
   d. As the CEO of Carolina Pneumatic, would you prefer that Ms. Jenks would or would not invest in the project?
   e. What nonfinancial performance measures could be used to supplement EVA as a performance measure that would serve to make Ms. Jenks more long-term oriented?

32. *(Throughput)* The Milwaukee Wave is a chain of microbreweries. The company evaluates its store managers on the basis of both financial and nonfinancial performance measures. One of the nonfinancial measures used is throughput. The following data pertain to the company's store in Atlanta. The unit of measurement is gallons.

Units started into production	360,000
Total good units completed	270,000
Total hours of value-added processing time	180,000
Total hours	240,000

   a. What was the manufacturing cycle efficiency?
   b. What was the process productivity of the store?
   c. What was the process quality yield of the store?
   d. What was the total throughput per hour?
   e. As the production manager of the Milwaukee Wave, how could you use the information on the component ratios of throughput to increase performance?

33. *(Nonfinancial performance measures)* For each of the following nonfinancial performance measures, indicate whether the measure captures performance in terms of quality (Q), customer service(CS), resource management (RM), or flexibility (F) and discuss the rationale for your answer.
   a. First-time-through rejection rate
   b. Percent on-time shipments
   c. Manufacturing cycle time
   d. Percent good output

e. Percent of units meeting design tolerance

f. Output per labor dollar

g. Number of crisis calls

h. Changeover time

i. Machine downtime

j. Supplier rejects

34. *(Financial and nonfinancial performance measures)* For the past three years, the highest divisional ROI within Lumar Corporation has been generated by the Winch Division, a very high-tech manufacturing division. The segment income and ROI for each year appear below. Lumar Corporation has specified a growth mission for Winch Division.

	1998	1999	2000
Segment income ($000)	$200,000	$195,000	$193,500
ROI	20%	23%	27%

a. Why do you think Winch Division has been so successful as measured by its ROI?

b. As controller of Lumar Corporation, what change or changes would you recommend to control the continued escalation in the ROI?

c. Assume that Lumar Division operates in a very competitive industry and its strategy is based on maintaining market share by delivering the best customer service in the industry. What nonfinancial performance measures could be used to capture Lumar's performance?

35. *(ROI)* Explain how each of the following items will affect the asset turnover ratio of a corporate division if asset amounts are determined by their net book values.

a. A new labor contract is negotiated that reduces labor costs by 10 percent.

b. Unused assets are carried on the books. These assets could be sold.

c. Obsolete inventory is carried on the books.

d. Uncollectible accounts receivable are carried on the books.

e. The rate of depreciation on plant and equipment is increased.

f. Fixed costs allocated to the division drop by 4 percent.

36. *(Defining performance measures)* The Institute of Management Accountants issued Statement on Management Accounting 4D, "Measuring Entity Performance," to help management accountants deal with the issues associated with measuring entity performance. Managers can use these measures to evaluate their own performance or the performance of subordinates, to identify and correct problems, and to discover opportunities. To assist management in measuring achievement, a number of performance measures are available. To present a more complete picture of performance, it is strongly recommended that several of these performance measures be utilized and that they be combined with nonfinancial measures such as market share, new product development, and human resource utilization. Five commonly used performance measures that are derived from the traditional historical accounting system are:

⊙ Gross profit margin (percentage)

⊙ Cash flows

⊙ Return on the investment in assets

⊙ Residual income

⊙ Total asset turnover

For each of the five performance measures just identified,

a. Describe how the measure is calculated.

b. Describe the information provided by the measure.

c. Explain the limitations of this information.

(CMA)

37. *(Delivering performance feedback)* Managers must be able to deliver both positive and negative feedback to employees. The method of delivering such feedback is often as important as the message in terms of its impact on the affected employee. Discuss

how, as a manager, you would deliver critical comments to an employee whose performance is unsatisfactory. How would you deliver feedback to an employee whose performance is superlative?

⊙ PROBLEMS

38. *(Divisional profit; nonfinancial performance measures)* Pueblo Division of the Southwest Fabrics Co. produces and markets floor covering products to wholesalers in Texas, New Mexico, Arizona, and California. The manager of Pueblo is Kara Forrester. Southwest Fabrics evaluates all of its division managers on the basis of a comparison of budgeted profit to actual profit achieved. The profit measure used is pre-tax income. For 1999, the budgeted income for Pueblo was as follows:

Sales	$12,000,000
Variable costs	(8,400,000)
Contribution margin	$ 3,600,000
Fixed costs	(2,400,000)
Segment income	$ 1,200,000

At the end of 1999, the actual results for Pueblo Division were determined. Those results follow.

Sales	$13,000,000
Variable costs	(9,750,000)
Contribution margin	$ 3,250,000
Fixed costs	(2,410,000)
Segment income	$ 840,000

a. Assume that you are the controller of Southwest Fabrics. Based on the preceding information, evaluate the performance of the Pueblo Division. What was the principal reason for the poor profit performance?

b. Explain how complete income statements provide a better basis to evaluate the profit performance of a manager than mere comparisons of the bottom lines of the budgeted and actual income statements.

c. Given your answer to Part a, describe some nonfinancial performance measures that could be used by the manager of the Pueblo Division in a strategy to improve divisional profit performance in the next year.

39. *(ROI)* Complete Solutions Inc. manufactures various production equipment. Corporate management has examined industry-level data and determined the following industry norms for producers of material handling systems:

Asset turnover   1.6 times
Profit margin   8%

The actual 1999 results for the company's Material Handling Division are summarized below:

Total assets at year end 1998	$ 9,600,000
Total assets at year end 1999	12,800,000
Sales	13,440,000
Operating expenses	12,499,200

a. For 1999, how did the Material Handling Division perform relative to industry norms?

b. As the divisional manager of Material Handling, how would you use the comparison in Part a to improve performance in the division?

40. *(ROI)* Johnson, First Star, and Nolan Bay are three companies that operate in the retail clothing industry. Some information on each of these companies for 1999 follows:

	JOHNSON	FIRST STAR	NOLAN BAY
Average total assets	$ 6,300,000	$ 5,400,000	$ 7,200,000
Revenues	12,600,000	16,200,000	14,400,000
Expenses	11,340,000	15,228,000	12,420,000

a. For each company, calculate profit margin, asset turnover, and return on investment.

b. As an investment analyst you are going to recommend that stock in one of these companies be purchased by your clients. Which of these companies would you recommend? Why?

c. Do the ratios indicate how any of the companies could improve their performance? How?

41. *(ROI)* The 1999 income statement for the Odessa Division of Industrial Services Corp. follows:

Sales	$3,200,000
Variable expenses	(1,600,000)
Contribution margin	$1,600,000
Fixed expenses	(800,000)
Segment income	$ 800,000

   Assets at the beginning of 1999 for Odessa Division were $3,600,000. Because of various capital investments during the year, the division ended 1999 with $4,400,000 of assets. Overall, Industrial Services Corp. experienced a 15 percent return on investment for 1999. It is company policy to award year-end bonuses to the managers whose divisions show the highest ROIs.

   The chief operating officer of Odessa is investigating a new product line for the division. The new line is expected to show the following approximate annual results: sales, $400,000; variable expenses, $200,000; and fixed expenses, $100,000. The product line would require a $620,000 average first-year investment in plant assets.

a. What was Odessa's 1999 ROI?

b. What is the expected ROI on the new product line?

c. If Odessa had invested in the new product line in 1999 and the expected results had occurred, what would have been the division's ROI?

d. Is the Odessa Division manager likely to want to add the new product line? Would the president of Industrial Services Corp. want Odessa to add the new product line? Discuss the rationale of each of the individuals.

42. *(ROI)* The numbers (1–9) in the following table identify missing data for three divisions of Big Creek Industries.

	PACKAGE DIVISION	TRANSPORT DIVISION	STORAGE DIVISION
Sales	$2,000,000	$16,000,000	$8,000,000
Segment income	$400,000	(4)	$1,000,000
Profit margin	(1)	15%	(7)
Asset turnover	(2)	1.4	(8)
Average assets	(3)	(5)	$4,000,000
Return on investment	10%	(6)	(9)

a. Determine the values for each of the missing items.

b. Identify the area where each division's performance is weakest and strongest relative to the other divisions.

43. *(ROI; RI)* Stolzer Wholesaling sells a broad line of clothing to specialty retail and department stores. For 1999, the company's Canadian Division had the following performance targets:

Asset turnover	1.5 times
Profit margin	8%

Actual information concerning the performance of the Canadian Division in 1999 follows:

Total assets at year-end 1998	$2,400,000
Total assets at year-end 1999	3,600,000
Sales for 1999	6,000,000
Operating expenses for 1999	5,640,000

a. For 1999, what was the Canadian Division's target objective for ROI? Show calculations.

b. For 1999, did the Canadian Division achieve its target objectives for ROI, asset turnover, and profit margin?

c. Where, as indicated by the performance measures, are the areas that are most in need of improved performance?

d. If the company has an overall target return of 13 percent, what was the Canadian Division's residual income for 1999?

44. *(Transaction effects on ROI; RI)* The following are a number of transactions affecting a specific division within a multiple-division company. Indicate whether each described transaction would increase (IN), decrease (D), have no effect (N) on, or have an indeterminate effect (I) on each of the following measures: asset turnover, profit margin, ROI, and RI for the present fiscal year. Each transaction is independent.

a. The division writes down an inventory of obsolete finished goods through the cost of goods sold expense account. The journal entry is:

Cost of Goods Sold	40,000	
Finished Goods Inventory		40,000

b. A special overseas order is accepted. The sales price for this order is well below the normal sales price but is sufficient to cover all costs traceable to this order.

c. A piece of equipment is sold for $70,000. The equipment's original cost was $400,000. At the time of sale, the book value of the equipment was $60,000. The sale of the equipment has no effect on product sales.

d. The division fires its research and development manager. The manager will not be replaced during the current fiscal year.

e. The company raises its target rate of return for this division from 12 percent to 14 percent.

f. At mid-year, the divisional manager decides to increase scheduled annual production by 2,000 units. This decision has no effect on scheduled sales.

g. Also at mid-year, the division manager spends an additional $150,000 on advertising. Sales immediately increase.

h. The divisional manager replaces a labor-intensive operation with machine technology. This action has no effect on sales, but total annual expenses of the operation are expected to decline by 12 percent.

45. *(Decisions based on ROI; RI)* The Canadian Yacht Company evaluates the performance of its two division managers using an ROI formula. For the forthcoming period, divisional estimates of relevant measures are:

	PLEASURE	COMMERCIAL	TOTAL COMPANY
Sales	$12,000,000	$48,000,000	$60,000,000
Expenses	10,800,000	42,000,000	52,800,000
Divisional assets	10,000,000	30,000,000	40,000,000

The managers of both operating divisions have the authority to make decisions regarding new investments. The manager of Pleasure Crafts is contemplating an investment in an additional asset that would generate an ROI of 14 percent, and the manager of Commercial Crafts is considering an investment in an additional asset that would generate an ROI of 18 percent.

a. Compute the projected ROI for each division disregarding the contemplated new investments.

b. Based on your answer in Part a, which of the managers is likely to actually invest in the asset under consideration?

c. Are the outcomes of the investment decisions in Part b likely to be consistent with overall corporate goals? Explain.

d. If the company evaluated the division managers' performances using a residual income measure with a target return of 17 percent, would the outcomes of the investment decisions be different from those described in Part b? Explain.

46. *(Decisions based on EVA)* You are a division manager of Luxwood Design Co. Your performance as a division manager is evaluated primarily on one measure: after-tax divisional segment income less the cost of capital invested in divisional assets. For existing operations in your division, projections for 1999 follow:

Sales	$40,000,000
Expenses	(35,000,000)
Segment income	$ 5,000,000
Taxes	(1,500,000)
After-tax segment income	$ 3,500,000

The invested capital of the division is $25,000,000, the required return on capital is 12 percent, and the tax rate is 30 percent.

At this moment, you are evaluating an investment in a new product line that would, according to your projections, increase 1999 pre-tax segment income by $400,000. The cost of the investment has not yet been determined.

a. Ignoring the new investment, what is your projected EVA for 1999?

b. In light of your answer in Part a, what is the maximum amount that you would be willing to invest in the new product line?

c. Assuming the new product line would require an investment of $1,100,000, what would be the revised projected EVA for your division in 1999 if the investment were made?

47. *(Throughput)* Bangor Spool Co. has historically evaluated divisional performance exclusively on financial measures. Top managers have become increasingly concerned with this approach to performance evaluation and are now actively seeking alternative measures. Specifically, they wish to focus on activities that generate value for customers. One promising measure is throughput. To experiment with the annual throughput measure, management has gathered the following historical information on one of its larger operating divisions:

Units started into production	200,000
Total good units completed	130,000
Total hours of value-added processing time	80,000
Total hours	120,000

a. What is the manufacturing cycle efficiency?

b. What is the process productivity of the division?

c. What is the process quality yield of the division?

d. Based on your answers to Parts a, b, and c, what is the total throughput per hour?

e. Which of the previous measures (Part a, b, or c) reflects the possible existence of a production bottleneck? Why?

f. Which of the previous measures (Part a, b, or c) reflects potentially poor quality in the production process as measured by the number of defective units? Why?

⊙ CASES

48. *(ROI; new investment evaluation)* Raddington Industries produces tool and die machinery for manufacturers. The company expanded vertically in 1995 by acquiring one of its suppliers of alloy steel plates, Reigis Steel Company. In order to manage the two separate businesses, the operations of Reigis are reported separately as an investment center.

Raddington monitors its divisions on the basis of both unit contribution and return on average investment (ROI), with investment defined as average operating assets employed. Management bonuses are determined based on ROI. All investments in operating assets are expected to earn a minimum return of 11 percent before income taxes.

Reigis's cost of goods sold is considered to be entirely variable, while the division's administrative expenses are not dependent on volume. Selling expenses are a mixed cost with 40 percent attributed to sales volume. Reigis's ROI has ranged from 11.8 percent to 14.7 percent since 1995. During the fiscal year ended November 30, 1999, Reigis contemplated a capital acquisition with an estimated ROI of 11.5 percent; however, division management decided that the investment would decrease Reigis's overall ROI.

The 1999 operating statement for Reigis follows. The division's operating assets employed were $15,750,000 at November 30, 1999, a 5 percent increase over the 1998 year-end balance.

REIGIS STEEL DIVISION
OPERATING STATEMENT
FOR THE YEAR ENDED NOVEMBER 30, 1999
($000 OMITTED)

Sales revenue		$25,000
Less expenses		
Cost of goods sold	$16,500	
Administrative expenses	3,955	
Selling expenses	2,700	(23,155)
Operating income before taxes		$ 1,845

a. Calculate the unit contribution for Reigis Steel Division if 1,484,000 units were produced and sold during the year ended November 30, 1999.

b. Calculate the following performance measures for 1999 for the Reigis Steel Division:
   (1) Pretax return on average investment in operating assets employed (ROI)
   (2) Residual income calculated in the basis of average operating assets employed

c. Explain why the management of the Reigis Steel Division would have been more likely to accept the contemplated capital acquisition if residual income rather than ROI was used as a performance measure.

d. The Reigis Steel Division is a separate investment center within Raddington Industries. Identify several items that Reigis should control if it is to be evaluated fairly by either the ROI or residual income performance measure.

(CMA)

49. *(Performance and compensation)* Northstar Offroad Co. (NOC), a subsidiary of Allston Automotive, manufactures go-carts and other recreational vehicles. Family recreational centers that feature go-cart tracks, miniature golf, batting cages, and arcade games have increased in popularity. As a result, NOC has been receiving some pressure from Allston Automotive top management to diversify into some of these other recreational areas. Recreational Leasing Inc. (RLI), one of the largest firms that leases arcade games to family recreation centers, is looking for a friendly buyer. Allston Automotive management believes that RLI's assets could be acquired for an investment of $3.2 million and has strongly urged Bill Grieco, division manager of NOC, to consider acquiring RLI.

Grieco has reviewed RLI's financial statements with his controller, Marie Donnelly, and they believe that the acquisition may not be in NOC's best interests. "If we decide not to do this, the Allston Automotive people are not going to be happy," said Grieco. "If we could convince them to base our bonuses on something other than return on investment, maybe this acquisition would look more attractive. How would we do if the bonuses were based on residual income using the company's 15 percent cost of capital?"

Allston Automotive has traditionally evaluated all of its divisions on the basis of return on investment, which is defined as the ratio of operating income to total assets; the desired rate of return for each division is 20 percent. The management team of any division reporting an annual increase in the return on investment is automatically eligible for a bonus. The management of divisions reporting a decline in the return on investment must provide convincing explanations for the decline to be eligible for a bonus, and this bonus is limited to 50 percent of the average bonus paid to divisions reporting an increase.

Presented below are condensed financial statements for both NOC and RLI for the fiscal year ended May 31, 1999.

	NOC	RLI
Sales revenue	$10,500,000	
Leasing revenue		$2,800,000
Variable expenses	(7,000,000)	(1,000,000)
Fixed expenses	(1,500,000)	(1,200,000)
Operating income	$ 2,000,000	$ 600,000
Current assets	$ 2,300,000	$1,900,000
Long-term assets	5,700,000	1,100,000
Total assets	$ 8,000,000	$3,000,000
Current liabilities	$ 1,400,000	$ 850,000
Long-term liabilities	3,800,000	1,200,000
Shareholders' equity	2,800,000	950,000
Total liabilities and shareholders' equity	$ 8,000,000	$3,000,000

a. Under the present bonus system, how would the acquisition of RLI affect Grieco's bonus expectations?
b. If Grieco's suggestion to use residual income as the evaluation criterion is accepted, how would acquisition of RLI affect Grieco's bonus expectations?
c. Given the present bonus arrangement, is it fair for Allston Automotive management to expect Grieco to acquire RLI?
d. Is the present bonus system consistent with Allston Automotive's goal of expansion of NOC into new recreational products?

(CMA)

50. *(Evaluating cash flow)* Major Currency, the controller of Texoma Meat Products, has become increasingly disillusioned with the company's system of evaluating the performance of profit centers and their managers. The present system focuses on a comparison of budgeted to actual income from operations. Major's concern with the current system is the ease with which the measure *income from operations* can be manipulated by profit center managers. The basic business of Texoma Meat Products consists of purchasing live hogs and cattle, slaughtering the animals, and then selling the various meat products and by-products to regional wholesalers and large retail chains. Most sales are made on credit, and all live animals are purchased for cash. The profit centers consist of geographical segments of Texoma Meat Products, and all profit center segments conduct both production and sales activities within their geographical territories. Following is a typical quarterly income statement for a profit center, which appears in the responsibility report for the profit center:

Sales	$5,000,000
Cost of goods sold	(3,000,000)
Gross profit	$2,000,000
Selling and administrative expenses	(1,500,000)
Income from operations	$ 500,000

Major has suggested to top management that the company replace the accrual income evaluation measure *income from operations* with a measure called *cash flow from operations*. He says that this measure will be less susceptible to manipulation by profit center managers. To defend his position, he compiles a cash flow income statement for the same profit center:

Cash receipts from customers	$4,400,000
Cash payments for production labor, livestock, and overhead	(3,200,000)
Cash payments for selling and administrative activities	(800,000)
Cash flow from operations	$ 400,000

a. If Major is correct about profit center managers' manipulating the income measure, where are manipulations likely taking place?

b. Is the proposed cash flow measure less subject to manipulation than the income measure? Explain.

c. Could manipulation be reduced if both cash flow and income measures were utilized? Explain.

d. Do the cash and income measures reveal different information about profit center performance? Explain.

e. Could the existing income statement be used more effectively in evaluating performance? Explain.

51. *(Performance and compensation)* Gulfland Chemical Corp. is a multinational firm that markets a variety of chemicals for industrial uses. One of the many autonomous divisions is the North America Petro-Chemical Division (NAPCD). The manager of NAPCD, Karyn Kravitz, was recently overheard discussing a vexing problem with her controller, William Michaels. The topic of discussion was whether the division should replace its existing chemical-handling equipment with newer technology that is safer, more efficient, and cheaper to operate.

According to an analysis by Mr. Michaels, the cost savings over the life of the new technology would pay for the initial cost of the technology several times over. However, Ms. Kravitz remained reluctant to invest. Her most fundamental concern involved the disposition of the old processing equipment. Because the existing equipment has been in use for only two years, it has a very high book value relative to its current market value. Ms. Kravitz noted that if the new technology were not purchased, the division would expect a segment income of $4 million for the year. However, if the new technology were purchased, the old equipment would have to be sold, and the division could probably sell it for only $1.2 million. This equipment had an original cost of $8 million, and $1.5 million in depreciation has been recorded. Thus, a book loss of $5.3 million ($6.5 − $1.2) would be recorded on the sale.

Ms. Kravitz' boss, Jim Heitz, is the president of the Western Chemical Group, and his compensation is based almost exclusively on the amount of ROI generated by his group, which includes NAPCD. After thoroughly analyzing the facts, Ms. Kravitz concluded, "The people in the Western Chemical Group will swallow their dentures if we book a $5.3 million loss."

a. Why is Ms. Kravitz concerned about the book loss on disposal of the old technology in her division?

b. What weaknesses in Western Chemical Group's performance pay plan are apparently causing Ms. Kravitz to avoid an investment that meets all of the normal criteria for acceptability (ignoring the ROI effect)?

⊙ ETHICS AND QUALITY DISCUSSIONS

52. A typical executive is in his mid-40s, frequently travels on business, says he values self-respect, and is very likely to commit financial fraud. That, anyway, is the conclusion of four business school professors, whose study on fraud was published in a recent issue of the *Journal of Business Ethics*.

    After getting nearly 400 people (more than 85 percent of them men) over the past seven years to play the role of a fictional executive named Todd Folger, the professors found that 47 percent of the top executives, 41 percent of the controllers, and 76 percent of the graduate-level business students surveyed were willing to commit fraud by understating write-offs that cut into their companies' profits.
    [SOURCE: Dawn Blalock, "Study Shows Many Execs Are Quick to Write Off Ethics," *Wall Street Journal*, March 16, 1996 pp. C1, C13.]

    a. What creates the incentive for managers to understate write-offs?
    b. How does the use of accounting as a performance measurement system of managers affect the objectivity of accounting information?
    c. What are the ethical obligations of accountants in dealing with managers who desire to manipulate accounting information for their personal benefit?

53. Nason Corporation manufactures and distributes a line of children's toys. As a consequence, the corporation has large seasonal variations in sales. The company issues quarterly financial statements, and first-quarter earnings were down from the same period last year.

    During a visit to the Preschool and Infant Division, Nason's president expressed dissatisfaction with the division's first-quarter performance. As a result, John Kraft, division manager, felt pressure to report higher earnings in the second quarter. Kraft was aware that Nason Corporation uses the LIFO inventory method, so he had the purchasing manager postpone several large inventory orders scheduled for delivery in the second quarter. Kraft knew that the use of older inventory costs during the second quarter would cause a decline in the cost of goods sold and thus increase earnings.

    During a review of the preliminary second-quarter income statement, Donna Jensen, division controller, noticed that the cost of goods sold was low relative to sales. Jensen analyzed the inventory account and discovered that the scheduled second-quarter material purchases had been delayed until the third quarter. Jensen prepared a revised income statement using current replacement costs to calculate cost of goods sold and submitted the income statement to John Kraft, her superior, for review. Kraft was not pleased with these results and insisted that the second-quarter income statement remain unchanged. Jensen tried to explain to Kraft that the interim inventory should reflect the expected cost of the replacement of the liquidated layers when the inventory is expected to be replaced before the end of the year. Kraft did not relent and told Jensen to issue the income statement using LIFO costs. Jensen is concerned about Kraft's response and is contemplating what her next action should be.

    a. Determine whether the actions of John Kraft are ethical and explain your position.
    b. Recommend a course of action that Donna Jensen should take in proceeding to resolve this situation.

    (CMA)

54. In a survey published in 1990, 649 managers responded to a questionnaire and provided their opinion as to the ethical acceptability of manipulating accounting earnings to achieve higher managerial compensation. One of the questions dealt with the acceptability of changing a sales practice to pull some of next year's sales into the current year so that reported current earnings can be pushed up. The results of the survey indicated that about 43 percent of the respondents felt this practice was ethically acceptable, 44 percent felt the practice was ethically questionable, and 13 percent felt the practice was ethically unacceptable.

Other results of the survey indicate that the managers considered large manipulations more unethical than small manipulations and income-increasing manipulations more ethically unacceptable than income-decreasing manipulations.

[SOURCE: Based on William J. Bruns and Kenneth A. Merchant, "The Dangerous Morality of Managing Earnings," *Management Accounting* (August 1990), pp. 22–25.]

a. If managers can manipulate earnings to effect changes in their pay, is this a weakness in the pay-for-performance plan? Explain.

b. In your view, does the materiality of a manipulation partly determine the extent to which the manipulation is ethically acceptable?

c. Describe any circumstances in which you believe manipulation would be ethically acceptable and provide justification for your decision.

Appendix A   The Management Accounting Profession

Management accountants may work in manufacturing, retail, or service companies or in government or not-for-profit enterprises. But, regardless of where they work, management accountants are essential members of the management team. As they gain experience and advance in their careers, management accountants must diversify their knowledge base and provide strategic, rather than repetitive, information. The following description is appropriate:

> Management accounting is a specialized discipline that goes far beyond the bounds of traditional accounting. Its objective is to provide management with dynamic information both for making operating decisions and for developing blueprints for business success. Using all manner of financial and nonfinancial information, the management accountant monitors and assesses real-time performance and helps businesses prepare for future needs by facilitating better decision making within the organization.[1]

In providing their services to organizations, management accountants recognize that their discipline, like that of public accounting, is a professional one. Professions around the world are generally characterized by certain features, including an organization of members, a process of certification or licensing, a set of standards or guidelines as foundation for practice, and a code of ethics. The profession of management accounting adheres to these commonalties.

MANAGEMENT ACCOUNTING ORGANIZATIONS AND CERTIFICATIONS

In the United States, over 78,000 individuals are members of a private-sector body called the Institute of Management Accountants (IMA). *Management Accounting* is a monthly journal published by the IMA; it contains articles on topics important to today's business, governmental, and service organizations.

Institute of Management Accountants (IMA)

The IMA's Certificate in Management Accounting (CMA) is a professional designation that recognizes the successful completion of a two-day examination,

---

[1]Society of Management Accountants of Canada, *Fact Sheet: Certified Management Accountants* (Hamilton, Ontario: Society of Management Accountants of Canada, October 1993).

NEWS NOTE

The Importance of a Professional Designation

A professional designation is a highly valued personal asset. Once acquired, a member has a choice—live off the principal value, probably for a short period of time, or increase the equity value of the designation.

Being a professional in today's markets is competitive. There is no certainty of employment, and standing still in career development is an invitation to redundancy.

Individually and collectively, we have a lot to gain in ensuring that equity growth underpins our professional designation. That equity growth is our competitive advantage. Like any other asset with value, it means we must ensure our reputation, our uniqueness, our investment, and our legal standing.

We believe that CMA designation is the starting point of a successful career, not the destination. Once the designation is earned, the skill base and knowledge surrounding it should be constantly updated and improved. In the same way that total quality is a process of continuous improvement in an organization, professionalism should be seen as a lifelong process of continuous improvement.

SOURCE: Doug Dodds, "A Professional Designation: The CMA's Competitive Edge," *CMA Magazine* (February 1995), p. 2.

acceptable work experience, and the satisfaction of certain continuing education requirements. The exam consists of four parts (Economics, Finance, and Management; Financial Accounting and Reporting; Management Reporting, Analysis, and Behavioral Issues; and Decision Analysis and Information Systems). There are approximately 21,000 CMAs in the United States.

Society of Management Accountants

The corresponding Canadian organization is the Society of Management Accountants. The Society publishes *CMA Magazine,* which is printed in both English and French and contains articles on areas such as quality, performance evaluation, information support systems, and management styles. The organization is composed of approximately 30,000 members, about 90% of whom are CMAs; the rest are professional program students. The Canadian CMA differs from the American one in that there are two exams (an entrance and a comprehensive final). Between taking these examinations, the aspiring CMA must obtain practical experience while participating in a demanding professional program that focuses on management theory and practice, professionalism, ethics, and emerging management accounting issues. The News Note above discusses the importance of the CMA designation, but the benefits are equally applicable to *any* professional designation, including the CPA (Certified Public Accountant), CA (Chartered Accountant), JD (Juris Doctorate), CFP (Certified Financial Planner), and CLU (Certified Life Underwriter).

MANAGEMENT ACCOUNTING STANDARDS

Cost Accounting Standards Board (CASB)

Financial accounting standards are established by the Financial Accounting Standards Board (FASB), a private-sector body. In the United States, no similar board exists to define *universal* management accounting standards. However, a public-sector board called the Cost Accounting Standards Board (CASB) was established in 1970 by the U.S. Congress to promulgate uniform cost accounting standards for all negotiated federal government contracts in excess of $500,000. Twenty cost accounting standards (one of which has been withdrawn) were issued by the CASB. These standards do not constitute a comprehensive set of rules, and compliance is required only for companies bidding on or pricing certain cost-related contracts for the federal government. Additionally, universities must follow CASB Disclosure statements in accounting for costs under federally sponsored agreements.

The CASB was discontinued for eight years because of a lack of funding but was recreated in 1988 as an independent board of the Office of Federal Procurement Policy, rather than as an agency of Congress. The board faces numerous controversial issues at a time when there is great interest in the abilities of entities doing business with the United States government to predict project costs. The new CASB has recodified some of the standards, rules, and regulations that were set by the original CASB.

The Institute of Management Accountants issues cost and management accounting guidelines called Statements on Management Accounting (SMAs). These pronouncements are not legally binding, but are issued after a rigorous developmental and exposure process meant to assure their wide support. The first SMAs concentrated on the development of a framework for management accounting and include objectives and terminology. Later SMAs have addressed management accounting practices and techniques such as determining direct labor cost, computing the cost of capital, and measuring entity performance.

Statements on Management Accounting (SMAs)

As of early 1995, the Society of Management Accountants of Canada had issued thirty Management Accounting Guidelines (MAGs) that advocate appropriate practices for specific management accounting situations. These MAGs cover issues such as post-investment audits of capital projects, cash and accounts receivable management, implementing JIT production systems and target costing, becoming ISO 9000 registered, and product life-cycle management. Like the SMAs, MAGs are not requirements for organizational accounting, but merely suggestions.

Management Accounting Guidelines (MAGs)

MANAGEMENT ACCOUNTING AND ETHICS

While neither the IMA nor the Society can issue comprehensive standards for management practices and cost accounting techniques, they do issue professional standards that are binding upon members. Because of the pervasive nature of management accounting, the IMA and the Society decided to formalize some basic ethical values held by the profession. The IMA's Code of Ethics, presented in Exhibit A-1 (page 738), reflects the areas of competence, confidentiality, integrity, and objectivity. In Canada, ethics is one of the themes in the Society's two-year professional program. Codes of professional ethics for CMAs vary in Canada among the provinces to comply with provincial legislation and the by-laws of the provincial societies whereas, in the United States, the IMA's code of ethics is nationwide. The code of ethics for the Society of Management Accountants of Ontario is given in Exhibit A-2 (page 739) as an illustration of the codes found in the various provinces.

When management accountants adhere to their codes of ethics, the behavior and ethical options of others may be influenced. A manager who has no support for potentially unethical activities from management accountants is limited in his or her ability to improperly record information, commit fraud, or "manage" earnings.

Top management should understand, interpret, and communicate the corporate value system to other employees. If top managers shun their responsibilities in this area, employees will often be quick to follow the managerial lead—as discussed in the News Note on page 740.

Like other codes of ethics, the IMA's and Society of Management Accountants's codes should be viewed as goals for professional behavior. Such codes cannot address every potential situation, and each individual operates under a personal code of ethics. Persons lacking high moral standards will not be deterred from unethical behavior by either a mandated or a voluntary code. However, these codes provide a benchmark by which management accountants can judge their conduct.

EXHIBIT A-1

Standards of Ethical Conduct for Practitioners of Management Accounting

Competence

Practitioners of management accounting have a responsibility to:

- ⊙ Maintain an appropriate level of professional competence by ongoing development of their knowledge and skills.
- ⊙ Perform their professional duties in accordance with relevant laws, regulations, and technical standards.
- ⊙ Prepare complete and clear reports and recommendations after appropriate analyses of relevant and reliable information.

Confidentiality

Practitioners of management accounting have a responsibility to:

- ⊙ Refrain from disclosing confidential information acquired in the course of their work except when authorized, unless legally obligated to do so.
- ⊙ Inform subordinates as appropriate regarding the confidentiality of information acquired in the course of their work and monitor their activities to assure the maintenance of that confidentiality.
- ⊙ Refrain from using or appearing to use confidential information acquired in the course of their work for unethical or illegal advantage either personally or through third parties.

Integrity

Practitioners of management accounting have a responsibility to:

- ⊙ Avoid actual or apparent conflicts of interest and advise all appropriate parties of any potential conflict.
- ⊙ Refrain from engaging in any activity that would prejudice their ability to carry out their duties ethically.
- ⊙ Refuse any gift, favor, or hospitality that would influence or would appear to influence their actions.
- ⊙ Refrain from either actively or passively subverting the attainment of the organization's legitimate and ethical objectives.
- ⊙ Recognize and communicate professional limitations or other constraints that would preclude responsible judgment or successful performance of an activity.
- ⊙ Communicate unfavorable as well as favorable information and professional judgments or opinions.
- ⊙ Refrain from engaging in or supporting any activity that would discredit the profession.

Objectivity

Practitioners of management accounting have a responsibility to:

- ⊙ Communicate information fairly and objectively.
- ⊙ Disclose fully all relevant information that could reasonably be expected to influence an intended user's understanding of the reports, comments, and recommendations presented.

SOURCE: Institute of Management Accountants (formerly National Association of Accountants), *Statements on Management Accounting Statement No. 1C (revised): Standards of Ethical Conduct for Practitioners of Management Accounting and Financial Management* (Montvale, N.J.: April 30, 1997).

All members shall adhere to the following "Code of Professional Ethics" of the Society:

i. A Member shall act at all times with

1. responsibility for and fidelity to public needs;
2. fairness and loyalty to his associates, clients and employers; and
3. competence through devotion to high ideals of personal honour and professional integrity.

ii. A Member shall

1. maintain at all times independence of thought and action;
2. not express his opinion on financial statements without first assessing his relationship with his client to determine whether he might expect his opinion to be considered independent, objective and unbiased by one who has knowledge of all the facts; and
3. when preparing financial statements or expressing an opinion on financial statements which are intended to inform management only, disclose all material facts known to him in order not to make such financial statements misleading, acquire sufficient information to warrant an expression of opinion and report all material misstatements or departures from generally accepted accounting principles.

iii. A Member shall

1. not disclose or use any confidential information concerning the affairs of his employer or client unless acting in the course of his duties or except when such information is required to be disclosed in the course of any defence of himself or any associate or employee in any lawsuit or other legal proceeding or against alleged professional misconduct by order of lawful authority of the Board or any committee of the Society in proper exercise of their duties but only to the extent necessary for such purpose;
2. inform his employer or client of any business connections or interests of which his employer or client would reasonably expect to be informed;
3. not, in the course of exercising his duties on behalf of his employer or client, hold, receive, bargain for or acquire any fee, remuneration or benefit without his employer's or client's knowledge and consent; and
4. take all reasonable steps, in arranging any engagement as a consultant, to establish a clear understanding of the scope and objectives of the work before it is commenced and will furnish the client with an estimate of cost, preferably before the engagement is commenced, but in any event as soon as possible thereafter.

iv. A Member shall

1. conduct himself toward other Members with courtesy and good faith;
2. not commit an act discreditable to the profession;
3. not engage in or counsel any business or occupation which, in the opinion of the Society, is incompatible with the professional ethics of a management accountant;
4. not accept any engagement to review the work of another Member for the same employer except with the knowledge of that Member, or except where the connection of that Member with the work has been terminated, unless the Member reviews the work of others as a normal part of his responsibilities;
5. not attempt to gain an advantage over other Members by paying or accepting a commission in securing management accounting work;
6. uphold the principle of adequate compensation for management accounting work; and
7. not act maliciously or in any other way which may adversely reflect on the public or professional reputation or business of another Member.

v. A Member shall

1. at all times maintain the standards of competence expressed by the academic and experience requirements for admission to the Society and for continuation as a Member;

EXHIBIT A-2

Code of Professional Ethics for the Society of Management Accountants of Ontario

EXHIBIT A-2
(*continued*)

2. disseminate the knowledge upon which the profession of management accounting is based to others within the profession and generally promote the advancement of the profession;

3. undertake only such work as he is competent to perform by virtue of his training and experience and will, where it would be in the best interests of an employer or client, engage, or advise the employer or client to engage, other specialists;

4. expose before the proper tribunals of the Society any incompetent, unethical, illegal or unfair conduct or practice of a Member which involves the reputation, dignity or honour of the Society; and

5. endeavour to ensure that a professional partnership or company with which such Member is associated as a partner, principal, director, or officer, abides by the Code of Professional Ethics and the rules of professional conduct established by the Society.

SOURCE: Society of Management Accountants of Ontario, *Code of Professional Ethics* (Ontario, Canada: Society of Management Accountants of Ontario, June 1991).

NEWS NOTE

The Small Ethical Decisions Help You Make the Big Ones

When the body of moral principles that govern your day-to-day life conflicts with the ethical practices of your company, clearing a path through the tangle can be slow, arduous work. Even though all ethical decisions deserve in-depth consideration, often there's no time for it.

There is a way to prepare yourself for making complex ethical judgments on the spot. It sounds corny, but the best way to meet these big challenges is to practice on the small ones you face every day. If you've been at a job for more than a week, you know the sorts of routine compromises that go with your professional territory. With just this information, you are well equipped to begin to establish where you feel comfortable drawing the line between personal standards and professional duty. Where ethical behavior is concerned, definitely sweat the small stuff—it's what will help you deal with tougher, more ambiguous situations later in your career.

Some things are out of the individual's control, however. Fundamentally, it's the chair, the chief executive, and the senior officers who set the underlying ethical tone for the company. They show what counts through hundreds of small actions that are highly visible to everyone else.

If the everyday compromises you are asked to make in a company seem to consistently clash with your own sense of propriety, look hard at your bosses. If they aren't the sort of people whose ethics you respect, then you're bound for a head-on collision.

SOURCE: Nancy K. Austin, "Ethics: Personal vs. Professional," *Working Woman* (September 1992), pp. 28, 32.

Appendix B   Using the Ethics Discussion Questions

There are few more difficult issues facing business graduates or people in the business world today than those pertaining to ethical dilemmas. Some of these situations are specifically covered by professional codes of conduct; others reflect the differences among what is ethical, what is legal, and what is professionally accepted. Most traditional coverage of ethics in accounting courses focuses on the teachings of the various professional codes of ethics. Although learning about codes of ethics is important, an ability to make ethical choices can be greatly enhanced by presenting cases involving questionable breaches of proper conduct in the myriad of everyday business transactions. By covering such situations, college faculty have an opportunity to make a significant contribution to their students' success and well-being in the area of day-to-day ethics.

The text provides a series of end of chapter situations that can be used to give students practice in recognizing ethical issues and opportunities to develop appropriate responses. Some questions address what appear to be fairly innocuous issues (such as where to place expenses on an income statement); others address mainstream environmental and ethical matters (such as the handling of environmentally destructive waste materials). But both types of situations have important underlying ethical conflicts and require a logical thought process to arrive at the most ethical solution rather than simply *rationalizing* any solution chosen. Students need to recognize that it may be easy to make an unethical decision when the stakes are not very high; when the stakes increase, the pattern of unethical decision making may already be in place and difficult to change. If minor ethical decisions can be analyzed and resolved ethically, major decisions are more likely to be addressed in a thoughtful and ethical manner.

It is important that students be prepared, while they are in school, for ethical conflicts with which they may be confronted in the workplace. An essential part of such preparation is developing the *ability to recognize* ethical problems before they become realities and learning how, when, and to whom to respond to such problems. The purpose of a managerial accounting course is not to provide a philosophy lecture, but it is an opportunity to provide students with an awareness of some major ethical theories and problem-solving models before being asked to analyze and resolve ethical conflict situations. Thus, the following information may be useful to both the faculty member teaching this course and the students taking it.

Ethics can be viewed and taught at two levels: (1) as a set of general theories and (2) as a set of specific principles.

ETHICS AS A SET OF THEORIES

Viewing ethics as a set of general theories allows people to learn the background used in developing specific principles and, therefore, be able to develop their own principles or guidelines when confronted with unique situations in which the existing principles seem to have no relevance. This type of teaching is usually performed in philosophy courses, but some of the basic theories can be briefly defined and illustrated at this point. Although these are not the only ethical theories that exist, they do provide a foundation from which to begin ethical discussions.

Utilitarianism. This theory holds that the primary method of determining what is right or ethical is the usefulness of an action or a policy in producing other actions or experiences that people value. It emphasizes the consequences that an action has on all the people directly and/or indirectly affected by that action. This theory reflects a societal viewpoint of the "greatest good for the greatest number." (Utilitarianism is a type of cost–benefit analysis.)

Although this theory may provide extremely valid ethical decisions, in practice it is highly unworkable in its theoretical state. This model would require determining *all* possible solutions to a dilemma, determining *all* possible stakeholders for each solution, determining *all* the costs and benefits of *each* solution to *each* stakeholder, summing such costs and benefits, and choosing the decision that maximized the benefits of the most stakeholders. Thus, when utilitarianism is applied as a model of ethical decision making, certain shortcuts are normally taken, such as considering only certain types of stakeholders or solutions within a certain type of framework. When such shortcuts are taken, however, the decision maker should occasionally review them to make sure that such simplifications have not automatically ignored important constituencies, reference points, interests, or values.

Categorical Imperatives. This set of rules requires that a person act on the premise that whatever he or she does would become a universal law. Categorical imperatives form the basis of duties that are considered inherently right. Actions are inherently right or wrong, regardless of any positive or negative consequences resulting from those actions. Thus, the model emphasizes treating all persons equally and as the person acting would like to be treated as well as emphasizing a respect for individuals and their freedoms. (Categorical imperatives reflect a "Do unto others as you would have them do unto you" concept.)

Theory of Rights. This theory asserts that people have some fundamental rights that must be respected in all decisions. Rights advocates suggest that there are liberty and welfare rights for all persons. Liberty rights have primarily been embedded in the U.S. Constitution and include:

- the right of free consent (people should be treated only as they knowingly and willing consent to be treated);
- the right to privacy (outside the work environment);

- ⊙ the right to freedom of conscience;
- ⊙ the right to free speech; and
- ⊙ the right to due process.

Welfare rights reflect the rights of all people to some minimum standard of living; these rights typically have fallen into the realm of governmental or corporate social responsibilities.

Theory of Justice.   This theory requires that people make decisions based on equity, fairness, and impartiality. This theory requires that people who are similar be treated in a similar manner and allows people who are different in a *relevant* way to be treated differently. Relevant ways affecting when people can be treated differently cannot relate to arbitrary characteristics; differences must be related to the task that is to be performed or differences in people's needs. In using the theory of justice, a decision maker must be careful to make certain that the characteristic(s) on which he or she is making the distinction is(are) relevant and not discriminatory.

ETHICS AS A SET OF PRINCIPLES

Teaching ethics as a set of specific principles provides individuals with a means to answer concrete, problem-oriented situations. This method is typically how ethics is treated in an auditing course or in discussions of codes of ethics.

In looking at ethics as a set of principles, one must distinguish between ethics and legality. Ethics can be viewed as a nonjurisdictional system of moral rights. It represents the moral rights that people have regardless of where or when they live, whether these rights are legally recognized or not. Legality merely refers to what is permissible under the law in a particular society. Sometimes society may condone an act as legal because of the surrounding circumstances even though the act itself may be viewed as unethical. (For example, it is unethical to kill another human being, but society may make it legal to do so under certain situations.) Legitimizing a "wrong" act because of circumstances does not make that act any more moral.

MAKING ETHICAL DECISIONS

In making ethical decisions, a person must first have the sensitivity to recognize that an ethical dilemma exists and must exert the self-control to attempt to resolve it. This conflict may be at the personal, organizational, or societal level. All feasible alternatives should be considered along with their influencing factors such as values, laws, resource constraints, pressures, and cultural mores. *Once all ramifications are considered and the decision maker selects an alternative using whatever theories or processes he or she chooses, the decision maker must also be willing to accept the outcomes from and responsibility for that choice.* An individual acts as an autonomous agent when he or she acts on the basis of principles that have been consciously evaluated and accepted by the individual as the correct principles to direct behavior; individuals cannot be considered autonomous when they act based on principles that have been imposed from the outside (through peer pressure or by some authority) or that have been internalized as a matter of mere habit.

The making of ethical choices is not a science; it is subjective and cannot be resolved from a societal point of view. Different individuals will always have different viewpoints as to what is ethical and what is the proper decision for an ethical dilemma. The challenge is to create a means for students to foresee potential problems, recognize they have an obligation to derive internal and personal criteria by which to resolve such dilemmas, and accept personal, organizational, societal, and legal determinations as to the ethical or unethical nature of solutions chosen when (or if) those solutions are made public.

Appendix C Present and Future Value Tables

TABLE 1   PRESENT VALUE OF $1

Period	1.00%	2.00%	3.00%	4.00%	5.00%	6.00%	7.00%	8.00%	9.00%	9.50%	10.00%	10.50%	11.00%
1	0.9901	0.9804	0.9709	0.9615	0.9524	0.9434	0.9346	0.9259	0.9174	0.9132	0.9091	0.9050	0.9009
2	0.9803	0.9612	0.9426	0.9246	0.9070	0.8900	0.8734	0.8573	0.8417	0.8340	0.8265	0.8190	0.8116
3	0.9706	0.9423	0.9151	0.8890	0.8638	0.8396	0.8163	0.7938	0.7722	0.7617	0.7513	0.7412	0.7312
4	0.9610	0.9239	0.8885	0.8548	0.8227	0.7921	0.7629	0.7350	0.7084	0.6956	0.6830	0.6707	0.6587
5	0.9515	0.9057	0.8626	0.8219	0.7835	0.7473	0.7130	0.6806	0.6499	0.6352	0.6209	0.6070	0.5935
6	0.9421	0.8880	0.8375	0.7903	0.7462	0.7050	0.6663	0.6302	0.5963	0.5801	0.5645	0.5493	0.5346
7	0.9327	0.8706	0.8131	0.7599	0.7107	0.6651	0.6228	0.5835	0.5470	0.5298	0.5132	0.4971	0.4817
8	0.9235	0.8535	0.7894	0.7307	0.6768	0.6274	0.5820	0.5403	0.5019	0.4838	0.4665	0.4499	0.4339
9	0.9143	0.8368	0.7664	0.7026	0.6446	0.5919	0.5439	0.5003	0.4604	0.4419	0.4241	0.4071	0.3909
10	0.9053	0.8204	0.7441	0.6756	0.6139	0.5584	0.5084	0.4632	0.4224	0.4035	0.3855	0.3685	0.3522
11	0.8963	0.8043	0.7224	0.6496	0.5847	0.5268	0.4751	0.4289	0.3875	0.3685	0.3505	0.3334	0.3173
12	0.8875	0.7885	0.7014	0.6246	0.5568	0.4970	0.4440	0.3971	0.3555	0.3365	0.3186	0.3018	0.2858
13	0.8787	0.7730	0.6810	0.6006	0.5303	0.4688	0.4150	0.3677	0.3262	0.3073	0.2897	0.2731	0.2575
14	0.8700	0.7579	0.6611	0.5775	0.5051	0.4423	0.3878	0.3405	0.2993	0.2807	0.2633	0.2471	0.2320
15	0.8614	0.7430	0.6419	0.5553	0.4810	0.4173	0.3625	0.3152	0.2745	0.2563	0.2394	0.2237	0.2090
16	0.8528	0.7285	0.6232	0.5339	0.4581	0.3937	0.3387	0.2919	0.2519	0.2341	0.2176	0.2024	0.1883
17	0.8444	0.7142	0.6050	0.5134	0.4363	0.3714	0.3166	0.2703	0.2311	0.2138	0.1978	0.1832	0.1696
18	0.8360	0.7002	0.5874	0.4936	0.4155	0.3503	0.2959	0.2503	0.2120	0.1952	0.1799	0.1658	0.1528
19	0.8277	0.6864	0.5703	0.4746	0.3957	0.3305	0.2765	0.2317	0.1945	0.1783	0.1635	0.1500	0.1377
20	0.8195	0.6730	0.5537	0.4564	0.3769	0.3118	0.2584	0.2146	0.1784	0.1628	0.1486	0.1358	0.1240
21	0.8114	0.6598	0.5376	0.4388	0.3589	0.2942	0.2415	0.1987	0.1637	0.1487	0.1351	0.1229	0.1117
22	0.8034	0.6468	0.5219	0.4220	0.3419	0.2775	0.2257	0.1839	0.1502	0.1358	0.1229	0.1112	0.1007
23	0.7954	0.6342	0.5067	0.4057	0.3256	0.2618	0.2110	0.1703	0.1378	0.1240	0.1117	0.1006	0.0907
24	0.7876	0.6217	0.4919	0.3901	0.3101	0.2470	0.1972	0.1577	0.1264	0.1133	0.1015	0.0911	0.0817
25	0.7798	0.6095	0.4776	0.3751	0.2953	0.2330	0.1843	0.1460	0.1160	0.1034	0.0923	0.0824	0.0736
26	0.7721	0.5976	0.4637	0.3607	0.2812	0.2198	0.1722	0.1352	0.1064	0.0945	0.0839	0.0746	0.0663
27	0.7644	0.5859	0.4502	0.3468	0.2679	0.2074	0.1609	0.1252	0.0976	0.0863	0.0763	0.0675	0.0597
28	0.7568	0.5744	0.4371	0.3335	0.2551	0.1956	0.1504	0.1159	0.0896	0.0788	0.0693	0.0611	0.0538
29	0.7493	0.5631	0.4244	0.3207	0.2430	0.1846	0.1406	0.1073	0.0822	0.0719	0.0630	0.0553	0.0485
30	0.7419	0.5521	0.4120	0.3083	0.2314	0.1741	0.1314	0.0994	0.0754	0.0657	0.0573	0.0500	0.0437
31	0.7346	0.5413	0.4000	0.2965	0.2204	0.1643	0.1228	0.0920	0.0692	0.0600	0.0521	0.0453	0.0394
32	0.7273	0.5306	0.3883	0.2851	0.2099	0.1550	0.1147	0.0852	0.0634	0.0058	0.0474	0.0410	0.0355
33	0.7201	0.5202	0.3770	0.2741	0.1999	0.1462	0.1072	0.0789	0.0582	0.0500	0.0431	0.0371	0.0319
34	0.7130	0.5100	0.3660	0.2636	0.1904	0.1379	0.1002	0.0731	0.0534	0.0457	0.0391	0.0336	0.0288
35	0.7059	0.5000	0.3554	0.2534	0.1813	0.1301	0.0937	0.0676	0.0490	0.0417	0.0356	0.0304	0.0259
36	0.6989	0.4902	0.3450	0.2437	0.1727	0.1227	0.0875	0.0626	0.0449	0.0381	0.0324	0.0275	0.0234
37	0.6920	0.4806	0.3350	0.2343	0.1644	0.1158	0.0818	0.0580	0.0412	0.0348	0.0294	0.0249	0.0210
38	0.6852	0.4712	0.3252	0.2253	0.1566	0.1092	0.0765	0.0537	0.0378	0.0318	0.0267	0.0225	0.0190
39	0.6784	0.4620	0.3158	0.2166	0.1492	0.1031	0.0715	0.0497	0.0347	0.0290	0.0243	0.0204	0.0171
40	0.6717	0.4529	0.3066	0.2083	0.1421	0.0972	0.0668	0.0460	0.0318	0.0265	0.0221	0.0184	0.0154
41	0.6650	0.4440	0.2976	0.2003	0.1353	0.0917	0.0624	0.0426	0.0292	0.0242	0.0201	0.0167	0.0139
42	0.6584	0.4353	0.2890	0.1926	0.1288	0.0865	0.0583	0.0395	0.0268	0.0221	0.0183	0.0151	0.0125
43	0.6519	0.4268	0.2805	0.1852	0.1227	0.0816	0.0545	0.0365	0.0246	0.0202	0.0166	0.0137	0.0113
44	0.6455	0.4184	0.2724	0.1781	0.1169	0.0770	0.0510	0.0338	0.0226	0.0184	0.0151	0.0124	0.0101
45	0.6391	0.4102	0.2644	0.1712	0.1113	0.0727	0.0476	0.0313	0.0207	0.0168	0.0137	0.0112	0.0091
46	0.6327	0.4022	0.2567	0.1646	0.1060	0.0685	0.0445	0.0290	0.0190	0.0154	0.0125	0.0101	0.0082
47	0.6265	0.3943	0.2493	0.1583	0.1010	0.0647	0.0416	0.0269	0.0174	0.0141	0.0113	0.0092	0.0074
48	0.6203	0.3865	0.2420	0.1522	0.0961	0.0610	0.0389	0.0249	0.0160	0.0128	0.0103	0.0083	0.0067
49	0.6141	0.3790	0.2350	0.1463	0.0916	0.0576	0.0363	0.0230	0.0147	0.0117	0.0094	0.0075	0.0060
50	0.6080	0.3715	0.2281	0.1407	0.0872	0.0543	0.0340	0.0213	0.0135	0.0107	0.0085	0.0068	0.0054

11.50%	12.00%	12.50%	13.00%	13.50%	14.00%	14.50%	15.00%	15.50%	16.00%	17.00%	18.00%	19.00%	20.00%
0.8969	0.8929	0.8889	0.8850	0.8811	0.8772	0.8734	0.8696	0.8658	0.8621	0.8547	0.8475	0.8403	0.8333
0.8044	0.7972	0.7901	0.7832	0.7763	0.7695	0.7628	0.7561	0.7496	0.7432	0.7305	0.7182	0.7062	0.6944
0.7214	0.7118	0.7023	0.6931	0.6839	0.6750	0.6662	0.6575	0.6490	0.6407	0.6244	0.6086	0.5934	0.5787
0.6470	0.6355	0.6243	0.6133	0.6026	0.5921	0.5818	0.5718	0.5619	0.5523	0.5337	0.5158	0.4987	0.4823
0.5803	0.5674	0.5549	0.5428	0.5309	0.5194	0.5081	0.4972	0.4865	0.4761	0.4561	0.4371	0.4191	0.4019
0.5204	0.5066	0.4933	0.4803	0.4678	0.4556	0.4438	0.4323	0.4212	0.4104	0.3898	0.3704	0.3521	0.3349
0.4667	0.4524	0.4385	0.4251	0.4121	0.3996	0.3876	0.3759	0.3647	0.3538	0.3332	0.3139	0.2959	0.2791
0.4186	0.4039	0.3897	0.3762	0.3631	0.3506	0.3385	0.3269	0.3158	0.3050	0.2848	0.2660	0.2487	0.2326
0.3754	0.3606	0.3464	0.3329	0.3199	0.3075	0.2956	0.2843	0.2734	0.2630	0.2434	0.2255	0.2090	0.1938
0.3367	0.3220	0.3080	0.2946	0.2819	0.2697	0.2582	0.2472	0.2367	0.2267	0.2080	0.1911	0.1756	0.1615
0.3020	0.2875	0.2737	0.2607	0.2483	0.2366	0.2255	0.2149	0.2049	0.1954	0.1778	0.1619	0.1476	0.1346
0.2708	0.2567	0.2433	0.2307	0.2188	0.2076	0.1969	0.1869	0.1774	0.1685	0.1520	0.1372	0.1240	0.1122
0.2429	0.2292	0.2163	0.2042	0.1928	0.1821	0.1720	0.1625	0.1536	0.1452	0.1299	0.1163	0.1042	0.0935
0.2179	0.2046	0.1923	0.1807	0.1699	0.1597	0.1502	0.1413	0.1330	0.1252	0.1110	0.0986	0.0876	0.0779
0.1954	0.1827	0.1709	0.1599	0.1496	0.1401	0.1312	0.1229	0.1152	0.1079	0.0949	0.0835	0.0736	0.0649
0.1752	0.1631	0.1519	0.1415	0.1319	0.1229	0.1146	0.1069	0.0997	0.0930	0.0811	0.0708	0.0618	0.0541
0.1572	0.1456	0.1350	0.1252	0.1162	0.1078	0.1001	0.0929	0.0863	0.0802	0.0693	0.0600	0.0520	0.0451
0.1410	0.1300	0.1200	0.1108	0.1024	0.0946	0.0874	0.0808	0.0747	0.0691	0.0593	0.0508	0.0437	0.0376
0.1264	0.1161	0.1067	0.0981	0.0902	0.0830	0.0763	0.0703	0.0647	0.0596	0.0506	0.0431	0.0367	0.0313
0.1134	0.1037	0.0948	0.0868	0.0795	0.0728	0.0667	0.0611	0.0560	0.0514	0.0433	0.0365	0.0308	0.0261
0.1017	0.0926	0.0843	0.0768	0.0700	0.0638	0.0582	0.0531	0.0485	0.0443	0.0370	0.0309	0.0259	0.0217
0.0912	0.0826	0.0749	0.0680	0.0617	0.0560	0.0509	0.0462	0.0420	0.0382	0.0316	0.0262	0.0218	0.0181
0.0818	0.0738	0.0666	0.0601	0.0543	0.0491	0.0444	0.0402	0.0364	0.0329	0.0270	0.0222	0.0183	0.0151
0.0734	0.0659	0.0592	0.0532	0.0479	0.0431	0.0388	0.0349	0.0315	0.0284	0.0231	0.0188	0.0154	0.0126
0.0658	0.0588	0.0526	0.0471	0.0422	0.0378	0.0339	0.0304	0.0273	0.0245	0.0197	0.0160	0.0129	0.0105
0.0590	0.0525	0.0468	0.0417	0.0372	0.0332	0.0296	0.0264	0.0236	0.0211	0.0169	0.0135	0.0109	0.0087
0.0529	0.0469	0.0416	0.0369	0.0327	0.0291	0.0258	0.0230	0.0204	0.0182	0.0144	0.0115	0.0091	0.0073
0.0475	0.0419	0.0370	0.0326	0.0289	0.0255	0.0226	0.0200	0.0177	0.0157	0.0123	0.0097	0.0077	0.0061
0.0426	0.0374	0.0329	0.0289	0.0254	0.0224	0.0197	0.0174	0.0153	0.0135	0.0105	0.0082	0.0064	0.0051
0.0382	0.0334	0.0292	0.0256	0.0224	0.0196	0.0172	0.0151	0.0133	0.0117	0.0090	0.0070	0.0054	0.0042
0.0342	0.0298	0.0260	0.0226	0.0197	0.0172	0.0150	0.0131	0.0115	0.0100	0.0077	0.0059	0.0046	0.0035
0.0307	0.0266	0.0231	0.0200	0.0174	0.0151	0.0131	0.0114	0.0099	0.0087	0.0066	0.0050	0.0038	0.0029
0.0275	0.0238	0.0205	0.0177	0.0153	0.0133	0.0115	0.0099	0.0086	0.0075	0.0056	0.0043	0.0032	0.0024
0.0247	0.0212	0.0182	0.0157	0.0135	0.0116	0.0100	0.0088	0.0075	0.0064	0.0048	0.0036	0.0027	0.0020
0.0222	0.0189	0.0162	0.0139	0.0119	0.0102	0.0088	0.0075	0.0065	0.0056	0.0041	0.0031	0.0023	0.0017
0.0199	0.0169	0.0144	0.0123	0.0105	0.0089	0.0076	0.0065	0.0056	0.0048	0.0035	0.0026	0.0019	0.0014
0.0178	0.0151	0.0128	0.0109	0.0092	0.0078	0.0067	0.0057	0.0048	0.0041	0.0030	0.0022	0.0016	0.0012
0.0160	0.0135	0.0114	0.0096	0.0081	0.0069	0.0058	0.0049	0.0042	0.0036	0.0026	0.0019	0.0014	0.0010
0.0143	0.0120	0.0101	0.0085	0.0072	0.0060	0.0051	0.0043	0.0036	0.0031	0.0022	0.0016	0.0011	0.0008
0.0129	0.0108	0.0090	0.0075	0.0063	0.0053	0.0044	0.0037	0.0031	0.0026	0.0019	0.0013	0.0010	0.0007
0.0115	0.0096	0.0080	0.0067	0.0056	0.0046	0.0039	0.0033	0.0027	0.0023	0.0016	0.0011	0.0008	0.0006
0.0103	0.0086	0.0077	0.0059	0.0049	0.0041	0.0034	0.0028	0.0024	0.0020	0.0014	0.0010	0.0007	0.0005
0.0093	0.0077	0.0063	0.0052	0.0043	0.0036	0.0030	0.0025	0.0020	0.0017	0.0012	0.0008	0.0006	0.0004
0.0083	0.0068	0.0056	0.0046	0.0038	0.0031	0.0026	0.0021	0.0018	0.0015	0.0010	0.0007	0.0005	0.0003
0.0075	0.0061	0.0050	0.0041	0.0034	0.0028	0.0023	0.0019	0.0015	0.0013	0.0009	0.0006	0.0004	0.0003
0.0067	0.0054	0.0044	0.0036	0.0030	0.0024	0.0020	0.0016	0.0013	0.0011	0.0007	0.0005	0.0003	0.0002
0.0060	0.0049	0.0039	0.0032	0.0026	0.0021	0.0017	0.0014	0.0011	0.0009	0.0006	0.0004	0.0003	0.0002
0.0054	0.0043	0.0035	0.0028	0.0023	0.0019	0.0015	0.0012	0.0010	0.0008	0.0005	0.0004	0.0002	0.0002
0.0048	0.0039	0.0031	0.0025	0.0020	0.0016	0.0013	0.0011	0.0009	0.0007	0.0005	0.0003	0.0002	0.0001
0.0043	0.0035	0.0028	0.0022	0.0018	0.0014	0.0012	0.0009	0.0007	0.0006	0.0004	0.0003	0.0002	0.0001

#1 @ end year 1
$1 @ end year 2
etc.

TABLE 2   PRESENT VALUE OF AN ORDINARY ANNUITY OF $1

Period	1.00%	2.00%	3.00%	4.00%	5.00%	6.00%	7.00%	8.00%	9.00%	9.50%	10.00%	10.50%	11.00%
1	0.9901	0.9804	0.9709	0.9615	0.0524	0.9434	0.9346	0.9259	0.9174	0.9132	0.9091	0.9050	0.9009
2	1.9704	1.9416	1.9135	1.8861	1.8594	1.8334	1.8080	1.7833	1.7591	1.7473	1.7355	1.7240	1.7125
3	2.9410	2.8839	2.8286	2.7751	2.7233	2.6730	2.6243	2.5771	2.5313	2.5089	2.4869	2.4651	2.4437
4	3.9020	3.8077	3.7171	3.6299	3.5460	3.4651	3.3872	3.3121	3.2397	3.2045	3.1699	3.1359	3.1025
5	4.8534	4.7135	4.5797	4.4518	4.3295	4.2124	4.1002	3.9927	3.8897	3.8397	3.7908	3.7429	3.6959
6	5.7955	5.6014	5.4172	5.2421	5.0757	4.9173	4.7665	4.6229	4.4859	4.4198	4.3553	4.2922	4.2305
7	6.7282	6.4720	6.2303	6.0021	5.7864	5.5824	5.3893	5.2064	5.0330	4.9496	4.8684	4.7893	4.7122
8	7.6517	7.3255	7.0197	6.7327	6.4632	6.2098	5.9713	5.7466	5.5348	5.4334	5.3349	5.2392	5.1461
9	8.5660	8.1622	7.7861	7.4353	7.1078	6.8017	6.5152	6.2469	5.9953	5.8753	5.7590	5.6463	5.5371
10	9.4713	8.9826	8.5302	8.1109	7.7217	7.3601	7.0236	6.7101	6.4177	6.2788	6.1446	6.0148	5.8892
11	10.3676	9.7869	9.2526	8.7605	8.3064	7.8869	7.4987	7.1390	6.8052	6.6473	6.4951	6.3482	6.2065
12	11.2551	10.5753	9.9540	9.3851	8.8633	8.3838	7.9427	7.5361	7.1607	6.9838	6.8137	6.6500	6.4924
13	12.1337	11.3484	10.6350	9.9857	9.3936	8.8527	8.3577	7.9038	7.4869	7.2912	7.1034	6.9230	6.7499
14	13.0037	12.1063	11.2961	10.5631	9.8986	9.2950	8.7455	8.2442	7.7862	7.5719	7.3667	7.1702	6.9819
15	13.8651	12.8493	11.9379	11.1184	10.3797	9.7123	9.1079	8.5595	8.0607	7.8282	7.6061	7.3938	7.1909
16	14.7179	13.5777	12.5611	11.6523	10.8378	10.1059	9.4467	8.8514	8.3126	8.0623	7.8237	7.5962	7.3792
17	15.5623	14.2919	13.1661	12.1657	11.2741	10.4773	9.7632	9.1216	8.5436	8.2760	8.0216	7.7794	7.5488
18	16.3983	14.9920	13.7535	12.6593	11.6896	10.8276	10.0591	9.3719	8.7556	8.4713	8.2014	7.9452	7.7016
19	17.2260	15.6785	14.3238	13.1339	12.0853	11.1581	10.3356	9.6036	8.9501	8.6496	8.3649	8.0952	7.8393
20	18.0456	16.3514	14.8775	13.5903	12.4622	11.4699	10.5940	9.8182	9.1286	8.8124	8.5136	8.2309	7.9633
21	18.8570	17.0112	15.4150	14.0292	12.8212	11.7641	10.8355	10.0168	9.2922	8.9611	8.6487	8.3538	8.0751
22	19.6604	17.6581	15.9369	14.4511	13.1630	12.0416	11.0612	10.2007	9.4424	9.0969	8.7715	8.4649	8.1757
23	20.4558	18.2922	16.4436	14.8568	13.4886	12.3034	11.2722	10.3711	9.5802	9.2209	8.8832	8.5656	8.2664
24	21.2434	18.9139	16.9355	15.2470	13.7986	12.5504	11.4693	10.5288	9.7066	9.3342	8.9847	8.6566	8.3481
25	22.0232	19.5235	17.4132	15.6221	14.0939	12.7834	11.6536	10.6748	9.8226	9.4376	9.0770	8.7390	8.4217
26	22.7952	20.1210	17.8768	15.9828	14.3752	13.0032	11.8258	10.8100	9.9290	9.5320	9.1610	8.8136	8.4881
27	23.5596	20.7069	18.3270	16.3296	14.6430	13.2105	11.9867	10.9352	10.0266	9.6183	9.2372	8.8811	8.5478
28	24.3164	21.2813	18.7641	16.6631	14.8981	13.4062	12.1371	11.0511	10.1161	9.6971	9.3066	8.9422	8.6016
29	25.0658	21.8444	19.1885	16.9837	15.1411	13.5907	12.2777	11.1584	10.1983	9.7690	9.3696	8.9974	8.6501
30	25.8077	22.3965	19.6004	17.2920	15.3725	13.7648	12.4090	11.2578	10.2737	9.8347	9.4269	9.0474	8.6938
31	26.5423	22.9377	20.0004	17.5885	15.5928	13.9291	12.5318	11.3498	10.3428	9.8947	9.4790	9.0927	8.7332
32	27.2696	23.4683	20.3888	17.8736	15.8027	14.0840	12.6466	11.4350	10.4062	9.9495	9.5264	9.1337	8.7686
33	27.9897	23.9886	20.7658	18.1477	16.0026	14.2302	12.7538	11.5139	10.4664	9.9996	9.5694	9.1707	8.8005
34	28.7027	24.4986	21.1318	18.4112	16.1929	14.3681	12.8540	11.5869	10.5178	10.0453	9.6086	9.2043	8.8293
35	29.4086	24.9986	21.4872	18.6646	16.3742	14.4983	12.9477	11.6546	10.5668	10.0870	9.6442	9.2347	8.8552
36	30.1075	25.4888	21.8323	18.9083	16.5469	14.6210	13.0352	11.7172	10.6118	10.1251	9.6765	9.2621	8.8786
37	30.7995	25.9695	22.1672	19.1426	16.7113	14.7368	13.1170	11.7752	10.6530	10.1599	9.7059	9.2870	8.8996
38	31.4847	26.4406	22.4925	19.3679	16.8679	14.8460	13.1935	11.8289	10.6908	10.1917	9.7327	9.3095	8.9186
39	32.1630	26.9026	22.8082	19.5845	17.0170	14.9491	13.2649	11.8786	10.7255	10.2207	9.7570	9.3299	8.9357
40	32.8347	27.3555	23.1148	19.7928	17.1591	15.0463	13.3317	11.9246	10.7574	10.2473	9.7791	9.3483	8.9511
41	33.4997	27.7995	23.4124	19.9931	17.2944	15.1380	13.3941	11.9672	10.7866	10.2715	9.7991	9.3650	8.9649
42	34.1581	28.2348	23.7014	20.1856	17.4232	15.2245	13.4525	12.0067	10.8134	10.2936	9.8174	9.3801	8.9774
43	34.8100	28.6616	23.9819	20.3708	17.5459	15.3062	13.5070	12.0432	10.8380	10.3138	9.8340	9.3937	8.9887
44	35.4555	29.0800	24.2543	20.5488	17.6628	15.3832	13.5579	12.0771	10.8605	10.3322	9.8491	9.4061	8.9988
45	36.0945	29.4902	24.5187	20.7200	17.7741	15.4558	13.6055	12.1084	10.8812	10.3490	9.8628	9.4163	9.0079
46	36.7272	29.8923	24.7755	20.8847	17.8801	15.5244	13.6500	12.1374	10.9002	10.3644	9.8753	9.4274	9.0161
47	37.3537	30.2866	25.0247	21.0429	17.9810	15.5890	13.6916	12.1643	10.9176	10.3785	9.8866	9.4366	9.0236
48	37.9740	30.6731	25.2667	21.1951	18.0772	15.6500	13.7305	12.1891	10.9336	10.3913	9.8969	9.4449	9.0302
49	38.5881	31.0521	25.5017	21.3415	18.1687	15.7076	13.7668	12.2122	10.9482	10.4030	9.9063	9.4524	9.0362
50	39.1961	31.4236	25.7298	21.4822	18.2559	15.7619	13.8008	12.2335	10.9617	10.4137	9.9148	9.4591	9.0417

11.50%	12.00%	12.50%	13.00%	13.50%	14.00%	14.50%	15.00%	15.50%	16.00%	17.00%	18.00%	19.00%	20.00%
0.8969	0.8929	0.8889	0.8850	0.8811	0.8772	0.8734	0.8696	0.8658	0.8621	0.8547	0.8475	0.8403	0.8333
1.7012	1.6901	1.6790	1.6681	1.6573	1.6467	1.6361	1.6257	1.6154	1.6052	1.5852	1.5656	1.5465	1.5278
2.4226	2.4018	2.3813	2.3612	2.3413	2.3216	2.3023	2.2832	2.2644	2.2459	2.2096	2.1743	2.1399	2.1065
3.0696	3.0374	3.0056	2.9745	2.9438	2.9137	2.8841	2.8850	2.8263	2.7982	2.7432	2.6901	2.6386	2.5887
3.6499	3.6048	3.5606	3.5172	3.4747	3.4331	3.3922	3.3522	3.3129	3.2743	3.1994	3.1272	3.0576	2.9906
4.1703	4.1114	4.0538	3.9976	3.9425	3.8887	3.8360	3.7845	3.7341	3.6847	3.5892	3.4976	3.4098	3.3255
4.6370	4.5638	4.4923	4.4226	4.3546	4.2883	4.2236	4.1604	4.0988	4.0386	3.9224	3.8115	3.7057	3.6046
5.0556	4.9676	4.8821	4.7988	4.7177	4.6389	4.5621	4.4873	4.4145	4.3436	4.2072	4.0776	3.9544	3.8372
5.4311	5.3283	5.2285	5.1317	5.0377	4.9464	4.8577	4.7716	4.6879	4.6065	4.4506	4.3030	4.1633	4.0310
5.7678	5.6502	5.5364	5.4262	5.3195	5.2161	5.1159	5.0188	4.9246	4.8332	4.6586	4.4941	4.3389	4.1925
6.0698	5.9377	5.8102	5.6869	5.5679	5.4527	5.3414	5.2337	5.1295	5.0286	4.8364	4.6560	4.4865	4.3271
6.3406	6.1944	6.0535	5.9177	5.7867	5.6603	5.5383	5.4206	5.3069	5.1971	4.9884	4.7932	4.6105	4.4392
6.5835	6.4236	6.2698	6.1218	5.9794	5.8424	5.7103	5.5832	5.4606	5.3423	5.1183	4.9095	4.7147	4.5327
6.8013	6.6282	6.4620	6.3025	6.1493	6.0021	5.8606	5.7245	5.5936	5.4675	5.2293	5.0081	4.8023	4.6106
6.9967	6.8109	6.6329	6.4624	6.2989	6.1422	5.9918	5.8474	5.7087	5.5755	5.3242	5.0916	4.8759	4.6755
7.1719	6.9740	6.7848	6.6039	6.4308	6.2651	6.1063	5.9542	5.8084	5.6685	5.4053	5.1624	4.9377	4.7296
7.3291	7.1196	6.9198	6.7291	6.5469	6.3729	6.2064	6.0472	5.8947	5.7487	5.4746	5.2223	4.9897	4.7746
7.4700	7.2497	7.0398	6.8399	6.6493	6.4674	6.2938	6.1280	5.9695	5.8179	5.5339	5.2732	5.0333	4.8122
7.5964	7.3658	7.1465	6.9380	6.7395	6.5504	6.3701	6.1982	6.0342	5.8775	5.5845	5.3162	5.0700	4.8435
7.7098	7.4694	7.2414	7.0248	6.8189	6.6231	6.4368	6.2593	6.0902	5.9288	5.6278	5.3528	5.1009	4.8696
7.8115	7.5620	7.3257	7.1016	6.8889	6.6870	6.4950	6.3125	6.1387	5.9731	5.6648	5.3837	5.1268	4.8913
7.9027	7.6447	7.4006	7.1695	6.9506	6.7429	6.5459	6.3587	6.1807	6.0113	5.6964	5.4099	5.1486	4.9094
7.9845	7.7184	7.4672	7.2297	7.0049	6.7921	6.5903	6.3988	6.2170	6.0443	5.7234	5.4321	5.1669	4.9245
8.0578	7.7843	7.5264	7.2829	7.0528	6.8351	6.6291	6.4338	6.2485	6.0726	5.7465	5.4510	5.1822	4.9371
8.1236	7.8431	7.5790	7.3300	7.0950	6.8729	6.6629	6.4642	6.2758	6.0971	5.7662	5.4669	5.1952	4.9476
8.1826	7.8957	7.6258	7.3717	7.1321	6.9061	6.6925	6.4906	6.2994	6.1182	5.7831	5.4804	5.2060	4.9563
8.2355	7.9426	7.6674	7.4086	7.1649	6.9352	6.7184	6.5135	6.3198	6.1364	5.7975	5.4919	5.2151	4.9636
8.2830	7.9844	7.7043	7.4412	7.1937	6.9607	6.7409	6.5335	6.3375	6.1520	5.8099	5.5016	5.2228	4.9697
8.3255	8.0218	7.7372	7.4701	7.2191	6.9830	6.7606	6.5509	6.3528	6.1656	5.8204	5.5098	5.2292	4.9747
8.3637	8.0552	7.7664	7.4957	7.2415	7.0027	6.7779	6.5660	6.3661	6.1772	5.8294	5.5168	5.2347	4.9789
8.3980	8.0850	7.7923	7.5183	7.2613	7.0199	6.7929	6.5791	6.3776	6.1872	5.8371	5.5227	5.2392	4.9825
8.4287	8.1116	7.8154	7.5383	7.2786	7.0350	6.8060	6.5905	6.3875	6.1959	5.8437	5.5277	5.2430	4.9854
8.4562	8.1354	7.8359	7.5560	7.2940	7.0482	6.8175	6.6005	6.3961	6.2034	5.8493	5.5320	5.2463	4.9878
8.4809	8.1566	7.8542	7.5717	7.3075	7.0599	6.8275	6.6091	6.4035	6.2098	5.8541	5.5356	5.2490	4.9898
8.5030	8.1755	7.8704	7.5856	7.3193	7.0701	6.8362	6.6166	6.4100	6.2153	5.8582	5.5386	5.2512	4.9930
8.5229	8.1924	7.8848	7.5979	7.3298	7.0790	6.8439	6.6231	6.4156	6.2201	5.8617	5.5412	5.2531	4.9930
8.5407	8.2075	7.8976	7.6087	7.3390	7.0868	6.8505	6.6288	6.4204	6.2242	5.8647	5.5434	5.2547	4.9941
8.5567	8.2210	7.9090	7.6183	7.3472	7.0937	6.8564	6.6338	6.4246	6.2278	5.8673	5.5453	5.2561	4.9951
8.5710	8.2330	7.9191	7.6268	7.3543	7.0998	6.8615	6.6381	6.4282	6.2309	5.8695	5.5468	5.2572	4.9959
8.5839	8.2438	7.9281	7.6344	7.3607	7.1050	6.8659	6.6418	6.4314	6.2335	5.8713	5.5482	5.2582	4.9966
8.5954	8.2534	7.9361	7.6410	7.3662	7.1097	6.8698	6.6450	6.4341	6.2358	5.8729	5.5493	5.2590	4.9972
8.6058	8.2619	7.9432	7.6469	7.3711	7.1138	6.8732	6.6479	6.4364	6.2377	5.8743	5.5502	5.2596	4.9976
8.6150	8.2696	7.9495	7.6522	7.3754	7.1173	6.8761	6.6503	6.4385	6.2394	5.8755	5.5511	5.2602	4.9980
8.6233	8.2764	7.9551	7.6568	7.3792	7.1205	6.8787	6.6524	6.4402	6.2409	5.8765	5.5517	5.2607	4.9984
8.6308	8.2825	7.9601	7.6609	7.3826	7.1232	6.8810	6.6543	6.4418	6.2421	5.8773	5.5523	5.2611	4.9986
8.6375	8.2880	7.9645	7.6645	7.3855	7.1256	6.8830	6.6559	6.4431	6.2432	5.8781	5.5528	5.2614	4.9989
8.6435	8.2928	7.9685	7.6677	7.3881	7.1277	6.8847	6.6573	6.4442	6.2442	5.8787	5.5532	5.2617	4.9991
8.6489	8.2972	7.9720	7.6705	7.3904	7.1296	6.8862	6.6585	6.4452	6.2450	5.8792	5.5536	5.2619	4.9992
8.6537	8.3010	7.9751	7.6730	7.3925	7.1312	6.8875	6.6596	6.4461	6.2457	5.8797	5.5539	5.2621	4.9993
8.6580	8.3045	7.9779	7.6752	7.3942	7.1327	6.8886	6.6605	6.4468	6.2463	5.8801	5.5541	5.2623	4.9995

TABLE 3 FUTURE VALUE OF $1

Period	3.00%	4.00%	5.00%	6.00%	7.00%	8.00%	9.00%	10.00%	11.00%	12.00%	13.00%	14.00%	15.00%
1	1.0300	1.0400	1.0500	1.0600	1.0700	1.0800	1.0900	1.1000	1.1100	1.1200	1.1300	1.1400	1.1500
2	1.0609	1.0816	1.1025	1.1236	1.1449	1.1664	1.1881	1.2100	1.2321	1.2544	1.2769	1.2996	1.3225
3	1.0927	1.1249	1.1576	1.1910	1.2250	1.2597	1.2950	1.3310	1.3676	1.4049	1.4429	1.4815	1.5209
4	1.1255	1.1699	1.2155	1.2625	1.3108	1.3605	1.4116	1.4641	1.5181	1.5735	1.6305	1.6890	1.7490
5	1.1593	1.2167	1.2763	1.3382	1.4026	1.4693	1.5386	1.6105	1.6851	1.7623	1.8424	1.9254	2.0114
6	1.1941	1.2653	1.3401	1.4185	1.5007	1.5869	1.6771	1.7716	1.8704	1.9738	2.0820	2.1950	2.3131
7	1.2299	1.3159	1.4071	1.5036	1.6058	1.7138	1.8280	1.9487	2.0762	2.2107	2.3526	2.5023	2.6600
8	1.2668	1.3686	1.4775	1.5938	1.7182	1.8509	1.9926	2.1436	2.3045	2.4760	2.6584	2.8526	3.0590
9	1.3048	1.4233	1.5513	1.6895	1.8385	1.9990	2.1719	2.3579	2.5580	2.7731	3.0040	3.2519	3.5179
10	1.3439	1.4802	1.6289	1.7908	1.9672	2.1589	2.3674	2.5937	2.8394	3.1058	3.3946	3.7072	4.0456
11	1.3842	1.5395	1.7103	1.8983	2.1049	2.3316	2.5804	2.8531	3.1518	3.4785	3.8359	4.2262	4.6524
12	1.4258	1.6010	1.7959	2.0122	2.2522	2.5182	2.8127	3.1384	3.4985	3.8960	4.3345	4.8179	5.3503
13	1.4685	1.6651	1.8856	2.1329	2.4098	2.7196	3.0658	3.4523	3.8833	4.3635	4.8980	5.4924	6.1528
14	1.5126	1.7317	1.9799	2.2609	2.5785	2.9372	3.3417	3.7975	4.3104	4.8871	5.5348	6.2613	7.0757
15	1.5580	1.8009	2.0789	2.3966	2.7590	3.1722	3.6425	4.1772	4.7846	5.4736	6.2543	7.1379	8.1371
16	1.6047	1.8730	2.1829	2.5404	2.9522	3.4259	3.9703	4.5950	5.3109	6.1304	7.0673	8.1372	9.3576
17	1.6528	1.9479	2.2920	2.6928	3.1588	3.7000	4.3276	5.0545	5.8951	6.8660	7.9861	9.2765	10.7613
18	1.7024	2.0258	2.4066	2.8543	3.3799	3.9960	4.7171	5.5599	6.5436	7.6900	9.0243	10.5752	12.3755
19	1.7535	2.1068	2.5270	3.0256	3.6165	4.3157	5.1417	6.1159	7.2633	8.6128	10.1974	12.0557	14.2318
20	1.8061	2.1911	2.6533	3.2071	3.8697	4.6610	5.6044	6.7275	8.0623	9.6463	11.5231	13.7435	16.3665

TABLE 4 FUTURE VALUE OF AN ORDINARY ANNUITY OF $1

Period	3.00%	4.00%	5.00%	6.00%	7.00%	8.00%	9.00%	10.00%	11.00%	12.00%	13.00%	14.00%	15.00%
1	1.0000	1.0000	1.0000	1.0000	1.0000	1.0000	1.0000	1.0000	1.0000	1.0000	1.0000	1.0000	1.0000
2	2.0300	2.0400	2.0500	2.0600	2.0700	2.0800	2.0900	2.1000	2.1100	2.1200	2.1300	2.1400	2.1500
3	3.0909	3.1216	3.1525	3.1836	3.2149	3.2464	3.2781	3.3100	3.3421	3.3744	3.4069	3.4396	3.4725
4	4.1836	4.2465	4.3101	4.3746	4.4399	4.5061	4.5731	4.6410	4.7097	4.7793	4.8498	4.9211	4.9934
5	5.3091	5.4163	5.5256	5.6371	5.7507	5.8666	5.9847	6.1051	6.2278	6.3528	6.4803	6.6101	6.7424
6	6.4684	6.6330	6.8019	6.9753	7.1533	7.3359	7.5233	7.7156	7.9129	8.1152	8.3227	8.5355	7.7537
7	7.6625	7.8983	8.1420	8.3938	8.6540	8.9228	9.2004	9.4872	9.7833	10.0890	10.4047	10.7305	11.0668
8	8.8923	9.2142	9.5491	9.8975	10.2598	10.6366	11.0285	11.4359	11.8594	12.2997	12.7573	13.2328	13.7268
9	10.1591	10.5828	11.0266	11.4913	11.9780	12.4876	13.0210	13.5795	14.1640	14.7757	15.4157	16.0853	16.7858
10	11.4639	12.0061	12.5779	13.1808	13.8164	14.4866	15.1929	15.9374	16.7220	17.5487	18.4197	19.3373	20.3037
11	12.8078	13.4864	14.2068	14.9716	15.7836	16.6455	17.5603	18.5312	19.5614	20.6546	21.8143	23.0445	24.3493
12	14.1920	15.0258	15.9171	16.8699	17.8885	18.9771	20.1407	21.3843	22.7132	24.1331	25.6502	27.2707	29.0017
13	15.6178	16.6268	17.7130	18.8821	20.1406	21.4953	22.9534	24.5227	26.2116	28.0291	29.9847	32.0887	34.3519
14	17.0863	18.2919	19.5986	21.0151	22.5505	24.2149	26.0192	27.9750	30.0949	32.3926	34.8827	37.5811	40.5047
15	18.5989	20.0236	21.5786	23.2760	25.1290	27.1521	29.3609	31.7725	34.4054	37.2797	40.4175	43.8424	47.5804
16	20.1569	21.8245	23.6575	25.6725	27.8881	30.3243	33.0034	35.9497	39.1899	42.7533	46.6717	50.9804	55.7175
17	21.7616	23.6975	25.8404	28.2129	30.8402	33.7502	36.9737	40.5447	44.5008	48.8837	53.7391	59.1176	65.0751
18	23.4144	25.6454	28.1324	30.9057	33.9990	37.4502	41.3013	45.5992	50.3959	55.7497	61.7251	68.3941	75.8364
19	25.1169	27.6712	30.5390	33.7600	37.3790	41.4463	46.0185	51.1591	56.9395	63.4397	70.7494	78.9692	88.2118
20	26.8704	29.7781	33.0660	36.7856	40.9955	45.7620	51.1601	57.2750	64.2028	72.0524	80.9468	91.0249	102.4436

GLOSSARY

A

ABC analysis an inventory control method that separates items into three groups based on annual cost-to-volume usage; items having the highest dollar volume are referred to as A items, while C items represent the lowest dollar volume

absorption costing a cost accumulation method that treats the costs of all manufacturing components (direct materials, direct labor, variable overhead, and fixed overhead) as inventoriable, or product, costs; also known as full costing

accounting rate of return (APR) the rate of accounting earnings obtained on the average capital investment over a project's life

activity a repetitive action, movement, or work sequence performed to fulfill a business function

activity center a segment of the production or service process for which management wants a separate report of the costs of activities performed

activity cost driver a measure of the demands placed on activities and, thus, the resources consumed by products and services; often indicates an activity's output

activity-based costing an accounting information system that identifies the various activities performed in an organization and collects costs on the basis of the underlying nature and extent of those activities

activity-based management a discipline that focuses on how the activities performed during the production/performance process can improve the value received by a customer and the profit achieved by providing this value

actual cost system costing system using the actual costs of production as the basis for determine the cost of work-in-process inventory

allocate assign based on the use of a cost driver, predictor, or an arbitrary method

annuity a series of equal cash flows occurring at equal time intervals

annuity due an annuity in which each cash flow occurs at the beginning of the period

applied overhead costs the amount of overhead assigned to Work in Process Inventory as a result of the occurrence of the activity that was used to develop the application rate; the result of multiplying the quantity of actual activity by the predetermined rate

appraisal cost A quality control cost incurred for monitoring or inspection;

compensates for mistakes not eliminated through prevention activities

appropriation a maximum allowable expenditure for a budget item (from appendix)

asset turnover a ratio that measures asset productivity; it is the number of sales dollars generated by each dollar of assets during a specific period

authority the right (usually by virtue of position or rank) to use resources to accomplish a task or achieve an objective; can be delegated or assigned to others

B

backflush costing a costing system that focuses on output and works backward through the system to allocate costs to cost of goods sold and inventory

Baldrige Award an award program administered by the U.S. Department of Commerce to recognize quality achievements by U.S. businesses

bar code groups of lines and spaces arranged in a special machine-readable pattern

batch-level cost a cost that is created by a group of similar things made, handled, or processed at a single time

benchmarking the process of investigating, comparing, and evaluating the company's products, processes, and/or services against those of companies believed to be the "best in class" so that the investigating company can imitate, and possibly improve on, their techniques

bill of materials a document that contains information about product material components, their specifications (including quality), and the quantities needed for production

bottleneck any resource whose ability to process is less than the need for processing

breakeven graph a graphical depiction of the relationships among revenues, variable costs, fixed costs, and profits (or losses) (from appendix)

breakeven point (BEP) that level of activity, in units or dollars, at which total revenues equal total costs

budget the quantitative expression of an organization's commitment to planned activities and resource acquisition and use

budget committee a group, usually composed of top management and the chief financial officer, that reviews and approves, or makes adjustments to, the master budget and/or the budgets submitted from operational managers

budget manual a detailed set of documents that provides information and guidelines about the budgetary process

budget slack the intentional underestimation of revenues and/or overestimation of expenses

budgeting the process of determining a financial plan for future operations

build mission a strategic mission that has the goal of increased market share, even at the expense of short-term earnings and cash flow; typically pursued by business units with low market share in high growth industries

business intelligence (BI) system a formal process for gathering and analyzing information and producing intelligence to meet decision making needs; requires knowledge of markets, technologies, and competitors; should also provide comprehensive information about internal functions and processes, including organizational strengths and constraints

business process reengineering (BPR) process innovation and redesign aimed at finding and implementing radical changes in how things are made or how tasks are performed to achieve substantial cost, service, or time reductions

business-value-added (BVA) activity an activity that is necessary for the operation of a business but for which a customer would not want to pay

C

capacity a measure of production volume or of some other cost driver related to plant production capability during a period

capacity utilization a measure of the extent to which actual production volume approaches potential production volume

capital asset an asset used to generate revenues or cost savings by providing production, distribution, or service capabilities for more than one year

capital budgeting a process for evaluating proposed long-range projects or courses of future activity for the purpose of allocating limited resources to desirable projects

carrying cost the variable cost of carrying one unit of inventory in stock for one year; consists of storage, handling, insurance charges, property taxes based on inventory size, possible losses from obsolescence or the like, and opportunity cost

cash flow the receipt or disbursement of cash

centralization an organizational structure in which top management makes most decisions and controls most activities of the organizational units from the company's central headquarters

committed cost the cost of the basic plant assets and personnel structure that an organization must have to operate

common cost a cost that cannot be associated with a particular cost object and is incurred because of general production activity.

compensation strategy a foundation for the compensation plan that addresses the role compensation should play in the organization

compound interest interest calculated on the basis of principal plus interest already earned

compounding period the time from one interest computation to the next

computer integrated manufacturing (CIM) a production system in which two or more flexible manufacturing systems are connected by a host computer and an information network

concurrent engineering see *simultaneous engineering*

confrontation strategy a strategy in which an organization tries to differentiate its products/services by introducing new features or tries to develop a price leadership position by dropping prices even though that organization knows that its competitors will rapidly bring out equivalent products and match price changes

constraint a restriction on the ability to reach an objective (from appendix)

continuous budget an ongoing twelve-month budget that is created by the addition of a new budget month (twelve months into the future) as each current month expires

continuous improvement small, but ongoing efforts to make positive adjustments in the status quo

contribution margin (CM) selling price per unit minus all variable production, selling, and administrative costs per unit

contribution margin ratio (CM%) contribution margin divided by revenue; indicates what proportion of selling price remains after variable costs have been covered

control chart a graphical presentation of the results of a specified activity; indicates the upper and lower control limits and those results that are out of control

control systems managerial tools for implementing plans

controlling exerting managerial influence on operations so that they will conform to plans

conversion transformation of organizational inputs into outputs

conversion cost the sum of direct labor and factory overhead costs; the cost incurred in changing direct materials or supplies into finished products or services

core competency any critical function or activity in which one organization has a higher proficiency than its competitors; are the roots of competitiveness and competitive advantage

correlation a statistical measure of the strength of relationship between two variables

cost a monetary measure of the resources given up to acquire a good or a service

cost accounting tools and methods applied to determine the cost of making products or performing services

cost avoidance a process of finding acceptable alternatives to high-cost items and not spending money for unnecessary goods or services

cost behavior the manner in which a cost responds to a change in a related level of activity

cost center an organizational unit in which the manager has the authority only to incur costs and is specifically evaluated on the basis of how well costs are controlled

cost consciousness a companywide employee attitude toward cost understanding, cost containment, cost avoidance, and cost reduction

cost containment the process of attempting, to the extent possible, to minimize period-by-period increases in per-unit variable and total fixed costs

cost control system a logical structure of formal and informal activities designed to influence costs and to enable management to analyze and evaluate how well expenditures were managed during a period

cost driver a factor that has a direct cause-effect relationship to a cost

cost leadership a competitive strategy in which an organization becomes the low-cost producer/provider and, thus, is able to charge low prices that emphasize cost efficiencies

cost management system set of formal methods developed for controlling an organization's cost-generating activities relative to its goals and objectives

cost object anything to which costs attach or are related

cost of capital (COC) the weighted average rate that reflects the costs of the various sources of funds making up a firm's debt and equity structure

cost of goods manufactured (CGM) the total cost of the goods that were completed and transferred to Finished Goods Inventory during the period

cost of production report a document used in a process costing system; details all manufacturing quantities and costs, shows the computation of cost per EUP, and indicates the cost assignment to goods produced during the period

cost reduction a process of lowering current costs, especially those in excess of necessary costs

cost structure relative proportions of variable and fixed costs

cost tables databases that provide information about how using different input resources, manufacturing processes, and design specifications would affect product costs

cost-volume-profit (CVP) analysis a process of examining the relationships among revenues, costs, and profits for a relevant range of activity and for a particular time frame

critical success factor an item that is so important to an organization that, without it, the organization would fail; quality, customer service, efficiency, cost control, and responsiveness to change are five basic critical success factors

cross-functional team a group of employees, each of whom possesses unique expertise, brought together to accomplish specific objectives

customer a generic term for the recipient or beneficiary of a process's output; can be internal or external

cycle time the time from when a customer places an order to the time that product or service is delivered or, using a full life-cycle approach, the time from the conceptualization of a product or service to the time the product or service is delivered to the market/customer

D

decentralization the downward delegation by top management of authority and decision making to the individuals who are closest to internal processes and customers

decision making using information to choose the best alternative from the options available to reach a particular goal or objective

Deming Prize Japan's premier quality award

dependent variable an unknown variable that is to be predicted by use of one or more independent variables

differentiation a competitive strategy in which an organization distinguishes its product or service from that of competitors by adding enough value (including quality and/or features) that customers are willing to pay a higher price

direct cost a cost that is clearly, conveniently, and economically traceable to a particular cost object

direct labor the time spent by individuals who work specifically on manufacturing a product or performing a service and whose efforts are conveniently and economically traceable to that product or service; can also be viewed as the cost of the direct labor time

direct material a readily identifiable, physical part of a product that is clearly, conveniently, and economically traceable to that product

discount rate the rate of return on capital investments required by the company; the rate of return used in present value computations

discounting the process of removing the portion of a future cash flow that represents interest, thereby reducing that flow to a present value amount

discretionary cost an optional cost that a decision maker must periodically review to determine whether it continues to be in accord with ongoing policies

distribution cost any cost incurred to fill an order for a product or service

downsizing management actions that reduce employment and restructure operations as a response to competitive pressures

Du Pont model a model that indicates the return on investment as it is affected by profit margin and asset turnover

dual pricing arrangement a transfer price method that allows a selling division to record the transfer of goods or services at a market-based or negotiated price and a buying division to record the transfer at a cost-based amount

E

economic integration the creation of multicountry markets through the development of transnational rules that reduce the fiscal and physical barriers to trade and, thus, encourage greater economic cooperation among countries

economic order quantity (EOQ) an estimate of the least costly number of units per order that would provide the optimal balance between ordering and carrying costs

economic production run (EPR) the quantity of units to produce that minimizes the total cost of setting up a production run and carrying costs

economic value added the difference between after-tax profits and the dollar cost of capital

effectiveness a measure of how well the firm's objectives and goals were achieved; involves comparing actual output results with desired results

efficiency the degree to which the relationship between outputs and inputs is satisfactory; performance of a task to produce the best outcome at the lowest cost from the resources used

electronic data interchange (EDI) the almost instantaneous computer-to-computer transfer of information

employee time sheet (time ticket) a source document that indicates, for each employee, what jobs were worked on during the day and for what amount of time

empowerment all practices that are designed to give workers the training, authority, and responsibility they need to manage their own jobs and make decisions about their work

environmental constraint any limitation on strategy caused by external cultural, fiscal (such as taxation structures), legal/regulatory, or political situations or by competitive market structures; tend to be long-run rather than short-run

equivalent units of production (EUP) an approximation of the number of whole units of output that could have been produced during a period from the actual effort expended during that period

ethical standard a norm that represents beliefs about moral and immoral behaviors; a norm for individual conduct in making decisions and engaging in business transactions

expatriate a parent company or third-country national assigned to a foreign subsidiary or a foreign national assigned to the parent company

expected activity a short-run concept representing the anticipated level of activity for the upcoming year

expected annual capacity a short-run concept representing the anticipated level of activity for the upcoming year

expected standard a standard that reflects what is actually expected to occur in a future period

F

facility-level cost see *organizational-level cost*

factory overhead any factory or production cost that is not directly or conveniently traceable to manufacturing a product or providing a service

failure cost A quality control cost associated with goods or services that have been found not to conform or perform to the required standards as well as the related costs (such as that of the complaint department); may be internal or external

feasible solution an answer to a linear programming problem that does not violate any of the problem constraints (from appendix)

FIFO method a method of process costing that computes an average cost per equivalent unit of production using only current period production and current cost information; units and costs in beginning inventory are accounted for separately

financial accounting generation of accounting information for external parties

financial budget a budget that reflects the funds to be generated or used during the budget period; includes the cash and capital budgets and the projected or pro forma financial statements

financing decision a judgment regarding how funds will be obrained to make an acquisition

fixed cost a cost that remains constant in total within a specified range of activity

fixed overhead spending variance the difference between actual and budgeted fixed overhead

flexible budget a series of financial plans that detail the individual variable and fixed cost factors comprising total cost and present those costs at different levels of activity according to cost behavior

flexible manufacturing system a production system in which a single factory manufactures numerous variations on products through the use of computer-controlled robots

Foreign Corrupt Practices Act (FCPA) an act passed in 1977 by the U.S. government that prohibits U.S. corporations from offering or giving bribes (directly or indirectly) to foreign officials to influence those individuals (or cause them to use their influence) to help businesses obtain or retain business; directed at payments that cause officials to act in a way specified by the firm rather than in a way prescribed by their official duties

functional classification a grouping of costs incurred for the same basic purpose

future value (FV) the amount to which one or more sums of money invested at a specified interest rate will grow over a specified number of time periods

G

global economy a business environment that encompasses the international trade of goods and services, movement of labor, and flows of capital and information

goal a desired result or condition that is expressed in qualitative terms

goal congruence a condition that exists when the personal and organizational goals of decision makers throughout a firm are consistent and mutually supportive

grade (of product or service) the addition or removal of product or service characteristics to satisfy additional needs, especially price

H

harvest mission a strategic mission that has the goal of maximizing short-term earnings and cash flow, even at the expense of market share; typically pursued business units with high market share in low growth industries

high–low method a technique for separating mixed costs that uses actual observations of a total cost at the highest and lowest levels of activity and calculates the change in both activity and cost; the levels chosen must be within the relevant range

hold mission a strategic mission that has the goal of protecting the business unit's market share and competitive position; typically pursued by business units with high market share in high growth industries

horizontal price fixing a practice by which competitors attempt to regulate prices through an agreement or conspiracy

hurdle rate the rate of return deemed by management to be the lowest acceptable return on investment

I

idle time storage time and time spent waiting at a production operation for processing

imposed budget a budget that is prepared by top management with little or no input from operating personnel, who are simply informed of the budget goals and constraints

incremental cost the additional cost of producing or selling a contemplated quantity of output

incremental revenue the additional revenue resulting from a contemplated sale of a quantity of output

independent project an investment project that has no specific bearing on any other investment project

independent variable a variable that, when changed, will cause consistent, observable changes in another variable; a variable used as the basis of predicting the value of a dependent variable

indirect cost a cost that cannot be clearly traced to a particular cost object;

innovation dramatic improvements in the status quo caused by radical new ideas, technological breakthroughs, or large investments in new technology or equipment

inspection time the time taken to perform quality control

intellectual capital the intangible assets of skill, knowledge, and information in an organization; encompasses human and structural capital

internal rate of return (IRR) the discount rate at which the present value of the cash inflows minus the present value of the cash outflows equals zero

investing decision a judgment regarding which assets an entity will acquire to achieve its stated objectives

investment center an organizational unit in which the manager is responsible for generating revenues, planning and controlling costs, and acquiring, disposing of, and using plant assets to earn the highest feasible rate of return on the investment base

ISO 9000 a set of standards established by the international community to define the minimum acceptable quality for processes that generate products and services offered in international trade

J

job a single unit or group of like units identifiable as being produced to distinct customer specifications

job order cost sheet a source document that provides virtually all the financial information about a particular job; the set of all job order cost sheets for uncompleted jobs composes the Work in Process Inventory subsidiary ledger

job order costing product costing method used by entities that produce limited quantities of custom-made goods or services that conform to specifications designated by the purchaser

just-in-time a philosophy about when to do something; the *when* is "as needed" and the *something* is a production, purchasing, or delivery activity

vertical price fixing collusion between producing businesses and their distributors to control the prices at which their products may be sold to consumers

volume variance the difference between budgeted and applied fixed overhead

W

weighted average method a method of process costing that computes an average cost per equivalent unit of production; combines beginning inventory units with current production and beginning inventory costs with current costs to compute that average

Z

zero-based budgeting a comprehensive budgeting process that systematically considers the priorities and alternatives for current and proposed activities in relation to organizational objectives (from appendix)

AUTHOR INDEX

ORGANIZATION INDEX

SUBJECT INDEX

A

ABB, 286, 288
ABC. *See* Activity-based costing (ABC)
ABC analysis, 496–497
ABCM, 551
ABM, 172–203, 204
Abramson, Leonard, 71–72
Absorption costing, 259–260
Accountants, 593, 595, 618
Accounting
  management, 735–740
  role in organizational strategy,
    22–28
  types of, 45–48
Accounting rate of return (ARR), 356,
    372–373, 374
Accounts, flow of product costs
    through, 142
Accounts Payable, in cash budget,
    303–305
Accounts Receivable
  in cash budget, 301–303
  in product cost accounting, 142
  "Achievement ratio," 415
Activity
  defined, 177
  relevant range of, 126
  value-added and non-value-added,
    178–180
Activity analysis, 82–83, 176–182
  for investment, 343–346
Activity-based budgeting (ABB), 286,
    288
Activity-based costing (ABC), 26, 100,
    173, 174, 180, 183–191, 202–203,
    204
  activity-based management and, 184
  appropriateness of, 191–199
  criticisms of, 199–201
  illustration of, 190–191, 192
  as performance measure, 704–706
  planning and, 198–199
  standard cost systems versus, 399
  at Teva Pharmaceutical Industries
    Ltd., 631, 658
Activity-based costing and manage-
    ment systems (ABCMs), 551
Activity-based management (ABM),
    172–203, 204
  activity-based costing and, 174, 184
  defined, 177
Activity-based management umbrella,
    177
Activity center, 189–190
Activity cost drivers, 189–190

Activity drivers, 190
Activity improvements, opportunities
    for, 182
Actual activity, 137
Actual cost system, 51–52
Actual overhead cost, 137
Advertising
  as capital expenditure, 343
  as discretionary cost, 556–557
  in oligopolies, 13–14
Advertising budgets, 251
Aesthetics, product quality and, 77
After-tax profits, in cost-volume-profit
    analysis, 234–235, 235–237
Alliances, in interorganizational cost
    management, 605–607
Allocated costs, 116–117
Allocation
  of costs, 116–117, 133, 190–191, 197
  traditional versus overhead, 193
  two-step, 189–190
American Management Association,
    survey on training budgets by, 96
Americans with Disabilities Act, 111
Analysis. *See also* Gap analysis
  ABC, 496–497
  activity, 82–83, 176–182
  breakeven, 257–259
  of downsizing decisions, 613
  high-tech investment, 364–365
  least-squares regression, 148–150
  of overhead costs, 131
  Pareto, 92–95, 107, 193–195
  payroll, 119
  profitability, 188
  of quality cost relationships, 91–95
  regression, 129
  sensitivity, 309
  value chain cost, 600–601
  variance, 408, 413–414, 416, 420,
    421, 644–645
Annuities, 348
  internal rate of return from, 353–
    355
  payback period and, 349
  present values of, 371–372
  table of future values for, 750
  table of present values for, 748–749
Annuity due, 371
Applied overhead, 136–137
Appraisal costs, 89, 90, 91, 93, 94, 704
Appropriateness, of standards,
    414–415, 421
Appropriations, in zero-based budget-
    ing, 314
ARR, 356, 372–373, 374

ASEAN, 18
Asia, ISO 9000 quality initiatives in, 86
Assembly lines, creation of, 398
Assessors, in control systems, 41–42
Assets. *See also* Capital asset selection
  in balance sheets, 140
  investment in, 343–346
Asset turnover, 694–697
Association of Southeast Asian Nations
    (ASEAN), 18
Assurance, 78, 89, 90
Attainability, of standards, 415–416,
    421
Audits, post-investment, 367
Authority, 6–7
  in cost centers, 642
  in decentralization, 632–634
  in organizational structures, 633
  in responsibility centers, 644, 647–
    648
Automobile industry, time-to-market
    reduction in, 55–56

B

Backflush costing, 521–522, 526
Balanced scorecard, 690–692
Balance sheets, 140
  cash budget and, 305–307
  for master budget, 294–295
Baldrige, Malcolm, 85
Baldrige Award, 85, 101
Bank loans, 309, 388
Banks, decentralization of, 637
Bar codes, 97–98, 145
Barnevik, Percy, 636
Barsczak, Vicki, 72
Basu, Radha, 614
Batch-level cost, 185–189
Bauerle, Jurgen, 712
Before-tax profits, in cost-volume-profit
    analysis, 233–234, 235
Beginning inventory balance, 296, 297
Benchmarking, 83–84, 106–107. *See*
    also Standards
  cost reduction with, 551–552
  in organizational and employee per-
    formance, 688–689
Benefits. *See also* Fringe benefits; Tax
    benefits
  from discretionary costs, 558–561
BEP. *See* Breakeven point (BEP)
Best investments, choosing, 344–346
Bill of materials, 396
BI system, 15, 28
Blystone, John B., 699